Applied Process Design

for Chemical and Petrochemical Plants

Volume 2
Second Edition

Applied Process

Volume 1
1. Process Planning, Scheduling, Flowsheet Design
2. Fluid Flow
3. Pumping of Liquids
4. Mechanical Separations
5. Mixing of Liquids
6. Ejector and Vacuum Systems
7. Pressure-Relieving Devices
   Appendix of Conversion Factors

Volume 2
8. Distillation
9. Packed Towers
   Appendix of Conversion Factors

Volume 3
10. Heat Transfer
11. Refrigeration Systems
12. Compression Equipment
13. Compression Surge Drums
14. Mechanical Drivers

Design for Chemical and Petrochemical Plants

Ernest E. Ludwig
Ludwig Consulting Engineers
Baton Rouge, Louisiana

Gulf Publishing Company
Houston, London, Paris, Zurich, Tokyo

To my wife, Sue, for her
patient encouragement and help

APPLIED PROCESS DESIGN FOR
CHEMICAL AND PETROCHEMICAL PLANTS
Volume 2
Second Edition

This edition was reviewed by the
author and reprinted January 1993.

Library of Congress Cataloging in Publication Data (Revised)

Ludwig, Ernest E
Applied process design for chemical and petrochemical
plants.

    Includes bibliographies and indexes.
     1. Chemical plants—Equipment and supplies.
2. Petroleum industry and trade—Equipment and supplies.
I. Title.
TP155.L8 1977   660.2'8   76-40867
ISBN 0-87201-755-9 (v. 1)
ISBN 0-87201-753-2 (v. 2)
ISBN 0-87201-754-0 (v. 3)
Series ISBN 0-87201-788-5

10 9 8 7 6 5 4

Contents

Preface to the
Second Edition vii

(Chapters 1 through 7 contained in Volume 1)

8. Distillation 1
   Part 1: Distillation Process Performance 1
   Equilibrium Basic Considerations, 1; Ideal Systems, 1; Non-Ideal Systems, 2; Azeotropes, 4; Binary System Material Balance: Constant Molal Overflow Tray to Tray, 6; Total Condenser, 7; Partial Condenser, 7; Thermal Condition of Feed, 7; Total Reflux: Minimum Plates, 8; Fenske Equation: Overall Total Trays with Total Condenser, 8; Relative Volatility, 10; Minimum Reflux Ratio: Infinite Plates, 10; Theoretical Trays at Actual Reflux, 11; Example 8-1: Graphical Design for Binary Systems, 11; Example 8-2: Thermal Condition of Feed, 13; Example 8-3: Minimum Theoretical Trays at Total Reflux, 15; Tray Efficiency, 18; Differential Distillation— Simple Batch, No Trays, Binary Mixtures, 18; Example 8-4: Binary Batch Distillation, 19; Differential Distillation—Simple Batch, Without Trays, Multicomponent Mixture, 20; Example 8-5: Multicomponent Batch Distillation, 20; Steam Distillation—Continuous Flash, Multicomponent or Binary, 21; Example 8-6: Multicomponent Steam Flash, 21; Steam Distillation—Continuous Differential, Multicomponent or Binary, 21; Steam Distillation—Continuous Flash, Two Liquid Phases, Multicomponent and Binary, 22; Batch Distillation with Fractionation Trays—Constant Overhead Product Composition, Multicomponent and Binary, 22; Open Live Steam Distillation—With Fractionation Trays, Binary, 23; Distillation with Heat Balance, 23; Unequal Molal Overflow, 23; Ponchon-Savarit Method—Binary Mixtures, 24; Example 8-7: Ponchon Unequal Molal Overflow, 25; Multicomponent Distillation, 28; Key Components, 29; Minimum Reflux Ratio—Infinite Plates, 29; Algebraic Plate-to-Plate Method, 29; Underwood Algebraic Method: Adjacent Key Systems, 29; Minimum Reflux Colburn Method: Pinch Temperatures, 31; Scheibel-Montross Empirical: Adjacent Key Systems: Constant or Variable Volatility, 32; Example 8-8: Scheibel-Montross Minimum Reflux, 34; Theoretical Trays at Opening Reflux, 34; Example 8-9: Operating Reflux Ratio, 39; Actual Number of Trays, 35; Feed Tray Location, 35; Tray-by-Tray, 36; Tray-by-Tray: Using a Digital Computer, 37; Example 8-10: Tray-to-Tray Design Multicomponent Mixture, 37; Heat Balance—Adjacent Key Systems with Sharp Separations, Constant Molal Overflow, 41; Example 8-11: Tray-by-Tray Multicomponent Mixture Using Digital Computer, 42; Computer Printout for Multicomponent Mixture, 42; Example 8-12: Multicomponent Examination of Reflux Ratio and Distillate to Feed Ratio, 46; Nomenclature for Part 1, 46.

Part 2: Hydrocarbon Absorption and Stripping 48
Kremser-Brown-Sherwood Method—No Heat of Absorption, 48; Absorption in Fixed Tray Tower, 48; Absorption—Determine Number Trays for Specified Product Absorption, 50; Stripping— Determine Theoretical Trays in Stripping Steam or Gas Rate for a Component Recovery, 50; Stripping—Determine Stripping-Medium Rate for Fixed Recovery, 51; Absorption—Edmister Method, 52; Intercooling for Absorbers, 56; Absorption and Stripping Efficiency, 57; Example 8-13: Determine Number Trays for Specified Product Absorption, 57; Example 8-14: Determine Component Absorption in Fixed-Tray Tower, 59.

Part 3: Mechanical Designs for Performance 61
Contacting Trays, 61; Tray Types and Distinguishing Application Features, 62; Bubble Cap Tray Design, 65; Bubble Cap Tray Tower Diameter, 67; Tray Layouts, 72; Flow Paths, 72; Liquid By-Pass Baffles, 88; Liquid Drainage or Weep Holes, 88; Bottom Tray Seal Plan, 89; Bubble Caps, 89; Tray Performance, 89; Tray Capacity Related to Vapor-Liquid Loads, 90; Tray Stability, 91; Flooding, 91; Pulsing, 91; Blowing, 91; Coning, 91; Entrainment, 91; Overdesign, 91; Total Tray Pressure Drop, 93; Liquid Height Over Outlet Weir, 93; Slot Opening, 93; Liquid Gradient Across Tray, 93; Riser and Reversal Pressure Drop, 95; Total Pressure Drop Through Tray, 101; Downcomer Pressure Drop, 101; Liquid Height in Downcomer, 101; Downcomer Seal, 101; Tray Spacing, 101; Residence Time in Downcomers, 102; Liquid Entrainment from Bubble Cap Trays, 102; Slot Seal, 103; Throw Over Outlet Segmental Weir, 103; Vapor Distribution, 103; Bubble Cap Tray Design and Evaluation, 103; Example 8-15: Bubble Cap Tray Design, 103; Sieve Trays with Downcomers, 106; Hydraulic Gradient, Δ, 109; Dry Tray Pressure Drop, 109; Static Liquid Seal on Tray, or Submergence, 109; Dynamic Liquid Seal, 110; Total Weight Tray Pressure Drop, 110; Liquid Back-Up or Height in Downcomer, 110; Minimum Vapor Velocity, Weep Point, 110; Maximum Hole Velocity: Flooding, 111; Design Hole Velocity, 111; Tray Stability, 112; Tray Layout, 112; Example 8-16: Sieve Tray Design (Perforated), with Downcomer, 112; Perforated Plates Without Downcomers, 116; Dump Point, Plate Activation Point, or Load Point, 118; Example 8-17: Design of Perforated Trays Without Downcomers, 119; Tower Specifications, 121; Nomenclature for Part 3, 121; Bibliography, 126; References (Absorbers), 128.

9. Packed Towers 129
Shell, 132; Packing, 134; Packing Supports, 138; Liquid Distribution, 140; Redistributors, 154; Hold-Down Grids, 155; Packing Installation, 155; Stacked, 155; Dumped, 156; Packing Selection and Perfor-

mance, 156; Minimum Liquid Wetting Rates, 157; Loading Point-Loading Region, 158; Flooding Point, 159; Packing Factors, 160; Recommended Design Capacity in Pressure Drop, 162; Design Criteria and Guide, 166; Loading and Flooding Regions, General Design Correlations, 167; Pressure Drop at Flooding, 167; Pressure Drop Below and at Flood Point, Liquid Continuous Range, 167; Pressure Drop Across Packing Supports and Redistribution Plates, 169; Example 9-1: Evaluation of Tower Condition in Pressure Drop, 170; Example 9-2: Alternate Evaluation of Tower Condition and Pressure Drop, 171; Example 9-3: Change of Performance with Change in Packing in Existing Tower, 172; Example 9-4: Stacked Packing Pressure Drop, 172; Liquid Hold-Up, 174; Correction Factors for Liquids Other Than Water, 176; Packing Wetted Area, 176; Effective Interfacial Area, 176; Entrainment from Packing Surface, 176; Example 9-5: Operation at Low Rate, Liquid Hold-Up, 177; Mass and Heat Transfer in Packed Towers, 179; Number of Transfer Units, N_{OG}, $N_{O}L$, 179; Example 9-6: Number of Transfer Units for Dilute Solutions, 182; Example 9-7: Use of Colburn's Chart for Transfer Units—Straight Line Equilibrium Curve, Constant Temperature Operation, 184; Example 9-8: Number Transfer Units—Concentrated Solutions, 184; Gas and Liquid-Phase Coefficients, k_G and k_L, 186; Height of a Transfer Unit, $H_{O}G$, $H_{O}L$, HTU, 186; Example 9-9: Design of Ammonia Absorption Tower, 188; Mass Transfer with Chemical Reaction, 197; I. Carbon Dioxide or Sulfur Dioxide in Alkaline Solutions, 197; Example 9-10: Design a Packed Tower Using Caustic to Remove Carbon Dioxide from a Vent Stream, 201; II. NH_3-Air-H_2O System, 203; III. SO_2-H_2O System (Dilute Gas), 203; IV. CL_2-H_2O System (for Dilute Gas Concentrations), 204; V. Air-Water System, 205; VI. Hydrogen Chloride-Water System, 205; Distillation in Packed Towers, 205; Height Equivalent to a Theoretical Plate (HETP), 205; Example 9-11: Transfer Units in Distillation, 210; Cooling Water with Air, 212; Cooling Tower Terminology, 214; Performance, 219; Ground Area Versus Height, 223; Pressure Losses, 224; Fan Horsepower for Mechanical Draft Tower, 225; Water Rates and Distribution, 225; Preliminary Design Estimate of New Tower, 225; Alternate Preliminary Design of New Tower, 225; Example 9-12: Wood Packing Cooling Tower with Recirculation, Induced Draft, 227; Cooling Tower Based on Ka Data, 239; Performance of Atmospheric and Natural Draft Towers, 239; Nomenclature, 239; Bibliography, 240; References, 242.

Appendix **244**

A-1: Alphabetical Conversion Factors, 244; A-2: Physical Property Conversion Factors, 251; A-3: Synchronous Speeds, 254; A-4: Conversion Factors, 254; A-5: Temperature Conversion, 257; A-6: Altitude and Atmospheric Pressures, 258; A-7: Vapor Pressure Curves, 259; A-8: Pressure Conversion Chart, 260; A-9: Vacuum Conversion, 261; A-10: Decimal and Millimeter Equivalents of Fractions, 262; A-11: Particle Size Measurement, 262; A-12: Viscosity Conversions, 263; A-13: Viscosity Conversions, 264; A-14: Commercial Wrought Steel Pipe Data (Based on ANSI B36.10 wall thicknesses), 265; A-15: Stainless Steel Pipe Data (Based on ANSI B36.19 wall thicknesses), 268; A-16: Properties of Pipe, 269; A-17: Equation of Pipes, 278; A-18: Circumferences and Areas of Circles (Advancing by eighths), 279; A-19: Capacities of Cylinders and Spheres, 285; A-20: Tank Capacities, Horizontal Cylindrical-Contents of Tanks with Flat Ends When Filled to Various Depths, 289; A-21: Tank Capacities, Horizontal Cylindrical-Contents of Standard Dished Heads When Filled to Various Depths, 289; A-22: Miscellaneous Formulas, 290; A-23: Decimal Equivalents in Inches, Feet and Millimeters, 291; A-24: Properties of the Circle, Area of Plane Figures, and Volume of a Wedge, 292, A-24 (continued): Trigonometric Formulas, Properties of Sections, 293; A-25: Wind Chill Equivalent Temperatures on Exposed Flesh at Varying Velocity, 297; A-26: Impurities in Water, 297; A-27: Water Analysis Conversions for Units Employed: Equivalents, 298; A-28: Parts Per Million to Grains Per U.S. Gallon, 298; A-29: Formulas, Molecular and Equivalent Weights, and Conversion Factors to $CaCO_3$ of Substances Frequently Appearing in the Chemistry of Water Softening, 299; A-30: Grains Per U.S. Gallons—Pounds Per 1000 Gallons, 301; A-31: Parts Per Million—Pounds Per 1000 Gallons, 301; A-32: Coagulant, Acid, and Sulfate—1 ppm Equivalents, 301; A-33: Alkali and Lime—1 ppm Equivalents, 302; A-34: Sulfuric, Hydrochloric Acid Equivalent, 302.

Author Index **303**

Subject Index **304**

Preface
to the Second Edition

The techniques of process design continue to improve as the science of chemical engineering develops new and better interpretations of fundamentals. Accordingly, this second edition presents additional, reliable design methods based on proven techniques and supported by pertinent data. Since the first edition, much progress has been made in standardizing and improving the design techniques for the hardware components that are used in designing process equipment. This standardization has been incorporated in this latest edition, as much as practically possible. Although most of the chapters have been expanded to include new material, some obsolete information has been removed. Chapter 8 has incorporated additional multicomponent systems information for distillation, and Chapter 9 has been significantly updated in the rapidly expanding packed tower field. Also, the new appendixes provide basic reference and conversion data.

The many aspects of process design are essential to the proper performance of the work of chemical engineers and other engineers engaged in the process engineering design details for chemical and petrochemical plants. Process design has developed by necessity into a unique section of the scope of work for the broad spectrum of chemical engineering.

The purpose of these 3 volumes is to present techniques of process design and to interpret the results into mechanical equipment details. There is no attempt to present theoretical developments of the design equations. The equations recommended have practically all been used in actual plant equipment design, and are considered to be the most reasonable available to the author, and still capable of being handled by both the inexperienced as well as the experienced engineer. A conscious effort has been made to offer guidelines to judgment, decisions and selections, and some of this will be found in the illustrative problems.

The text material assumes that the reader is a graduate or equivalent chemical or related engineer having a sound knowledge of the fundamentals of the profession. From this background the reader is led into the techniques of design required to actually design as well as mechanically detail and specify. It is the author's philosophy that the process engineer has not adequately performed his function unless the results of a process calculation for equipment are specified in terms of something that can be economically built, and which can by visual or mental techniques be *mechanically interpreted* to actually perform the process function for which it is being designed. This concept is stressed to a reasonable degree in the various chapters.

As a part of the objective the chapters are developed by the *design function* of the designing engineer and not in accordance with previously suggested standards for unit operations. In fact some chapters utilize the same principles, but

require different interpretations when recognized in relation to the *process* and the function the equipment performs in this process.

Due to the magnitude of the task of preparing such material in proper detail, it has been necessary to drop several important topics with which every designing engineer must be acquainted, such as corrosion, cost estimating, economics and several others. These are now left to the more specialized works of several fine authors. Recognizing this reduction in content, it is still the hope of the author that in many petrochemical and chemical processes the designer will find design techniques adaptable to 75-80 percent of his requirements. Thus an effort has been made to place this book in a position of utilization somewhere between a handbook and a fundamentals teaching text. The present work is considered suitable for graduate courses in detailed process design, and particularly if a general course in plant design is available to fill in the broader factors associated with overall plant layout and planning.

The author is indebted to the many industrial firms which have so generously made available certain valuable design data and information. This credit is acknowledged at the appropriate locations in the text, except for the few cases where a specific request was made to omit this credit.

The author was encouraged to undertake this work by Dr. James Villbrandt together with Dr. W.A. Cunningham and Dr. J.J. McKetta. The latter two together with the late Dr. K.A. Kobe offered many suggestions to help establish the usefulness of the material to the broadest group of engineers. Dr. P.A. Bryant, professor at Louisiana State University, contributed significantly to updating this second edition's Absorption and Stripping section.

In addition, the author is deeply appreciative of the courtesy of The Dow Chemical Co. for use of certain noncredited materials, and their release for publication. In this regard particular thanks are given to Mr. N.D. Griswold and Mr. J.E. Ross, The valuable contribution of associates in checking material and making suggestions is gratefully acknowledged to H.F. Hasenbeck, L.T. McBeth, E.R. Ketchum, J.D. Hajek, W.J. Evers, D.A. Gibson.

The contribution of Western Supply Co. through Mr. James E. Hughes is also acknowledged with appreciation.

The courtesy of the Rexall Chemical Co. to encourage continuation of this work is also gratefully appreciated.

Ernest E. Ludwig
Baton Rouge, Louisiana

Applied Process Design

for Chemical and Petrochemical Plants

Distillation

Part 1: Distillation Process Performance

Efficient and economical performance of distillation equipment is vital to many processes. Although the art and science of distillation has been practiced for many years, studies still continue to determine the best design procedures for multicomponent, azeotropic, batch, multidraw, multifeed and other types. Some short cut procedures are adequate for many systems, yet have limitations in others; in fact the same might be said even for more detailed procedures.

The methods outlined in this chapter are considered adequate for the stated conditions, yet some specific systems may be exceptions to these generalizations. The process engineer often "double checks" his results by using a second method to verify the "ball-park" results, or short-cut recognized as being inadequate for fine detail.

Current design techniques using computer programs allow excellent prediction of performance for complicated multi-component systems such as azeotropic or high hydrogen hydrocarbon as well as extremely high purity of one or more product streams. Of course, the more straightforward, uncomplicated systems are being predicted with excellent accuracy also. The use of the digital computer provides capability to examine a useful array of variables, which is invaluable in selecting optimum or at least preferred modes or conditions of operation.

The expense of fabrication and erection of this equipment certainly warrants recognition of the quality of methods as well as extra checking time prior to initiating fabrication. The general process symbol diagram of Figure 8-1 will be used as reference for the systems and methods presented. Nomenclature for (1) distillation performance and design is on page 46 (2) absorption and stripping on page 60 and (3) tray hydraulic design on page 121.

Equilibrium Basic Considerations

Distillation design is based on the theoretical consideration that heat and mass transfer from stage to stage (theoretical) are in equilibrium. Actual columns with actual trays are designed by establishing column tray efficiencies, and applying these to the theoretical trays or stages determined by the calculation methods to be presented in later sections.

It is essential to calculate, predict or experimentally determine vapor-liquid equilibrium data in order to adequately perform distillation calculations. These data need to relate composition, temperature, and system pressure.

Basically there are two types of systems; ideal and nonideal. These terms apply to the simplier binary or two component systems as well as to the often more complex multicomponent systems.

Figure 8-2 illustrates a typical normal volatility vapor-liquid equilibrium curve for a particular component of interest in a distillation separation, usually for the more volatile of the binary mixture, or the one where separation is important in a multicomponent mixture.

Ideal Systems

The performance of these systems can be predicted by Raoult's Law, applying to vapors and liquids.

$$K_i = \frac{y_i}{x_i} = \frac{p_i{}^*}{p}$$

where: K_i = equilibrium distribution coefficient for system's component, i

$p_i{}^*$ = Vapor pressure of component, i, at temperature

p = Total pressure of system = ¶

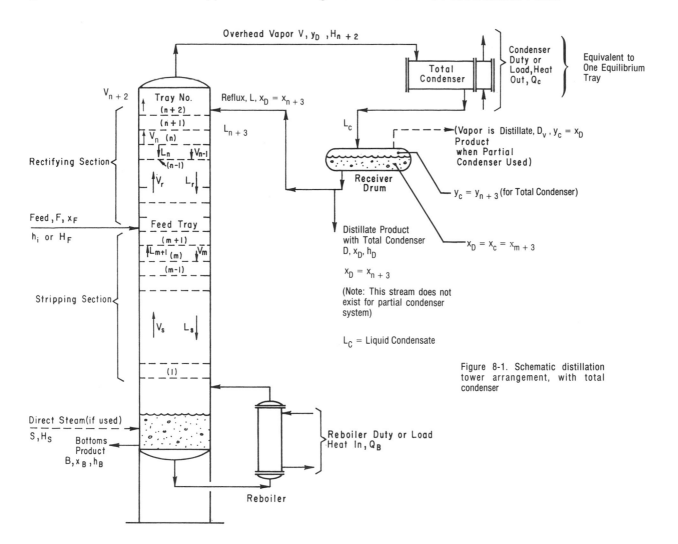

Figure 8-1. Schematic distillation tower arrangement, with total condenser

The ideal concept is usually a good approximation for close boiling components of a system, wherein the components are all of the same "family" of hydrocarbons or chemicals; for example paraffin hydrocarbons. When "odd" or non-family components are present, the possibility of deviations from non-ideality becomes greater, or if the system is a wide boiling range of components.

Often for preliminary calculation, the ideal conditions are assumed, followed by more rigorous design methods. The first approximation ideal basis calculations may be completely satisfactory, particularly when the activities of the individual components are 1.0 or nearly so.

Although it is not the intent of this chapter to evaluate the methods and techniques for establishing the equilibrium relationships, selected references will be given for the benefit of the designer's pursuit of more detail. This subject is so detailed as to require specialized books for adequate reference such as Prausnitz.[54]

Many process components do not conform to the ideal gas laws for pressure, volume and temperature relationships. Therefore, when ideal concepts are applied by

calculation, erroneous results are obtained—some not serious when the deviation from ideal is not significant, but some can be quite serious. Therefore, when data is available to confirm the ideality or non-ideality of a system, then the choice of approach is much more straightforward and can proceed with a high degree of confidence.

Non-Ideal Systems

Systems of two or more hydrocarbon, chemical and water components may be non-ideal for a variety of reasons. In order to accurately predict the distillation performance of these systems, accurate, experimental data is necessary. Second best is the use of specific empirical relationships that predict with varying degrees of accuracy the vapor pressure-concentration relationships at specific temperatures and pressures.

Prausnitz[54] presents a thorough analysis of the application of empirical techniques in the absence of experimental data.

The heart of the question of non-ideality deals with the determination of the distribution of the respective

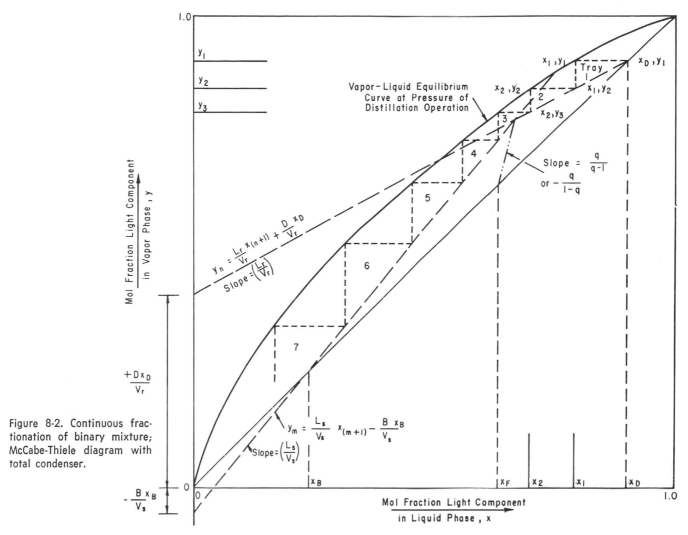

Figure 8-2. Continuous fractionation of binary mixture; McCabe-Thiele diagram with total condenser.

system components between the liquid and gaseous phases. The concepts of fugacity and activity are fundamental to the interpretation of the non-ideal systems. For a pure ideal gas the fugacity is equal to the pressure, and for a component, i, in a mixture of ideal gases it is equal to its partial pressure $y_i P$, where P is the system pressure. As the system pressure approaches zero, the fugacity approaches ideal. For many systems the deviations from unity are minor at system pressures less that 25 psig.

The ratio f/f° is called activity, a. Note this is *not* the activity coefficient. The activity is an indication of how "active" a substance is relative to its standard state (not necessarily zero pressure), f°. The standard state is the reference condition which may be anything; however, most references are to constant temperature, with composition and pressure varying as required. Fugacity becomes a corrected pressure, representing a specific component's deviation from ideal. The fugacity coefficient is:

$$\Omega_i = \frac{f_i}{y_i P}$$

The Virial Equation of State for gases is generally:

$$Z = \frac{Pv}{RT} = 1 + \frac{B}{v} + \frac{C}{v^2} + \frac{D}{v^3} + \cdots$$

where: B, C, D, etc. = virial coefficients, independent of pressure or density, and for pure components are functions of temperature only
v = molar volume
Z = Compressibility factor

Fugacities and activities can be determined using this concept.

Other important equations of state which can be related to fugacity and activity have been developed by Redlich-Kwong[56] with Chueh[10], which is an improvement over the original Redlich-Kwong, and Palmer's summary of activity coefficient methods[51].

Activity coefficients are equal to 1.0 for an ideal solution when the mole fraction is equal to the activity. The activity (a) of a component, i, at a specific temperature,

pressure and composition is defined as the ratio of the fugacity of i at these conditions to the fugacity of i at the standard state.[54]

$$a\ (T,\ P,\ x) = \frac{f_i\ (T,\ P,\ x)}{f_i\ (T,\ P^o,\ x^o)},\ \text{liquid phase}$$

(Zero superscript indicates a specific pressure and composition)

The activity coefficient γ_i is

$$\gamma_i = \frac{a_i}{x_i} = 1.0\ \text{for ideal solution}$$

The ideal solution law, Henry's Law, also enters into the establishment of performance of ideal and non-ideal solutions.

The Redlich-Kister[55, 57] equations provide a good technique for representing liquid phase activity and classifying solutions.

The Gibbs-Duhem equation allows the determination of activity coefficients for one component from data for those of other components.

Wilson's[77] equation has been found to be quite accurate in predicting the vapor-liquid relationships and activity coefficients for miscible liquid systems. The results can be expanded to as many components in a multicomponent system as may be needed without any additional data other than for a binary system. This makes Wilson's and Renon's techniques valuable for the complexities of multicomponent systems and in particular the solution by digital computer.

Renon's[58] technique for predicting vapor-liquid relationships is applicable to partially miscible systems as well as those with complete miscibility. This is described in the reference above and in Reference[54].

There are many other specific techniques applicable to particular situations, and these should often be investigated in order to select the method for developing the vapor-liquid relationships most reliable for the system. These are often expressed in calculation terms as the effective "K" for the components, i, of a system. Frequently used methods are: Chao-Seader, Peng-Robinson, Renon, Redlich-Kwong, Soave Redlich-Kwong, Wilson.

Azeotropes

Azeotrope mixtures consist of two or more components, and are surprisingly common in distillation systems. Therefore it is essential to determine if the possibility of an azeotrope exists. Fortunately, if experimental data is not available, there is an excellent reference which lists known azeotropic systems, with vapor pressure information.[20, 28, 43] Typical forms of representation of azeotropic data are shown in Figure 8-3 and 8-4. These are homogeneous, being of one liquid phase at the azeotrope point. Figure 8-5 illustrates a heterogeneous azeotrope where two liquid

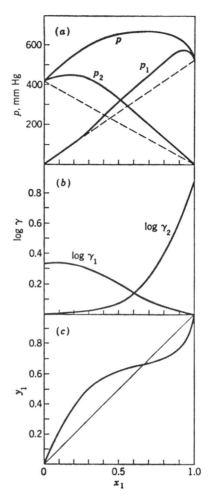

Figure 8-3. Chloroform (1)-methanol (2) system at 50° C. Azeotrope formed by positive deviations from Raoult's law (dashed lines). (Data of Sesonke, Dissertation, University of Delaware. By permission, B. D. Smith, "Design of Equilibrium Stage Processes." New York: McGraw-Hill, 1963.)

phases are in equilibrium with one vapor phase. The system butanol-water is an example of the latter, while chloroform-methanol and acetone-chloroform are examples of homogeneous azeotropes with "minimum boiling point" and "maximum boiling point" respectively.

A "minimum" boiling azeotrope exhibits a constant composition as shown by its crossing of the x = y, 45° line in Figure 8-6, which boils at a lower temperature than either of its pure components. This class of azeotrope results from positive deviations from Raoult's Law. Likewise, the "maximum" Figure 8-7, boiling azeotrope represents negative deviations from Raoult's Law and exhibits a constant boiling point which is greater than either pure component. At the point where the equilibrium curve crosses x = y, 45° line, the composition is constant and cannot be further purified by normal distillation. Both the minimum and maximum azeotropes can be modified by changing the system pressure and/or addition of a third component which should form a minimum boiling azeotrope with one of the original pair. To be effective the new azeotrope should boil well below or above the original azeotrope. By this technique one of the original components can often be recovered as a pure product, while still obtaining the second azeotrope for separate purification.

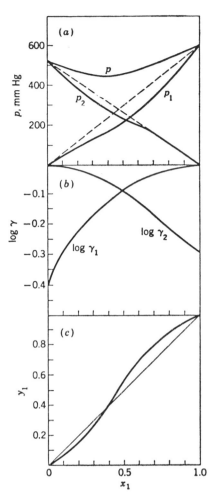

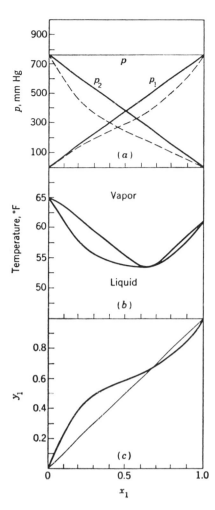

Figure 8-4. Acetone (1)-chloroform (2) system at 50° C. Azeotrope formed by negative deviations from Raoult's law (dashed lines). (Data of Sesonke, Dissertation, University of Delaware. By permission, B. D. Smith, "Design of Equilibrium Stage Processes." New York: McGraw-Hill, 1963.)

Figure 8-6. Chloroform (1)-methanol (2) system at 757 mm Hg. Minimum boiling azeotrope formed by positive deviations from Raoult's law (dashed lines). (By permission, B. D. Smith, "Design of Equilibrium Stage Processes." New York: McGraw-Hill 1963.)

For a "minimum" boiling azeotrope the partial pressures of the components will be greater than predicted by Raoult's Law, and the activity coefficients will be greater than 1.0.

$$\gamma = y_i p / x_i p_i *$$

where $p_i *$ = vapor pressure of component i, at temperature

$p = P$ = total pressure = ¶

$\gamma = a_i / x_i$ = activity coefficient of component, i

p_i = partial pressure of component i.

Raoult's Law; $p_i = x_i p_i * = x_i P_i = y_i P$

For "maximum" boiling azeotropes the partial pressures will be less than predicted by Raoult's Law and the activity coefficients will be less that 1.0.

In reference to distillation conditions, the azeotrope represents a point in the system where the relative volatilities reverse. This applies to either type of azeotrope, the direction of reversal is just opposite. For example in Figure 8-3 the lower portion of the x-y diagram shows that $y_i > x_i$, while at the upper part, the $y_i < x_i$. In actual distillation, without addition of an azeotrope "breaker" or solvent to change the system characteristics, if a feed of composition 30% x_i were used, the column could only produce

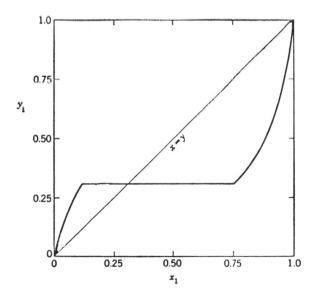

Figure 8-5. System with heterogeneous azeotrope—two liquid phases in the equilibrium with one vapor phase. (By permission, B. D. Smith, "Design of Equilibrium Stage Processes," New York: McGraw-Hill, 1963.)

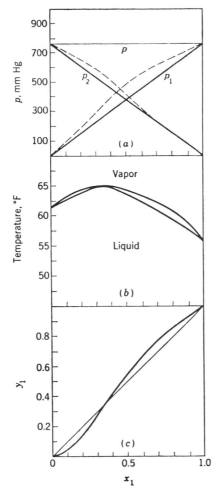

Figure 8-7. Acetone (1)-chloroform (2) system at 760 mm Hg. Maximum boiling azeotrope formed by negative deviations from Raoult's law (dashed lines). (By permission, B. D. Smith, "Design of Equilibrium Stage Processes." New York: McGraw-Hill, 1963.)

(or approach) pure x_2 out the bottom while producing the azeotrope composition of about 65% x_i and 35% x_2 at the top. The situation would be changed only to the extent of recognizing that if the feed came in above the azeotropic point, the bottoms product would be the azeotrope composition, Smith[65] discusses azeotropic distillation in detail.

Binary System Material Balance: Constant molal overflow tray to tray

- Rectifying Section

$$V_r = L_r + D \qquad (8\text{-}1)$$

For any component in the mixture; using total condenser see Figures 8-2 and 8-8.

$$V_n y_{ni} = L_{n+1} x_{(n+1)i} + D x_{Di} \qquad (8\text{-}2)$$

$$y_{ni} = \frac{L_{n+1}}{V_n} x_{(n+1)i} + \frac{D}{V_n} x_{Di} \qquad (8\text{-}3)$$

- Operating Line Equation:

$$y_{ni} = \frac{L_r}{V_r} x_{(n+1)i} + \frac{D}{V_r} x_{Di} \qquad (8\text{-}4)$$

For total condenser: y (top plate) = x_D

- Stripping Section

$$L_s = V_s + B \qquad (8\text{-}5)$$

$$L_{(m+1)} x_{(m+1)i} = V_m y_{mi} + B x_{Bi} \qquad (8\text{-}6)$$

- Operating Line Equation:

$$y_{mi} = \frac{L_s}{V_s} x_{(m+1)i} - \frac{B}{V_s} x_{Bi} \qquad (8\text{-}7)$$

Conditions of Operation: usually fixed

1. Feed composition, and quantity.

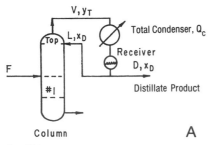

Total Condenser

Conditions: $y_T = x_D$

y_T in Equilibrium with Top Tray

D is Liquid

Partial Condenser

Conditions: y_D in Equilibrium with x_0

y_D is Vapor

D is Vapor Product
Partial Condenser acts as One Plate with
y_D in Equilibrium with Top Tray Condensate, x_0

Fig 8-8. Total and partial condenser arrangements.

2. Reflux Ratio (this may be a part of the initial unknowns).

3. Thermal condition of feed (at boiling point, all vapor, sub-cooled liquid).

4. Degree, type or amount of fractionation or separation, including compositions of overhead or bottoms.

5. Column operating pressure or temperature of condensation of overhead (determined by temperature of cooling medium), including type of condensation, i.e., total or partial.

6. Constant molal overflow from stage to stage (theoretical) for simple ideal systems following Raoult's Law. More complicated techniques apply for non-ideal systems.

Total Condenser

In a total condenser all of the overhead vapor is condensed to the liquid state. When the heat load or duty on the condenser is exactly equal to the latent heat of the saturated or dew point of the overhead vapor from the distillation column, the condensed liquid will be a saturated bubble point liquid. The condenser and accumulator pressure will be the total vapor pressure of the condensate. If an inert gas is present the system total pressure will be affected accordingly. When using a total condenser, the condensed stream is split into one going back into the column as reflux and the remaining portion leaving the system as distillate product.

Partial Condenser

The effect of the partial condenser is indicated in Figure 8-8 and is otherwise represented by the relations for the rectifying and stripping sections as just given. The key point to note is that the product is a vapor which is in *equilibrium* with the reflux to the column top tray, and hence the partial condenser is actually serving as an "external" tray for the system and should be considered as the *top* tray when using the equations for total reflux conditions. This requires just a little care in step-wise calculation of the column performance.

In a partial condenser there are two general conditions of operation:

1. All condensed liquid is returned to column as reflux, while all vapor is withdrawn from the accumulator as product. In this case the vapor $y_c = x_D$; Figure 8-1 and Figure 8-9.

2. Both liquid and vapor products are withdrawn, with liquid reflux composition being equal to liquid product composition. Note that on an equilibrium diagram the partial condenser liquid and vapor stream's respective compositions are in equilibrium, but only when *combined* do they represent the intersection of the operating line with the 45° slope. (Figure 8-9)

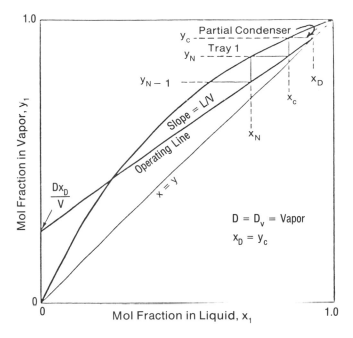

Figure 8-9. Diagram of partial condenser, only a vapor product is withdrawn.

Thermal Condition of Feed

The condition of the feed as it enters the column has an effect on the number of trays, reflux requirements and heat duties for a given separation. Figure 8-10 illustrates the possible situations, i.e., sub-cooled liquid feed, feed at the boiling point of the column feed tray, part vapor and part liquid, all vapor but not superheated, and superheated vapor. The thermal condition is designated as "q," and is approximately the amount of heat required to vaporize one mol of feed at the feed tray conditions, divided by the latent heat of vaporization of the feed.

$$L_s = L_r + qF \qquad (8-8)$$

$$q = (L_s - L_r)/F \qquad (8-8A)$$

The slope of a line from the intersection point of the feed composition, x_F, with the 45° line on Figure 8-2 is given by $q/(q-1) = -q/(1-q)$. Physically this gives a good approximation of the mols of saturated liquid that will form on the feed plate by the introduction of the feed, keeping in mind that under some thermal conditions the feed may vaporize liquid on the feed plate rather than condense any.

As an alternate to locating the "q" line, any value of x_1 may be substituted in the "q" line equation below, and a corresponding value of y_1 determined, which when plotted will allow the "q" line to be drawn in. This is the line for SV — I, V — I, PV — I, BP — I and CL — I of Figure 8-10

$$y_1 = -\frac{q}{1-q} x_1 + \frac{x_F}{1-q} \qquad (8-9)$$

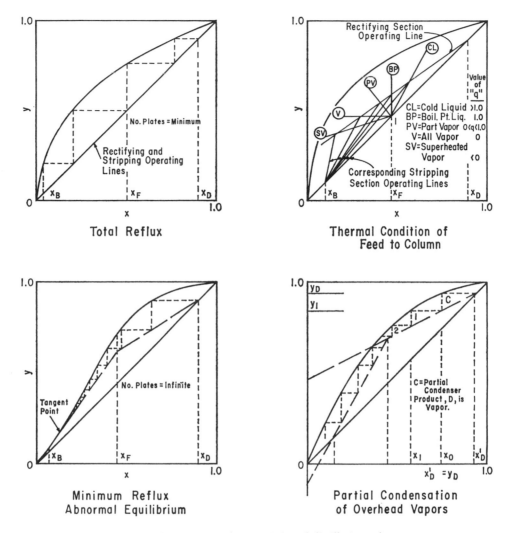

Figure 8-10. Operating characteristics of distillation columns.

Total Reflux; Minimum Plates

Total reflux exists in a distillation column, whether a binary or multicomponent system, when all the overhead vapor from the top tray or stage is condensed and returned to the top tray. Usually a column is brought to equilibrium at total reflux for test or for a temporary plant condition which requires discontinuing feed. Rather that shut down, drain and then re-establish operating conditions later, it is usually more convenient and requires less energy in the form of reboiler heat and condenser coolant to maintain a total reflux condition with no feed, no overhead and no bottoms products or withdrawals.

The conditions of total liquid reflux in a column also represent the minimum number of plates required for a given separation. Under such conditions the column has zero production of product, and infinite heat requirements, and $L_s/V_s = 1.0$ as shown in Figure 8-10. This is the limiting condition for the number of trays and is a convenient measure of the complexity or difficulty of separation.

Fenske Equation: Over-all Total Trays with Total Condenser

$$S_m = (N_{min} + 1) = \frac{\log\left(\frac{x_{Dl}}{x_{Dh}}\right)\left(\frac{x_{Bh}}{x_{Bl}}\right)}{\log \alpha \text{ avg.}} \quad (8\text{-}10)$$

Note that N_{min} does not include the reboiler as a tray, the "+ 1" adds it in. Since the feed tray is essentially non-effective it is suggested that an additional tray be added to allow for this, making N + 2. This can be conveniently solved by the nomograph[21] of Figures 8-11 and 12. If the minimum number of trays in the rectifying section are needed, they can be calculated by the Fenske equation substituting the limits of x_{Fl} for x_{Bh} and x_{Bl}, and the stripping section can be calculated by difference.

For a condition of overall total trays with partial condenser, replace $(N_{min} + 1)$ above by $(N_{min} + 2)$, and if allowance is made for feed tray effect, add one more tray, making $N_{min} + 3$.

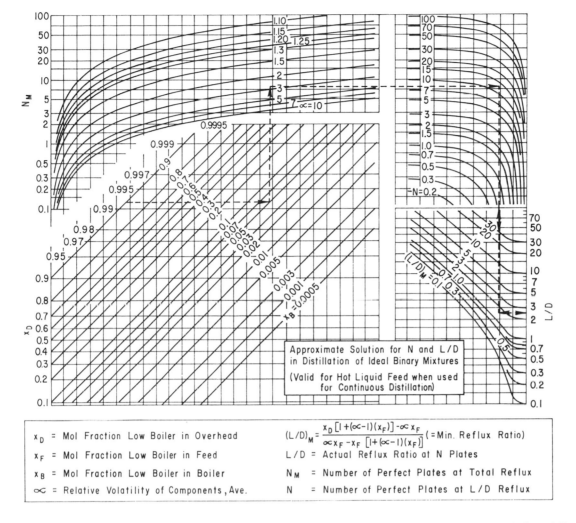

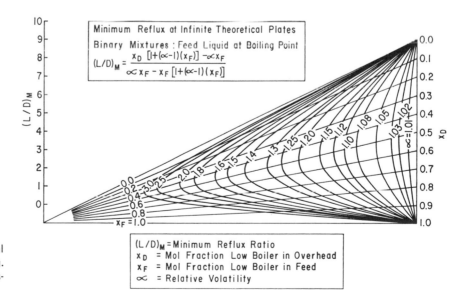

Figure 8-11. Approximate solution for N and L/D in distillation of ideal binary mixtures. (Courtesy J. W. Faasen, Ind. and Eng. Chem. Vol. 36, p. 248 (1944), reprinted by permission American Chemical Society.)

Figure 8-12. Minimum reflux at infinite theoretical plates. (Courtesy of E. H. Smoker, Ind. and Eng. Chem., Vol. 34, p 510 (1942) reprinted by permission American Chemical Society.)

Relative Volatility

For ideal systems following Raoult's Law; relative volatility $\alpha_{1h} = p_1/p_h$, ratio of partial pressures.

For a binary distillation, α is calculated at top and bottom conditions and a geometric mean used where the differences are relatively small.

$$\alpha_{avg.} = \sqrt{\alpha_D(\alpha_B)} \qquad (8\text{-}11)$$

For values of α near 1.0, extreme care must be used in establishing data, as a small change in the value of $\alpha_{avg.}$ may double the number of trays.

The exact procedure is to estimate a temperature profile from top to bottom of the column and then calculate α for each theoretical tray or stage by assuming a temperature increment from tray to tray. For many systems this, or some variation, is recommended to achieve good separation calculations.

For non-ideal systems:

$$\alpha_{1h} = \frac{y_1\, x_h}{x_1\, y_h} \qquad (8\text{-}12)$$

$$\alpha_{1h} = \frac{K_1}{K_h} \qquad (8\text{-}13)$$

The vapor-liquid equilibrium relationship may be determined from

$$y_1 = \frac{\alpha_{1h}\,(x_1)}{1 + (\alpha_{1h} - 1)\, x_1} \qquad (8\text{-}14)$$

By assuming values of x_1, the corresponding y_1 may be calculated.

Minimum Reflux Ratio: Infinite Plates

As the reflux ratio is decreased from infinity for the total reflux condition, more theoretical steps or trays are required to complete a given separation, until the limiting condition of Figure 8-13 is reached where the operating line touches the equilibrium line and the number of steps to go from the rectifying to stripping sections becomes infinite. This graphical representation is easier to use for non-ideal systems than the calculation method. This is another limiting condition for column operation, i.e., below this ratio the specified separation cannot be made even with infinite plates. This minimum reflux ratio can be determined graphically from Figure 8-13, as the line with smallest slope from x_D intersecting the equilibrium line at the same point as the "q" line for mixture following Raoult's Law.

External reflux ratio = L/D

Slope of line from x_D:

$$\left(\frac{L}{V}\right)_{min} = \frac{(L/D)_{min}}{(L/D)_{min} + 1} = \frac{x_D - y_c}{x_D - x_c} \qquad (8\text{-}15)$$

$$L/V = \text{internal reflux ratio}$$

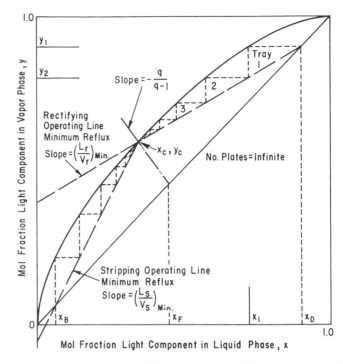

Figure 8-13. Fractionation of binary mixture minimum reflux condition.

For non-ideal mixtures the minimum L/V may be as indicated in Figure 8-10, and hence not fixed as indicated above.

Figure 8-12 presents a convenient and acceptably accurate nomogram of Smoker's.[66]

$$\left(\frac{L}{D}\right)_{min} = \frac{x_D - y_c}{y_c - x_c}$$

Where: x_c and y_c are coordinates of intersection of minimum reflux "operating" line with equilibrium curve. At Boiling Point $x_c = x_F$.

Underwood's algebraic evaluation[73] for minimum reflux ratio is acceptable for handling ideal or near ideal systems:

Bubble Point Liquid, q = 1.0

$$(L/D)_{min} = \frac{1}{\alpha - 1}\left[\frac{x_{1D}}{x_{1F}} - \frac{\alpha(1 - x_{1D})}{(1 - x_{1F})}\right] \qquad (8\text{-}16)$$

All vapor feed, no superheating, q = 0

$$(L/D)_{min} = \frac{1}{\alpha - 1}\left[\frac{\alpha x_{1D}}{x_{1F}} - \frac{(1 - x_{1D})}{(1 - x_{1F})}\right] - 1 \qquad (8\text{-}17)$$

For the general case the relation is more complex in order to solve for $(L/D)_{min}$.

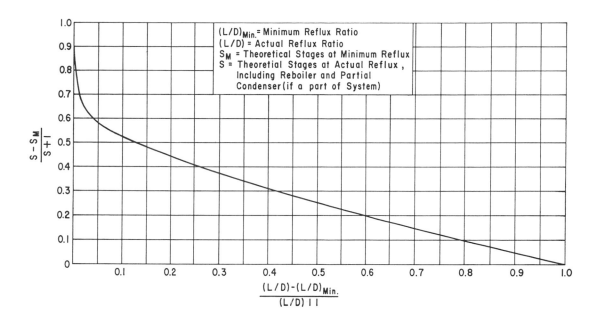

Figure 8-14. Correlation of theoretical plates with reflux ratio.

$$\frac{(L/D)_{min}(x_{1F}) + q\,x_{1D}}{L/D_{min}(1 - x_{1F}) + q(1 - x_{1D})}$$

$$= \frac{\alpha[((L/D)_{min} + 1)y_{1F} + (q-1)x_{1D}]}{[(L/D)_{min} + 1](1 - x_{1F}) + (q-1)(1 - x_{1D})} \quad (8\text{-}18)$$

Theoretical Trays at Actual Reflux

The Gilliland correlation[23] of Figure 8-14 has proven satisfactory for many binary as well as multicomponent mixtures over a wide range of reflux ratios and number of plates.

Many systems appear to be economically designed for

$$\frac{(L/D) - (L/D)_{min}}{(L/D) + 1} = 0.1 \text{ to } 0.33 \text{ and using actual reflux}$$

ratios of 1.2 to 1.5 times the ratio at minimum reflux. For systems of greatly varying relative volatility this should not be used; instead, a Ponchon or enthalpy method must be followed.

Example 8-1: Graphical Design for Binary Systems[59]

The benzene-toluene example of Robinson and Gilliland[59] has been elaborated on and expanded after the advanced distillation course of Holland[25], Figure 8-15.

It is desired to separate an equimolal mixture of benzene and toluene into a top product containing 95 mol percent benzene and a bottom product containing 95 mol percent toluene. The distillation is to be carried out at atmospheric pressure. Use a total condenser.

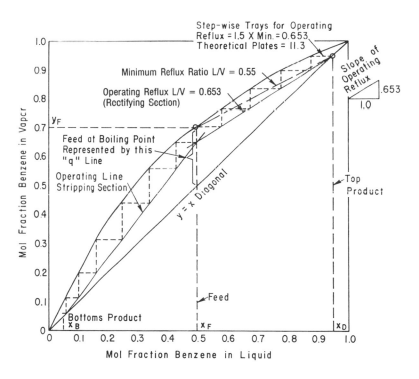

Figure 8-15. Equilibrium curve: Benzene-toluene for example No. 1. (Curve data only by permission C. S. R. Robinson and E. R. Gilliland "Elements of Fractional Distillation," 4th Ed. McGraw-Hill Book Co. (1950).)

A. Calculate the minimum reflux ratio if the feed is liquid at its boiling point.

B. Calculate the theoretical plates required if a reflux ratio (L/D) of 1.5 times the minimum is employed.

Feed   = 50 mols benzene + 50 mols toluene

Overhead = 95% benzene

Bottoms   = 95% toluene

Material balance with respect to benzene:

$$0.50 \ (100) = \ (0.95) \ (D) + 0.05B$$
$$50 = .95D + .05(100 - D)$$
$$50 = .95D + 5 - .05D$$
$$45 = .90D$$
$$D = 45/.90 = 50 \text{ mols overhead } product$$
$$D = \text{overhead } product, \text{ mols}$$
$$B = \text{bottoms, mols}$$

A. For a Feed at its Boiling Point:

$$\frac{L_n}{V_n} = \frac{L/D}{L/D+1} \text{ or } \frac{L}{V} = \frac{x_D - y_F}{x_D - x_F}, \ y_F = 0.70 \text{ (from curve)}$$

$$= \frac{0.95 - 0.70}{0.95 - 0.50}$$

Minimum L/V = 0.55 mols reflux/mol vapor up

substituting: $0.55 = \dfrac{L/D}{L/D+1}$

$$0.55 \ L/D + 0.55 = L/D$$

$$0.45 \ L/D = 0.55$$

Reflux/Product = L/D = 0.55/0.45 = 1.22

The value of L/D minimum should be equal to:

$$\frac{L_{12}}{D} = \frac{x_D - y_c}{y_c - x_c} = \frac{0.95 - 0.70}{0.70 - 0.50} = \frac{.25}{.20} = 1.25$$

The slight difference is probably due to inaccuracy in reading $y_c = 0.70$ from equilibrium curve.

B. Theoretical Plates at L/D = 1.5 Times Minimum.

Operating Reflux Ratio = (1.5) (1.25) = 1.878 = L/D

Slope of operating line at this reflux ratio:

$$\frac{L}{V} = \frac{L/D}{L/D+1}$$

$$\frac{L}{V} = \frac{1.878}{1.878+1} = 0.653$$

From Graph, L/V = 0.653 was plotted based on feed at its boiling point, No. of theoretical plates (step-wise graph) = 11.3

Now, to *calculate* theoretical plates:

Rectifying section:

$$y_n = \frac{L_n + 1}{V_n} x_{n+1} + \frac{D}{V_n} x_D \quad \text{operating line}$$

At: L/D = 1.878, D = 50 mols overhead

L = (1.878) (50) = 93.9 mols reflux to column

V = L + D = 93.9 + 50 = 143.9 mols to vapor overhead

$$y_n = \frac{93.9}{143.9} x_{n+1} + \frac{50}{143.9} (0.95) = 0.652 \ x_{n+1} + 0.331$$

For a total condenser: $y_{top} = x_D = x_R = 0.95$

From the equilibrium curve at $y_t = 0.95$

then: $x_t = 0.88$

$$y_{(t-1)} = 0.651 \ (x_t) + 0.331$$

$$y_{(t-1)} = 0.651 \ (0.88) + 0.331 = 0.903$$

$y_{t-1} = 0.903$, then x_{t-1} from equilibrium curve = 0.788

Now calculate y_{t-2}

$$y_{t-2} = 0.651 \ (.788) + 0.331 = 0.844$$

At $y_{t-2} = 0.844$, curve reads: $x_{t-2} = 0.69$

Then: $y_{t-2} = 0.651 \ (0.69) + .331 = 0.780$

At y_{t-3}, curve reads: $x_{t-3} = 0.60$

Then: $y_{t-4} = 0.651 \ (0.60) + .331 = 0.722$

At y_{t-4}, curve reads: $x_{t-4} = 0.52$ (Feed Tray)

Then: $y_{t-5} = 0.651 \ (0.52) + .331 = 0.669$ (too far below feed).

Now go to *stripping section curve:*

$$y_m = \frac{L_{m+1} x_{m+1}}{V_m} - \frac{W}{V_m} x_B$$

The feed was at its boiling point:

$$V_n = V_m = 143.9$$

$$B = \text{Bottoms} = 50$$

$$L_m = B + V = 50 + 143.9 = 193.9$$

$$y_m = \left(\frac{193.9}{143.9} \right) x_{m+1} - \frac{50}{143.9} (0.50)$$

$$= 1.35 \ x_{m+1} - .01736$$

Starting at t-4 = feed tray:

$$x_{t-4} = 0.52$$

$$\begin{array}{l} y \ (\text{feed} - 1) = 1.35 \ x_f - 0.0176 \\ (f - 1) \end{array}$$

$$y_{(t-1)} = 1.35 \ (0.52) - 0.01736 + 0.685$$

At $y_{f-1} = 0.685$, $x_{f-1} = 0.475$,

Note: This is not too accurate due to switched operating line equations before the feed compositions were reached, yet, one more calculation on the stripping line would have placed us below the feed plate composition. Hence a change in reflux ratio is necessary in order to split right at the feed composition.

continuing:

$$y_{f-2} = 1.35 \ (0.475) - .01736 = 0.624$$

From curve at $y_{f-2} = 0.624$

$$x_{f-2} = 0.405$$

$y_{f-3} = 1.35 \,(.405) - .01736 = 0.531$

From curve, $x_{f-3} = 0.32$

$y_{f-4} = 1.35 \,(.32) - .01736 = 0.416$

$\quad x_{f-4} = 0.23$

$y_{f-5} = 1.35 \,(.23) - .01736 = 0.294$

$\quad x_{f-5} = 0.15$

$y_{f-6} = 1.35 \,(.15) - .01736 = 0.186$

$\quad x_{f-6} = 0.092$

$y_{f-7} = 1.35 \,(.092) - .01736 = 0.107$

$\quad x_{f-7} = 0.05$ (The desired bottoms composition)

Total theoretical trays:

rectifying section	= 4
feed tray	= 1
stripping section	= 7
total	= 12 Trays

Example: 8-2 Thermal Condition of Feed

Using the same operating reflux (same fraction times the minimum) as was used in Example 8-1, calculate the theoretical plates required for feed of the following thermal conditions: Use Figure 8-16

(a) $q = 1.5$

(b) $q = 0$

(c) $q = -1.5$

A. For $q = 1.5$

Slope of "q" line $= -q/1-q$

Substituting: slope $= \dfrac{-1.5}{1-1.5} - \dfrac{-1.5}{-0.5} = +3$

Referring to calculations of Example 8-1, for an equimolal mixture of benzene and toluene in feed:

overhead product, D = 50 mols/100 mols feed

calculate: $\left(\dfrac{L_R}{D}\right)_{min} = \dfrac{x_D - y_c}{y_c - x_c}$,

where: $x_D = 0.95$

$\quad y_c = 0.774^*$

$\quad x_c = 0.59^*$

$$= \dfrac{0.95 - 0.774}{0.774 - 0.59}$$

$$= \dfrac{0.176}{0.184}$$

$(L/D)_{min} = (L_R/D)_{min} = 0.956$ Min. Reflux ratio, Reflux/Product

---

*Read from graph at intersection of "q" line for 1.5 and minimum reflux operating line.

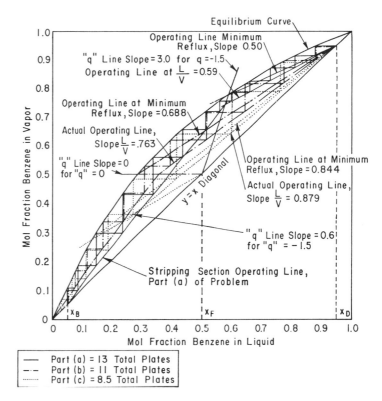

Figure 8-16. Equilibrium curve: Benzene-toluene, for example No. 2. (Curve data only by permission C. S. R. Robinson and E. R. Gilliland "Elements of Fractional Distillation," 4th Ed. McGraw-Hill Book Co. (1950).)

Slope of operating line at Min. Reflux:

$$\left(\frac{L}{V}\right) = \left(\frac{L_R}{V}\right)_{min} = \frac{L/D}{L/D + 1} = \frac{0.956}{0.956 + 1} = 0.49$$

(Graph reads 0.59 but this depends much on accuracy of plot).

calculating

$$\left(\frac{L}{V}\right)_{min} = \frac{x_D - y_c}{x_D - x_c}$$

$$= \frac{.95 - .774}{.95 - .59} = 0.49$$

Actual Operating Line

Operating reflux ratio $= (1.5)\,(L/D) = 1.5(0.956) = 1.432$ reflux/product

Slope of actual operating line:

$$\frac{L}{V} = \frac{L/D}{L/D + 1} = \frac{1.432}{1.432 + 1} = 0.59$$

Graphically, read 13 steps or theoretical plates from the top plate through bottom reboiler (assuming a total condenser).

rectifying section	= 5
feed plate	= 1
stripping section	= 7 (includes reboiler)
	13 Plates including reboiler.

To calculate this stepwise:

Operating line of rectifying section:

$$y_{n+1} = \frac{L_r}{V_r} x_n + \frac{D_{xD}}{V_r}$$

$L/V = 0.59$

$L/D = 1.432$, $D = 50$ mols product

$L = (50)\ 1.432 = 71.6$ mols liquid reflux

$V_r = L_r + D = 71.6 + 50 = 121.6$ mols

then: $y_{n+1} = 0.59\ x_n + 50\ (.95)/121.6$

$y_{n+1} = 0.59\ x_n + 0.39$, operating line equation

At top: $y_{n+1} = x_D = 0.95$

So: From equilibrium curve at $y_{n+1} = 0.95$, read the liquid in equilibrium, which is x_n (or top plate in this case) $x_n = x_{top} = 0.88$.

Now substitute this value $x = 0.88$ into the equation and calculate the vapor coming up from the first plate below the top $(t - 1)$. Thus, if $x_n =$ top plate, $y_{n+1} =$ vapor from plate below top. Now, read equilibrium curve at $y_{(t-1)}$ and get $x_{(n+1)}$ or x_{t-1} which is liquid on plate below top. Then using x_{t-1}, calculate y_{t-2} (second plate below top, etc.). Then, read equilibrium curve to get corresponding liquid x_{t-2}. Continue until feed plate composition is reached, then switch to equation of stripping section and continue as before until desired bottoms composition is reached.

Operating line of stripping section:

$$y_m = \frac{L_s\ x_{m+1}}{V_s} - \frac{B_{xB}}{V_s}$$

Since the feed is a super cooled liquid, L_s/V_s is *not* equal to L_r/V_r. From definition of "q":

$$L_s = L_r + qF$$

$$L_s = 71.6 + (1.5)\ (100)$$

$$L_s = 221.6$$

Also: $$\frac{V_r - V_s}{F} = 1 - q$$

$$\frac{121.6 - V_s}{100} = 1 - 1.5$$

$$121.6 - V_s = -50$$

$$V_s = 171.6$$

So: $$\frac{L_s}{V_s} = \frac{221.6}{171.6} = 1.29$$

$$\frac{B}{V_s} = \frac{50}{171.6} = 0.291$$

Stripping section operating line:

$$y_m = 1.29\ x_{m+1} - 0.291\ x_B$$

$$x_B = 0.05$$

$$y_m = 1.29\ x_{m+1} - 0.01455$$

Use this equation as described above following down from the feed plate cross-over from the rectifying equation to the stripping equation.

B. For q = 0

This represents feed as all vapor (not superheated). Slope of "q" line:

$$= \frac{-q}{1-q} = \frac{-0}{1-0} = 0$$

This represents no change in overflow from the feed plate, and the increase in vapor flow is equal to the mols of feed.

$$\text{Minimum reflux:} \left(\frac{L}{D}\right)_{min} = \frac{x_D - y_c}{y_c - x_c},$$

where: $x_D = 0.95$

$\left.\begin{array}{l} y_c = 0.50 \\ x_c = 0.29 \end{array}\right\}$ read from graph

$$= \frac{0.95 - 0.50}{0.50 - 0.29}$$

$$= 2.14\ \text{Min. Reflux Ratio, Reflux/Product}$$

Slope of operating line at minimum reflux:

$$\left(\frac{L}{V}\right)_{min} = \frac{L/D}{L/D + 1} = \frac{2.14}{2.14 + 1} = 0.682$$

Slope from graph $= 0.688$

Operating reflux ratio $= (1.5)\ (2.14) = 3.21$, Reflux/Product, $(L/D)_{op.}$

Slope of operating line $= (L/V)_{op.} = 3.21/(3.21 + 1) = 0.763$

No. of theoretical plates from graph $= 11$

No. plates rectifying section $= 5$

feed plate $= 1$

stripping section $= 5$ (includes reboiler)

total $= 11$ (includes reboiler)

Rectifying Section Equation for Operating Line:

$$y_{n+1} = \frac{L_r}{V_r} x_n + \frac{D_{xD}}{V_r}$$

$L/V = 0.763$

$L/D = 3.21$

$L = (3.21)\ (50\ \text{Mol product, D}) = 160.6$ mols, (Reflux liquid)

$V_r = L_r + D = 160.6 + 50$

$V_r = 210.6$ mols vapor up column

then: $y_{n+1} = 0.763\ x_n + \frac{50}{210.6}\ (0.95)$

$y_{n+1} = 0.763\ x_n + 0.225$

Liquid down Stripping Section:

$$L_s = L_r + qF$$
$$L_s = 160.6 + (0) \ (100 \text{ mols feed})$$
$$L_s = 160.6 = L_r$$

Vapor up Stripping Section:

$$\frac{V_r - V_s}{F} = 1 - q$$
$$\frac{210.6 - V_s}{100} = 1 - 0$$
$$210.6 - V_s = 100$$
$$V_s = 110.6 \text{ mols}$$

Stripping Section Equation for Operating Line

$$y_m = \frac{L_s}{V_s} x_{m+1} - \frac{B}{V_s} x_B$$
$$y_m = \frac{160.6}{110.6} x_{m+1} - \frac{50}{110.6} (0.05)$$
$$y_m = 1.452 \ x_{m+1} - 0.0226$$

Use these equations as described for the (a) part of problem in solving for number of theoretical plates stepwise.

C. For q = —1.5

This represents feed as a superheated vapor, and there is a decrease in liquid overflow from feed plate.

Slope of "q" line $= \dfrac{-q}{1-q} = \dfrac{-(-1.5)}{1-(-1.5)} = 0.60$

Minimum Reflux: $(L/D)_{min} = \dfrac{x_D - y_c}{y_c - x_c}$

where: $x_D = 0.95$

$\left.\begin{array}{l} y_c = 0.277 \\ x_c = 0.138 \end{array}\right\}$ read from graph

$$= \frac{.95 - .277}{.277 - .138}$$

$(L/D)_{min} = 4.84 \text{ Reflux/Product.}$

Slope of operating line at Min. Reflux:

$$(L/V)_{min} = \frac{L/D}{L/D + 1} = \frac{4.84}{4.84 + 1}$$
$$= 0.830 \text{ (graph reads 0.844)}$$

Actual Operating Line:

Operating reflux ratio $= (1.5) \ (4.84) = 7.26 \text{ Reflux/Product.}$

Slope of actual operating line $= (L/V) = \dfrac{7.26}{7.25 + 1} = 0.879$

Graphically we read *8.5* total plates thru bottom reboiler.

rectifying section	= 5
feed plate	= 1
stripping section	= 2.5 (includes reboiler)
total	= 8.5 (includes reboiler)

Equations for Stepwise Tray to Tray Calculations Rectifying Section Operating Line

$$y_{n+1} = \frac{L_r}{V_r} x_n + \frac{D_{xD}}{V_r}$$
$$L_r/V_r = 0.879$$

$L/D = 7.26$
$L_r = (7.26) \ (50) = 363 \text{ mols liquid reflux}$
$V_r = L_r + D = 363 + 50 = 413$

$$y_{n+1} = 0.879 \ x_n + \frac{50}{413} (0.95)$$
$$y_{n+1} = 0.879 \ x_n + 0.115$$

Liquid down Stripping Section:

$$L_s = L_r + qF$$
$$L_s = 363 + (-1.5) \ (100) = 213 \text{ mols liquid}$$

Vapor up Stripping Section:

$$\frac{V_r - V_s}{F} = 1 - q$$
$$\frac{413 - V_s}{100} = 1 - (-1.5) = 2.5$$
$$-V_s = 250 - 413$$
$$V_s = 163 \text{ mols vapor}$$

Stripping Section Operating Line:

$$y_m = \frac{L_s}{V_s} x_{m+1} - \frac{B}{V_s} x_B$$
$$y_m = \frac{213}{163} x_{m+1} = \frac{50}{163} (.05)$$
$$y_m = 1.307 \ x_{m+1} - 0.01535$$

Use these equations as described for Part (a) in solving for theoretical plates.

Example 8-3: Minimum Theoretical Trays at Total Reflux

A finishing column is required to produce 99.9 percent (vol.) trichlorethylene purity from 10,000 Lbs./hour of a feed of 40 percent (wt.) trichlorethylene and 60 percent (wt.) perchlorethylene. Only 1 percent (vol.) of the trichlorethylene can be accepted in the bottoms.

Since the process system which will receive vents from this condensing system is operating at 5 psig, allow 5 psi pressure drop to insure positive venting and set top of tower pressure at 10 psig.

Feed (158° F.)	(1) Wt. %	(2) Mol. Wt.	(1) (2) Mols.	Mol Fraction
Trichlorethylene	40	131.4	0.00304	0.456
Perchlorethylene	60	165.9	0.00362	0.544
	100		0.00666	1.000

Avg. mol. wt. 1.00/.00666 = 150.0

Overhead

Overhead temperature for essentially pure products at 10 psig = 223° F. from vapor pressure curve.

Bottoms

Allow 10 psi tower pressure drop, this makes bottom pressure = 20 psig = 1800 mm Hg.

Material Balance:

$$\text{Feed rate: mols/hr.} = \frac{10,000 \text{ lbs./hr.}}{(150.0)} = 66.7$$

$$x_1 F = x_1 D + x_1 B$$
$$0.456(66.7) = 0.999\ D + 0.01\ B$$
$$30.4 = .999\ D + .01\ (66.7 - D)$$
$$D = 30.05 \text{ mols/hr.}$$
$$\text{bottoms: } B = F - D$$
$$B = 66.7 - 30.05 = 36.65 \text{ mols/hr.}$$

Bottoms Composition:	Mol Fraction	Mols/hr.	V. P. (316 F.) mm Hg	V. P. Frac.
Trichlor	0.01	0.3665	4200	42
Perchlor	0.99	36.2835	1780	1762
	1.00	36.65		1804 mm

The 1804 mm compares to the balance value of 1800 mm ≅ 20 psig.

Overhead Composition	Mol Fraction	Mols/Hr.
Trichlor	0.999	30.02
	0.001	0.03
	1.000	

Relative Volatility: overhead conditions

$$\frac{\alpha \text{ tri/per}}{(223° F)} = \frac{\text{v.p. (tri)}}{\text{v.p. (per)}} = \frac{1280 \text{ mm}}{385 \text{ mm}} = 3.32$$

Bottom Conditions

$$\frac{\alpha \text{ tri/per}}{(316° F)} = \frac{\text{v.p. (tri)}}{\text{v.p. (per)}} = \frac{4200}{1780} = 2.36$$

$$\text{mean } \alpha \atop \text{top/bottom} = \sqrt{(3.32)(2.36)} = 2.80$$

Thermal Condition of the Feed at 158° F.

At conditions of feed tray, assume pressure is 15 psig ≅ 1533 mm Hg. Determine bubble point:

Component	x_{iF}	assume t= 266 F. v.p. mm Hg	Partial Press. x(v.p.)
Trichlor	0.456	2350	1072
Perchlor	0.544	880	478
			1550

This is close enough to 1533 mm; actual temperature might be 265° F., although, plotted data is probably not that accurate. Since the feed enters at 158° F., and its bubble point is 266° F., the feed is considered sub-cooled.

Heat to vaporize one mol of feed,

Component	x_{iF}	Latent Ht. @ 266° F.	$(x_F)(L_v)$	Btu/Mol (°F.) Cp @ 158° F.	$(x_F)(C_p)$ (266-158)
Trichlor	0.456	12,280 Btu/Mol	5600	30.9	1523
Perchlor	0.544	14,600 Btu/Mol	7950	36.4	2180
		13550 Btu/Mol			3703 Btu/Mol

$$q = \frac{\text{heat required to vaporize one mol of feed}}{\text{latent heat of one mol of feed}}$$

$$q = \frac{13,550 + 3703}{13,550} = \frac{17,253}{13,550} = 1.272$$

Minimum Number Tray at Total Reflux

$$x_{Dl} = 0.999$$
$$x_{Dh} = 0.001$$
$$x_{Bl} = 0.01$$
$$x_{Bh} = 0.99$$
$$\alpha_{Avg} = 2.8$$

For a total condenser system:

$$(N_{Min} + 1) = \frac{\log(x_{Dl}/x_{Dh})\ (x_{Bh}/x_{Bl})}{\log \alpha_{Avg.}}$$

$$= \frac{\log(.999/.001)\ (.99/.01)}{\log 2.8}$$

$$N_{Min} + 1 = 11.18$$
$$N_{Min} = 10.18 \text{ Trays, not including reboiler}$$

Summary:

Min. total physical trays in column	= 10.18
Reboiler	1.0
For conservative design, add feed tray	1.0
Minimum total theoretical stages	12.18, Say 12

Minimum Reflux Ratio

Since this is not feed at its boiling point, but subcooled liquid, the convenient charts cannot be used with accuracy. Using Underwood's general case:

$$\frac{(L/D)(x_{lF}) + q\, x_{lD}}{(L/D)(1 - x_{lF}) + q(1 - x_{lD})}$$

$$= \frac{\alpha\{[(L/D)+1]y_{lF} + (q-1)(x_{lD})\}}{[(L/D)+1](1-x_{lF}) + (q-1)(1-x_{lD})}$$

Solve first for y_{lF}, assuming that the system follows the ideal (as it closely does in this instance).

$$y_{lF} = \frac{x_{lF}(\alpha_F)}{1 + (\alpha_F - 1)x_{lF}}$$

This takes the place of drawing the equilbrium curve and solving graphically, and is only necessary since the "q" is not 1.0 or zero.

The α should be for the feed tray. However, the value of $\alpha = 2.8$ should be accepted for *feed tray* conditions (not 158° F.). It would not be if this were predominantly a rectifying or a stripping operation.

$$y_{lF} = \frac{0.456\,(2.8)}{1 + (2.8 - 1)(0.456)} = 0.70$$

Now, substituting to solve for $(L/D)_{min}$.
$$\frac{(L/D)(0.456) + 1.272(0.999)}{(L/D)(1 - 0.456) + 1.272(1 - 0.999)}$$

$$= \frac{2.8\{[(L/D)+1]\,0.70 + (1.272 - 1)(0.999)\}}{((L/D)+1)(1 - 0.456) + (1.272 - 1)(1 - 0.999)}$$

$$\frac{(L/D)(0.456) + 1.271}{L/D\,(0.544) + 0.00127} = \frac{2.8[(L/D)(0.70) + 0.70 + 0.271]}{(L/D)(0.544) + 0.544 + 0.000271}$$

Solving this quadratic:

$$(L/D)_{Min} = 0.644$$

Reading Figure 8-12 for $(L/D)_{Min}$ *assuming* a liquid feed at the boiling point, $(L/D)_{Min} = 1.2$. This demonstrates the value of taking the thermal condition of the feed into account.

Actually, any point on one of the curves represents a condition of reflux and number of trays that will perform the required separation.

Theoretical Trays at Actual Reflux:

Assume actual reflux ratios of 1.2, 1.8, 2.25, 3.0 times the minimum and plot the effect on theoretical plates using Gilliland plot.

Actual Reflux Ratio	$\dfrac{(L/D)-(L/D)_{Min}}{L/D + 1}$	(From Fig. 8-14 $\dfrac{N-N_{Min}}{N + 1}$	N (Theo.)	Conservative Add 1 For Feed, Total N
0.772	0.0722	0.552	26.2	27
1.16	0.239	0.416	19.8	21
1.45	0.329	0.356	17.9	19
1.93	0.439	0.288	16.1	17

$$\frac{(L/D) - (L/D)_{Min}}{(L/D) + 1} = \frac{0.772 - 0.644}{0.772 + 1} = 0.0722$$

Read value from curve Figure 8-14.

$$\frac{N - N_{Min}}{N + 1} = 0.552$$

$$\frac{N - 11.18}{N + 1} = 0.552$$

$$N = 26.2$$

Note that these values for theoretical trays *do not* contain corrections in overall efficiency, and hence *are not* the *actual* trays for the binary distillation column. Efficiencies generally run 50-60 percent for systems of this type which will yield a column of actual trays almost twice the theoretical at the operating reflux.

Figure 8-17 presents the usual determination of *optimum* or *near* optium theoretical trays at actual reflux based on performance. It is not necessarily the point of least cost for all operating costs, fabrication costs or types of trays. A cost study should be made to determine the merits of moving to one side or other of the so-called optimum point. From the Figure 8-17.

First choice actual reflux ratio, L/D = 1.33

Corresponding theoretical trays or stages, N = 18.6

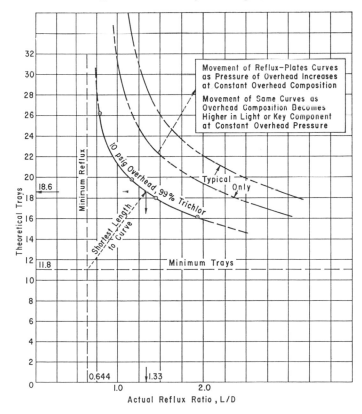

Figure 8-17. Relationship of reflux ratio and theoretical trays.

Note that the 18.6 includes the reboiler, so physical trays in column = 17.6. Do not round-off decimal or fractions of trays until after efficiency has been included.

Tray Efficiency

Base at average column temperature of $(158 + 266)/2 = 212°$ F.

Component	x_{iF}	Viscosity, cp	$(\mu)(x_i)$
Trichlor	0.456	0.27	0.123
Perchlor	0.544	0.36	0.196
			0.319 cp.

From Figure 8-18;

$$\text{Efficiency} = 47.5\%$$

Actual Trays at Actual Reflux

Actual L/D = 1.33

Actual trays = 18.6/0.475 = 39.2 (including reboiler)

Physical trays: 39.2 — 1 (reboiler) + 1 (conservative, feed) = 39.2

Round-off to: 40 trays plus reboiler plus total condenser.

Note: If there is any reason to know that the efficiency of this system is usually lower (or in same chemical family), then either the efficiency should be reduced to account for this or the trays should have an additional allowance. In practice, this same column might be installed as 40 trays in one plant, 45 in another and 50 in another.

Tray Details

Tray details will be considered in a later example.

Tray Efficiency

Several empirical efficiency correlations have been developed from commercial equipment and some laboratory data and serve the majority of design problems for the average hydrocarbon and chemical systems. They are empirical correlations and the application in new systems is unpredictable. For this reason results for efficiencies are evaluated by more than one method to obtain some idea of the possible spread. Even so, in the light of the AIChE study discussed below, some of these empirical methods can be off by 15-50 percent. Comparisions indicate these deviations are usually on the safe or low side. The relation of Drickamer and Bradford[16] of Figure 8-18 has been found to agree quite well for hydrocarbon, chlorinated hydrocarbons, glycols, glycerine and related compounds, and some rich hydrocarbon absorbers and strippers.

The relation of O'Connell[49] (Figure 8-18) has generally also given good results for the same systems but generally the values are high. The absorber correlation of O'Connell (Figure 8-18) should be used as long as it generally gives lower values than the other two relations. It can be used for stripping of gases from rich oils provided care is exercised to not accept too high values.

The area of absorption and stripping is difficult to correlate for the wide range of peculiarities of such systems. The correlation of Gautreaux and O'Connell[22] allows a qualitative handling of tray mixing to be considered with overall and local efficiencies. In general it agrees with the Drickamer correlation at least for towers to seven feet in diameter. Although the effect of liquid path apparently needs to be considered, the wide variety of tray and cap designs makes this only generally possible, and the overall correlations appear to serve adequately.

The American Institute of Chemical Engineer's Distillation Tray Efficiency Research[2] program has produced a method more detailed than the short-cut methods, and correspondingly is believed to produce reliable results. This method produces information on tray efficiencies of new systems without experimental data. At present there is not enough experience with the method and its results to evaluate its complete range of application.

Differential Distillation; Simple Batch, No Trays, Binary Mixtures

For systems of high (above approximately 3.0) constant relative volatility the Raleigh equation can be expressed:

$$\ln \frac{B_{T1}}{B_{To}} = \frac{1}{\alpha - 1} \ln \frac{(1-x_o)x_1}{(1-x_1)x_o} + \ln \frac{(1-x_o)}{(1-x_1)}$$

$$\text{or: } \ln \frac{B_{T1}}{B_{To}} = \int_{x_o}^{x_1} \frac{d_x}{y^* - x} \tag{8-19}$$

where: B_{To} = total moles liquid in bottom of still at start, T_o

B_{T1} = total moles liquid in bottom of still at time, T_1

x_o = mol fraction of component, i, in bottoms B_{To} at start, time T_o

x_1 = mol fraction of component, i, bottoms B_T, at time, T

α = Relative volatility of light to heavy components

y^* = Equilibrium value of x_i

The results of either relation allow the plotting of an instantaneous vapor composition for given percents of material taken overhead.

The outline of Teller[70] suggests using the differential form above.

1. Calculate or obtain an x-y equilibrium diagram for the light component.

2. Plot x versus 1/y-x.

3. Determine area under curve between the starting x_o and any selected value in the bottoms at any later time, x_1.

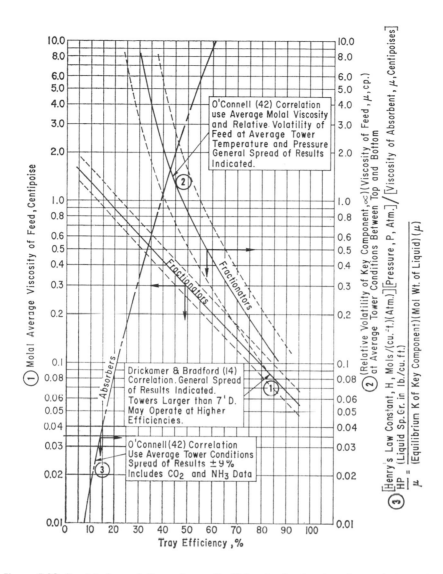

Figure 8-18. Empirical correlations of overall efficiencies for fractionation and absorption.

4. This area of each interval is equal to $\ln\left(\dfrac{B_{To}}{B_{T1}}\right)$

5. For each value of x, and the values of (B_{To}/B_{T1}) found above, calculate $\dfrac{(B_{To} - B_{T1})}{B_{To}}$ (100), the percent of material taken overhead.

6. A plot of the distillate composition, y versus Percent Distilled (from (5)) will show the value of the instantaneous vapor composition.

Example 8-4: Binary Batch Distillation

Dimethyl either is to be separated from methanol. A batch type operation is to be tried to see if an existing coil-in-tank can be used. The pressure of the system will be about 55 psia. How many total mols will remain in the bottoms when the bottoms liquid composition contains 0.5 mol percent dimethyl ether? What is the composition of the total overhead collected?

Component	Initial Charge		At 104° F Vap. press. psia	$K = P/\pi$	$y^* = Kx$
	Mols	Mol Fraction			
Dimethyl ether..	61	0.427	125.0	2.27	0.97
Methanol.......	82	0.573	5.1	0.093	0.05
	143	1.000			$\Sigma = 1.02$

Initial boiling point of mixture = 104° F.

$$\ln \frac{B_{T1}}{B_{To}} = \frac{1}{\alpha - 1} \ln \frac{(1 - x_o)x_1}{(1 - x_1)(x_o)} + \ln \frac{(1 - x_o)}{1 - x_1}$$

$$B_{To} = 143 \text{ mols}$$

$$x_o = 0.427$$

$$x_1 = 0.005$$

$$\alpha = 125/5.1 = 24.5$$

$$\ln \frac{B_{T1}}{143} = \frac{1}{24.5 - 1} \ln \frac{(1 - 0.427)(0.005)}{(1 - .005)(.427)} + \ln \frac{(1 - 0.427)}{(1 - 0.005)}$$

$$= 0.0426 \ln \frac{.00286}{.425} + \ln \frac{0.573}{0.995}$$

$$= 0.0426 \ln 148.5 - \ln 1.73$$

$$= 0.0426 (\ln 1.485 + \ln 100) - \ln 1.73$$

$$= -0.0426 (0.395 + 4.605) - 0.548$$

$$\ln \frac{B_{T1}}{143} = -0.761$$

$$\ln \frac{143}{B_{T1}} = 0.761$$

$B_{T1} = 143/2.14 = 67$ mols remaining in bottom when dimethyl ether is 0.5 mol percent.

Total vapor collected overhead $= 143 - 67 = 76$ mols

Mols dimethyl ether in bottoms $= 0.005 (67) = 0.335$

Mols dimethyl ether overhead $= 61 - 0.335 = 60.665$

Composition of total overhead collected:

Dimethyl ether $= \frac{60.665}{76.0} (100) = 79.82$

Methanol $= 100.0 - 79.82 = 20.18\%$

Differential Distillation—Simple Batch, without Trays, Multicomponent Mixture

For multicomponent systems, the relation of the system can be expressed using the relative volatility:

$$B_i = B_{io} \left(\frac{B_b}{B_{bo}} \right)^{\alpha_i} \qquad (8\text{-}20)$$

where: $B_i = $ mols of component, i, after a given time of distillation

$B_{io} = $ mols of component, i, at start of distillation

$B_b = $ mols of component, b, used as reference for volatility after a given time of distillation

$B_{bo} = $ mols of component, b, used as reference for volatility, at start of distillation.

Knowing the amount of components present at the beginning, the quantity remaining after the distillation can be calculated.

Example 8-5: Multicomponent Batch Distillation

A mixture of hydrocarbons at 80 psia is to be differentially distilled until the mols of propane is reduced to 10 mols per 100 mols of bottom feed material. A kettle with bottom coil is to be used, and no trays.

Material in kettle at start of distillation:

Component	Mol Fraction
C_2H_6	0.10
C_3H_8	0.25
$N - C_4H_{10}$	0.35
$i - C_4H_{10}$	0.30
	1.00

Basis: 100 mols of bottoms feed

Bubble Point of Initial Charge

Component	x_i Mol. Fract	@ 50° F K_i	$y = k_x$	Assumed 105°, K_i	α_i 50° K_i/K_p	α 105 K_i/K_p	α Avg
C_2H_6	0.10	4.5	0.45	7.2	3.81	3.28	3.54
C_3H_8	0.25	1.18	0.295	2.2	1.0	1.0	1.0
$n\text{-}C_4H_{10}$	0.35	0.33	0.115	0.75	0.28	0.341	0.310
$i\text{-}C_4H_{10}$	0.30	0.48	0.144	1.0	0.407	0.454	0.430
	1.00			1.004 O.K.			

Note: K values at 80 psia from *Natural Gasoline Supply Man's Assoc. Data Book, 1957.*[48]

Propane is reference material.

$$\alpha_{i 50}° = \frac{K_i}{K_{propane}} = \frac{4.5}{1.18} = 3.81$$

$$\alpha_{i 105}° = \frac{K_i}{K_{propane}} = \frac{7.2}{2.2} = 3.28$$

$$B(\text{Total}) = \Sigma B_i = \Sigma B_{io} \left(\frac{B_b}{B_{bo}} \right)^{\alpha_i}$$

$$B(\text{ethane}) = (10) \left(\frac{10}{25} \right)^{3.54} = \frac{10}{25.6} = 0.39 \text{ mols in bottoms}$$

Component	B_i	Final Bottoms x_i	Vapor Press. at 105°, P_i	$p_i = P_i x_i$
C_2H_6	0.39	0.00686	840 psia	5.75
C_3H_8	10.00	0.176	200	35.2
$n\text{-}C_4H_{10}$	26.30	0.463	57	26.4
$i\text{-}C_4H_{10}$	20.20	0.355	78	27.6
	56.89	1.000		94.9 (Too high, assume lower temperature and recalculate)

$x_i = 0.39/56.89 = 0.00686$

Vapor pressure from N. K. Rector chart in Reference.[48]

Second Try

Component	Initial x_i	α_i 50°	Assume 95°, K_i	$\alpha 95$ K_i/K_p	α Avg.
C_2H_6............	0.10	3.81	6.7	3.35	3.58
C_3H_8............	0.25	1.0	2.0	1.0	1.0
$n\text{-}C_4H_{10}$.........	0.35	0.28	0.67	0.335	0.307
$i\text{-}C_4H_{10}$.........	0.30	0.407	0.92	0.46	0.432

Component	Final B_i	Vapor Press @ 95° P_i	Final x_i	$\Sigma\, p_i = P_i x_i$
C_2H_6......................	0.378	750	0.0066	4.8
C_3H_8......................	10.0	174	0.175	30.4
$n\text{-}C_4H_{10}$...................	26.4	47	0.464	21.8
$i\text{-}C_4H_{10}$....................	20.2	67	0.354	23.7
	56.97			80.7 psia

Therefore the final temperature should be close to 95° F., since 80.7 psia compares satisfactorily with the operating pressure of 80 psia.

Total mols of bottoms remaining at end: 56.9 mols liquid

Total mols vaporized = $100 - 56.9 = 43.1$

Liquid composition mol fraction is given in column "Final x_i," and corresponds to the actual mols B_i, noting that there are the required 10 mols of propane in the bottoms under these conditions.

Steam Distillation—Continuous Flash, Multicomponent or Binary

This system requires direct steam injection into the still with the liquid, all the steam leaves overhead with the boiled-up vapors (no internal condensation) in a steady-state operation, system at its dew-point. Steam is assumed immiscible with the organics. Steam distillation is usually applied in systems of high boiling organics, or heat sensitive materials which require separation at vacuum conditions.

$$\frac{M_s}{B_{To}} = \frac{\pi}{P_b B_{To}}\left[\sum \frac{B_{io}}{\alpha_i}\right]_{i\neq s} - 1 \qquad (8\text{-}21)$$

b is more volatile reference component.

$i\neq s$ = components, i, are not to include steam, s.

M_s = total mols steams required

B_{To} = total mols hydrocarbons at start (not including the steam)

B_{io} = mols of component, i, at start

α_i = relative volatility of more volatile to each of other components

P_b = vapor pressure of reference more volatile component, b.

π = total system pressure, absolute

Example 8-6: Multicomponent Steam Flash

A mixture of bottoms material of composition B_{io} below has accumulated in the run-down tank. It is necessary to separate the volatile organic heavies from the tarry polymerized residue (heavy liquid). Steam is to be injected into the insulated tank containing heating coils. The system is to operate at 200 mm. Hg. absolute pressure and 250° F. with no condensation of the steam. The organic volatile heavies contain:

Component	Vapor Pressure @ 250° F.	$\alpha = P_i/P_A$	Mols B_{io}	B_{io}/α_i
A.........	35 mm Hg	1.0	45	45
B.........	20	0.57	40	70
C.........	6	0.171	26	152
			111 mols	267

$$\frac{M_s}{B_{To}} = \frac{\pi}{P_b B_{To}}\left[\sum \frac{B_{io}}{\alpha_i}\right] - 1$$

$$\frac{M_s}{111} = \frac{200}{35(111)}[267] - 1$$

$$= 13.75 - 1 = 12.75$$

$M_s = 1417$ total mols steam required for 111 mols mixture

Mols steam/mol of mixture organic volatiles = $1417/111 = 12.8$

Steam Distillation—Continuous Differential, Multicomponent or Binary

The results of the differential distillation end the same as the flash distillation, although the mechanism is somewhat different. This is a batch type operation distilling differentially. All sensible and latent heat are supplied separately from the steam or by superheat in the steam. Steam acts as an inert in the vapor phase, and quantity will vary as the distillation proceeds, while temperature and pressure are maintained.

$$\frac{M_s}{B_{T1}-B_{To}} = 1 - \frac{\pi}{P_b(B_{T1}-B_{To})}\left[\sum \frac{B_{io}}{\alpha_i}\left[\left(\frac{B_b}{B_{bo}}\right)^{\alpha_i}-1\right]\right] \qquad (8\text{-}22)$$

If all the volatile materials are distilled: $\left(\dfrac{B_b}{B_{bo}}\right)=0$

and $B_{T1}=0$

This relation is handled very similar to the flash steam separation.

If all of the material is not to be removed as overhead vapors from the still, leave a percentage of a particular compound in the bottoms, then select the particular compound as the reference material "b" for α determinations.

$$B_b = (\text{Fraction retained})\,(B_{bo})$$

$$\text{and}\ \left(\frac{B_b}{B_{bo}}\right) = (\text{Fraction retained})$$

substitute and solve for B_{Ti}.

$$B_{T1} = \sum_{i \neq s} B_{io}\left(\frac{B_b}{B_{bo}}\right)^{\alpha_i} \qquad (8\text{-}23)$$

Knowing B_{T1}, the relation for M_s can be solved to determine mols of steam to reduce initial material to percentage of a compound in the remaining bottoms. If steam condenses, the requirement for steam increases by this amount.

Steam Distillation—Continuous Flash, Two Liquid Phases, Multicomponent and Binary

Since water will be present in this system, and is assumed immiscible with the other components, it will exert its own vapor pressure. This situation is similar to many systems where the liquid to be flashed enters below its dew point, and hence requires the use of steam to heat (sensible + latent) as well as steam for the partial pressure effect.

Mols steam in vapor phase only:

$$M_s\ (\text{vapor}) = P_s \sum \frac{B_{io}}{P_i}\ (\text{at assumed flash temperature})$$

where: $P_s =$ vapor pressure of steam

$P_i =$ vapor pressure of each component at the flash temperature

Mols steam to heat is sum of sensible plus latent.

Total mols steam is sum of M_s (vapor) plus heating steam. System total pressure:

$$\pi = \frac{M_s + B_{To}}{\displaystyle\sum_{i \neq s} \frac{B_{io}}{P_i}},\ \text{absolute} \qquad (8\text{-}24)$$

$B_{To} =$ mols (total) volatile material at start

Batch Distillation With Fractionation Trays—Constant Overhead Product Composition, Multicomponent and Binary

The method of Bogart[4] is useful in this case. The basic relation is:

$$\theta = \frac{B_{To}\,(x_{1D} - x_{1B})}{V} \int_{x_B}^{x_F} \frac{dx}{(1 - L/V)\,(x_{1D} - x_{1B})^2} \qquad (8\text{-}25)$$

Application may be (1) to determine a column diameter and number of plates or (2) to take an existing column and assume a operating reflux for the fixed trays and determine the time to separate a desired cut or product.

where: $\theta =$ time from start when given L/V will produce constant overhead composition, x_{1D}

$B_{To} =$ mols total batch charge to still

$V =$ total mols per hour vapor overhead

$x_{1D} =$ mol fraction light key component in overhead product

$x_{1B} =$ mol fraction light key component in original charge

Suggested procedure for situation (2) above: using existing column:

1. Calculate minimum number of plates and minimum reflux ratio

   (a) For multicomponent mixture, select key components, light and heavy

   (b) Calculate relative volatility, α_i, referenced to heavy key component, at top and bottom temperatures, and determine geometric average α.

   (c) Calculate minimum theoretical plates at total reflux by Fenske's equation (8-10).

   (d) Use Gilliland correlation to determine actual reflux ratio, using an *estimated* number of actual plates, and a minimum reflux ratio from:

   $$(L/D)_{min} = \left(\frac{1}{\alpha - 1}\right)\left[\left(\frac{x_{1D}}{x_{1B}}\right) - \alpha\left(\frac{x_{hD}}{x_{hB}}\right)\right]$$

   (e) Calculate:

   $$\text{Internal } (L/V) = \frac{L/D}{L/D + 1}$$

2. Set up table: Keep x_{1D} values constant

**Assumed "x_1" values	(L/V)	(1 — L/V)	$(x_{1D} - x_1{}^*)$	A	B
x (Bottoms)	.	.	.	.	.
x_2	.	.	.	.	.
x_3	.	.	.	.	.
:	.	.	.	.	.
x (Feed)	.	.	.	.	.

$$A = (1 - L/V)\,(x_{1D} - x_1{}^*)^2$$

$$B = \frac{1}{(1 - L/V)\,(x_{1D} - x_1{}^*)^2}$$

**Assume "x_1" values of bottoms compositions of light key for approximate equal increments from final bottoms to initial feed charge. Calculate L/V values corresponding to the assumed "x_1" values by inserting the various "x_1" values in the Fenske equation for minimum reflux ratio of 1-(d). The "x_1" values replace the x_{1B} of this relation as the various assumptions are calculated. The actual (L/D) are calculated as in 1-(d) keeping the minimum number of trays constant. Complete the table values.

* = assumed values

3. Plot $\dfrac{1}{(1 - L/V)\,(x_{1D} - x_1{}^*)^2}$ vs $(x_1)^*$

The total area, ΣA, under the curve may be obtained in several ways; the rectangular or trapezoidal rules are generally quite satisfactory. The area concerned is between the original feed and the final bottoms composition for the particular component.

4. Time required for a batch

$$\theta = B_{T_0} \frac{(x_{1D} - x_{iB})}{V} (\Sigma A)$$

V is an assumed or known value, based on reboiler capacity.

5. Plot of reflux quantity versus time.

From the L/D values of 1-(e), knowing the L/V, using V assumed as constant, calculate the necessity reflux fluid, L. Figure 8-19 indicates a plot of time to produce a constant product composition and the necessary external reflux returned to the tower.

The batch distillation of a binary is somewhat simplified, as L/V values can be assumed, and since there is only enrichment of the overhead involved, only one operating line is used per operating condition. Theoretical trays can be stepped off and x_{iB} values read to correspond. The plots involved are the same as described above.

Open Live Steam Distillation—With Fractionation Trays, Binary

Open or direct injection of steam into a distillation system at the bottom may be used to heat the mixture as well as to reduce the effective partial pressure of the other materials. In general, if steam is used to replace a reboiler, one tray is added to replace the reboiler stage, and from one-third to one or more trays may be needed to offset the dilution of the system with water in the lower portion. Of course, where steam is acceptable, it replaces the cost of a reboiler and any cleaning associated with this equipment. For most columns, quite a few trays can be purchased to offset this cost.

When one of the components of the binary is water, and steam is used, the following equation is used for the operating stripping line (there is no rectifying section):
For component not including water:

$$V_s y_{i\,(m)} = L_s x_{i\,(m+1)} - B x_{iB}$$

Slope of operating line $(L/V)_m = B/S$

Operating line intersects the x-axis at x_{iB}.

The step-off of trays starts at x_{iB} on the x-axis, y $= 0$.

Open steam is used for stripping of dissolved or absorbed gases from an absorption oil, with all of the steam going overhead, and the stripped oil leaving at the bottom. This absorption coefficient of the oil for the component must be known in order to construct the equilibrium curve. The operating curve is constructed from several point material balances around the desired component, omitting the oil as long as its volatility is very low. The trays can be stepped off from a plot of y vs. x as in other binary distillations, again using only the stripping section.

Distillation With Heat Balance

This type of evaluation of a distillation system involves a material and heat balance around each tray. It is extremely tedious to do by conventional means, and is now handled with digital computers. But even with this untiring worker, the amount of calculations is large and require relatively long time. Only those special systems which defy a reasonable and apparently economical solution by other approaches are even considered for this type of solution.

The detailed method involves trial and error assumptions on both the material balance as well as the heat balance.

Unequal Molal Overflow

This is another way of expressing that the heat load from tray to tray is varying in the column to such an extent as to make the usual simplifying assumption of equal molal overflow invalid. The relations to follow do not include heats of mixing. In general they apply to most hydrocarbon systems.

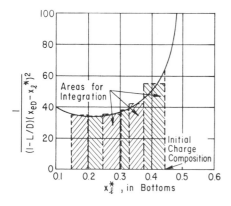

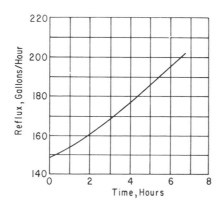

Figure 8-19. Batch distillation with trays; constant overhead product.

(1) Equation of operating line in rectifying section, light component.[59]

$$L_{n+1} = V_n - D$$

$$y_n = \left(\frac{M_D - H_n}{M_D - h_{n+1}}\right) x_{n+1} + \left(\frac{H_n - h_{n+1}}{M_D - h_{n+1}}\right) x_D$$

$$\frac{L_{n+1}}{V_n} = \frac{M_D - H_n}{M_D - h_{n+1}} = 1 - \frac{H_n - h_{n+1}}{M_D - h_{n+1}} \qquad (8\text{-}26)$$

(2) Equation of operating line in stripping section, light component

$$L_{m+1} = V_m + B$$

$$y_m = \left(\frac{M_B - H_m}{M_B - h_{m+1}}\right) x_{m+1} + \left(\frac{H_m - h_{m+1}}{M_B - h_{m+1}}\right) x_B$$

$$\frac{L_{m+1}}{V_m} = 1 - \frac{H_m - h_{m+1}}{M_B - h_{m+1}} \qquad (8\text{-}27)$$

where: $M_B = h_B - Q_B/B$

$M_D = Q_c/D + h_D$

H_n = total molal enthalpy of vapor at conditions of plate n, $H_n = \Sigma H_{ni} (y_{ni})$

h_n = total molal enthalpy of liquid at conditions of plate n, $h_n = \Sigma h_{ni} (x_{ni})$

s = lbs. (or mols) steam per lb. (or mol) bottoms.

Ponchon-Savarit Method—Binary Mixtures

This graphical method allows solution of many distillation systems which would require considerable work if attempted by rigorous methods. Robinson and Gilliland have technical and descriptive details substantiating the method.[8, 59] Figure 8-20 presents a summary of the use of this method and appropriate interpretations.

The basic method allows the non-ideal heat effects of the system to be considered as they affect the plate-to-plate performance. The systems as represented in the diagrams are usually at constant pressure, but this is not necessarily the case. The equilibrium tie lines connect points fixed by the x-y values to corresponding saturated liquid and saturated vapor conditions at a constant temperature, such as "a" °F. or "b" °F. The mol fractions are obtained from the usual x-y diagram for the system, and the enthalpy values are relative to a fixed datum for the available heat data of the particular components. For such systems as ammonia-water and ethanol-water the data are readily available. The saturated liquid line represents the enthalpies of liquid mixtures at the various compositions all at a constant pressure. This is the bubble point curve. The dew point curve is produced by plotting the enthalpies of the various vapor mixtures at the saturation temperature at a constant pressure.

An effort has been made to present the basic understanding of the method as it applies to systems involving

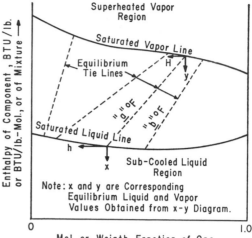

Figure 8-20A

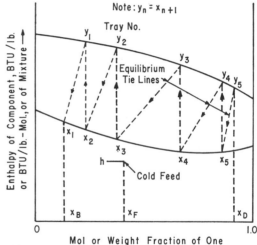

Figure 8-20B

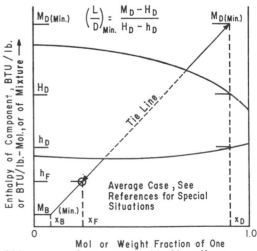

Figure 8-20C

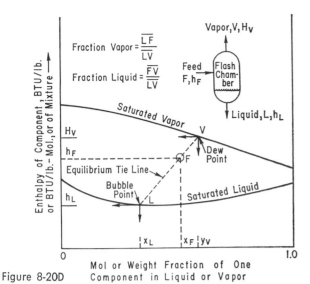

Figure 8-20D

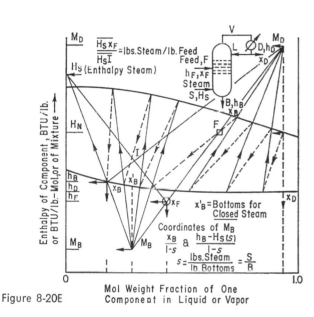

Figure 8-20E

Figure 8-20. Performance analysis of unequal modal overflow for binary system. (Parts A, B, C, D, E.)

unequal molal overflow, open steam distillation and single flash vaporization in Figures 8-20 and 8-21.

In order to obtain extreme or even necessary accuracy for some design conditions, the end portions of the graphi-cal representation may require enlargement from the usual size for graphical plotting. In most cases a size of 11 x 17 inches is suggested.

Example 8-7: Ponchon Unequal Molal Overflow

An ammonia-water recirculating solution of 62 weight percent is to be stripped of the ammonia for recovery by condensation at 260 psia with river water cooling. The overhead ammonia product is to be at least 99.5 weight percent and the bottoms should approach 0.05 weight percent ammonia. The feed enters as a liquid at its boiling point, with an enthalpy of 42 BTU/lb.

Enthalpy Diagram

Prepared by reading the h and H values from the Jennings and Shannon Aqua-Ammonia Tables[35] at 260 psia and various weight percents of ammonia in the liquid. The tie lines connect the vapor compositions with the equilibrium liquid values, Figure 8-22.

Vapor-Liquid Equilibrium Diagram

Prepared from corresponding x and y values in reference[35], at 260 psia, Figure 8-23.

Number of Trays

$x_F = 0.62$ weight fraction ammonia

$x_D = 0.995$ weight fraction ammonia

$x_B = 0.0005$ weight fraction ammonia

1. Minimum Reflux

$$\left(\frac{L}{D}\right)_{min} = \frac{(M_D)_{min} - H_D}{H_D - h_D}$$

From enthalpy-composition diagram:

$H_D = 590$ BTU/lb.

$h_D = 92$ BTU/lb. (assuming no subcooling)

$(M_D)_{min} = 596$ BTU/lb.

$(M_D)_{min}$ is determined by reading the equilibrium y value corresponding to the feed composition 0.62 from the x-y diagram, noting it on the enthalpy diagram on the saturated vapor curve, and connecting the tie line, then extending it on to intersect with the x_D ordinate 0.995, reading $(M_D)_{min} = 596$ BTU/lb.

$$(L/D)_{min} = \frac{596 - 590}{590 - 92} = 0.012$$

2. Operating reflux ratio, L/D

Select $(L/D)_{actual} = 10(L/D)_{min} = 10(0.012) = 0.12$

This is not unusual to select an operating reflux ratio ten, or even fifty times such a low minimum. Selecting a

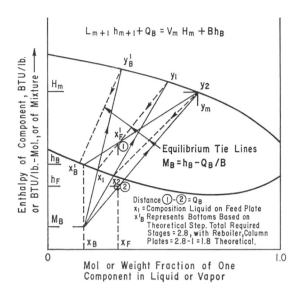

Figure 8-21A

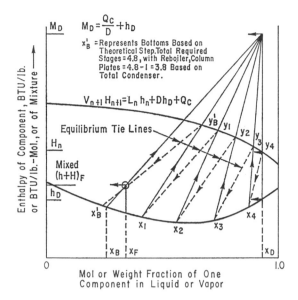

Figure 8-21B

Figure 8-21. Graphical solution of unequal molal overflow; binary system. (Part A above, parts B and C in next column.)

higher reflux can reduce the number of trays required, and this becomes a balance of the reduction in trays versus operating and capital expense in handling the increased liquid both external to the column and internally.

3. Operating M_D

$$(L/D)_{act.} = 0.12 = \frac{M_D - 590}{590 - 92}$$

$$M_D = 649.8 \text{ BTU/lb.}$$

Locate this value on the diagram and connect it to the feed point, x_F. Extend this line to intersect the bottoms condition ordinate (extended), x_B. In this case it is impossible to represent the value, $x = 0.005$, accurately, but construct it as close as possible to the required condition. M_B is now located. Improvement of this accuracy will be shown later in the problem.

Following the procedures shown in Figures 8-21, 8-22, and 8-23, the trays are constructed from the top or overhead down toward the bottom. The x values are read to correspond to the y values constructed. This establishes the tie line. When the x value tie line points (representing the trays) cross the feed ordinate, the construction is shifted from using the point M_D to the point M_B. Note that only 1½ theoretical trays are required above the feed, since this is predominantly a stripping type operation. The number of theoretical trays or stages which can be easily plotted is six to seven counting down from the top. The

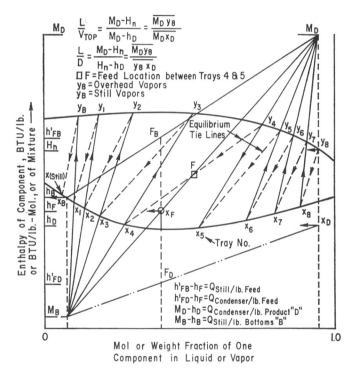

Figure 8-21C

sixth tray is too inaccurate to use graphically. Instead of calculating the balance of the trays assuming a straight line equilibrium curve from tray seven to the end, the plot could be enlarged in this area and the trays stepped off. By reference to the x-y diagram it can be seen that the equilibrium line from $x = 0.02$ to $x = 0$ is straight.

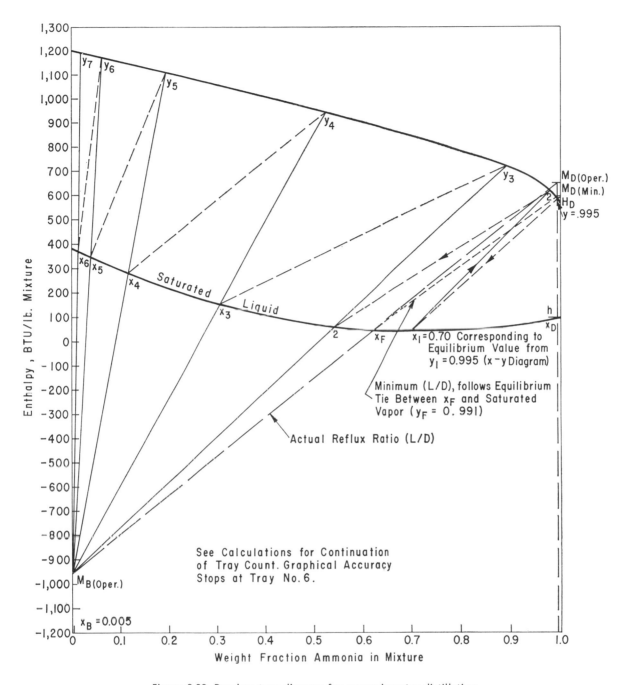

Figure 8-22. Ponchon type diagram for ammonia-water distillation.

For the condition of straight operating and equilibrium curves, the number of plates can be calculated including the "reference" plate (number seven in this case):[59]

$$N_B = \frac{\ln\left[\dfrac{[(VK/L)-1][(x_m/x_{1B})-1]}{(V/L)(K-1)}+1\right]}{\ln\,VK/L}$$ (8-28)

where: N_B = number of trays from tray m to bottom tray, but not including the still or reboiler.

x_m = tray liquid mol fraction for start of calculations (most volatile component).

x_{1B} = mol fraction most volatile component in bottoms.

For the lower end of the equilibrium curve.

$y_m = 5.0\,x_m$ (by slope calculation of x-y diagram)

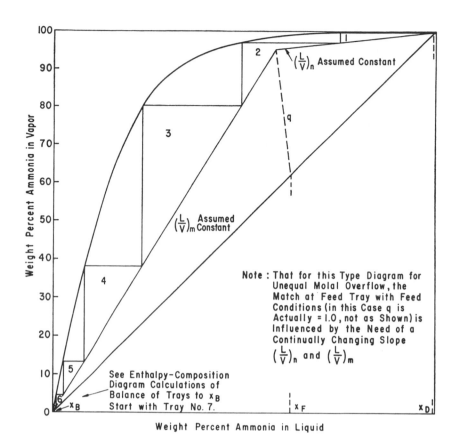

Figure 8-23. McCabe-Thiele diagram for ammonia-water system.

For the stripping section: consider top seven trays, vapor entering tray No. 6, $y_7 = 0.02$. m = tray 7, m + 1 = tray 6, reading from diagram,

$$(L/V)_m = 1 - \frac{H_m - h_{m+1}}{M_B - h_{m+1}} = 1 - \frac{(1190 - 369)}{-960 - 369} = 1.618$$

use: $H_m = 1190$

$h_{m+1} = 369$

$M_B = -960$

$x_7 = \frac{y_7}{5.0} = \frac{0.02 \text{ (from graph)}}{5.0} = 0.004$

$$N_B = \frac{\ln \left[\frac{(5.0/1.618 - 1)\ 0.004/0.0005 - 1)}{(1/1.618)\ (5.0 - 1)} + 1 \right]}{\ln 5/1.618}$$

$N_B = 1.71$ trays (theoretical) not including reboiler, but including tray number 7, the one used as reference.

Total trays = 7 (from diagram plus $(1.71 - 1) = 7.7$ theoretical, plus a reboiler, on 8.7 including a reboiler.

Tray efficiency is calculated as previously demonstrated and will not be repeated, except, that normally stripping tray efficiencies run lower than rectification efficiencies. For ammonia-water stripping such as this example most over-all efficiencies run 50-60 percent.

Note that if the problem of accurate graphical representation occurs in the rectification end of the diagram, the corresponding relation to use to calculate the balance of the trays, assuming straight line operating and equilibrium lines in the region is:[59]

Rectifying section:

$$N_n = \frac{\ln \left[\frac{(1 - L/V) + x'_n/y'_D(L/V - K')}{1 - K'} \right]}{\ln L/K'V} - 1$$

(8-29)

where: $K' =$ equilibrium constant for the *least* volatile component, $K' = y/x$

$N_n =$ number of plates above (but not including) reference plate n.

$y', x' =$ mol fractions *least* volatile component.

Multicomponent Distillation

The basic background and understanding of binary distillation applies to a large measure in multicomponent problems. Reference should be made to Figure 8-1 for the symbols.

Multicomponent distillations are more complicated than binary systems due primarily to the actual or potential involvement or interaction of one or more components of the multicomponent system on other components of

the mixture. These interactions may be in the form of vapor-liquid equilibriums such as azeotrope formation, or chemical reaction, etc., any of which may affect the activity relations, and hence deviations from ideal relationships. For example, some systems are known to have two azeotrope combinations in the distillation column. Sometimes these, one or all, can be "broken" or changed in the vapor pressure relationships by addition of a third chemical or hydrocarbon.

To properly handle the changing composition relationships it is almost essential to utilize some electronic computer techniques if good accuracy is to be achieved. Even three component systems become tedious using desk size electronic calculators without significant internal memory. The large computers can be well programmed to handle the complexities of trial and check for convergence to a preset acceptable limit.

Techniques for convergence of the digital computer program are often the heart of an efficient multicomponent calculation. There are several techniques incorporated into many programs.[07, 76]

Key Components

The two components in a feed mixture whose separations will be specified.

1. Adjacent keys: key components that are adjacent with respect to their volatilities.

2. Split keys: key components that are separated in volatilities by a non-key component, i.e., the system of components contains one or more whose volatilities fall between the volatilities of the designated keys.

3. Light key: the designation of the key component with the highest volatility of the two key components.

4. Heavy key: the designation of the key component with the lowest volatility of the two key components.

5. Example: component Designations

Component	Relative Volatility $\alpha_{l/h}$ — 7° F. and 550 psia	Designation
Hydrogen	11.7	Lighter than Key
Methene	3.7, α_l	*Light Key,* l
Ethylene	1.0, α_h	*Heavy Key,* h
Ethane	0.72	Heavier than Key
Propylene	0.23	Heavier than Key
Propane	0.19	Heavier than Key

Minimum Reflux Ratio—Infinite Plates

This is the smallest value of external reflux ratio (L/D) which can be used to obtain a specified separation. This is not an operable condition. Knowledge of the minimum reflux ratio aids considerably in establishing an economical and practical operating ratio. Ratios of 1.2 to 2.0 times the minimum are often in the economical range for hydro-

carbon chemical systems. However, it is well to recognize that high reflux rates increase column size, (but reduce number of trays required) reboiler size, steam rate, condenser size and coolant rate.

For adjacent key systems, all components lighter than the light key appear only in the overhead, and all components heavier than the heavy key appear only in the bottoms, and the keys each appear in the overhead and bottoms in accordance with specifications.

For a split key system the lights and heavies distribute the same as for adjacent key systems. However, the component(s) between the keys also distribute to overhead and bottoms.

At minimum reflux, the regions in which the number of trays approaches infinity (called the pinch zones and region of constant compositions) are:

1. Binary system: pinch zone adjacent to feed plate

2. Multicomponent:

a. Three components with no component lighter than light key: pinch zone in stripping section adjacent to feed plate.

b. Three components with no component heavier than heavy key: pinch zone in rectifying section adjacent to feed plate.

c. Three components mixture: pinch zones may be above and below feed plate.

d. Greater than four components: pinch zones appear in rectifying and stripping sections.

Algebraic Plate-to-Plate Method

Like any plate-to-plate calculation this is tedious, and in most instances does not justify the time since shorter methods give reasonably acceptable results. VanWinkle[75] outlines the steps necessary for such calculations.

Underwood Algebraic Method: Adjacent Key Systems[72]

This system for evaluating multicomponent adjacent key systems, assuming constant relative volatility and constant molal overflow, has proven generally satisfactory for many chemical and hydrocarbon applications. It gives a rigorous solution for constant molal overflow and volatility, and acceptable results for most cases which deviate from these limitations.

Over-all Column — Constant α

$$(L/D)_{min} + 1 = \frac{(\alpha_a x_a)_D}{\alpha_a - \Theta} + \frac{(\alpha_b x_b)_D}{\alpha_b - \Theta} + \cdots \frac{(\alpha_l x_l)_D}{\alpha_l - \Theta} \tag{8-30}$$

In arriving at $(L/D)_{min}$ the correct value of Θ is obtained from:

$$1 - q = \frac{(\alpha_a x_a)_F}{\alpha_a - \Theta} + \frac{(\alpha_b x_b)_F}{\alpha_b - \Theta} + \cdots \frac{(\alpha_l x_l)_F}{\alpha_l - \Theta} = \sum \frac{x_{Fi}}{1 - \Theta/\alpha_i} \tag{8-31}$$

The "q" value is the same as previously described for the thermal condition of the feed.

Rectifying section only:

$$V_r = \sum_{i=1,h,L} \frac{Dx_{Di}}{1 - \Theta/\alpha_i} \qquad (8\text{-}32)$$

Stripping section only:

$$V_s = \sum_{i=1,h,H} \frac{Bx_{Bi}}{1 - \Theta/\alpha_i} \qquad (8\text{-}33)$$

At the minimum reflux condition all the Θ values are equal, and generally related:

$$\alpha_h < \Theta < \alpha_l$$

Suggested Procedure:

1. From equation 8-31 expressing Θ and q evaluate Θ by trial and error, noting that Θ will have a value between the α of the heavy key and the α of the light key evaluated at or near pinch temperatures, or at α avg. Suggested tabulation, starting with an assumed Θ value, Θ_a:

Component	x_{Fi}	$\alpha_i \, x_{Fi}$	$\alpha_i - \Theta$	$\alpha_i \, x_{Fi}/(\alpha_i - \Theta)$	$\alpha_i \, x_{Fi}/(\alpha_i - \Theta)^2$
a	x_{Fa}	$\alpha_a \, x_{Fa}$	$\alpha_a - \Theta_a$	$\alpha_a \, x_{Fa}/(\alpha_a - \Theta_a)$	$\alpha_a \, x_{Fa}/(\alpha_a - \Theta_a)^2$
b	x_{Fb}	$\alpha_b \, x_{Fb}$	$\alpha_b - \Theta_a$	$\alpha_b \, x_{Fb}/(\alpha_b - \Theta_a)$	$\alpha_b \, x_{Fb}/(\alpha_b - \Theta_a)^2$
.	.	.	.	.	.
.	.	.	.	.	.
				$\Sigma\,\Psi\,(\Theta_a)$	$\Sigma\,\Psi'\,(\Theta_a)$

Ψ, Ψ', represents function.

Corrected Θ by Newton's approximation method:

$$\Theta_c = \Theta \text{ (assumed)} - \frac{\Psi\,(\Theta_a)}{\Psi'\,(\Theta_a)}$$

Repeat the same type of tabular computation, substituting the corrected Θ_c for the Θ_a. If the second corrected Θ'_c checks closely with Θ_c, the value of Θ has been obtained, if not, a third recalculation should be made using the Θ'_c value as the new assumed value.

Note that average α values should be used (constant) for each component unless the values vary considerably through the column. In this later case follow the discussion given elsewhere in this section.

2. Calculate $(L/D)_{min}$ by substituting the final Θ value in Equation 8-30 solving for $(L/D)_{min}$. Note that this requires evaluating the functions associated with Θ at the composition of the distillate product. The α values are the constant values previously used above.

Underwood Algebraic Method: Adjacent Key Systems; Variable α

For varying α systems, the following procedure is suggested:

1. Assume $(L/D)_{min}$ and determine the pinch temperature by Colburn's method.

2. At this temperature, evaluate α at pinch and α at overhead temperature, obtaining a geometric average α. As an alternate, Shiras[63] indicates a $t_{avg.}$ value which gives acceptable results when compared to pinch and stepwise calculations. This suggestion calculates,

$$t_{avg.} = (Dt_o + Bt_B)/F$$

3. Determine Underwood's Θ value as previously described, using the average α value.

4. Calculate $(L/D)_{min}$ and compare with assumed value of (1) above. If check is satisfactory, $(L/D)_{min}$ is complete; if not, reassume new $(L/D)_{min}$ using calculated value as basis, and repeat (1) through (4) until satisfactory check is obtained.

where: t_o = overhead temp. °F, t_B = bottoms temp. °F.

$t_{avg.}$ = avg. temp., °F.

Underwood Algebraic Method: Split Key Systems: Constant Volatility[72]

Although this method appears tedious, it is not so unwieldy as to be impractical. It does require close attention to detail. However, a value of $(L/D)_{min}$ can be obtained with one trial that may be satisfactory for "order of magnitude" use, which is quite often what is desired before proceeding with detailed column design and establishment of operating L/D

1. Assume Θ_t values and check by

$$\sum \frac{\alpha_i \, x_{Fi}}{\alpha_i - \Theta_{ti}} = 1 - q \qquad (8\text{-}34)$$

There are a total solutions of Θ_{ti} equal to one more than the number of split components between the keys. The Θ_t values will be spaced:

$$\alpha_{l3} \quad \Theta_{t3} \quad \alpha_4 \quad \Theta_{t4} \quad \alpha_5 \quad \Theta_{t5} \quad \alpha_{h6}$$

where α_l is the light key and component number 3, and correspondingly for the heavy key, component number 6. Determine Θ values as for constant volatility case of adjacent keys.

For some systems, the Θ values can be assumed without further solution of the above relation, but using these assumed values as below.

2. Calculate,

$$v = \frac{\displaystyle\frac{1}{(P)\,(\Theta_{ti})}\Big|_{i=h-1}}{1 + \displaystyle\frac{1}{(P)\,(\alpha_i)}\Big|_{i=h-1}} \qquad (8\text{-}35)$$

which represents (for the hypothetical system set up in (1)) the product of (Θ_{t5}) (Θ_{t4}) (Θ_{t3}) divided by the product of (α_5) (α_4), based upon the lightest component being numbered one, the next two, etc., the heaviest components having the higher numbered subscripts. $\overline{P}$ means product, and l, i = h — 1, i = 1 + 1 are limits for evaluation referring to components between the keys, and the light and heavy keys.

3. Calculate,

$$\omega_j = \frac{\dfrac{1+1}{\overline{(P)}}\left(1 - \dfrac{\alpha_1}{\alpha_j}\right)}{\dfrac{1}{\overline{(P)}}\left(1 - \dfrac{\Theta_{ti}}{\alpha_j}\right)} \qquad (8\text{-}36)$$

$$\underset{i=h-1}{}$$

For the Θ example shown in (1) above:

$$\underset{\text{(light key)}}{\omega_3} = \frac{(1 - \alpha_5/\alpha_3)(1 - \alpha_4/\alpha_3)}{(1 - \Theta_{t5}/\alpha_3)(1 - \Theta_{t4}/\alpha_3)(1 - \Theta_{t3}/\alpha_3)}$$

$$\underset{\text{(heavy key)}}{\omega_6} = \frac{(1 - \alpha_5/\alpha_6)(1 - \alpha_4/\alpha_6)}{(1 - \Theta_{t5}/\alpha_6)(1 - \Theta_{t4}/\alpha_6)(1 - \Theta_{t3}/\alpha_6)}$$

Also calculate ω for all components lighter than light key.

Component, j	ω_j	$\alpha_j \dfrac{\omega_j}{\alpha_j} x_{Dj}$	$\omega_j x_{Dj}$	$\dfrac{\omega_j}{\alpha_j}(x_{Dj})$
l (light key)	·	· · ·	·	·
h (heavy key)	·	· · ·	·	·
L_{l+1} lighter				
L_{l+2} than light	·	· · ·	·	·
L_{l+3} key, etc.			$\Sigma\, \omega_j\, x_{Dj}$	$\Sigma\, \dfrac{\omega_j}{\alpha_j}(x_{Dj})$

4. Calculate $(L/V)_{min}$: (internal)

$$(L/V)_{min} = (v)\frac{\underset{j=h,l,L}{\Sigma}\,D\left(\dfrac{\omega_j}{\alpha_j}\right)(x_{Dj})}{\underset{j=h,l,L}{\Sigma}\,D\,(\omega_j)\,x_{Dj}} \qquad (8\text{-}37)$$

5. Calculate External $(L/D)_{min}$:

$$(L/D)_{min} = \frac{1}{(V/L)_{min} - 1} \qquad (8\text{-}38)$$

For variable α conditions, the pinch temperature can be used for α determinations as previously described.

Minimum Reflux Colburn Method: Pinch Temperatures[12]

This method has also found wide usage and might be considered less tedious by some designers. It also yields an approximation of the rectifying and stripping section pinch temperatures.

Rectifying:

$$(L/D)_{min} = \frac{1}{\alpha - 1}\left(\frac{x_D}{x_n} - \alpha\,\frac{x_{hD}}{x_{hn}}\right) \qquad (8\text{-}39)$$

where: $\alpha =$ relative volatility of any component referenced to the heavy key component.

$x_{hD} =$ overhead composition of heavy key component, mol frac.

$x_{hn} =$ pinch composition of heavy key component, mol frac.

$x_D =$ overhead composition of any light component, mol frac.

$x_n =$ pinch composition of any light component, mol frac.

1. Calculate D, B, Dx_{D1} and Bx_{B1} from problem specification.

2. Assume or set the operating pressure and overhead temperature (may be calculated).

3. Calculate the liquid and vapor quantities and their respective compositions in the feed to the column.

4. Calculate estimated ratio of key components on feed plate based on the liquid portion of the feed.

$$r_f = \frac{\text{Mol fraction light key}}{\text{Mol fraction heavy key}}$$

(a) For all liquid feed at feed tray temperature (boiling point) $r_f =$ mol fraction ratios in feed.

(b) For a part or all vapor feed just at its dew point, $r_f =$ ratio of key components in the equilibrium liquid phase of feed.

(c) For all liquid feed below feed plate temperature $r_f =$ ratio of key components at intersection point of operating line (from a McCabe-Thiele diagram).

5. Determine approximate pinch zone liquid composition for light key component

$$x_{ln} = \frac{r_f}{(1 + r_f)(1 + \Sigma\alpha_i x_{Fi})_H} \qquad (8\text{-}40)$$

$\Sigma\alpha_i x_{Fi} =$ sum of $\alpha_{h+1} x_{Fh+1} + \alpha_{h+2} x_{Fh+2} + \cdots$ for all components in liquid portion of feed *heavier* than heavy key. Note that x_{Fi} values are the mol fractions of the component in the liquid portion of feed only and the Σx_{Fi} equal to 1.0.

6. Calculate approximate value for $(L/D)_{min}$.

$$(L/D)_{min} = \frac{1}{\alpha_1 - 1}\left(\frac{x_{1D}}{x_{1n}} - \alpha\,\frac{x_{hD}}{x_{hn}}\right)$$

The second term in the right hand parenthesis can be omitted unless the mol fraction of the heavy key in the distillate, x_{hD}, is 0.1 or greater. Use $x_{hn} = x_{1n}/r_f$.

7. Estimate stripping and rectifying pinch temperatures at values one-third and two-thirds of the interval between the column bottoms and overhead respectively.

8. Calculate internal vapor and liquid flows.

$$(L_r/D)_{min} = \text{assumed}$$

Solve for $(L_r/V_r)_{min}$:

$$(L_r/V_r)_{min} = \frac{1}{1 + (D/L_r)_{min}}$$

$$L_r = (\text{number}) \quad (V_r) = (L_r/D)_{min}(D)$$

D is known

Calculate V_r and L_r from above.

In stripping section:

Solve directly for L_s.

$$L_s = L_r + qF$$

Solve for V_s:

$$\frac{V_r - V_s}{F} = 1 - q$$

Calculate L_s/B

9. Evaluate pinch compositions at the assumed temperatures of Step 7. If this temperature does not give a balance, other temperatures should be assumed and a balance sought as indicated below. Either of the following balances can be used, depending upon the convenience of the designer:

Rectifying:

$$\sum x_{pr_i} = \sum x_n = \sum_{i = h, l, L'} \left(\frac{Dx_{Di}/V_r}{\alpha_i \ K_h - L_r/V_r} \right) = 1 \quad (8\text{-}41)$$

$$\text{or} \quad \sum x_n = \sum_{i = h, l, L'} \left(\frac{Dx_{Di}/V_r}{K_i - L_r/V_r} \right) = 1$$

$$\text{or} \quad \sum x_n = \sum_{i = h, l, L'} \frac{x_{Di}}{(\alpha_i - 1)(L_r/D)_{Min.} + \alpha_i \ x_{hDi}/x_{hn}} = 1$$

When the heavy key in the overhead is very small, less than 0.1 mol fraction, the last term of the denominator can be omitted.

$$\text{or} \quad \sum x_n = \sum_{i = h, l, L'} \frac{x_{Di}}{K_i + (K_i - 1)(L_r/D)_{Min.}} = 1$$

Note that the calculations are only made for the heavy key, h; light key, 1; and all components lighter than it, L'. If there are split keys, the calculation is to include all components lighter than the heavy key.

Stripping pinch compositions:

$$\sum x_{ps_i} = \sum x_m = \sum_{i = H, h, l} \frac{Bx_{Bi}/V_s}{\dfrac{L_s}{V_s} - \alpha_i K_h} = 1 \quad (8\text{-}42)$$

$$\text{or} \quad \sum x_m = \sum_{i = H, h, l} \frac{Bx_{Bi}/V_s}{\dfrac{L_s}{V_s} - K_i} = 1$$

$$\text{or} \quad \sum x_m = \sum_{i = H, h, l} \frac{\alpha_i \ x_{Bi}}{(\alpha_i - \alpha_i)(L_s/B)_{Min.} + \alpha_i x_{iB}/x_{ip}} = 1$$

Since the second term of the denominator is usually negligible when the light key in the bottoms is very small, less than 0.1 mol fraction, this term is often omitted.

$$\text{or} \quad \sum x_m = \sum_{i = H, h, l} \frac{x_{Bi}}{K_i + (1 - K_i)(L_s/B)_{Min.}} = 1$$

Note that these calculations are made for the light key, 1; heavy key, h; and all components heavier than the heavy key, H. For split key systems, the calculations are made for all components heavier than the light key.

10. Calculate mol fraction ratio:

   (a) Stripping pinch

$$r_{ps} = \frac{\text{light key}}{\text{heavy key}}$$

   (b) Rectifying pinch

$$r_{pr} = \frac{\text{light key}}{\text{heavy key}}$$

   (c) $p = r_{ps}/r_{pr}$

11. Calculate for each component in pinch.

Rectifying: apply only to components lighter than light key, $i = L'$

$$\frac{(\alpha_1 - 1)\alpha_1}{\alpha_1}$$

Read from Figure 8-24, value of C_{n_i} for each component.

Calculate for each component:

$$(C_{n_i}) \ (x_{i_{pr}})$$

Sum these values:

$$\sum_{i = L'} C_{ni} \ x_{ip}$$

Stripping: apply only to components heavier than heavy key, $i = H$.

$$(\alpha_1 - 1) \ (\alpha_i)$$

Read from Figure 8-24, value of C_{m_i} for each component.

Calculate for each component:

$$C_{m_i} \ \alpha_i \ x_{i_{ps}}$$

Sum these values:

$$\sum_{i = H} C_{mi} \ \alpha_i \ x_{ips}$$

12. Calculate:

$$p' = \frac{1}{[1 - \Sigma \ C_n \ x_{ipr}] \ [1 - \Sigma \ C_m \ \alpha_i \ x_{ips}]} \quad (8\text{-}43)$$

If the two values of p are not very nearly equal, this requires a retrial with a new $(L/D)_{min}$, and a follow through of the steps above.

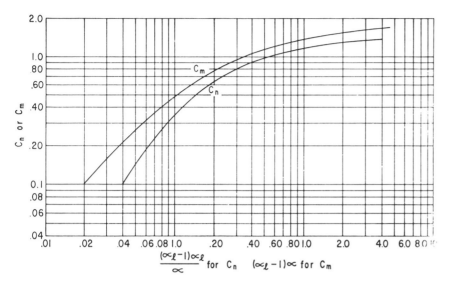

Figure 8-24. Colburn minimum reflux factors, above (C_n) and below (C_m) feed point. (By permission A. P. Colburn, Trans. Amer. Inst. Ch. Engrs., Vol. 37, p 805 (1941).)

When $r_{ps}/r_{pr} > p'$; the assumed $(L/D)_{min}$ is too high. Note that r_{ps}/r_{pr} changes rapidly with small changes in $(L/D)_{min}$. p' changes slightly. When $p = p'$, the proper $(L/D)_{min}$ has been found. Colburn reports the method accurate to one percent. It is convenient to graph the assumed $(L/D)_{min}$ versus p and p' in order to facilitate the selection of the correct $(L/D)_{min}$.

Scheibel-Montross Empirical: Adjacent Key Systems: Constant or Variable Volatility[61]

Although this method has not found as much wide acceptance when referenced to use by designers or controversial discussion in the literature, it nevertheless allows a direct approximate solution of the average multicomponent system with accuracy of 1-8 percent average. If the key components are less than 10 percent of the feed, the accuracy is probably considerably less than indicated. If a split key system is considered, Scheibel reports fair accuracy when the split components going overhead are estimated and combined with the light key, the balance considered with the heavy key in the L/D relation.

$$(L/D)_{Min.} = \frac{1}{x_{lF} + \Sigma x_{FL}}\left[x_{lF} R' + (x_{hF} + \Sigma x_{FH})\Sigma \frac{\frac{x_{FH}}{\alpha_l}}{\frac{\alpha_l}{\alpha_H} - 1} + \Sigma \frac{x_{FL}}{\alpha_L}\left(1 + \frac{\alpha_l}{\alpha_L}\right) \right] \quad (8\text{-}44)$$

where: x_{lF} = mol fraction of light key in feed
Σx_{FL} = sum of all mol fractions lighter than light key in feed
R' = pseudo minimum reflux
Σx_{FH} = sum of all mol fractions heavier than heavy key in feed
x_{hF} = mol fraction heavy key in feed.

α_l = relative volatility of light key to heavy key at feed tray temperature.

α_H = relative volatility of components heavier than heavy key at feed tray temperature.

α_L = relative volatility of components lighter than light key at feed tray temperature.

x_{lt} = mol fraction liquid at intersection of operating lines at minimum reflux. (Calculated or from graph).

x_{lo} = mol fraction light key in overhead expressed as fraction of total *keys* in overhead.

Pseudo minimum reflux:

$$R' = \frac{x_{lo}}{(\alpha_l - 1)x_l} - \frac{(1 - x_l)(\alpha_l - 1)}{(1 - x_{lo})\alpha_l}$$

When the overhead contains only a very small amount of heavy key, the second term in the equation may be neglected.

Intersection of operating lines at Equilibrium Curve:

$$x_{lt} = \frac{\left[(\alpha_l - 1)(1 + m)\left(\frac{x_{lF}}{x_{lF} + x_{hF}}\right) - \alpha_l - m \pm \sqrt{\left\{ \left[(\alpha_l - 1)(1 + m)\left(\frac{x_{lF}}{x_{lF} + x_{hF}}\right) - \alpha_l - m \right]^2 + 4m(\alpha_l - 1)(1 + m)\left(\frac{x_{lF}}{x_{lF} + x_{hF}}\right) \right\}} \right]}{2m(\alpha_l - 1)}$$

$$(8\text{-}45)$$

The proper value for x_{lt} is positive and between zero and one. Actually this is fairly straight forward and looks more difficult to handle than is actually the case.

Pseudo ratio of liquid to vapor in feed:

$$m = \frac{x_L - \Sigma x_{FH}}{x_v - \Sigma x_{FL}} = \frac{F_L - \Sigma F_H}{F_v - \Sigma F_L}$$

where: x_L = mol fraction of feed as liquid

x_v = mol fraction of feed as vapor

F_L = mols of liquid feed

F_v = mols of vapor feed

ΣF_H = total mols of components heavier than heavy key in feed

ΣF_L = total mol of components lighter than light key in feed.

Example: 8-8 Scheibel-Montross Minimum Reflux, (from Ref. 61. A tower has the following all liquid feed composition:

Component	Feed Mols/hr.	Overhead Mols/hr.	Bottoms Mols/hr.
A	30	30.0	—
B (light key)	20	19.5	0.5
C (heavy key)	20	0.5	19.5
D	30	—	30.0
	100	50.0	50.0

Relative volatilities referenced to the heavy key, C:

$$\alpha_A = 4.0$$
$$\alpha_B = 2.0 = \alpha_l$$
$$\alpha_C = 1.0 = \alpha_h$$
$$\alpha_D = 0.5$$

Calculate: $m = \dfrac{x_L - \Sigma x_{FH}}{x_v - \Sigma x_{FL}} = \dfrac{1.0 - 0.30}{0 - 0.30} = -2.33$

Intersection of Operating Lines:

$$x_{it} = \frac{(2-1)(1-2.33)\left(\dfrac{0.2}{0.2+0.2}\right) - 2 - (-2.33) \pm}{\sqrt{\left\{ \begin{array}{l} \left[(2-1)(1-2.33)\left(\dfrac{0.2}{0.2+0.2}\right) - 2 - (-2.33)\right]^2 \\ + 4(-2.33)(2-1)(1-2.33)\left(\dfrac{0.2}{0.2+0.2}\right) \end{array} \right\}}}{2(-2.33)(2-1)}$$

$x_{it} = 0.610$, or -0.459 (not acceptable)

Pseudo minimum reflux ratio:

$$x_{lo} = \frac{19.5}{19.5 + 0.5} = 0.975$$

$$R' = \frac{0.975}{(2-1)(0.610)} - \frac{(1.0 - 0.975)(2)}{(1 - 0.610)(2 - 1)}$$

$$R' = 1.472$$

Minimum reflux ratio:

$(L/D)_{min}$

$$= \frac{1}{0.2 + 0.3}\left[0.2\,(1.472) + (0.2 + 0.3)\left(\frac{0.3}{\frac{2}{0.5} - 1}\right) + \frac{0.3}{4}\left(1 + \frac{2}{4}\right) \right]$$

$(L/D)_{min} = 0.912$

Minimum Number of Trays: Total Reflux—Constant Volatility

The minimum theoretical trays at total reflux can be determined by the Fenske relation as previously given

$$S_m = N_{min} + 1 = \frac{\log\left(\dfrac{x_{Dl}}{x_{Dh}}\right)\left(\dfrac{x_{Bh}}{x_{Bl}}\right)}{\log \alpha_{Avg.}}$$

Note that N_{min} is the number of trays in the column and does not include the reboiler. When α varies considerably through the column, the results will not be accurate using the α avg. as algebraic average, and the geometric means is used in these cases.

$$\alpha_{Avg.} = [(\alpha_t)\,\alpha_b)]^{1/2}$$

For extreme cases it may be necessary to calculate down from the top and up from the bottom until each section shows a fairly uniform temperature gradient from tray to tray. Then the Fenske relation is used for the remaining trays, using the conditions at the trays calculated as the terminal conditions instead of the actual overhead and bottoms.

Theoretical Trays at Operating Reflux

The method of Gilliland,[23] (Figure 8-14) is also used for multicomponent mixtures to determine theoretical trays at a particular operating reflux ratio, or at various ratios.

The Brown and Martin[9] curve of Figure 8-25 is also used in about the same manner, and produces essentially the same results, but is based on internal vapor and liquid flows.

The values needed to use the graph include:

$$(L/V)_r = \frac{1}{1 + (D/L)}$$

where $(D/L) = 1/(L/D)$

$$L_s = L_r + qF$$
$$L_r = (L/D)\,(D_r)$$
$$V_r = (L/D)D_r/(L/V)$$
$$V_s = V_r - F(1 - q)$$

Note that when $(L/D)_{min}$ is used as the starting basis, the L_r, L_s, V_r, V_s and their ratios will be for the minimum condition, and correspondingly so when the operating reflux is used.

Example 8-9: Operating Reflux Ratio

The minimum reflux ratio $(L/D)_{min}$ has been determined to be 1.017. Using the Brown and Martin graph, evaluate the theoretical number of trays at an operating reflux of 1.5 times the minimum. The minimum number of stages was determined to be 22.1 including the reboiler.

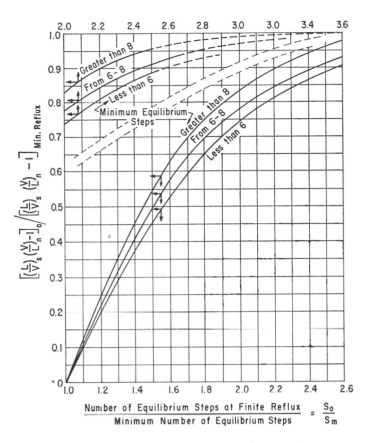

Figure 8-25. Operating reflux and stages correlated with minimum reflux and stages. (Adapted from Van Winkle, M., Oil & Gas Jour. 182, Mar. 23 (1953).

The column will have a total condenser. Product rate D is 0.664 mols/mol feed, and the feed is a boiling point liquid.

Minimum values:

$$\left(\frac{L}{V}\right)_{min} = \frac{1}{1 + (D/L)_{min}} = \frac{1}{1 + 1/1.017} = 0.506$$

$$0.506\, V_r = 1.017 (D_r) = 1.017\,(0.664)$$

$$V_r = 1.332 \text{ mols per mol of feed}$$

$$L_r = 1.017\,(0.664) = 0.674 \text{ mols/mol feed}$$

$$q = 1.0$$

$$L_s = (0.674) + (1)(1) = 1.674 \text{ mols/mol feed}$$

$$V_s = 1.332 - (1)(1-1) = 1.332 \text{ mols/mol feed}$$

$$\left(\frac{L}{V}\right)_s = \frac{1.674}{1.332} = 1.255$$

Operating values:

$$\text{Operating } (L/D)_o = (1.5)(1.017) = 1.525$$

$$\left(\frac{L}{V}\right)_o = \frac{1}{1 + 1/1.525} = 0.603$$

$$V_r = \frac{(1.525)\,(0.664)}{0.603} = 1.68 \text{ mols/mol feed}$$

$$L_r = (1.525)\,(0.664) = 1.013 \text{ mols/mol feed}$$

$$q = 1.0$$

$$L_s = 1.013 + (1)(1) = 2.013$$

$$V_s = 1.68 - (1)(1-1) = 1.68$$

$$(L/V)_s = 2.013/1.68 = 1.198$$

For graph:

$$\left[\left(\frac{L}{V}\right)_s \left(\frac{V}{L}\right)_r - 1\right]_o = 1.198\left(\frac{1}{0.603}\right) - 1 = 0.985$$

$$\left[\left(\frac{L}{V}\right)_s \left(\frac{V}{L}\right)_r - 1\right]_{min} = (1.255)\left(\frac{1}{0.506}\right) - 1 = 1.48$$

Read curve for "greater than 8" minimum equilibrium steps:

$$\text{at } 0.985/1.48 = 0.666$$

$$\text{Curve reads: } S_o/S_M = 1.64$$

Theoretical stages at reflux $(L/D) = 1.525$

$$S_o = S_M\,(1.64) = 22.1\,(1.64)$$

$$S_o = 36.2 \text{ stages}$$

Theoretical trays at the operating reflux $(L/D) = 1.525$;

$$N_o = 36.2 - 1 \text{ (for reboiler)} = 35.2 \text{ trays in column.}$$

Actual Number of Trays

From the theoretical trays at operating reflux the actual trays for installation is determined:

$$N_{Aot.} = N_o/E_o \qquad (8\text{-}46)$$

The reboiler is considered 100 percent efficient, and likewise any partial condenser, if used. Therefore the value N_o represents the *theoretical* trays or stages in the column proper, excluding the reboiler and partial condenser. E_o represents the over-all tray efficiency for the system based upon actual test data of the same or similar systems, or from the plot of Figures 8-18, giving operating information preference (if reliable).

Feed Tray Location

The approximate location can be determined by the ratio of the total number of theoretical stages above and below the feed plate from the Fenske total reflux relation:

$$\frac{S_r}{S_s} = \frac{n+1}{m+1} = \frac{\log\,(x_l/x_h)_D\,(x_h/x_l)_F}{\log\,(x_l/x_h)_F\,(x_h/x_l)_B} \qquad (8\text{-}47)$$

The relation is solved for S_r/S_s. The results are not exact, since the feed tray composition is very seldom the same as the feed; which is the assumption in this relation. Actually the feed point or correct location for the feed may be off by two or three theoretical trays. This will vary with the system. It does mean, however, that when

this approach is used for feed plate location, alternate feed nozzles should be installed on the column to allow for experimental location of the best feed point. These extra nozzles are usually placed on alternate trays (or more) both above and below the calculated location. A minimum of three alternate nozzles should be available.

When the feed point is located by a match from tray-by-tray calculation, the correct point can be established with greater confidence, but still alternate nozzles are suggested since even these detailed calculations can be off to a certain extent.

The actual number of trays in the rectifying section $(N_{Act})_r$ can be determined by:

$$S = S_r + S_s \qquad (8\text{-}48)$$
$$S_M = S_s(S_r/S_s) + S_s$$

Solve for S_s, since S_M and S_r/S_s are known.

Obtain S_r by difference.

$(N_{Act})_r = S_r/E_o$ (for total condenser; if partial condenser use $(S_r - 1)/E_o$

$(N_{Act})_s = (S_s - 1)/E_o$ (for columns with reboilers)

For systems with wide variation in relative volatility, the suggestion of Cicalese, et. al.[9] is often used to evaluate the theoretical total equilibrium stages in the rectifying and stripping sections:

$$S_r = \frac{\log \dfrac{(x_l/x_h)_D}{(x_l/h_h)_F}}{\log \alpha \text{ (average above feed)}} \qquad (8\text{-}49)$$

$$S_s = \frac{\log \dfrac{(x_l/h_h)_F}{(x_l/x_h)_B}}{\log \alpha \text{ (average below feed)}} \qquad (8\text{-}50)$$

Tray-by-Tray

Rigorous tray-by-tray computations for multicomponent mixtures of more than three components can be very tedious, even when made omitting a heat balance. Electronic digital computers are quite adaptable to this detail and several computation methods are in use.

The direct-solution method of Akers and Wade[1] is among several which attempt to reduce the amount of trial-and-error solutions. This has been accomplished and has proven quite versatile in application. The adaptation outlined modifies the symbols and rearranges some terms for convenient use by the designer.[3] Dew point and bubble point compositions and the plate temperatures can be determined directly. Constant molal overflow is assumed, and relative volatility is held constant over sections of the column.

Rectifying section: reference component is heavy key, x_h

$$\left(\frac{x_l}{x_h}\right)_n = \frac{1}{\alpha_l}\left[\frac{(L/D)(x_l)_{n+1} + x_{Dl}}{(L/D)(x_h)_{n+1} + x_{Dh}}\right] \qquad (8\text{-}51)$$

$$\Sigma\, x_l = 1.0 \text{ (including } x_h)$$

$$\Sigma\left(\frac{x_l}{x_h}\right)_n = \left(\frac{1}{x_h}\right)_n$$

The compositions of each component are obtained from the $(x_l/x_h)_n$ ratio.

The tray temperature is obtained from:

$$K_h = \frac{1}{\Sigma\, \alpha_l\, x_l} \qquad (8\text{-}52)$$

K_h is evaluated at the column pressure by use of suitable K charts.

Stripping section: reference component is heavy key, x_h, y_h.

$$\left(\frac{y_l}{y_h}\right)_m = \alpha_l\left[\frac{(V_s/B)(y_l)_{m-1} + x_{Bl}}{(V_s/B)(y_h)_{m-1} + x_{Bh}}\right] \qquad (8\text{-}53)$$

$$\Sigma(y_l/y_h)_m = 1.0 \text{ (including } y_b)$$

The composition of each component on a tray is obtained from $(y_l/y_h)_m$.

The tray temperature is obtained from:

$$K_h = \Sigma y_l/\alpha_l \qquad (8\text{-}54)$$

at the column pressure using K charts for the heavy key or reference component.

Procedure:

A. Rectifying Section

1. Determine material balance around column, including reflux L, distillate product D, bottoms product B.

  (a) With total condenser, the reflux composition is equal to the condensed distillate product composition.

  (b) With a partial condenser, the product D is a vapor, so a dew point must be run on its composition to obtain the liquid reflux composition.

2. Determine top tray temperature for use in relative volatility calculations by running a dew point on the overhead vapor. For total condenser its composition is same as distillate product. For a partial condenser, run a dew point on the column overhead vapor composition as determined by a material balance around the partial condenser, reflux and product.

3. Determine $(x_l/x_h)_2$, for tray No. 2 (second from top), for each component, using the x values for the reflux as the initial x_l $(n + 1)$.

4. Total this column to yield $\Sigma(x_l/x_h)$. This equals $1/x_h$.

5. Determine x_i for each component by:

$$x_i = \frac{(x_i/x_h)}{\Sigma(x_i/x_h)} \qquad (8\text{-}55)$$

This is liquid composition on tray.

6. Continue down column using the composition calculated for tray above to substitute in Equation 8-51 to obtain the (x_i/x_h) for the tray below.

7. Test to determine if α is varying to any great extent by calculating $\alpha_i x_i$ for a test tray. $\Sigma \alpha_i x_i = 1/K_h$. Determine temperature and evaluate corresponding values. Use new α_i if significantly different.

8. Continue step-wise calculations until the ratio of light to heavy key on a tray equals (or nearly so) that ratio in the liquid portion of the feed. This is then considered the feed tray.

9. If there are components in the feed and bottoms which do not appear in the overhead product, they must gradually be introduced into the calculations. The estimated position above the feed tray to start introducing these components is determined by:

$$\frac{x_{Fi}}{x_a} = \left[\frac{1}{(1 + D/L)K_i}\right]^{p''} \qquad (8\text{-}56)$$

where: x_{Fi} = mol fraction of a component in feed that does not appear in overhead

x_a = small arbitrary mol fraction in the liquid p'' plates above the feed plate

p'' = number of plates above the feed where introduction of components should begin

B. Stripping Section:

1. Determine bubble point temperature of bottoms and composition of vapor, y_{Bi}, up from liquid. Calculate relative volatility of light to heavy component at this temperature.

2. From these calculate vapor compositions, using Equation 8-53 calculate the ratio (y_i/y_h) for the first tray at the bottom.

3. Total $\Sigma (y_i/y_h)$ to obtain $1/y_h$.

4. Calculate y_i for tray one

$$y_i = \frac{(y_i/y_h)_1}{\Sigma y_i/y_h}, \qquad \qquad \Sigma y_i/y_h = 1/y_h$$

$$\Sigma y_i = 1.0$$

5. Calculate (y_i/y_h) for next tray, using the y_i values of tray one (m-1) in the equation to solve for $(y_i/y_h)_m$.

6. Test to determine if α is varying significantly by $K_h = \Sigma (y_i/\alpha_i)$. Evaluate temperature of heavy component

at the column bottoms pressure (estimated) using K charts or the equivalent. If necessary, calculate new α_i values for each component at the new temperature. Recheck every two or three trays if indicated.

7. Introduce components lighter than the light key which are not found in the bottoms in the same general manner as discussed for the rectifying section.

$$x_{Fi}/x_a = [(1 + D/L)K_i]^{p'} \qquad (8\text{-}57)$$

where p' is the number of trays below the feed tray where the component, i, is introduced in an assumed amount (usually small) x_a. Then x_{Fi} is the mol fraction of the component in the feed.

8. Continue step-wise calculations until ratio of light to heavy keys in the liquid portion of the feed essentially matches the same component ratio in the liquid on one of the trays.

9. The total of theoretical trays in the column is the sum of those obtained from the rectifying calculations, plus those of the stripping calculations, plus one for the feed tray. This does not include the reboiler or partial condenser as trays in the column.

Tray-by-Tray: Using a Digital Computer

Multicomponent distillation is by far the common requirement for process plants and refineries, rather than the simpler binary systems. There are many computer programs which have been developed to aid in accurately handling the many iterative calculations required when the system involves three to possibly ten individual components. In order to properly solve a multicomponent design, there should be both heat and material balance at every theoretical tray throughout the calculation.

To accommodate the step-by-step, recycle and check for convergences requires input of vapor pressure relationships (such as Wilson's, Renon's, etc.) through the previously determined constants, latent heat of vaporization data (equations) for each component, (or enthalpy of liquid and vapor) specific heat data per component, and possibly special solubility or Henry's Law deviations when the system indicates.

There are several valuable references to developing and applying a multicomponent distillation program, including Holland,[26, 27] Prausnitz,[52, 53] Wang and Henke,[76] and Boston and Sullivan.[6] Convergence of the iterative trials to reach a criterion requires careful evaluation. There are several convergence techniques with some requiring considerably less computer running time than others.

Example 8-10: Tray-to-Tray Design Multicomponent Mixture

A column is to be designed to separate the feed given below into an overhead of 99.9 mol percent trichloroethylene. The top of the column will operate at 10 psig. Feed temperature is 158° F.

FEED		Overhead		Bottoms	
Feed	Mol Fraction	Mols	Mol Fraction	Mols	Mol Fraction
(A) Trichloroethylene..........	0.456	0.451	0.999	0.00549	0.010
(B) β Trichloroethane.........	0.0555	0.00045	0.001	0.05505	0.101
(C) Perchloroethylene.........	0.3625	....	.....	0.36250	0.661
(D) Tetras (1).................	0.0625	....	.....	0.0625	0.114
(E) Tetras (2).................	0.0635	....	.....	0.0625	0.114
	1.0000	0.45145	1.000	0.54804	1.000

Note: the material balance for overhead and bottoms is based on:

(a) 99.9 mol % trichlor in O'hd.

(b) 1.0 mol % trichlor in bottoms.

(c) 1.0 mol feed total

(d) Light key = trichloroethylene
Heavy key = β trichloroethane

Determine Overhead Temperature

Since trichlor is 99.9 percent overhead, use it only to select boiling point from vapor pressure curves at 10 psig overhead pressure = 223° F. (1280 mm Hg abs.)

Determine Bottoms Temperature (Bubble Point)

Allowing 10 psig column pressure drop, bottoms pressure = 20 psig (1800 mm Hg abs.)

Component	x_{iB}	Try t = 320° F, Vapor Press. mm Hg	x_1 (vp.)	$(y_i)_B$
A..........	0.01	4500	45	0.0249
B..........	0.101	2475	250	0.1382
C..........	0.661	1825	1210	0.67
D..........	0.114	1600	183	0.1012
E..........	0.114	1050	120	0.0664
			1808, mm Hg abs.	1.0007

This compares quite well with the selected 1800 mm bottoms pressure. Bottoms temperature is 320° F.

Relative Volatilities: Light to Heavy key

$$\text{At top: } \alpha = \frac{\text{v.p. Tri}}{\text{v.p. } \beta \text{ Tri}} = \frac{1280}{600} = 2.13$$

$$\text{At bottoms: } \alpha = \frac{\text{v.p. Tri}}{\text{v.p. } \beta \text{ Tri}} = \frac{4500}{2275} = 1.98$$

$$\alpha \text{ (average)} = [(2.13)(1.98)]^{\frac{1}{2}} = 2.06$$

Minimum Stages at Total Reflux

$$S_M := N_{Min.} + 1 = \frac{\log(x_{D1}/x_{Dh})(x_{Bh}/x_{B1})}{\log \alpha_{avg.}}$$

$$= \frac{\log(0.999/0.001)(0.101/0.01)}{\log 2.06}$$

$$= \frac{4.003}{0.318} = 12.6 \text{ theoretical stages}$$

Minimum Stages Above Feed:

$$S_r = \frac{\log(0.999/0.001)(0.0555/0.456)}{\log 2.13}$$

$$= \frac{2.082}{0.328} = 6.35 \text{ theoretical stages}$$

Thermal Condition of Feed

Feed temperature = 158° F.

Calculated Bubble Point of feed = 266° F. at assumed feed tray pressure of 15 psig.

$$q = \frac{\text{Heat to bring feed to boiling point} + \text{Heat to vaporize feed}}{\text{Latent Heat of one mol of feed}}$$

q = 1.298 (Calculations not shown, but handled in same manner as for example given in binary section, however all feed components considered, not just keys.)

Minimum Reflux—Underwood Method, Determination of α Avg.

Assume pinch temperatures (usually satisfactory since α does not vary greatly) at ⅓ and ⅔ of over-all column temperature differences:

Lower pinch = 320 — ⅓ (320-223) = 288° F.

Upper pinch = 320 — ⅔ (320-223) = 255° F.

Component	@ 255° F.		@ 288° F.		α_i (avg).
	v.p.	α	v.p.	α	
A	2050	2.00	3050	1.91	1.955
B	1025	1.00	1600	1.00	1.00
C	750	0.732	1180	0.737	0.735
D	650	0.634	1035	0.647	0.641
E	390	0.380	650	0.406	0.393

To start, assume θ = 1.113 (It must lie between 1.00 and 1.955)

Component	x_{Fi}	$\alpha_i x_{Fi}$	$(\alpha_i - \theta)$	$\alpha_i x_{Fi}/(\alpha_i - \theta)$	$\alpha_i x_{Fi}/(\alpha_i - \theta)^2$
A	0.456	0.891	0.842	1.058	1.252
B	0.0555	0.0555	—0.113	—0.491	4.33
C	0.3625	0.266	—0.378	—0.704	1.86
D	0.0625	0.0401	—0.472	—0.085	0.18
E	0.0625	0.0246	—0.720	—0.0342	0.0472
				Σ= —0.2562	Σ7.669

$\theta_c = 1.113 - (-0.2562/7.669) = 1.113 + 0.0334$

$\theta_c = 1.146$ (this is close enough check to original, to not require recalculation.

The correct value of 1.146 should be used.

Check for balance:

$$1 - q = \sum \frac{x_{Fi}}{1 - \Theta/\alpha_i} = \sum \frac{\alpha_i \, x_{Fi}}{\alpha_i - \Theta} = -0.256$$

$$1 - 1.298 = -0.298 = -0.256$$

This could be corrected closer if a greater accuracy were needed. This is not as good a match as ordinarily desired.

$$(L/D)_{min.} + 1 = \frac{(\alpha_a \, x_a)_D}{\alpha_a - \Theta} + \frac{(\alpha_b \, x_b)_D}{\alpha_b - \Theta}$$

(for all distillate components)

$$(L/D)_{min} + 1 = \frac{(1.955)(0.999)}{(1.955 - 1.146)} + \frac{1.00 \, (0.001)}{(1.00 - 1.146)}$$

$$= 2.41 + (-0.00685)$$

$$= 2.404$$

$$(L/D)_{min} = 2.404 - 1.0 = 1.40$$

Operating Reflux and Theoretical Trays—Gilliland Plot

Min trays $= S_M = 12.6$

$(L/D)_{min} = 1.4$

Assume $(L/D)_o$	$\dfrac{(L/D)_o - (L/D)_M}{(L/D)_o + 1}$	Read: $S - S_M/(S+1)$	Theo Stages S
1.4	0	∞	∞
1.6	0.0768	0.546	29
2.0	0.20	0.445	23.5
3.0	0.40	0.312	18.8
4.0	0.52	0.245	17
∞	—	—	12.6

These values are plotted in Figure 8-26. From the curve, the operating $(L/D)_o$ was selected, and the theoretical stages corresponding are 19.

Tray-by-Tray Calculation—Ackers and Wade Method

Rectifying Section, $(L/D)_o = 3:1$

Light key = Trichlor; Heavy key = β Tri

Relative Volatilities to start: Use average of top and feed

$$\propto avg.$$

A	2.05
B	1.00
C	0.734

Neglect the heavier than perchlor components in the rectifying section.

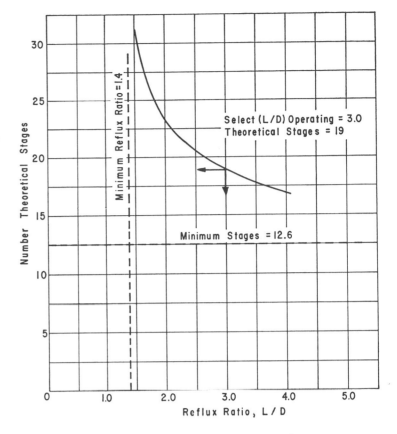

Figure 8-26. Gilliland plot for multicomponent example.

In order to carry the perchlor it is assumed at 0.0001 mol fraction in overhead and reflux, the β-Tri is reduced to 0.0005 mol fraction for these calculations being tighter specifications than the initial calculated balance. The overall effect will be small.

Component	$x_{iD} = x_i$ (Reflux)	$(x_i/x_h)_1$	$(x_i)_1$	$(x_i/x_h)_2$	$(x_i)_2$
A	0.9994	975.02	0.9984	545.5	0.9971
B	0.0005	1.00	0.001024	1.0	0.001828
C	0.0001	0.273	0.000280	0.359	0.000656
		$\Sigma = 976.293$	0.999704 (close enough)	546.859	

Typical calculations:

$$\left(\frac{x_i}{x_h}\right)_1 = \frac{1}{\alpha_i}\left[\frac{(L/D)(x_i)_{n+1} + x_{Di}}{L/D \, (x_h)_{n+1} + x_{Dh}}\right]$$

For component A: Tray 1

$$\left(\frac{x_i}{x_h}\right)_1 = \frac{1}{2.05}\left[\frac{(3)(0.9994) + 0.9994}{(3)(0.0005) + 0.0005}\right] = 975.02$$

Component B:

$$\left(\frac{x_i}{x_h}\right)_1 = \frac{1}{1.00}\left[\frac{3(0.0005) + 0.0005}{3(0.0005) + 0.0005}\right] = 1.00$$

Component C:

$$\left(\frac{x_i}{x_h}\right)_1 = \frac{1}{0.734}\left[\frac{3(0.0001) + 0.0001}{3(0.0005) + 0.0005}\right] = 0.272$$

$$(x_A)_1 = 975.02/976.293 = 0.9984$$
$$(x_B)_1 = 1.00/976.293 = 0.001024$$
$$(x_C)_1 = 0.273/976.293 = 0.000280$$

Tray 2: Component A

$$\left(\frac{x_i}{x_h}\right)_2 = \frac{1}{2.05}\left[\frac{3(0.9984) + 0.9994}{3(0.00102) + 0.0005}\right] = 545.5$$

Component B

$$\left(\frac{x_i}{x_h}\right)_2 = \frac{1}{1.00}\left[\frac{3(0.00102) + 0.0005}{3(0.00102) + 0.0005}\right] = 1.00$$

Component C

$$\left(\frac{x_i}{x_h}\right)_2 = \frac{1}{0.734}\left[\frac{3(0.00028) + 0.0001}{3(0.0005) + 0.0005}\right] = 0.359$$

	$(x_i/x_h)_3$	$(x_i)_3$	$(x_i/x_h)_4$	$(x_i)_4$	$(x_i/x_h)_5$	$(x_i)_5$
A	325.24	0.9952	200.81	0.9916	126.61	0.9851
B	1.0	0.00306	1.0	0.004938	1.0	0.007781
C	0.514	0.001573	0.682	0.00337	0.908	0.007065
	326.754		202.492		128.518	

	$(x_i/x_h)_6$	$(x_i)_6$	$(x_i/x_h)_7$	$(x_i)_7$	$(x_i/x_h)_8$	$(x_i)_8$
A	80.60	0.9736	52.05	0.9520	33.97	0.9138
B	1.0	0.01208	1.0	0.01829	1.0	0.0269
C	1.213	0.01465	1.633	0.02987	2.21	0.05945
	82.813		54.683		37.18	

	$(x_i/x_h)_9$	$(x_i)_9$	$(x_i/x_h)_{10}$	$(x_i)_{10}$	$(x_i/x_h)_{11}$	$(x_i)_{11}$
A	22.47	0.8491	15.196	0.7501	7.716	0.5421
B	1.0	0.03779	1.0	0.04936	1.0	0.07026
C	2.994	0.1131	4.061	0.2005	5.516	0.3876
	26.464		20.257		14.232	

Ratio of keys in feed = 0.456/0.0555 = 8.2

Ratio of keys on Tray No. 10 = 0.7501/0.04936 = 15.2

Ratio of keys on Tray No. 11 = 0.5421/0.07026 = 7.7

Tray No. 11 should be used as feed tray, (counting down from the top). Note that since the relative volatility did not change much from top to feed, the same value was satisfactory for the range.

Stripping Section

Determine V_s: per mol of feed

$$(L/V)_r = \frac{1}{1 + D/L} = \frac{1}{1 + \frac{1}{3}} = 0.75$$

$$V_r = \frac{(L/D)D}{(L/V)} = \frac{3(0.45145)}{0.75} = 1.806$$

$$L_r = (L/D)(D) = 3(0.45145) = 1.35 \text{ mols/mol feed}$$

$$L_s = L_r + qF = 1.35 + 1.298(1.0) = 2.648$$

$$V_s = V_r - F(1 - q) = 1.806 - (1.0)(1 - 1.298) = 2.104$$

$$V_s/B = 2.104/0.54804 = 3.84$$

Relative volatilities, α_i, determined at average temperature between bottom and feed of column. Usually the pinch temperature gives just as satisfactory results.

Component	x_{iB}	y_{iB}	(α_i)avg	$(y_i/y_h)_1$	$(y_i)_1$	$(y_i/y_h)_2$	$(y_i)_2$
A	0.010	0.0249	1.905	0.319	0.0543	0.552	0.107
B	0.101	0.1382	1.00	1.000	0.170	1.00	0.194
C	0.660	0.6700	0.740	3.800	0.647	3.08	0.597
D	0.114	0.1012	0.648	0.517	0.088	0.389	0.0754
E	0.114	0.0664	0.411	0.241	0.0411	0.1476	0.0286
				5.877		5.1686	

Typical calculations: starting at bottom and working up the column.

Tray 1: Component A

$$(y_i/y_h)_1 = \alpha_i\left[\frac{(V_s/B)(y_i)_{m-1} + x_{Bi}}{(V_s/B)(y_h)_{m-1} + x_{Bh}}\right]$$

$$= 1.905\left[\frac{(3.84)(0.0249) + 0.010}{3.84(0.1382) + 0.101}\right]$$

$$(y_i/y_h)_1 = 0.319$$

$$(y_i)_1 = 0.319/5.877 = 0.0543$$

Tray 2: Component A

$$(y_i y_h)_2 = 1.905\left[\frac{3.84(0.0543) + 0.010}{3.84(0.170) + 0.101}\right]$$

$$= 0.552$$

Continuation of the calculations gives an approximate match of ratio of keys in feed to those on plate 10. Then feed tray is number 10 from bottom and this is also number 11 from top.

Liquid mol fraction ratio from vapor mol fraction ratio:

$$(x_i/x_h) = \frac{(y_i/y_h)}{\alpha_{i/h}}$$

Ratio on tray no. 9 = 15.018/1.905 = (x_i/x_h) = 7.9

Ratio on tray no. 10 = 19.16/1.905 = 10.05

Ratio in feed = 8.2

Total theoretical trays = 11 + 10-1 (common feed tray count)

= 20 not including reboiler

Total theoretical stages = 20 + 1 (reboiler) = 21

This compares with 19 theoretical stages from **Gilliland** plot.

Tray Efficiency

Use average column temperature of 271° F. and feed analysis.

Component	x_{iF}	μ, cp	μx_{iF}	vp.	$\alpha_{1/h}$
A	0.456	0.28	0.128	2500	1.94
B	0.0555	0.36	0.020	1290	
C	0.362	0.37	0.134		
D	0.0625	0.40	0.025		
E	0.0625	0.48	0.030		

$$\Sigma = 0.337 \text{ cp}$$

$$\alpha \Sigma (\mu)(x_{iF}) = 1.94\,(0.337) = 0.654$$

Using Figure 8-18

Drickamer and Bradford curve, $E_o = 46\%$

O'Connell curve, $E_o = 53.8\%$

In this case, recommend using:

$$E_o = (46 + 53.8)/2 = 49.6\%$$

Actual trays in column:

$$N_{Act} = 20/0.496 = 40.3 \text{ trays}$$

From tray-by-tray calculations, feed tray is $10/0.496 = 20.1$ trays from bottom, use 20.

Generally, practice would be to select a column allowing a few extra trays, making column total trays = 45.

	No.
Rectifying trays =	22
Feed =	1
Stripping =	22
	45

Feed nozzles should be located on trays No. 21, 23 and 25 counting up from the bottom tray as no. 1.

Heat Balance—Adjacent Key Systems with Sharp Separations, Constant Molal Overflow

Total Condenser Duty

Refer to Figure 8-27 (System (1)).

1. Assume or set condenser liquid product temperature, t_D.

2. Calculate condensing pressure, with t_D as bubble point (if subcooling exists, and t_D is below bubble point, use bubble point temperature for pressure calculation only).

3. $V_1 = L + D$

$$H_1 V_1 = [L\,h_D + D\,h_D] + Q_c \qquad (8\text{-}58)$$

$$H_1 = \sum_1^i H_{1i}\, y_{1i} \text{ at } t_1 \qquad (8\text{-}59)$$

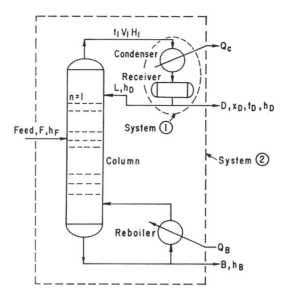

Figure 8-27. Heat balance diagram.

$$h_D = \sum_1^i h_{Di}\, x_{Di} \qquad (8\text{-}60)$$

$$Q_c = V_1\,(H_1 - h_D) \qquad (8\text{-}61)$$

4. Calculate t_1 and x_1 by dew point on vapor V_1. Then determine H_1, referring to top tray as number one in this case.

where: H_1 = total vapor enthalpy above reference datum for sum of all contributing percentages of individual components, i, in stream, Btu/lb., or Btu/mol

h_D = total liquid enthalpy above reference datum for sum of all contributing percentages of individual components, i, in product stream. (Also same as reflux), Btu/lb. or Btu/mol

5. For partial condenser: replace Dh_D by DH_D in Step 3. A dewpoint on compositions of y_D (vapor) give t_D or total pressure. Also get liquid composition x_p (liquid reflux in equilibrium with product vapor y_D. Overhead vapor is sum of compositions of y_D and x_p. A dewpoint on this vapor (overhead from tray one (top)) gives top tray temperature, t_1.

$$V_1 H_1 + Q_c = Lh_D + DH_D$$

Reboiler Duty

Refer to Figure 8-27 (System (2))

1. Determine bottoms temperature by bubble point on liquid x_B.

2. From feed condition, determine enthalpy.

$$h_F = \frac{\Sigma V_F (H_1 y_1)_F + \Sigma L_F (h_1 x_1)_F}{F} \qquad (8\text{-}62)$$

3. Solve for Q_B, reboiler duty, Btu/hr.

$$F \; h_F + Q_B = Dh_D + Bh_B + Q_c \qquad (8\text{-}63)$$

where: h_D = total enthalpy of distillate product, Btu/mol or Btu/lb.

h_B = total enthalpy of bottoms product, Btu/mol or Btu/lb.

h_F = total enthalpy of feed, Btu/mol or Btu/lb.

Example 8-11: Tray-By-Tray Multicomponent Mixture using Digital Computer

This example summarizes a typical short multicomponent distillation utilizing the techniques previously cited (see Computer Printout).

The problem was to separate component 4 from component 5 while keeping component 5 losses into the overhead at less than 5 weight % of the total overhead or to recover in the bottoms better than 90% (weight) of the component 5 entering in the feed.

The feed composition is:

Component	Mols	Pounds	Boil Point, °F
1	0.623	53.68	155.7
2	7.234	130.36	313.0
3	80.223	7423.03	244.2
4	1.717	127.20	332.6
5	9.678	1395.28	380.3
6	0.525	85.37	476.6
	100.000	9214.91	

Enthalpy, BTU/unit flow 2901.076 31.48
Feed temperature: 90° F, liquid at stage 5 from top, Equimolal overflow not assumed.
Column Pressure: 0.39 (top) to 0.86 (bottom) psia, distributed uniformly to each tray
Reflux Ratio: 0.50 (assumed)
Assumed No. Theoretical Stages: 8 including condenser and reboiler

Summary of input data to computer:

1. Molecular weights
2. Boiling points
3. "K" value equations for each component as a function of pressure
4. Equations for calculating enthalpy of liquid of each component as a function of temperature
5. Equations for calculating enthalpy of vapor of each component as a function of temperature
6. *Initial* values for stages to start calculations
   a. linear temperature gradient
   b. linear pressure gradient

The results of the computer calculation are as summarized by copies of the print out sheets. Note that Stage *one* is the product from an overhead condenser and is liquid, as is the bottoms or reboiler outlet product. The results show that the initial criteria have been met for recovery of component 5; however, this does not reflect any optimization of reflux or final number of stages (theoretical trays) that might be required to accomplish the separation in a final design.

As an example, if this were the final column selection, then the column trays = 8-condenser-reboiler = 6 theoretical. Actual trays at an estimated 65% tray efficiency = 6/0.65 = 9.23 or use 10 *actual* trays in the column itself.

Computer Printout for Multicomponent Distillation

```
NUMBER OF STAGES =    8       (INCLUDING CONDENSER AND REBOILER)
NUMBER OF COMPONENTS = 6
COMPONENTS                MOLECULAR WEIGHT     NORMAL BOILING POINT, DEG.F.
      1                      86.170                  155.70
      2                      18.020                  212.00
      3                      92.530                  244.20
      4                      74.080                  332.60
      5                     144.170                  380.30
      6                     162.610                  476.60
COLUMN PRESSURE =     0.39    TO     0.86 PSIA
REFLUX RATIO =    0.5000

EQUIMOLAL OVERFLOW NOT ASSUMED

FEED STREAMS


    STAGE   5 (LIQUID FEED STREAM), TEMP. =    90.00 DEG.F.
      COMPONENT                          MOLS              LBS.
      1                                  0.623             53.68
      2                                  7.234            130.36
      3                                 80.223           7423.03
      4                                  1.717            127.20
      5                                  9.678           1395.28
      6                                  0.525             85.37
                     TOTAL            100.000           9214.91
            ENTHALPY, BTU/ UNIT FLOW    2901.076          31.48


                                    SUM OF FEEDS   =    100.000 MOLS
```

PRODUCT STREAMS

OVERHEAD RATE =   89.797 MOLS LIQUID
                   0.0   MOLS VAPOR

BOTTOMS RATE =   10.203 MOLS LIQUID

SUM OF PRODUCTS =   100.000 MOLS

INITIAL VALUES FOR STAGE VARIABLES (LINEAR TEMP. GRADIENT, LINEAR PRESSURE GRADIENT, EQUIMOLAL OVERFLOW,
SPECIFIED HEAT LOSSES NOT INCLUDING OVERHEAD CONDENSER AND BOTTOMS REBOILER)

STAGE	TEMP.DEG.F.	PRESS.PSIA	L(MOLS)	V(MOLS)	Q(BTU)
1	85.00	0.39	44.898	0.0	0.0
2	102.86	0.46	44.898	134.695	0.0
3	120.71	0.52	44.898	134.695	0.0
4	138.57	0.59	44.898	134.695	0.0
5	156.43	0.66	144.898	134.695	0.0
6	174.29	0.73	144.898	134.695	0.0
7	192.14	0.79	144.898	134.695	0.0
8	210.00	0.86	10.203	134.695	0.0

STAGE NO.   1 ...... OVERHEAD CONDENSER

TEMPERATURE =   81.75 DEG.F
PRESSURE =   0.39 PSIA

	-----MOL FRACTIONS----		K	----LIQUID PRODUCT---- 81.75 DEG.F.		----VAPOR PRODUCT---- 81.75 DEG.F.	
	X	Y		---MOLS----	----LBS----	---MOLS----	----LBS----
1	0.693787E-02	0.579909E-01	0.835864E+01	0.62300	53.684	0.0	0.0
2	0.805591E-01	0.111028E+00	0.137823E+01	7.23397	130.356	0.0	0.0
3	0.893344E+00	0.829924E+00	0.929014E+00	80.21964	7422.723	0.0	0.0
4	0.180887E-01	0.101670E-02	0.562068E-01	1.62431	120.329	0.0	0.0
5	0.106980E-02	0.384860E-04	0.359752E-01	0.09607	13.850	0.0	0.0
6	0.608310E-07	0.566475E-09	0.931235E-02	0.00001	0.001	0.0	0.0
	1.000000	0.999998		89.79700	7740.937	0.0	0.0

ENTHALPY, BTU/UNIT FLOW =   2318.02881   26.890   20467.7891   244.037

CONDENSER HEAT DUTY =   2499393.0 BTU

-----LIQUID REFLUX------ (R =   0.500000)
--- 81.75 DEG.F.----
---MOLS----   ----LBS----

		---MOLS----	----LBS----
1	N-HEXANE	0.31150	26.842
2	WATER	3.61698	65.178
3	EPICHLOROHYDRIN	40.10982	3711.361
4	GLYCIDOL	0.81216	60.165
5	GMA	0.04803	6.925
6	MCM	0.00000	0.000
		44.89850	3870.471

ENTHALPY, BTU/UNIT FLOW =   2318.02881   26.890

STAGE NO.   2

TEMPERATURE =   95.98 DEG. F
PRESSURE =   0.46 PSIA

	-----MOL FRACTIONS----		K	--------LIQUID--------		--------VAPOR--------	
	X	Y		---MOLS----	----LBS----	---MOLS----	----LBS----

INTERNAL STREAMS LEAVING STAGE

1	0.702365E-03	0.693785E-02	0.987776E+01	0.03030	2.611	0.93450	80.526
2	0.438818E-01	0.805594E-01	0.183580E+01	1.89314	34.114	10.85099	195.535
3	0.738175E+00	0.893351E+00	0.121019E+01	31.84622	2946.731	120.33041	11134.172
4	0.196187E+00	0.180890E-01	0.922004E-01	8.46386	627.003	2.43651	180.496
5	0.210494E-01	0.106981E-02	0.508229E-01	0.90811	130.922	0.14410	20.775
6	0.462302E-05	0.608316E-07	0.131582E-01	0.00020	0.032	0.00001	0.001
	1.000000	1.000007		43.14185	3741.413	134.69550	11611.500

ENTHALPY, BTU/UNIT FLOW =   2958.33154   34.112   20873.9062   242.141

STAGE NO.   3

TEMPERATURE =   115.04 DEG. F
PRESSURE =   0.52 PSIA

	-----MOL FRACTIONS----		K	--------LIQUID--------		--------VAPOR--------	
	X	Y		---MOLS----	----LBS----	---MOLS----	----LBS----

INTERNAL STREAMS LEAVING STAGE

1	0.379421E-03	0.491427E-02	0.129519E+02	0.01563	1.347	0.65330	56.295
2	0.245430E-01	0.686564E-01	0.279735E+01	1.01098	18.218	9.12711	164.471
3	0.470701E+00	0.842987E+00	0.179089E+01	19.38924	1794.086	112.06575	10369.441
4	0.414043E+00	0.758873E-01	0.183279E+00	17.05534	1263.460	10.08837	747.346
5	0.902625E-01	0.755377E-02	0.836849E-01	3.71812	536.041	1.00419	144.774
6	0.711249E-04	0.154139E-05	0.216712E-01	0.00293	0.476	0.00020	0.033
	1.000000	1.000000		41.19226	3613.627	132.93884	11482.352

ENTHALPY, BTU/UNIT FLOW =   4063.29980   46.318   21326.8906   246.916

STAGE NO.   4   TEMPERATURE =   131.91 DEG. F
                    PRESSURE =   0.59 PSIA

	-----MOL FRACTIONS----		K	--------LIQUID--------		--------VAPOR--------	
	X	Y		---MOLS----	----LBS----	---MOLS----	----LBS----
INTERNAL STREAMS LEAVING STAGE							
1	0.303078E-03	0.487530E-02	0.160854E+02	0.01203	1.037	0.63861	55.029
2	0.159964E-01	0.629432E-01	0.393465E+01	0.63502	11.443	8.24489	148.573
3	0.309609E+00	0.760431E+00	0.245599E+01	12.29079	1137.266	99.60825	9216.750
4	0.442138E+00	0.142611E+00	0.322527E+00	17.55190	1300.244	18.68048	1383.850
5	0.231266E+00	0.291193E-01	0.125906E+00	9.18075	1323.588	3.81431	549.909
6	0.687129E-03	0.224091E-04	0.326110E-01	0.02728	4.436	0.00294	0.477
	1.000000	1.000001		39.69777	3778.014	130.98926	11354.582
		ENTHALPY, BTU/UNIT FLOW =		5421.28906	56.965	21947.7500	253.195

STAGE NO.   5   TEMPERATURE =   144.67 DEG. F
                    PRESSURE =   0.66 PSIA

	-----MOL FRACTIONS----		K	--------LIQUID--------		--------VAPOR--------	
	X	Y		---MOLS----	----LBS----	---MOLS----	----LBS----
TOTAL FEEDS TO STAGE							
1				0.62300	53.684	0.0	0.0
2				7.23400	130.357	0.0	0.0
3				80.22301	7423.031	0.0	0.0
4				1.71700	127.195	0.0	0.0
5				9.67800	1395.277	0.0	0.0
6				0.52300	85.370	0.0	0.0
				99.99998	9214.906	0.0	0.0
		ENTHALPY, BTU/UNIT FLOW =		2901.07593	0.0	0.0	0.0
INTERNAL STREAMS LEAVING STAGE							
1	0.266697E-03	0.490374E-02	0.183858E+02	0.03452	2.975	0.63501	54.719
2	0.123573E-01	0.607659E-01	0.491700E+01	1.59954	28.824	7.86887	141.797
3	0.237150E+00	0.714384E+00	0.301213E+01	30.69696	2840.390	92.50896	8559.852
4	0.312228E+00	0.148094E+00	0.474257E+00	40.41512	2993.952	19.17737	1420.659
5	0.433081E+00	0.716411E-01	0.165407E+00	56.05843	8081.941	9.27715	1337.486
6	0.491682E-02	0.210695E-03	0.428481E-01	0.63644	103.491	0.02728	4.437
	1.000000	0.999999		129.44102	14051.566	129.49477	11518.941
		ENTHALPY, BTU/UNIT FLOW =		6947.83984	64.003	22570.4453	253.735

STAGE NO.   6   TEMPERATURE =   188.49 DEG. F
                    PRESSURE =   0.73 PSIA

	-----MOL FRACTIONS----		K	--------LIQUID--------		--------VAPOR--------	
	X	Y		---MOLS----	----LBS----	---MOLS----	----LBS----
INTERNAL STREAMS LEAVING STAGE							
1	0.820382E-05	0.289519E-03	0.352913E+02	0.00105	0.091	0.03452	2.975
2	0.107639E-02	0.134144E-01	0.124627E+02	0.13827	2.492	1.59951	28.823
3	0.358612E-01	0.257415E+00	0.717825E+01	4.60658	426.246	30.69373	2840.090
4	0.167536E+00	0.338163E+00	0.201852E+01	21.52092	1594.270	40.32170	2987.031
5	0.788222E+00	0.389783E+00	0.494524E+00	101.25171	14597.457	46.47696	6700.582
6	0.729625E-02	0.935050E-03	0.128159E+00	0.93725	152.405	0.11149	18.130
	1.000000	0.999998		128.45580	16772.957	119.23819	12577.629
		ENTHALPY, BTU/UNIT FLOW =		11524.1094	88.257	27816.3281	263.704

STAGE NO.   7   TEMPERATURE =   213.25 DEG. F
                    PRESSURE =   0.79 PSIA

	-----MOL FRACTIONS----		K	--------LIQUID--------		--------VAPOR--------	
	X	Y		---MOLS----	----LBS----	---MOLS----	----LBS----
INTERNAL STREAMS LEAVING STAGE							
1	0.189382E-06	0.891154E-05	0.470578E+02	0.00003	0.002	0.00105	0.091
2	0.611520E-04	0.116901E-02	0.191176E+02	0.00808	0.146	0.13824	2.491
3	0.365365E-02	0.389279E-01	0.106551E+02	0.48272	44.666	4.60334	425.947
4	0.447734E-01	0.181203E+00	0.404748E+01	5.91546	438.217	21.42773	1587.366
5	0.935284E+00	0.775205E+00	0.828903E+00	123.56973	17815.047	91.67026	13216.098
6	0.162273E-01	0.348651E-02	0.214363E+00	2.14403	348.640	0.41229	67.043
	1.000000	1.000000		132.12006	18646.711	118.25296	15299.031
		ENTHALPY, BTU/UNIT FLOW =		14190.3711	100.545	32961.2969	254.772

STAGE NO.   8   (REBOILER ----- LIQUID STREAM IS BOTTOMS PRODUCT)

TEMPERATURE =   224.68 DEG. F
PRESSURE =   0.86 PSIA

	-----MOL FRACTIONS----		K	--------LIQUID--------		--------VAPOR--------	
	X	Y		---MOLS----	----LBS----	---MOLS----	----LBS----

INTERNAL STREAMS LEAVING STAGE

1	0.400988E-08	0.204898E-06	0.510988E+02	0.00000	0.000	0.00002	0.002
2	0.299190E-05	0.660195E-04	0.220665E+02	0.00003	0.001	0.00805	0.145
3	0.324473E-03	0.393227E-02	0.121192E+02	0.00331	0.306	0.47941	44.360
4	0.908419E-02	0.477594E-01	0.525762E+01	0.09269	6.866	5.82269	431.344
5	0.939133E+00	0.934957E+00	0.995584E+00	9.58198	1381.433	113.98735	16433.555
6	0.514552E-01	0.132798E-01	0.258093E+00	0.52500	65.370	1.61904	263.271
	1.000000	0.999995		10.20300	1473.976	121.91722	17172.676

ENTHALPY, BTU/UNIT FLOW =   15248.2773   105.550   35206.3750   249.947

REBOILER HEAT DUTY =   2573009.0 BTU
CONDENSER HEAT DUTY=   2499393.0 BTU

OVERALL COMPONENT BALANCES (MOLS) ---- BEFORE FINAL FORCING ----

	IN	OUT	IN/OUT
1	0.62300	0.62300	1.00000000
2	7.23400	7.23400	1.00000000
3	80.22301	80.22293	1.00000000
4	1.71700	1.71700	1.00000000
5	9.67800	9.67804	0.99999583
6	0.52500	0.52500	0.99999529
	99.99998	99.99995	1.00000000

NORMALIZED PRODUCT STREAMS ---- AFTER COMPONENT BALANCES FORCED ----

STAGE NO.   1 `...... OVERHEAD CONDENSER

TEMPERATURE =   81.75 DEG.F
PRESSURE =   0.39 PSIA

	----------------LIQUID PRODUCT----------------				----------------VAPOR PRODUCT----------------			
	MOLS	MOL FRACTION	LBS	MASS FRACTION	MOLS	MOL FRACTION	LBS	MASS FRACTION

COMPONENT

1	0.62300	0.693787E-02	53.684	0.693506E-02	0.0	0.0	0.0	0.0
2	7.23397	0.805591E-01	130.356	0.168398E-01	0.0	0.0	0.0	0.0
3	80.21964	0.893345E+00	7422.723	0.958892E+00	0.0	0.0	0.0	0.0
4	1.62431	0.180887E-01	120.329	0.155445E-01	0.0	0.0	0.0	0.0
5	0.09606	0.106980E-02	13.850	0.178914E-02	0.0	0.0	0.0	0.0
6	0.00001	0.608307E-07	0.001	0.114746E-06	0.0	0.0	0.0	0.0
	89.79697		7740.937		0.0		0.0	

STAGE NO.   8 (REBOILER)

TEMPERATURE =   224.68 DEG.
PRESSURE =   0.86 PSIA

	----------------LIQUID PRODUCT----------------				----------------VAPOR PRODUCT----------------			
	MOLS	MOL FRACTION	LBS	MASS FRACTION	MOLS	MOL FRACTION	LBS	MASS FRACTION

COMPONENT

1	0.00000	0.400989E-08	0.000	0.239181E-08	0.0	0.0	0.0	0.0
2	0.00003	0.299191E-05	0.001	0.373200E-06	0.0	0.0	0.0	0.0
3	0.00331	0.324474E-03	0.306	0.207826E-03	0.0	0.0	0.0	0.0
4	0.09269	0.908423E-02	6.866	0.465829E-02	0.0	0.0	0.0	0.0
5	9.58194	0.939133E+00	1381.427	0.937216E+00	0.0	0.0	0.0	0.0
6	0.52499	0.514551E-01	85.369	0.579180E-01	0.0	0.0	0.0	0.0
	10.20296		1473.969		0.0		0.0	

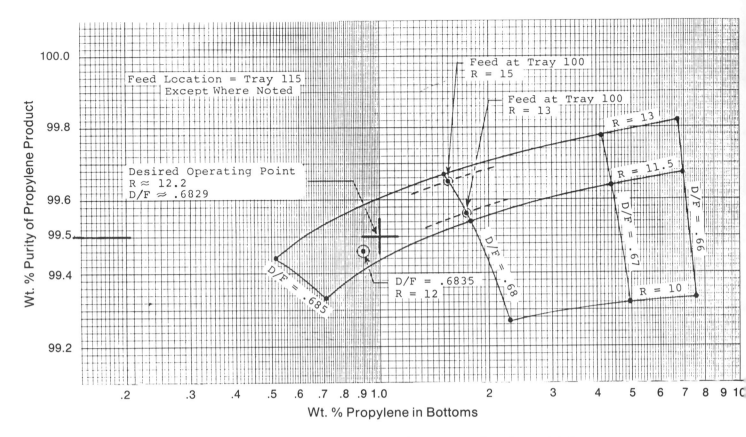

Figure. 8-28. Effect of reflux ratio and distillate—feed ratios on propylene content of product and bottoms.

Example 8-12: Multicomponent Examination of Reflux Ratio and Distillate to Feed Ratio

The detailed calculations of Figure 8-28 present an example of the excellent performance analysis information that can be developed by an orderly or systematic study of the variables in a multicomponent system. There are other variables to be studied as well.

This design is targeted to produce 99.5 weight percent propylene overhead while not allowing more than 1 weight percent in the bottoms.

Note that in a high purity condition as is represented in this example, the system is quite sensitive to the overhead withdrawal rate (product from the system). This system is for the purification of propylene from a feed high in propylene, with lessor amounts of propane, butane, and ethane.

Without a digital computer the detail of Figure 8-28 would be practically impossible and cost prohibitive in terms of time involved.

Nomenclature For Part 1: Distillation Process Performance

a = Activity of component

B = Bottoms product or waste, lb. mols/hour

B_b = Mols of component, b, used as reference for volatility, after a given time of distillation

B_{bo} = Mols of component, b, used as reference for volatility, at start of distillation

B_i = Mols of component, i, after a given time of distillation

B_{io} = Mols of component, i, at start of distillation

B_{Ti} = Total mols liquid in bottom of still at time, T_1

B_{To} = Total mols liquid (not including any steam) in bottom of still at start time, T_0.

C_{mi} = Factor in Colburn Minimum Reflux Method, Pinch condition, stripping

C_{ni} = Factor in Colburn Minimum Reflux Method, Pinch conditions, rectifying

C_p = Specific heat, BTU/lb. (° F.)

D = Distillate or overhead product, lb. mols/hour

E_o = Overall tray efficiency, fraction

F = Feed rate to tower, lb. mols/hour

f = Fugacity at a specific condition

f^o = Fugacity at reference standard condition

H = Total enthalpy, above reference datum, of vapor mixture at tray or specified conditions, BTU/lb. mol, or BTU/lb.

H' = Henry's Law constant, lb. mols/(cu. ft.) (atm)

H_n = Total molal enthalpy of vapor at conditions of tray n, $H_n = \Sigma H_{ni} (y_{ni})$

H_s = Total enthalpy of steam, BTU/lb. mol, or BTU/lb.

h = Enthalpy of liquid mixture or pure compound at tray conditions of temperature and pressure, or specified point or condition BTU/lb. mol, or BTU/lb.

h_n = Total molal enthalpy of liquid at conditions of tray, n, $h_n = \Sigma h_{ni} (x_{ni})$

K = Equilibrium constant for a particular system ($= y/x$)

K' = Equilibrium constant for least volatile component

L = Liquid flow rate return to tower as reflux, lb. mols/hour

L_r = Liquid flow rate down rectifying section of distillation tower, lb. mols/hr.

L_s = Liquid flow rate down stripping section of distillation tower, lb. mols/hr.

L/D = Actual external reflux ratio

$(L/D)_{Min}$ = Minimum external reflux ratio

M_s = Total mols steam required

N = Number of theoretical trays in distillation tower (not including reboiler) at operating or finite reflux. For partial condenser system N includes condenser

N_{Act} = Actual number of trays excluding reboiler and partial condenser

N_B = Number of trays from tray m to bottom tray, but not including still or reboiler

N_{Min} = Minimum number theoretical trays in distillation tower (not including reboiler) at total or infinite reflux. For partial condenser system, N_{Min} includes condenser

N_n = Number of trays above reference plate n, but *not* including n

P = Pressure, atmospheres; or vapor pressure of component, atm.

P_i = Vapor pressure of each component

P_s = Vapor pressure of steam, absolute

p = Partial pressure, absolute units, or ratio r_{ps}/r_{pr}

p = Total pressure of system

p' = Number of trays below feed where introduction of light components should begin, Akers-Wade Calculation method

p_i^* = Vapor pressure component, i, at temperature

p'' = Number of trays above feed where introduction of heavy components should begin, Akers-Wade Calculation method

Q_B = Net heat in through reboiler, reboiler duty, BTU/hr.

Q_c = Net heat out of overhead condenser, BTU/hr., $= w c_p (t_i - t_o)$

q = Thermal condition of feed, dimensionless

R' = Pseudo minimum reflux ratio

r_{ps} = Ratio light to heavy keys, stripping pinch

r_{pr} = Ratio light to heavy keys, rectifying pinch

r_f = Ratio mol fraction light key to heavy key in feed

S = Steam flow rate, lbs./hr. or lb. mols/hr., or theoretical stages at actual reflux (Figure 8-14)

S_M = Minimum theoretical stages at total reflux from bottoms composition through overhead product composition, including reboiler and any partial condenser (if used)

S_o = Theoretical stages at a finite operating reflux

S_r = Theoretical stages in total rectifying section, including partial condenser (if used)

S_s = Theoretical stages in total stripping section, including reboiler

s = Pounds (or mols) steam per pound (or mol) of bottoms

t_B = Bottoms temperature, ° F.

t_i = Temperature in, ° F.

t_o = Temperature out, ° F., or overhead temperature, °F.

V = Total overhead vapor from tower, lb. mols/hour

V_r = Vapor flow rate up rectifying section of tower, lb. mols/hour

V_s = Vapor flow rate up stripping section of tower, lb. mols/hour

v = Molar volume

w = Pounds coolant/hour

x = Mol fraction of component in liquid phase

x' = Mol fractions of least volatile component

x_1 = Mol fraction of component, i, in bottoms, B_T, at time, T_1

x_{it} = Mol fraction liquid at intersection of operating lines at minimum reflux, Scheibel-Montross equation

x_L = Mol fraction of feed as liquid, Scheibel-Montross

x_{lo} = Mol fraction light key in overhead expressed as fraction of total keys in overhead, Scheibel-Montross equation

x_m = Tray liquid mol fraction for start of calculations (most volatile component)

x_o = Mol fraction of component, i, in bottoms B_{To} at start time, T_0

x_v = Mol fraction of feed as vapor, Scheibel-Montross equation

y = Mol fraction of component in vapor phase

y' = Mol fraction of least volatile component

y^* = Equilibrium value corresponding to x_i

α, α_1 = Relative volatility of light key to heavy key components

α_{Avg} = Average relative volatility between top and bottom sections of distillation tower

α_H = Relative volatility of components heavier than heavy key

$\alpha_i =$ Relative volatility of more volatile to each of other components

$\alpha_L =$ Relative volatility of components lighter than light key

$\Theta =$ Time from start of distillation, or value of relative volatility to satisfy Underwood Algebraic method

$\mu =$ Viscosity, centipoise

$\gamma =$ Activity coefficient

$\pi =$ Total system pressure, absolute; atm, mm Hg, psia

$\Sigma =$ Sum

$\Psi =$ First derivative function

$\Psi' =$ Second derivative function

$\omega_j =$ Function in Underwood's Algebraic method for Minimum Reflux Ratio

Subscripts

a, b, c, etc. $=$ Specific components in a system or mixture

Avg., Av. $=$ Average

B $=$ Any consistent component in bottoms product

b $=$ bottom

D $=$ Any consistent component in condensed overhead product

F $=$ Feed

FH $=$ All mol fractions lighter than light key in feed, Scheibel-Montross Method

FL $=$ All mol fractions lighter than light key in feed, Scheibel-Montross method

H $=$ Components heavier than heavy key

h $=$ Heavy or high boiling component in mixture, also heavy key component

i $=$ Any individual component in mixture, may be specifically identified by subscripts 1, 2, 3, etc. or subscripts a, b, c, etc.

j $=$ Specific components in a system or mixture

L $=$ Liquid, Scheibel-Montross method only

L $=$ Components lighter than light key

l $=$ Light or low boiling component in mixture, also light key component

lh $=$ Refers to light component referenced to heavy component

m $=$ No. trays in stripping section, or tray number

n $=$ No. trays in rectifying section, or tray number

o $=$ Operating condition

$p_r =$ Pinch condition in rectifying section

$p_s =$ Pinch condition in stripping section

r $=$ Rectifying section

s $=$ Stripping section

t $=$ Top

v $=$ Vapor

1, 2, 3, etc. $=$ Specific components in a system or mixture

Part 2: Hydrocarbon Absorption and Stripping
(With Contributions by Dr. P. A. Bryant)

Many operations in petrochemical plants require the absorption of components from gas streams into "lean" oils or solvents. The resultant "rich" oil is then stripped or denuded of the absorbed materials. The greatest use of this operation utilizes hydrocarbon materials, but the basic principles are applicable to other systems provided adequate equilibrium data is available.

Several methods[17, 18, 29, 40, 62, 67] for handling this design have been offered and each has introduced a concept to improve some feature. An approximation method combination of Kremser-Brown[40, 67] and a more complete method of Edmister[18] will be summarized. Figure 8-29 summarizes the system and terminology. The accepted nomenclature for absorption and stripping is located on page 60.

Kremser-Brown-Sherwood Method— No Heat of Absorption[18]

This method gives reasonably good results for systems involving relatively lean gas and small quantities being absorbed. For rich gases the error can be considerable (more than 50 percent for some components). It has given generally good results on natural gas and related systems.

Absorption—Determine component Absorption in Fixed Tray Tower (Adapted in part from Ref. 18).

1. Calculate the total mols of gas inlet to the absorber identifying the quantities of individual components.

2. Assuming the tower pressure as set and an average of top and bottom temperatures can be selected (these may become variables for study), read equilibrium K_i values from charts for each component in gas.

3. Assume or fix a lean oil rate.

4. Calculate

$$\frac{L_o}{V_{N+1}} = \frac{\text{Mols/hr. lean oil in}}{\text{Mols/hr. rich gas in}}$$

Assume this value constant for tower design.

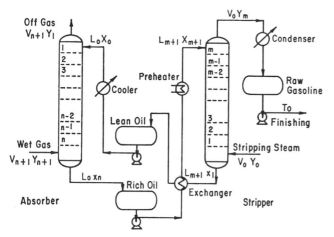

Figure 8-29 Flow diagram of absorption-stripping system for hydrocarbon recovery from gaseous mixture. (By permission of W. C. Edmister, Petroleum Engineer, Sept. 1947, series to January 1948.)

5. Calculate absorption factor, $A_i = L_o/(V_{N+1}) (K_i)$, using values of (2) and (4) above for each component.

6. Calculate fraction absorbed for each component, assuming a fixed overall tray efficiency for an assumed number of actual trays (or an existing column with trays)

(a) Theoretical trays, $N =$ (tray efficiency, E_o,) (no. actual trays)

(b) Fraction absorbed

$$E_{ai} = \frac{Y_{N+1} - Y_1}{Y_{N+1} - Y_o{}^*} = \frac{A_i{}^{N+1} - A_i}{A_i{}^{N+1} - 1} \qquad (8\text{-}64)$$

Where $Y_o{}^*$ is often considered zero or very small. Solve using A_i values.

7. Mols each component absorbed/hr.

$$= (V_o Y_{(n+1)i}) (E_{ai})$$

8. Mols each component absorbed/(mol inlet lean oil) (hr.) $= X_{iR}$

9. Mols of each component in gas out top of absorber: $=$ (mols component in inlet gas) — (mols component absorbed)

10. Mols of component in gas out top of absorber/mol of inlet rich gas:

$$E_{ai} = \frac{Y_{N+1} - Y_1}{Y_{N+1} - Y_o{}^*}$$

Solve for Y_1

11. Correct values from first calculation, Steps 1 thru 10, using the ΣX_{iR} values of Step 8, as follows.

12. Calculate A_i:

$$A_i = \frac{L_o}{V_{N+1} K_i} (1 + \Sigma X_{iR}) \qquad (8\text{-}65)$$

13. Calculate absorption efficiency, E_{ai}, using new A_i value

$$E_{ai} = \frac{A_i{}^{N+1} - A_i}{A_i{}^{N+1} - 1}, \text{ read Figure 8-30}$$

14. Calculate mols absorbed/hr:
$= (E_{ai})$ mols component in inlet rich gas)

15. Mols of each component in gas out top of absorber/ hr. = (mols component in) — (mols component absorbed)

16. Mols of component in outlet gas/mol inlet rich gas Solve for Y_{1i}

$$E_{ai} = \frac{Y_{N+1} - Y_{1i}}{Y_{N+1} - Y_o{}^*}$$

If the X_1 in equilibrium with Y_1 is desired:

$$X_1 = \frac{Y_1 (1 + \Sigma X_{iR})}{K \Sigma Y_1} \qquad (8\text{-}66)$$

17. Improved values can be obtained by recalculation from Step 11 if there is too great a difference between the "Σ mols absorbed" from trial no. 1 and trial no. 2

First Trial

Component	Inlet $Y_{(N+1)i}$	Mols/Hr. In	K_i	$A = \dfrac{L}{V K_i}$
•	•	•	•	•
•	•	•	•	•
•	•	•	•	•
	1.00	Σ •		

Component	Fraction Absorbed, E_{ai}	Mols Absorbed	X_{iR}	Mols/Hr. Off Gas	$Y_{1i\,(out)}$
•	•	•	•	•	•
•	•	•	•	•	•
•	•	•	•	•	•
		Σ •	Σ •	Σ •	

For second trial, see Step 11.

18. A graphical stepwise procedure offered by Sherwood[62] is also summarized by Reference 18. Y and X are plotted and handled stepwise as in distillation. The equilibrium line equation is for any single component:

$$\frac{Y_i}{X_i} = K_i \left(\frac{\Sigma Y_i}{1 + \Sigma X_i} \right) \qquad (8\text{-}67)$$

For a complete denuded inlet solvent at the top $\Sigma X = 0$, using K at top column conditions. The slope of the operat-

ing ling $= L_o/V_{N+1} =$ mols lean oil entering/mols wet gas entering.

Absorption—Determine Number Trays For Specified Product Absorption

1. For fixed tower temperature, pressure, gas feed rate, specified or assumed operating (L_o/V_{N+1}) times minimum value, specified component recovery out of inlet gas.

2. Calculate:

   (a) Mols component in inlet gas/ hr.

   (b) Mols in outlet gas
   $$= \frac{100 - (\% \text{ recovery})(\text{total mols in})}{100}$$

   (c) Mols component absorbed $=$ inlet $-$ outlet

3. Calculate: E_{ai} for specified component (specified in 1.)

$$E_{ai} = \frac{\text{mols component in} - \text{mols component out}}{\text{mols component in}}$$

$$= \text{specified fraction recovery}$$

4. Minimum (L/V) for specified component:

$$(L_o/V_{N+1})_{Min.} = K E_a \left[\frac{\Sigma Y}{1 + \Sigma X} \right]$$

Assuming equilibrium at bottom, $\Sigma Y = 1$. Ignoring ΣX gives slightly conservative value,

$$\left(\frac{L_o}{V_{N+1}} \right)_{min.} = K_1 E_{ai}$$

5. Operating $(L_o/V_{N+1})_o$
   $= $ (specified unit) $(L_o/V_{N+1})_{Min}$

6. Operating

$$A_{1o} = \left(\frac{L_o}{V_{N+1}} \right)_o \left(\frac{1}{K_1} \right) \qquad (8\text{-}68)$$

7. Theoretical plates at operating (L_o/V_{N+1}): solve for N.

$$E_{ai} = \frac{A_{1o}^{N+1} - A_{1o}}{A_{1o}^{N+1} - 1} \qquad (8\text{-}69)$$

$$(N + 1) \log (A_{1o}) = \log \left[\frac{(A_{1o} - E_{ai})}{(1 - E_{ai})} \right]$$

8. Actual trays at operating (L_o/V_{N+1}):
$$N_o = N/E_o$$

E_o values may be calculated from Figure 8-18 or assumed at 20 to 50 percent as an estimating value for hydrocarbon oil and vapors, pressures atmospheric to 800

psig, and temperatures of 40° F. to 130° F. (see Table 8-2).

9. Lean oil rate:
$$L_o = (A_1)(K_1)(V_{N+1})_o, \text{ mols/hr.} \qquad (8\text{-}70)$$

10. For other components: E_{ai} is estimated by

$$E_{ai} = (E_{a1}) \left(\frac{K_1}{K_2} \right), \text{ with} \qquad (8\text{-}71)$$

a limiting value of unity.

Stripping—Determine Theoretical Trays and Stripping Steam or Gas Rate For A Component Recovery[18]

The rich gas from the absorption operation is usually stripped of the desirable components and recycled back to the absorber (Figure 8-29). The stripping medium may be steam or a dry or inert gas (methane, nitrogen, carbon oxides—hydrogen, etc.). This depends upon the process application of the various components.

1. The rich oil flow rate and absorbed component compositions (this is the only composition of concern, not the oil composition, unless reaction or change takes place under the system conditions) are known. From the temperature levels of the available condensing fluids (water, refrigerant, etc.), determine a column operating pressure which will allow proper condensation of the desirable components at the selected temperature, allowing for proper Δt for efficient heat transfer. The condensing pressure (and column operating pressure) may be dictated by the available steam pressure used in stripping or the pressure on the inert stripping gas.

2. From K charts, determine K_1 values for each component at the column temperature and pressure.

3. From a fixed percentage of recovery for key component ($= E_{s1}$ for key component), Mols component stripped/hr. $= G_{m1} = (L_{m+1})(X_{m+1})(E_{s1})$

4. Estimate stripping efficiency for components other than the key by:

$$E_{s2} = E_{s \text{ key}} \left(\frac{K_{\text{key}}}{K_2} \right)$$

Note that no recovery can be greater than 1.00, so any value so calculated is recorded as 1.00, indicating that the component is completely stripped from the rich oil. Calculate mols stripped per hour for each component as in Step (2).

5. The minimum stripping medium (steam or gas)—lean oil ratio is estimated by a trial and error procedure based on key component:

Assume Known			$\Sigma X_i =$			
V_o	L_o	V_o/L_o	$(LX_i)_{m+1}/L_o$	$1 + \Sigma X_i$	$E_{s, key} (1 + \Sigma X_i)$	
—	Same	—	—	—	—	
—	for	—	—	—	—	
—	all	—	—	—	—	
—	trials	—	—	—	—	

$\Sigma Y_i =$				
G_{m1} (step 3)/V_o	$1 + \Sigma Y_i$	$K_{key} (1 + \Sigma Y_i)$	$\dfrac{E_{s, key}(1 + \Sigma X_i)}{K_{key}(1 + \Sigma Y_i)}$	
——	——	——	——	
——	——	——	——	
——	——	——	——	
——	——	——	——	

By assuming several values of V_o, plot V_o/L_o versus $E_{s, Key} (1 + \Sigma X_i)/K_{Key} (1 + \Sigma Y_i)$. The point where they are equal gives the minimum value for V_o/L_o. This calculation can be thought of as assuming equilibrium at the gas outlet end and being slightly conservative by including the $(1 + \Sigma X_i)$ term. Operation at this point requires infinite plates; therefore values larger than the minimum should be used. For economical as well as reasonable operation several values of $(V_o/L_o)_{oper.}$ should be tried and corresponding plates evaluated.

V_o (operating)
$$= (\text{assumed } (V_o/L_o)_{oper.}) (L_o \text{ inlet}), \text{mols/hr.}$$

6. Calculate S_i for the key component, using the value of $(1 + \Sigma X_i)$ calculated in Step 5. Calculate

$$(1 + \Sigma Y_i) = 1 + \Sigma \frac{Y_{m1} \text{ (step 3)}}{V_o \text{ (oper.)}}$$

then, $S_{io} = K_i \left(\frac{V_o}{L_o} \right)_{oper.} \left(\frac{1 + \Sigma Y_i}{1 + \Sigma X_i} \right)$ (8-72)

Sometimes the last term on right can be neglected.

7. Calculate number of theoretical trays, M.

$$E_{si} = \frac{S_{io}^{M+1} - S_{io}}{S_{io}^{M+1} - 1}$$ (8-73)

$$(M_o + 1) \log S_{io} = \log \left[\frac{S_{io} - E_{si}}{1 - E_{si}} \right]$$ (8-74)

8. Actual trays at operating reflux:

$$M_{act.} = \frac{M_o}{E_o}$$

9. Calculate for each component corrected amount stripped:

For each component:

$$S_i = K_i \left[\left(\frac{V_o}{L_o} \right)_{oper.} \left(\frac{1 + \Sigma Y_i}{1 + \Sigma X_i} \right) \right]$$

$(V_o/L_o)_{oper.} = $ fixed in Step 5.

$(1 + \Sigma Y_i)$ and $(1 + \Sigma X_i)$ come from Step 6.

10. From Figure 8-30, read $(S^{M+1} - S)/S^{M+1} - 1) = E_{si}$ for each component at the fixed *theoretical* required trays and at individual S_i values.

11. For final detail, recalculate mols stripped per hour from new E_{si} values and the total quantities of each component in the incoming rich oil. If values do not check exactly, adjustments can be made in steam rate and ΣY_i to give exact values. In many cases this accuracy is not justified since the method is subject to some deviation from theoretically correct values.

12. A graphical solution is presented by Edmister[18] and handled like step-wise distillation.

Equilibrium line: starts at origin of X-Y plot.

For assumed X values, calculate Y corresponding for key component from

$$\frac{X_i}{Y_i} = \frac{1}{K_i} \left(\frac{1 + \Sigma X_i}{1 + \Sigma Y_i} \right)$$

At lean oil end of tower: $\Sigma X_i = 0$ and $\Sigma Y_i = 0$.

Slope of equilibrium line is $Y/X = K_i$

At rich oil end of tower:

$$Y_i = K_i X_i \left(\frac{1 + \Sigma Y_i}{1 + \Sigma X_i} \right)_R$$ (8-75)

Where X_i, ΣX_i and ΣY_i are known. R = rich end.

Operating line:

$$\text{Slope} = L_o/V_o = \frac{\text{Mols lean oil leaving stripper}}{\text{Mols stripping steam (or gas) entering}}$$

At lean end, $Y_i = 0$ (or nearly so in most cases), if not plot accordingly.

Stripping—Determine Stripping-Medium Rate For Fixed Recovery[18]

1. The composition and quantity of rich oil, and percent recovery of a specified key component are known, also column pressure and temperature.

2. Using Figure 8-30 assume a value for theroetical plates, read S_e corresponding to specified value of recovery E_{si} for key component, since:

$$E_s = (S^{M+1} - S)/(S^{M+1} - 1)$$

Note that with this procedure, the effect of the number of theoretical plates available can be determined. In an existing column where the number of trays are fixed, the theoretical trays can be obtained by evaluating an efficiency for the system.

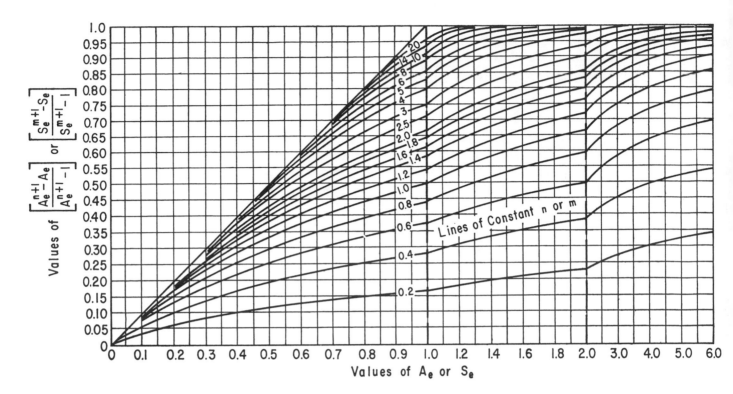

Figure 8-30. Absorption and stripping factors, E_a or E_s versus effective values A_e or S_e (Efficiency functions). (By permission W. C. Edmister, Pet. Engr. Sept. (1947) series to Jan. (1948).)

3. The value of $S_e = S_i$ for key component obtained in Step (2) is equal to

$$S_i = K_i \frac{V_o}{L_o} \left(\frac{1 + \Sigma Y_i}{1 + \Sigma X_i} \right)$$

Using key component:

$$\frac{V_o}{L_o} \left(\frac{1 + \Sigma Y_i}{1 + \Sigma X_i} \right) = \left(\frac{S_i}{K_i} \right), \text{known}$$

Set up table: use K_i for each component to calculate Column 4.

Component	Mols/hr. in Rich Oil	K_i at Col. Cond.	$K_i \left[\frac{V_o \ (1 + \Sigma Y_i)}{L_o \ (1 + \Sigma X_i)} \right]$	E_{si}	Mols/hr. Stripped
—	—	—	—	—	—
—	—	—	—	—	—
—	—	—	—	—	—
	Σ				Σ

From values of S_i calculated $(=S_e)$, read E_{si} values from Figure 8-30 at the number of theoretical trays assumed in Step (2). Note that the S_e corresponds to the number of trays selected, hence will give a value for performance of the system under these particular conditions.

4. Calculate the mols of each component stripped/hr.

$$= (L_{M+1} X_{M+1})_R (E_{si})$$

5. Calculate, V_o, mols/hr. of stripping medium required (steam or gas)

From Step (3), $\dfrac{V_o}{L_o} \left(\dfrac{1 + \Sigma Y}{1 + \Sigma X} \right)$ is known (equals S_i/K_i)

for key component.
   Multiply by L_o.

Then, multiply result by $\dfrac{(1 + \Sigma \ \text{Mols/hr. in rich oil}/L_o)}{(1 + \Sigma \ \text{Mols/hr. stripped (step 3)} /V_o)}$

This is equal to V_o. Note that V_o also is in the right hand side of the denominator, so fractions must be cleared.

Absorption—Edmister Method

This method[18], is well suited to handling the details of a complicated problem, yet utilizing the concept of average absorption and stripping factors. It also allows for the presence of solute components in the solvent and the loss of lean oil into the off gas. Reference 18 presents more details, than are included here. Reference 18 is Edmister's original publication of the basic method for absorbers and strippers. Reference 18 also generates the treatment to include distillation towers and presents the same graphical relationships in a slightly modified form.

Absorption:
Lean Oil Requirement for Fixed Component Recovery in Fixed Tower[18]

1. The rich gas is known, the theoretical trays are fixed (or assumed and corresponding result obtained), the operating pressure and temperature can be fixed.

2. For key component and its fixed recovery, E_a, read A_e from Figure 8-30 at the fixed theoretical trays, N.

$$E_a = \frac{A_e^{N+1} - A_e}{A_e^{N+1} - 1} \qquad (8\text{-}76)$$

3. Assume: (a) Total mols absorbed

　　　(b) Temperature rise of lean oil (Normally 20-40° F.)

　　　(c) Lean oil rate, mols/hr., L_o

4. Using Horton and Franklin's[29] distribution relation for amount absorbed (or vapor shrinkage), per tray:

$$= \left(\frac{V_1}{V_{N+1}}\right)^{1/N}$$

or:
$$\left(\frac{V_1}{V_{N+1}}\right)^{1/N} = \frac{V_1}{V_{i+1}} \qquad (8\text{-}77)$$

Mols off gas leaving top tray
$$= V_1 = V_{N+1} - \text{Mols absorbed (assumed)}$$

Mols gas leaving bottom tray No. N
$$= V_N = V_{N+1} (V_1/V_{N+1})^{1/N}$$

Mols gas leaving Tray No. 2 (from top) $= V_2 = \dfrac{V_1}{\left(\dfrac{V_1}{V_{N+1}}\right)^{1/N}}$

Liquid leaving top tray No. $1 = L_1 = L_0 + V_2 - V_1$

where:

$V_2 =$ Vapor leaving tray No. 2 from top, mols/hr.

$L_0 =$ Lean oil entering (assumed completely free of rich gas components), Mols/ Hr.

$L_N =$ Liquid leaving bottom tray, Mols/hr.

$V_N =$ Vapor leaving bottom tray, Mols/hr.

Liquid leaving bottom tray
$$= L_4 = L_0 + \text{Mols absorbed (assumed)}$$

5. Calculate: At top, L_1/V_1

　　　At bottom, L_N/V_N

6. Use Horton-Franklin method to estimate temperatures at tower trays:

$$\frac{T_N - T_i}{T_N - T_o} = \frac{V_{N+1} - V_{i+1}}{V_{N+1} - V_1} \qquad (8\text{-}78)$$

where:

$T_o =$ Lean oil temperature, °F.

$T_N =$ Bottom tray temperature, °F.

$T_i =$ Tray, i, temperature, °F.

$T_{N+1} =$ Inlet rich gas temperature, °F.

These relations assume constant percent absorption per tray, and temperature change proportioned to the vapor contraction per tray. For estimating use only.

Temperature bottom tray $= T_N = T_{N+1} +$ (assumed rise)

Temperature top tray

$$= T_N - \text{(assume rise)} \left(\frac{V_{N+1} - V_{\text{Tray 2}}}{V_{N+1} - V_1}\right)$$

7. Read K values from equilibrium charts for components in feed at temperatures of (a) top tray and (b) bottom tray.

8. Calculate A_{Ti} and A_{Bi} for each component.

　　A_{Ti} (for top conditions) $= L_1/(K_i V_1)$

　　A_{Bi} (for bottom conditions) $= L_N/(K_i V_N)$

where: $A_{Ti} =$ Absorption factor for each component at conditions of top tray

　　$A_{Bi} =$ Absorption factor for each component at conditions of bottom tray.

9. Read A_e values corresponding to A_{Ti} and A_{Bi} values from Figure 8-31.

10. Read E_{ai} values for fraction absorbed from Figure 8-30 using the A_e values of Step (9) and the fixed or assumed theoretical trays.

11. Calculate the mols of each component absorbed by:

　　(Mol component in inlet rich gas) (E_{ai})

Suggested tabulation:

Component	Mols Rich Gas In.	K		Absorption Factors			Eai, Frac. Absorbed	Mols Absorbed
		Top	Bottom	A_T	A_B	A_e		
—	—	—	—	—	—	—	—	—
—	—	—	—	—	—	—	—	—

12. If the result does not yield the desired amount of the key component absorbed, then reassume the lean oil quantity, L_0, and recalculate. Adjustments may have to be made separately or simultaneously in the assumed absorption quantity until an acceptable result is obtained. After two or three trials a plot of the key variables will assist in the proper assumptions.

Absorption: Number of Trays for Fixed Recovery of Key Component

Here we also consider the more general case when the lean oil contains some of the components to be absorbed from the entering gas. The relationships are most conveniently written as follows[18], for a given component:

$$v_1 = f_s l_o + (1 - f_a) v_{n+1} \qquad (8\text{-}79)$$

$$f_s = \frac{S_e^{n+1} - S_e}{S_e^{n+1} - 1} \qquad (8\text{-}80)$$

$$f_a = \frac{A_e^{n+1} - A_e}{A_e^{n+1} - 1} \qquad (8\text{-}81)$$

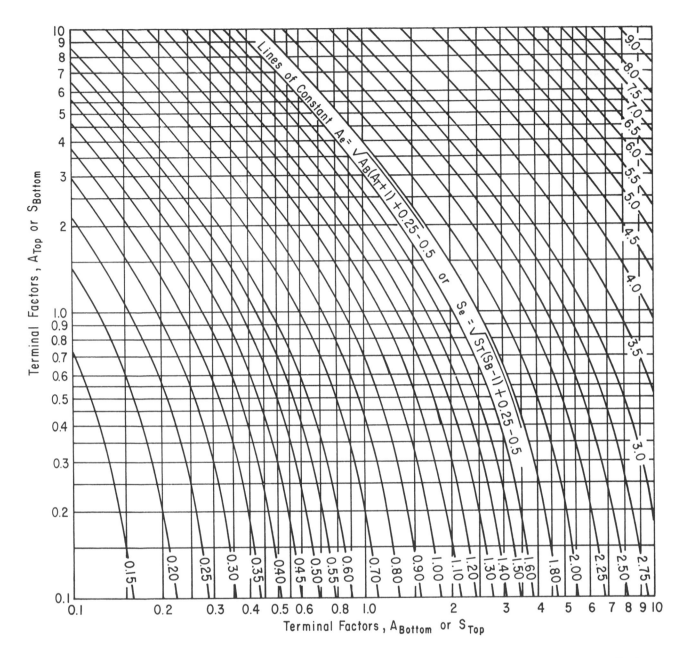

Figure 8-31. Effective absorption and stripping factors used in absorption, stripping and fractionation as functions of Effective Factors. (By permission W. C. Edmister, Pet. Engr., Sept. 1947 series to Jan. 1948.)

Rearranging 8-81 yields

$$1 - f_a = \frac{A_e - 1}{A_e^{n+1} - 1} \qquad (8\text{-}82)$$

Combining Equations 8-79, 8-80, and 8-82 results in

$$v_1 = \left(\frac{S_e^{n+1} - S_e}{S_e^{n+1} - 1} \right) l_o + \left[1 - \left(\frac{A_e^{n+1} - A_e}{A_e^{n+1} - 1} \right) \right] v_{n+1} \qquad (8\text{-}83)$$

which can be written as

$$v_1 = \left[1 - \left(\frac{S_e - 1}{S_e^{n+1} - 1} \right) \right] l_o + \left(\frac{A_e - 1}{A_e^{n+1} - 1} \right) v_{n+1} \qquad (8\text{-}84)$$

where: v_{1i} = Molar gas flow rate of component "i" leaving plate 1 in absorber.

l_{oi} = Molar flow of component "i" in entering liquid to absorber.

v_{n+1_i} = Molar gas flow rate of component "i" in entering gas to absorber.

f_{s_i} = The fraction of V_{n+1_i} that is absorbed by the liquid phase.

f_{a_i} = The fraction of V_{n+1} that is absorbed by the liquid

n = Absorber theoretical trays, also = N

m = Stripper theoretical trays, also = M

A material balance on the key component fixes v_1, l_0 and v_{n+1} for the key. A_e is estimated after A_T and A_B are calculated using approximate conditions at the top and bottom, with a multiple of the minimum solvent rate, which is estimated by assuming equilibrium at the bottom of the tower. S_e is estimated from S_T and S_B. Note that $S_T = 1/A_T$ and $S_B = 1/A_B$. A trial and error solution for the number of theoretical stages is effected by using Equation 8-84 (or 8-83 and Figure 8-30). Values of v_1 for the non-keys can be calculated by using these relationships directly with the calculated value of n. If necessary, the entire procedure can be repeated, using the better estimates of the component flow rates in the leaving streams that were estimated in the first iteration.

Example for Absorption

The gas stream shown in Table 8-1 is fed to an isothermal absorber operating at 90° F and 75 psia. 90% of the n-butane is to be removed by contact with a lean oil stream consisting of 98.7 mol% non-volatile oil and the light components shown in Column 2 of Table 8-1. Estimate the composition of the product streams and the required number of theoretical stages if an inlet rate of 1.8 times the minimum is used.

Solution:

1. Initial estimates of extent of absorption of non-keys.

As a rough approximation, assume the fraction absorbed of a given component is inversely proportional to its K value (Eq. 8-71). For example:

n-C_4, in off gas = $33.6 - (0.9)(33.6) = 3.36$

C_1, in off gas = $1639 - (0.9)\left(\dfrac{0.65}{42.5}\right)(1639.2) = 1616.6$

C_2, in off gas = $165.8 - (0.9)\left(\dfrac{0.65}{7.3}\right)165.8 = 152.5$

The other estimates in column 5 of Table 8-1 are calculated in a similar manner. Note that the C_5's are assumed to be completely absorbed for this first iteration.

2. Inlet rate of rich oil.

The maximum mol fraction n-C_4 in the leaving liquid is taken as that in equilibrium with the incoming gases. Thus, for n-C_4,

$$\frac{l_n}{(L_n)_{min.}} = \frac{0.017}{0.65} = = 0.02617$$

A material balance on n-C_4 yields

$$l_n = 0.002\, L_0 + (0.9)\,33.6$$

With the absorption efficiencies assumed above,

$$L_n = L_0 + 126.34$$

Combining the above equations yields the estimate of the minimum lean oil rate:

$$\frac{0.002\,(L_o)_{min} + (0.9)\,33.6}{(L_o)_{min} + 126.38} = 0.02617$$

Table 8-1

| Component | 90° F
K
75 psia | Feed
Gas In
(mols/hr) | Lean Oil
in
(Mol.
Fraction) | Initial
Estimate
Of Net
Amount
Absorbed
(mols/hr) | Initial
Estimate
(mols/hr) | Off-Gas | | | Lean Oil
In
(mols/hr) | Rich Oil
Out
(mols/hr) |
						After First Iteration (mols/hr)	After Second Iteration (mols/hr)	After Third Iteration (mols/hr)		
Methane	42.5	1639.2	—	22.6	1616.6	1597.5	1598.4	1598.4	—	40.8
Ethane	7.3	165.8	—	13.3	152.5	141.2	141.8	141.8	—	24.0
Propane	2.25	94.9	—	24.67	70.23	49.84	50.76	50.76	—	44.14
i - Butane	0.88	17.8	0.001	11.83	5.97	3.10	3.13	3.13	1.91	16.58
n - Butane	0.65	33.6	0.002	30.24	3.36	3.36	3.36	3.36	3.83	34.07
i - Pentane	0.28	7.9	0.004	7.9	0	2.08	2.03	2.03	7.66	13.53
n - Pentane	0.225	15.8	0.006	15.8	0	2.51	2.44	2.44	11.49	24.85
Heavy Oil	0	—	0.987	0	0	0	0.	0.	1889.83	1889.83
		1975.0	1.000	126.34	1848.66	1799.57	1801.92	1801.92	1914.72	2087.78

or $(L_o)_{min} = 1114.3$ mols/hr

Thus, $L_o = 1.8 (1114.3) = 2005.7$ mols/hr

3. Effective Absorption Factor for n-C$_4$.

The total rich oil out is estimated as

$$L_n = 1975 + 2005.7 - 1848.66 = 2132.04$$

The absorption factors are calculated by

$$A_T = 2005.7/(.65)(1848.66) = 1.669$$
$$A_B = 2132.04/(.65)(1975) = 1.661$$
$$A_e = \sqrt{1.661(2.669) + .25} - 0.5 = 1.664$$

The stripping factor, S_e, is taken as $1/A_e = 0.6010$

4. Calculation of required number of theoretical stages.

Using Equation 8-83 for n-butane,

$$3.36 = \left(\frac{0.601^{n+1} - 0.601}{0.601^{n+1} - 1}\right)4.0 + \left[1 - \left(\frac{1.664^{n+1} - 1.664}{1.664^{n+1} - 1}\right)\right] 33.6$$

which is equivalent to

$$3.36 = \left[1 - \left(\frac{0.601 - 1}{0.601^{n+1} - 1}\right)4.0 + \left(\frac{1.664 - 1}{1.664^{n+1} - 1}\right)\right] 33.6$$

Solving for n by trial and error yields, n = 5.12

5. Calculation of absorption of non-keys.

Equation 8-84 is used with n = 5.12 to calculate v_1, as for example, for i-butane,

$A_T = 1.233$
$A_B = 1.227$
$A_e = \sqrt{1.227(2.333) + 0.25} - 0.5 = 1.229$
$S_e = \dfrac{1}{1.229} = 0.8137$
$v_o = 17.8$
$l_o = (0.001)(2005.7) = 2.01$
$v_1 = \left[1 - \left(\dfrac{0.8137 - 1}{0.8137^{6.12} - 1}\right)2.01 + \left(\dfrac{1.229 - 1}{1.229^{6.12} - 1}\right)\right] 17.8 = 3.10$
$l_n = 17.8 + 2.01 - 3.10 = 16.71$

The remaining non-keys in the off-gas are calculated in a similar manner and are tabulated in Column 6 of Table 8-1. Note that the calculated values are somewhat different from the assumed values in Column 5.

6. Second Iteration.

Using the previous calculated values, the net amount absorbed is $1975 - 17999.95 = 175.41$ mols/hr. The minimum rate of lean oil is calculated from

$$\frac{(0.002)(L_o)_{min} + 0.9(33.6)}{(L_o)_{min} + 175.41} = 0.02617$$

from which $(L_o)_{min} = 1061.2$ mols/hr. and

$$L_o = 1.8 (1061.2) = 1910.2 \text{ mols/hr.}$$

An overall material balance gives $L_n = 2085.6$. The effective absorption factor for n-C$_4$ is $A_e = 1.627$, and $S_e = 0.6145$, n is calculated from

$$3.36 = \left[1 - \frac{0.6145 - 1}{0.6145^{n+1} - 1}\right] 3.82 + \left(\frac{1.627 - 1}{1.627^{n+1} - 1}\right) 33.6$$

from which n = 5.20 theoretical stages.

The non-key components are computed and tabulated in column 7 of Table 8-1.

7. Third Iteration.

A third iteration gave $(L_o)_{min} = 1063.73$, $L_o = 1914.72$, $L_n = 2087.8$, and $V_1 = 1801.92$, with no change in the calculated off gas component flows.

The stripping calculations are handled in a manner similar to the steps above, and using the figures indicated.

Intercooling For Absorbers

Most absorbers require some intercooling between some stages or trays to remove heat of absorption and to provide internal conditions compatable with proper or required absorption. Some temperature rise $(10 - 30°$ F.) is usually designed into the initial conditions. The rise above this must be handled with intercoolers.

The total intercooler duty is the difference between the total heat in of the rich gas and lean oil and the total heat out of the off gas and rich oil all at the terminal calculated or design conditions. The total duty is often divided between several coolers placed to re-cool the oil as it passes down the column. If intercoolers are not used, then the absorption cannot meet the design terminal outlet conditions and the quantity of material absorbed will be reduced. If the intercooling is too great so as to sub-cool, then greater absorption may be achieved, but this can be controlled by the intercooler operation.

A second approach to the same result involves the same requirements as for a balanced "heat" design; the heat of absorption of the actual components absorbed must equal the sum of the heat added to the lean oil and to the lean gas. For hydrocarbon materials these factors can be developed by using total heats.

The relation of Hull and Raymond[32] takes into account heat loss through the column wall, and indicates that either the total heat of absorption or the rich oil outlet temperature for system balance can be calculated. Thus if a reasonable temperature balance is not obtained, the heat load for the intercoolers can be set.

$$W_{Lo} C_{pLo} (T_{Ro} - T_{Lo}) + W_{DG} C_{pDG} (T_{DG} - T_{IG}) +$$

$$W_s C_{ps} (T_{RO} - T_{IG} = \Delta H_s - 0.024 U A'' (T_{AV} - A_{AMB})$$
(8-85)

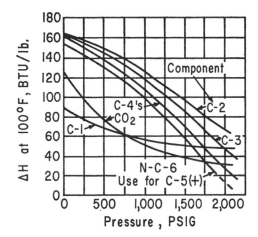

Figure 8-32. Component heats of absorption. (By permission R. J. Hull and K. Raymond, Oil & Gas Journal, Nov. 9, 1953 thru March 15, 1954.)

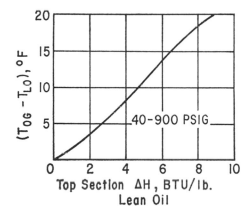

Figure 8-33. Hydrocarbon systems: overhead gas minus lean oil temperature for components absorbed in top "theoretical" tray (or top actual three trays). (By permission R. J. Hull and K. Raymond, Oil & Gas Journal, Nov. 9, 1953 thru March 15, 1954.)

Figure 8-32 presents actual total heats of absorption based on experimental studies.[32] As long as the hydrocarbon absorption is in the range of 80-120° F., the values read from the graph should apply.

Estimation of discharge gas temperature may be made from Figure 8-33, based on test data.

The design of absorbers has not received the empirical design guidelines study so prevalent in distillation problems. The graph of Hutchinson[34], Figure 8-34, is convenient to examine a problem to determine preliminarily the effects of design. This curve is compatible with the conventional absorption factor graphs. The percent extraction gives a quick evaluation of the possibilities of accomplishing the desired absorption. As the number of trays in the absorber is increased, the amount of heavier material (larger A values) absorbed increases greater than the lighter components (lower A values). More heavier materials are also absorbed as the temperature of absorption is lowered. Thus,

a cold lean oil has more capacity per gallon than a warm oil. This requires a study of the entire process and not just the one unit. Heat economy, oil flows, and tower costs all enter into a full evaluation of the absorber as it fits into the plant system.

Many designs are set up by assuming the number of theoretical trays, using best available information for tray efficiencies and then calculating the expected performance. A series of such studies might be made.

Absorption and Stripping Efficiency

Unfortunately the efficiencies for tray and overall column operation are incomplete and nullify to a certain extent some very high quality theoretical performance design. Tray efficiencies may be estimated by Figure 8-18 or Table 8-2.

Example 8-13: Determine Number Trays for Specified Product Absorption

A gas stream is to have the ethylene removed by absorption in a lean oil of molecular weight 160, Sp. Gr. 0.825. The inlet gas is at 70 psig and 100° F. and the oil is at 80° F. The gas rate is 16,000,000 std. cu. ft./day (60° F.). Examine the tower performance for 98 percent ethylene recovery at 1.25 times the minimum L_o/V_N.

Feed Gas

Component	Mol or Volume %
H_2	18.5
CH_4	22.3
C_2H_4	20.5
C_2H_6	0.5
C_3H_6	22.0
C_3H_8	0.7
n, C_4H_{10}	2.5
n, C_5H_{12}	13.0
	100.0

Determine the oil rate and the number of theoretical and actual trays required. (Note this example illustrates that unreasonable results must be examined, not just accepted).

1. Inlet rich gas rate $= \dfrac{16,000,000}{359 \left(\dfrac{14.7}{14.7}\right)\left(\dfrac{460+60}{460+32}\right)}$ (24)

$= 1756$ mols/hr.

Mols ethylene in $= (20.5/100)(1756) = 360$ mols/hr.

Mols ethylene in outlet gas $= (100\text{-}98/100)(360)$
$= 7.20$ mols/hr.

Mols ethylene absorbed in oil $= 360$ -7.2 $= 352.8$ mols/hr.

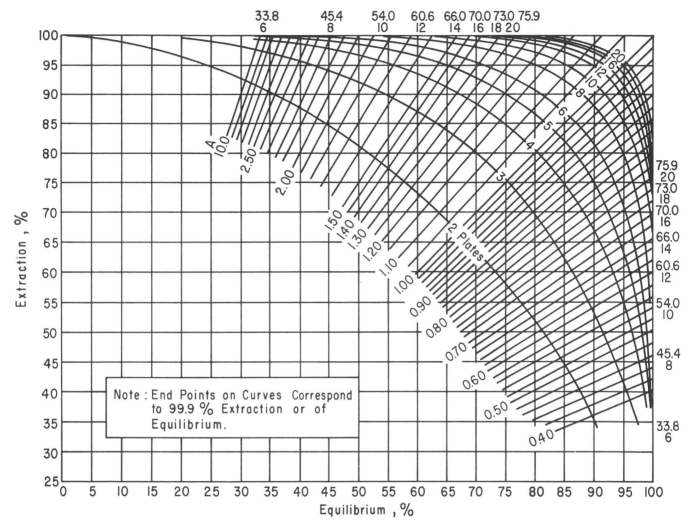

Figure 8-34. Absorption equilibrium curve. (By permission of Petroleum Refiner, Reference No. 28.).

Table 8-2

Absorption-Stripping Approximate Tray Efficiencies**

Type	Pressure Range, psig	Temp., °F.	Range Efficiency %
Absorption			
Hydrocarbon Oils & Vapors	0 - 800	30 - 130	35 - 50
Propane-key	100 - 2100	-	30 - 37* - 38
Butane-key	100 - 2100	-	28 - 33* - 36
Stripping			
Hydrocarbon Oils with Steam	0 - 130	300 - 550	50 - 80
Unsaturates in Oil with closed reboiler	0 - 50		25 - 35

* Average value
** Hull, R. J. and K. Raymond, Oil and Gas Journal, Nov. 9 1953—March 15, 1954.

2. Specified ethylene separation $= 0.98 = E_{ai}$

$$= \frac{\text{Mols in} - \text{Mols out}}{\text{Mols in}}$$

3. Minimum L/V for ethylene:

$$\left(\frac{L_o}{V_{N+1}}\right)_{min} = K_i E_{ai}$$

Average tower conditions for K:
    Temperature $= (100 + 80)/2 = 90°$ F.

Pressure: allow 20 psi pressure drop, then top pressure would be $70 - 20 = 50$ psig

Average: $(50 + 70)/2 = 60$ psig.

K (ethylene) at 60 psig and 90° F. $= 11.5$ (from equilibrium charts).

$$\left(\frac{L_o}{V_{N+1}}\right)_{min} = (11.5)\ (0.98) = 11.28$$

4. Operating $(L_o/V_{N+1})_o = (1.25)\ (11.28) = 14.1$

5. Operating $A_{io} = \left(\dfrac{L_o}{V_{N+1}}\right)_o \left(\dfrac{1}{K_i}\right) = \dfrac{14.1}{11.5} = 1.227$

6. Theoretical trays at operating (L_o/V_{N+1}):

$$E_{ai} = \dfrac{A^{N+1} - A_i}{A^{N+1} - 1} = \dfrac{(1.227)^{N+1} - 1.227}{(1.227)^{N+1} - 1} = 0.98$$

$$(N+1) \log 1.227 = \log \left[\dfrac{1.227 - 0.98}{1 - 0.98}\right]$$

$$N = 11.22$$

7. Actual plates at operating (L_o/V_{N+1}):

Efficiency of oil at 90° F., and Sp. Gr. of 0.825 corresponding to API of 40.

Viscosity = 0.81 centipoises

For O'Connell's efficiency correlation, Figure 8-18.

$$\dfrac{0.825 \ (62.3 \ \text{lb./cu. ft.})}{(11.5)\ (160)\ (0.81)} = 0.0345$$

Reading curve (3), Eff. = 14%

This value is low, but agrees generally with the specific data in O'Connell's[49] report.

Although Drickamer's data is not so specific for absorption, the graph of this correlation gives Eff. = 20% for the 0.81 cp. Since no better information is available, use Eff. = 15%.

$$\text{Actual trays, } N_o = N/E_o = 11.22/0.15 = 74.8$$

$$\text{Use } N_o = 75 \text{ trays}$$

8. Lean oil rate $= L_o = A_i(K_i)(V_{N+1})_o$

$$= (1.227)\ (11.25)\ (1756)$$

$$L_o = 24,200 \text{ mols/hr.}$$

$$\text{GPM oil} = \dfrac{24,200\ (160)}{(8.33)\ (0.825)\ (60)} = 9400$$

This is unreasonable, and is due to the effect of

a. Operating pressure being too low thus giving a high K value

b. Ethylene being light component and difficult to absorb

c. Temperature too high.

9. Recalculation of Steps 3 thru 8.

Assume operating pressure is 700 psig, K = 1.35. Note that this same K value could have been achieved by lowering the operating temperature to −90° F. This is also not practical from the oil standpoint or even from the economics of operating the entire system and refrigeration system at this level, unless (1) the refrigeration is available and (2) a suitable oil is available.

Min. $(L/V) = (1.35)\ (0.98) = 1.32$

Operating $(L/V_{N+1})_o = (1.25)\ (1.32) = 1.65$

Operating $A_{io} = 1.65/1.35 = 1.222$

Theoretical trays at operating (L_o/V_{N+1}):

$$(N+1) \log 1.222 = \log \left[\dfrac{1.222 - 0.98}{1 - 0.98}\right]$$

$$N = 11.2 \text{ trays}$$

Efficiency: $\dfrac{(0.825)\ (62.3)}{(1.35)\ (160)\ (0.81)} = 0.294$

Reading curve (3), Eff. = 29%

Actual trays = 11.1/0.29 = 38.6. Say 40 trays.

Lean oil rate = $(1.222)(1.35)(1756) = 2900$ mols/hr.

$$\text{GPM} = \dfrac{(2900)\ (160)}{(8.33)\ (0.825)\ (60)} = 1122$$

This is still a large quantity of oil to absorb the ethylene. Under some circumstances it might be less expensive to separate the ethylene by low-temperature fractionation.

Example 8-14: Determine Component Absorption in Fixed-Tray Tower

An existing 40-tray tower is to be examined to determine the absorption of a rich gas of the following analysis:

Component	Mols/hr.	Mol wt.	104° K_i 176 psia
H_2	500.0	2	59.0
CH_4	20.9	16	56.0
C_2H_4	131.5	26	8.1
CO	230.0	28	12.3
C_3H_4	3.5	40	0.07
C_4H_2	4.1	50	0.009
	890.0		

1. The key component is methyl acetylene, C_3H_4. Recovery will be based on 96.5 percent of this material.

The tower average temperature will be assumed = 104° F.

The operating average pressure will be = 161 psig.

2. The K_i values are tabulated for the conditions of (1), and were determined from laboratory test data for the special solvent oil being considered.

$K_i = 14.7\ (H_i)/176$, where H_i is Henry's constant expressed as atm./mol. fraction for each component. Note that conventional K charts are only applicable to hydrocarbon oil systems, and do not apply for any special solvents.

3. Calculate tray efficiency for C_3H_4.

Using O'Connell's correlation:

(solvent) at 104° F. = 2.3 cp

Sp. Gr. = 1.0

Mol. wt. solvent 180

K = 0.07

$$HP = \frac{\text{Sp. Gr. solvent}}{(K_{C_3H_4})\,(\text{M. W. solvent})} = \frac{(1.0)\,(62.3)}{(0.07)\,(180)} = 4.94$$

$$\frac{HP}{\mu} = \frac{4.9}{2.3} = 2.13$$

Efficiency = 46.5% (From Figure 8-18)

Use: 45%

Actual number trays in column = 40

Theoretical trays based on 45% efficiency = (40) (.45) = 18

4. Using $E_{ai} = 96.5\%$ for C_3H_4, read A_i from Figure 8-30.

At n = 18

$A_e = A_i = 1.04$

$A_i = L_o/KV_{N+1}$

$V_{N+1} = 890$ mols/hr.

$L_o = (1.04)\,(0.07)\,(890) = 64.8$ mols/hr.

$L_o/V_{N+1} = 64.8/890.0 = 0.0728$

5.

Component	Inlet		$A_i = \dfrac{L_o}{V_{N+1}\,K_i}$	E_{ai}
	$Y_{(N+1)i}$	Mols/Hr. In.		
H$_2$	0.562	500.0	0.001235	0.001235
CH$_4$	0.0235	20.9	0.00130	0.00130
C$_2$H$_2$	0.1478	131.5	0.009	0.009
CO	0.258	230.0	0.00592	0.00592
C$_3$H$_4$	0.00393	3.5	1.04	0.965
C$_4$H$_2$	0.00462	4.1	8.1	1.000
	0.99985	890.0		

Component	Mols/Hr. Absorbed	X_{iR}	Mols/Hr. Off Gas	Y_{1i} (out)
H$_2$	0.617	0.00953	*499.383	0.561
CH$_4$	0.0272	0.00042	20.8728	0.02348
C$_2$H$_2$	1.185	0.0183	130.315	0.14647
CO	1.36	0.021	228.64	0.2565
C$_3$H$_4$	3.37	0.052	0.13	0.00014
C$_4$H$_2$	4.1	0.0633	0	0
	10.659	0.1645		

*These are subtraction differences and do not infer that the results are this accurate.

Typical calculations: for hydrogen

$$A_i = 0.0728/59.0 = 0.001235$$

From Figure 8-30 at n = 18 trays theoretical, and $A_i = 0.001235$ read E_{ai}, except that in this low region some values cannot be read accurately. When A_i is considerably less than 1.0, use $E_{ai} = A_i$ (very little light material recovered), and when A_i is quite a bit larger than 1.0, use $E_{ai} = 1.0$ (heavy material mostly recovered).

Mols component absorbed/hr. $= (V_{N+1})\,(Y_{(N+1)i})E_{ai}$

$$= (890)\,(0.562)\,(0.001235)$$

$$= 0.617$$

Mols component absorbed/mol lean oil $= X_{iR} = 0.0617/64.8$

$$= 0.00953$$

Mols of component in off gas out top of absorber:

$$= 500.0 - 0.617 = 499.383 \text{ mols/hr.}$$

Mols component in, out top of absorber/mol inlet rich gas

$$E_{a1} = \frac{Y_{N+1} - Y_{11}}{Y_{N+1} - Y_o{}^*}, \qquad \text{let } Y_o{}^* = 0$$

$$0.001235 = \frac{0.562 - Y_1}{0.562}$$

$$Y_{1i} = 0.5614$$

6. Correcting values and recalculating

Component	Inlet		$A_i = \dfrac{L_o\,(1 + \Sigma X_{iR})}{V_{N+1}\,K_i}$	E_{ai}
	$Y_{(N+1)i}$	Mols/Hr.		
H$_2$	0.562	500.0	0.00144	0.00144
CH$_4$	0.0235	20.9	0.001513	0.001513
C$_2$H$_2$	0.1478	131.5	0.01048	0.01048
CO	0.258	230.0	0.00689	0.00689
C$_3$H$_4$	0.00393	3.5	1.21	0.98
C$_4$H$_2$	0.00462	4.1	9.43	1.00

Component	Mols/Hr. Absorbed	X_{iR}	Off Gas	
			Mols/Hr.	Y_{1i}
H$_2$	0.72	0.0111	499.28	0.561
CH$_4$	0.0317	0.000488	20.869	0.0232
C$_2$H$_2$	1.38	0.0213	130.12	0.1463
CO	1.585	0.0244	228.415	0.257
C$_3$H$_4$	3.43	0.0529	0.07	0.00008
C$_4$H$_2$	4.1	0.0633	0	0
	11.246	0.1734	878.754	0.9775

Typical calculations, using hydrogen:

$$A_i = \frac{L_o}{V_{N+1}\,(K_i)}\,(1 + \Sigma X_{iR}) = \frac{0.0728}{59.0}\,(1 + 0.1645) = 0.00144$$

Mols component absorbed/hr. $= (0.00144)\,(500) = 0.72$

Mols component absorbed/mol lean oil

$$= 0.72/64.8 = 0.0111$$

Mols of component in off gas out top of absorber:

$$= 500.0 - 0.72 = 499.28$$

These results do not justify recalculation for greater accuracy. Note that 98 percent of the C_3H_4 is absorbed instead of 96.5 percent as initially specified. This could be revised by reassuming a lower (slightly) oil rate, but this is not considered necessary.

The off gas analysis Y_1 represents mols gas out per mol entering rich gas.

For a new design a study should be made of number of trays against required lean oil for a given absorption.

Nomenclature For Part 2, Absorption and Stripping

(Special notations, all others same as for Distillation Performance nomenclature, Part 1)

A' = Edmister's effective absorption factor

A'' = Outside surface area of absorber, sq. ft.

A = Absorption Factor, average

A_e = Effective absorptive factor

A_{Bi} = Absorption factor for each component at conditions of bottom tray

A_{Ti} = Absorption factor for each component at conditions of top tray.

c_p = Specific heat, BTU/lb. (° F.)

E_a = Absorption Efficiency, or fraction absorbed

E_o = Overall tray efficiency, fraction

E_s = Stripping Efficiency, or fraction stripped

f_{ai} = Fraction of v_{n+1i} absorbed by the liquid

f_{si} = Fraction of l_{oi} stripped out of the liquid

G_{mi} = Mols individual components stripped per hour

ΔH = Total heat of absorption of absorbed components, thousand BTU/day

K = Equilibrium constant, equals y/x, at average tower conditions

L_{M+1} = Mols/hour rich oil entering stripper

L_N = Liquid leaving bottom absorber tray, mols/hr.

L_o = Mols/hr. lean oil entering absorber, or leaving stripper

l_{oi} = Molar flow of component "i" in entering liquid to absorber

M = Number theoretical stages in stripper

m = M (see above)

N = Number theoretical stages in absorber

n = N (see above)

S, Se = Stripping factor, average and effective resp.

S' = Edmister's effective stripping factor

T_i = Tray i, temperature, ° F.

T_N = Bottom tray temperature, ° F.

T_{N+1} = Inlet rich gas temperature, ° F.

T_o = Lean oil temperature, ° F.

U = Overall heat transfer coefficient between absorber outside surface and atmosphere, BTU/(sq. ft.) (° F.) (hr.) Usual value = 3.0

V_1 = Mols/hr. lean gas leaving absorber

V_i = Gas leaving tray i, mols/hr.

V_{i+1} = Gas leaving tray, i + 1, mols/hr.

V_N = Vapor leaving bottom absorber tray, mols/hr.

V_{N+1} = Mols/hr. rich gas entering absorber

V_o = Mols/hr. stripping medium (steam or gas) entering stripper

v_{1i} = Molar gas flow rate of component "i" leaving plate 1 in absorber

v_{n+1i} = Molar gas flow rate of component "i" in entering gas to absorber

W = Rate of flow, thousand pounds/day

X = Number mols absorbed component or stripped per mol lean oil entering column

X_1 = Number mols liquid phase component in equilibrium with Y_1

X_{iR} = Mols of a component in liquid absorbed per mol of lean oil entering column

ΣX_i = Total mols of all liquid phase components absorbed per mol of lean oil (omitting lean oil present in liquid phase, considered = 1.0)

X_{M+1} = Number liquid phase mols of component entering stripper per mol of lean oil

X_{oi} = Number liquid phase mols of component entering absorber with lean oil per mol of lean oil

Y_1 = Number vapor phase mols of component leaving top plate of absorber per mol rich gas entering absorber

Y_i = Mols component in vapor phase from tray "i"/mol rich gas entering absorber

ΣY_i = Total mols of all vapor phase components stripped per mol of stripping medium

Y_{N+1} = Number vapor phase mols of component entering absorber per mol rich gas entering

Y_o^* = Number vapor phase mols of component in equilibrium with lean oil per mol of rich gas entering

Subscripts

1, 2, etc. = Components in a system

Amb = Ambient

A_{vg}, A_v = Arithmetic average

DG = Discharge gas

e = Effective

i = Individual components in mixture

IG = Intake gas

Key = Key component

L = Lean concentration end of column

LO = Lean oil

Min = Minimum condition

o = Operating condition

R = Rich concentration end of column

RO = Rich oil

S = Absorbed components

Part 3: Mechanical Designs for Performance

The determination of the number of trays in a distillation column is only part of the design necessary to insure system performance. The interpretation of distillation, absorption or stripping requirements into a mechanical vessel with internal components (trays) to carry out the function requires use of theoretical and empirical data. The costs of this equipment are markedly influenced by the column diameter and the intricacies of the trays, such as caps, risers, weirs, downcomers, perforations, etc. Calcu-

lated tray efficiencies for determination of actual trays can be lost by any unbalanced and improperly designed tray.

Contacting Trays

The particular tray selection and its design can materially affect the performance of a given distillation, absorption, or stripping system. Each tray should be designed so as to give as efficient a contact between the vapor and

Figure 8-35. Bubble cap tray in large column. (Courtesy F. W. Glitsch & Sons, Dallas, Texas.)

Figure 8-36. Slip-type assembly for bubble cap in small column 1'-10 13/16" I.D. (Courtesy F. W. Glitsch & Sons, Dallas, Texas.)

liquid as possible, within reasonable economic limits. It is not practical in most cases to change the design of each tray to fit calculated conditions. Therefore, the same tray design is usually used throughout the column, or the top section may be of one design (or type) while the lower section is of another design. The more individual tray designs included in a column, the greater the cost.

Tray Types and Distinguishing Application Features

Bubble Cap

Vapor rises up through "risers" or "up-takes" into bubble cap, out through slots as bubbles into surrounding liquid on tray. Bubbling action effects contact. Liquid flows over caps, outlet weir, and downcomer to tray below, Figures 8-35, 36, and 48.

Capacity: moderately high, maintains efficiency.

Efficiency: most data is for this type, as high as other tray designs.

Entrainment: about three times that of perforated type plate or sieve tray. Jet-action accompanies bubbling.

Flexibility: most flexible of tray designs for high and low vapor and liquid rates. Allows positive drain of liquid from tray. Liquid heads maintained by weirs.

Application: all services except extremely coking, polymer formation or other high fouling conditions. Use for extremely low flow conditions where tray must remain wet and maintain a vapor seal.

Tray Spacing: 18-inch average, 24 to 36-inch for vacuum conditions.

Figure 8-37. Sieve tray with integral downcomer. (Courtesy Hendrick Mfg. Co., Carbondale, Pa.)

Sieve Tray or Perforated Tray With Downcomers:

Vapor rises through small holes (⅛ to 1-inch) in tray floor, bubbles through liquid in fairly uniform manner. Liquid flows across tray floor over weir (if used), through downcomer to tray below. Figures 8-37 and 38.

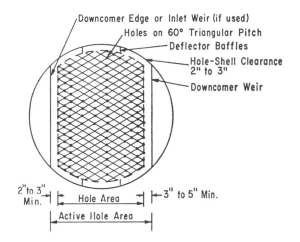

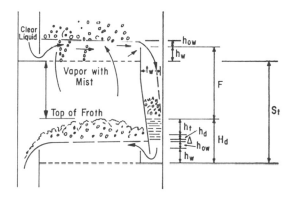

Figure 8-38. Sieve or perforated tray with downcomers.

Capacity: as high or higher than bubble cap at design or down to 60 percent of design rates with good efficiency. At lower throughputs performance drops as efficiency falls off rapidly.

Efficiency: As high as bubble caps in region of design, but falls to unacceptable values when capacity reduces below 60 percent. (approximately)

Entrainment: Only about one-third that of bubble cap trays.

Flexibility: Not generally suitable for columns operating under variable load, falling below 60 percent of design. Tray weeps liquid at low vapor rates.

Application: Systems where high capacity near-design rates to be maintained in continuous service. Handles suspended solid particles flushing them down from tray to tray. Holes become plugged in salting-out systems where trays run hot and dry (as underside of bottom tray).

Tray Spacing: Can be closer than bubble cap due to improved entrainment. Fifteen inches is average, 9-inch, 10-inch and 12-inch are acceptable, with 20 to 30 inches for vacuum.

Perforated Plate Without Downcomers:

Vapor rises through holes (³⁄₁₆ to 1-inch) in tray floor and bubbles through liquid. At the same time liquid head forces liquid countercurrent through these holes and onto tray below. Liquid flow forms random patterns in draining and does not form continuous streamlets from each hole. See Figure 8-39.

Capacity: Quite similar to sieve tray, as high or higher than bubble cap tray from 50 percent up to 100 percent design rate (varies with system and design criteria). Performance at specification quality falls off at lower rates.

Efficiency: Usually not quite as high as bubble caps in region of design, but falls to unacceptable values below 60 percent design rate.

Figure 8-39. Perforated tray without downcomer. (Courtesy Hendrick Mfg. Co., Carbondale, Pa.)

Figure 8-40. Type "T" flexitray. (Courtesy Koch Engineering Co. Inc. Wichita, Kansas.)

Figure 8-42. Nutter float valve tray with downcomer. (Courtesy Nutter Engineering Co., Tulsa, Okla.)

Figure 8-43. Nutter float valve detail. (Courtesy Nutter Engineering Co., Tulsa, Okla.)

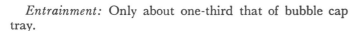

Figure 8-41. Type "A" flexitray with double pass. (Courtesy Koch Engineering Co. Inc., Wichita, Kansas.)

Entrainment: Only about one-third that of bubble cap tray.

Application: Systems where high capacity near-design rates to be maintained in continuous service. Handles suspended crystal and small solid materials, as well as polymer forming materials. Holes become plugged in salting-out systems where trays run hot and dry (as underside of bottom tray). Good in vacuum or low pressure drop design.

Tray Spacing: Can be closer than bubble cap due to improved entrainment. Twelve-inch is average; 9 to 18-inch acceptable; 18 to 30 inches for vacuum.

Proprietary Trays

There are many special tray designs which solve special problems and exceed the capabilities of the conventional trays. The comments regarding performance are those claimed by the manufacturer.

Tray	Manufacturer	Comments
Flexitray Type T Figure 8-40	Koch Engineering Co.	Low pressure drop, high capacity, high efficiency, high flexibility
Flexitray Type A Figure 8-41	Koch Engineering Co.	Very low pressure drop, low tray spacing, extremely high capacity
Figure 8-42 Figure 8-43	Nutter Engineering Co. Nutter Engineering Co.	Low pressure drop, high capacity, high efficiency
Type V-1 Ballast Cap Figure 8-44	F. W. Glitsch & Sons	High capacity, wide flexibility of operating range, high efficiency over wide range.
Type A-1 Ballast Cap Figure 8-45	F. W. Glitsch & Sons	Increased capacity, high flexibility, high efficiency
Turbogrid	Shell Development Co.	High capacity, low pressure drop
Multiple Downcomer Figure 8-47	Union Carbide Corp., Linde Div.	High capacity, low pressure drop, high efficiency

Figure 8-44. Type V-1 ballast tray. (Courtesy F. W. Glitsch & Sons Dallas, Texas.)

Figure 8-45. Type A-1 ballast tray. (Courtesy F. W. Glitsch & Sons, Dallas, Texas.)

Figure 8-46. Ripple tray. (Courtesy Stone & Webster Engineering Corp., Boston, Mass.)

Figure 8-47. Linde Multiple-Downcomer Tray. (By permission Union Carbide-Linde Division.)

Bubble Cap Tray Design

The bubble cap has been studied extensively and several design recommendations have been presented over the years. The most complete and generally applicable is that of Bolles.[5] It should be stressed that proper mechanical interpretation of process requirements is essential in design for efficient and economic operation. There is not just one result, but a multiplicity of results, each unique to a particular set of conditions, and some more economical than others. Yet at the same time, many of the mechanical design and fabrication features can be identical for these various designs.

The tray and caps operate as a unit or system; therefore they must be so considered in design (Figures 8-48 and 8-49.)

Standardization

The custom design of the trays for each application is usually unnecessary and uneconomical. Instead most designers utilize a standard reference tray layout and cap size to check each system. If the results of the tray hydraulics study indicate operation unsatisfactory for the standard tray, then alterations of those features controlling the out-of-line performance is in order, utilizing the same method as will be outlined for the initial design of a custom tray. It is understood that such a standard tray cannot be optimum for every application but experience

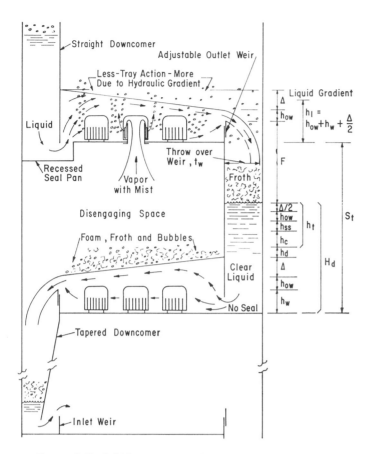

Figure 8-48. Bubble cap tray schematic—dynamic operation.

has demonstrated that many applications fit. The economic advantages of utilizing a limited number of bubble cap sizes and designs are reflected in warehouse stocks. The standardization of layouts, downcomer areas, weir lengths and many other features are reflected in savings in engineering mechanical design time.

At the same time, systems which do not adapt themselves to this standardization should be recognized and handled as special designs.

Design Objectives

Each tray design should ultimately resolve and achieve the following:

1. Capacity: high for vapor and/or liquid as required. This yields the smallest column diameter for a given throughput. Flexibility or adaptability to high and low fluctuations in vapor and liquid rates.

2. Pressure Drop: low pressure drop is necessary to reduce temperature gradients between top and bottom of the column. High pressure drop is usually (but not always) associated with uneconomical design. In some systems pressure drop is not a controlling feature, within reasonable limitations.

3. Efficiency: high efficiency is the objective of each tray performance. The better the contact over a wide range of capacities, the higher will be the efficiency throughout this range.

4. Fabrication and Installation Costs: details should be simple to maintain low costs.

5. Operating and Maintenance Costs: mechanical details must account for the peculiarities of the system fluids (coking, suspended particles, immiscible fluids, etc.) and accommodate the requirements for drainage, cleaning (chemical or mechanical), corrosion, etc., in order to keep the daily costs of operation and downtime to a minimum.

Bubble-Cap-Tray Tower Diameter

Column diameter for a particular service is a function of the physical properties of the vapor and liquid at the tray conditions, the efficiency and capacity characteristics of the contacting mechanism (bubble trays, sieve trays, etc.) as represented by velocity effects including entrainment, and the pressure of the operation. Unfortunately the inter-relationship of these is not clearly understood. Therefore diameters are determined by relations correlated by empirical factors. The factors influencing bubble cap and similar devices, sieve tray and perforated plate columns are somewhat different.

The Souders-Brown[67] empirically correlated maximum allowable mass velocity is represented in Figure 8-50 for "C" Factor determination, and in Figure 8-51 for solution of the relation:

$$W = C \left[\rho_v \left(\rho_L - \rho_v\right)\right]^{\frac{1}{2}} \qquad (8\text{-}86)$$

Figure 8-49. Bubble cap performance.

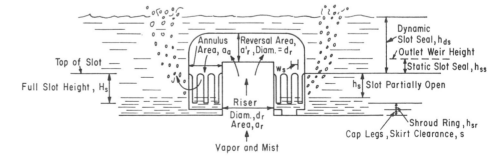

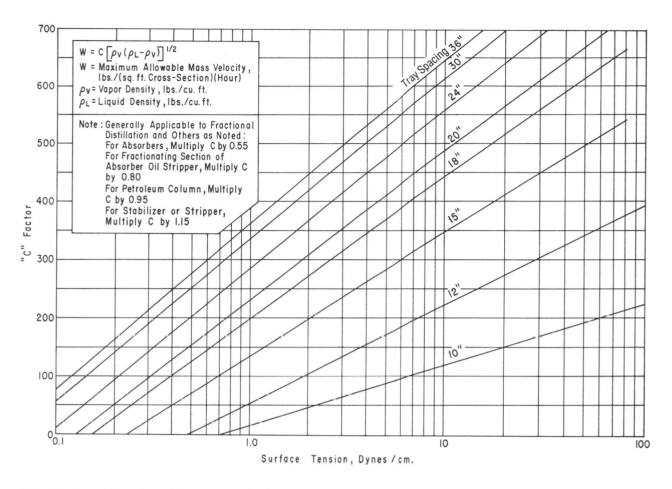

Figure 8-50. "C" factors for column diameter using bubble cap trays. (Adapted by permission M. Souders, Jr., and G. G. Brown, Ind. and Eng. Chem. Vol. 26, p. 98 (1934), copyright The American Chemical Society.)

where: W = Maximum allowable mass velocity through column using bubble cap trays, lbs./(sq. ft. cross-section) (hour)

C = Factor from Figure 8-50 related to entrainment

ρ_v = Vapor density, lbs./cu. ft.

ρ_L = Liquid density, lbs./cu. ft.

The "C" factor is determined at the top and bottom (or intermediate) positions of the column in order to evaluate the point of maximum required diameter. The "W" rate obtained in this solution is the maximum allowable, and hence corresponds to the minimum acceptable diameter for operation with essentially no entrainment carryover from plate to plate. Normally a factor of "safety" or "ignorance" of 1.10 to 1.25 would be applied (W divided by 1.10 to 1.25) if irregularities in capacity, system pressure or other significant variables can be anticipated. Recent experience indicates that the relation is somewhat conservative for pressure (5 to 250 psig) operated distillation systems, and the maximum allowable rate can be increased by 5-15 percent (W times 1.05 to 1.15)

exercising judgment and caution. Basically this reflects the satisfactory operation at conditions tolerating some entrainment with no noticeable loss in fractionating efficiency. In any case the shell diameter should be rounded to the nearest inches on the diameter for fabrication standardization. Diameters such as 3 ft., 8⅝ in. inside diameter are to be avoided, but can be used if conditions warrant. Standard tray layouts for caps, weirs, etc. are usually set at 6-inch intervals of diameter starting about 24 to 30 inches.

The diameter based on vapor flow rate, V', in the region of greatest flow:

$$D = \left[\frac{4}{\pi} \left(\frac{V'}{W} \right) \right]^{\frac{1}{2}}$$

Entrainment may not be the controlling factor in proper design. In cases of high liquid load or with extremely foamy or frothy fluids the tendency to flood is generally increased by close tray spacing. The hydraulics of the tray operation must be evaluated and the liquid height in the downcomer reviewed for approach to flooding. If

(Text continued on page 72)

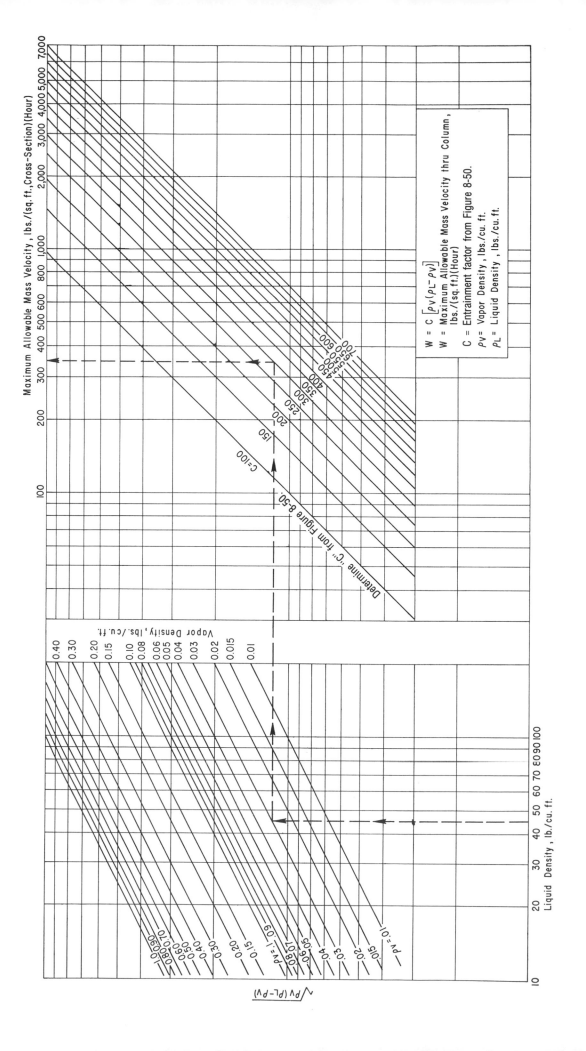

Figure 8-51. Allowable mass velocity for fractionation, absorption and stripping columns.

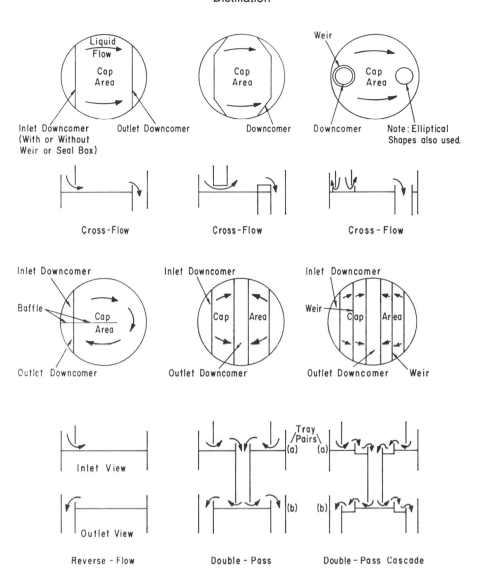

Figure 8-52. Tray types by liquid paths.

Table 8-3[5]
Guide for Tentative Selection of Tray Type

Estimated Tower Dia. Ft.	Range of Liquid Capacity, GPM			
	Reverse Flow	Cross Flow	Double Pass	Cascade Double-Pass
3.........	0–30	30–200	....	....
4.........	0–40	40–300	....	....
6.........	0–50	50–400	400–700	....
8.........	0–50	50–500	500–800	....
10........	0–50	50–500	500–900	900–1400
12........	0–50	50–500	500–1000	1000–1600
15........	0–50	50–500	500–1100	1100–1800
20........	0–50	50–500	500–1100	1100–2000

Table 8-4[5]
Approximate Distribution of Areas as Percent of Tower Area
(Allocated cap area is determined by difference)

Tower Diameter Ft.	Downflow Area		Liquid Distribution Area			
	Cross Flow	Double Pass	Cross Flow	Double Pass	Cascade Double	End Wastage
3......	10–20	.....	10–25	.....	.....	10–30
4......	10–20	.....	8–20	.....	.....	7–22
6......	10–20	20–30	5–12	15–20	.....	5–18
8......	10–20	18–27	4–10	12–16	.....	4–15
10......	10–20	16–24	3–8	9–13	20–30	3–12
12......	10–20	14–21	3–6	8–11	15–25	3–10
15......	10–20	12–18	2–5	6–9	12–20	2–8
20......	.....	10–15	.....	5–7	9–15	2–6

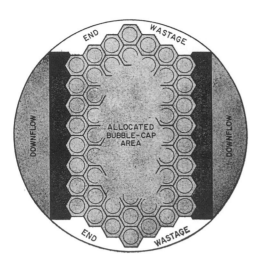

Figure 8-53. Classification of tray area. (By permission W. L. Bolles, Reference 5.)

Table 8-5
Tray Design Guide for Bubble Caps**

Materials of Construction
Type ....Light gage metal*
Material..........Determined by corrosion conditions

Tray Type
General use ....Cross-flow
Low L/V ratio......................Reverse-flow
High L/V or large towers...............Double-pass
Very high L/V or very
   large towers.................Double-pass, cascade

Downcomers and Weirs
Downcomer type ....Segmental
Downflow baffle ....Vertical
Weirs for normal loads.....................Straight
Weirs for low loads......................Notched
Weir adjustment ....1-3 in.*
Length: Cross-flow trays, % Tower Dia. 60-70%*
Length: Double pass trays, % Tower Dia. 50-60%*
Downcomer width for double-pass trays.......8-12 in.*

Bubble-Caps
Nominal size for:
  2.5-3 ft. towers ....4 in.*
  4-10 ft. towers ....4 in.
  10-20 ft. towers ....6 in.
Design.....................Use suggested standards*
Pitch..........Equil. triangular, rows normal to flow
Spacing ....1-3 in.

Table 8-5 (Cont'd)

Bubble-Caps (Cont.)
Skirt height ....0.25-1.5 in.*
Fastening ....Removable design
Clearances
  Cap to tower wall...............1.5 in. minimum
  Cap to weir..................... 3 in. minimum
  Cap to downcomer or downflow baffle..3 in. minimum*

Tray Dynamics
Mean slot opening
  Maximum ....100% slot height
  Minimum .... 0.5 in.
Mean dynamic slot submergence
  Vacuum operation ....0.25-1.5 in.*
  Atmospheric ....0.50-2.0 in.*
  50-100 psig .... 1.0-3.0 in.*
  200-500 psig .... 1.5-4.0 in.*
Vapor distribution ratio (Δ/h_c)...........0.5 maximum
Height clear liquid
  in downcomers.....50% downflow height, maximum
Downflow residence time.........5 seconds, minimum
Liquid throw over weir..60% downflow width, maximum
Entrainment
  As mol/mol dry vapor..............0.10 maximum
Pressure drop.................As limited by process

Tray Spacing
For towers 2.5-10 ft.* ....18 in.
For towers 4-20 ft.* ....24 in.

Miscellaneous Design Factors
Inlet weirs
  ....Use as required for liquid distribution*
Intermediate weirs:
     Minimum height > height liquid downstream
Reverse-flow baffles:
      Minimum height twice clear liquid
Redistribution baffles
  Location:
  All rows where end space is 1-in. > cap spacing
  Clearance to caps.............Same as cap spacing
  Height.................Twice height clear liquid
Downflow baffle seal
  Weir to baffle < 5 ft. .... 0.5 in.
  Weir to baffle 5-10 ft. .... 1.0 in.
  Weir to baffle > 10 ft. .... 1.5 in.
Tray design deflection (structural)........... ⅛ in.
Drain holes
  Size ....⅜-⅝ in.
  Area...............4 sq. in./100 sq. ft. tray area
Leakage:
  ......Max. fall 1.0 in. from top of weir in 20 min.
    with drain holes plugged

Construction Tolerances
Tray levelness*.......⅛-inch Max. under 36-inch Dia.*
            ³⁄₁₆-inch Max. 36-60-inch Dia.*
            ¼-inch Max. over 60-inch. Dia.*
Weir levelness ....± ¹⁄₁₆-in.*

** Bolles, W. L., *Petroleum Processing*,[5]
and as modified by this author.*

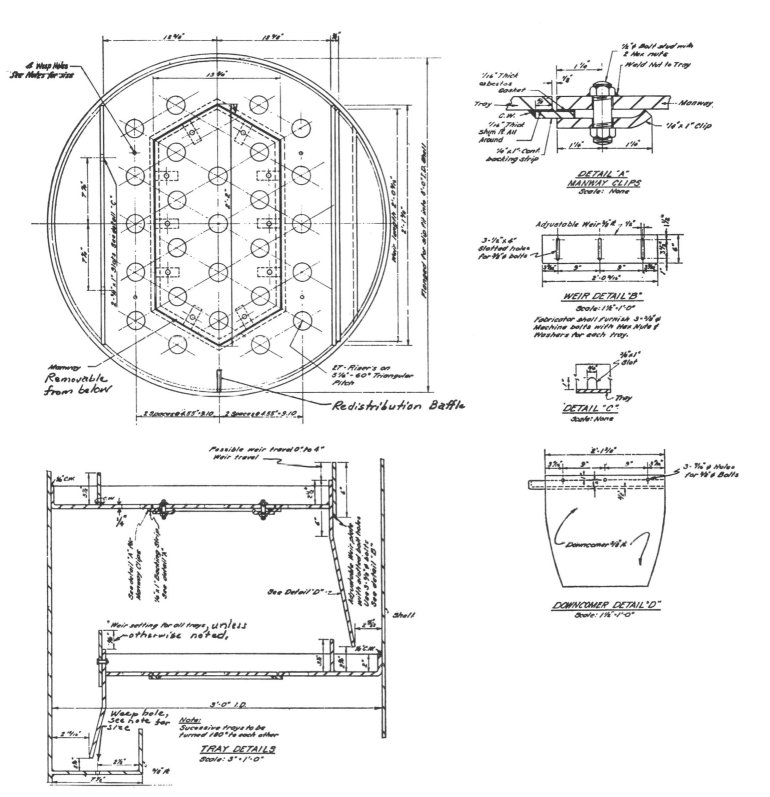

Figure 8-54. Typical bubble cap tray details. 3'-0" diameter column; 4" caps.

liquid height in the downcomer exceeds one-half the tray spacing, the spacing should be increased and the column rechecked. In such cases entrainment is of no worry as the allowable entrainment vapor capacity will be greater than needed to satisfy the increased tray spacing.

Tray Layouts
Flow Paths

The simplest tray arrangement considering fluid flow and mechanical details is the cross-flow shown in Figure 8-52. It fits the majority of designs. When liquid flows become small with respect to vapor flows the reverse flow tray is recommended; when liquid load is high with respect to vapor, the double pass tray is suggested, as the path is cut in half and the liquid gradient reduced; and for the extremely high liquid loads the double-pass cascade is suggested. These last two are usually encountered only in large-diameter towers.

The liquid flow paths across the tray are important, as channelling to one area or another prevents efficient vapor contact. Short tray baffles are often installed to prevent short circuiting, particularly near the column shell wall. The segmental downcomer with straight chordal type weirs provides an efficient initial distribution pattern for liquid. Circular or pipe-type downcomers with corresponding shaped weirs require careful attention to the liquid path as it leaves or enters such a downcomer. For small liquid flows they serve very well. A guide for tentative selection of the tray type for a given capacity is given in Table 8-3.[5]

Figure 8-53 and Table 8-4 identify the distribution of areas of a tray by the action of the tray area.

A tray design guide is given in Table 8-5 and is as presented by Bolles[5] except with modifications where noted.

Figure 8-54 is a 3-foot 0-inch diameter tray, and is representative of details associated with tray design.

A typical 4-inch pressed cap is shown in Figure 8-55.

The details of these figures are only one set of many which will adequately serve as a general purpose tray. Since such a tray is adaptable to many services, it cannot be as specific for optimum design, as the designer of a particular system might prefer. Table 8-6 gives bubble cap and riser layout data and weir lengths for other sizes of general purpose trays.

Caps suitable for particular tray designs are shown in Figures 8-56, 57, and 58. The rectangular caps require layouts differing from the bell caps, but similar in design principles of flow path evaluation.

Layout Helps

The scheme for arranging caps and downcomers as proposed by Bolles[5] is one of several. Plain drafting using the suggested guides is a bit longer than the short cuts. The layout sheet of Figures 8-59 and 8-60 is convenient once cap-pitch master layouts are made for the sizes normally used. Figure 8-61—8-68 and 8-54 present tray layouts to

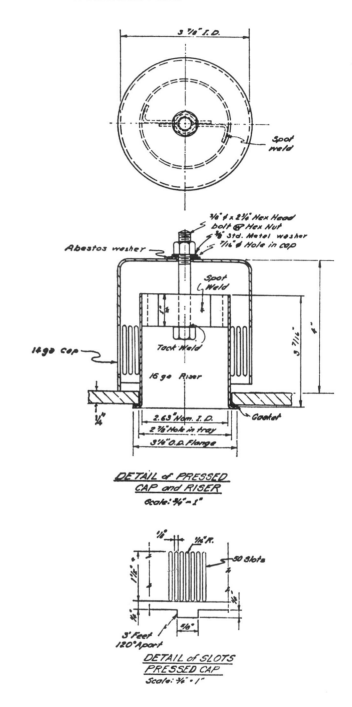

Figure 8-55. Typical 3⅞" I.D. (Nominal 4") pressed bell bubble cap.

match the data given in Table 8-6. These have successfully fitted many different processing situations.

Cap Layout

Caps should be arranged on the plate in 60° equilateral layout, with the liquid flowing into the apex of the triangle rather than parallel to the base. The liquid flows normal to each row of caps.

(Text continued on page 87)

GENERAL NOTES

(1) "a" dimension should not be less than metal thickness on closed tooth slots, and preferable 1.5 times metal thickness. (Does not apply on open tooth slots if slots are tapering to a top tooth width of 2 times metal thickness.)

(2) Bubble cap I.D. has been set as a fixed dimension with the O.D. of the cap a minor variable. This permits the use of a standard slotting mandrel for various gauges of material used on a cap with a fixed I.D. dimension. Fixing the cap I.D. will also maintain a constant inside area and its relationship to annular area.

(3) Riser O.D. has been set as a fixed dimension to prevent disturbing balance between riser area and annular area and allow ease of fitting of risers to deck sections irrespective of metal thickness used on risers. This is important principally on a "pull-up" riser inserted through the deck from beneath the tray.

(4) Columns "U", "V" and "W" are assumed and established to give a cap slot area of approximately 1.7 to 1.85 times the riser area. The size and shape of the slots have been arbitrarily selected so that column "Z" could be calculated. These columns are of academic interest and may be of value as a comparison in selecting a slot shape or area of greater desirability.

(5) Formula to find riser I.D. "D" (with a wall thickness $= t_r$) when annular area $= \phi$. Vapor uptake area. $\phi =$ any desired ratio of vapor uptake area to annular area. ($J = \phi E$)

$$D = \frac{2}{\phi + 1} \sqrt{\frac{N(\phi + 1)}{\pi} - \phi t_r{}^2} - \frac{2 t_r}{\phi + 1}$$

BUBBLE CAP FIXED I.D.		RISER #1		VAPOR RISER SIZE FOR AN APPROXIMATE VALUE OF ANNULAR (OR REVERSAL) AREA − RISER (VAPOR UPTAKE) AREA. J (or H) = E +					RISER #2		VAPOR RISER SIZE FOR AN APPROXIMATE VALUE OF ANNULAR (OR REVERSAL) AREA = 1.25 RISER (VAPOR UPTAKE) AREA. J_1 (or H_1) = 1.25 E_1					CAP SPACING (Δ) FOR AN APPROXIMATE VALUE OF FREE SPACE AREA = 2.0 : AREA RISER #1 OR 2.4 : AREA RISER #2				
A	B	C	D	E	F	G	H	J	C_1	D_1	E_1	F_1	G_1	H_1	J_1	K	L	M	N	P
O.D.	I.D.	O.D.	I.D.	INTERNAL RISER AREA	EXTERNAL RISER AREA	VERTICAL SPACE RISER TO CAP	REVERSAL AREA	ANNULAR AREA	O.D.	I.D.	INTERNAL RISER AREA	EXTERNAL RISER AREA	VERTICAL SPACE RISER TO CAP	REVERSAL AREA	ANNULAR AREA	CAP Δ SPACING	DISTANCE BETWEEN ADJACENT CAPS	DISTANCE BETWEEN CAP ROWS	INTERNAL AREA OF CAP (FIXED)	EXTERNAL AREA OF CAP (16 GA.)
	(2)	(3)	(5)						(3)	(5)										
FOR 16 ga. (.062)	FIXED FOR ALL GAUGES	FIXED FOR ALL GAUGES	FOR 16 ga. (.062)	$\frac{\pi D^2}{4}$	$\frac{\pi C^2}{4}$	FOR H : E = 1 MIN.	$\pi D G$	N−F	FIXED FOR ALL GAUGES	FOR 16 ga. (.062)	$\frac{\pi D_1{}^2}{4}$	$\frac{\pi C_1{}^2}{4}$	FOR $H_1 : E_1 = 1.25$ MIN.	$\pi D_1 G_1$	N−F_1	FOR S : E = 2 MIN.	K−A	.866 K	$\frac{\pi B^2}{4}$	$\frac{\pi A^2}{4}$
9.00	8½	6¾	6.187	30.069	31.296	1⅜	21.588	30.566	6	5.875	27.109	28.274	1⅝	34.607	33.588	12½	3½	10.5	61.862	63.617
8.50	8⅛	5⅞	5.812	26.535	27.688	1½	27.39	27.40	5⅝	5.50	23.758	24.85	1⅝	30.238	30.238	11½	3	9.96	55.088	56.745
8.00	7⅝	5⅜	5.50	23.758	24.850	1¾	24.83	23.857	5¼	5.187	21.135	22.166	1⅝	26.483	26.541	10¹³⁄₁₆	2¹³⁄₁₆	9.36	48.707	50.265
7.50	7⅛	5¼	5.125	20.629	21.648	1¾	21.12	21.07	5	4.875	18.665	19.635	1½	22.973	23.083	10¼	2¾	8.822	42.718	44.179
7.00	6⅝	4⅞	4.750	17.721	18.665	1¼	18.65	18.457	4⅝	4.50	15.904	16.80	1½	21.21	20.322	9½	2½	8.23	37.122	38.485
6.50	6⅛	4⅞	4.437	15.466	16.349	1⅜	15.68	15.571	4¼	4.187	13.772	14.607	1⅝	17.26	17.313	8¹³⁄₁₆	2⁵⁄₁₆	7.63	31.92	33.183
6.25	6¼	4⅜	4.250	14.186	15.033	1⅜	15.02	14.432	4¼	4.00	12.566	13.364	1⅝	16.487	16.101	8⁵⁄₁₆	2⁵⁄₁₆	7.31	29.465	30.68
6.00	5⅞	4⅝	4.062	12.962	13.772	1¾	13.55	13.338	4	3.875	11.793	12.566	1½	15.218	14.544	8⅛	2⅛	7.03	27.11	28.274
5.75	5⅜	4	3.875	11.793	12.566	1	12.174	12.284	3¹⁵⁄₁₆	3.687	10.680	11.416	1⅝	13.75	13.434	7¾	2	6.72	24.85	25.967
5.50	5⅜	3¹³⁄₁₆	3.687	10.68	11.416	1	11.585	11.275	3⅝	3.50	9.621	10.321	1¾	12.371	12.37	7⅛	1¹¹⁄₁₆	6.44	22.691	23.758
5.25	5⅛	3⅞	3.50	9.621	10.321	· ¹³⁄₁₆	10.30	10.308	3½	3.375	8.946	9.621	1¾	11.26	11.008	7½	1¾	6.17	20.629	21.648
5.00	4⅞	3½	3.375	8.946	9.621	⅞	9.278	9.044	3⅜	3.187	7.9798	8.6179	1	10.014	10.047	6⅝	1¾	5.84	18.665	19.635
4.75	4⅝	3¾	3.187	7.98	8.618	¹³⁄₁₆	8.234	8.182	3¼	3.00	7.069	7.67	1	9.425	9.13	6¾	1¹¹⁄₁₆	5.58	16.8	17.721
4.50	4⅜	3⅛	3.00	7.069	7.67	¹³⁄₁₆	7.65	7.363	3	2.875	6.492	7.069	¹³⁄₁₆	8.463	7.964	6¼	1⅝	5.31	15.033	15.904
4.25	4⅛	2¹³⁄₁₆	2.812	6.213	6.777	¾	6.63	6.587	2¹³⁄₁₆	2.687	5.673	6.213	⅞	7.388	7.151	5¾	1½	4.98	13.364	14.186
4.00	3⅝	2¾	2.625	5.412	5.94	¾	6.185	5.853	2⅝	2.50	4.909	5.412	¹³⁄₁₆	6.381	6.381	5¾	1¾	4.71	11.793	12.566
3.75	3⅝	2½	2.50	4.909	5.412	⅝	4.909	4.909	2½	2.375	4.430	4.909	¾	5.596	5.412	5½	1⅜	4.45	10.321	11.05
3.50	3⅜	2⅜	2.312	4.20	4.667	⅝	4.54	4.279	2⅜	2.187	3.76	4.20	¹³⁄₁₆	4.721	4.746	4¾	1¼	4.12	8.9467	9.6211
3.25	3⅛	2¼	2.125	3.547	3.976	⅝	4.172	3.694	2¼	2.00	3.1416	3.547	¹¹⁄₁₆	4.316	4.123	4¾	1⅜	3.84	7.6699	8.2958
3.00	2⅞	2⅜	1.968	3.042	3.44	½	3.092	3.052	2	1.875	2.761	3.1416	⅝	3.68	3.35	4⅛	1⅛	3.57	6.4918	7.0686
2.75	2⅝	1¹⁵⁄₁₆	1.781	2.491	2.853	½	2.798	2.559	1¹³⁄₁₆	1.687	2.236	2.580	⁵⁄₁₆	2.979	2.832	3¹⁵⁄₁₆	1⅛	3.5	5.4119	5.9396
2.50	2⅜	1¹³⁄₁₆	1.5937	1.995	2.32	¾	2.19	2.11	1¹³⁄₁₆	1.531	1.841	2.153	½	2.41	2.277	3½	1	3.15	4.4301	4.9087
2.25	2⅛	1⅝	1.437	1.623	1.917	⅜	1.694	1.6296	1¹⁵⁄₁₆	1.3437	1.418	1.694	¾	1.845	1.853	3¼	⅞	2.71	3.5466	3.9761
2.00	1⅞	1⅜	1.250	1.227	1.485	⅜	1.473	1.2762	1¾	1.187	1.108	1.353	¾	1.40	1.408	2¾	¾	2.38	2.7612	3.1416
1.75	1⅝	1¼	1.062	.887	1.108	¼	1.04	.966	1¼	1.00	.785	.994	¾	1.19	1.080	2⅜	¹³⁄₁₆	2.11	2.0739	2.4053
1.50	1⅜	1½	.906	.645	.835	¼	.71	.650	⁷⁄₃₂	.8434	.559	.7371	⅜	.827	.748	2¼	¾	1.788	1.4849	1.7671
1.25	1¼	⁷⁄₈	.730	.418	.576	¾	.429	.418	¹³⁄₁₆	.6875	.371	.5185	¼	.540	.4755	1⅜	½	1.52	.994	1.2272
1.00	⅞	⁵⁄₈	.553	.2401	.361	⁵⁄₃₂	.271	.2403	⁷⁄₃₂	.525	.2164	.3318	¾	.309	.2695	1⅜	⁷⁄₁₆	1.19	.6013	.7854

Figure 8-56. Bubble cap and riser comparison data. (Courtesy of F. W. Glitsch & Sons, Dallas, Texas.)

(Figure continued on next page)

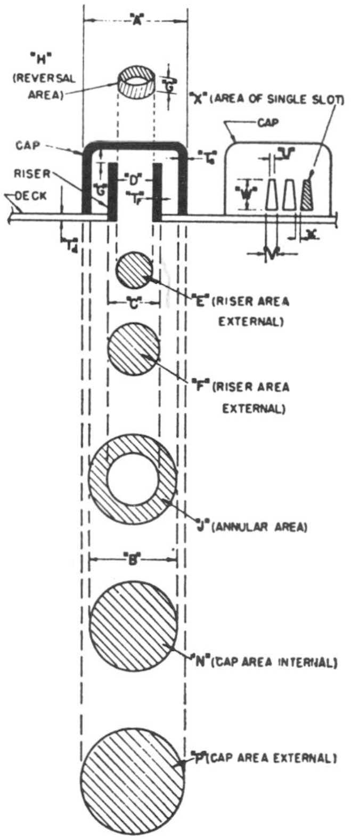

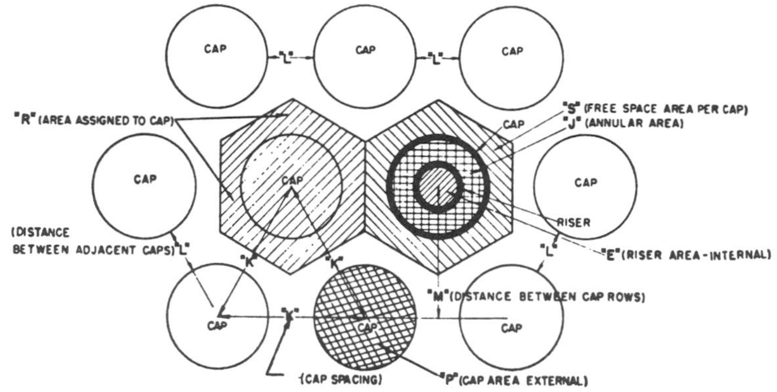

R	S	FREE SPACE AREA RATIO TO #1 RISER AREA	FREE SPACE AREA RATIO to #2 RISER AREA	TOTAL CAP SLOT AREA (Z) FOR AN APPROXIMATE VALUE OF CAP SLOT AREA = 1.7 AREA RISER #1 OR 1.85 AREA RISER #2(1) (a = SLOT LIGAMENT) T	U(4)	V(4)	W(4)	X	Y		Z(4)	CAP SLOT AREA RATIO TO #1 RISER AREA	CAP SLOT AREA RATIO TO #2 RISER AREA	FOR 16 ga. RISERS: ACTUAL D = $\sqrt{.636N-.004}-.062$ (5)	FOR 16 ga. RISERS: ACTUAL D_1 = $.889\sqrt{.916N-.005}-.055$ (5)	CIRCUMFERENCE OF RISER D = INSIDE DIAM.	CIRCUMFERENCE OF RISER D_1 = INSIDE DIAM.	ACTUAL G	ACTUAL G_1
AREA ASSIGNED TO CAP	FREE SPACE AREA			OUTSIDE CIRCUM OF CAP	SLOT WIDTH AT TOP	SLOT WIDTH AT BOTTOM	SLOT LENGTH	AREA OF SINGLE SLOT	NUMBER OF SLOTS PER CAP		TOTAL SLOT AREA								
$.866 K^2$	R − P			π A	AS-SUMED	AS-SUMED	CALCU-LATED	$\frac{W(U+V)}{2}$	(1) a	$\frac{T}{a+V}$	XY								
127.31	63.693	2.118	2.350	28.274	¼	¾	3¾	1.875	¼	28	52.6	1.749	1.940	6.213	5.865	19.439	18.457	1.572	1.82
114.53	57.785	2.178	2.432	26.703	¼	¾	3½	1.751	¼	26	45.6	1.718	1.919	5.865	5.532	18.260	17.279	1.50	1.75
101.2	50.935	2.144	2.410	25.133	¼	¾	3¼	1.625	¼	25	40.6	1.709	1.921	5.50	5.190	17.28	16.297	1.38	1.629
89.87	45.691	2.215	2.448	23.562	¼	¾	3	1.50	¼	23	34.5	1.672	1.848	5.148	4.861	16.10	15.315	1.31	1.51
78.16	39.672	2.239	2.494	21.991	¼	¾	2¾	1.375	¼	22	31.3	1.766	1.968	4.798	4.523	14.923	14.137	1.24	1.44
67.25	34.167	2.209	2.481	20.42	¼	½	2⅜	.882	3/16	30	26.75	1.730	1.942	4.458	4.194	13.941	13.155	1.12	1.32
61.7	31.02	2.187	2.469	19.635	¼	½	2⅜	.882	3/16	28	24.75	1.745	1.970	4.268	4.025	13.352	12.556	1.08	1.28
57.2	28.926	2.232	2.453	18.85	¼	⅜	1⅞	.585	⅛	38	22.20	1.713	1.882	4.088	3.861	12.763	12.174	1.05	1.20
52.0	26.033	2.207	2.438	18.064	¼	⅜	1¾	.546	⅛	36	19.70	1.670	1.845	3.913	3.697	12.174	11.585	1.01	1.16
47.9	24.142	2.260	2.509	17.279	¼	⅜	1¾	.546	⅛	34	18.55	1.737	1.928	3.738	3.528	11.585	10.996	.973	1.13
44.2	22.552	2.344	2.521	16.494	3/16	5/16	1¾	.437	⅛	38	16.62	1.727	1.858	3.548	3.359	10.996	10.603	.937	1.04
39.5	19.865	2.221	2.489	15.708	3/16	5/16	1 11/16	.425	⅛	36	15.20	1.699	1.905	3.383	3.195	10.603	10.014	.85	1.00
35.9	18.179	2.278	2.572	14.923	3/16	5/16	1⅝	.407	⅛	34	13.82	1.732	1.955	3.208	3.03	10.14	9.425	.81	.969
33.5	17.596	2.489	2.710	14.137	3/16	5/16	1½	.375	⅛	32	12.00	1.698	1.848	3.028	2.861	9.425	9.032	.78	.882
28.62	14.434	2.323	2.544	13.352	3/16	5/16	1 7/16	.359	⅛	30	10.78	1.735	1.900	2.853	2.697	8.836	8.443	.745	.847
25.55	12.984	2.399	2.645	12.566	3/16	5/16	1 5/16	.3285	⅛	28	9.2	1.700	1.874	2.676	2.528	8.247	7.854	.710	.8125
22.75	11.70	2.383	2.641	11.781	3/16	5/16	1¼	.313	⅛	27	8.44	1.719	1.905	2.50	2.362	7.854	7.461	.625	.725
18.57	9.949	2.369	2.646	10.996	3/16	5/16	1⅛	.2825	⅛	25	7.04	1.676	1.872	2.32	2.196	7.265	6.872	.589	.691
17.04	8.744	2.465	2.783	10.21	3/16	5/16	1 1/16	.266	⅛	23	6.13	1.728	1.951	2.15	2.025	6.676	6.283	.583	.656
14.72	7.651	2.515	2.771	9.4248	3/16	5/16	1	.250	⅛	21	5.25	1.726	1.901	1.968	1.861	6.183	5.890	.494	.569
12.62	6.680	2.682	2.987	8.6394	⅛	¼	1	.187	⅛	23	4.3	1.726	1.923	1.793	1.692	5.595	5.301	.457	.534
10.6	5.691	2.853	3.091	7.854	⅛	¼	⅞	.164	⅛	21	3.45	1.729	1.874	1.618	1.527	5.007	4.81	.421	.473
8.46	4.484	2.763	3.162	7.0686	⅛	¼	13/16	.152	⅛	18	2.74	1.688	1.932	1.44	1.359	4.516	4.22	.361	.439
6.56	3.418	2.786	3.085	6.2832	⅛	¼	¾	.141	⅛	15	2.11	1.720	1.904	1.263	1.192	3.927	3.731	.325	.377
5.13	2.72	3.067	3.465	5.4978	⅛	3/16	9/16	.0862	⅛	18	1.55	1.747	1.975	1.086	1.03	3.338	3.1416	.259	.344
3.682	1.915	2.969	3.426	4.7124	⅛	3/16	½	.078	⅛	15	1.17	1.814	2.093	.908	.849	2.846	2.65	.228	.282
2.65	1.42	3.397	3.827	3.927	⅛	3/16	⅜	.0585	⅛	12	.703	1.682	1.895	.730	.693	2.293	2.16	.182	.220
1.64	.854	3.557	3.946	3.1416	⅛	3/16	¼	.039	⅛	10	.390	1.624	1.802	.553	.525	1.737	1.65	.138	.163

Figure 8-56 continued.

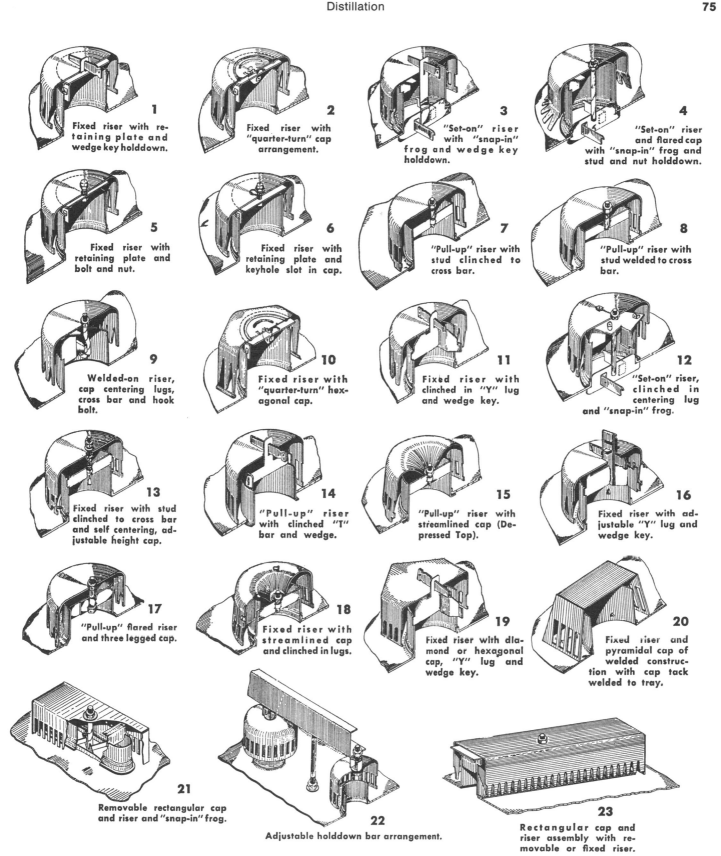

1. Fixed riser with retaining plate and wedge key holddown.

2. Fixed riser with "quarter-turn" cap arrangement.

3. "Set-on" riser with "snap-in" frog and wedge key holddown.

4. "Set-on" riser and flared cap with "snap-in" frog and stud and nut holddown.

5. Fixed riser with retaining plate and bolt and nut.

6. Fixed riser with retaining plate and keyhole slot in cap.

7. "Pull-up" riser with stud clinched to cross bar.

8. "Pull-up" riser with stud welded to cross bar.

9. Welded-on riser, cap centering lugs, cross bar and hook bolt.

10. Fixed riser with "quarter-turn" hexagonal cap.

11. Fixed riser with clinched in "Y" lug and wedge key.

12. "Set-on" riser, clinched in centering lug and "snap-in" frog.

13. Fixed riser with stud clinched to cross bar and self centering, adjustable height cap.

14. "Pull-up" riser with clinched "T" bar and wedge.

15. "Pull-up" riser with streamlined cap (Depressed Top).

16. Fixed riser with adjustable "Y" lug and wedge key.

17. "Pull-up" flared riser and three legged cap.

18. Fixed riser with streamlined cap and clinched in lugs.

19. Fixed riser with diamond or hexagonal cap, "Y" lug and wedge key.

20. Fixed riser and pyramidal cap of welded construction with cap tack welded to tray.

21. Removable rectangular cap and riser and "snap-in" frog.

22. Adjustable holddown bar arrangement.

23. Rectangular cap and riser assembly with removable or fixed riser.

Figure 8-57. Bubble cap and riser design. (Courtesy, F. W. Giltsch and Sons, Inc., Dallas)

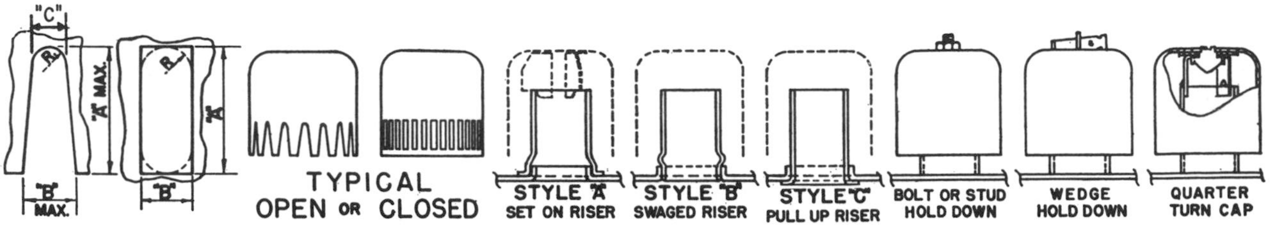

BUBBLE CAP AND RISERS - TYPES AND HOLD DOWNS

EXPLANATION

The slots shown below for various cap diameters may be furnished in any of the riser styles and holddown styles shown above with either open or closed slot arrangement as limited in the chart.

Cap I.D.	NO. SLOTS	A CLOSED	A OPEN	B	C	R
1 7/8	30	3/4	11/16	3/32	3/32	—
	30	1 1/4	1 3/16	3/32	3/32	—
2 1/16	12	1/2	7/16	3/8	1/4	1/8
2 3/16	28	3/4	11/16	5/16	0	0
2 3/4	38	7/8	13/16	1/8	1/8	—
	38	3/4	11/16	1/8	1/8	—
	18	3/4	11/16	1/4	1/4	—
2 7/8	25	1/2	7/16	3/16	3/16	—
	38	5/8	9/16	1/8	1/8	—
	48	3/4	11/16	3/32	3/32	—
	50	3/4	11/16	3/32	3/32	—
	18	3/4	11/16	9/32	9/32	—
	21	1	15/16	1/4	1/4	—
	38	3/4	11/16	1/8	1/8	1/16
	25	1 1/2	1 7/16	1/4	1/4	—
	18	1 1/16	1	5/16	1/4	1/8
	14	1 1/4	1 3/16	1/2	1/4	1/8
	18	1	15/16	5/16	1/8	1/16
	21	1	15/16	5/16	1/8	1/16
	38	1/2	7/16	1/8	1/8	—
	25	3/4	11/16	1/4	1/4	—
	48	1 3/16	1 1/8	3/32	3/32	—
	18	1 1/4	1 3/16	3/16	3/16	3/32
	40	13/16	3/4	3/32	3/32	—
	18	1 1/4	1 3/16	1/8	1/8	1/16
3	38	1/2	7/16	1/8	1/8	—
	16	1	15/16	5/32	5/32	5/64
	24	1	15/16	5/32	5/32	5/64
	32	1	15/16	5/32	5/32	5/64
	18	1	15/16	1/4	1/4	—
	21	1	15/16	1/4	1/4	—
	28	1 1/4	1 3/16	3/16	3/16	—
	40	1 3/16	1 1/8	3/32	3/32	—
3 1/16	25	1 5/16	1 1/4	1/4	1/4	—
	24	1	15/16	5/16	5/16	—
3 3/8	45	1 1/2	1 7/16	1/8	1/8	1/16
3 5/8	18	1 13/16	1 3/4	3/8	1/4	1/8
3 3/4	40	23/32	5/8	5/32	5/32	5/64
	12	15/16	5/8	5/8	5/8	5/16
	18	1	15/16	3/8	1/4	1/8
	18	1 3/16	1 1/8	13/32	5/16	5/32
	19	1 1/2	1 7/16	3/8	1/4	1/8
3 7/8	21	1 1/2	1 7/16	3/8	5/16	5/32
	19	1 5/8	1 1/2	13/32	11/32	11/64
	21	1 3/8	1 5/16	3/8	3/8	3/16
	34	1	15/16	3/16	3/16	—
	21	1	15/16	3/8	3/8	—
	34	1 1/4	1 3/16	3/16	3/16	—
	32	1 7/16	1 3/8	7/32	7/32	—
	24	1 1/2	1 7/16	3/16	3/16	—
	30	1 1/4	1 3/16	1/4	3/16	3/32
	18	1 1/4	1 3/16	3/8	9/32	9/64
	20	1 1/4	1 3/16	1/2	1/4	1/8
	52	27/32	25/32	3/32	3/32	3/64
	50	1	15/16	1/8	1/8	1/16
	51	1 1/2	1 7/16	1/8	1/8	1/16
	40	3/4	11/16	1/8	1/8	1/16
	32	1 1/2	1 7/16	3/16	3/16	3/32
	38	1 1/2	1 7/16	1/8	1/8	1/16
	40	3/4	11/16	1/8	1/8	—
	28	1 1/2	1 7/16	1/4	1/4	—
	16	1 1/2	1 3/8	1/2	1/4	1/8
	28	1 3/16	1 1/8	1/4	1/4	—
	66	7/8	13/16	3/32	3/32	3/64
4 1/8	28	1	15/16	3/16	3/16	—
	32	1	15/16	3/16	3/16	—
	26	1 1/2	1 7/16	5/16	5/16	—
	32	1 1/8	1 1/16	5/16	1/4	1/8
	26	1	15/16	5/16	5/16	—
4 1/4	32	1 1/2	1 7/16	1/4	1/4	—
	24	1 5/16	1 1/2	3/8	1/4	1/8
	24	1 1/4	1 3/16	3/8	3/16	3/32
4 3/8	32	1	15/16	3/16	3/16	—
	40	1	15/16	3/16	3/16	—
4 3/8	18	1 11/16	1 5/8	5/8	7/32	7/64
	32	1	15/16	1/4	1/4	—
	36	1 1/8	1 1/16	1/4	1/4	—
	25	1 1/2	1 7/16	3/8	3/16	3/32
4 7/8	20	1 9/16	1 1/2	9/16	1/4	1/8
	27	1 9/16	1 1/2	3/8	5/16	5/32
	30	2 1/16	2	9/32	1/4	1/8
	18	1 1/2	1 7/16	3/8	1/4	1/8
	20	1 3/4	1 11/16	5/8	1/4	1/8
5 1/8	20	1 1/4	1 3/16	9/16	1/4	1/8
5 3/8	30	1 1/2	1 7/16	3/8	1/4	1/8
5 5/8	20	1 27/32	1 25/32	5/8	1/4	1/8
5 3/4	48	1 3/4	1 11/16	1/4	3/16	3/32
5 7/8	26	3/4	11/16	1/2	1/2	—
	48	7/8	13/16	1/4	1/4	—
	32	1	15/16	1/4	1/4	—
	33	1 11/16	1 5/8	3/8	1/4	1/8
	30	1 3/4	1 11/16	3/4	1/4	1/8
	60	1 1/2	1 7/16	5/32	5/32	5/64
	25	1 1/2	1 7/16	1/2	1/4	1/8
	48	1 3/16	1 1/8	1/4	3/16	3/32
	20	2 1/8	2 1/16	5/8	1/4	1/8
	38	2 1/8	2 1/16	3/8	1/4	1/8
	48	9/16	5/8	1/4	1/4	—
	30	1 3/16	1 1/8	3/8	3/8	—
6	50	1 1/8	1 1/16	1/4	1/4	—
	28	1 1/2	1 7/16	3/8	1/4	1/8
	32	1 1/2	1 7/16	3/8	1/4	1/8
6 1/8	40	1 7/8	1 13/16	1/4	1/4	—
	32	1 1/2	1 7/16	3/8	5/32	5/64
	32	2	1 15/16	3/8	5/16	5/32
	32	1 9/16	1 1/2	23/32	7/32	7/64
	32	1 9/16	1 1/2	3/8	1/4	1/8
6 1/2	40	1 3/4	1 11/16	5/16	3/16	3/32
6 7/8	28	1 9/16	1 1/2	9/16	3/8	3/16
7	22	3	2 15/16	11/16	1/4	1/8
7 7/8	24	1 9/16	1 1/2	11/16	7/16	7/32

Figure 8-58. Bubble cap and risers—types and hold-downs. (Courtesy of F. W. Glitsch & Sons, Inc., Dallas, Texas.)

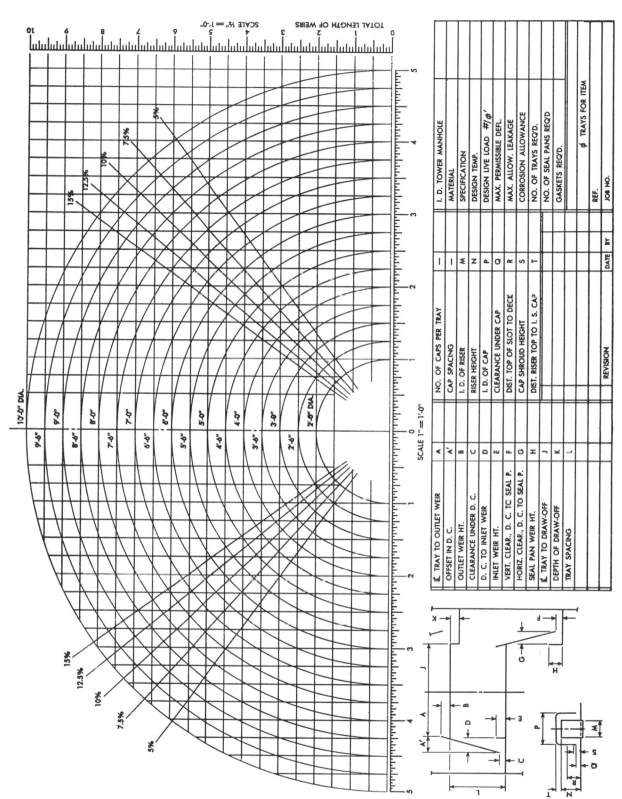

Figure 8-59. Distillation tray layout form (use with Figure 60. Not reproduced to scale. (By permission Wyatt Metal & Boiler Works, Inc., Copyright 1956.)

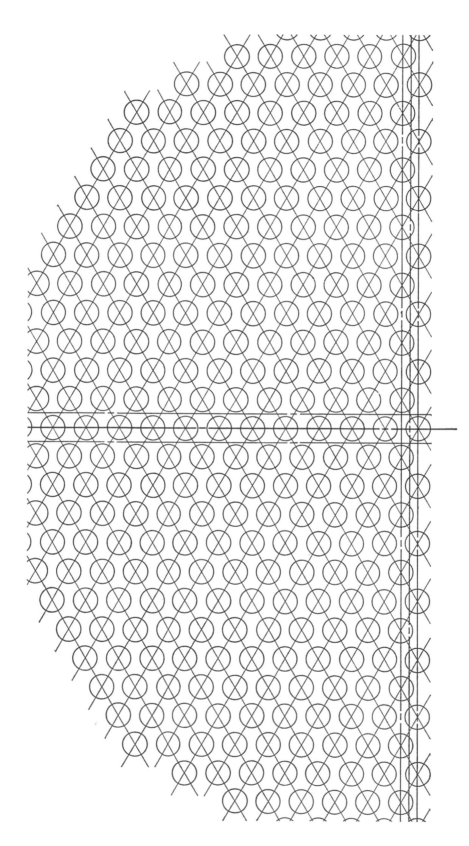

Figure 8-60. 4" Dia. bubble caps on 5.5" △ pitch. (By permission Wyatt Metal & Boiler Works, Inc., Copyright 1956.)

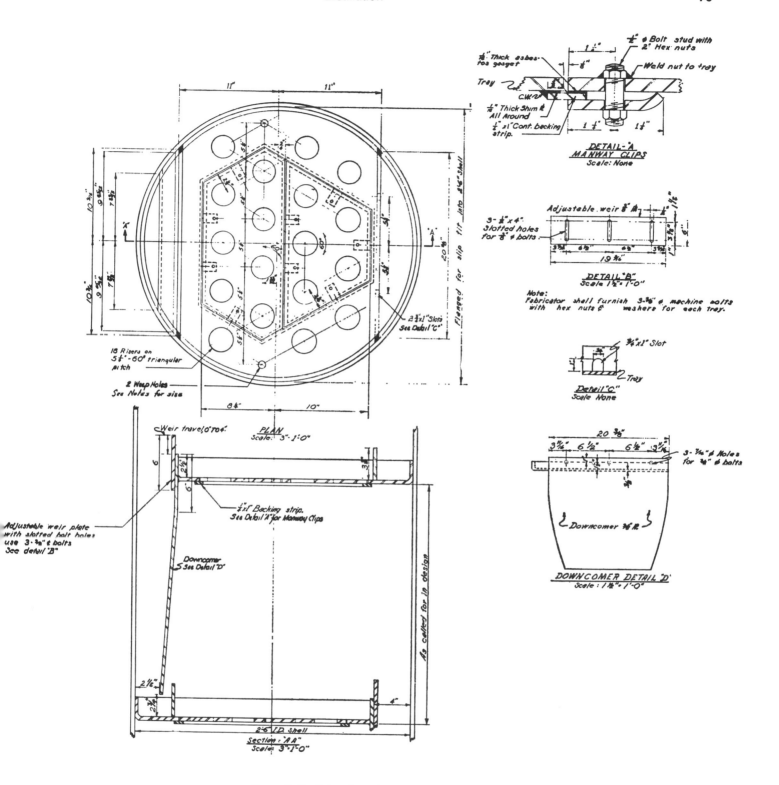

Figure 8-61. 2'-6" Dia. column—4" caps.

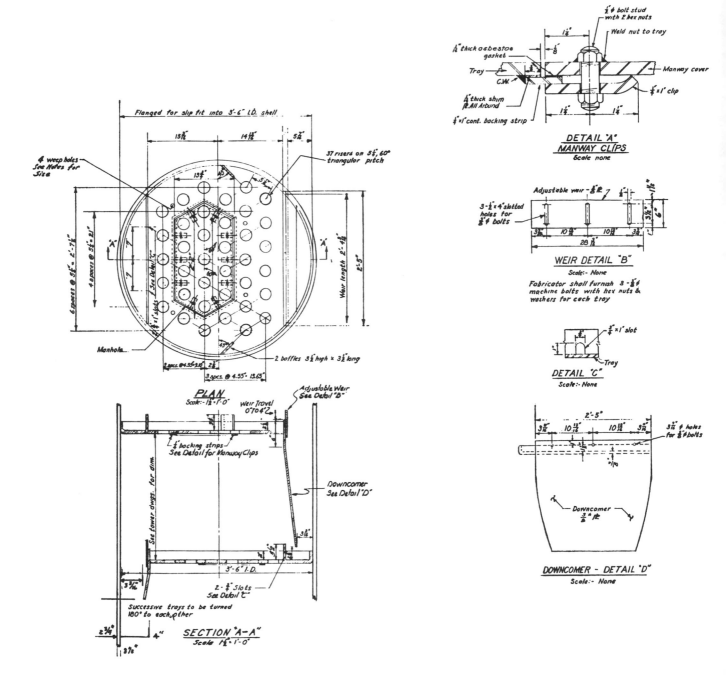

Figure 8-62. 3'-6" Dia. column—4" caps.

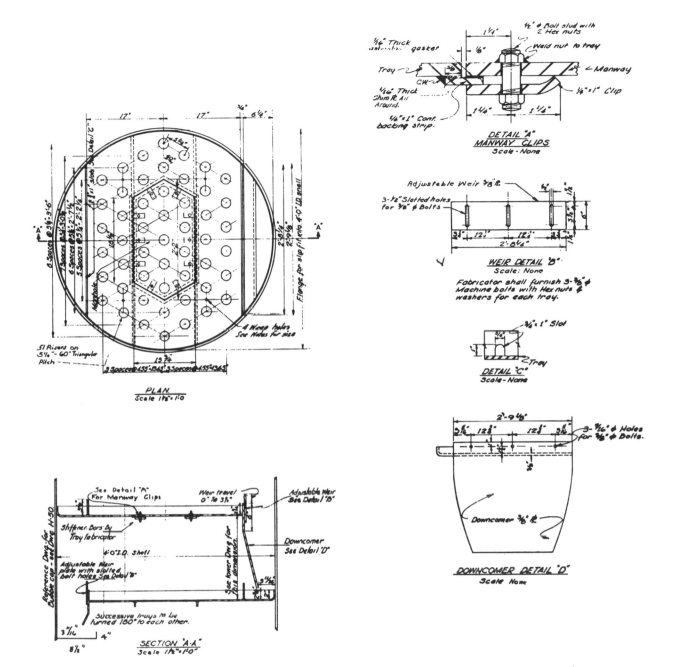

Figure 8-63. 4'-0" Dia. column—4" caps.

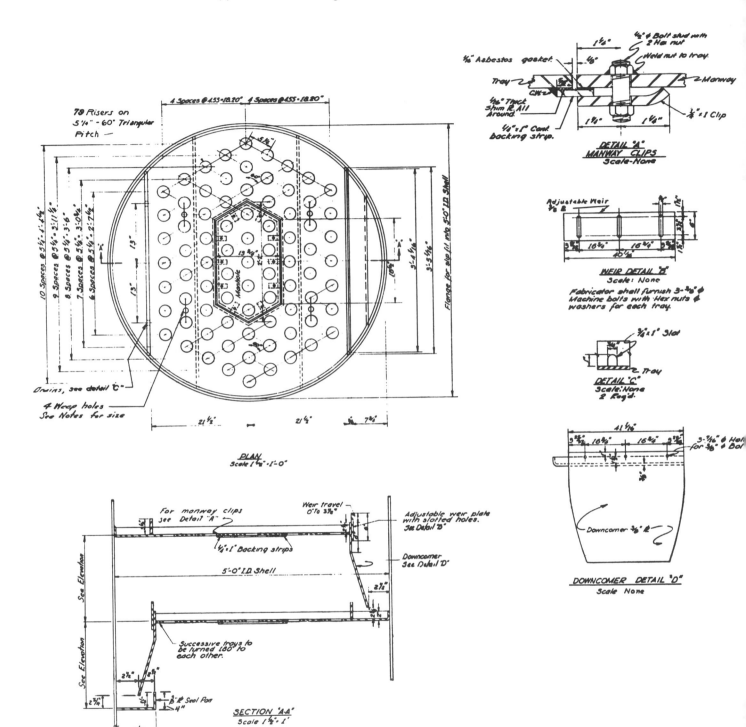

Figure 8-64. 5'-0" Dia. column—4" caps.

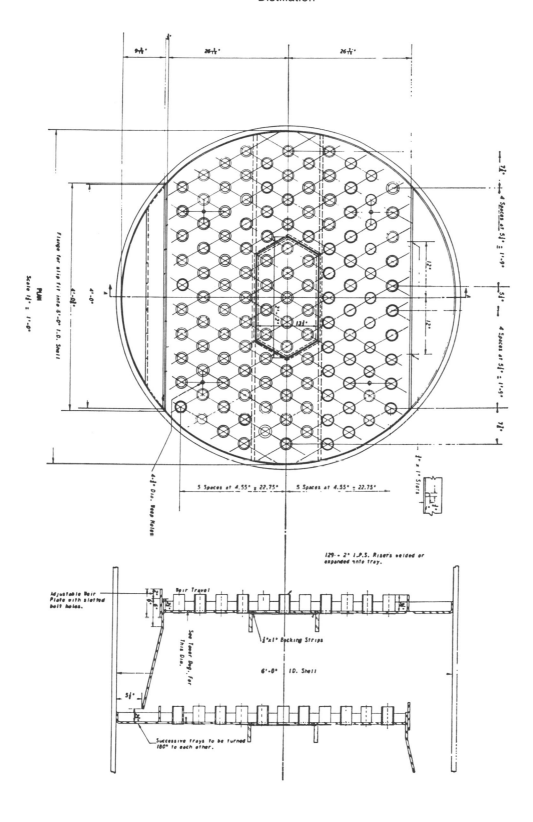

Figure 8-65. 6'-0" Dia. column—4" caps.

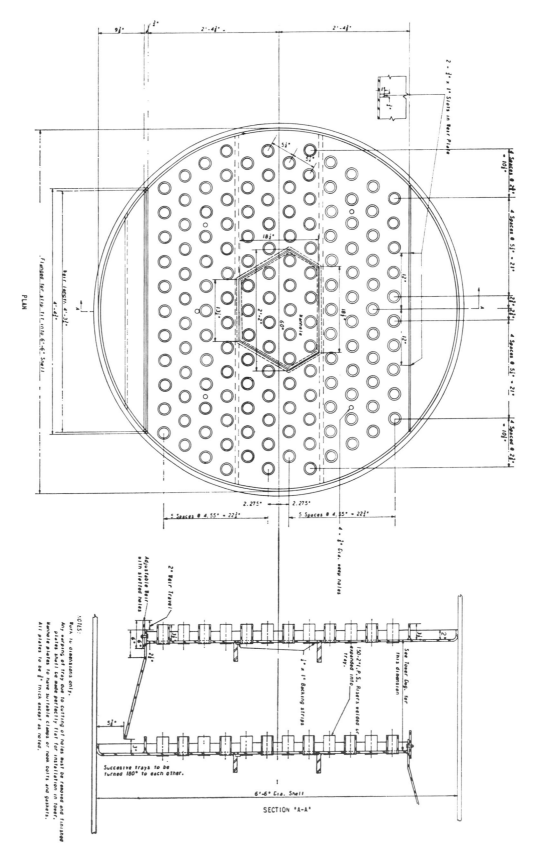

Figure 8-66. 6'-6" Dia. column—4" caps.

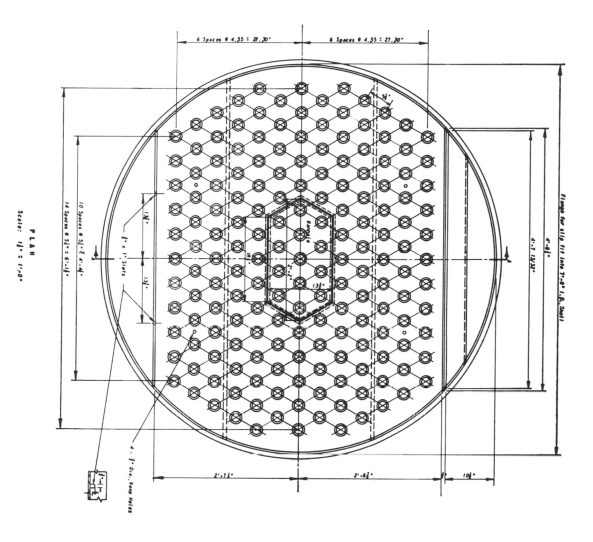

PLAN
Scale: 1½" = 1'-0"

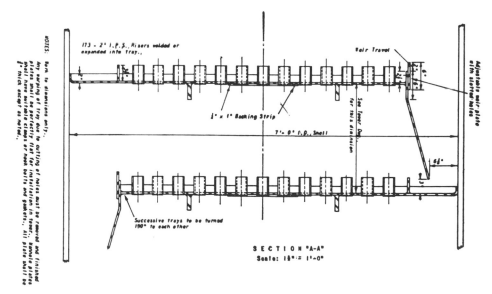

SECTION "A-A"
Scale: 1½" = 1'-0"

Figure 8-67. 7'-0" Dia. column—4" caps.

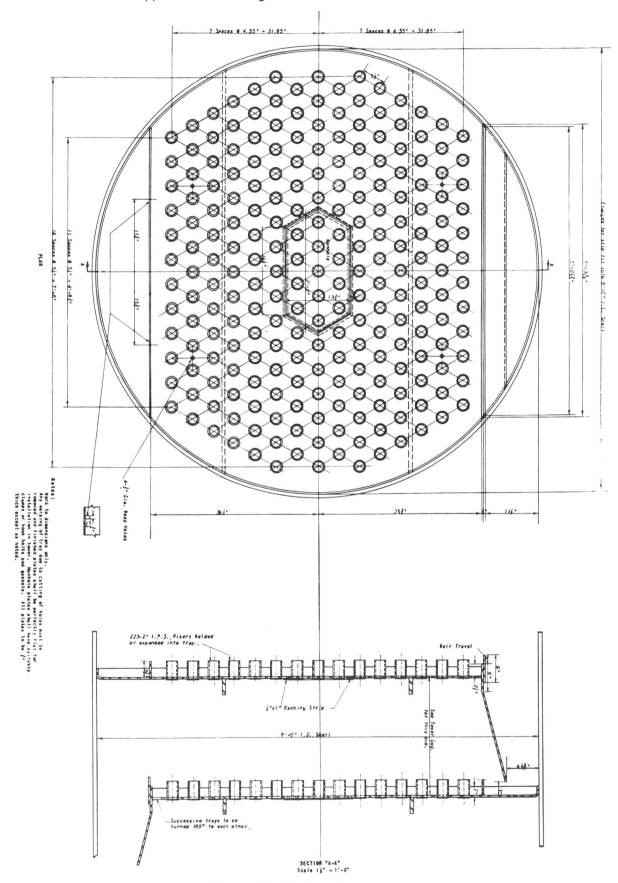

Figure 8-68. 8'-0" Dia. column—4" caps.

Table 8-6

General Purpose Distillation Trays Using 3⅞-Inch I.D. Pressed Metal Bell Caps on 5¼-Inch Centers

Inside Diameter	2'-6"	3'-0"	3'-6"	4'-0"	5'-0"	6'-0"	6'-6"	7'-0"	8'-0"
Total Area, Sq. Ft............	4.91	7.07	9.62	12.56	19.63	28.28	33.18	38.48	50.26
Liquid Flow..................	Cross	Cross	Cross	Cross	Cross	Cross	Cross	Cross	Cross
No. Downflow Weirs (1).....	One	One	One	One	One	One	One	One	One
No. Downflow Seals (2)......	One	One	One	One	One	One	One	One	One
No. Caps & Risers/Tray.......	18	27	37	51	79	129	150	173	223
No. Rows/Tray..............	4	5	6	7	9	11	12	13	15
Total Slot Area, Sq. Ft. (3)....	1.15	1.73	2.38	3.27	5.08	8.29	9.64	11.1	14.29
Percent of Tower Area	23.4	24.5	24.8	26.0	25.9	29.3	29.1	28.9	28.50
Total Riser Area, Sq. Ft. (4) ...	0.683	1.04	1.42	1.96	3.00	4.95	5.56	6.64	8.57
Percent of Tower Area.......	13.9	14.7	14.8	15.6	15.3	17.5	16.75	17.25	17.05
Overflow Weir Length, Ft. (1)..	1.625	2.05	2.35	2.686	3.35	4.0	4.31	4.62	5.21
Percent of Tower Diameter...	65.0	68.0	67.1	67.0	67.0	66.7	66.0	66.05	65.1
Downflow Segment Area (5)									
Maximum Area, Sq. Ft......	0.338	0.642	0.80	0.96	1.41	2.12	2.39	2.85	3.50
Minimum Area, Sq. Ft.......	0.167	0.225	0.33	0.45	0.69	0.886	1.027	1.14	1.47
Under Flow Clearance, In......	2½	2¾	2¾	2¾	2¾	2¾	3	3	3
Under Flow Area, Sq. Ft.......	0.274	0.354	0.426	0.473	0.604	0.710	0.750	0.887	1.01
Up Flow Area, Minimum Sq. Ft. (6)........	0.137	0.365	0.335	0.552	0.795	0.740	0.882	1.000	1.21

(1) 2½″ minimum height above tray floor, with adjustable weir 0 to 3½″ additional.
(2) 3½″ high above tray floor.
(3) Slots are 50—⅛″ x 1½″ per cap. Caps on triangular pitch.
(4) Riser inside diameter = 2.68″.
(5) Design uses tapered segmental downcomer and inlet weir.
(6) Area between downcomer and inlet weir for up-flow of inlet liquid. All trays included access manway.

Cap Pitch Center to Center

Cap sizes 2-inch, 3-inch, and 4-inch: recommended cap lane distance of 1½ inches (with 1¼-inch minimum, 1¾-inch maximum) plus cap outside diameter.

For cap sizes of 6 and 8 inches: recommended cap lane distance of 1½ inches, (1½-inch minimum, 2½-inch maximum) plus cap outside diameter.

Weirs

Figure 8-69 is convenient for arriving at weir lengths relative to their effect on segmental downcomers.

(a) Inlet

These contribute to the uniform distribution of liquid as it enters the tray from the downcomer. There are about as many tray designs without weirs as with them. The downcomer without inlet weir tends to maintain uniform liquid distribution itself. The tray design with recessed seal pan insures against vapor backflow into the downcomer, but this is seldom necessary. It is not recommended for fluids that are dirty or tend to foul surfaces. The inlet weir is objectionable for the same reason.

The first row of caps next to the weir or inlet downcomer must be set back far enough to prevent bubbling into the downcomer. The inlet weir prevents this, although it can be properly handled by leaving about 3 inches between inlet downcomer and the nearest face of the first row of caps.

The height of an inlet weir, if used, should be 1 to 1½ inches above the top of the slots of the bubble caps when installed on the tray.

If inlet weirs are used they should have at least two slots ¾-inch by 1-inch flush with the tray floor to aid in flushing out any trapped sediment or other material. There should also be weep or drain holes below the downcomer to drain the weir seal area. The size should be set by the type of service, but a minimum of ⅜-inch is recommended.

(b) Outlet

These are necessary to maintain seal on the tray, thus insuring bubbling of vapors through liquid. The lower the submergence, i.e., the distance between top of slots of bubble caps and liquid flowing on the tray, the lower the tray pressure drops. However, this submergence must

be some reasonable minimum value (¼ to ⅜-inch) to avoid excessive by-passing of vapor through void spots in the surging, moving liquid body as it travels across the tray from inlet to outlet.

The adjustable weir feature of many tray designs allows a standard tray to be utilized in different services by re-adjusting the weir height as needed. The fixed portion of the weir should never be lower than the top of the slots of the bubble caps. Depending upon service the adjustable weir should be capable of traveling a minimum of 2 inches, with designs for some trays being 4 to 6 inches.

Downcomer

Figure 8-69 is convenient for determining the down-comer area and width for a given weir length (see Table 8-6 also).

The downcomer from a tray must be adequate to carry the liquid flow plus entrained foam and froth. This foamy material is disengaged in the downcomer as only clear liquid flows onto the tray below. The vertical and straight segmental downcomer is recommended, although the seg-mental tapered design has been used quite successfully. In the latter design the wide mouth of the inlet as com-pared to the outlet is considered to provide better foam disengagement conditions.

The downcomer seal on the tray is recommended[5] based on the liquid flow path:

Liquid path, Downcomer to outlet Weir, Feet	Downcomer Seal, In.
Below 5	0.5
5-10	1.0
Above 10	1.5

Liquid By-Pass Baffles

Also known as redistribution baffles, these short stub baffles guide the liquid flow path to prevent excessive by-passing of the bubble cap field or active tray area. Unfortunately this action is overlooked by many designers with resulting low tray efficiencies. Table 8-5 gives recom-mendations for layout.

Liquid Drainage or Weep Holes

Holes for drainage must be adequate to drain the column in a reasonable time, yet not too large to interfere with tray action. Draining of the column through the trays is necessary before any internal maintenance can be started or before fluid services can be changed, when mixing is not desirable. The majority of holes are placed adjacent to the outlet or downcomer weir of the tray. However, some holes are placed in the downcomer inlet area or any suspected low point in the mechanical layout of the column.

The study of Broaddus et. al,[7] can be used to develop the following drainage time relation, and is based on fluids of several different densities and viscosities:

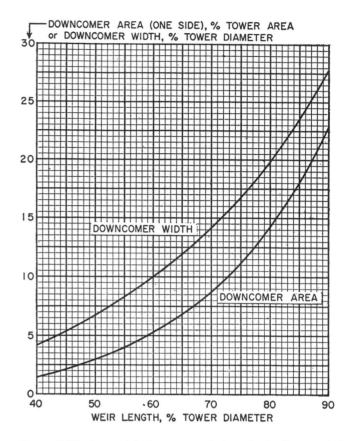

Figure 8-69. Segmental downcomer design chart. (By permission W. L. Bolles, Reference 5.)

$$\theta = \frac{(0.18\ N + 0.15)(\mu)^{0.12}\ (A_n)}{(\rho)^{\frac{1}{4}}\ (d_h/h')^{1.2}} \qquad (8\text{-}87)$$

where: θ = Time to drain tower, minutes

A_n = Net open liquid area of one tray, equal to total tower cross section minus area occupied by caps and minus area of segmental or other downcomer at outlet of tray, sq. ft.

ρ = Liquid density, grams/cc. at liquid temperature in tower

μ = Viscosity of liquid at tower temperature, centipoise

d_h = Weep hole diameter inches. Note that this is the diameter equivalent to the area of all the weep holes/tray

h' = Height of overflow weir or bubble cap riser, which-ever is smaller, inches

N = Total number of trays in tower

The accuracy of this relation is given as 14 percent maximum, 6 percent average.

A general recommendation[5] is to provide four square inches of weep hole area per 100 sq. ft. of net open liquid tray area in the tower. This latter refers to the total of all trays in the tower.

Bottom Tray Seal Pan

The bottom tray of a tower must have its downcomer sealed to prevent upflow of reboiled vapors. The downcomer of this tray is usually equal to or 6 inches longer than the other downcomers to insure against bottom vapor surges or pulses in pressure breaking the seal. The seal pan is designed to avoid liquid back pressure and minimum restrictions to liquid flow.

Bubble Caps

Although there are many styles and dimensions of caps in use, the round bell shaped bubble cap is quite practical and efficient. It is recommended as a good basis for the contacting requirements. This selection does not infer that other contacting caps are not acceptable, in fact many are in use in the chemical and petroleum industry. Their design criteria is limited to the proprietary knowledge of the manufacturer and not available to the designer.

Dimensions

The most popular and perhaps most adaptable size is about 4 inches O.D. ($3\frac{7}{8}$ inches I.D.). The 3-inch and 6-inch are also in common use for the smaller and larger diameter towers, although it is not necessary to change cap size with change in tower diameter. For a given active cap area the cost of installing the smaller diameter caps is 10-15 percent greater than the 4-inch, while the larger (and fewer number) 6-inch caps are about 15 percent cheaper. There is usually less waste tray area with the 3-inch caps than the 4-inch or 6-inch caps. Table 8-7.

For the sake of standardization and developing a feel on the part of the designer for the effect of various design variables on tray performance, the 4-inch cap (or $3\frac{3}{4}$-inch or $4\frac{3}{8}$-inch) caps are recommended as good general purpose units. This means that any application from a 2.5-foot dia. to 10-foot dia. tower is first evaluated using the 4-inch cap. If there are points of poor performance, cap sizes can be changed and the performance re-evaluated to adjust in the direction of optimum performance.

Pressed steel caps of 12 to 14 U.S. Standard gage are the most frequently used, although cast iron caps are used in some services such as corrosive chlorinated hydrocarbons, drying with sulfuric acid, etc. Alloy pressed caps maintain the light weight desirable for tray construction, yet frequently serve quite well in corrosive conditions. Special caps of porcelain, glass and plastic are also available to fill specific applications. The heavier caps require heavier trays or more supports in the lighter trays. The use of hold-down bars on caps is not recommended for the average installation; instead, individual bolts and nuts are preferred. Some wedge type holding mechanisms are satisfactory as long as they will not vibrate loose.

Slots

The slots are the working part of the cap, i.e., the point where the bubbling action is initiated. Slots are usually rectangular or trapezoidal in shape, either one giving good performance. A single comparison[5] indicates the rectangular slots give slightly greater capacity than the trapezoidal, while the trapezoidal slots give slightly better performance at low vapor rates (flexibility). This study shows that triangular slots are too limited in capacity, although they would be the better performers at low vapor rate. Generally, the capacity range offered by the rectangular and trapezoidal slots is preferred.

Table 8-7
General Purpose Guide For Pressed Cap Size Selection

Tower Diameter, In Feet	General Purpose Size, I.D. In Inches	Possible Alternate In Inches
2.5, 3	$3\frac{7}{8}$	$2\frac{3}{4}$; 3; $3\frac{5}{8}$
3.5, 4	$3\frac{7}{8}$	3; $5\frac{5}{8}$
5, 6, 7, 8, 9, 10	$3\frac{7}{8}$	6
11, 12, 13, 14	6	$3\frac{7}{8}$

Slot Sizes

Width: $\frac{1}{8}$-$\frac{1}{2}$-inch, $\frac{1}{8}$-inch recommended rectangular $\frac{1}{8}$-inch x $\frac{1}{4}$-inch to $\frac{1}{4}$-inch x $\frac{3}{4}$-inch, $\frac{3}{16}$-inch x $\frac{5}{16}$-inch recommended trapezoidal

Height: $\frac{3}{4}$-inch to $1\frac{7}{8}$-inch, $1\frac{1}{4}$-inch to $1\frac{1}{2}$-inch recommended

Shroud Ring

This is recommended to give structural strength to the prongs or ends of the cap. The face of the ring may rest directly on the tray floor, or it is recommended to have three short legs of $\frac{1}{4}$-inch for clean service. For all materials the skirt clearance is often used at $\frac{1}{2}$ to 1-inch, and for dirty service with suspended tarry materials it is used as high as $1\frac{1}{2}$ inches. These legs allow fouling or sediment to be washed out of the tray, and also allow emergency cap action under extremely overloaded conditions—at lower efficiencies.

Tray Performance

A bubble cap tray must operate in dynamic balance, and the closer all conditions are to optimum, the better the performance for a given capacity. Evaluation of performance requires a mechanical interpretation of the relationship of the tray components as they operate under a given set of conditions. This evaluation includes the determination of:

1. Tray pressure drop
   a. Slot opening
   b. Static and dynamic slot seals
   c. Liquid height over weir
   d. Liquid gradient across tray

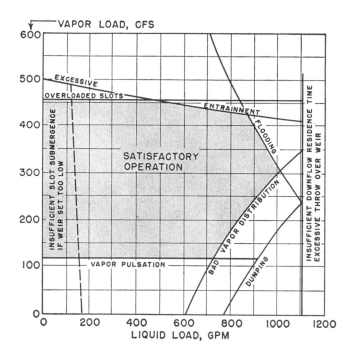

Figure 8-70. Qualitative effect of liquid and vapor loads on bubble cap tray performance. (By permission W. L. Bolles, Reference 5.)

2. Downcomer conditions
   a. Liquid height
   b. Liquid residence time
   c. Liquid throw over weir into downcomer
3. Vapor distribution
4. Entrainment
5. Tray efficiency

The evaluation is made in terms of pressure drops (static and friction) through the tray system. Figures 8-48 and 8-49 diagrammatically present the tray action.

An understanding of the action of the bubble cap tray is important to good design judgment in deciding upon the acceptance of a particular design. The passage of vapor through the caps and liquid across the tray is complicated by fluid actions associated with the mechanical configuration and with the relative velocities of the fluids at various points on the tray. The quantitative considerations will be given in more detail in later paragraphs. However, the qualitative interpretation is extremely valuable. The following descriptions are presented for this purpose.

Tray Capacity Related to Vapor-Liquid Loads

Figure 8-70 presents a generalized representation of the form useful for specific tray capacity analysis. Instead of plotting actual vapor load versus liquid load, a similar form of plot will result if actual vapor load per cap (here the cap row relative to inlet or outlet of tray is significant) versus the liquid load per inch or foot of outlet weir length.

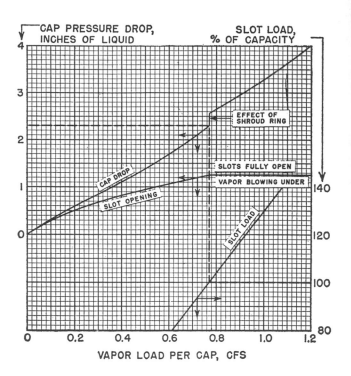

Figure 8-71. Effect of vapor load on slot opening, slot load and cap pressure drop. (By permission W. L. Bolles, Reference 5.)

Although each plot must be for a specific system of conditions, Figures 8-71 and 8-72 are extremely valuable in analyzing the action of a bubble tray.

For Figure 8-72 Bolles points out that the cap loads for inlet and outlet rows will be essentially balanced or "lined out" when the shaded areas are equal.

From Figure 8-70, the region of satisfactory tray operation is bounded by performance irregularities. Here all the caps are flowing vapor; the bubbling action is acceptable from an efficiency standpoint; entrainment is within design limits; there is no dumping (or back flow) of liquid down the risers, and no undesirable vapor jetting around the caps.

Tray Balance

A tray is in balance when it operates with acceptable efficiency under conditions at or very near those of design.

Tray Flexibility

A tray is flexible when it operates with acceptable efficiency under conditions which deviate significantly from those established for design. The usual changes affecting flexibility are vapor and/or liquid loading. A tray may operate down to 50 percent and up to 120 percent of vapor load, and down to 15 percent and up to 130 percent of liquid load and still be efficient. Beyond these points its efficiency may fall off, and the flexible limits of the tray would be established.

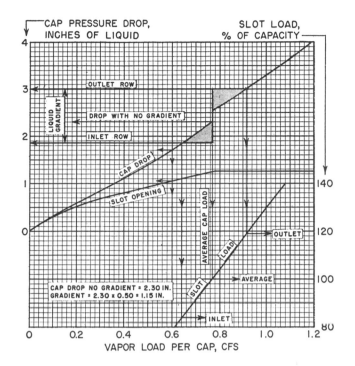

Figure 8-72. Effect of liquid gradient on vapor distribution with 0.50 vapor distribution ratio. (By permission W. L. Bolles, Reference 5.)

Tray Stability

A tray is stable when it can operate with acceptable efficiencies under conditions which fluctuate, pulse, or surge, developing unsteady conditions. This type of operation is difficult to anticipate in design, and most trays will not operate long without showing loss in efficiency.

Flooding

A bubble tray tower floods when the froth and foam in the downcomer back up to the tray above and begin accumulating on this tray. The downcomer then contains a mixture of lower density than the clear liquid, its capacity becomes limited, disengagement is reduced, and the level rises in the downcomer. This level finally extends onto the tray above, and will progress to the point of filling the column, if not detected and if the liquid and vapor loads are not reduced. Flooding is generally associated with high liquid load over a rather wide range of vapor rates. The foaming tendencies of the liquid influence this action on the tray. The design condition for height of clear liquid in the downcomer for flooding is usually set at 0.60 to 0.80 of $(S_t + h_w)$. See Figure 8-48.

Pulsing

A bubble tray pulses when the vapor rate is low and unsteady, when the slot opening is low (usually less than ½

inch), and when the liquid dynamic seal is low. With irregular vapor flow entering the caps, the liquid pulses or surges, even to the point of dumping or back-flowing liquid down the risers. The best cure is a steady vapor rate and good slot opening to allow for reasonable upsets.

Blowing

A bubble tray blows when the vapor rate is extremely high, regardless of the liquid rate, causing large vapor streams or continuous bubbles to be blown through the liquid. The efficiency and contact is low and entrainment is usually high. Here also low slot seals contribute to the sensitivity of the tray to such action.

Coning

A bubble tray cones when the liquid seal over the slot is low and the vapor rate is so high as to force the liquid completely away from the cap, thus bypassing the liquid entirely. Obviously, efficiency is unsatisfactory. The dynamic slot seals recommended in Table 8-8 normally will prevent such action.

Entrainment

A bubble tray has high entrainment when mist and liquid particles carry up in the vapor from the liquid on one tray through the riser and cap on to the tray above. Bubble caps tend to entrain by jetting liquid-vapor mixtures high above the tray. Sufficient tray spacing must be available to prevent the quantity of material from significantly affecting the efficiency of the system. The quantitative presentation of entrainment in later paragraphs is designed to work to this end.

Overdesign

Overdesign is often necessary in designing a tray, although caution must be exercised to prevent a piling-up or accumulation of safety factors resulting in numbers which are totally unrealistic for performance. In other words, the magnitude, effect, and significance of overcapacity figures must be continuously monitored as each

Table 8-8

Suggested Slot Seals

Tower Operating Pressure	Static Slot Seal[15] Inches	Dynamic Slot Seal[5] Inches
Vacuum, 30-200 mm Hg. abs	0-0.25	0.5-1.5
Atmospheric	0.5	1.0-2.0
50-100 psig	1.0	1.5-3.0
300 psig	1.5	2.0-4.0
500 psig	1.5	2.0-4.0

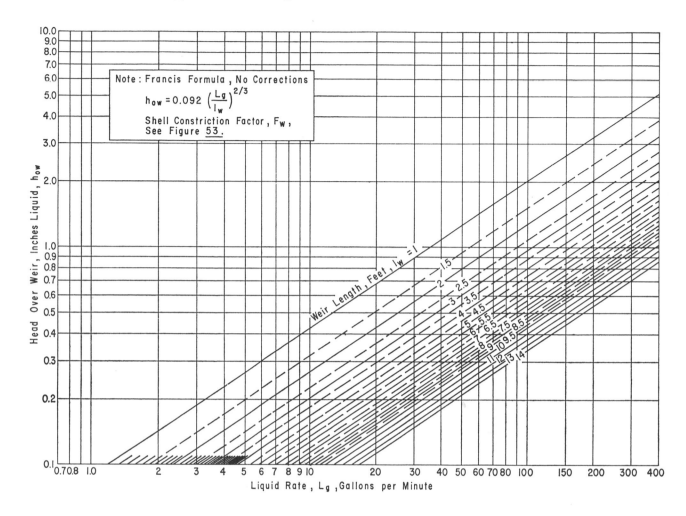

Figure 8-73. Liquid height over straight weir.

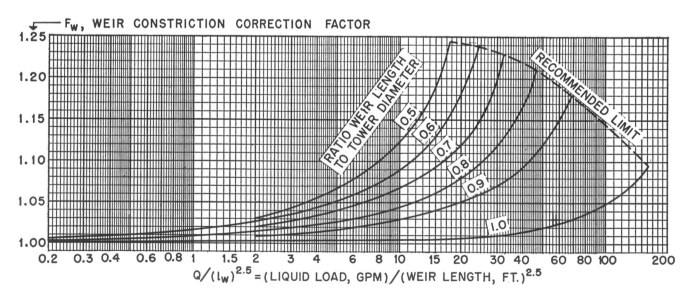

Figure 8-74. Weir formula correction factor for segmental type weirs. (By permission W. L. Bolles, Reference 5.)

factor is calculated. A factor of 10-15 percent on liquid and vapor rates is usually acceptable. However, each should be checked relative to the effect on maximum cap vapor capacity and entrainment, and on liquid gradient and buildup in the downcomer.

Total Tray Pressure Drop

This is normally taken as the wet bubble cap pressure drop plus the "mean dynamic slot seal" in inches of clear or unaerated liquid on the tray.

Guide values for normal operations, drop per tray.

Pressure	*Vacuum (500 mm Hg and below)*
2-4 inches *water*	2-4 mm Hg

Liquid Height Over Outlet Weir

For a straight (non-circular) weir, the head of liquid over its flat top is given by the modified[5] **Francis Weir** relation (Figure 8-73):

$$h_{ow} = 0.092 \ F_w \ (L_g/l_w)^{2/3} \qquad (8\text{-}88)$$

The modifying factor F_w developed by Bolles[5] for restriction at the shell due to segmental downcomer application is determined from Figure 8-74.

When h_{ow} values exceed 1¾ to 2 inches, consider special downcomers or down pipes to conserve cap area for high vapor loads.

Notched outlet weirs are only used for low liquid flow rates, and the head over this type of weir with notches running full.[18]

$$L_g = 14.3 \ (1_w/n) \left[h_{ow'}{}^{5/2} - (h_{ow'} - h_t)^{5/2} \right] \quad (8\text{-}89)$$

For notches not running full

$$L_g = 13.3 \ (l_w/n) \ (h_{ow'})^{5/2} \qquad (8\text{-}90)$$

where: h_{ow} = Height of liquid crest over flat weir, inches

l_w = Length of weir (straight), feet

L_g = Liquid flow rate, gallons per minute

n = Depth of notches in weir, inches

$h_{ow'}$ = Height of liquid above bottom of notch in weir, inches

For circular weirs (pipes) $h_{ow} = L_g/10 \ d_w$ (8-91)

where: d_w = diameter of circular weir, inches

Slot Opening

The slot opening is the vertical opening available for vapor flow during operation of the cap under a given set of conditions. It has been found to be essentially independent of surface tension, viscosity and depth of liquid over the cap. When the required opening exceeds the available, the vapor will either flow under the cap, create greater pressure drop or both.

A. Caps with Rectangular Slots[60]

$$h_s = 32 \left(\frac{\rho_v}{\rho_L - \rho_v} \right)^{1/3} \left(\frac{V}{N_c (N_s) (w_s)} \right)^{2/3} \quad (8\text{-}92)$$

where: h_s = Slot opening, or pressure drop through slot, inches liquid

V = Total vapor flow through tray, cu. ft./sec.

N_c = Number of caps per tray

N_s = Number of slots per cap

w_s = Width of slot (rectangular), inches

Figure 8-75 ppresents a quick solution of this relation. Maximum slot capacity[5]:

$$V_m = 0.79(A_s) \left[H_s \left(\frac{\rho_L - \rho_v}{\rho_v} \right) \right]^{1/2} \quad (8\text{-}93)$$

where: A_s = Total slot area per tray, sq. ft.

H_s = Slot height, in.

V_m = Maximum allowable vapor load per tray, cu. ft./sec.

B. Caps with Trapezoidal Slots

A trial solution is involved in determining the slot opening for trapezoidal slots.[5] The relation for maximum capacity at full slot opening is:

$$V_m = 2.36 \ (A_s) \ [\text{continued}$$

$$\left[\frac{2}{3} \left(\frac{R_s}{1 + R_s} \right) + \frac{4}{15} \left(\frac{1 - R_s}{1 + R_s} \right) \right] \left[H_s \left(\frac{\rho_L - \rho_v}{\rho_v} \right) \right]^{1/2}$$
$$(8\text{-}94)$$

where: R_s = ratio of top to bottom widths of trapezoid slot.

Figure 8-76 is useful in solving for the slot height as a percentage of the vapor capacity and of full opening.

Whenever possible, the slots should be designed to be 50-60 percent open to allow for pulses and surges in vapor flow.

Liquid Gradient Across Tray

The difference in height of liquid between the liquid inlet and liquid outlet sides of a tray is the liquid gradient. This is the result of frictional drag on the caps and internals plus resistance created by the bubbling action. A tray with high liquid gradient may be operating inefficiently and at reduced capacity if the rows of caps covered by high liquid are not bubbling, thus forcing all the vapor through the rows of caps nearer the tray outlet where the liquid head is lower. Liquid gradient is one of the criteria which must be checked to assure proper understanding of a tray design and its performance.

The recommendation of Bolles[5] is based on the work of Davies[14, 15] and serves the average design adequately. It assumes an I.D. of bubble cap to I.D. of riser of 1.42 and this

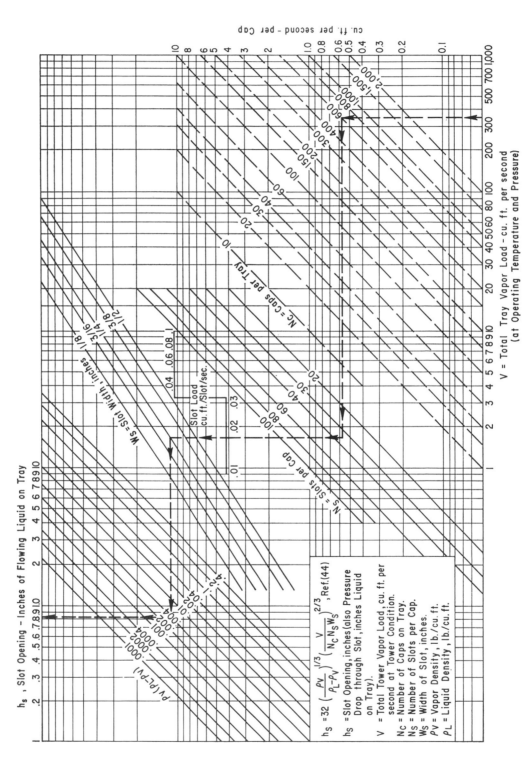

Figure 8-75. Opening of rectangular-vertical slots for bell type bubble cap. (By permission Stone & Webster Engineering Corp.)

$$h_S = 32 \left(\frac{\rho_V}{\rho_L - \rho_V}\right)^{1/3} \left(\frac{V}{N_C N_S W_S}\right)^{2/3}, \text{Ref.(44)}$$

h_S = Slot Opening, inches (also Pressure Drop through Slot, inches Liquid on Tray).

V = Total Tower Vapor Load, cu. ft. per second at Tower Condition.

N_C = Number of Caps on Tray.

N_S = Number of Slots per Cap.

W_S = Width of Slot, inches.

ρ_V = Vapor Density, lb./cu. ft.

ρ_L = Liquid Density, lb./cu. ft.

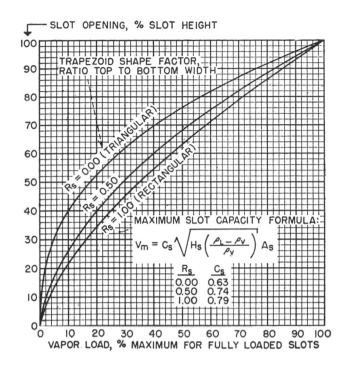

SLOT OPENING, % SLOT HEIGHT

TRAPEZOID SHAPE FACTOR, RATIO TOP TO BOTTOM WIDTH

$R_s = 0.00$ (TRIANGULAR)

$R_s = 0.50$

$R_s = 1.00$ (RECTANGULAR)

MAXIMUM SLOT CAPACITY FORMULA:

$$V_m = C_s \sqrt{H_s \left(\frac{\rho_L - \rho_v}{\rho_v} \right)} \, A_s$$

R_s	C_s
0.00	0.63
0.50	0.74
1.00	0.79

VAPOR LOAD, % MAXIMUM FOR FULLY LOADED SLOTS

Figure 8-76. Trapezoidal slot generalized correlation. (By permission W. L. Bolles, Reference 5.)

is close to the range for 85 percent of the installations. Small deviations will be negligible. It must be remembered that the agreement between the several investigators is good [24, 38, 44] but still lacks a final solution to all situations. In general, calculated values should not be considered better than ± 0.2-in.

The relation:

$$\frac{L_g / 1_{tw}}{C_d} = 25.8 \left(\frac{\gamma}{1 + \gamma} \right) (\Delta'_r)^{\frac{1}{2}} \left[1.6 \, \Delta'_r + 3 \left(h_1 + \frac{0.3 \, s}{\gamma} \right) \right]$$

(8-95)

where: L_g = Total liquid load in tray or tray section, gpm

1_{tw} = Total flow width across tray normal to flow, ft.

C_d = Liquid gradient factor (Ref. 5, Figure 7)

γ = Ratio of distance between caps to cap diameter

Δ'_r = Liquid gradient per row of caps, uncorrected, in.

h_1 = Depth of clear liquid on tray, in.

s = Cap skirt clearance, in.

$$h_1 = h_W + h_{ow} + \Delta/2$$

(8-96)

Some designers use $\Delta/5$ to $\Delta/3$ in place of $\Delta/2$.

The charts of Figures 8-77, 78, 79, 80 were developed[5] from the modified Davies equation to simplify the solution of a tedious problem. The mean tray width is usually taken as average of weir length and column diameter. Special tray patterns may indicate another mean value.

The values of liquid gradient read from these charts are uncorrected for vapor flow. This correction is a multiplier read from Figure 8-81.

$$\text{Corrected } \Delta = \Delta' \, C_v \qquad (8\text{-}97)$$

Although this method appears to be conservative for the average case, it is not strictly correct for towers with liquid flowing over the cap. Therefore it would be well to check the results of gradients over 1.0 inches by comparing with some of the other methods and with the tabulation of data of Reference 38.

Adjustments to the tray or caps is usually not considered unless the calculated gradient exceeds ½ to 1 inch liquid. Several schemes are in use:

1. Raise cap in inlet half of tower by one-fourth to one-half the calculated gradient, but not exceeding 1 inch.

2. For large towers (usually over 8 feet in diameter) check the hydraulic gradient for sections of the tray normal to liquid flow, adjusting each section by not more than one-half the gradient.

3. Slope the trays downward from liquid inlet to outlet, with the total drop from inlet to outlet weir not exceeding one-half the calculated gradient.

4. Cascading the tray by using weirs as dams to divide the tray in steps, each step or section of the tray having no significant gradient from its inlet to outlet. This is usually only considered for trays 10 feet in dia. and larger, as it adds considerable to the cost of each tray.

5. More elaborate tests and adjustments can be made.[5] However, they are usually unnecessary except in unusual cases of very high liquid loads and/or large columns.

In any case, the average head over the cap slots for the section should approximately equal the average head over the adjoining sections, and the inlet and outlets of the section should not be extreme, even though the average is acceptable. The object of fairly uniform head over the slots should be kept in mind when reviewing the gradient adjustments.

Riser and Reversal Pressure Drop

The method proposed by Bolles fits the average design problem quite satisfactorily. However, for low pressure drop designs as in vacuum towers, it may well require checking by the more detailed method of Dauphine.[13]

A. Bolles' Design Method:[5]

Solve for the combined riser, reversal, annulus, and slot pressure drop by:

$$h_{pc} = K_c \left(\frac{\rho_V}{\rho_L - \rho_V} \right) \left(\frac{V}{A_r} \right)^2 \qquad (8\text{-}98)$$

(Text continued on page 100)

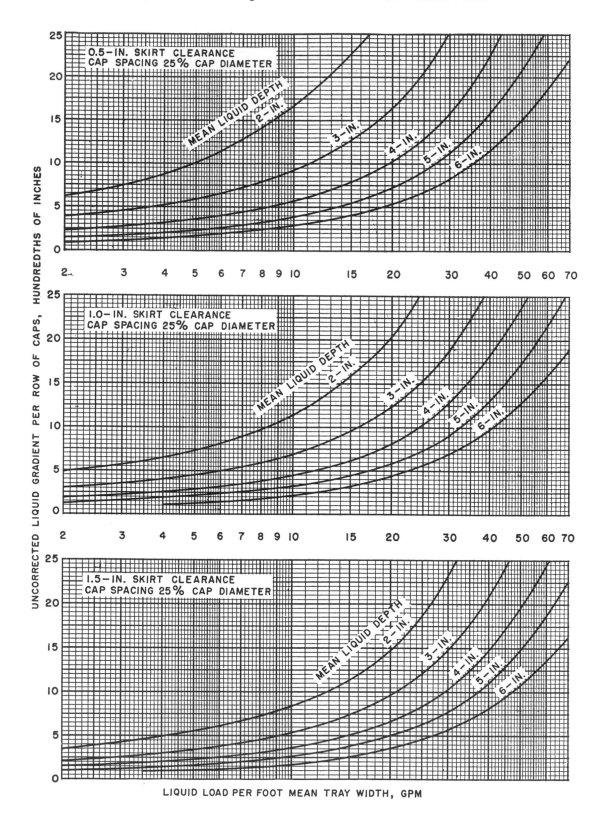

Figure 8-77. Liquid gradient chart—cap spacing 25% cap diameter. (By permission W. L. Bolles, Reference 5.)

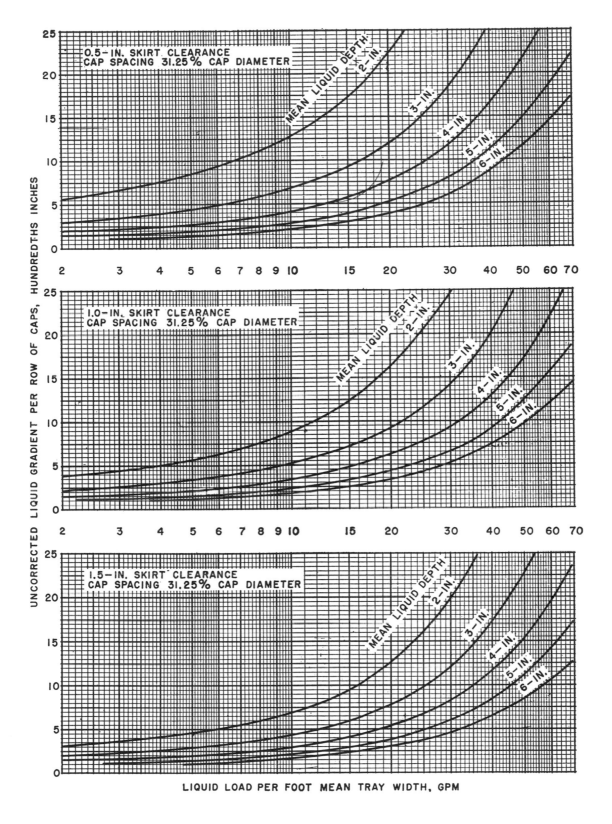

Figure 8-78. Liquid gradient chart—cap spacing 31.25% cap diameter. (By permission W. L. Bolles, Reference 5.)

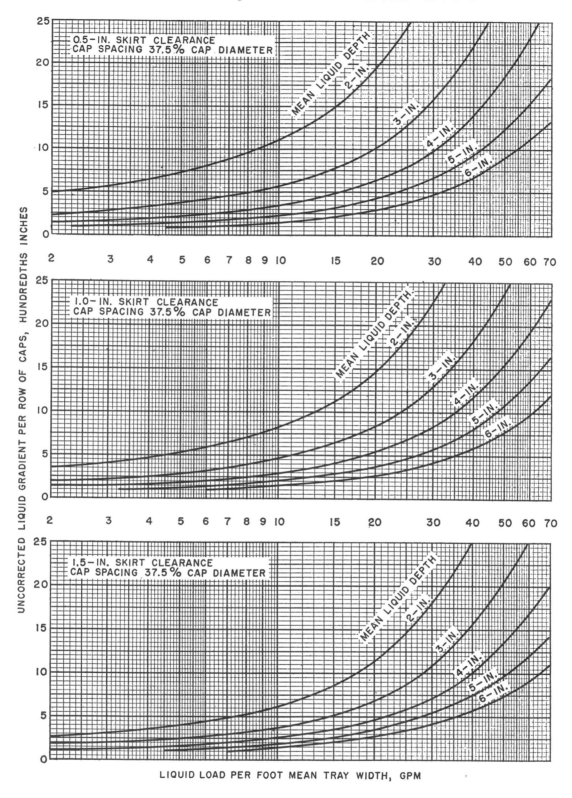

Figure 8-79. Liquid gradient chart—cap spacing 37.5% cap diameter. (By permission W. L. Bolles, Reference 5.)

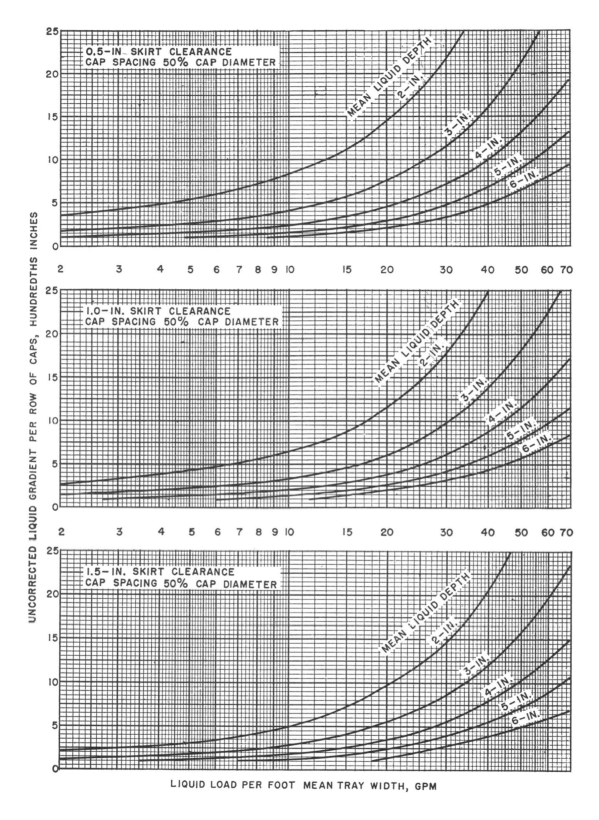

Figure 8-80. Liquid gradient chart—cap spacing 50% cap diameter. (By permission W. L. Bolles, Reference 5.)

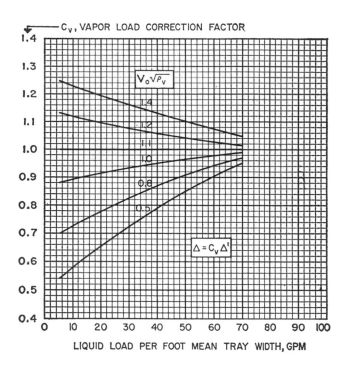

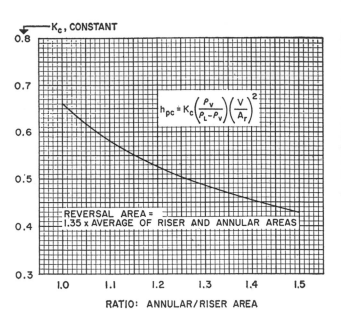

Figure 8-82. Bubble cap pressure drop constant (Bolles method). (By permission W. L. Bolles, Reference 5.)

Figure 8-81. Correction of liquid gradient for vapor load. (By permission J. A. Davies, Ind. and Eng. Chem. Vol. 39, p. 774 (1947), copyright The American Chemical Society.)

The constant, K_c, is obtained from Figure 8-82, noting that the annular area between riser and cap must always be larger than the riser area for K_c to be valid.

where: h_{pc} = Cap assembly pressure drop, including drop through riser, reversal, annulus, slots, in. liquid

A_r = Total riser area per tray, sq. ft.

K_c = Constant for Bolles Bubble Cap pressure drop equation

B. Modified Dauphine Relations[5, 11]:

1. Riser pressure drop

   (1) Reversal Area Greater than Riser Area

   $$h_r = 0.111 \frac{d_r}{\rho_L} \left[(\rho_V)^{1/2} \left(\frac{V}{A_r} \right) \right]^{2.09} \qquad (8\text{-}99)$$

   (2) Reversal Area Less than Riser Area

   $$h_r = 0.099 \frac{d_r}{\rho_L} (a_r/a_{r'})^{1/2} \left[(\rho_V)^{1/2} \left(\frac{V}{A_r} \right) \right]^{2.1} \qquad (8\text{-}100)$$

2. Reversal and annulus pressure drop

The reversal area is the area of the cylinderical vertical plane between the top of the riser and the underside of the bubble cap through which the incoming vapor must pass. The vapor then moves into the annulus area between

the inside diameter of the cap and the outside diameter of the riser before entering the slots in the cap.

The pressure drop due to reversal is independent of slot height and riser height as long as riser height is greater than 2 inches and the cap slot height does not exceed the riser height.[13] When riser height is less than 2 inches, the reversal pressure drop increases as long as the slot height is less than the riser height.

For riser height greater than 2.5 inches:

$$h_{ra} = \frac{0.68}{\rho_L} \left[\left(\frac{2a_r^2}{a_x a_c} \right) (\rho_V)^{1/2} \left(\frac{V}{A_r} \right) \right]^{1.71} \qquad (8\text{-}101)$$

3. Dry cap pressure drop: rectangular slots.

The slot pressure drop through the dry cap increases nearly linearly with cap diameter.

$$h'_s = \frac{0.163}{\rho_L} \left[(d_c \rho_V)^{1/2} \left(\frac{V}{A_s} \right) \right]^{1.73} \qquad (8\text{-}102)$$

4. Total dry cap pressure drop

$$h'_c = h_r + h_{ra} + h'_s \qquad (8\text{-}103)$$

5. Wet cap pressure drop

$$h_c = h'_c / C_w \qquad (8\text{-}104)$$

The correction factor, C_w, is obtained from Figure 8-83. Figure 8-83 applies to cap slots 1 inch through 2 inches, and if slots are smaller (around ½ inch) the C_w factor increases about 25 percent average (50-10 percent). **The** relation applies only to the pressure drop attributable to **the conditions of liquid on the tray up to the top of the** slots.

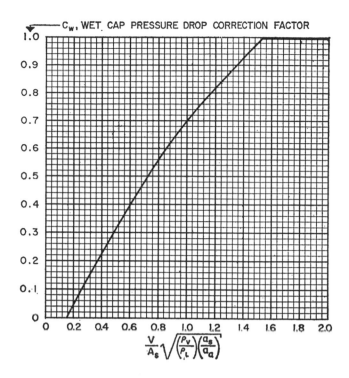

C_w, WET CAP PRESSURE DROP CORRECTION FACTOR

Figure 8-83. Correction for wet cap pressure drop (after Dauphine. (By permission W. L. Bolles, Reference 5, using data of Reference 13.)

Total Pressure Drop Through Tray

A. Bolles Method

$$h_t = (h_{pc} + h_s) + h_{ss} + h_{ow} + \Delta/2 \qquad (8\text{-}105)$$

B. Dauphine Method

$$h_t = h_c + h_{ss} + h_{ow} + \Delta/2 \qquad (8\text{-}106)$$

Downcomer Pressure Drop

The head loss in liquid flowing down the downcomer, under its underflow edge (and up over an inlet weir, if used) and onto the tray is important in determining the back up of liquid in the downcomer. There are many suggested relations representing this head loss.

A. Segmental Type Downcomer

1. Downcomer friction loss plus underflow loss

$$h_{du} = 0.56 \left[\frac{L_g}{449\,(A_d)} \right]^2 \qquad (8\text{-}107)$$

2. Loss through inlet weir

When an inlet weir is used, the additional resistance to flow may be approximated by:

$$h'_d = 0.3\, v^2{}_{du} \qquad (8\text{-}108)$$

Table 8-9
Downcomer Liquid Seal[15]

Tower Diameter Feet	Seal, Outlet Weir Height minus Distance Downcomer Off Tray Floor, Inches
6 and below	0.5
7-12	1
13 and above	1.5

B. Circular or Pipe-Type Downcomer

These downcomers are suggested only where liquid flow is relatively small for the required tower diameter, allowing a maximum of space for bubble caps.

$$h_{dc} = 0.06\,(L_g/a_d)^2 \qquad (8\text{-}109)$$

Liquid Height in Downcomer

The back-up of liquid during flowing conditions must be determined in order to set the proper tray spacing. Tray spacing is usually set at twice the liquid height in the downcomer. This can be adjusted to suit the particular system conditions.

$$H_d = h_w + h_{ow} + \Delta + h_d + h_t \qquad (8\text{-}110)$$

Downcomer Seal

The bottom of the downcomer must be sealed below the operating liquid level on the tray. Due to tolerance in fabrication and tray level, it is customary to set the downcomer seal referenced to the weir height on the outlet side of the tray. Recommended seals, based on no inlet weir adjacent to the downcomer, and referenced as mentioned are given in Table 8-9.

For trays with inlet weirs, seal values may be reduced if necessary for high flow conditions. A good tray design is centered about a 1.5 inch clearance distance between tray floor and bottom of downcomer edge.

Tray Spacing

Adequate tray spacing is important to proper tray operation during normal as well as surging, foaming, and pulsing conditions. Since the downcomer is the area of direct connection to the tray above, the flooding of a tray carries to the tray above. In order to dampen the response, the tray must be adequately sealed at the downcomer and the spacing between trays must be approximately twice the backup height of liquid in the downcomer. Thus for normal design:

$$S_t \geqq 2\,H_d$$

where: S_t = Tray spacing, inches

H_d = Height of liquid in downcomer

Once foam or froth in the downcomer backs up to the tray above, it tends to be re-entrained in the overflowing liquid, making it apparently lighter, and accentuating this height of liquid-foam mixture in the downcomer. The downcomer must be adequate to separate and disengage this mixture, allowing clear liquid (fairly free of bubbles) to flow under the downcomer seal.

A tray inlet weir tends to insure sealing of the downcomer, preventing the bubbling caps from discharging a mixture into the downcomer.

The residence time in the downcomers is another criteria of adequate tray spacing.

Residence Time in Downcomers

In order to provide reasonably adequate time for disengagement of foam and froth from the liquid in the downcomer, the total downcomer volume is checked against a minimum allowable average residence time of 5 seconds. Table 8-10 gives suggested downcomer clear liquid velocities based on relative foaming characteristics of the fluid on the tray at tray conditions.

Liquid Entrainment From Bubble Cap Trays

The work of Simkin, Strand, and Olney[64] correlates the majority of the work of other investigators, and can be used for estimation of probable entrainment from bubble cap trays as shown in Figure 8-84. It is recommended that the liquid entrainment for design be limited to 0.10 mols/mol dry vapor.

Eduljee's[19] correlation of literature data appears to offer a route to evaluating the effect of entrainment on tray spacing and efficiency. It is suggested as another check on other methods. Figure 8-85 may be used as recommended:

1. Assume or establish a level of acceptable entrainment, such as 10 mols liquid/100 mols vapor.

2. Determine effect on efficiency by Colburn's relation (see Efficiency section).

3. Calculate total entrainment as pounds of liquid per hour, based on total vapor flow in tower.

4. Determine area of tray above caps (equals tower area minus area of two downcomers for cross-flow tower).

5. Calculate liquid entrainment, W'_e, as pounds of liquid per square foot of net tray area, equals (Step 3)/(Step 4), lbs./hr. (sq.ft.).

6. Calculate vapor velocity, v_f, based on area of (Step 4), ft./sec.

7. Calculate density factor, $[\rho_v/(\rho_L - \rho_v)]^{1/2}$

8. Calculate $v_f [\rho_v/(\rho_L - \rho_v)]^{1/2}$

9. From Figure 8-85, read Log W_e^*

Table 8-10

Suggested Downcomer Velocities[5]

Approximate Tray Spacing, Inches	System Foaming Characteristics Allowable Clear Liquid Velocities, Ft./sec.		
	High	Medium	Low
18............	0.15–0.2	0.35–0.42	0.45–0.52
24............	0.25–0.32	0.48–0.52	0.55–0.60
30............	0.30–0.35	0.48–0.52	0.65–0.70
Typical Representative System	Amine, Glycerine	Oil systems	Gasoline, Light Hydrocarbons

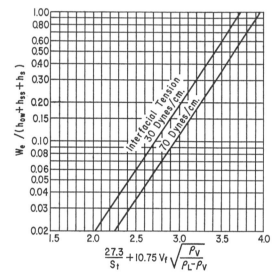

Figure 8-84. Correlation of entrainment. (By permission W. L. Bolles, Reference 5, using data of Reference 64.)

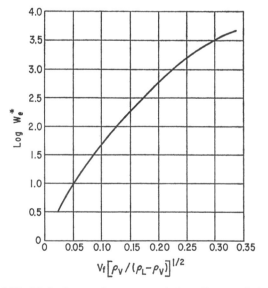

Figure 8-85. Eduljee's entrainment correlation. (By permission H. E. Eduljee, British Chemical Engineering, Sept. 1958.)

10. Calculate S″ from

$$\text{Log } W^*_e = \text{Log } W'_e + 2.59 \text{ Log } S'' + \text{Log } \mu + 0.4 \text{ Log } \sigma$$

11. Assume a foam height, h_f, of approximately twice the height of the dynamic tray seal, inches. This agrees with several investigators for *medium* foaming systems.

12. Minimum tray spacing $S_t = h_f + S'$, inches

where: v_f = Vapor velocity based on free area above caps (not including two downcomers), ft./sec.

W_e^* = Entrainment corrected for liquid properties and plate spacing

S'' = Clear height above foam or froth, (equals tray spacing minus foam height above tray floor), feet

μ = Viscosity of liquid, centipoise

σ = Surface tension of liquid, dynes/cm.

W_e' = Entrainment (based on assumed allowance) lbs. liquid/(sq. ft. free plate area) (Hr.)

h_f = Height of top of foam above tray floor, inches

Free Height in Downcomer

$$F = S_t + h_w - H_d$$

Slot Seal

The static slot seal is the fixed distance between the top of the outlet weir and top of the bubble cap slots.

The actual operating or dynamic slot seal is more indicative of conditions pertaining to the tray in operation and is:[5]

$$h_{ds} = h_{ss} + h_{ow} + \Delta/2 \qquad (8\text{-}111)$$

Note that this seal varies across the tray, although the tray design must be such as to make the value of h_{ds} nearly the same for each row of caps.

In order to insure good efficiencies and yet a definite seal consistent with allowable pressure drops, suggested values for h_{ds} are modified from the references and shown in Table 8-8.

Throw Over Outlet Segmental Weir

In order to insure unobstructed vapor passage above the froth and liquid in the downcomer from a tray, the liquid mixture must not throw against the shell wall. The distance of throw the weir is given by:[5] See Fig. 8-48

$$t_w = 0.8 \left[h_{ow} (F) \right]^{\frac{1}{2}} \qquad (8\text{-}112)$$

$$h_t' = S_t + h_w - H_d \qquad (8\text{-}113)$$

Vapor Distribution

The vapor distribution approximation

$$R_v = \Delta/h_c \qquad (8\text{-}114)$$

is an indication of the uniformity of vapor flow through the caps on the inlet side of the tray to those on the outlet side and the tendency of inlet caps to stop bubbling. Davies [14, 15] recommends values for the ratio of 0.4, not to exceed 0.6; Bolles recommends 0.5. Only at values around 0.1 is essentially uniform vapor flow maintained through all the caps. As the R_v ratio increases, a smaller percentage of the vapor flows through the inlet tray caps and a larger percentage is shifted to the outlet caps. This cross-flow of vapor increases the effect of Δ on the tray and accentuates the problem. Unfortunately it is often overlooked in many tray examinations. When the ratio reaches the value equal to the cap drop at full slot capacity (usually 1.75 to 2.5 inches) liquid will flow or dump back down the risers at the inlet row of caps. This is definitely improper tray operation, providing markedly reduced tray efficiencies.

For stepped caps (tray level, risers of different heights) or cascade tray (tray consisting of two or more levels) care must be taken to analyze all the conditions associated with level changes on the tray. Reference 5 discusses this in some detail.

Bubble Cap Tray Design and Evaluation

Example 8-15: Bubble Cap Tray Design

Check the trays for a finishing tower operating under vacuum of 75 mm mercury at the top. The estimated pressure drop for the twenty trays should not exceed 50-60 mm. Hg. Fifteen trays are in the rectifying section, five in the stripping section.

Following the suggested form, and starting with the standard tray design existing in the unit, the calculations will be made to check this tray, making modifications if necessary. The 6-ft., 0-in, diameter tower was designed originally for a significantly different load, but is to be considered for the new service. The tray features are outlined in Table 8-6. It becomes obvious that the tray is too large for the requirements, but should perform reasonably well. The weakest point in performance is the low slot velocity.

*Tray Design**

Tower application or service: *Product Finishing*

Tower Inside Diameter; 6 feet, 0 inches

Tray Type; Cross Flow

Tray Spacing, inches 24; Type outlet weir; *End*

Note: Tray spacing was set when the 6-foot, 0-inch diameter was determined.

No. downcomers/tray *1;* Located: *End*

Cap Data:

(1) Cap I.D., dc, inches *3⅞ inches,* Spacing: *5½ inches Δ 60° centers*

(2) Total height, inches *3¹⁵⁄₁₆ inches*

(3) No./tray, N_c, *129*

(4) Slots: No., N_s *50*

---

* Adapted from Ref. 15, modified to suit recommendations offered in this presentation.

(5) Height, H_s, in. *1½ inches*

(6) Width, w_s, in. *⅛ inch*

(7) Skirt Height, s, in. *¼ inch*

(8) Shroud Ring height, h_{sr}, in. *¼ inch*

(9) Height of inside surface of cap above tray, in. *3.94 inches*

(10) Riser I. D., dr, *2.68* in.

(11) Riser height above tray floor, *3 inches*

Areas:

(12) Riser inside cross-sectional, a_r, sq. in. *5.43* per riser

(13) Total riser inside cross-sect. area/tray, A_r, sq. ft. *4.95*

(14) Riser outside cross-sectional area a_{ro}, sq. in. *5.94* per riser. Riser is 2¾-in O.D.; $\pi 2.75^2/4 = 5.94$

(15) Cap inside cross-sectional area, a_c, sq. in. *11.79* per cap. Cap is 3⅞-inch I.D., $\pi(3⅞)^2/4 = 11.79$

(16) Total cap inside cross-sectional area, A_c, sq. ft. *10.53*

(17) Annular area per cap, a_a, sq. in., $(11.79)—(5.94) = 5.85$

(18) Total annular area per tray, A_a, sq. ft. *5.24*

(19) Reversal area per cap, a'_r, sq. in. $= \pi(2.69)(3.94) — 3.0) = 7.95$. d $= (2.75 + 2.63)/2 = 2.69$ in.

(20) Total reversal area, per tray, A'_r, sq. ft., $(129/144)(7.95) = 7.12$

(21) Slot area per cap, a_s, sq. in. $(50)(⅛)(1.5) = 9.39$

(22) Total slot area per tray, A_s, sq. ft. *8.40*

Tray Details

(23) Length of outlet overflow weir, l_w, feet *4.0*

(24) Height of weir (weir setting) above tray floor, inches, h_w, 2.5

(25) Inlet weir (downcomer side) length (if used), feet *4.0*

(26) Inlet weir height above tray floor, inches, *3*

(27) Height of top of cap slots above tray floor, inches *2*

(28) Static slot submergence or static slot seal (2.5-2.0), h_{ss}, inches, *0.5*

(29) Height of bottom of downcomer above tray floor, *2¾ inches*

(30) Downcomer flow areas: (a) Between downcomer and tower shell, sq. ft. *0.886*

(31) (b) Between bottom downcomer and tray floor, sq. ft. *0.710*

(32) (c) Between downcomer and inlet weir, sq. ft. *0.740*

(33) Riser slot seal, (3.0-2), inches *1.0*

Tray Operations Summary and Pressure Drop	Top	Bottom
A. Tray number	20	1
B. Operating pressure, mm. Hg	75	100
C. Operating temperature, °F	60	100
D. Vapor flow, lbs./hr.	6565	6565
E. Vapor volume, cu. ft./sec. @ operating conditions, V	132.2	105
F. Vapor density, lbs./cu. ft. operating conditions	0.0138	0.01735
G. Liquid flow, gallons/minute, L_g	3.74	3.74
H. Liquid flow, lbs./hr., L'	1515	1515
I. Liquid flow, cu. ft./sec. @ operating conditions	0.00834	0.00776
J. Liquid density, lbs./cu. ft. @ operating conditions	50.5	54.2
K. Superficial vapor velocity, based on Tower I.D., ft./sec., 132.2/28.28	4.67	3.7
L. Vapor velocity based on cap area between inlet and outlet weirs, ft./sec., 132/[28.28-2(2.12)]	5.49	4.37
M. Volume of downcomer; Area top segment, Perry's Hdbk. 3rd Ed. pg. 32. h/D = 9³⁄₁₆ inch /72 = 0.1276, A = 0.05799(6)² = 2.08 sq. ft.	4.04	4.04
Lower taper, use h @ 2/3 of vert. taper for estimate. 8/72 = 0.111, A = 0.04763(6)² = 1.71 sq. ft. Volume = (2.08)(0.5) + (1.71)(21/12) = 4.04 cu. ft.		
N. Liquid residence time in downcomer, seconds, (4.04)/0.00834 = 485	485	520
O. Throw over downcomer weir (sideflow), inches	1.17	1.17
P. Throw over downcomer weir (center flow), min. =	——	——
Q. Tray layout, actual downcomer width, inches	9³⁄₁₆ 5½	9³⁄₁₆ 5½
Taper downcomer has 6″ vertical dimension at 9³⁄₁₆ inches wide. Tapers to 5½ inches, 24 inches below tray.		
R. Slot velocity: minimum 3.4/$(\rho_G)^{1/2}$ ft./sec.	29	25.9
S. Slot velocity: maximum = 12.1/$(\rho_G)^{1/2}$ = 12.1/(.0138)$^{1/2}$ and 12.1/(.01735)$^{1/2}$, ft. sec.	103.1	92
T. Slot velocity: Superficial, $u_o = V/A_s =$ 132.2/8.40 and 105/8.4 ft./sec.	15.7	12.5
Pressure Drop, Inches Liquid on Tray	**Top**	**Bottom**
a. Height of liquid over weir (straight weir) $L_g/(l_w)^{2.5} = 3.74/(48/12)^{2.5} = 0.1168$ $l_w/D = 4/6 = 0.667$ Read $F_w = 1.018$ from Figure 8-74. $h_{ow} = 0.092(1.018)(3.74/4)^{⅔}$	0.0989	0.0989
Use ¼ inch-V-notched weir, 2.5 inches from tray floor to bottom of notch. This is necessary because of low liquid flow.		
b. Static submergence, h_{ss}, inches	0.5	0.5
c. Caps Modified Dauphine and Cicalese, [11,13] dry cap basis.		
1. Riser pressure drop, reversal area greater than riser area.		

$$h_r = 0.111\left(\frac{2.63}{50.5}\right)\left[(0.0138)^{1/2}\left(\frac{132.2}{4.95}\right)\right]^{2.09}$$

= 0.06333	0.0633	0.0462

Pressure Drop, Inches Liquid on Tray   **Top**   **Bottom**

2. Reversal and annulus pressure drop
Riser height > 2.5 inches

$$h_{ra} = \frac{0.68}{50.5} \left[\frac{2(5.43)^2}{(7.95)(11.79)} (0.0138)^{1/2} \left(\frac{132.2}{4.95} \right) \right]^{1.71}$$

$= 0.045$ 0.045   0.0322

3. Rectangular slot dry pressure drop

$$h'_s = \frac{0.163}{50.5} \left[[3.875 \ (0.0138)]^{1/2} \left(\frac{132.2}{8.40} \right) \right]^{1.73}$$

$= 0.0308$ 0.0308   0.0231

4. Total Dry cap pressure drop
$h'_e = h_r + h_{ra} + h_s' = 0.0633$
$+0.045 + 0.0308 = 0.139$ 0.1391   0.1015

5. Wet cap pressure drop

$$\frac{V}{A_s} \left[\frac{\rho_v}{\rho_L} \left(\frac{a_s}{a_s} \right) \right]^{1/2}$$

$$= \frac{132.2}{8.40} \left[\frac{0.0138}{50.5} \left(\frac{9.39}{5.85} \right) \right]^{1/2} = 0.33$$

From Figure 8-59, $C_w = 0.16$
$h_e = h_e'/C_w = 0.1391/0.16 = 0.87$ 0.87   0.847

6. Check maximum pressure drop
through wet caps:
h_e max. $= 0.0633 + 0.045 + (1.5 +$
0.25), inches 1.8   1.3
Since h_e is less than h_e max., cap is
O.K. and not blowing under shroud
ring

Bolles' recommendation

7. Riser, reversal, annulus pressure drop
$a_s/a_r = 5.85/5.43 = 1.075$
From Figure 8-58, $K_e = 0.598$

$$h_{pc} = 0.598 \left(\frac{0.0138}{50.5 - 0.0138} \right) \left(\frac{132.2}{4.95} \right)^2$$

0.118   0.0861

8. Slot pressure drop, Rectangular slots

$$h_s = 32 \left(\frac{0.0138}{50.5 - 0.0138} \right)^{1/3} \left(\frac{132.2}{129 \ (50) \ (1/8)} \right)^{2/3}$$

$= 0.626$ 0.626   0.566

d. Liquid Gradient
Mean tray width $= (4 + 6)/2 = 5$ feet
GPM/ft. mean tray width $= 3.74/5 =$
0.75
Assumed mean liquid depth, $h_l =$
$2.5 + 0.0989 + 0.1$
Uncorrected Δ'/row caps $=$ approx.
0.02 inches
$v_o \ (\rho_v)^{1/2} = 4.67 \ (0.0138)^{1/2} = 0.548$
C_v, from Figure 8-81, $=$ estimated
0.55 (off chart)
No. cap rows $= 11$
Corrected $\Delta = (0.02) \ (0.548) \ (11)$
$= 0.1206$ inches 0.12   0.12
$\Delta/2$, inches (essentially negligible in
this case) 0.06   0.06

e. Total pressure drop per tray, inches
liquid
1. Modified Dauphine
$h_t = h_e + h_{ss} + h_{ow} + \Delta/2$
$h_t = 0.87 + 0.5 + 0.0989 + 0.06$ ... 1.528   1.505

2. Bolles
$h_t = h_{pc} + h_s + h_{ss} + h_{ow} + \Delta/2$
$= 0.118 + 0.626 + 0.5 + 0.0989 +$
0.06 .... 1.502   1.310

f. Pressure drop for *15 trays* in rectifying
Section
1. Modified Dauphine, 15 (1.528) $=$
22.9 inches liquid $= 34.2$ mm Hg.. 34.2 mm
2. Bolles, 15 (1.502) $= 22.4$ inches
liquid $= 33.4$ mm Hg .... 33.4 mm

Pressure drop for *5 trays* in stripping
section
1. Modified Dauphine, 5 (1.505) $= 7.52$
inches liquid $=$ ....   11.1 mm
2. Bolles, 5 (1.42) $= 6.56$ inches
liquid $=$ ....   9.7 mm

Total pressure drop for *20 trays*
1. Modified Dauphine ....   45.3 mm
2. Bolles ....   43.1 mm

g. Height liquid in downcomer
1. Segmental, underflow plus friction.. 0.000077   0.000077

$$h_{du} = 0.56 \left(\frac{3.74}{449 \ (0.710)} \right)^2$$

2. Segmental, upflow when inlet weir
used .... Neg.   Neg.
$h_d' = 0.3 \ v_{du}^2$
3. Total segmental loss, h_d 0.000077   0.000077
4. Circular downspout ....
5. Liquid height in downcomer
$H_d = h_w + h_{ow} + h_d + h_t + \Delta$
$= 2.5 + 0.0989 + 0.000077 +$
$1.638 + 0.35$ 4.58   4.56
6. Free height in downcomer
$F = S_t + h_w - H_d = 24 + 2.5 -$
4.58 .... 21.69   21.71
7. Throw over weir
$t_w = 0.8 \ [h_{ow} \ (F)]^{1/2}$
$= 0.8 \ [0.0989(21.69)]^{1/2}$ 1.17   1.17

h. Vapor distribution ratio
$R_v = \Delta/h_e = 0.12/0.87$ 0.138   0.141

i. Slot seal
Dynamic, $h_{ds} = h_{ss} + h_{ow} + \Delta/2 =$
$0.5 + 0.0989 + 0.06$ 0.65   0.65

Liquid Velocity in Downcomer

Minimum cross-section area of downcomer $= 0.886$ sq. ft.

Liquid rate $= 0.00834$ cu.ft./sec.

Velocity $= 0.00834/0.886 = 0.00942$ ft./sec.

This is very low and confirms that there should be ample disengaging capacity in the downcomers. The downcomers are too large for good design.

Slot Velocity

The results of lines R, S, and T indicate that the vapor velocity through the cap slots is lower than desirable for good bubbling.

Slot Opening

The slot opening, h_s, given in line c8 is only slightly lower than the normal design of 50-60% of H_s, or 0.75″ to 0.90″.

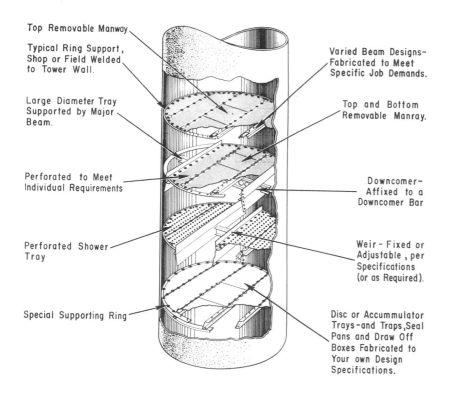

Figure 8-86. Sieve tray with downcomers. Tower assembly (Courtesy of Hendrick Mfg. Co.)

Vapor Distribution Ratio

The values of line (h) are quite in line with good vapor flow through all the caps. This is as would be expected, since the hydraulic gradient is low; too low to require any compensation.

Liquid Entrainment

$$v_f = 132.2/[28.28 - 2(2.12)] = 5.5 \text{ ft./sec.}$$

$$\frac{27.3}{s_t} + 10.75\, v_f \left(\frac{\rho_V}{\rho_L - \rho_V}\right)^{\frac{1}{2}}$$

$$= \frac{27.3}{24} + 10.75(5.5)\left(\frac{0.0138}{50.5 - 0.0138}\right)^{\frac{1}{2}}$$

$$= 1.13 + 0.978 = 2.108$$

Reading Figure 8-84

For 27 dynes/cm surface tension

$$W_e/h_{ow} + h_{ss} + h_s = 0.026$$

$$W_e = (.026)(0.098 + 0.5 + 0.626) = 0.0317 \text{ Lbs./Min. (sq. ft.)}$$

Entrainment $= (0.0317)[28.28 - 2(2.12)] = 0.764$ lbs./min.

Entrainment ratio $= 0.764/(6565/60) = .00698$

This value of entrainment is negligible. For a new column design, this would indicate that the tower was too large, and a smaller shell should be considered.

Conclusion

This is not a good tray design, but it should operate. However, a reduced efficiency is to be expected due to low vapor velocities.

Since the liquid flow is low also, $\frac{1}{4}$-inch v-notched weirs should be used to ensure uniform flow and level across the tray. The bottom of the notches should be 2.5″ above the tray floor.

Sieve Trays With Downcomers

The performance analysis of these trays is quite similar to bubble caps, since the tray has the same basic mechanical features. The difference being that bubble caps are replaced by perforations or holes in the tray for entrance of the gas to the liquid on the tray. Figures 8-38 and 8-86 and -87 represent the general construction of a sieve tray.

Sieve trays have been used in both clean and fouling service, including solutions of suspended particles. The bubbling action seems to wash the solids down from tray to tray provided there are no corners or "dead" spots on the tray. Sieve trays are preferably selected for applications which can be operated at from 50-100 percent of capacity without too sudden a surge from one rate to another significantly different. When operating within the design range, the efficiency of these trays for many systems is better than for bubble cap trays, although without specific test data it is still impossible to safely take advantage of this feature of performance.

In some sieves the capacity is 1.5 to as much as 3 times that of a bubble cap tray provided careful consideration has been given to all design features.

The "type tray" guide proposed by Huang and Hodson[30] serves to identify the major breaks in type of tray design (Figure 8-88). In the region between types, the

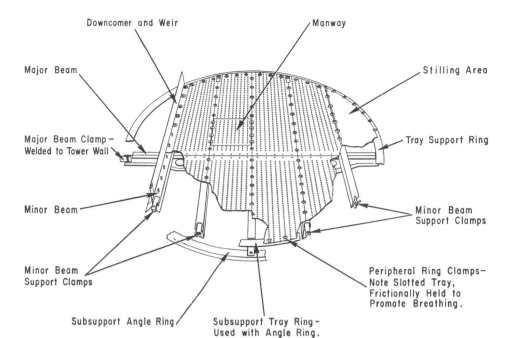

Figure 8-87. Sieve tray with downcomers. Tray components. (Courtesy of Hendrick Mfg. Co.)

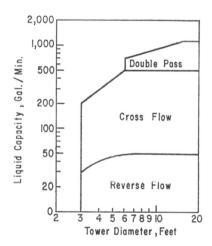

Figure 8-88. Selection guide, perforated trays with downcomers. (By permission Chen-Jung Huang and J. R. Hodson, Pet. Ref., Vol. 37, (1958), 104.)

Figure 8-89. The "Linde Tray" is a proven tray design for new installations, as well as for improving the performance of existing distillation columns.

selection is not sharp and the design should be evaluated based on other criteria.

Various aspects of sieve tray performance have been studied[30, 31, 33, 36, 41, 42, 45, 71, 78] and several design methods have been recommended.[30, 31, 41, 42] The following composite method has given good performance in operating towers, and is based on satisfying the three critical capacity features, i.e., entrainment, flooding and weeping.

The action on this type of tray seems to produce fewer jets of liquid froth than a bubble cap tray. The entrainment from the surface of the bubbling liquid-froth mixture is less (about 1/3) than a bubble cap tray for the same superficial tower velocity and tray spacing. Generally the

trays will flood before capacity reaches a limitation set by entrainment.

The proprietary "Linde Tray," Figure 8-89, is a proven tray design used for new installations, and also often for improving the performance of existing distillation columns by replacing the older and possibly less efficient trays. One of the advantages of this type tray is its capability of being installed at tray spacings as low as 9 to 10 inches, and frequently at 12 inches. The tray efficiency varies with the distillation system, but as a general guide, will be equal to that of a multipass tray.

Tower Diameter

The tower diameter may be calculated for first approximation by the Souders-Brown method; however, this has been found to be conservative, since it is based on no liquid entrainment between trays. Actually some entrainment can be tolerated at negligible loss in efficiency or capacity.

There are several approaches to column diameter design[65, 74] as well as the proprietary techniques of major industrial and engineering designers. Some of these use the proprietary Fractionation Research Institute methods which are only available on a membership basis and do not appear in the technical literature.

In general, a better first approximation and often a more economical tower diameter is determined using

Figure 8-90 (Reference 33)

$$e_w = 0.22 \left(\frac{73}{\sigma}\right)\left(\frac{v_c}{S'}\right)^{3.2} \qquad (8\text{-}115)$$

$$S' = S_t - 2.5\,h_c \qquad (8\text{-}116)$$

where: e_w = Weight of liquid entrained/unit weight of vapor flowing in sieve tray column
σ = Liquid surface tension, dynes/cm.
v_c = Vapor velocity based on column cross-section, ft./sec.
S' = Effective tray spacing, distance between top of foam and next plate above, inches
h_c = Height of clear liquid in bubbling zone, inches

This is based on a frothed mixture density of 0.4 that of the clear liquid on the tray, and has been found to be a reasonable average for several mixtures.

Entrainment values of 0.05 lbs. liquid/lb. vapor are usually acceptable, with 0.001 and 0.5 lbs./lb. being the extremes. The specific design dictates the tolerance on entrainment. From the calculated vapor velocity, v_c, the diameter of the column can be calculated using:

$$D = \left[\frac{4}{\pi}\left(\frac{V}{v_c}\right)\right]^{\frac{1}{2}}, \text{ feet}$$

Entrainment does not usually become a problem until the tray is operating at 85-100 percent of the flooding condition. Figure 8-90 is convenient for solving for e_w.

Tray Spacing

Tray spacing can usually be about 6″ less than for a corresponding bubble tray. Sieve trays are operating on spacings of 9 inches and up to 30 inches. The latter being necessary for high vacuum service. Spacing of 12-16 inches is common.

Minimum spacing is the same as recommended for bubble cap trays, i.e., $S_t = 2\,H_d$.

Downcomer

Downcomers are designed for the same conditions as bubble tray towers.

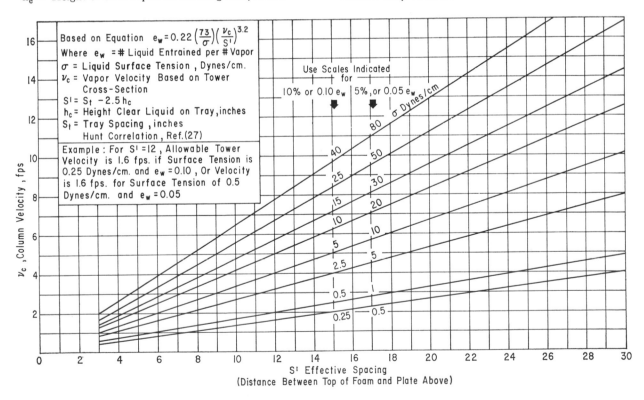

Figure 8-90. Sieve tray entrainment correction. (By permission C. D'A. Hunt, D. N. Hanson and C. R. Wilke, Am. Inst. Chem. Engrs. Jour Vol. 1, p. 441 (1955).)

Hole Size and Spacing

The majority of the literature has presented data for trays with holes of ⅛-inch through ¼-inch diameter. The work of Hunt et. al.,[27] includes ½-inch holes. Some commercial units have used ¾ and 1-inch holes, although these sizes should be used with caution when adequate data is not available. The recommended hole size for the average clean service is 3/16-inch based on present published data. Holes of ½-inch may be used for any service including fouling and fluids containing solids with no loss in efficiency. Holes of ⅛-inch dia. are often used in vacuum service.

Holes spaced closer than twice the hole diameter lead to unstable operation. The recommended spacing is 2.5 d_o to 5 d_o with 3.8 d_o being preferable.[42] Holes are usually placed on 60° equilateral triangular pitch with the liquid flowing normally to the rows. Holes should not be greater than 2.5-3 inches apart for effective tray action

The percentage hole area in a tray varies according to the needs of the design; the usual range is 4-15 percent of the total tower cross-section. Experience has indicated that this is a questionable basis, and it is clearer to refer areas to the active bubbling section of the tray, provided liquid cannot by-pass this area. Thus, rather arbitrarily, but referenced to test literature, the effective tray action area might be the area enclosed by encircling the perforated hole area a distance 2-3 inches from the periphery holes. On this basis, the hole area would be 6-25 percent with a usual value range of 7-16 percent with about 10 percent being preferred.

Height of Liquid Over Outlet Weir, h_{ow}

This may be calculated as recommended for bubble cap trays. Minimum weir height is 0.5-inches, with 1-3 inches preferred. See Figure 8-38.

Hydraulic Gradient, Δ

Tests have indicated that the hydraulic gradient is negligible or very small for most tray designs. Usual design practice is to omit its effect unless the value of Δ is expected to be greater than 0.75 in. If hydraulic gradient is appreciable, then the holes nearer to the tray inlet (liquid) will tend to weep before those nearer the tray outlet. This creates the same type of cross-flow and improper distribution as was discussed for bubble cap tray operation. The recommendation of Hughmark and O'Connell[31] includes corrections to the friction factor of Klein.[39]

For stable tray operation, the hydraulic gradient should be less than one half the dry tray pressure drop. For conditions of high weir height and high $v_o (\rho_v)^{1/2}$ the greater the friction factor affecting the hydraulic gradient.[25] Also, the greater the liquid flow the higher the pressure drop and gradient.

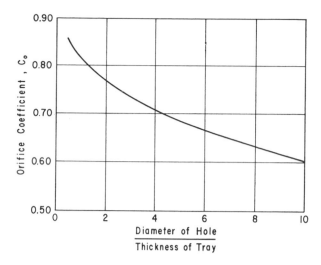

Figure 8-91. Orifice coefficient for perforated trays. (By permission G. A. Hughmark and H. E. O'Connell, Chem. Engr. Prog., Vol. 53, p. 127-M (1957).)

Dry Tray Pressure Drop

This is the drop occurring when the vapor passes through the holes on the tray. The relation below[25] correlates the data of several of the major investigators with a maximum deviation of less than 20 percent and an average deviation of 10 percent.

$$h_{dt} = 0.003 \, [v_o^2 \, \rho_V] \left(\frac{\rho_{water}}{\rho_L} \right) (1 - \beta^2)/C_o^2 \quad (8\text{-}117)$$

$$F_s = v_o(\rho)^{1/2}, \, F^2 = v_o^2(\rho_V) \quad (8\text{-}118)$$

where: h_{dt} = Pressure drop through dry perforated tray, inches liquid on tray

v_o = Vapor velocity through perforated holes, ft./sec.

β = Fraction perforated hole area in perforated tray area only

C_o = Orifice coefficient from Figure 8-91.

Note that β is not the fraction of hole area in the active tray region, but is limited to the perforated section only.

Static Liquid Seal on Tray, or Submergence

Aeration of the liquid by gas bubbles reduces density. The usual and somewhat conservative approach recommends that this aeration effect be neglected. Many successful towers have trays operating on this design basis.[45]

A.

$$h_{sl} = (f)h_w + h_{ow} \quad (8\text{-}119)$$

$$f = 1.0$$

where: f = aeration factor

h_{sl} = Static liquid seal on sieve tray, inches liquid

B. A second and also successful method accounts to a certain extent for the aeration effect, based on test data from many references. This method is not quite as conservative when estimating total tower pressure. This follows the effective head concept of Hughmark et. at.[31] Effective head, h_e, is the sum of the hydrostatic head plus the head to form the bubbles and to force them through the aerated mixture. Figure 8-92 is the correlation for h_e plotted against submergence, h_{s1}.[31] See Dynamic Liquid Seal.

Dynamic Liquid Seal

When hydraulic gradient is a factor in the tray design, the dynamic liquid seal should be used in place of h_{s1} for the determination of effective head.

$$h_{d1} = (f)h_w + h_{ow} + \Delta/2 \qquad (8\text{-}120)$$

where: h_{d1} = Dynamic liquid seal for sieve tray, in. liquid
h_e = Effective liquid head taking aeration of liquid into account, in. liquid, from Figure 8-92

Total Wet Tray Pressure Drop

A. Conservative

$$h_t = (f)h_w + h_{ow} + h_{dt} + \Delta/2$$

This will give a higher pressure drop per tray than the method (B).

B. Hughmark and O'Connell method

The results of this approach agree with a considerable number of tests reported over a wide range of operation.

$$h_t = h_{dt} + h_e \qquad (8\text{-}121)$$

Pressure Drop through Downcomer, h_d

Calculate as for bubble cap tray.

Liquid Back-up or Height in Downcomer

$$H_d = h_t + h_w + h_{ow} + \Delta + h_d \qquad (8\text{-}122)$$

Note that if an inlet tray weir is used, the $(h_w + h_{ow})$ group is replaced by the corresponding $(h_w{}' + h_{ow}{}')$ calculated for the inlet weir using the same algebraic relations.

Free Height in Downcomer

$$F = S_t + h_w - H_d \qquad (8\text{-}123)$$

Minimum Vapor Velocity: Weep Point

The "weep point" is considered to be the minimum vapor velocity that will provide a stable tray operation, preventing liquid from passing through the holes and by-passing the overflow weir and downcomer.

This point is generally considered the lower point of operation for the tray while maintaining acceptable efficiency. Some systems are known to operate at only slight

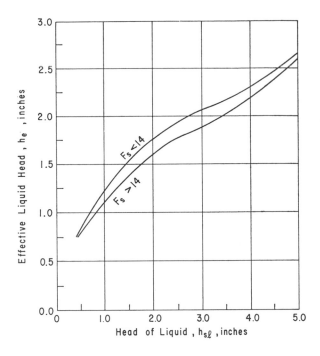

Figure 8-92. Effective liquid head for sieve trays with downcomers (By permission G. A. Hughmark and H. E. O'Connell, Chem. Egnr Prog. Vol. 53, p. 127-M (1957).)

reduction in efficiency while vapor velocities are well below the weep point values. It is impossible to predict this behavior at present. Weeping is usually the limiting condition in design for low vapor rate, high liquid rate systems. Some factors affecting the weep point of any system are as follows.

Weep Point (Velocity)

1. Increases as the liquid surface tension decreases

2. Decreases as the hole size decreases

3. Increases as the plate thickness decreases

4. Increases as the percentage free area increases

5. Increases for hole spacing close to $2d_o$ and smaller. Spacing of $3d_o$ and $4d_o$ give better operation. Only the 1/8 inch holes of Hunt[33] indicate that $2d_o$ spacing may be acceptable if the holes are very small.

6. Decreases with increasing wetability of liquid on plate surface. Kerosene, hexane, carbon tetrachloride, butyl alcohol, glycerine-water mixtures all wet the test plate better than pure water. The critical tray stability data of Hunt et. al.,[33] is given in Table 8-11 for air-water, and hence the velocities for other systems which wet the tray better than water should be somewhat lower than those tabulated. The data of Zenz[78] are somewhat higher than these tabulated values by 10-60 percent.

These values are to be used as guides in establishing first estimates of lower limiting vapor velocities. Actual values should be calculated as outlined below.

Table 8-11[33]

Tray Stability With Varying Liquid Head,
Air-Water System

Hole Diam., In. Spacing, In.	Calculated Critical Gas Velocity in Holes Ft./Sec.			
	$h_{dl} = h_w + h_{ow} + \Delta/2$			
	1.0 In.	1.8 In.	2.8 In.	3.8 In.
⅛ x 4d₀	5	25	32	35
¼ x 4d₀	20	30	45	55
¼ x 3d₀	27	40	55	70
½ x 4d₀	25	27	27	30
½ x 6d₀	30	35	40	45

The two approaches to determining the weep point are:

A. *Conservative Design*

1. Assume a minimum vapor velocity through the holes.

2. Calculate h_{dt}., Eq. 8-117

3. Compare calculated h_{dt} with value of dry tray pressure drop as given:

$$h_{dt} \text{ (weep)} = 0.2 + 0.067 (h_w + h_{ow})$$

This is based on the correlation of Mayfield[45] where: h_{dt} (weep) = dry tray pressure drop at tray weep point, in. liquid.

4. Set minimum design dry tray pressure drop 30 percent above the value of h_{dt} (weep).

B. *Normal Design*[31]

1. Assume a minimum vapor velocity through the holes. Calculate $v_{om} (\rho_v)^{½}$ (minimum)

2. Calculate wet tray pressure drop, determine effective head from Figure 8-92.

3. Read weep point velocity factor, $v_{om} (\rho_v)^{½}$, from Figure 8-93.

The assumed value of v_{om} must be greater than the value read from the curve for $v_{om} (\rho_v)^{½}$.

4. Minimum design vapor velocity through the holes may be used a calculated, or if additional safety is required, increase the value by 20 percent.

Maximum Hole Velocity: Flooding

The maximum hole velocity will give a liquid build up in the downcomer of 50 percent of the tray spacing.

To determine the maximum velocity:

1. Assume a hole velocity

2. Calculate liquid height in downcomer, H_d by Equation 8-122.

3. If $H_d = ½ S_t$, the assumed hole velocity is satisfactory; if not, repeat until a close balance is obtained.

Design Hole Velocity

The design velocity for selection of the holes also sets the minimum tower diameter. In order to take advantage of as much flexibility in operation as possible throughout the expected operating range, the following points should be considered in setting this velocity.

A. Select a design velocity near the weep point if:

1. The design vapor rate is, or is very close to the minimum rate.

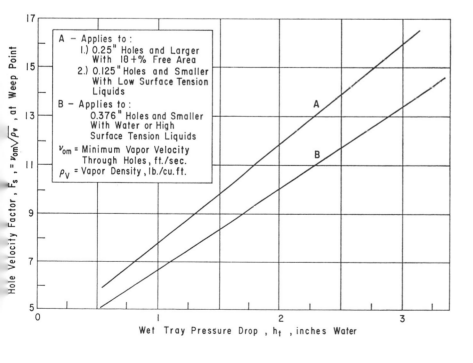

A – Applies to :
  1.) 0.25" Holes and Larger
    With 18 +% Free Area
  2.) 0.125" Holes and Smaller
    With Low Surface Tension
    Liquids
B – Applies to :
    0.376" Holes and Smaller
    With Water or High
    Surface Tension Liquids
v_{om} = Minimum Vapor Velocity
  Through Holes, ft./sec.
ρ_V = Vapor Density, lb./cu. ft.

Figure 8-93. Weeping correlation for sieve trays with downcomers. (By permission G. A. Hughmark and H. E. O'Connell. Chem. Engr. Prog. Vol. 53, p 127-M (1957).)

2. All change in capacity is to be as an increase over design rate.

3. Reduction in efficiency can be tolerated if vapor rate falls to weep point minimum or below.

4. Low tray pressure drop is required, as for vacuum systems. Design with extra caution under vacuum, since data correlations have not been checked in this region.

B. Select a design velocity near the maximum velocity if:

1. The design vapor rate is the maximum expected. All change will be to lower rates.

2. High efficiency is required.

3. High pressure drops are acceptable.

Tray Stability

Figure 8-94 of Huang and Hodson[30] can be prepared from an evaluation of limits of tray performance using the relations set forth herein, or as presented in the original reference using slightly different analysis.

Tray Layout

Some of the details of tray layout are given in Figure 8-38. The working details can be set by the required performance.

1. A tower diameter is selected based on Souders-Brown (20-50 percent conservative, usually) or Hunt's relation, Eq. 8-115.

2. Assume a tray layout: downcomer areas, non-perforated area; perforated area. Base downcomer requirements on bubble cap tray information of Figure 8-69.

3. Determine the percent hole area in the active tray portion for pressure drop calculation. Note that hole size does not have to be set at this point. (Figure 8-95.)

4. Calculate the expected tray performance.

5. From the selected design hole velocity and the total vapor rate corresponding, the total number of holes can be determined for a given assumed hole diameter.

$$\text{No. holes} = V/(v_d) \; (\text{sq.ft/hole}) \qquad (8\text{-}124)$$

From Figure 8-96 or by calculation determine the plate area required for the holes on the pitch selected. Several selections may be tried to be used with the tray layout. These should be checked to agree with the assumed per cent hole area of Step 3.

6. If the tray does not balance area-wise, assume a new area arrangement or even diameter, if indicated, and re-check the procedure.

Example 8-16: Sieve Tray Design (Perforated) with Downcomer

The conditions for tray design in a chlorinated hydrocarbon finishing tower are:

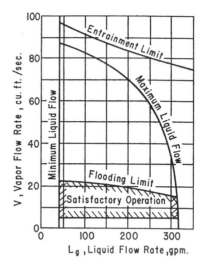

Figure 8-94. Typical performance chart: sieve (perforated) tray with downcomer. (By permission Chen-Jung Huang and J. R. Hodson, Pet. Ref., Vol. 37, p. 104 (1958).)

1. Clean service, no fouling or suspended material

2.

	Top	Bottom
Vapor rate, cu.ft./sec.	5.23	5.58
Liquid rate, GPM	9.57	22.1
Vapor Density, Lb./cu.ft	0.582	0.674
Liquid Density, Lb./cu.ft.	83	85
Surface tension, dynes/cm	20	20+

3. Tray spacing is to be close as possible, since vertical installation space is a premium.

Estimated Tower Diameter

Souders-Brown method

$$W = C[\rho_V(\rho_L - \rho_V)]^{1/2}$$

From Figure 8-50, C = 100 for 9-inch tray spacing

In this case rates are close and ρ_v does not change much from bottom to top of tower.

$$W = 100 \,[0.674(85 - 0.674)]^{1/2} = 753 \text{ lbs./hr. (sq. ft.)}$$

$$\cong \frac{753}{(3600)(0.582)} = 0.36 \text{ cu. ft./sec. (sq. ft.)}$$

Tower cross-section area = 5.23/0.36 = 14.5 sq. ft.

$$\text{Diameter} = [(4/\pi)(14.5)]^{1/2} = 4.28 \text{ ft.}$$

Using Hunt equation:

$$\text{Assume: } h_w + h_{ow} = 1.5''$$

$$S' = S_t - 2.5 \, h_c = 9 - 2.5(1.5) = 5.25''$$

At surface tension = 20 dynes/cm,

For $e_w = 5\% = 0.05$

Figure 8-90 reads: allowable tower velocity = 2.2 ft./sec.

Required tower area = 5.58/2.2 = 2.54 sq. ft. (bottom, largest)

$$\text{Diameter} = [(4/\pi)(2.54)]^{1/2} = 1.8 \text{ ft.}$$

Select: tower diameter = 2.5 feet

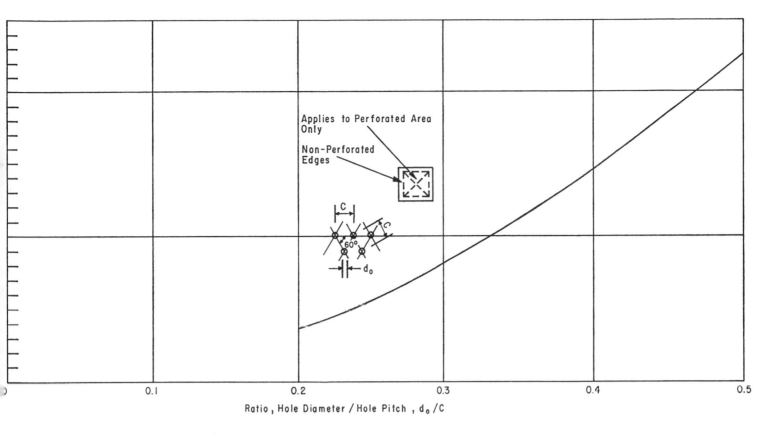

Figure 8-95. Percent open hole area for perforated and sieve trays.

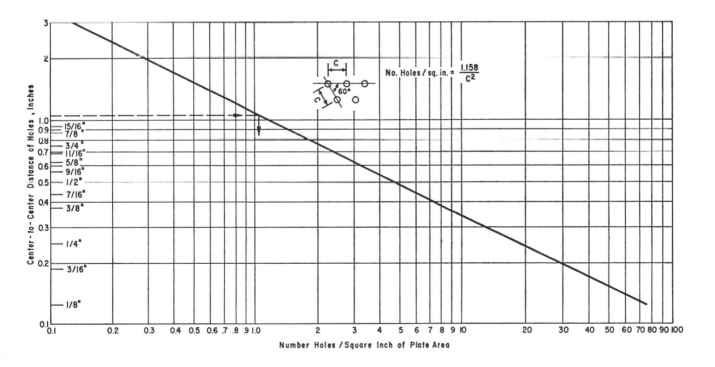

Figure 8-96. Number of holes in perforated plates.

A 2-ft. tower would be expected to perform satisfactorily with properly designed trays. However, a 2.5-ft. tower is the minimum diameter suitable for internal inspection and maintenance. The cost of a tray tower of 2.5-ft. has been found to be no more, and from some bids 5 percent less, than the smaller 2-ft. tower. A 2-ft. tower would either be used with packing or with trays inserted from the top on rods with spacers. This would allow removal of the trays for inspection and maintenance.

Tray Layout based on 2.5 Diameter Tower

Use a segmental downcomer on a cross-flow tray.

From the residence time in downcomers for bubble cap trays, and at the very low tray spacing of 9 inches, select an allowable liquid velocity of 0.1 ft./sec.

$$\text{Downcomer area} = \frac{22.1 \text{ gpm}}{7.48\,(60)\,(0.1)} = 0.492 \text{ sq.ft.}$$

Total tower area $= \pi\,(2.5)^2/4 = 4.91$ sq.ft.

Percent of tower area $= 0.492\,(100)/4.91 = 10.01\%$

Using Figure 8-69 for segmental downcomers, at 10 percent downcomer area, the weir length is 72.8 percent of tower diameter.

Weir length $= 72.8\,(30)/100 = 21.8$ in.

Since standard details for fabrication are already available for a tray with a 19.5 inch weir in a 30 inch tower (65% of dia.), try this as first tray examined. This is 6.8 percent of tower cross-sectional area. Downcomer area $= 0.068\,(4.91) = 0.334$ sq.ft.

Hole Size

Try 3/16-inch dia. on ½-inch pitch

This is spacing of 2.66 d_o, and is as close as good design would suggest. Use ⅛-inch tray thickness.

Ratio $d_o/c = \frac{3}{16}/\frac{1}{2} = \frac{3}{8} = 0.375$

Percent hole area $= 12.8\%$ (of perforation area only) as shown in Figure 8-95.

Minimum Hole Velocity: Weeping

Assume: $v_o\,(\rho_v)^{\frac{1}{2}} = 13$

Assume: Submergence $= 1.5$-inch $= h_{s1} = h_{d1}$ (neglecting $\triangle/2$)

Dry Tray Pressure drop, h_{dt}

$$= 0.003\,(v_o^2\rho_v)\left(\frac{\rho_{water}}{\rho_L}\right)(1-\beta^2)/C_o^2$$

The hole diam./tray thickness ratio $= \frac{3}{16}/\frac{1}{8} = 1.5$

From Figure 8-91, orifice coefficient, $C_o = 0.78$, $\beta = 0.128$

$$h_{dt} = \frac{0.003(13)^2\,(62.3/85)\,(1-(0.128)^2)}{(0.78)^2} = 0.608 \text{ in. liquid}$$

Effective head

For $h_{s1} = 1.5$, $F_s < 14$

Read Figure 8-92; effective head $= 1.58$ in. liquid

Total Wet tray pressure drop

$h_t = 0.608 + 1.58 = 2.188$ in. liquid

Weep Point

Using Figure 8-93 Curve A, and $h_t = 2.19$ in. liquid
Read weep point velocity $= 12.5 = v_{om}\,(\rho_v)^{\frac{1}{2}}$

Curve A is used when in doubt, and it gives a higher minimum v_{om}, which is on safer side for design.

Since $v_{om}\,(\rho_v)^{\frac{1}{2}} = 12.5$ is less than the assumed value of 13, the 13 will be used.

Maximum Hole Velocity at Flood Conditions

Assume $F_s = v_o\,(\rho_v)^{\frac{1}{2}} = 20$ max.
Dry tray pressure drop

$$= 0.003\,F_s^2\left(\frac{\rho_{water}}{\rho_L}\right)(1-\beta^2)/C_o^2$$
$$= 0.003\,(20)^2\,(62.3/85)\,(1-(0.128)^2)/(0.78)^2$$
$$= 1.44 \text{ in. liquid}$$

Effective head, h_e
$$= 1.4 \text{ in. liquid, for } F_s > 14 \text{ and } h_{s1} = 1.5$$

Total wet tray pressure drop, $h_t = 1.44 + 1.4 = 2.84$ inches liquid

Liquid Back-up or Height in Downcomer

$H_d = h_t + (h_w + h_{ow}) + \triangle + h_d$
$H_d = 2.84 + 1.5 + 0 + 0$ (assumed, to be confirmed)
$H_d = 4.34$ inches liquid

The limit on H_d for flooding is $S_t/2 = 9/2 = 4.5$ inches
Therefore $F_s = 20$ appears to be close to minimum.

Design Hole Velocity

Select a velocity represented by F_s factor between minimum and maximum limits.

$20 > \text{Design} > 13$

Select a median value of $F_s = 17$, since freedom to operate above and below the design value is preferred in this case.

Design Basis

$F_s = 17$

1. Weir Height selected $= h_w = 1.0$ inch

2. Height of liquid over weir, $h_{ow} = 0.52$ inch
From Figure 8-73 at 22.1 gpm and $l_w = 1.62$ feet

3. Submergence, $h_{s1} = (f)\,(h_w) + h_{ow} = (1)\,(1.0) + 0.52 = 1.52$ in. liquid

4. Downcomer pressure loss. Clearance between bottom of downcomer and plate = 1-inch max. Underflow area = (9.5 inches) (1 inch)/144 = 0.065 sq.ft. Since this is less than the downflow area (of 0.334 sq.ft.), it must be used for pressure drop determination. No inlet weir used on this design.

$$h_{du} = 0.56 \left[\frac{L_g}{449(A_d)} \right]^2 = 0.56 \left[\frac{22.1}{449(0.065)} \right]^2 = 0.312 \text{ in liquid across restriction}$$

5. Dry tray pressure drop
$h_{dt} = 0.003 (17)^2 (62.3/85) (1 - (0.128)^2)/(0.78)^2$
   $= 1.04$ in. liquid

6. Effective head
$h_{s1} = 1.52$ inches
$h_e = 1.4$ in. liquid for $F_s > 14$, Figure 8-92.

7. Total wet tray pressure drop
$h_t = 1.04 + 1.4 = 2.44$ inches liquid

8. Total tower pressure drop for 45 trays:
$$\Delta P(\text{tower}) = \frac{(2.44)(45)}{1728 \text{ cu. in./cu. ft.}} \left(\frac{83+85}{2} \right) = 5.33 \text{ psi}$$

An actual operating tower measured 5 psi ±. It is satisfactory to average the conditions for top and bottom of tower when flows do not vary significantly. Otherwise, parallel determinations must be carried through for top and bottom (and even feed in some cases) conditions.

9. Number of holes required
   Hole size selected = 3/16-inch
   Hole spacing or pitch = ½-inch
   From Figure 8-96, Holes/sq.in. plate area = 4.62
   Area of a 3/16-inch hole = 0.0276 sq. in.

Calculation Summary

Maximum Velocity	Design Velocity	Weep Point
$F_s = 20$	17	13
v_o top = 20/(0.582)½ = 26.2 ft./sec.	= 17/(.582)½ = 22.3	= 13(0.582)½ = 17
v_o Bot. = 20/(0.674)½ = 24.4 ft./sec.	= 17/(0.674)½ = 20.7	= 13/(0.674)½ = 15.8
No. Holes required: CFS at *top* = 5.23 No. holes = $\frac{5.23(144)}{26.2(0.0276)}$ = 1040	= $\frac{5.23(144)}{22.3(0.0276)}$ = 1223	= $\frac{5.23(144)}{17(0.0276)}$ = 1605
CFS at *bottom* = 5.58 No. holes = $\frac{5.58(144)}{24.4(0.0276)}$ = 1195	= $\frac{5.58(144)}{20.7(0.0276)}$ = 1410	= $\frac{5.58(144)}{15.8(0.0276)}$ = 1845

The selected design $F_s = 17$ gives the number of holes to operate at these conditions. Note that the values of 1223 and 1410 holes for the top and bottom respectively indicated operations somewhat closer to the tower maximum than to the weep point. This usually insures as good an efficiency as is obtainable for a given system. It may limit the flexibility of the tower, since there will not be enough holes to operate down to the weep point at the given design flow rates.

On the other hand the tower should be able to operate at changing vapor and liquid loads without serious upset. In this type of tray the designer has a selection of holes, in this case: For the top select 1100 to 1500; for the bottom, select 1300 to 1750, and still expect acceptable performance.

The fabrication of all trays may be punched or drilled (more expensive) with 1410 holes, and those in the lower section have blank strips placed over the inlet and outlet edge rows until approximately 1223 holes are left open in the top section above the feed tray.

For close examination of systems having varying latent heats and flow rates, it is wise to examine several points in the tower, even tray by tray in some cases, to be certain that the number of holes in that tray does not place its performance too close to the weep or flood conditions. Towers have been built and operated at rated peak loads with every tray having a significantly different number of holes.

10. Mechanical tray Layout details. Allow a total of 3½-inches on diameter for extension of tray ring-type support into the tower. This reduces available tray area. Other support details might make more area available. Each must be examined.

Allow 5 inch clearance (no holes) between inlet downcomer and first row of holes. The 5 inches could be reduced to 3 inches minimum if an inlet weir were used.

Allow 3 inch clearance (no holes) between outlet weir and adjacent row of holes.

Downcomer width = 3.6 inches (From Figures 8-69 and 8-97 at 65% weir length).

Area determinations: Figure 8-97
Area of segment of circle (2) with chord AD:
   Diameter circle (2) = 30 — 3.5 = 26.5 inches
   Height of chord = 13.25 — (15 — 3.6 — 5) = 6.85 inches
   Chord height/circle dia. = 6.85/26.5 = 0.258
   Referring to *Perry's Handbook*, pg. 32, 3rd Ed.
   Area = 0.161 (26.5)² = 113.2 sq. in.
Area of segment of circle (2) width chord BC:
   Height of chord = 13.25 — (15 — 3.6 — 3) = 4.85
      h/D = 4.85/26.5 = 0.183
      Area = 0.0984 (26.5)² = 69.1 sq. in.
Area of circle (2) = π (26.5)²/4 = 552 sq. in.
Area available for holes
      = 552 — 113.2 — 69.1 = 369.7 sq.in.
Area required for holes
      = (1410)/4.62 holes/sq.in. = 305 sq.in.

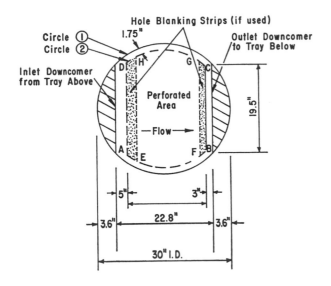

Figure 8-97. Sieve tray with downcomer layout for example problem No. 14.

Actually not all of the tray needs to be drilled. However, the location of "dead" or unperforated areas must be carefully selected, preferable next to weirs. A special punching (or drilling)arrangement for the holes can run the cost of the trays quite high. It will probably be preferable to check effect of punching holes in entire area A B C D of Figure 8-97.

$$Area = 369.7$$

$$No. holes = 369.7 (4.62) = 1710 holes$$

This number is in the range of acceptable performance for bottom section and should be punched. If performance indicates fewer holes are preferable, blanking strips can be added (or even added before the trays are installed). The top trays definitely require blanking of holes.

Perforated Plates Without Downcomers

Perforated plates without downcomers have only recently been included in commercial equipment. The data for rating the performance is not adequately covered in the literature, since the present developments in industrial equipment have not been released. The information included here is based only on available data and experience, yet it may serve as a basis for rating, since the basic nature of the contact is quite analogous to the sieve tray. The limits of performance are not well defined; therefore the methods outlined cannot be considered firm. However, they are adequate for many applications and as the basis for further study.

The action of the perforated tray (Figure 8-98) is one of simultaneous flow of vapor and liquid through different holes on a tray; they do not flow countercurrently and simultaneously through the same holes. For a tray in its operating range, the liquid-vapor bubble mixture is in constant agitation. There is usually a level of relatively clear liquid on the tray followed on top by a bubbling, agitated mass, part of which becomes frothy and/or foamy in appearance depending upon the tray operation and the fluid system properties. There are wavelets of froth-liquid mixture moving from one place to another over the tray. As the head builds up sufficient to overcome the tray hole pressure drop, the vapor stops flowing in the region and liquid drips and drains through. As soon as the head is reduced, the draining stops and bubbling starts. This action is taking place randomly over the tray. Sutherland[69] observed that vapor was flowing through 70-90 percent of the holes, well distributed over the plate. Liquid flowed through the 30-10 percent of the holes.

The only available data for correlation is that of Sutherland on air-water[69] and of Myers[47] on two hydrocarbon systems. The latter data being at close tray spacings for laboratory columns.

These trays are somewhat sensitive to rapid changes in tower conditions. Towers over 40 trays must be controlled within fine limits.

The perforated plate, punched plate, or Dual-Flow plate are terms used to refer to a tray operating without downcomers, with vapor and liquid passing countercurrent through perforations in the tray. The Dual-Flow term has been coined by Fractionation Research, Inc., and its design know-how is restricted to contributing members, and cannot be presented in this book.

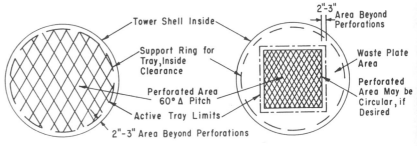

Figure 8-98. Perforated trays without downcomers.

Diameter

There is essentially no published work on specific tests with these trays as relates to entrainment, etc. However, the very close similarity between a perforated plate without downcomers and one with downcomers is sufficient to justify using some data for one in the design of the second.

This is the case with diameter determination. The relation of Equation 8-115 for the perforated tray or sieve tray with downcomers can be used for the plate without downcomers. Generally, the liquid level and foam-froth height will be higher on this tray, hence the value of h_c, clear liquid on the tray, may range from 1-inch to 6-inches, depending on the service.

Capacity

In general, the vapor capacity for a given tray diameter is 10-35 percent greater than bubble cap trays and somewhat greater than sieve trays with downcomers. The flexibility or range is limited since reasonable efficiencies fall-off near the dump point for most systems. Usual designs limit the lower operating point to 60-70 of the flood point, unless particular data is available to safely allow reduction in lower limits without the accompanying loss in tray efficiency.

Pressure Drop

The pressure drop of these trays is usually quite low. They can be operated at an effective bubbling condition with acceptable efficiencies and low pressure drops. For more efficient operation the clear liquid height on the tray appears to be similar to the sieve tray, i.e., 1.5-2-inches minimum. This is peculiar to each system, and some operate at 1 inch with as good an efficiency as when a 2-inch is used. When data is not available, 2 inches is recommended as a median design point.

Dry Tray Pressure Drop

As should be expected, the relation of Hughmark[31] correlated the data of Sutherland[69] quite well.

$$\text{thus: } h_{dt} = 0.003 \ (v_o^2 \ \rho_v) \left(\frac{\rho_{water}}{\rho_L} \right) (1 - \beta^2)/C_o^2$$

$$F_h^2 = v_o^2 \ \rho_v \qquad (8\text{-}125)$$

The orifice coefficient can be read from Figure 8-91. Sutherland used $C_o = 0.85$ and 0.73 for $\frac{3}{16}$-inch and $\frac{3}{4}$-inch holes respectively, in $\frac{1}{4}$-inch plate.

Effective Head, h_e

Although Sutherland did not obtain an equation for total tray pressure drop, correlation at this time indicates that it follows the effective head concept of Hughmark. This is a limited evaluation since the data available did not indicate any clear liquid heights over about 0.75 inches.

When "head of liquid" is considered "clear liquid on the tray," Figure 8-92 may be used to read the effective head, h_e. Values of h_{cl} beyond 1 inch have not been checked for lack of data, but do agree generally with the plotted results of Sutherland.[52]

Total Wet Tray Pressure Drop

For the data checked,

$$h_t = h_{dt} + h_e \qquad (8\text{-}126)$$

These results cannot be expected to correlate for a tray just becoming active (very low liquid on tray, 0.1″ ±), but have been satisfactory at 0.2-inches for clear liquid height, h_{cl}.

To determine a tray operation with respect to pressure drop, the value of h_{cl} must be assumed at a reasonable value, — the larger the better the contact, and higher the pressure drop. Values of h_{cl} should be limited to about 4 inches, following sieve tray practice.

Hole Size, Spacing, Percent Open Area

Hole size is as important in perforated plates without downcomers as far the sieve tray. Published data limits a full analysis of the relationships; however, the smaller holes, $\frac{1}{8}$-inch, 3/16-inch, $\frac{1}{4}$-inch appear to give slightly higher efficiencies for the same tray spacing.[47] Unfortunately the data[69] for the larger $\frac{3}{4}$-inch holes was not evaluated for efficiencies. Experience has indicated efficiencies equal to or only slightly, 10-15 percent, less for $\frac{3}{4}$-inch holes when compared to 3/16-inch holes for some systems. Holes as small as 1/16-inch, 3/32-inch and 7/16-inch were considered unsatisfactory for high surface tension materials such as water.[47]

Sutherland reports frothy type contact for 3/16-inch holes and jetting spray bubbly action for $\frac{3}{4}$-inch holes.

Percent open tray areas of 20-30 percent appear to be optimum for hydrocarbon systems.[47]

The larger holes are recommended for high surface tension liquids.

Holes are usually spaced a minimum of 2 d_o, with 3 d_o to 4 d_o being preferable. The distance between holes should never exceed 3 inches. Thin plates appear to be preferable to thick.

Tray Spacing

The height of the liquid-froth mixture on the tray is important in determining tray spacing, as tray flooding moves up the column as the liquid mixture of one tray approaches the underside of the tray above. Tray spacing is recommended as twice the maximum design height of liquid-froth mixture on the tray h_{al}. Spacing of 9, 12, 15, 18 and 24 inches have been used with good success. The closer the spacing, the less the tray flexibility. The 15-inch spacing is usually a good design value.

The height of aerated liquid-froth mixture on the tray, h_{al}, (inches) was determined to agree with the following relation[52] for air-water for 23 percent and 40 percent open trays.

$$h_{al} = 1.25 \, F_c + 0.0005 \, L + (0.54/\beta) - 2.45 \quad (8\text{-}127)$$

$$F_c = v_c \, \rho_v^{1/2} \quad (8\text{-}128)$$

L = Liquid rate, pounds/(hr.) (sq.ft. of active plate)

This relation does not hold for plates having 10 percent open hole area, as the heights are several times the corresponding heights for 23 percent and 40 percent trays at the same vapor rate, F_c.

For water, the total height of aerated mixture relative to the height of clear liquid on the tray, h_{al}/h_{cl}, had values of 10 to 3. The higher values being obtained from the 3/16-inch (smaller) holes. Liquid flow rate does not appear to influence these values to any extent.

Higher open tray areas tend to produce a spray rather than a froth. High vapor rates produce a spray, while the higher liquid rates produce a froth.[69]

If these trays are used in systems with exceedingly high foaming tendencies, tray action may be impaired to the extent of improper performance. In such cases, the foaming tendency should be examined experimentally. Anti-foam agents have proven quite helpful in some problem cases using these trays.

Entrainment

Data is not available to distinguish between the entrainment of sieve and perforated trays without downcomers. The relation of Hunt et. al.,[33] given for sieve trays is recommended, and should apply quite well. Sutherland[69] reports for air-water entrainment of 0.0001 to 0.1 pounds liquid/pound vapor, averaging 0.01 for 15-inch tray spacing at hole velocity F_s values of 3 to 15. $F_h = v_o \, \rho_v^{1/2}$. These values are 1-10 percent of bubble cap plates. Simkin et. al.,[64] reports a comparison with the Turbogrid tray giving only 3-60 percent of the entrainment of bubble caps over a wide range of operation.

Sutherland's[69] relation for air-water on 15-inch tray spacing correlating ¾-inch holes on 40 percent and 23 percent open area, and ³⁄₁₆-inch holes with 23 percent open area is:

$$e_w = 6.31 \, (10^{-7}) \, (F_s)^{4.57} \quad (8\text{-}129)$$

where e_w = entrainment, pounds liquid/pound vapor.
The correlation of ³⁄₁₆-inch holes in 40 percent open trays is

$$e_w = 2.37 \, (10^{-4}) \, (F_s)^{1.73} \quad (8\text{-}130)$$

Why this deviates from the previous correlation is not understood.

Dump Point, Plate Activation Point, or Load Point

These trays will dump liquid excessively through the perforations giving exceeding low efficiencies[47] unless a minimum vapor rate is maintained for a given liquid capacity. The smaller the holes the lower the dump point (vapor velocity).

Figure 8-99 indicates minimum values of F_h to initiate acceptable bubbling tray action. Efficiency at this activation or load point might be expected to be low; however Myers results indicate good values at this rate.

It is recommended that trays be designed for a minimum of 10 percent above the lower plate activation values. Below these values the tray will dump liquid and become inoperable.

Efficiency

Tray efficiency is as high as for bubble caps and almost as high as sieve trays. It is higher than bubble caps in some systems. Performance indicates a close similarity to sieve trays, since the mechanism of bubble formation is almost identical. The real point of concern is that the efficiency falls off quickly as the flow rate of vapor through the holes is reduced close to the minimum values represented by the dump point, or point of plate initial activation. Efficiency increases as the tray spacing increases for a given throughput.

Myers found only a slight decrease in efficiency with an increase in hole size. Industrial experience indicates that large holes of ½-inch and ¾-inch can be designed to operate as efficiently as a small hole, say ³⁄₁₆-inch.

Efficiency appears to fall off significantly for open tray areas above 30 percent. The higher efficiencies are usually obtained in the 20-25 percent range of open hole area[47]

Higher efficiencies are obtained for operating conditions within 85-95 percent of the tray flood point.

Flood Point

At the flood point, liquid continues to flow down the column, but builds up at a greater rate from tray to tray. Sutherland demonstrated that flooding moves up the column from the point of origin. For this reason it is important to design perforated trays without downcomers with extra care, as changing internal rates are quickly reflected in performance if the proper hole requirements are not met. They are a useful tray for steady state operations.

Tray Designs and Layout

1. Establish a tower design diameter using the Souders-Brown method or the relation of Hunt, both given previously.

2. Determine the vapor and liquid rates in the tower at all possible critical points of change. The anticipated maximum and minimum values must be defined.

3. Determine the values of the plate activation velocities (or load points), F_h^2, for the minimum as well as maximum liquid loads at top and bottom of the tower and any intermediate points exhibiting significant change in flow rates. For partial column area trays of Figure 8-98, the

v_c refers to the area of active tray limits. If the minimum rates are more than 20 percent below the maximum, the smaller hole sizes and open areas should be selected.

4. Select a design hole vapor rate, v_o, of 1.25 to 1.5 times the minimum values of the plate activation point, or about 25 percent below the hole velocity at flood conditions.

5. Check the number of holes required at each maximum rate to determine if the required holes can be placed in the tower area.
Use Figure 8-96 to aid in the determination. If more plate area is required than is available, back-calculate the necessary maximum hole velocity. Check if this is reasonable (say not over twice the minimum). If so, the diameter is still acceptable; or change the hole spacing to allow more or fewer holes to be placed in the given diameter of the tower. Use limiting values previously given on hole spacing.

6. Calculate the total wet tray pressure drop, using an assumed height of clear liquid on the tray of 0.5-inch minimum to 4-inch maximum (1 to 2-inch are usual values).

7. Determine height of aerated liquid on the tray, h_{al}.
If foaming characteristics of the system are less than air-water, results will be conservative. For systems tending to greater foam and bubbles than the air-water system, approximate a value of h_{al} by multiplying calculated value by 2, or 3 or known relative relationship.

8. Set tray spacing at twice the selected value of h_{al}.

9. Check entrainment at maximum vapor rate.

10. Physical arrangement: refer to Figure 8-98.

For new towers, the designs will usually develop to utilize the entire tower cross-section. However, for existing towers with perforated trays being installed to replace bubble caps or packing, the optimum active tray area may not utilize the entire cross-section. If the number of holes required is small compared to available area, it is better to group the holes on 2.5 d_o to 3.5 d_o than to exceed these limits. Holes separated by more than 3 inches are not considered effective in tray action so necessary for good efficiency. Blanking strips may be used to cover some holes when more than required have been perforated in the tray.
If trays are punched, the sharp hole edge side should face the entering vapor.

Example 8-17: Design of Perforated Trays Without Downcomers

A tower separates a weak ammonia solution. Design trays using perforated plates without downcomers for the following conditions as determined from the column performance calculations.

	Top Tray	Bottom Tray
Liquid, gpm	40.8	17.8
Lb./cu. ft.	38.8	54.2
Dynes/cm	<13	59
Vapor, cu. ft./sec.	5.22	4.3
Lb./cu. ft.	0.593	0.408

Estimated Tower Diameter

$$e_w = 0.22(73/\sigma)(v_c/S')^{3.2}$$

Allowable velocity: assume $S' = 15$ inches — 2.5(1.5 inches)
= 11.25 inches

From Figure 8-90 for $e_w = 0.05$ and assumed 15-inch tray spacing
at top, tower velocity $v_c = 4$ ft./sec.
at bottom, $v_c = 6.4$ ft./sec.
Tower area at 4'/sec. limiting: $= 5.22/4 = 1.30$ sq. ft.
Diameter $= [(4/\pi)\ 1.30]^{1/2} = 1.29$ ft. Say 1 ft. 6 in.

Comparison:
Souders-Brown, Figure 8-51, at top tray conditions, which are limiting.
$W = 2000$ Lbs./hr. (sq. ft.) Max. allowable vapor velocity
Top vapor rate $= 5.22(0.593)(3600) = 11,130$ lbs. vapor/hr.
Required area $= 11,130/2000 = 5.5$ sq. ft.
Diameter $= 2.64$ ft., Say 2 ft., 8 inches.

Since it is known that the entrainment from perforated trays is considerably less than for bubble caps, the 2-foot, 8-inch diameter would be very conservative and perhaps excessively large.
Tower diameters in the 1-foot, 6-inch to 2-foot range are not usually economical as tray installations. A packed tower might prove the best economically. Trays can be installed on a central rod and spacer arrangement, with seals between trays and tower shell. Such an arrangement usually brings the cost of the installation up to that of a 2-foot, 6-inch tower. This is the smallest practical size that a man can crawl through.
For the purpose of this design, assume that a cost study has verified the above remarks, and a 2-foot, 6-inch tower will be used. This means that entrainment will be very low on a 15-inch tray spacing. Therefore, a smaller spacing should be considered. From usual fabrication costs, 12-inch spacing is about the closest spacing to consider.
The allowable velocity by Hunt for this spacing, $S' = 8.25$, $v_c = 4(8.25/11.25) = 2.94$ ft./sec.
Tower area $= \pi(2.5)^2/4 = 4.9$ sq. ft.
Actual tower velocity $= 5.22/4.9 = 1.06$ ft./sec.
Therefore 12-inch spacing should be O.K. entrainment-wise, check aeration later.

Plate Activation Velocities (Minimum)
Top:
Liquid rate, $L = (40.8\ \text{gpm}/7.48)(38.8)(60)$
$= 12,200$ lbs./hr. (sq. ft.)

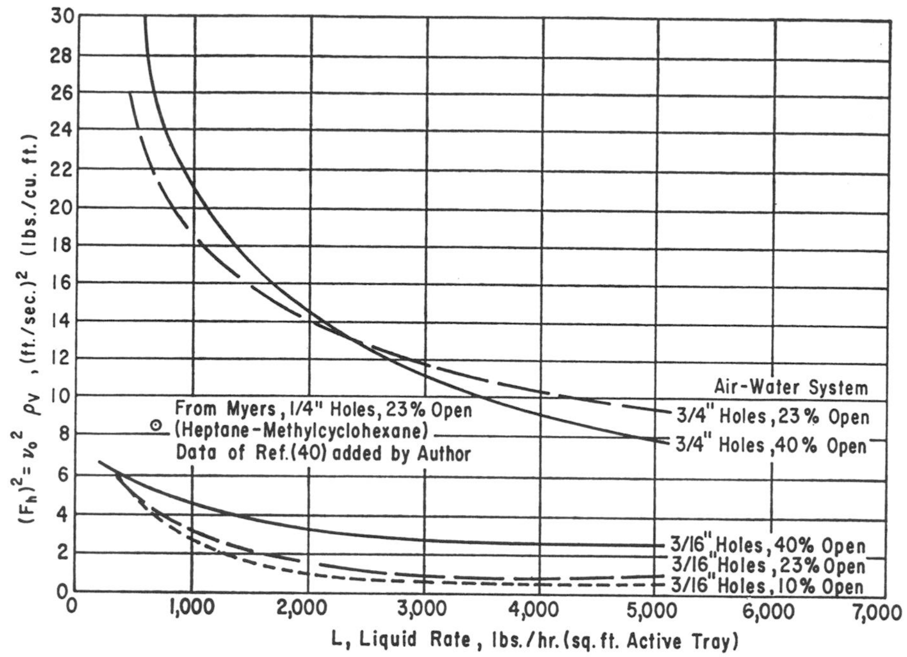

Figure 8-99. Vapor and liquid rates for tray activation; perforated trays, no downcomers. (Compiled from data of Sutherland, Reference 69 and Myers, Reference 47.)

From Figure 8-99, read $F_h{}^2 = 1.0$ @ $\frac{3}{16}$-inch holes, 23 percent open area.

$$(v_o \rho_v{}^{\frac{1}{2}})^2 = 1.0 = v^2{}_h \rho_v$$

$$v_o = (1/\rho_v)^{\frac{1}{4}} = (1/0.593)^{\frac{1}{4}} = 1.298 \text{ ft./sec.}$$

Bottom:

$$L = 17.8 \ (54.2) \ (60)/7.48 = 7,730 \text{ lbs./hr. (sq. ft.)}$$

From Figure 8-99, read $F_h{}^2 = 1.0$ @ $\frac{3}{16}$-inch holes, 23% open

$$\text{area } v_h = (1/0.408)^{\frac{1}{4}} = 1.56 \text{ ft./sec.}$$

Note that Figure 8-99 indicates the operating liquid minimum range is quite stable in the region of design for these trays. The vapor rate must never fall below the above values or instability will immediately set in and dumping will result.

Design Hole Velocity

Set at 1.5 times the activation velocity, or 2.34 ft./sec. at the top and 1.95 ft./sec. at the bottom.

Hole Arrangement

$\frac{3}{16}$-inch Dia. on 60° $\triangle$ pitch, spaced on $\frac{3}{8}$-inch centers This gives 22.6% open area (Figure 8-95), close enough to the 23% selected.

No. holes/sq. in. = 8.3

Area required for holes:

Top: 5.22/2.34 = 2.23 sq. ft.

No. holes = 2.23(144)(8.3) = 2670

Bottom: 4.3/1.95 = 2.2

No. holes = 2.2(144)(8.3) = 2640

Since these are so close the same number of holes can be perforated in all plates. These should be drilled (punched) in a 1-foot, 6-inch x 1-foot, 6-inch square area as per Figure 8-97. This will reduce costs of trays slightly as compared to custom perforating to different number of holes.

The tower area is 4.9 sq. ft.; therefore the entire tray will not be perforated for the conditions of design.

If there is the possibility of vapor and liquid rates being reduced to 50 percent of the indicated values, this would place the trays as selected above at the dumping point, or activation point, which is not a good operating condition. In this situation the number of holes should be reduced in order to maintain a velocity of vapor through the holes greater by at least 15 percent than the activation velocity.

Wet Tray Pressure Drop

(a) Dry Tray Pressure Drop

$$h_{dt} = 0.003 \ (v_o{}^2 \, \rho_v) \left(\frac{\rho_{water}}{\rho_L}\right) (1 - \beta^2)/C_o{}^2$$

Top appears to be region of greatest pressure drop

$$h_{dt} = 0.003[(2.34)^2(0.593)] \ (62.3/38.8) \ (1 - (0.226)^2)/(0.82)^2$$

$C_o = 0.82$ for $\frac{3}{16}$-inch hole in $\frac{3}{16}$-inch tray (Figure 8-91)

$$h_{dt} = 0.0222 \text{ in. liquid}$$

(b) Effective Head

Assume clear liquid height on tray = 1 inch (note, 1 inch may be a slightly better value than the 1.5 inches assumed when determining e_w).

From Figure 8-92, effective head, $h_e = 1.1$ inches liquid at $F_s = 2.34 \ (0.593)^{\frac{1}{2}} = 1.81$

(c) Total wet tray pressure drop

$$h_t = 0.022 + 1.1 = 1.12 \text{ in. liquid}$$

Total Tower Tray Pressure Drop

For 15 trays, the *maximum* expected drop using the expected tray drop at the top:

$$= 15(1.12) = 16.8'' \text{ liquid}$$

$$= \left(\frac{16.8}{12}\right)\frac{(38.8)}{2.31(62.3)} = 0.38 \text{ psi}$$

A more precise approach requires evaluation of the wet tray drop for the bottom condition also. However, since it will give a lower value (by inspection), the higher result is preferred as long as a vacuum tower is not being designed. Here, the careful approach is justified.

It must also be remembered that the data used in establishing the design criteria are not accurate to better than ± 10-20 percent.

Height of aerated liquid on tray

$$h_{al} = 1.25 F_c + .0005 L + (0.54/\beta) - 2.45$$

At top:

$$= 1.25[(1.06)(0.593)^{1/2}] + .0005(12,200) + 0.54/0.226 - 2.45$$

$$= 1.002 + 6.1 + 2.39 - 2.45$$

$$h_{al} = 7.06 \text{ in. (evaluated as air-water)}$$

Tray Spacing

From this value of h_{al} it is essential that the trays be spaced no closer than 2(7.06), say 15 inches. If lab tests indicate these mixtures foam more than water-air, the value of 15 inches should be increased in relative proportion.

Tower Specifications

After making proper calculations for performance, they must be interpreted for mechanical construction and for summary review by others concerned with the operation and selection of equipment. Typical specification sheets are given in Figures 8-100 and 8-101 for the tower and internal trays respectively. Suggested manufacturing tolerances are given in Figure 8-102. A composite cut-a-way view of tower trays assembled is shown in Figure 8-103.

The calculation of nozzle connections has not been demonstrated, but normally follows line sizing practice, or some special velocity limitation, depending upon nozzle purpose.

Tower shells may be ferrous, non-ferrous, stainless alloys or clad (such as monel-clad-steel). The trays are usually light gage metal consistent with the corrosion and erosion problems of the system. The velocity action of vapors flowing through holes and slots accentuates the erosion-corrosion problems, and often a carbon steel tower will use stainless, alloy steel, monel or nickel trays, caps

and all internal parts. Sometimes just the cap or hole portion of the trays are of expensive construction.

When clad metal is used, it is often specified as 1/8-inch or 1/4-inch minimum clad thickness. This is usually sufficient to allow proper weld connections. Care must be used in sealing all internal joints of clad material to prevent exposure of the base metal.

The towers are designed in accordance with the particular code (such as ASME Unfired Pressure Vessel) used by the company or required by law. To provide stiffness and bending strength in high winds, design normally figures a wind load recommended for the area. It is not unusual to design for 75 to 100 mph winds, taking into account the external insulation, piping, ladders and platforms in computing the effective force areas. Foundations must be adequate to carry the total dead weight of the erected tower, platforms, etc. plus the weight of water (or perhaps other fluid) to allow for in-place testing, or complete tower flooding.

Tray types are selected for performance. However, when a particular type is not specifically required, it is well to consider that, in carbon steel, the trays installed (not including tower shell) cost approximately:

Bubble Caps, 25% > Sieve, 10% > Perforated without downcomers.

Nomenclature For Part 3: Tray Hydraulics Design

A_a = Total annular cap area per tray, sq. ft.
A_c = Total cap inside cross section area per tray, sq. ft.
A_d = Minimum flow area at bottom of downcomer per tray, sq. ft.
A_n = Net open liquid area of one tray, equal to total tower cross section minus area occupied by caps and minus area of segmental or other downcomer at outlet of tray, sq. ft.
A_s = Total slot area per tray, sq. ft.
A_r = Total riser inside area per tray, sq. ft.
A'_r = Total reversal area per tray, sq. ft.
a_a = Annular area per cap, sq. in.
a_c = Inside cross section area of cap, sq. in.
a_d = Cross-section flow area, minimum, of down-pipe clearance area between tray floor and down-pipe bottom edge, or up-flow area between outer circumference down-pipe and any inlet tray weir, sq. in.
a_r = Riser inside cross-section area per riser, sq. in.
$a_{r'}$ = Reversal area per cap assembly, sq. in.
a_{ro} = Riser outside cross-section area, based on O.D., sq. in. per riser
a_s = Slot area per cap, sq. in.
a_x = Smaller area value; a_a or $a_{r'}$, for use in Eq. 8-96.
C = Factor for Souders-Brown maximum entrainment relation
C_d = Liquid gradient factor
C_o = Orifice coefficient
C_v = Liquid gradient vapor load correction factor
C_w = Wet cap pressure drop correction factor
c = Hole spacing center to center, inches
D = Tower inside diameter, feet
d_c = Inside diameter of cap, inches
d_h = Diameter of weep hole, inches. Note that this is the diameter equivalent to area of all the weep holes per tray

(Text continued on page 126)

Job No.	
B/M No.	

TOWER SPECIFICATIONS

Page _____ of _____ Pages
No. Units _One_
Item No. _T-3_

Service _Methanol Finishing_   Size _4'-0" I.D. x 45 Trays_
No. Trays _45_ Type _Bubble_ Caps _4" Pressed St._ Feet Packing _____ Size _____ Sprays _____
Tower Internals Spec. Dwg. No. _A_

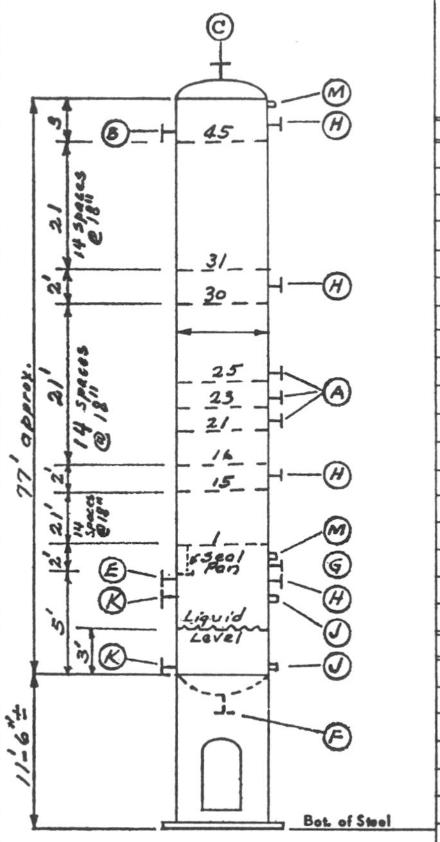

OPERATING AND MECHANICAL CONDITIONS

Oper. Press. _1 to 5.0_ PSIG.   Oper. Temp. _220_ °F
Des. Press. _30.0_ PSIG.   Des. Temp. _350_ °F
Code _ASME_ Stamp. Req'd. _Yes_   Density of Contents _47_ lbs./cu. ft.
Lethal Construction _No_   Self Supporting _Yes_
Materials: Shell _Carbon Steel_ Heads _C.S._ Skirt _C.S._
Lining; Metal _None_   Rubber or Plastic _None_
Brick _None_   Cement _None_
Internal Corrosion Allowance _1/32" to 1/16" max._
Insulation ? ☑ Yes ☐ No   Class _Standard for 200°F_

NOZZLES

SERVICE	NO. REQ'D.	SIZE	PRESS. CL.	FACING	MARK NO.
Feed*	3	2"	150	Raised F.	A
Reflux	1	2"	150	RF	B
Vapor Out	1	6"	150	RF	C
Liquid Out	1	2"	150	RF	D
Reboiler Vapor	1	6"	150	RF	E
Reboiler Liquid	1	3"	150	RF	F
Drain	on piping				
Safety Valve	1	4"	150	R.F.	G
Manhole	4	18"	150	R.F.	H
Gage Glass	2	3/4"	6000#	Coupling	J
Level Control	2	2"	150	RF	K
Thermowell Pts.	9	1"	6000#	Coupling	L
Pressure Taps	2	3/4"	6000#	Coupling	M
Sample Conn.	4	3/4"	6000#	Coupling	N

* Feed Points to be located in: ☐ Vapor Space ☑ Downcomer _to tray_

REMARKS

1. TW Points in Vapor Located- _Tray #1, 21, 23, 25, 27, 44_
2. TW Points in Liquid Located- _Tray #1, 21, 44_
3. Sample Points in Vapor Located-
4. Sample Points in Liquid Located- _Tray #20, 22, 24, 44_
5. Pressure Taps Located in Vapor Space as Follows: _Below tray #1, above tray #45_

Locate nozzle Ⓔ 3' below tray #1.
Seal pan for tray #1 to be 2' high downcomer with 1" extra seal depth over normal.

By.	Chk'd.	App.	Rev.	Rev.	Rev.
Date					

P.O. To:

Figure 8-100. Tower specifications form.

Job No. _____

B/M No. _____

TOWER INTERNALS SPECIFICATIONS
TRAY TYPE COLUMNS

Page	of	Pages
No. Units	*one*	
Item No.	*T-3*	

Contacting Device -- Bubble Cap, Sieve, Dualflow *Bubble Cap*

No. of Trays __*45*__   Type: *Fixed*, ~~Removable~~ (From Top, Bottom) *Welded* (Bolted, Clamped)

Tray Spacing *18" except as noted*, Manway (Yes, ~~No~~)   (Removable from Top, ~~Bottom~~)

Bubble Cap: Number/Tray __*51*__ , Size *3⅜" I.D.* ~~O.D.~~, *60° Δ* Spacing *5¼" C to C*.   Gauge __*14*__

Riser: Diameter *2¾ O.D.* .   Gauge __*16*__ .

Holes: Number _____ , Size _____ Diam.,   Spacing _____ C to C

Clearance Between Holes and Tower Wall _____

Clearance Between Holes and Weirs _____

Tray Thickness (Not Required for Bubble Caps) _____

Type of Flow: Split, *Cross* ✓

Inlet Weirs: (*Yes*, No):   Height Above Tray Floor __*3½*__ Inches

Outlet Weirs: Length __*2'-9⅛"*__

(a). Fixed Weir Height Above Tray Floor __*2½*__ Inches

(b). Weir Adjustable From __*2½*__ To __*4*__ Inches Above Tray Floor

(c). Weir Set __*3*__ Inches Above Tray Floor; Weir Slots Covered (Yes,) (*No*) ✓

Downcomer: (*Yes*, No)   Type: _____ Pipe, *Segmental* (Straight, *Tapered*)

Downcomers (*Fixed*, Removable):   Clearance Above Tray Floor __*2¾*__ Inches

Seal Pan Distance Below Bottom Tray *24"* .   Seal __*4½*__ Inches

Weep Holes: No./Tray __*4*__   Size __*⅜"*__

Hydraulic Gradient Provision: *None required, all caps same height above tray*

Standards:

(a). Bubble Cap *Drawing No. A-XYZ*

(b). Tray Layout *Drawing No. B-XYZ*

(c). Tower Tolerances *Drawing No. C-XYZ*

MATERIALS OF CONSTRUCTION

Bubble Cap and Riser: *Carbon steel*   Gaskets: *asbestos*

(a). Bolts, Nuts and Washers: *carbon steel*

Trays: *Carbon steel*   Gaskets *asbestos*   Bolting: *Carbon steel*

Tray Supports, Downcomers and Seal Pan: *Carbon steel*

REMARKS

Trays to be standard design and layout with removable center section for access through tower from above. Caps to be assembled and mounted on trays in fabricator's shop.

By	Chk'd	App.	Rev.	Rev.	Rev.
Date					

P.O. To: _____

Figure 8-101. Tower internals specifications form, tray type columns.

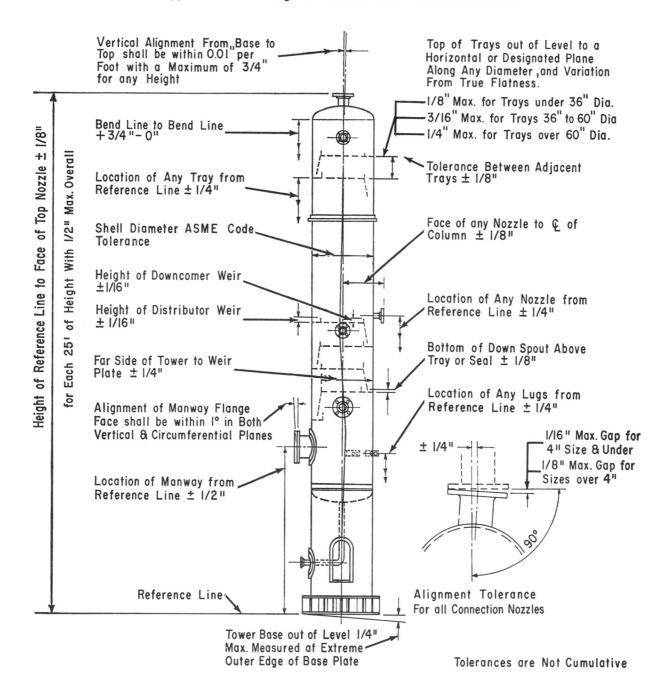

Vertical Alignment From Base to Top shall be within 0.01" per Foot with a Maximum of 3/4" for any Height

Bend Line to Bend Line +3/4"–0"

Location of Any Tray from Reference Line ± 1/4"

Shell Diameter ASME Code Tolerance

Height of Downcomer Weir ± 1/16"

Height of Distributor Weir ± 1/16"

Far Side of Tower to Weir Plate ± 1/4"

Alignment of Manway Flange Face shall be within 1° in Both Vertical & Circumferential Planes

Location of Manway from Reference Line ± 1/2"

Reference Line

Height of Reference Line to Face of Top Nozzle ± 1/8"

for Each 25' of Height With 1/2" Max. Overall

Top of Trays out of Level to a Horizontal or Designated Plane Along Any Diameter, and Variation From True Flatness.

1/8" Max. for Trays under 36" Dia.
3/16" Max. for Trays 36" to 60" Dia
1/4" Max. for Trays over 60" Dia.

Tolerance Between Adjacent Trays ± 1/8"

Face of any Nozzle to ₵ of Column ± 1/8"

Location of Any Nozzle from Reference Line ± 1/4"

Bottom of Down Spout Above Tray or Seal ± 1/8"

Location of Any Lugs from Reference Line ± 1/4"

± 1/4"

1/16" Max. Gap for 4" Size & Under
1/8" Max. Gap for Sizes over 4"

90°

Alignment Tolerance For all Connection Nozzles

Tower Base out of Level 1/4" Max. Measured at Extreme Outer Edge of Base Plate

Tolerances are Not Cumulative

Figure 8-102. Suggested tolerances for distillation type towers.

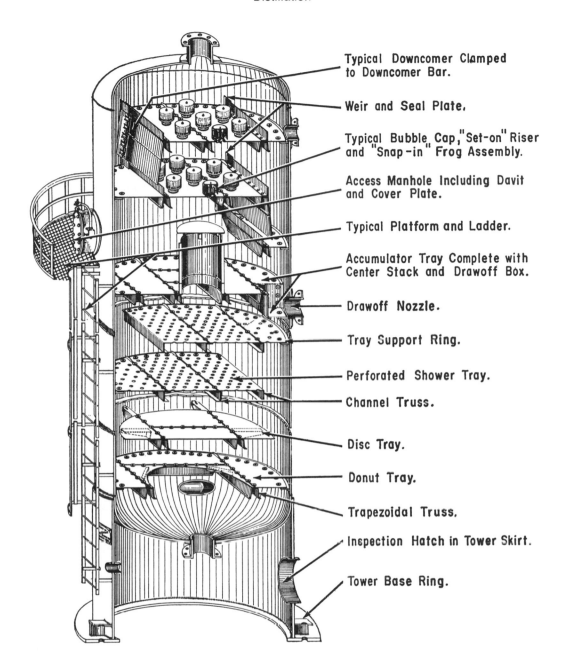

Figure 8-103. Composite tower-tray assembly illustrating special trays with corresponding nozzles. (Courtesy F. W. Glitsch & Sons, Inc.)

d_o = Hole diameter, inches

d_r = Inside diameter of riser, inches

d_w = Diameter of circular weir, inches

e_w = Weight of liquid entrained per unit weight of vapor flowing, Lbs./lb.

F = Free height in downcomer above clear liquid level (not froth level), inches

F_c = Tower velocity factor

$F_h = v_o \sqrt{\rho_v}$, for perforated trays, no downcomers

F_s = Hole velocity factor $= v_o \sqrt{\rho_v}$

F_w = Modification factor to weir formula

f = Aeration factor (usually = 1.0)

H_d = Height of clear liquid in downcomer, inches

H_s = Slot height of bubble cap, inches

h' = Height of overflow weir or bubble cap riser, which ever is smaller, inches

h_{al} = Height of aerated liquid on tray, inches

h_{cw} = Wet cap pressure drop (riser, reversal, annulus, slots), inches liquid

h_c = Head of liquid in bubbling zone, wet cap pressure drop, taken as inches of clear liquid on tray

h'_c = Total dry cap pressure drop, inches liquid

h_{cl} = Height of clear liquid on tray, inches

h_d = Total head loss under downcomer, in. liquid

h'_d = Head loss between segmental downcomer and inlet weir, inches liquid

h_{dc} = Head loss of circular down-pipe at point of greatest restriction, inches liquid

h_{dl} = Dynamic liquid seal on sieve or perforated tray, inches liquid

h_{ds} = Dynamic slot seal, inches liquid

h_{dt} = Pressure drop through dry perforated or sieve tray, inches liquid

h_{du} = Downcomer head loss due to friction and underflow, inches liquid

h_e = Effective liquid head taking aeration of liquid into account, inches liquid

h_f = Height of top of foam above tray floor, inches

$h_{f'}$ = Height of free fall of liquid, inches

h_l = Depth of clear liquid on tray, inches

h_{ow} = Height of liquid crest over flat weir, inches

h'_{ow} = Height of liquid above bottom of notch in notched weir, inches

h_{pc} = Cap assembly partial pressure drop, including drop through riser, reversal, annulus, slots inches liquid

h_r = Pressure drop through risers, inches liquid

h_{ra} = Pressure drop through reversal and annulus, inches liquid

h_s = Slot opening, or pressure drop through slot, inches liquid

h'_s = Pressure drop through dry slots, inches liquid

h_{sl} = Static liquid seal on sieve tray, inches liquid

h_{ss} = Static slot seal, inches

h_{sr} = Height of cap shroud ring, inches

h_t = Total pressure drop per tray, inches liquid (wet tray)

h_w = Height of weir above tray floor, inches. (To top of flat weir, or bottom of notch in notched weir)

K_c = Constant for Bolles' bubble cap equation

L' = Liquid flow, lbs./hr.

L = Liquid rate, lbs./(hr.) (sq. ft. of active plate)

L_g = Liquid flow rate, gallons per minute, gpm

l_{fw} = Total flow width across tray normal to flow, feet

l_w = Length of straight weir, feet

N = Total number actual trays in tower

N_c = Number of caps per tray

N_s = Number slots per bubble cap

n = Depth of notches in weir, inches

Q = Liquid load, gpm $= L_g$

R_s = Ratio of top to bottom widths of trapezoidal slot, bubble cap dimensionless

R_v = Vapor distribution ratio, dimensionless

Δ'_r = Liquid gradient per row of caps, uncorrected, inches

S' = Effective tray spacing, distance between top of foam, froth or bubbles and tray above, inches. (For Hunt's relation S' = tray spacing minus 2.5 h_c)

S'' = Same as S', except units, feet

S_t = Tray spacing, inches

s = Cap skirt clearance between cap and tray floor, inches

t_w = Liquid throw over weir, inches

V = Total vapor flow through tray or tower, cu. ft./sec.

V' = Internal vapor flow, lbs./hr.

V_m = Maximum allowable vapor load per tray, cu. ft./sec.

v_c = Superficial vapor velocity in tower, ft./sec. (Based on tower cross-section)

v_d = Design hole vapor velocity, ft./sec.

v_{du} = Velocity of liquid flowing between segmental downcomer and inlet weir, ft./sec.

v_f = Vapor velocity through equivalent net tray area, based on tower area minus twice downcomer area, ft./sec.

v_o = Vapor velocity through holes, ft./sec.

v_{om} = Minimum velocity through holes at weep point, ft./sec.

W = Maximum allowable mass velocity through column using bubble cap trays, lbs./(hr.) (sq. ft. tower cross-section)

W_e = Liquid entrainment mass velocity, lbs. entrainment/(minute) (sq. ft.), based on net tray area of tower area minus twice downcomer area

W'_e = Assumed allowable liquid entrainment mass velocity derived from assumed allowable loss mols liquid/mol vapor, lbs./hr. (sq. ft.), based on net tray areas same as for W_e

W_e^* = Liquid entrainment mass velocity corrected for liquid properties and plate spacing, lbs. entrainment/(hour) (sq. ft.), based on net tray area same as for W_e

w_s = Width of slot (rectangular), inches

α = Relative volatility, dimensionless

β = Fraction perforated or open hole area in perforated area of tray (not fraction hole area in tower area)

γ = Ratio of distance between caps to cap diameter, dimensionless

Δ = Liquid gradient (corrected) for tray or tray section, inches

Δ' = Uncorrected liquid gradient for tray or tray sections, inches

Δ'_r = Liquid gradient per row of caps, uncorrected, inches

Θ = Time to drain tower, minutes

μ = Viscosity of liquid at tower temperature, centipoise

π = 3.14

ρ = Liquid density at temperature of tower, grams/cc.

ρ_L = Liquid density, lbs./cu. ft.

ρ_v = Vapor density, lbs./cu. ft.

σ = Surface tension of liquid, dynes/cm.

Bibliography

1. Akers, W. W. and D. E. Wade, "New Plate-to-Plate Method," Pet. Ref. 36, 199 (1954)
2. American Institute of Chemical Engineers, "Bubble Tray Design Manual, Prediction of Fractionation Efficiency," Amer. Inst. Chem. Engrs. (1958)
3. Biggers, M. W., Private communications

4. Bogart, M. J. P., "The Design of Equipment for Fractional Batch Distillations," Trans. A.I.Ch.E. **33**, 139 (1937

5. Bolles, W. L., "Optimum Bubble-Cay Tray Design, *"Pet. Processing;* Feb. through May 1956

6. Boston and Sullivan, *Canadian Jour. of Chem. Engr.,* **50**, Oct. (1972)

7. Broaddus, J. E., A. J. Moose, R. L. Huntington, "How to Drain Bubble Cap Columns," *Pet. Ref.,* Feb. (1955)

8. Brown, G. G. and Associates, *Unit Operations,* 4th Ed. John Wiley and Sons, New York, N. Y., (1953)

9. Brown, G. G. and H. Z. Martin, "An Empirical Relationship Between Reflux Ratio and the Number of Equilibrium Plates in Fractionating Columns," Trans. A.I.Ch.E. **38**, No. 5 (1939)

10. Chueh, P. L. and J. M. Prausnitz, I.&E.C. Fundamentals 6, (1967) p. 492.

11. Cicalese, J. J., J. J. Davis, P. J. Harrington, G. S. Houghland, A. J. L. Hutchinson, and T. J. Walsh, *Pet. Ref.* **26**, May 127 (1947)

12. Colburn, A. P., "Calculation of Minimum Reflux Ratio in Distillation of Multicomponent Mixtures," Trans. A.I.Ch.E. **37**, 805 (1941)

13. Dauphine, T. C. "Pressure Drops in Bubble Trays," Sc. D. Thesis, Mass. Inst. Technology (1939)

14. Davies, J. A., "Bubble Tray Hydraulics," Ind. Eng. Chem. **39**, 774 (1947)

15. Davies, J. A., "Bubble Trays—Design and Layout," *Pet. Ref.* **29**, 93, 121 (1950)

16. Drickhamer, H. G. and J. B. Bradford, *"Overall Plate Efficiency of Commercial Hydrocarbon Fractionating Columns,"* Trans. A.I.Ch.E. **39**, 319 (1943)

17. Edmister, W. C., "Design for Hydrocarbon Absorption and Stripping," *Ind. Eng. Chem.* **35**, 837 (1943)

18. Edmister, W. C., "Hydrocarbon Absorption and Fractionation Process Design Methods," *Pet. Engr.* May 1947-March 1949 and, "Absorption and Stripping—Factor Functions for Distillation Calculations by Manual and Digital—Computer Methods," *A. I. Ch. E. Journal,* 3, No. 2 (1957) pg. 165.

19. Eduljee, H. E. "Entrainment From Bubble-Cap Distillation Plates," *British Chem. Engr,* pg. 474, Sept. (1958)

20. Ewell, R. H., J. M. Harrison, and Lloyd Berg, "Hydrocarbon Azeotropes," *Pet. Engr.,* (installment, Oct., Nov., Dec. (1944))

21. Faassen, J. W., "Chart For Distillation of Binary Mixtures," *Ind. Eng. Chem.* **36**, 248, (1944)

22. Gautreaux, M. F., H. E. O'Connell, "Effect of Length of Liquid Path on Plate Efficiency," *Chem. Eng. Prog.* **51**, 232 (1955)

23. Gilliland, E. R., "Multicomponent Rectification," *Ind. Eng. Chem.* **32**, 1101 and 1220 (1940)

24. Good, A. J., M. H. Hutchinson, W. C. Rousseau, "Liquid Capacity of Bubble Cap Plates," *Ind. Eng. Chem.,* **34**, 1445 (1942)

25. Holland, C. D., Advanced Distillation Course in Extension, Texas A. & M. College (1954)

26. Holland. C. D., *Multicomponent Distillation,* Prentice-Hall (1963)

27. Holland, C. D., *Unsteady State Processes with Applications in Multicomponent Distillation,* Prentice-Hall

28. Horsley, L. H., "Azeotropic Data," Advances in Chemistry Series, American Chemical Society, Washington, D. C.

29. Horton, G., W. B. Franklin, "Calculation of Absorber Performance and Design," *Ind. Eng. Chem.* **32**, 1384 (1940)

30. Huang, Chen-Jung, and J. R. Hodson, "Perforated Trays Designed This Way," *Pet. Ref.* **37**, 104, 1958

31. Hughmark, G. A., and H. E. O'Connell, "Design of Perforated Plate Fractionating Towers," *Chem. Eng. Prog.* **53**, 127-M (1957)

32. Hull, R. J. and K. Raymond. "How To Design and Evaluate Absorbers," *Oil and Gas Jour.,* Nov. 9, 1953 through Mar. 15, 1954

33. Hunt, C. D'A., D. N. Hanson and C. R. Wilke, "Capacity Factors in the Performance of Perforated Plate Columns," *A.I.Ch.E. Jour.* **1**, 441 (1955)

34. Hutchinson. A. J. L., "A System of Calculations for Light Hydrocarbons, *Pet. Ref.* Oct. 1950-April 1951

35. Jennings, B. H. and F. P. Shannon, "Aqua-Ammonia Tables," Lehigh University, Part 1, Science and Technology Series No. 1, Bethlehem, Pa.

36. Jones, J. B. and C. Pyle, "Relative Performance of Sieve and Bubble Cap Plates," *Chem. Eng. Progress,* **51**, 424 (1955)

37. Kelly, R. G., *Oil and Gas Journal,* April 18, pg. 128, (1955)

38. Kemp, H. S. and C. Pyle, "Hydraulic Gradient Across Various Bubble Cap Plates," *Chem. Eng. Prog.* **45**, 435 (1949)

39. Klein, J. H., D. Sc. Thesis, Mass. Inst. Technology, (1950)

40. Kremser, A., "Theoretical Analysis of Absorption Process, *Nat. Pet. News,* **22**, 48 (1930)

41. Lee, D. C., Jr., "Sieve Trays," *Chem. Eng.* pg. 179, May 1954 Leibson, I., R. E. Kelley and L. A. Bullington, "How to Design Perforated Trays," *Pet. Ref.* **36**, 127 (1957)

43. Martin, G. Q., "Guide To Predicting Azeotropes," *Hydrocarbon Processing,* No. 1, (1975) p. 241

44. May, J. A. and J. C. Frank, "Compensation for Hydraulic Gradient in Large Fractionator," *Chem. Eng. Prog.* **51**, 189 (1955)

45. Mayfield, F. D., W. L. Church, Jr., A. C. Green, D. C. Lee, Jr. and R. W. Rasmussen, "Perforated-Plate Distillation Columns," *Ind Eng. Chem.* **44**, 2238 (1952)

46. Munk, Paul, "Design of Bubble Cap Trays," *Pet. Ref.* **34**, 104 (1955)

47. Myers, H. S., "A Versatile Fractionating Column," *Ind. Eng. Chem.* **50**, 1671 (1958)

48. *Natural Gasoline Supply Men's Association, Engineering Data Book,* 7th Ed. 1957, Tulsa, Oklahoma

49. O'Connell, H. E., "Plate Efficiency of Fractionating Columns and Absorbers," *Trans. A.I.Ch.E.* **42**, 741 (1946)

50. Oryc, R. V. and J. M. Prausnitz, *Ind. Eng. Chem.* **57**, 5, p. 19 (1965)

51. Palmer, D. A., "Predicting Equilibrium Relationships for Maverick Mixtures," *Chem. Eng.,* June 9, (1975) p. 80

52. Prausnitz, J. M. and P. L. Cheuh, *Computer Calculations for High Pressure Vapor-Liquid Equilibrium,* Prentice-Hall Inc. (1968)

53. Prausnitz, J. M., C. A. Eckert, R. V. Orye and J. P. O'Connell, *Computer Calculations for Multicomponent V-L Equilibria,* Prentice-Hall (1967)

54. Prausnitz, J. M., *Molecular Thermodynamics of Fluid Phase Equilibria,* Prentice-Hall (1969)

55. Redlich, O., and A. T. Kister, *Ind. Eng. Chem.,* **40**, p. 345 (1948)

56. Redlich, O.. and J. N. S. Kwong, *Chem. Rev.* **44** (1949), p. 233

57. Redlich, O., T. Kister, and C. E. Turnquist, *Chem. Engr. Progr. Sym. Ser.* **48**, 2, (1952) p. 49.

58. Renon, H. and J. M. Prausnitz, *A.I.Ch.E. Jour.,* **14**, (1968) p. 135

59. Robinson, C. S. R. and E. R. Gilliland, *Elements of Fractional Distillation,* McGraw-Hill, 4th Ed., (1950)

60. Rogers, M. C. and E. W. Thiele, "Pressure Drop in Bubble-Cap Columns," *Ind. Eng. Chem.* **26**, 524 (1934)

61. Scheibel, E. G. and C. F. Montross, "Empirical Equation for Theoretical Minimum Reflux." *Ind. Eng. Chem.* **38**, 268 (1946)

62. Sherwood, T. K., *Absorption and Extraction,* McGraw-Hill Book Co., Inc., New York, N. Y. (1937)

63. Shiras, R. N., D. N. Hansen, C. H. Gibson, "Calculation of Minimum Reflux in Distillation Columns," *Ind. Eng. Chem.* **42**, 871 (1950)

64. Simkin, D. J., C. P. Strand and R. B. Olney, "Entrainment from Bubble Caps," *Chem. Eng. Prog.* **50**, 565 (1954)

65. Smith, B. D., *Design of Equilibrium Stage Processes*, McGraw-Hill (1963)

66. Smoker, E. H., "Nomographs for Minimum Reflux Ratio and Theoretical Plates for Separation of Binary Mixtures," *Ind. Eng. Chem.* **34**, 509 (1942)

67. Souders, M., Jr., G. G. Brown, "Fundamental Design of Absorbing and Stripping Columns for Complex Vapors." *Ind. Eng. Chem.* **24**, 519 (1932)

68. Souders, M., Jr., G. G. Brown, "Design of Fractionating Columns," *Ind. Eng. Chem.* **26**, 98 (1934)

69. Sutherland, S., Jr., "Characteristics of Countercurrent Vapor Liquid Flow at a Perforated Plate. M. S. Thesis, Jan. 1958. Texas A. & M. College

70. Teller, A. J., "Binary Distillation." *Chem. Eng.* pg. 168, Sept. (1954)

71. Umholtz, C. L. and M. Van Winkle, "Effect of Hole Free Area. Hole Diameter, Hole Spacing Weir Height. and Downcomer Area," *Pet. Ref.* **34**, 114 (1955)

72. Underwood, A. J. V.. "Fractional Distillation of Multicomponent Mixtures," *Chem. Eng. Prog.* **44**, 603 (1948)

73. Underwood. A. J. V.. Trans. Inst. Ch. E. (London) 10, 112 (1932)

74. Van Winkle. M.. *Distillation*, McGraw-Hill, Inc. (1967)

75. Van Winkle. M., "Multicomponent Distillation." *Oil and Gas Journal,* 182. Mar. 23, (1953)

76. Wang, J. C. and G. E. Henke, "Tridiagonal Matrix for Distillation," *Hydrocarbon Processing*, **45**, 8, (1966) p. 155

77. Wilson, G. M., *J. Am. Chem. Soc.,* **86**, (1964) p. 127

78. Zenz, F. A., "Calculate Capacity of Perforated Plates." *Pet. Ref.* **33**, 99 (1954)

References (Absorbers)

Burningham, D. W. and F. D. Otto, "Which Computer Design for Absorbers?" *Hydrocarbon Processing,* **46**, Oct. (1967), p. 163

Coates, Jesse and B. S. Pressburg, "Analyze Absorption in Gas Separations," *Chem. Engr.* Oct. 3 (1960) p. 99

Zenz, F. A., "Designing Gas-Absorption Towers." *Chem. Engr.* Nov. 13 (1972), p. 120

Packed Towers

Packed towers are used as contacting equipment for gas-liquid and liquid-liquid systems. Figure 9-1 presents a cross-section of a typical unit. The shell is usually cylindrical, although square wooden, light metal, or reinforced plastic towers are used. The basic unit consists of:

1. Shell
2. Packing (one or more sections)
3. Packing support(s)
4. Liquid distributor(s)

Figure 9-1. Cross-section of typical packed tower.

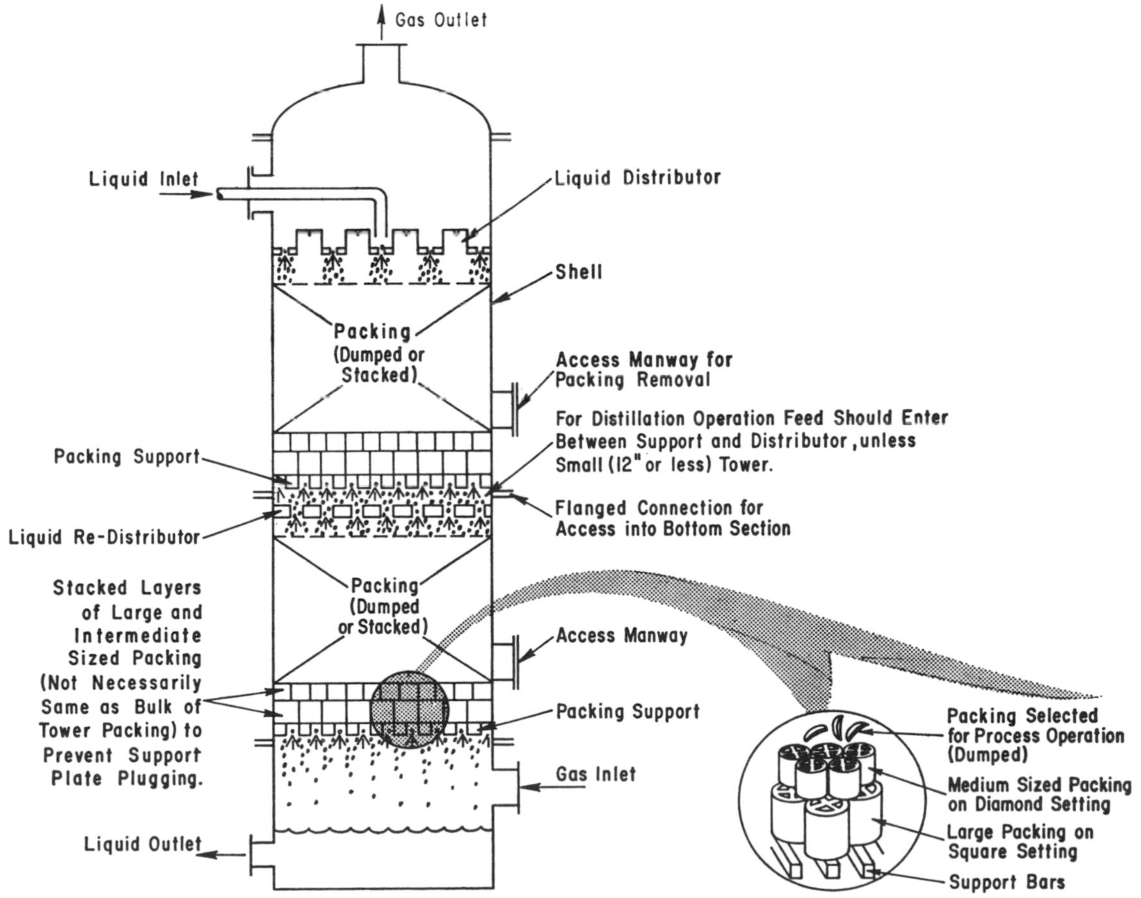

Labels on figure:
- Gas Outlet
- Liquid Inlet
- Liquid Distributor
- Shell
- Packing (Dumped or Stacked)
- Access Manway for Packing Removal
- For Distillation Operation Feed Should Enter Between Support and Distributor, unless Small (12" or less) Tower.
- Packing Support
- Flanged Connection for Access into Bottom Section
- Liquid Re-Distributor
- Stacked Layers of Large and Intermediate Sized Packing (Not Necessarily Same as Bulk of Tower Packing) to Prevent Support Plate Plugging.
- Packing (Dumped or Stacked)
- Access Manway
- Packing Support
- Gas Inlet
- Liquid Outlet
- Packing Selected for Process Operation (Dumped)
- Medium Sized Packing on Diamond Setting
- Large Packing on Square Setting
- Support Bars

(Text continued on page 132)

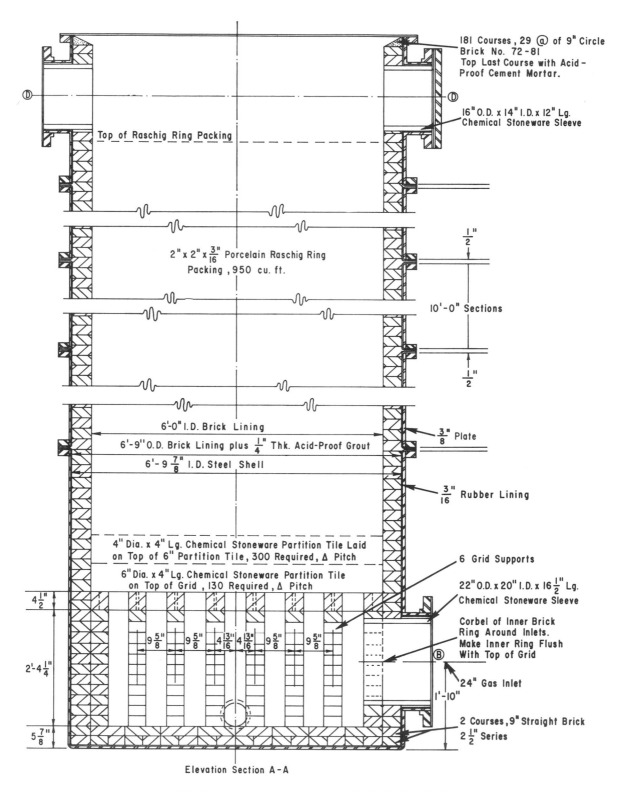

Figure 9-2A Cross-section of membrane and brick lined packed tower.

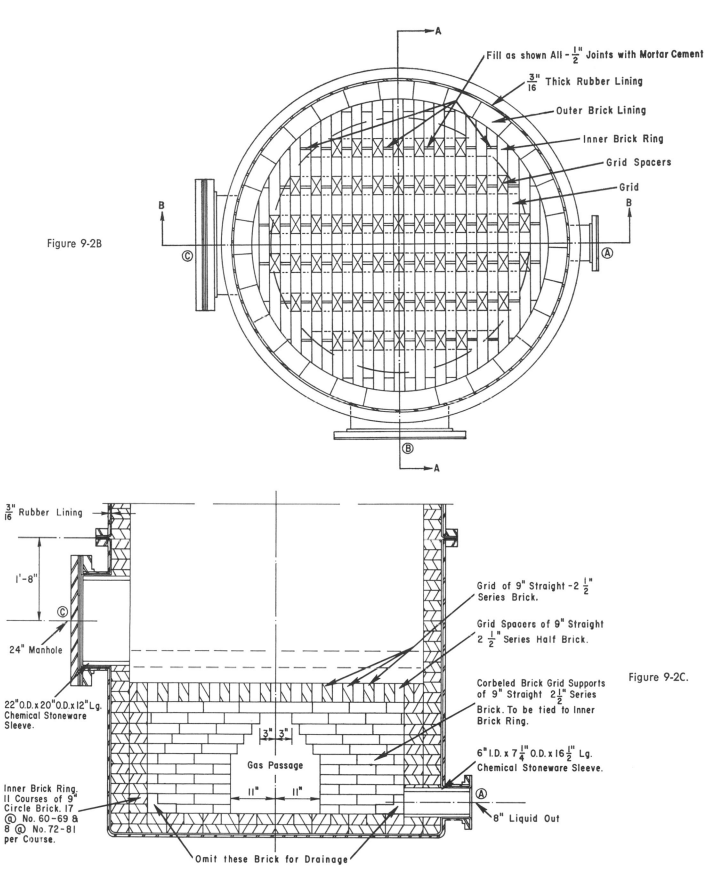

Figure 9-2B

Fill as shown All - $\frac{1}{2}$" Joints with **Mortar Cement**

$\frac{3}{16}$" Thick Rubber Lining

Outer Brick Lining

Inner Brick Ring

Grid Spacers

Grid

$\frac{3}{16}$" Rubber Lining

1'-8"

24" Manhole

22" O.D. x 20" O.D. x 12" Lg. Chemical Stoneware Sleeve.

Inner Brick Ring. II Courses of 9" Circle Brick. 17 @ No. 60-69 & 8 @ No. 72-81 per Course.

Grid of 9" Straight - 2 $\frac{1}{2}$" Series Brick.

Grid Spacers of 9" Straight 2 $\frac{1}{2}$" Series Half Brick.

Corbeled Brick Grid Supports of 9" Straight 2 $\frac{1}{2}$" Series Brick. To be tied to Inner Brick Ring.

6" I.D. x 7 $\frac{1}{4}$" O.D. x 16 $\frac{1}{2}$" Lg. Chemical Stoneware Sleeve.

8" Liquid Out

Figure 9-2C.

Gas Passage

3" 3"

II" II"

Omit these Brick for Drainage

Elevation Section B-B

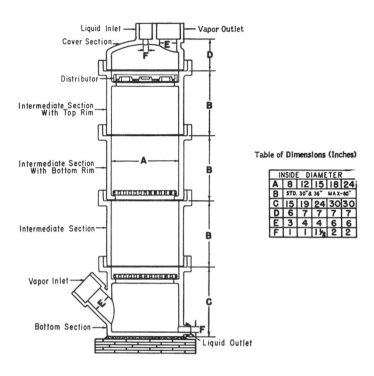

Figure 9-3 Bell and spigot ceramic tower. (By permission General Ceramics and Steatite Corp.)

Table of Dimensions (Inches)

INSIDE DIAMETER					
A	8	12	15	18	24
B	STD. 30"& 36"			MAX-60"	
C	15	19	24	30	30
D	6	7	7	7	7
E	3	4	4	6	6
F	1	1	1½	2	2

5. Intermediate supports and redistributors

6. Gas and liquid entrance and exit nozzles

Many of the mechanical aspects of tower construction and assembly have an influence upon the design and interpretation of tower performance. Every effort should be made to increase the effectiveness of contact between the process streams and to reduce losses by entrainment or wall effects at a minimum expenditure of pressure drop. At the same time the design must be consistent with the economics dictated by the process and type of construction.

Shell

The shell may be of metal (steel, alloy, or non-ferrous), plastic, wood or some combination which may require the addition of liners or inner layers of rubber, plastic or brick. The mechanical problems of attaching inner nozzles, supports and brick require considerable attention that is not an integral part of sizing the equipment. Figure 9-2A shows a typical large steel brick-lined-membrane lined tower with corbeled brick support locations. In these towers, temperature and/or corrosive conditions usually dictate the internal lining, and the selection of the proper acid-(or alkali-) proof cements.

Ceramic, plastic and other non-metal tower shells are used quite often (Figures 9-3, 4, and 5). It is important

Table 9-1

Chemical Stoneware and Porcelain Raschig Rings

Nominal Size Inch	Wall Thickness, Inch	O.D. and Length, Inch	Approx. Avg. Number per Cubic Foot	Approx. Avg. Weight per Cu. Ft., Lb. **	Approx. Avg. Surface Area F.²/Ft.³	Per Cent Free Gas Space	Equivalent Spher. Diam. Dp (Inch)
¼ *	¹⁄₃₂	¼	85600	60	233	62	0.22
⅜ *	¹⁄₁₆	⅜	24700	61	137	67	0.35
½	³⁄₃₂	½	10700	55	124	64	0.48
⅝	³⁄₃₂	⅝	5600	48-52	100	68	0.57
¾	³⁄₃₂	¾	3090	50	78	72	0.65
1	⅛	1	1350	42	58	74	0.87
1¼	³⁄₁₆	1¼	670	46	44	71	1.10
1½	¼	1½	387	43	36	73	1.40
2	¼	2	164	41	28	74	1.75
3	⅜	3	50	35	19	78	2.65
‡3(D)	⅜	3	74	67	29	60	2.65
‡3(S)	⅜	3	64	58	25	66	2.65
4	½	4	25	40			

⅝", 2½", 4" and 6" available on special order. The 3-in., 4-in., and 6-in. O. D. sizes are also made with ribbed or corrugated outside surfaces. The 3-in., 4-in., and 6-in. sizes can be made in lengths up to 12 inches, on special order.

**Porcelain Rings are about 5% heavier than Stoneware. These weights are the average for both.

‡ Data for stacked arrangement. "D" indicates diamond pattern. "S" indicates square pattern.

Original by permission, M. Leva, Ref. 40 and Bulletin TP-54, U.S. Stoneware Co., Akron, O.; updated 1978 to present latest data, by permission Norton, Bull. TP-78.

*Porcelain only

DIMENSIONS OF STANDARD TOWERS						
Inside Diameter of Tower A	24 in.	30 in.	36 in.	40 in.	48 in.	60 in.
A	24	30	36	40	48	60
A¹	23¼	29¼	35	39	47½	58
B	27½	34	41½	45	54½	67½
C	36	36	36	36	36	36
C¹	30	30	36	36	40	40
D	6	6	6	6	6	6
E	15	15	15	15	15	15
F	10	12	14	14	18	18
G	6	8	12	12	18	18
H	8	10½	14¾	14¾	21	21
I	1	1	1	1½	1½	1½
J	2½	2½	2½	3	3	3
L	4	4	4	4	4	4
M	3	3	3	3	3	3
O	7	9⅜	11½	11⅝	13¾	18
P	3	3	3	3	3	3
Q	7	8	11	11	14	16
R	1⅛	1¼	1⅜	1½	1¾	2
R¹	1½	1⅝	1¾	1¾	2	2
S	¾	¾	1	1	1¼	1¼

S is inside diameter of ground in faucet.

WEIGHTS						
	Diameter					
	24 in.	30 in.	36 in.	40 in.	48 in.	60 in.
Tower Cover, Fig. 360 Weight, lbs.	80	130	215	300	500	700
Tower Distributor, Fig. 401 and 401a Weight, lbs.	36	60	100	120	170	250
Plain Tower section, Fig. 356 Weight, lbs.	220	300	430	520	700	1000
Tower Section with Rim Fig. 356a and 356b Weight, lbs.	225	310	445	540	750	1100
Supporting Plate, Fig. 279 Weight, lbs.	30	80	140	160	250	400
Tower Section with branch, Fig. 355 Weight, lbs.	230	320	530	630	900	1800
Tower Saucer, Fig. 354 Weight, lbs.	120	200	250	340	500	800
Tower Bottom Section, Fig. 355a Weight, lbs.	260	370	610	730	1000	1500

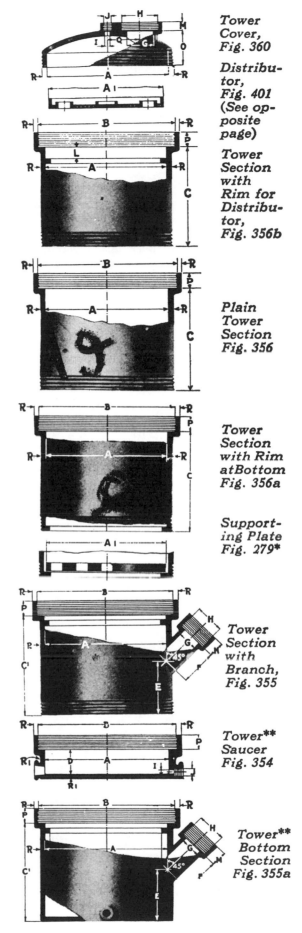

Tower Cover, Fig. 360

Distributor, Fig. 401 (See opposite page)

Tower Section with Rim for Distributor, Fig. 356b

Plain Tower Section Fig. 356

Tower Section with Rim at Bottom Fig. 356a

Supporting Plate Fig. 279*

Tower Section with Branch, Fig. 355

Tower** Saucer Fig. 354

Tower** Bottom Section Fig. 355a

Figure 9-4. Physical dimensions of stoneware tower sections, bell and spigot design. (By permission of General Ceramics and Steatite Corp.)

to consider in ceramic construction that the main inlet or outlet nozzles or any other large connections should be oriented 90° to each other to reduce the possibility of cracking the walls, as most cracks go one-half diameter. Preferably there should only be one nozzle at any one horizontal plane. The nozzles should never carry any piping or other stress load.

The bell and spigot type tower, Figures 9-3 and 4, is satisfactory for 2 to 2.5 psi in 12-inches dia. to 30-inches dia. towers when the joints are packed with asbestos and caulking compound. For operating pressures of 5 psi in 18-inches through 48-inches dia., use asbestos and silicate cement. Special hold-down packing gland-type rings will allow operation at slightly higher pressure. The porcelain towers should be used for the higher pressures rather than the weaker stoneware.

The rate of heating or cooling a stoneware or porcelain tower should not exceed 15° F. per minute.

Packing

The packing is the heart of the performance of this equipment. Its proper selection entails an understanding of packing operational characteristics and the effect on performance of the points of significant physical difference between the various types. The types and corresponding physical data are given in Figure 9-6 and Tables 9-1 through 9-16. The evaluation of these materials for various conditions of service is given later. However, Table 9-17 outlines packing service applications and Table 9-18 summarizes packing type applications.

(Text continued on page 138)

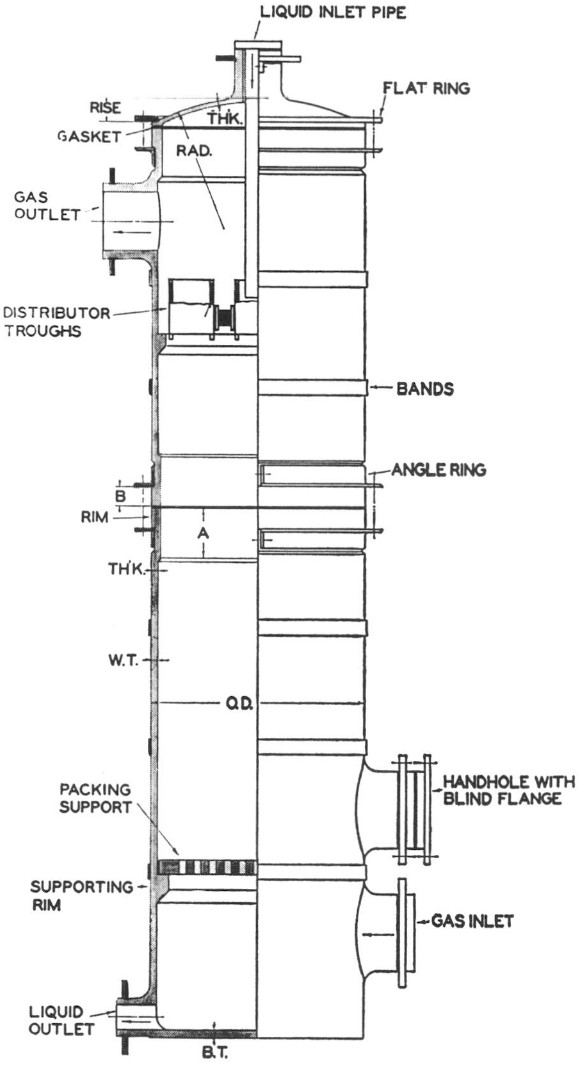

Figure 9-5. Typical reinforced plastic packed tower construction. **(By permission Haveg Corp., Bul. F-7.)**

DESIGN INFORMATION FOR SINGLE OR MULTIPLE SECTION CYLINDRICAL HAVEG TOWERS

Size	O.D.	Max. Height of Section	Wall & Bottom Thickness		Support Rim	Joint for Section Towers										COVER							Staves and Hoops	
						Rim			Angle Ring			Gasket		Bolts		Head			Flat Ring			Bolts		
			W.T.	B.T.	I.D. x Tk.	A	B	Th'k.	Size	I.D.	B.C.	I.D.	O.D.	No.	Size	Rad.	Rise	Th'k.	I.D.	O.D.	Th'k.	Size	Size Hoops	No. of Staves
12"	13½	15'-0"	⅝	¾	......	4	1	1⅛	2 x2 x3/16	12⅞	15⅛	11¼	13½	12	½x3½	8⅝	2¼	½	11¼	16¾	⅜	½x3		
15"	16¼	15'-0"	⅝	¾	11⅝x1	4	1	1⅛	2 x2 x3/16	15⅝	17⅞	14	16¼	12	½x3½	12⅛	2¼	½	14	19½	⅜	½x3		
18"	19¼	15'-0"	⅝	¾	14 x1	4½	1½	1⅛	2 x2 x3/16	18⅝	20⅞	17	19¼	12	½x4½	16½	2	½	17½	23	½	½x3½	......	......
20"	21½	15'-0"	⅝	¾	16¼x1¼	4½	1½	1⅛	2 x2 x¼	20⅞	23⅛	19¼	21½	16	½x4½	18	2¾	½	19¼	24¾	½	½x3½	......	......
2'	25¼	15'-0"	⅝	¾	20 x1¼	4½	1½	1⅛	2 x2 x¼	24½	26¾	23	25¼	16	½x4½	25	2⅞	⅝	23½	28½	½	½x3½	......	......
2'-6"	31½	15'-0"	¾	1	24 x1½	5	1½	1¼	2½x2½x7/16	30¾	33½	29	31½	20	½x5	32⅜	3¼	⅝	29	36	⅝	½x4	......	......
3'	37¼	14'-6"	¾	1	29¾x1½	5	1½	1¼	2½x2½x7/16	36½	39¼	34¾	37¼	28	½x5	39	3⅞	¾	34¾	41¾	⅝	½x4	......	......
3'-6"	43½	14'-6"	¾	1	36 x1½	6½	3	1¼	2½x2½x7/16	42¾	45½	41	43½	28	½x8	47¾	4⅜	¾	41	48	⅝	½x5½	⅝	25
4'	49½	14'-6"	1	1¼	40¾x2	7	3	1⅝	3 x3 x½	48½	51½	46¼	49½	32	⅝x8	48½	6	¾	47	54	¾	⅝x6	⅝	28
5'	61½	14'-0"	1	1¼	53½x2	7	3	1⅝	3 x3 x½	60½	63½	58¼	61½	40	⅝x8	58⅝	7¼	1	59	66	¾	⅝x6½	⅝	35
6'	74	14'-0"	1	1¼	65 x2½	7½	3	1⅝	3½x3½x½	73	76¼	70¾	74	48	⅝x8	75	8¾	1	71½	79½	¾	⅝x6½	⅝	42
7'	86⅜	13'-6"	1¼	1⅜	......	7½	3	2	3½x3½x½	85⅜	88⅝	82⅜	86⅜	52	⅝x8	87½	10	1	83⅜	91⅜	⅞	⅝x6½	¾	49
8'	98⅜	13'-0"	1¼	1⅜	......	8	3	2	4 x4 x⅝	97⅜	100⅞	94⅜	98⅜	60	¾x8½	91¼	12⅞	1¼	95⅜	104⅜	⅞	¾x7	¾	56
9'	110⅜	12'-6"	1¼	1⅜	......	9	3	2	5 x5 x⅝	109⅛	112⅞	106⅜	110⅜	72	¾x8½	108½	13⅛	1¼	107⅜	117⅜	⅞	¾x7	¾	63
10'	120	12'-0"	1½	1⅝	......	9	3	2¼	5 x5 x⅝	118¾	122½	115½	120	80	¾x8½	119½	15	1¼	116¾	126¾	⅞	¾x7	¾	69

All dimensions are in inches unless otherwise noted.

Table 9-2
Carbon Raschig Rings

Nominal Size Inch	Wall Thickness, Inch	O.D. and Length, Inch	Approx. Avg. Number per Cubic Foot	Approx. Avg. Weight per Cu. Ft., Lb.	Approx. Avg. Surface Area F.²/Ft.³	Per Cent Free Gas Space	Equivalent Spher. Diam. Dp (Inch)
¼	¹⁄₁₆	¼	85000	46	212	55	0.27
½	¹⁄₁₆	½	10600	27	114	74	0.42
¾	⅛	¾	3140	34	74	67	0.72
1	⅛	1	1325	27	57	74	0.87
1¼	³⁄₁₆	1¼	678	31	45	69	1.10
1½	¼	1½	392	34	37.5	67	1.40
2	¼	2	166-157*	27	28.5	74	1.75
3	⁵⁄₁₆	3	49-44*	33	19	78	2.50
3(D)	⁵⁄₁₆	3	74	49.5	29	66	2.50
3(S)	⁵⁄₁₆	3	64	43	25	71	2.50

S = Square pattern
D = Diamond pattern } Stacked

From: M. Leva, U. S. Stoneware Co., Akron, Ohio, Ref. 40, and Bulletin CP-2512, National Carbon Co., New York, N.Y.
* Varies with supplier

Table 9-3
Metal Raschig Rings

Nominal Size Inch	Wall Thickness, Inch	O.D. and Length, Inch	Approx. Avg. Number per Cubic Foot	Approx. Avg. Weight per Cu. Ft., Lb.*	Approx. Avg. Surface Area F.²/Ft.³	Per Cent Free Gas Space	Equivalent Spher. Diam. Dp (Inch)
¼	¹⁄₃₂	¼	88000	133	236	72	0.22
⅜	¹⁄₃₂	⅜	27000	94	....	81	....
½	¹⁄₃₂	½	11400	75	123	85	0.34
½	¹⁄₁₆	½	11000	132	118	73	0.44
¹⁹⁄₃₂	¹⁄₃₂	¹⁹⁄₃₂	7300	66	112	86	0.40
¹⁹⁄₃₂	¹⁄₁₆	¹⁹⁄₃₂	7000	120	106.5	75	0.50
¾	¹⁄₃₂	¾	3340	52	81.7	89	0.46
¾	¹⁄₁₆	¾	3140	94	70.6	80	0.58
1	¹⁄₃₂	1	1430	39	62.2	92	0.56
1	¹⁄₁₆	1	1310	71	55.2	86	0.70
1¼	¹⁄₁₆	1¼	725	62	49.3	87	0.75
1½	¹⁄₁₆	1½	400	49	39.2	90	0.90
2	¹⁄₁₆	2	168	37	29.3	92	1.15
3	¹⁄₁₆	3	51	25	19.8	95	
3(D)	¹⁄₁₆	3	74	35	29	93	
3(S)	¹⁄₁₆	3	64	30	25	94	

* Based upon Carbon Steel Rings; other weights are: Stainless Steel 105%; Copper 120%; Aluminum 37%; Monel and Nickel 115%.
Usually metal Raschig rings are made with fitted butted-joints.
Original by permission, M. Leva, Reference 40, U. S. Stoneware Co., Akron, O.; updated 1978 to present latest data from Norton Bull. TP 78, by permission.
Note: Sizes availability varies with manufacturers.

Table 9-4
Metal Lessing Rings

Size, Inch	Wall Thickness, Inch	O. D. and Length, Inch	Approximate Number per Cu. Ft.	Approximate Weight per Cu. Ft. Lbs*	Approximate Surface Area Sq. Ft./Cu. Ft.	Percent Free Gas Space	Equivalent Spherical Dia., Dp, Inch
1/4	1/32	1/4	81,840	195	306.8	60	0.24
3/8	1/32	3/8	25,110	114	217.1	76	0.31
1/2	1/32	1/2	10,974	100	166.4	81	0.38
1/2	1/16	1/2	10,230	172	153.4	66	0.46
5/8	1/32	5/8	6,789	86	145.6	82	0.45
5/8	1/16	5/8	6,510	150	138.4	68	0.57
3/4	1/32	3/4	3,171	71	108.5	85	0.52
3/4	1/16	3/4	2,967	130	93.3	71	0.63
1	1/32	1	1,339	52	81.5	90	0.62
1	1/16	1	1,251	95	73.7	80	0.77
1 1/4	1/16	1 1/4	674	81	64.1	82	0.99
1 1/2	1/16	1 1/2	391	65	53.6	87	1.02
1 3/4	1/16	1 3/4	246	58	46.0	89	1.13
2	1/16	2	167	49	40.8	90	1.24

All figures are on a dumped basis. Metal Lessing Rings are also made in stainless steel, copper, and aluminum.
*Weights shown are for carbon steel.
By permission: U. S. Stoneware Co. Bul. TP54, Ref (5)
except column 8, Ref. (40)

Table 9-5
Ceramic Lessing Rings

O.D. and Length, Inch	Wall Thickness, Inch	Approx. No. of Rings per Ft.^{3}, Dumped	Approx. Wt. Per Cubic Foot, Dumped	Per Cent Free Gas Space	Approx. Surface Area per Cubic Foot	Equiv. Spher. Diameter Dp (Inch)
1	1/8	1300	50	66	69	0.95
1 1/4	3/16	650	56	62	53	1.20
1 1/2	1/4	350	58	60	40	1.55
2	3/8	150	49	68	32	1.90

From M. Leva, U. S. Stoneware Co., Ref. 40, by permission.

Table 9-6A
Ceramic Berl Saddle Packings

Nominal Size	Approx. Average Number/ft.^{3}	Approx. Wt./ft.^{3}, lb.	Approx. Average Surface Area ft.^{2}/ft.^{3}	Per Cent Free Gas Space	Equivalent Spher. Diam. D_P (Inch)
1/4	113000	56	274	60	0.23
1/2	16200	54	142	63	0.42
3/4	5000	48	82	66	0.58
1	2200	45	76	69	0.76
1 1/2	580	38	44	75	1.10
2	250	40	32	72	1.55

From M. Leva, U. S. Stoneware Co., Ref. 40, by permission.

Table 9-6B
Steel* Berl Saddles

1	2,500	87	85	83
1 1/2	825	60	58	88

* Other metals available.
Courtesy Maurice A. Knight Co., Akron, Ohio, Bulletin No. 11, by permission.

Table 9-7

Ceramic Intalox* Saddles

Nominal Size, Inch	Approximate Number per Cu. Ft.	Approximate Weight per Cu. Ft., Lbs.	Approximate Surface Area Sq. Ft./Cu. Ft.	Per Cent Free Gas Space	Equivalent Spherical Diameter D_P (Inch)
¼	117,500	54	300	65	0.20
⅜	49,800	50	—	67	—
½	18,300	46	190	71	0.32
¾	5,640	44	102	73	0.48
1	2,150	42	78	73	0.68
1½	675	39	59.5	76	0.96
2	250	38	36	76	1.38
3	52	36	—	79	—

Data shown applies to Intalox Saddle made either from chemical stoneware or chemical porcelain. Weights per cubic foot are based on chemical porcelain. Chemical stoneware Intalox Saddles will weigh approximately 5% less.
* Trade name Norton Co.
Orig. By permission: U. S. Stoneware Co., Akron, Ohio, Ref. 5, except column 6, frem Ref. 40; updated 1978 from Bull. CI 17, Norton Co. by permission

Table 9-8

Stoneware Cross-Partition Rings

Outside Diameter (Inches)	Outside Length (Inches)	Wall Thickness (Inches)	Number of Rings per Cubic Foot		Weight of Rings per Cubic Foot (Lbs.)		Per Cent Free Gas Space		Square Feet of Surface Area per Cubic Foot of Packing		Net Cross-Section Area of Packing in Sq. Ft.— Per Square Foot	
			D Setting	S Setting	D Setting	S Setting	D Setting	S Setting	D Setting	S Setting	D Setting	S Setting
3	3	⅜	74	64	73	63	47-48	54-55	41-43	35-37	.53	.46
4	3	½	41	36	81-72	71-63	46-49	52-55	31-33	27-29	.54	.47
4	4	⁷⁄₁₆	31	27	81-62	71-54	45-56	52=61	30-32	26-29	.54	.47
6	4	⅝	14	12	73-70	62-60	51-50	58-57	22	19	.49	.42
6	6	⅝	9	8	70	62	53-50	58-56	20	18	.49	.42

Also made with outer surfaces ribbed or corrugated, and in lengths up to 12 inches. Rings with different wall thicknesses than above can be made on special order. Porcelain rings weigh about 5% more than above. For D and S patterns, see Figure 9-11. Compiled from Ref. 40, U. S. Stoneware Bull. TP-54, and Maurice A. Knight Co., Chemical Equipment Bulletin, by permission.

Table 9-9

Stoneware Spiral Packing Rings*

	Outside Diam. (In.)	Outside Length (In.)	Wall Thickness (In.)	Number of Rings per Cubic Foot		Weight of Rings per Cubic Foot		Per Cent Free Gas Space		Square Feet of Surface Area per Cubic Foot of Packing		Net Cross-Section Area of Packing in Sq. Ft. per Square Foot	
				D Setting	S Setting	D Setting	S Setting	D Setting	S Setting	D Setting	S Setting	D Setting	S Setting
Single Spiral	3¼ -3	3	⁵⁄₁₆	63-74	54-64	60-67	52-58	58-52	66-59	40-41	34-36	.32	.27
	4	4	⅜	31	27	61-60	55-52	60-57	67-64	32	28	.33	.28
	6	6	½	9	8	59-54	51-48	66-61	70-66	21	19	.28	.25
Double Spiral	3¼	3	⁵⁄₁₆	63	54	67	58	56	63	44	37	.37	.32
	4	4	⅜	31	27	64	58	59	64	35	31	.38	.33
	6	6	½	9	8	65	58	64	68	23	21	.32	.29
Triple Spiral	3¼	3	⁵⁄₁₆	63	54	69	60	50	57	50	42	.51	.44
	4	4	⅜	31	27	65	59	53	58	40	35	.46	.40
	6	6	½	9	8	68	60	60	64	24	21	.32	.29

* Basic data in table for U. S. Stoneware "Cyclohelix" spiral packing, Bul. TP 54, Ref. 5. Data for other spiral packings shown set to right from Maurice A. Knight Co. Bulletin No. 11, by permission. For D and S patterns, see Figure 9-11.

Relative Packing Costs

Packing costs referenced to carload quantities of 1 inch porcelain Raschig rings as 1.0 (as of Jan. 1979)

Size	Intalox® Saddles
½ inch	0.995
1 inch	0.973
1½ inch	0.968

Base price 1 inch unglazed porcelain R.R. approximately $19.00/cu.ft. F.O.B. factory.

Table 9-10
Pall Rings

Metal

Size O.D. & Length	Wall † Thickness, In.	Approximate Number per cu. ft.	Approximate Weight, Lbs/cu.ft.	Surface Area sq.ft/cu.ft.	Percent Free Gas Space
⅝″	0.018	5,865	37	104	93
1″	0.024	1,400	30	63	94
1½″	0.030	375	24	39	95
2″	0.036	165	22	31	96
3½″	0.048	33	17	20	97

Plastic

Size O.D. & Length	Wall † Thickness, In.	Approximate Number per cu. ft.	Approximate Weight, Lbs/cu.ft.	Surface Area sq.ft/cu.ft.	Percent Free Gas Space
⅝″	—	6,050	7‡	104	87
1″	—	1,440	5.5	63	90
1½″	—	390	4.75	39	91
2″	—	180	4.25	31	92
3½″	—	33	4	26	92

By permission, Norton Co., TP-78 and PR-16; other manufacturer's data is equivalent
†Standard gauge carbon steel
‡Weights referenced to polypropylene; other plastics available, high density polyethylene, glass reinforced polypropylene and fluorinated vinyls

Table 9-11
Teller Rosette (Tellerette) Plastic*

Nominal Size	No. Units per Cu. Ft.	Weight per Cu. Ft., Lbs.	Surface Area Sq. Ft./Cu. Ft.	Per Cent Free Gas Space
1″	1125	10	76	83

* Harshaw Chemical Co. "Tellerette" bulletin, and Dr. A. J. Teller.

Table 9-12
Dowpac Plastic Packing—FN-90

3¾″	56	5.6	25	92

The Dow Chemical Co., Bulletin (1955).
Refer to section on cooling towers for application.

Packing Supports

The packing support may be anything from cross-grid bars spaced to prevent fall-through of packing to more refined speciality units designed to direct the flow of gas and liquid. Good tower performance is definitely linked to proper packing support. The net free flow cross-sectional area of the support should be 65 percent (or larger) of the tower area, and greater than the free area of the packing itself. In addition, the effect of the free area "blocking" by the positioning of the packing on the support must be considered. To allow for this, every effort should be made to obtain as large a support-free area as possible and yet remain consistent with the structural strength of the material being used. If this area is too

Table 9-13
Super Intalox® Saddles: Ceramic†

Size No. Designation	Approximate Number per cu. ft.	Weight‡ Lbs/cu. ft.	Surface Area sq. ft./cu. ft.	Percent Free Gas Space
1	1490	39	76	79
2	180	37	32	81

Plastic

Size No. Designation	Approximate Number per cu. ft.	Weight‡ Lbs/cu. ft.	Surface Area sq. ft./cu. ft.	Percent Free Gas Space
1	1620	6	63	90
2	190	3.75	33	93
3	42	3.25	27	94

By permission, Norton Co., Bull. SI-72; other manufacturer's data is equivalent.
†Also available in polypropylene (including glass reinforced); high density polyethylene, rigid PVC, fluoronated vinyls.
‡Weights for polypropylene; others are times PP: 1.03 for high density polyethylene: 1.54 for PVC: 1.87 to 1.95 for fluoronated vinyls.

Table 9-14
Hy-Pak* Metal Packing

Size No. Designation	Approximate Number Per Cubic Foot	Weight, ** Lbs./cu. ft.	Percent Free Gas Space
1	850	19	96
2	107	14	97
3	31	13	97

*By permission, Norton Co., Bull. HY-30, reg. trademark.
**Weight for standard gauge carbon steel, available in most other common metals.

Table 9-15
Chempak® Metal Packing*

1	950	19	96

*By permission, Chem-Pro Equipment Corp., Licensed from Dr. Max Levo, Bull. 702. Weight is for carbon steel

Table 5-10: Grid Tile (Drip Point)*

ARRANGEMENT OF TILE IN STACKED PACKING		SURFACE CONTACT PER CU. FT.		FREE AREA PER SQ. FT. HOR. SURFACE		NUMBER PCS. PER CU. FT.		WEIGHT PER CU. FT. LBS		PRESSURE DROP
		TILE SHAPE		TILE SHAPE		TILE SHAPE		TILE SHAPE		TILE SHAPE
		6295 SQFT.	6897 SQFT.	6295 SQFT	6897 SQFT	6295 PCS	6897 PCS	6295 LBS	6897 LBS	6295 / 6897 GAL/MIN/SQFT
CONTINUOUS FLUE	GRID	24.01	34.09	.435	.420	6.88	6.88	79.12	79.12	SEE MFG'S LITERATURE FOR CHARTS SHOWING PRESSURE DROP IN INCHES OF WATER PER FT. OF HEIGHT
	CHECKER'D	14.5	22.0	.67	.67	3.36	3.36	38.64	38.64	
CROSS FLUE	GRID	24.01	34.09			6.88	6.88	79.12	79.12	
	CHECK'RD	14.5	22.0			3.36	3.36	38.64	38.64	
DUMPED										

CROSS FLUE ARRANGEMENT

CONTINUOUS FLUE ARRANGEMENT

↳ of Tower volume

CRUSHING STRENGTH ALLOWABLE LBS/FT2

SPRAY CHAMBERS = 41% OF TOTAL VOL.

OPEN OPEN OPEN OPEN — ELEVATION

OPEN OPEN OPEN OPEN — PLAN CHECKER ARRANG'T

ELEVATION

PLAN GRID ARRANGMNT

4-1/2"

7-15/32"

SHAPE #6295 PLAN

SHAPE #6897 PLAN SIDE

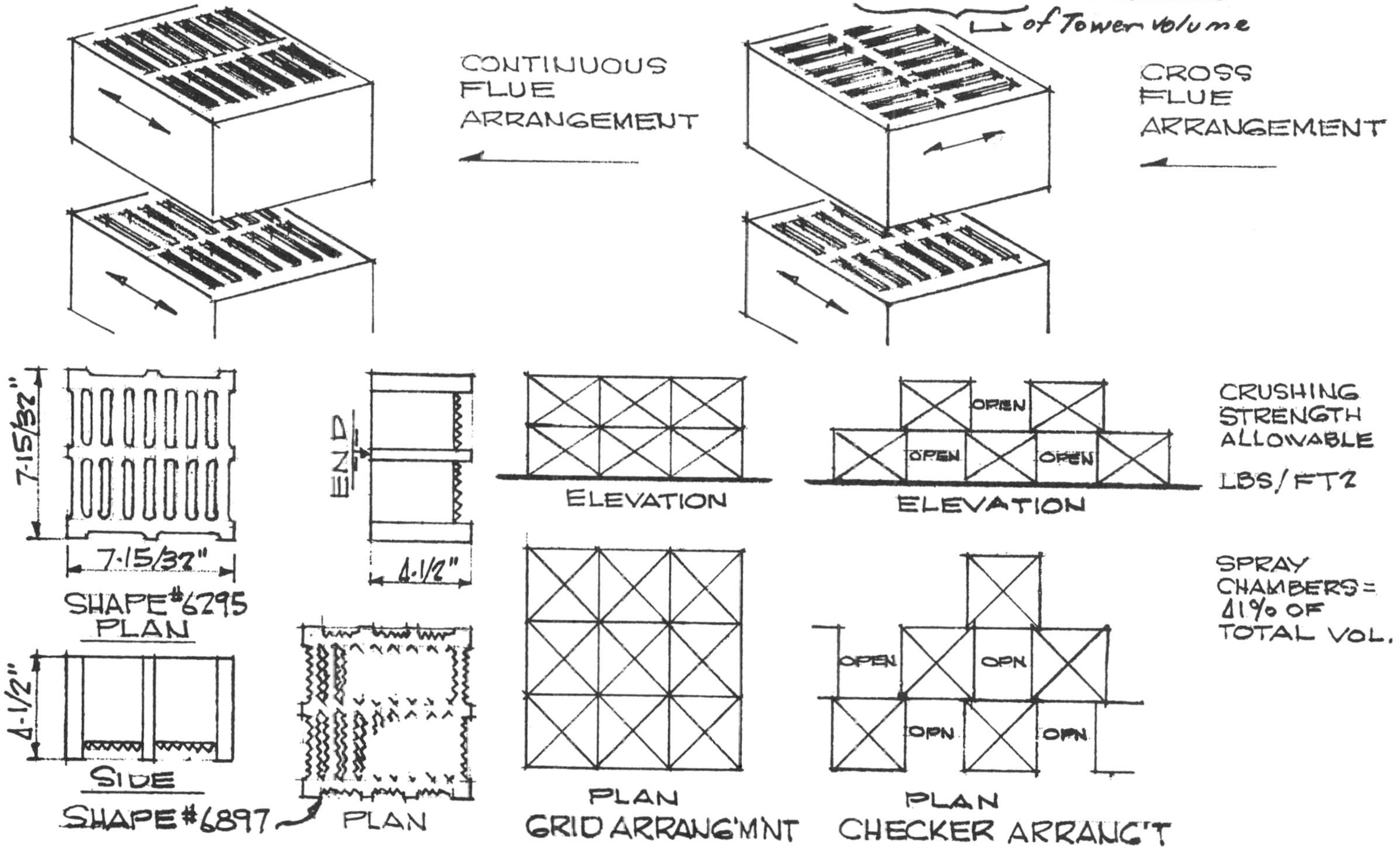

* By permission, General Refractories Co.

Table 9-17

Packing Service Application

Packing Material	General Service Application	Remarks
Glazed and unglazed, Porcelain or Chemical Stoneware	Neutral and acid conditions except hydrofluoric, solvents. Not good in hot caustic (above 70° F.)	Unglazed usual type specified except special requirement of low adsorption on surface. Special ceramics available for mild caustic. Porcelain stronger and more resistant than stoneware.
Carbon	Hot alkali, all acids except nitric, no oxidizing atmospheres.	Stand Thermal shock, low cubic weight
Plastic	Alkali, salts, aqueous and acids depending on resin	Light weight
Steel and other light gauge metals	Hot alkali for steel, other service to suit metals	May be heavier than ceramic, more expensive

restricted, liquid build-up will occur at the plate, reducing efficiency and increasing pressure drop of the tower, and leading to a flooding condition. A lot depends on the material of construction that the system requires; for example, carbon or graphite bar grids, brick grid piers, some steel grating grids and most rubber or plastic covered metal grids have inherently low free cross-sectional areas. These may be less than 65% free area.

In some large towers the support grid is built up from supporting brick arches coming from the bottom (see Figure 9-2. Quite often in large towers, drip point grid tile is used as the supporting first layer, either as a support "plate" itself, or as the support for other packing stacked on it. This initial stacking of the first and perhaps second courses of packing prevents the blocking of free area usually associated with dumping packing on support plates. The resultant net free area "balance" around the support grid or plate and its first two courses of packing (whether dumped or stacked) should be calculated to evaluate the effect on tower performance. Figures 9-1 and 9-4 show a typical arrangement of several support plates.

The weight to be carried by the support plate is the sum of the weight of the packing plus the weight of the flooded liquid volume of the packing voids plus any pressure surges that might be imposed on the system. The effect of side thrust of the packing in reducing the dead packing load on the support should be ignored, as it is an indeterminate figure. Normally each support is required to support only the weights of the packed section directly above it and not those separately supported above or below it. If any intermediate supports or redistributors are not separately supported on the tower wall but rest on the packing itself, the bottom support would carry the entire

tower load of packing as mentioned, plus the weights of intermediate support and redistribution plates. This is not good practice as it complicates the packing and repacking of the tower in addition to possibly imposing heavy loads on the bottom supports.

As a general rule packing heights per support plate should not exceed 12 feet for Raschig rings or 15-20 feet for most other packing shapes. Other types fit within these limits. The mechanical, vibrational and thermal shock loads become important and sometimes affect the tower operation beyond these limits.

Liquid Distribution

Liquid distribution plays an important part in the efficient operation of a packed tower. A good packing from the process viewpoint can be reduced in effectiveness by poor liquid distribution across the top of its upper surface. Poor distribution reduces the effective wetted packing area and promotes liquid channeling.

The final selection of the mechanism of distributing the liquid across the packing depends upon the size of the tower, type of packing (exposed surface, configuration), tendency of packing to divert liquid to tower walls, and materials of construction for distribution. Table 9-19 summarizes a few typical distributors and some pertinent points affecting selection. Figure 9-8 illustrates a few distribution types. Spray nozzles are used, but care must be taken in evaluating the percent of the total liquid that hits the walls and never enters the packing. Full cone nozzles with spray angles which will keep most of the liquid on the center portion of the packing for initial contact will perform quite well.

There are many other types and variations in addition to those listed, although, they are usually special-purpose trays and not necessarily generally adaptable.

Good design generally considers that the streams of liquid should enter onto the top of the packing on 3 to 6-inch square centers for small towers less than 36 inches in diameter, and should number $(D/6)^2$ streams for 36-inches and larger, where D is the tower inside diameter in inches.[22] When the liquid stream spacings exceed 6-inch square pitch, consideration should lean to this figure. Most manufacturers make some type of distributor giving one stream every 6 sq. in. of tower area.

For stacked packing the liquid usually has little tendency to cross-distribute, and thus moves down the tower in the cross-sectional area that it enters. In the dumped condition most packings follow a conical distribution down the tower, with the apex of the cone at the liquid impingement point. After about 12 ft. vertical height, the liquid flows vertically downward unless redistributed. For uniform liquid flow and reduced channeling of gas and liquid with as efficient use of the packing bed as possible the impingement of the liquid onto the bed must be as uniform as possible.

Since the liquid tends to flow to the wall, and any that reaches it is reduced in effective contact possibilities, ne

(Text continued on page 154)

Table 9-18

Packing Type Application

Packing	Application Features	Packing	Application Features
Raschig Rings	Earliest type, usually cheaper per unit cost, but sometimes less efficient than others. Available in widest variety of materials to fit service. Very sound structurally. Usually packed by dumping wet or dry, with larger 4-6-inch sizes sometimes hand stacked. Wall thickness varies between manufacturers, also some dimensions; available surface changes with wall thickness. Produce considerable side thrust on tower. Usually has more internal liquid channeling, and directs more liquid to walls of tower. Low efficiency.	Grid Tile	Available with plain side and bottom or serrated sides and drip-point bottom. Used stacked only. Also used as support layer for dumped packings. Self supporting, no side thrust. Pressure drop lower than most dumped packings and some stacked, lower than some ¼-inch x 1-inch and ¼-inch x 2-inch wood grids, but greater than larger wood grids. Some HTU values compare with those using 1-inch Raschig rings.
Berl Saddles	**More efficient than Raschig Rings in** most applications, but more costly. Packing nests together and creates "tight" spots in bed which promotes channeling but not **as much as Raschig rings. Do not produce** as much side thrust, has lower HTU and unit pressure drops with higher flooding point than Raschig rings. **Easier to break in bed than Raschig rings.**	Teller Rosette (Tellerette)	Available in plastic, lower pressure drop and HTU values, higher flooding limits than Raschig rings or Berl saddles. Very low unit weight, low side thrust.
Intalox Saddles (1) And Other Saddle-Designs	One of most efficient packings, but more costly. Very little tendency or ability to nest and block areas of bed. Gives fairly uniform bed. Higher flooding limits and lower pressure drop than Raschig rings or Berl saddles; lower HTU values for most common systems. Easier to break in bed than Raschig rings, as ceramic.	Spraypak (3)	Compared more with tray type performance than other packing materials. Usually used in large diameter towers, above about 24-inch dia., but smaller to 10-inch dia. available. Metal only.
		Panapak (4)	Available in metal only, compared more with tray type performance than other packing materials. About same HETP as Spraypak for available data. Used in **towers 24 inches and larger. Shows some** performance advantage over bubble cap trays up to 75 psia in fractionation service, but reduced advantages above this pressure or in vacuum service.
Pall Rings (2)	Lower pressure drop (less than half) than Raschig rings, also lower HTU (in some systems also lower than Berl saddles), higher flooding limit. Good liquid distribution, high capacity. Considerable side **thrust on column wall. Available in metal,** plastic and ceramic.	Stedman Packing	Available in metal only, usually used in batch and continuous distillation in small diameter columns not exceeding 24-inches dia. High fractionation ability per unit height, best suited for laboratory work. **Conical and triangular types available.** Not much industrial data available.
Metal Intalox (1) Hy-Pak (1) Chempak (8)	High efficiency, low pressure drop, reportedly good for distillations.	Sulzer, Flexipac, and similar	High efficiency, generally low pressure drop, well suited for distillation of clean systems, very low HETP.
		Goodloe Packing (5) and Wire mesh Packing	Available in metal and plastic, used in large and small towers for distillation, absorption, scrubbing, liquid extraction. High efficiency, low HETP, low pressure drop. Limited data available.
Spiral Rings	Usually installed as stacked, taking advantage of internal whirl of gas-liquid and offering extra contact surface over Raschig ring, Lessing rings or crosspartition rings. Available in single, double and triple internal spiral designs. Higher pressure drop. Wide variety of performance data not available.	Cannon Packing	**Available in metal only, low pressure drop, low HETP, flooding limit probably higher than Raschig rings. Not much literature data available. Used mostly in small laboratory or semi-plant studies.**
Lessing Rings	Not much performance data available, but in general slightly better than Raschig ring, pressure drop slightly higher. High side wall thrust.	Wood Grids	Very low pressure drop, low efficiency of contact, high HETP or HTU, best used in atmospheric towers of square or rectangular shape. Very low cost.
Cross-Partition Rings	Usually used stacked, and as first layers on support grids for smaller packing above. Pressure drop relatively low, channeling reduced for comparative stacked packings. No side wall thrust.	Dowpac FN-90 (6)	Plastic packing of very low pressure drop (just greater than wood slats), transfer **Coefficients about same as 2-inch Raschig** rings. Most useful applications in gas cooling systems or biological trickling filters.
		Poly Grid (7)	Plastic packing of very low pressure drop, developed for water-air cooling tower applications.

(1) Trade name, Norton Co.
(2) Introduced by Badische Anilin and Sodafabrik, Ludwigshafen am Rhein
(3) Trade name of Denholme Inc., Licensed by British Government

(4) Trade name of Packed Column Corp.
(5) Trade name Packed Column Corp.
(6) **Trade name of The Dow Chemical Co.**
(7) **Trade name The Fluor Products Co.**
(8) Trade name Chem-Pro Equip. Corp.

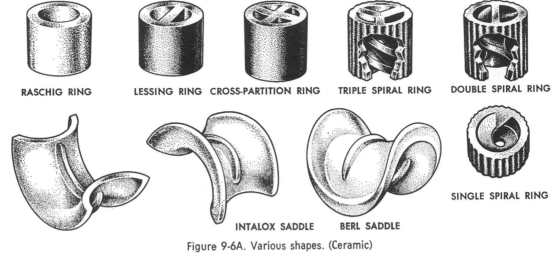

RASCHIG RING   LESSING RING   CROSS-PARTITION RING   TRIPLE SPIRAL RING   DOUBLE SPIRAL RING

INTALOX SADDLE   BERL SADDLE   SINGLE SPIRAL RING

Figure 9-6A. Various shapes. (Ceramic)

Figure 9-6B. Raschig rings. (Ceramic, Carbon and Metal)

Figure 9-6D. Berl saddles, dumped.

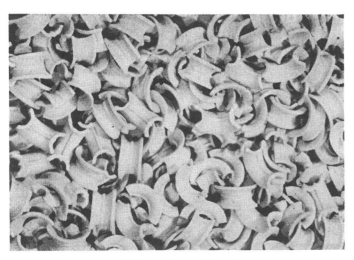

Figure 9-6C. Intalox saddles, dumped.

Figure 9-6E. Pall rings, dumped.

Figure 9-6. Packing shapes.

(Figure continued on next page)

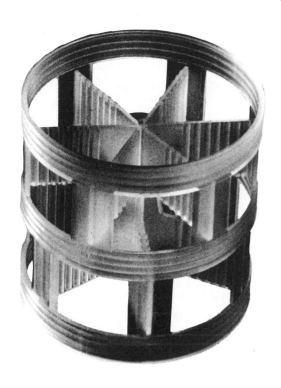

Figure 9-6F. Koch Plastic Flexiring. (Courtesy of Koch Engineering Co., Inc., Bul. PFR-1.)

gure 9-6G. Metal Hy-Pak®. (By permission, Norton Company, Bul. ?-11.)

Figure 9-6H. Plastic Pall Ring. Note: Ballast Ring® of Glitsch, Inc. is quite similar. (By permission, Norton Co., Bul. DC-11.)

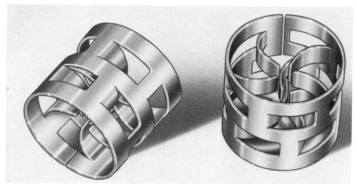

Figure 9-6I. Metal Pall Ring. Note: Ballast Ring® of Glitsch, Inc. is quite similar, also Koch Engineering Flexiring®. (By permission, Norton Co., Bul. N-60D.)

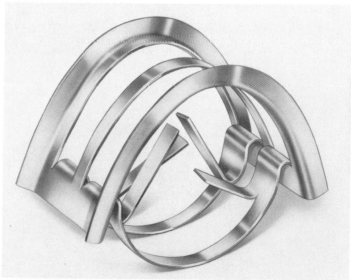

Figure 9-6J. Metal Intalox®. (By permission, Norton Co., Bul. N-60D.)

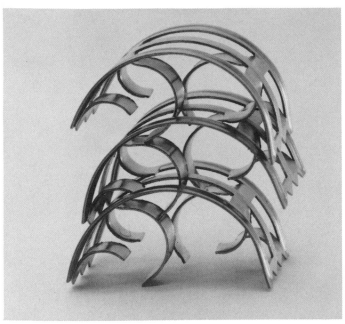

Figure 9-6K. Chempak® packing. (By permission, Chem-Pro Equipment Corp., licensed from Dr. Max Leva.)

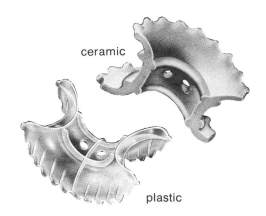

ceramic

plastic

Figure 9-6L. Super Intalox® saddles. Note Ballast Saddle® of Glitsch Inc. is similar, also Koch Engineering Flexisaddle®. (By permission, Norton Co., Bul. N-60D.)

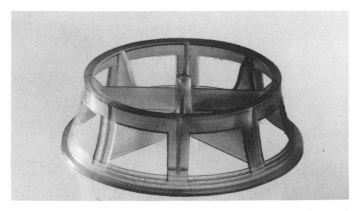

Figure 9-6M. Cascade Mini-ring®. (By permission, Mass Transfer, Inc.)

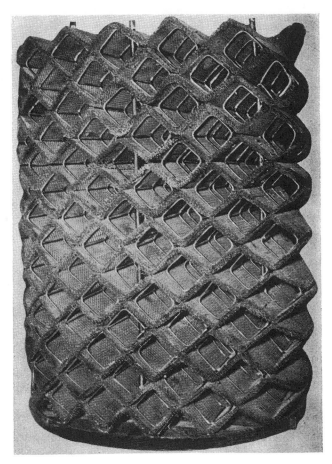

Figure 9-6N. Panapak packing for a 6-foot diameter column (original design).

Figure 9-6O. Panapak packing for a 6-foot diameter column, latest design) (By permission Packed Column Corp.)

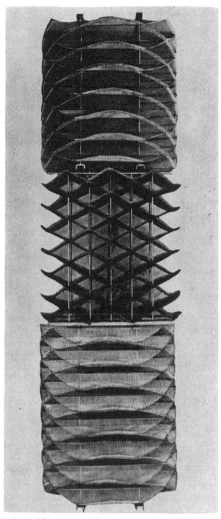

Figure 9-6P. Cartridges 8½ feet high of 32-inch I.D. spraypak packing. (By permission Denholme, Inc., Bul. No. 8.)

Figure 9-6R. Teller Rosette. (By permission Dr. A. J. Teller.)

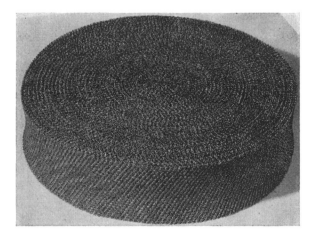

Figure 9-6Q. Goodloe packing. (By permission Packed Column Corp.)

Figure 9-6S. Koch Sulzer packing. (By permission, Koch Engineering, Inc.)

Figure 9-6T. Koch Flexipac packing. (By permission, Koch Engineering, Inc., Bul. KFP-1.)

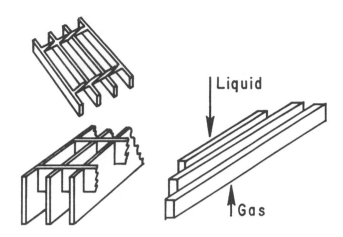

Figure 9-7A. Bar-grid support.

Figure 9-7B. (Drawing and table below). Perforated support plates. (By permission U. S. Stoneware Co.)

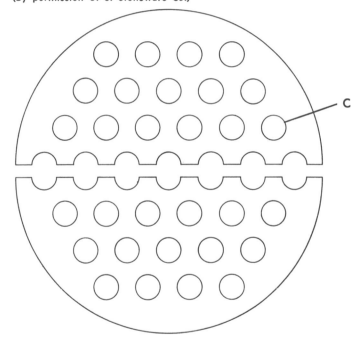

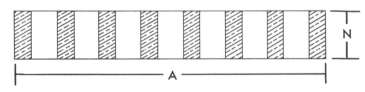

DIMENSIONS PERFORATED SUPPORT PLATE

Tower Diameter in Inches......	12	15	18	20	24	30	36	42	48	60
Diameter of Plate "A"........	11	14	17	19	23	29	35	40	45½	57½
Height of Plate "N"..........	1	1	1	1	1	1½	2	2½	3	4
Diameter of Holes "C"........	1	1¼	1¼	1½	2	2	2½	3	3½	3½
Number of Holes.............	22	31	31	38	37	61	61	55	61	101
Approximate Weight (lbs.).....	16	19	23	28	35	85	150	185	260	425

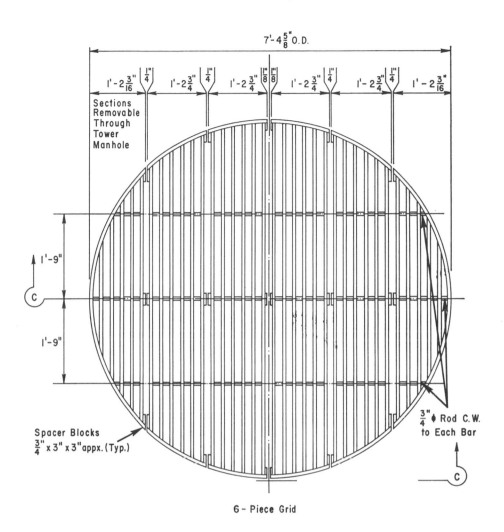

7'-4⅝" O.D.

1'-2³⁄₁₆" | ¼" | 1'-2¾" | ¼" | 1'-2¾" | ⅛" ⅛" | 1'-2¾" | ¼" | 1'-2¾" | ¼" | 1'-2³⁄₁₆"

Sections
Removable
Through
Tower
Manhole

1'-9"

C

1'-9"

Spacer Blocks
¾" x 3" x 3" appx. (Typ.)

¾" ⌀ Rod C.W.
to Each Bar

C

6- Piece Grid

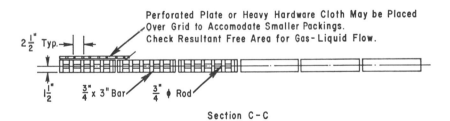

Perforated Plate or Heavy Hardware Cloth May be Placed
Over Grid to Accomodate Smaller Packings.
Check Resultant Free Area for Gas- Liquid Flow.

2½" Typ.

1½"

¾" x 3" Bar   ¾" ⌀ Rod

Section C-C

Figure 9-7C. Bar-grid support plate, typical details.

Figure 9-7 continued on next page

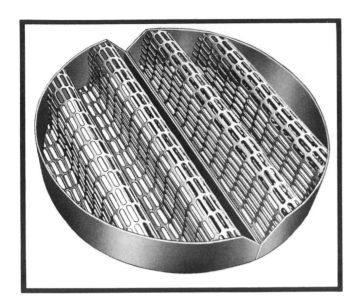

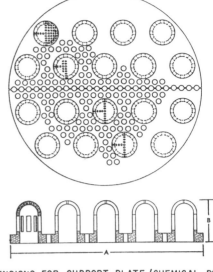

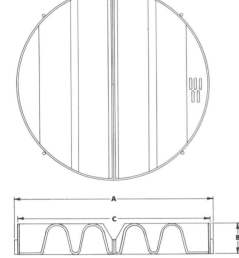

DIMENSIONS FOR SUPPORT PLATE (CHEMICAL PORCELAIN)

Tower Diam. (Inside)	Plate Diam. "A"	No. of Risers	Overall Height "B"	Per Cent of Free Area	Packing Size (Min.)	Support Ledge (Min.) ‡	Approx. Net Wt. (lbs.)
12"	11-1/4"	4	5-3/4"	52.5	1/2"	3/4"	10
14"	13-1/4"	4	6-7/8"	58.0	1/2"	3/4"	14
15"	14-1/4"	4	6-7/8"	54.6	1/2"	3/4"	16
16"	15-1/4"	4	7"	56.8	1/2"	3/4"	18
18"	17-1/4"	4	7-9/16"	53.0	1/2"	3/4"	28
20"	19"	4	7-9/16"	51.4	3/4"	1"	30
24"	23"	6	7-11/16"	54.6	3/4"	1"	38
30"	29"	10	7-7/8"	55.2	3/4"	1"	76
*36"	35"	18	8"	64.2	1"	1"	98
*42"	40-1/2"	20	8-1/4"	60.2	1"	1-1/2"	180
*48"	46-1/2"	24	8-1/2"	52.9	1-1/2"	1-1/2"	292
*60"	58"	40	9"	60.6	1-1/2"	2"	400

*For these sizes use no more than 10 feet of packed depth unless designed for specific load requirement.

‡In order to avoid blocking any free area of the support plate the maximum width of the support ledge should not be appreciably greater than the minimum width shown. In prefabricated ceramic towers, 24" and 30" towers have a 1½" support ledge, the 36" tower a 1¾" ledge and the 42" and 48" towers a 2" support ledge.

Figure 9-7D. Typical efficient metal and porcelain support plate designs for gas injection into packing. Designs also available in plastic—FRP, polypropylene, PVC, etc. (By permission, Norton Co., Bul. TA-80.)

MODEL 818 "GAS - INJECTION" METAL SUPPORT PLATE						
TOWER I.D.		DIA. OVER SPACERS A	HEIGHT B	PLATE DIA. C	SUPPORT LEDGE (MIN.)	MIN. DIA. OF ACCESS	APPROX. NET WEIGHT (LBS.)*
INCHES	MM						
12	305	------	4½"	11¾"	¾"	8"	7
13¼	337	------	4½"	12¾"	¾"	9"	8
14¼	362	------	4½"	13¾"	¾"	9"	9
15¼	388	------	4½"	14¾"	¾"	10"	10
17¼	438	------	4½"	16¾"	¾"	10"	11
19¼	489	------	4½"	18¾"	1"	11"	12
21¼	540	------	4½"	20¾"	1"	12"	17
23¼	591	------	4½"	22¾"	1"	13"	19
29¼	743	------	4½"	28¾"	1"	16"	25
36	914	35½"	4½"	34¾"	1"	14"	40
42	1067	41½"	4½"	40¾"	1½"	16"	52

*Weights shown are for standard construction and material thickness, carbon steel.

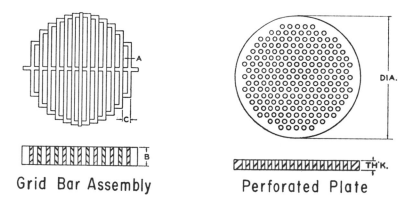

Grid Bar Assembly   Perforated Plate

Haveg Packing Supports

Tower Dia.	GRID BARS					PERFORATED PLATE				
	No.	Size			%·Free			Holes		%Free
		A	B	C	Area	Dia.	Th'k.	No.	Dia.	Area
12"	7	½	2½	1½	48	13½	1	33	¾	6
15"	9	¾	2½	1½	30	13⅝	1¼	55	¾	10
18"	9	¾	2½	1½	34	16½	1½	65	¾	8
20"	9	¾	2½	1½	37	19½	1⅝	95	¾	9
2'	13	¾	3½	1½	39	23¼	1¾	134	¾	9
2'-6"	15	¾	3½	1½	36	29¼	2	188	¾	7
3'	19	¾	3½	1½	38	35	2	299	¾	9
3'-6"	21	¾	3½	1¾	41	41¼	2	402	¾	9
4'	27	¾	5	1¾	41	47	2¼	544	¾	10
5'	31	¾	5	1¾	45	58½	2½	843	1	19
6'	37	¾	5	1¾	46	71	3	1277	1	20
7'	43	¾	6	1¾	46	..	...	....	...	..
8'	51	¾	6	1¾	47	..	...	....	...	..
9'	57	¾	6	1¾	48	..	...	....	...	..
10'	61	¾	6	1¾	50	..	...	....	...	..

Note: All Dimensions are in inches unless Otherwise Noted.
Perforated Plate Free Area Should Be increased when Possible

Figure 9-7E. Reinforced plastic support plates. (By permission, Haveg Corp., Bulletin F-7.)

(Figure continued on next page)

Figure 9-7F. Typical me... full cross-section redistri... utor. (By permission, N... ton Co., Bul. TA-80.)

Metal "Rosette" Redistributor

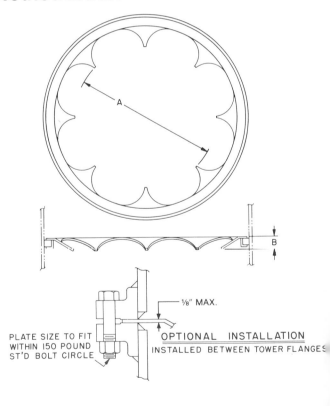

MODEL 858 "ROSETTE" METAL REDISTRIBUTOR				
TOWER I.D.		PLATE DIA.	DIAMETER A	HEIGHT B
INCHES	MM			
4	102	OUTSIDE DIAMETER OF SEALING STRIP WILL BE 1/16 INCH GREATER THAN TOWER I.D.	$2\frac{13}{16}$"	$\frac{1}{4}$"
$6\frac{1}{16}$	154		$4\frac{7}{16}$"	$\frac{1}{4}$"
$7\frac{15}{16}$	202		$5\frac{7}{8}$"	$\frac{7}{16}$"
10	254		$7\frac{5}{8}$"	$\frac{3}{8}$"
$11\frac{15}{16}$	303		$8\frac{1}{2}$"	$\frac{9}{16}$"
$13\frac{1}{8}$"	333		$9\frac{1}{2}$"	$\frac{5}{8}$"
15	381		$11\frac{1}{4}$"	$\frac{11}{16}$"
$16\frac{7}{8}$"	429		$12\frac{3}{8}$"	$\frac{13}{16}$"
$18\frac{13}{16}$	478		$13\frac{3}{8}$"	1"
$21\frac{1}{4}$"	540		$15\frac{7}{8}$"	1"
$22\frac{5}{8}$"	575		$16\frac{1}{2}$"	$1\frac{1}{4}$"

⅛" MAX.

PLATE SIZE TO FIT WITHIN 150 POUND ST'D BOLT CIRCLE

OPTIONAL INSTALLATION
INSTALLED BETWEEN TOWER FLANGES

Figure 9-7G. Metal Rosette style redistributor. (By permission, Nort... Co., Bul. TA-80.)

Table 9-19
Effect of Liquid Distributor Performance in Packed Towers

Type	Usually Acceptable in	Limitations	Other Conditions	Relative Tower Performance using 1-in. Ceramic Raschig rings	
				Stacked	Dumped
(1) Level Troughs, distributing stream every 4″	Towers through 42 Inch dia.	Difficult to install level. Can limit gas flow in large towers.	Cheap, can be improved by V-Notching sides. No splashing of liquid.	1.0*	1.2
(2) Single inlet pipe dumping liquid on top of packing, 9″ off top.	Small towers not over 18 Inch dia.	In large towers top section packing ineffective due to diversion of liquid to walls.	Cheap, easy to install. Splashing of liquid important to performance.	0.16*	0.63*
(3) Single inlet as (2), except liquid impinged on flat plate rather than packing.	Small towers not over 18 Inch—24 Inch dia.	In large towers essentially same objection as (2)	Cheap, easy to install. Splashing of liquid important.	0.76*	0.63
(4) Single inlet spray nozzle, full cone, non-atomizing.	Small towers not over 36 Inch dia. Takes several nozzles for large towers.	Gas velocities must be low to keep down liquid entrainment. Often large amount of liquid hits wall and is ineffective.	Angle of spray must be small, and not too high above packing for effective use.	0.3	0.5
(5) Single inlet pipes impinging about ½ inch off packing surface.	Small towers not over 18 inch.	Severly limits liquid in horizontal movement near top of packing. Large towers very in-effective due to reduced splash distribution.	Cheap, easy to install. Very reduced splashing of liquid.	<0.16	0.59* (small towers only)
(6) Multiple inlet pipes impinging 6 inch off packing, 4 inch centers.	Small and large diameter towers.	Too much splash may create liquid entrainment in out-going gas. Can cause considerable internal piping problems.	Not expensive, splashing of liquid important.	1.0	1.2*
(7) Single inlet sparger pipe with holes on 1 inch centers extend across tower.	Small towers not over 24 inch dia.	Gives fair distribution in one direction but limits at 90°. Not good in large towers.	Cheap, easy to install. Splashing of liquid important.	0.50	0.70
(8) Cross pipe inlet with 90° arms, holes on 1 inch centers extend across tower.	Towers to 42 inch—48 inch dia.	Does not give good distribution at 45° to arms in large diameter towers.	Cheap, better than some more expensive types. Splashing of liquid important.	0.70	0.85
(9) Spider pipe inlet with multiple arms, holes spaced to give distribution points on 4 to 6 inch squares throughout tower crosssection.	Large Towers above 42 inch dia.	Too bulky for small towers.	Splashing of liquid neces-sary but not all-impor-tant. Some designs may induce liquid entrainment in gas.	1.0	1.2
(10) Circular pipe inlet with holes spaced to spread liquid from center to about 60% of diameter.	Large towers above 36 inch dia.	May create liquid en-trainment if holes point above 45°.	Splashing of liquid neces-sary but not all-impor-tant.	0.9	1.1
(11) Inlet terminates at face of tower, no extending pipe.	No tower	Creates channeling down wall of tower. Poor dis-tribution pattern.		0.05	0.2
(12) Flat plate sealed at edges, with holes on 4 to 6 inch spacing for dual passage of gas and liquid, inlet liquid at edge or center wall.	Small towers to 24 inch dia.	Uneven level causes all liquid to enter one sec-tion of tower in prefer-ence to others. This is too great a problem in large towers. Not too good for liquid overload.	Velocity of gas through holes must be kept low.	0.9	1.0
(13) Flat plate with liquid containing rim, holes through piers of various levels, gas around outside of plate, between plate and tower shell.	Small and large towers with low liquid loads, or low varying liquid loads, clean liquid.	Not good for high liquid. Holes may be too small for solids or dirt and tend to plug.	Suitable in ceramic, metal or plastic.	1.2	1.2
(14) Flat plate with liquid through holes, gas through risers.	Small and large towers with medium to large liquid loads.	Not good for very low liquid load, as all holes might not be effective, leading to poor distri-bution.	Suitable in ceramic, metal or plastic. High liquid loads can restrict gas passage.	1.2	1.2
(15) Notched troughs us-ing one or more to receive inlet liquid and several be-low to redistribute liquid every 3 to 6 inches in more or less square pattern.	Large towers 42 inch dia. and greater. Install through manway if neces-sary. Good for large liquid and gas rates.	Difficult to handle in small tower. Should be level, but slight variation han-dled by V-notches.	Suitable in ceramics, metal, plastic. Not im-paired by suspended mat-ter to any great extent.	1.2	1.2

* Compiled from data in M. Leva, *Tower Packings and Packed Tower Design*, 2nd Ed. pg. 20, U.S. Stoneware Co., Akron, Ohio (1953) Ref. 35, by permission.   Other values estimated by this author.

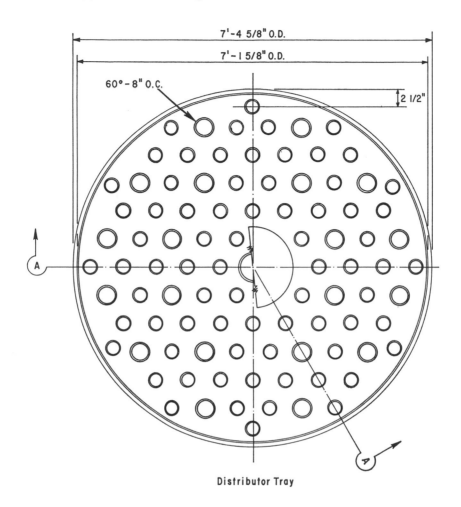

Distributor Tray

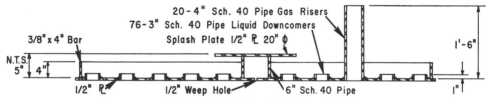

Section A-A
Figure 9-8A. Multilevel distributor with splash plate.

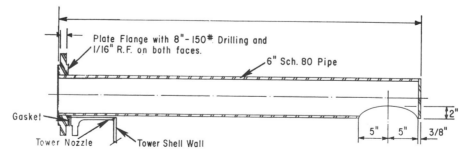

Figure 9-8B. Inlet pipe for distributor Figure 9-8A.

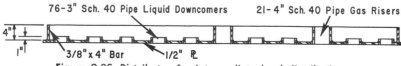

Figure 9-8C. Distributor for intermediate level distribution.

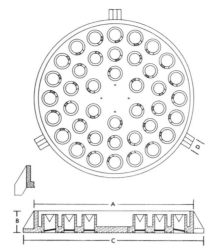

DIMENSIONS FOR "WEIR FLOW" DISTRIBUTOR (CERAMIC)

Tower Dia.	Plate Dia. "A"	Overall Dia. "B"	Overall Dia. "C"	Width of Lugs "D"	No. of Weirs	Flow (Gallons Per Minute)	Approx. Net Weight
24"*	20"	23"	5¾"	3"	8	16	55
30"	25"	29"	5¼"	3"	18	36	70
36"	30"	35"	5¼"	3"	18	36	120
42"	35"	41"	5½"	3"	36	72	150
48"	40"	46"	5½"	3"	40	80	190
60"	50"	58"	6"	4"	48	96	270

*Raised lugs standard on this size only.

Figure 9-8D. Weir-flow distributor. (By permission U. S. Stoneware Co. Bul. TA-40.)

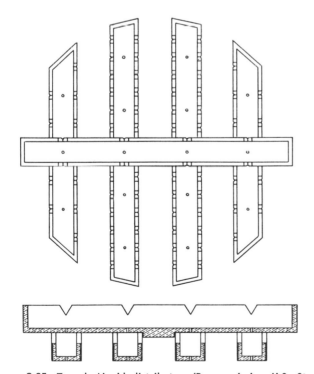

Figure 9-8E. Trough Liquid distributor. (By permission U.S. Stone-ware Co.)

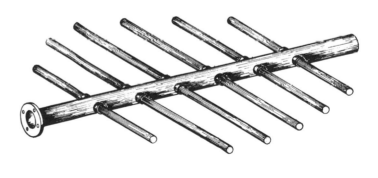

Figure 9-8F. Typical design for inlet liquid distributor using holes (orifices) on underside of distribution pipe. Note: Number of side pipes adjusted to provide uniform stream entry across packing area, thus avoiding dropping any stream closer than 3" to wall of column.

large percentage (not over 10 percent) of the total liquid should enter the packing at the top packing-wall circumference, or within 5-10 percent of the tower diameter from the tower wall. With this approach the bulk of the liquid starts down the tower somewhat away from the wall.

When using plate-type distributors, an out-of-level condition can cause serious channeling of liquid down one part of the column and gas up the other. Provision should be made for self-adjusting levels of liquid, such as v-notches, which will allow for shifting of tower alignment, brick walls, etc. Gas velocities through the tower at the point of leaving the packing and/or through the distributor plate gas risers should be low to reduce liquid carry-through. This can be calculated by using liquid entrainment limitations. From limited tests it appears that there is essentially no entrainment off a packing until the flooding point is reached.

The various packings have different characteristics for distributing the liquid throughout the bed. Leva[40] shows the results of Baker, et al.[8] which illustrates the effect of various types of distribution on the liquid pattern inside the packing. A general summary is given in Table 9-20.

Redistributors

The liquid coming down through the packing and on the wall of the tower should be redistributed after a bed depth of approximately 3 tower diameters for Raschig

rings and 5-10 tower diameters for saddle packings. As a guide, Raschig rings usually have a maximum of 10-15 feet of packing per section, while saddle packing can use 12-20 feet. This redistribution brings the liquid off the wall and outer portions of the tower and directs it toward the center area of the tower for a new start at distribution and contact in the next lower section.

The height of packing before redistribution is a function of the liquid flow pattern through the packing, and this is a function of the size and type of packing. Some towers have 20-30 feet of packing with no redistribution; however, the reasons may be economic as well as operational. The exact amount of performance efficiency sacrificed is subject to question, although with 20-35 percent of the liquid flowing down the walls after 10 feet of ring packing depth, it appears reasonable to consider that performance is lost for most of this liquid. Redistribution is usually not necessary for stacked bed packings as the liquid flows essentially in vertical streams.

Physically the redistributions may be a simple and relatively inefficient side wiper as in Figure 9-7G and 9-9; a conventional support grid or plate plus regular distribution plate as used at the top; a combination unit similar to

Table 9-20*

Liquid Distribution Patterns in Packed Columns
(Data in 6-inch, 12-inch and 24-inch Dia. Towers)

Packing	Tower Dia. In.	Type Liquid Feed	Per Cent Liquid Distribution in Inner ¾ Tower Area	
			2 Feet from Top	8 Feet from Top
½ Inch Raschig Rings	6	Center Point	40	40
	12	Center Point	90	78 (4 Feet down)
	12	4 Point	70	65 (4 Feet down)
1 Inch Raschig Rings	12	Center Point	95	70 (4 Feet down)
	12	4 Point	70	60 (4 Feet down)
½ Inch Berl Saddles	6	Center Point	60	50
	12	Center Point	95	88 (4 Feet down)
	12	4 Point	70	60 (4 Feet down)
1 Inch Berl Saddles	12	Center Point	85	65 (4 Feet down)
	12	4 Point	75	55 (4 Feet down)
1 Inch Lessing Rings	12	Center Point	90	55
	12	4 Point	70	55
	12	19 Point	70	50
	24	Center Point	100	90
	24	12 Point	80	70
½ Inch Glass Rings	6	Center Point	90	70 (7 Feet down)
	6	Center Point	83	75 (7 Feet down) 3 Feet/sec., air
	6	4 Point	75	70 (7 Feet down)
	6	4 Point	75	75 (7 Feet down, 3 Feet/sec., air)
½ Inch Spheres	6	Center Point	83	85 (4 Feet down)
	6	Center Point	90	90 (4 Feet down, 2.5 Feet/sec., air)

* Compiled from M. Leva, *Tower Packings and Packed Tower Design,* 2nd Ed., pg. 21, U. S. Stoneware Co., Akron, Ohio (1953), Ref. 40, by permission.

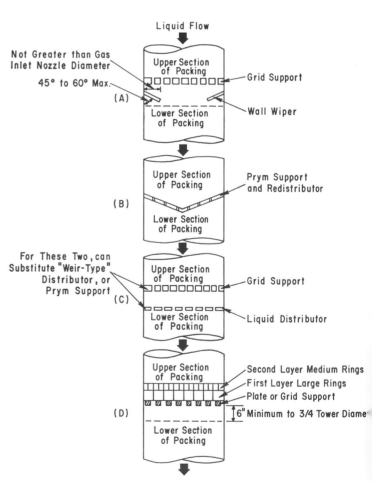

Figure 9-9. Liquid redistribution in packed towers.

Figure 9-10A. Hold-down plate for packed tower. (By permission U.S. Stoneware Co.)

Prym support and distributor; or a support plate as shown in Figures 9-7D and E.

The possibility of causing flooding in the tower at the redistribution point must not be overlooked, as too much restriction by a wall wiper, or by packing on a plate can be the focal point for poor tower performance. The velocity conditions should be checked for the smallest cross-section.

Hold-down Grids

To reduce ceramic or carbon packing breakage and blowing out of light weight plastic packing when a tower surges due to gas pockets, uneven loading, etc., it is sometimes helpful to have heavy hardware cloth or other stiff but open grid resting (floating) at the top of the tower and on the top of the packing (Figure 9-10A and B). This grating or grid must be heavy enough to hold down about the top five feet of packing, yet must be able to move down as the packing settles, always resting at the top of the packing. If the packing is restricted in upward movement, it usually will not be crushed. If the packing does break and crush, the bed settles and its characteristics change considerably.

Bed-limiters are usually lighter weight and must be bolted in place, not resting on the packing.

They are used with metal and plastic packings to prevent the bed lifting, or the entrainment of individual pieces of packing from being carried out of the tower. These packings usually do not break, and as long as the bed temperature is below the softening or deflection point for plastic packing, the bed should not compress or consolidate to create operational limitations.

Packing Installation

Stacked

Stacked packing is a hand operation and rather costly. It is avoided where possible except for the initial layers on

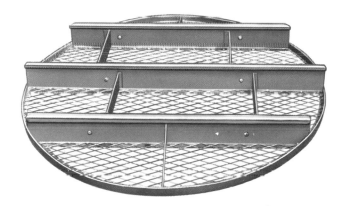

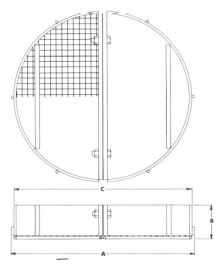

METAL HOLD - DOWN PLATE							
TOWER I.D.		DIA. OVER SPACERS	HEIGHT	PLATE DIA.	NUMBER OF	MIN. DIA. OF	APPROX. NET WEIGHT
INCHES	MM	A	B	C	PIECES	ACCESS	(LBS.)*
17¼	438	17"	4"	16½"	2	10"	36
19¼	489	19"	4"	18½"	2	11"	45
21¼	540	21"	4"	20½"	2	12"	52
23¼	591	23"	4"	22½"	2	13"	59
29¼	743	28½"	4"	27½"	2	16"	98
36	914	35¼"	4"	35¼"	3	14"	140
42	1067	41¼"	4"	41¼"	3	16"	188

*Weights shown are for standard construction and material thickness.

Figure 9-10B. Typical metal hold-down plate for use with ceramic or carbon packing; it rests directly on top of packing. Note: Bed-limiters are similar in design in metal or plastic, bolted to column wall above packing. (By permission, Norton Co., Bul. TA-80.)

supports. Liquid distributed on a stacked packing usually flows straight down through the packing immediately adjacent to the point of contact. There is very little horizontal liquid flow. Packing patterns perform differently, and are illustrated in Figure 9-11A-C.

Dumped

Dumping is the most common method of packing installation. If possible, the tower should be filled with water for ceramic packings after installation of the bottom support arrangement, including any stacked rings, and the loose packing floated down to rest on top of the support. The fall should be as gentle as possible since broken packing tightens the bed and increases pressure drop.

One manufacturer[22] suggests loading ceramic ring type packing using a sheet metal cone in the tower thereby causing the rings to slide off the cone and fill to the edges first. The cone is lifted as the rings are floated or dropped in. This technique is believed to reduce the tendency for rings to channel liquid to the tower wall. Saddle-type packing does not require the use of the cone.

In packing a tower dry, high hydrostatic heads are thus avoided on joint connections; however, extra care must be taken to avoid breakage. The packing will probably settle after installation, but it should not be pressed or tamped in place. This will cause extra breakage. The packing should not be allowed to fall more than two feet to the bed surface. It should be dumped at random to avoid developing any pattern. The dry packed tower will be more dense than the wet packed and should not be pressed or tamped in place. The pressure drop for dry packed beds can be as much as 50-60 percent greater than for wet packed.

Metal and plastic packing can be dumped dry into the tower; however, reasonable care must be exercised.

Repacking a tower will usually show a variation in pressure drop. For small 8-inch dia. units the variation may be as much as 100 percent. In larger columns 24-inches dia. and up, this variation is noticed, but only to about 50 percent.

Packing Selection and Performance

Any of the available packings will usually perform the operation of another; the differences being in efficiency of contact, expressed as HTU, HETP or Kga, and pressure drop for the *particular* packing-fluid system. Therefore, system data is very important and helpful in selecting a packing. When it is not available, an effort should be made to find any analogous system as far as process type, fluids, physical properties, pressure and temperature conditions, etc. If this is not possible, then the best judgment of the designer must be used.

The number of packing sizes, types (designs), and materials of construction currently available to the de-

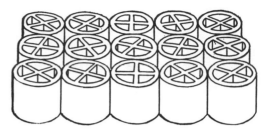

Figure 9-11A. Square pattern(S)

Figure 9-11B. Diamond pattern(D)

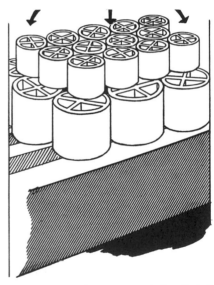

Figure 9-11C. Packing assembly. (By permission U. S. Stoneware Co.)

Figure 9-11. Stacked packing patterns

signer has increased considerably. To select a packing for a process application requires a weighing of information and an evaluation of the closest comparable data. The key factors to consider:

1. *Contacting Efficiency, Expressed as Kg_a, HTU, HETP*

   When specific data on system is not available, and often it will not be, then close comparisons should be

sought. If nothing more can be done, tabulate the relative efficiency for other systems and apply judgement to select a value.

2. *Packing Size*

This affects contact efficiency; usually, the smaller packing is more efficient; however, pressure drop increases.

As a general guide, use:

Packing Size, Nominal, inches	Column Diam., inches
½″ — ⅝″	6″ — 12″
⅝″ — 1″	12″ — 18″
¾″ — 1″	18″ — 24″
1″ — 2″	24″ — 48″
1½ — 2″ — 3″	36″ — larger

3. *Pressure Drop*

This is important to most column designs. Recognize that pressure drop will increase due to:

a. Unsteady column operations
b. Increased liquid/vapor loads
c. Breakage of ceramic packings (this can be serious)
d. Compaction/Deflection of plastic packings

4. *Materials of Construction*

Give careful consideration to fluids, temperatures of systems, aeration. Plastic materials may be quite good for the application; however, carefully determine the recommended *long-term heat deflection* characteristics. With time, many plastics will deform, thereby changing the packing bed characteristics, and the column pressure drop. As a general rule, do not select a plastic to operate at any time within 50° F of the softening or deflection temperature of the plastic.

5. *Particle versus Compact Preformed Packings*

Particle packings are usually (not always) less efficient than the pre-packaged/preformed assemblies; however, particle types are generally more flexible in loading and the ability to handle "dirty" fluids.

Cost of the packing and its effect on the system costs must be considered, as some packings are much more expensive than others, yet produce very little improved performance. Table 9-18 presents some comparative information. The most common packings and hence the ones with the most available data are Raschig rings, Berl saddles, several saddle types and Pall Rings® (Norton Co.) or equivalent.

As a guide with only rough experimental backing, the ratio of maximum random packing size to tower diameter is

Raschig rings:	1:20 (Reference 5)
	1: 8 (Reference 52)
Berl saddles:	1:10
Intalox saddles:	1: 8 to 1:10 (Reference 6)

The 1:8 ratio is in more common use for most packings; however recent data indicated that Raschig rings require a larger ratio approaching 1:20.

These ratios are useful in dealing with small towers, and serve as guides for the borderline cases of others. There are no guides to the smallest sized packing to place in a tower. However, ½-inch is about the smallest ceramic used with ¾-inch and 1-inch being the most popular. Operating and pressure drop factors will usually control this selection.

Packed towers are not limited to small units; in fact the largest processing towers for absorption and stripping operations are probably in these towers. Some units are 40 and 50 feet in diameter using 2-inch and larger packings to heights of 20-30 ft. Other units are 5-6 feet in diameter with 60 feet of packing. Towers with a 24-inch dia. and smaller are most often used with packing rather than trays.

Minimum Liquid Wetting Rates

In order to feed enough liquid into the tower to effectively place a wet film of liquid over all the packing, a minimum wetting rate (MWR) has been evaluated for guidance in operation and design. Morris and Jackson[52] recommended the MWR shown in Table 9-21.

A minimum liquid rate for any tower packing is used by some designers as 1500 lbs. liquid/(hr.) (sq. ft. tower) referencing to liquid of properties of water.

$$L_{Min} = (MWR) (a_t) \qquad (9-1)$$

where: L_{Min} = liquid rate, cu.ft./(hr.) (sq. ft. cross-section)

MWR = value of minimum wetting rate from Table 9-21

Table 9-21

Minimum Wetting Rate*

Packing	MWR Rate, Liquid, cu.ft./(hr.) (sq.ft. Cross Sect.) Packing Surface area per tower volume, sq.ft./cu.ft.
Rings (Raschig, Lessing, etc.), thru 3-inches Dia.	0.85
Grid Type (Wooden, etc.) (pitch 2 inches)	0.85
All Packings larger than 3 inches	1.3
Polished metal packings and poor wetting surfaces (some plastics, glazed porcelain, etc.)	1.3, estimate to 2.5 Preferably etch surfaces to reduce problem).

* Compiled by permission from Morris and Jackson, *Absorption Towers*, Butterworth Scientific Pub. (1953) London and Imperial Chemical Industries, Ltd., Ref. 52.

a_t = packing surface area per unit volume, sq. ft./cu.ft.

Another expression of "reasonable minimum wetting rate,"[48] is given in Table 9-22. The surface characteristics of the packing material are important in the type of liquid film (or droplets) that flow across, around, and drip off of the surface. The better the specific liquid wets the packing surface and forms a moving film the more efficient will be the packing for distillation, absorption, etc. In general, from the table it can be noted that the surfaces that tend to wet easily have the lower minimum wetting rates. The data given in Table 9-22 does not agree too well with the recommendations of Table 9-21. Although there is no validation, it is believed that the information in Table 9-22 is more current and represents a more recent evaluation of available data. However, the fact that the results are not identified by packing design types, suggests there probably still needs to be more evaluation of this factor.

Note that when packing is changed from one material of construction to another, it is important to recognize the effect on minimum wetting rate for the new condition.

Loading Point—Loading Region

Examination of Figure 9-12 shows the pressure drop of the packed bed with gas flow and no liquid flow as the dry curve. As liquid is added to the top of the packing the effect on pressure drop is immediately noticeable. Note that the lower part of all the liquid rate curves parallel the slope of the "dry" bed curve; however, at a point a noticeable change in the slope of the pressure drop curve occurs. This is attributed to the transition

of liquid hold-up in the bed from being only a function of liquid rate to a condition of liquid hold-up also being a function of gas rate. Although the change seems to occur for some packings at a point, it is difficult to determine accurately for all packings, and is perhaps

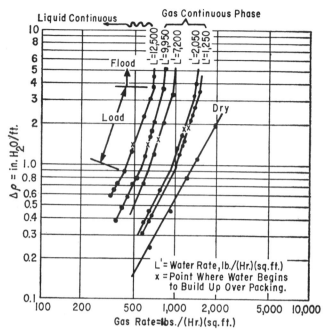

Pressure Drop Data on 1-inch Raschig Rings

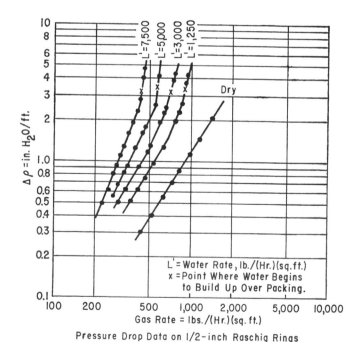

Pressure Drop Data on 1/2-inch Raschig Rings

Figure 9-12. Pressure drop-flow characteristics in conventional packed towers. (By permission B. R. Sarchet, "Trans." Amer. Inst. Chem. Engrs. Vol. 38, No. 2, page 293 (1942).)

Table 9-22
Packing Wetting Rates Related to Packing Material Surface

Surface	Reasonable minimum wetting rate		Materials
	ft³/ft²hr	m³/m²h	
Unglazed ceramic	1.5	0.5	Chemical stoneware
Oxidized metal	2.2	0.7	Carbon steel, copper
Surface treated metal	3.2	1.0	Etched stainless steel
Glazed ceramic	6.4	2.0	
Glass	8.0	2.5	
Bright metal	9.6	3.0	Stainless steel, tantalum
PVC — CPVC	11.6	3.5	
Polypropylene	12.8	4.0	
PTFE/FEP	16.0	5.0	

By permission Mass Transfer, Inc., Bul. TP/US/Bl (1978)

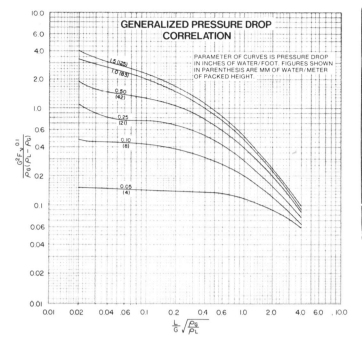

Figure 9-13A. Latest generalized pressure drop correlation. (By permission, Norton Co.)

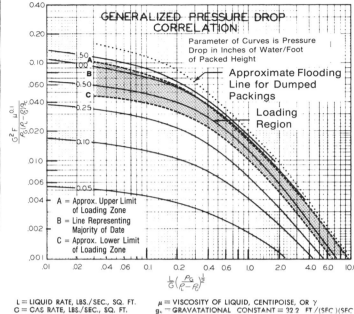

L = LIQUID RATE, LBS./SEC., SQ. FT.
C = GAS RATE, LBS./SEC., SQ. FT.
ρ_L = LIQUID DENSITY, LBS./CU. FT.
ρ_G = GAS DENSITY, LBS./CU. FT.
F = PACKING FACTOR = $2/\epsilon^3$

μ = VISCOSITY OF LIQUID, CENTIPOISE, OR γ
g_c = GRAVATATIONAL CONSTANT = 32.2 FT./(SEC.)(SEC.)
L' = LIQUID RATE, LBS./HR.
G' = GAS RATE, LBS./HR.

Figure 9-13B. Generalized pressure drop correlation essentially equivalent to Figure 9-13A. (By permission, Norton Co.)

Figure 9-13C. Loading, flooding and pressure drop correlation. (Adapted by permission M. Leva, "Tower Packings & Packed Tower Design, 2nd ed." U. S. Stoneware Co., additions by this author.)

ρ_L = Liquid density, Lb./cu. ft.
ν = Liquid viscosity, centistokes
ψ = Density water/Density liquid
G = Gas (vapor)
Lb./(sec.)(sq. ft. tower section)
g = 32 ft./(sec.)(sec.)
(a/ϵ^3) = Packing factor, F
ρ_g = Gas Density, Lb./cu. ft.
L = Liquid rate,
Lb./(sec.)(sq. ft. tower section)

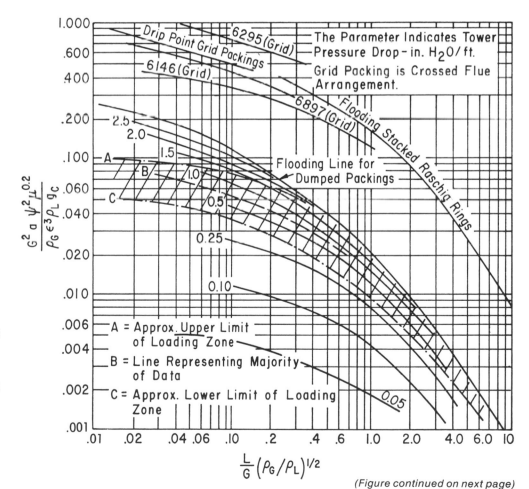

(Figure continued on next page)

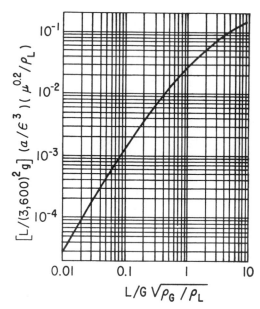

Figure 9-13D. Sherwood-type correlation for flooding gas rate at a given liquid rate. (By permission, F. A. Zenz, "Chem. Engr.," Aug., p. 181, 1953.)

better considered a region—from the first point of inflection of the curve to its second. Towers are usually designed to operate with gas-liquid rates in the loading region or within about 60-80 per cent of its lower point. As will be discussed later, it is necessary to operate farther from the loading point for some situations than others due to the relative proximity of the loading to the flooding point.

For Figure 9-13A the loading region is centered about the 0.75 inch/foot pressure drop curve; the preferred design range being 0.35 to a maximum of 1.0 inch of water/foot.

Figure 9-13B indicates the loading region as centered about line B, which is a reasonable upper design condition.

Some recent evaluations of data by other investigators indicate that a so-called loading region does not exist as clearly as may be suggested by some data, and therefore they suggest operations essentially up to the flooding point. For a good, reliable design which must allow for fluctuations in feed, and possibly column back-pressure up sets, designing to the flood region cannot be recommended. Design limits are suggested below, and in later sections.

Flooding Point

At the second sharp change in the slope of the pressure drop curve, Figure 9-12, the packing tends to hold up more and more liquid. This creates a rapid increase in pressure drop. The flooding point of the system is said to be the point of the second inflection of the pressure drop curve. Here the liquid build-up on top of the packing becomes in-

creasing higher and the pressure drop essentially goes to infinity for a finite increase in gas rate. In many actual cases operation can be maintained at the flooding point, but it will be erratic, the performance (efficiency) of operation poor, and the entrainment carry-over excessively high. It is obvious that towers are not designed for flood point operations, but at 40-60 per cent of gas and liquid rates associated with this point. Figure 9-13B indicates that the flooding region usually is above 2.5 in. water/foot, but note how cramped and much more sensitive this condition becomes as the extreme right hand side of the graph is approached.

Packing Factors

The use of "packing factors" is established in the design concepts of evaluating packed tower performance. This factor is a unique characteristic of each packing size and style/design. Although these factors can be determined by calculation from the physical dimensions, they are more accurately determined experimentally.

Packing factor selection significantly affects the performance of a packed tower system. These factors are only suitable for discreet particle type packing, and their values vary depending on how the packing is installed in the tower. For example, the factors for a ceramic packing are different for packing floated (dumped) into a tower full of water and the particles allowed to float down when compared to the same packing dumped into a dry empty tower where significant breakage can occur and consolidate the packing, or even to packing "hand-placed" or stacked dry.

Often it is only necessary to change a packing size or type to modify the capacity and/or contacting efficiency of an existing tower, since this change affects the packing factor. Table 9-23A-D presents specific packing factors from the manufacturers.

Many of the packings of the various manufacturers are essentially identical in shape, size, and performance factors. Some packing manufacturers suggest adjusting packing factors for vacuum and pressure distillations; however, this should only be done after consultation.

The experimentally determined packing factors are the only reliable values to use for design calculations; although estimates can be made for packing shapes when no data are available. The packing factor is expressed as:

$$F = a/\varepsilon^3$$

where: a_t = Specific surface of packing, sq. ft/cu. ft.

    a = Effective interfacial area for contacting, sq. ft./cu. ft.

    ε = Fractional voids

The values of a/ε^3 determined experimntally by Lobo et al. are indicated.[47] These are the values in the develop-

Table 9-23A
Packing Factors*
DUMPED PACKING

Packing Type	Material	1/4	3/8	1/2	5/8	3/4	1 or #1	1 1/4	1 1/2	2 or #2	3	3 1/2 or #3
							Nominal Packing Size (Inches)					
Intalox®	Metal						41		25	16		13
Hy-Pak™	Metal						43		26	18		15
Super Intalox® Saddles	Ceramic						60			30		
Super Intalox Saddles	Plastic						33			21		16
Pall Rings	Plastic				97		52		40	24		16
Pall Rings	Metal				70		48		33	20		16
Intalox® Saddles	Ceramic	725	330	200		145	92		52	40	22	
Raschig Rings	Ceramic	1600	1000	580	380	255	155	125	95	65	37	
Raschig Rings	1/32" metal	700	390	300	170	155	115					
Raschig Rings	1/16" metal			410	290	220	137	110	83	57	32	

*By permission Norton Co., from data compiled in Norton Co. Laboratories, Copyright 1977.
Packing factors determined with an air-water system in 30" I.D. Tower.

Table 9-23B
Packing Factors*

Packing Type	Material	1/4	3/8	1/2	5/8	3/4	1 or #1	1 1/4	1 1/2	2 or #2	3	3 1/2 or #3
							Nominal Packing Size (Inches)					
Flexisaddles	Plastic						30			20		15
Flexirings	Plastic†				78		45		28	22		18
Flexisaddles	Ceramic	600		200		145	98		52	40	22	

*By permission, Koch Engineering Co. Inc.
†Use for plastic or metal.

Table 9-23C
Packing Factors*

Packing Type	Material	1/4	3/8	1/2	5/8	3/4	1 or #1	1 1/4	1 1/2	2 or #2	3	3 1/2 or #3
							Nominal Packing Size (Inches)					
Ballast™ Ring	Metal						48	28	20		15	
Ballast™ Ring	Plastic				97		52	32	25		16	
Ballast™ Saddle	Plastic						30		20		15	

*By permission, Glitsch Inc.

Table 9-23D
Packing Factors*

Packing Type	Material	1/4	3/8	1/2	5/8	3/4	1 or #1	1 1/4	1 1/2	2 or #2	3	3 1/2 or #3
							Nominal Packing Size (Inches)					
Cascade Mini-Ring	Plastic					30‖	25	18¶		15		12
Cascade Mini-Ring	Metal			55†		34				22	14	10‡
Cascade Mini-Ring	Ceramic									38	24	18§

*By permission, Mass Transfer, Inc.
†Designated No. 0
‡Designated No. 4
§Designated No. 5, value for No. 7 size is 15.
‖Designated No. 1A
¶Designated No. 2 A

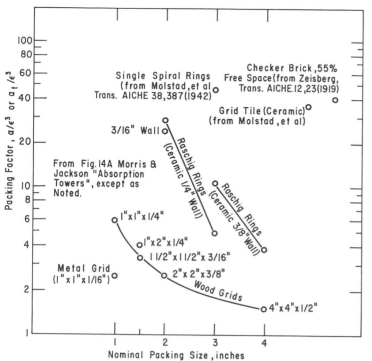

Figure 9-14A. Packing factors (stacked packings and grids). (By permission Morris & Jackson, "Absorption Towers," Butterworth Scientific Publications, and Imperial Chemical Industries, Ltd., and as adapted by U. S. Stoneware Co.)

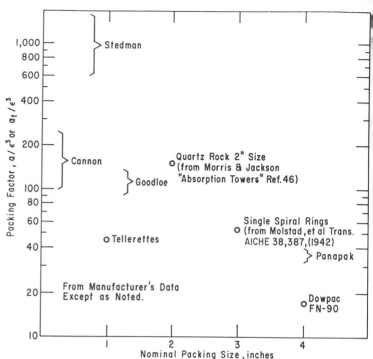

Figure 9-14B. Packing factors (screen packing and random dumped packing). (By permission U. S. Stoneware Co.)

ment of the basic relation expressed in Figure 9-13 with correction of ψ^2 suggested by Leva.[41] These a/ϵ^3 values were found to correlate a considerable amount of the literature data within 12 percent. This would mean about a 6 percent error in tower diameter determined at flooding conditions. Values calculated using surface area per cubic foot and percent free gas space from manufacturer's tables can be as much as 40 percent off. The values are dependent upon the method of packing the tower, i.e., dry dumped, wet dumped, or wet, dumped an shaken. The latter condition may approximate the situation after a tower has been running a while and the packing settled.

Experience definitely indicates that the packing factor increases with hours of operation for ceramic materials up to some limit. This is due to settling, breakage, plugging, etc. For design of commercial towers, values of a/ϵ^3 should be increased from 15 to 75 percent for ceramic materials, over values read from Table 9-23A-D. The percent increase depends upon the tendency of the shape to disintegrate into smaller pieces during operations—flooding, gas surging, etc. In general, circular shapes exhibit the least tendency to break up. As a reasonable value where data is available, the average of the wet dumped, and wet dumped and shaken values for tower voidages is recommended.

As a general guide, plastic packings should not be selected to operate any closer than 40-50° F of their

softening point or the manufacturers recommended use temperature. These packings also deflect with time and temperature and compress, thereby changing performance and increasing pressure drop.

Leva[40] has correlated the data of Lubin into correction factors to apply to a non-irrigated bed pressure drop to end up with pressure drop for a liquid-gas system in the loading to flooding range. In general this does not appear any more convenient to use than Figure 9-13B.

Relations expressing the fractional voids in a ring packed bed are useful in estimating the "ϵ" values for a/ϵ^3 determinations.[47] The average deviation is ± 2.6 percent.

Dry packed tower:

$$\epsilon = 1.046 - 0.658\,\phi \qquad (9\text{-}2)$$

Wet packed, unshaken tower:

$$\epsilon = 1.029 - 0.591\,\phi \qquad (9\text{-}3)$$

Wet packed and shaken tower:

$$\epsilon = 1.009 - 0.626\,\phi \qquad (9\text{-}4)$$

where:

$\phi = \dfrac{1 - (d_i/d_o)^2}{(ld_o^2)^{0.0170}}$, not valid if $\phi < 0.20$ or for extra thick walls or solids

$1 =$ ring height, inches

$d_o =$ outside diameter of ring, inches

$d_i =$ inside diameter of ring, inches

The generalized correlations of Sakiadis and Johnson[59] are reported to satisfy a wide variety of systems.

Manufacturers of commercial packings provide packing factors for their products. Many of the commonly used (not necessarily all) packing factors are presented in Table 9-23. These values are to be used with the application of Figures 9-13A and 9-13B. Factors presented in Figures 9-14A and 9-14B can also be used where the design requires them.

Recommended Design Capacity and Pressure Drop

The relationships in packed tower performance which are concerned specifically with the gas and liquid flows through a bed are expressed as a function of pressure drop. Pressure drop may be created by poor packing arrangements, i.e., tight and open sections in the bed, breakage of packing and settling of the bed, or plugging of void spaces by solids or reaction products. All of these are in addition to the inherent characteristic resistance of a *particular* packing to flow of fluids. This resistance will be different if the system is single phase as contrasted to two phase for most adsorption, scrubbing, or desorption operations. The basic pressure drop performance pattern of nearly all packings can be shown as in Figure 9-12.

Below the loading region, the pressure drop can be read from appropriate system curves if they are available, as Figure 9-12. However, for general use the data has been well correlated, Figures 9-13A and 9-13B. The slope of most of the curves for pressure drop indicate a proportionality of 1.8 to 2.8 power of the superficial gas mass velocity up the tower. This performance is typical of the gas-continuous range of packed tower operation. In Figure 9-12 the curves for performance at water rates of $L' = 1250$ through $L' = 9950$ all seem to be a part of the same family. The curve $L' = 12,500$ will be discussed later. The pressure drop information to follow is valid only for the gas-continuous type of operation. Fortunately the majority of packed towers operate in this condition; however, the liquid-continuous will be considered later.

Pressure drop data for several styles and arrangements of drip point grid tile are given in Figures 9-15A, B, C, D, E, F. These are not included in the general correlations to follow.

Figure 9-13A is one of the latest general purpose correlations presented by several manufacturers of packing materials. The relative differences between the various correlations appear to be minor; thereby allowing any packing performance to be evaluated on any chart; as long as the packing factors, F or (a/ε^3), have been determined on the same basis. Packing factors are presented

(Text continued on page 166)

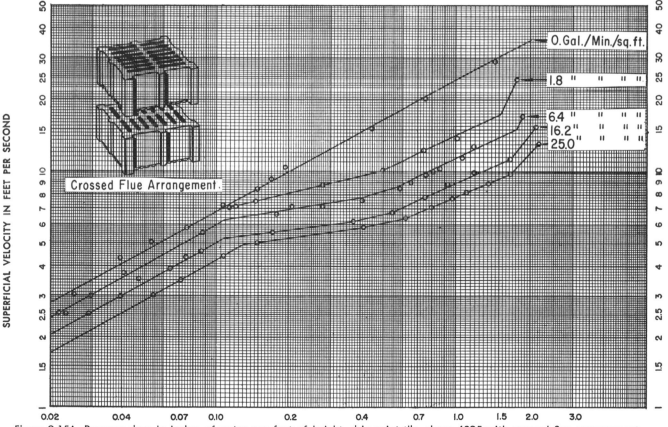

Figure 9-15A. Pressure drop in inches of water per foot of height, drip point tile, shape 6295 with crossed flue arrangement.

Figures 9-15A – 9-15E by permission General Refractories

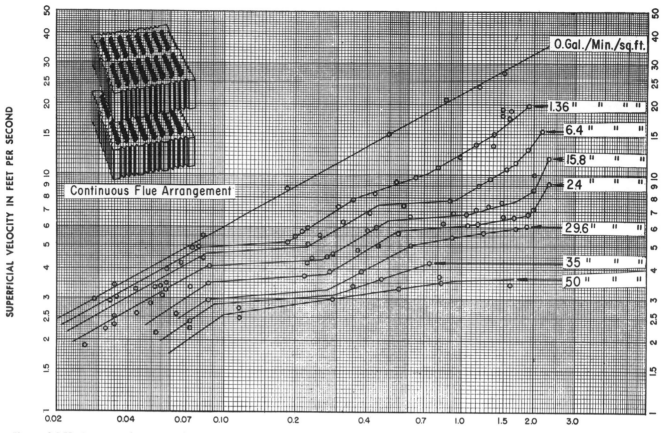

Figure 9-15B. Pressure drop in inches of water per foot of height, drip point tile, shape 6897 with continuous flue arrangement.

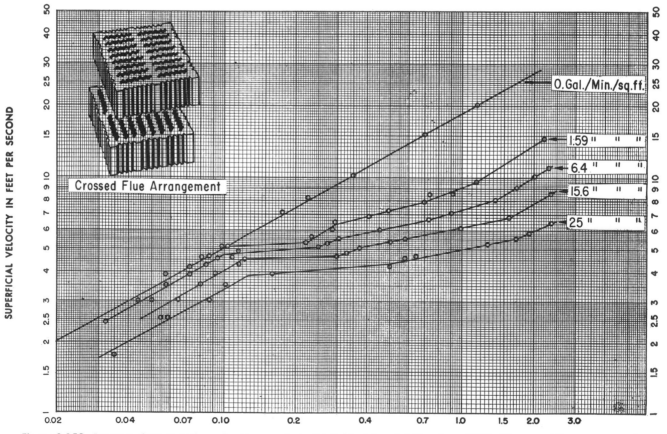

Figure 9-15C. Pressure drop in inches of water per foot of height, drip point tile, shape 6897 with crossed flue arrangement.

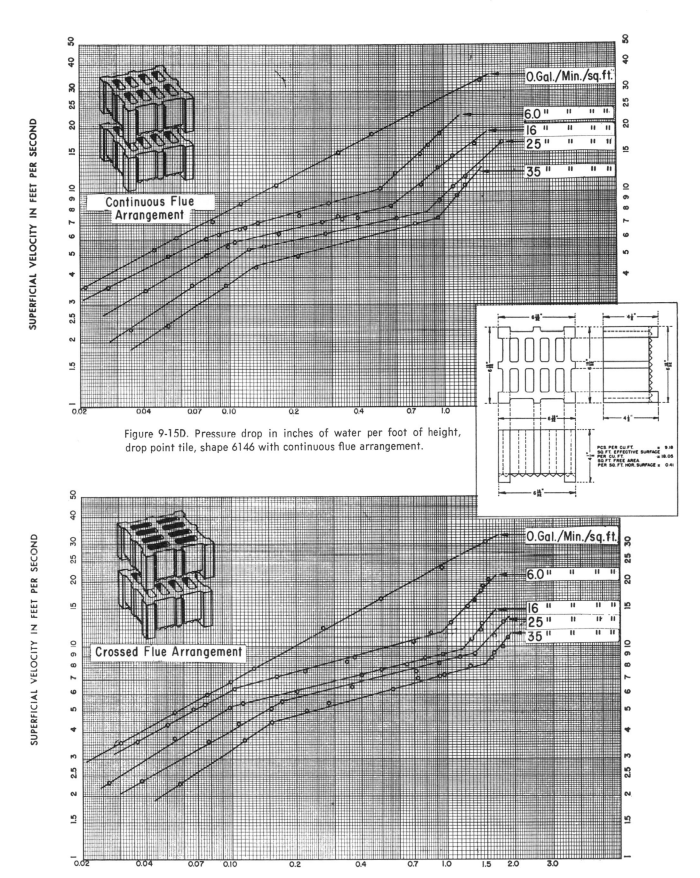

Figure 9-15D. Pressure drop in inches of water per foot of height, drop point tile, shape 6146 with continuous flue arrangement.

Figure 9-15E. Pressure drop in inches of water per foot of height, drop point tile, shape 6146 with crossed flue arrangement.

in Table 9-23A-D and are identified for the discreet particle packings similar to those illustrated in Figure 9-6, since the compacted or assembled packing materials such as are shown in Figures 9-6S and T do not use the packing factor concept for design evaluation. Therefore, since each proprietary material such as those in Figure 9-6 S or T has its own design/rating technique, the respective manufacturer should be consulted, as they cannot be rated using Figures 9-13A or 13B.

Design Criteria and Guide

A. Calculate the abscissa of Figures 9-13A or -13B,

$$\frac{L}{G} \sqrt{\frac{\rho_G}{\rho_L}}$$

B. Select a design/operating pressure drop, as shown on the curves of Figures 9-13A or 13-B. Suggested selection basis is as follows:
  1. Low to medium pressure column operation, select pressure drop of 0.75 to 1.0 inches water/foot of packing height, although towers will operate at 1½"-2.0" water/foot.
  2. Absorption and similar systems, select pressure drop of 0.20 to 0.75 inches water/foot.
  3. Atmospheric or pressure distillation, select pressure drop of 0.50 - 1.0 inches water/foot.
  4. Vacuum distillation, varies with system, normally select low pressure drop in the 0.10 to 0.25 inches water/foot range. Several other factors must be considered, such as variability of gas and liquid rates.
  5. Foaming materials should be operated at 0.1 - 0.25 water/foot.
  6. Vacuum service requires recognition of minimum liquid flow; refer to section on minimum wetting rate. Pressure drops are designed to be low, but normally not lower than 0.10 inches water/foot.
C. Select a packing and determine its packing factor from Table 9-23A-D. Packing is selected for its expected process performance, pressure drop and materials of construction for the system. Table 9-18 presents summary comments for applications. Selection guides are as follows:
  1. As packing factor, F or (a/ε^3), becomes larger by selection of smaller sized packing; gas capacity for the column is reduced; and pressure drop will increase for a fixed gas flow.
  2. Some packings are sized by general dimensions in inches, while some shapes are identified by numbers, #1, #2, #3 for increasing size.
  3. Not all packings are manufactured in all materials of construction, i.e. ceramic, various plastics, various metals.
  4. Packing size versus tower diameter recommendations:

Tower Diam., Feet	Nominal Packing Size, Inches
< 1.0	< 1
1.0 — 3.0	1 — 1½
> 3.0	2 — 3

D. Referring to Figure 9-13A or (13-B), read up from the abscissa to the pressure drop line selected, and read across to the ordinate

$$\frac{CG^2F\mu^{0.1}}{\rho_G(\rho_L - \rho_G)} = \text{Ordinate number}$$

Substitute F and the other knowns into the equation and solve for G, the gas mass flow rate, Lbs./sec.-sq. ft.

Then, determine the required tower cross-section area and diameter:

$$\text{Diameter, foot} = 1.1283 \left[\frac{\text{Gas Rate, lbs./sec, } G''}{G} \right]^{1/2}$$

E. Effects of physical properties.

For nonfoaming liquids, capacity of packing is independent of surface tension. Foaming conditions reduce capacity significantly and design should recognize by selecting operating pressure drop at only 50% of normal non-foaming liquid.

For liquids of viscosity of 30 centipoise and lower, effect on capacity is small. For higher viscosity select larger packing to reduce pressure drop, and also consult packing manufacturer.

Dumped Packing: Gas-Liquid System Below Loading

A. Water-Gas System[40]

$$\Delta P = \alpha(10^{\beta L}) \left(\frac{G^2}{\rho_g} \right) \quad (9-5)$$

where: ΔP = Pressure drop in "below loading" region, inches water/foot of packing height

  G = Gas superficial mass velocity, lb./(second) (sq.ft. tower cross-section)

  L = Liquid superficial mass velocity, lb./(second) (sq. ft. tower cross-section)

  ρ_g = Gas density, lb./cu.ft.

  α = Constant from Table 9-24.

  β = Constant from Table 9-24.

This relation is valid for operation in nearly any water-gas system (including above atmospheric) if it is well below the loading region. It gives low values when used in the loading region.

B. Liquid - Gas System: below, but approaching loading use relation above for (A.) but use:

$$L = (\text{Liquid mass velocity}) \left(\frac{\rho \text{ Water}}{\rho \text{ liquid}} \right), \text{ Lb./(second) (sq.ft.)}$$

This correction by Leva[41] produces a better agreement of Equation 9-5 for liquids with density different than water and a viscosity below two centipoise.

Dumped Packing: Loading and Flooding Regions, General Design Correlations

Figure 9-13A may be used for any system to obtain a good estimate of pressure drop for practically any packing material. The relative state of liquid loading and liquid flooding may be identified from the position of the point on the graph, and the approximate pressure drops per foot of packing depth may be read as parameters. It is important to recognize that the load upper limit, line A, is essentially coincident with the flooding condition. It is also apparent that the relative relation of the operating point to the flooding and loading conditions is quite different at the extreme right of the figure for large values of the abscissa than for low values to the left.

The rearranged form of the same Sherwood[61, 62] equation allows the curve for flooding of dumped packings to be conveniently presented to facilitate calculation of the flooding gas rate, G_f, corresponding to a given liquid flow L.[81] Figure 9-13D.

The packing factors to use with Figures 9-13A and B are given in Table 9-23A-D and Figure 9-14A and B.

Dumped Packing: Pressure Drop at Flooding

As a comparison or alternate procedure, the pressure drop at the flooding point as indicated by the upper break in the pressure drop curve can be estimated from Table 9-25 and Figure 9-16 for rings and saddles.[81] The values in the table multiplied by the correction ratio gives the pressure drop for the liquid in question, expressed as inches of water.

Dumped Packing: Pressure Drop Below and at Flood Point, Liquid Continuous Range

For a particular liquid-gas system and tower packing, performance indicates a region where the *liquid phase becomes continuous* and the gas phase discontinuous. This is obviously at relatively high liquor rates, but not beyond the range of satisfactory performance for the equipment. This region is characterized by proportionally higher pressure drops than the gas-continuous region, and the existence of a critical liquid rate as this pressure drop deviation takes place.

Equation 9-5 and Tables 9-24A and 9-24B can be used as a rough approximation provided it is understood that the actual pressure drops may be 10-50 percent higher. Referring to Figure 9-12 the curve for L' - 12,500 shows the beginning of the "move to the left," swinging away from the uniform slope of the curves for lower L' values.

This probably is not the L_c value for the system. The study of Zenz suggests that the critical liquid rate, L_c, is the minimum liquid rate which *completely* wets the packing thus having essentially all packing surface effective for gas contact. Rates above this value should be determined by allowable pressure drop and the limitation that the tower often begins to approach the flooding conditions more rapidly than in the gas-continuous region. Figure 9-17 correlates this L_c for Raschig rings and Berl saddles as a function of liquid viscosity.

More work is needed to fully understand this feature of tower performance and extend the information to

Table 19-24A

Pressure Drop Correlation for Irrigated Towers*

(Valid for water-gas systems only when operating below loading point)

General form of equation: $\Delta p = (\alpha)\,(10^{\beta L})\left(\dfrac{G^2}{\rho_G}\right)$ where

ΔP = Pressure drop, inches H_2O/ft. of packing height.
ρ_G = Gas density, lb./(cu.ft.)
G = Gas mass velocity, lb./(sec) (sq.ft.)
L = Liquid mass velocity, lb./(sec) (sq.ft.)
α and β are constants, given below.

Packing type and nominal size		α	β	Equation valid for liquor range, L (lb./ft.² ,sec.)	Valid for bed voidage, (percent)
Standard	3/8	4.70	0.41	0.2 -1.2	57.0
Wall thickness	1/2	3.10	0.41	0.08-2.4	58.6
Raschig rings	5/8	2.35	0.26	0.3 -1.8	67.0
	3/4	1.34	0.26	0.5 -3.0	72.0
	1	0.97	0.25	0.1 -7.5	69.2
	1¼	0.57	0.23	0.2 -3.0	75.6
	1½	0.39	0.23	0.2 -4.0	75.9
(Dumped)	2	0.24	0.17	0.2 -5.5	81.6
(Stacked)	2	0.06	0.12	0.2 -9.0	80.0
Spiral (Dumped)	3	0.18	0.15	0.2 -5.0	70.5
rings (Stacked)	3	0.15	0.15	0.2 -6.5	63.2
Berl saddles	1/2	1.20	0.21	0.08-6.0	63.2
	3/4	0.48	0.17	0.1 -4.0	71.0
	1	0.39	0.17	0.2 -8.0	70.9
	1½	0.21	0.13	0.2 -6.0	70.0
Intalox saddles	1/2	0.82	0.20	0.15-4.0	77
	3/4	0.48	0.16	0.1 -4.0	75
	1	0.31	0.16	0.7 -4.0	74
	1½	0.14	0.14	0.2 -8.0	78
	2	0.08	0.14		80
Pall Rings	1	0.15	0.15		93.4
(Carbon Steel)	1½	0.08	0.16		94.0
	2	0.06	0.12		94.0

* Basic Table from: M. Leva, "Tower Packings and Packed Tower Design," 2nd Ed. (1953) U. S. Stoneware Co., Akron, Ohio; with additions for Intalox Saddles and Pall rings by this author, Ref. 5, 6, 22, by permission.

Table 9-24B

Revised Packed Tower Pressure Drop Correlation Constants For Towers Operating Below Flooding Region

Type of Packing	Mat'l		1/4	3/8	1/2	5/8	3/4	1	1 1/4	1 3/8	1 1/2	2	3
						NOMINAL PACKING SIZE (Inches)							
Intalox Saddles	Ceramic	α			1.04		0.52	0.52			0.13	0.14	
		β			0.37		0.25	0.16			0.15	0.10	
Raschig Rings	Ceramic	α			1.96	1.31	0.82	0.53			0.31	0.23	0.18
		β			0.56	0.39	0.38	0.22			0.21	0.17	0.15
Berl Saddles	Ceramic	α			1.16		0.56	0.53			0.21	0.16	
		β			0.47		0.25	0.18			0.16	0.12	
Pall Rings	Plastic	α						0.22	0.14			0.10	
		β						0.14	0.13			0.12	
Pall Rings	Metal	α			0.43		0.15				0.08	0.06	
		β			0.17		0.15				0.16	0.12	
Raschig Rings 1/32" Wall	Metal	α			1.20								
		β			0.28								
Raschig Rings 1/16" Wall	Metal	α			1.59	1.01	0.80	0.53			0.29	0.23	
		β			0.29	0.39	0.30	0.19			0.20	0.14	

Equation

By permission J. Eckert, U.S. Stoneware Co. Copyright 1958.

$$\Delta p = \alpha \times 10^{\beta L} \left(\frac{G^2}{\rho_G} \right) \text{ (Limited to Region Below Flooding).}$$

Δp = Pressure Drop—Inches of H_2O/Ft. of Packing.
G = Gas Mass Velocity—Lbs./Sec. Ft^2.
L = Liquid Mass Velocity—Lbs./sec. Ft^2.
ρ_G = Gas Density—Lbs./Ft^3.
α and β = Constants.

Table 9-25

Pressure Drop at Upper Break Point (Flood) With Water As the Flowing Liquid*

Raschig Rings, In Inches	ΔP_f, In. H_2O/ft. of Packed Bed		Berl Saddles In Inches	ΔP_f, In. H_2O/ft. of Packed Bed
2	2.5		1 1/2	2.2
1 1/2	2.5		1	2.5
1 1/4	4.0		3/4	2.5
1 (ribbed)	3.0		1/2	2.0
1	4.0		1/4	1.25
3/4	3.0			
5/8	2.5			
1/2	3.5			
3/8	4.0			
1/4	4.0			

*By permission, F. A. Zenz, Chem. Eng., Aug., 176 (1953), Ref. 73.

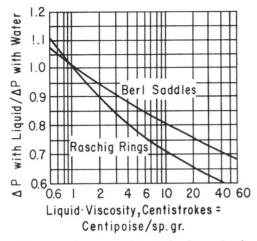

Figure 9-16. Pressure drop correction at flooding point for use with Table 9-20. (By permission F. A. Zenz, "Chem. Eng." Aug. p, 176, 1953).

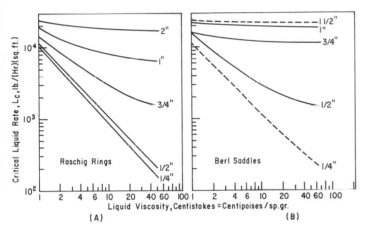

Figure 9-17. Values of liquid rate when the system becomes liquid-continuous, L_c. (By permission F. A. Zenz, Chem. Eng., Aug. p. 176, 1953).

other common packings. Determination of L_c from the figures will indicate whether the tower is operating under gas-continuous (values of L lower than L_c) or liquid-continuous (values equal to or larger than L_c). The approximate degree of wetting of the packing can be evaluated as the ratio of L/L_c.[73] The pressure drop is evaluating using Figure 9-13 to determine the flooding liquid rate, L_f. Then calculate the ratio of L_f to actual L. Read Figure 9-18 to obtain ΔP actual/ΔP_f. Thus, ΔP actual is the ratio value times $\triangle P_f$ calculated using Figure 9-16 and Table 9-25.

Pressure Drop Across Packing Supports and Redistribution Plates

Useful correlated information on pressure drop across packing supports and redistribution plates is practically not available. Some order of magnitude guide data is given in Figures 9-19, 20, 21, 22, and 23.

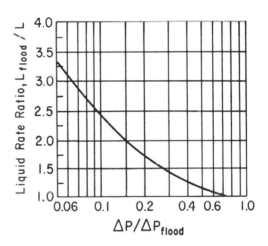

Figure 9-18. Pressure drop correlation at flooding. (By permission F. A. Zenz, Chem. Eng., Aug., p. 181, 1953.)

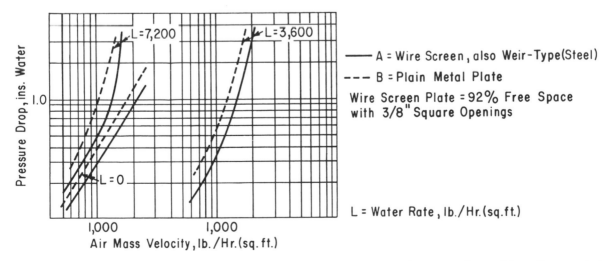

Figure 9-19. Comparison effect of pressure drop across support plates and bed of 1½-inch intalox saddles. (By permission M. Leva, J. M. Lucas, H. H. Frahme, "Ind. Eng. Chem." Vol. 46, No. 6, 1954.)

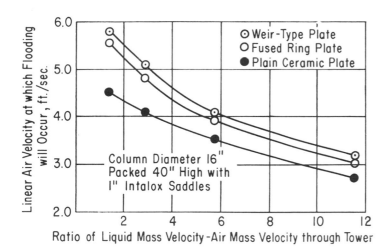

Figure 9-20. Effect of choice of support plate on flooding rate. (By permission U. S. Stoneware Co.)

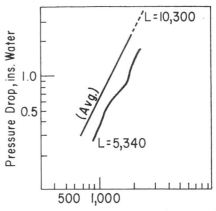

Pressure Drop Through Fused Raschig Ring Plate, with Plate Covered with One inch of 1" Size Intalox Saddles (L = Liquid Mass Rate Parameter)

Plate = 58 % Free Area

Figure 9-21. Pressure drop through fused raschig ring plate with plate covered with one inch of one inch size Intalox saddles. (By permission M. Leva, J. M. Lucas, H. H. Frahme, "Ind. Eng. Chem." Vol. 46, No. 6, 1954.)

Since this data is peculiar to the supports studied, it can serve only as a good estimate for other situations. It is important to remember that the results obtained with a bare plate, and one holding a layer of packing can be quite different. The latter being the more realistic condition.

The only available test data[44] indicate that the plain flat plate (26 - 45 percent free area) has a decided detrimental effect on the allowable flooding conditions of the tower; whereas the wire screen, weir-type, and fused Raschig ring designs have very little effect when using Intalox saddles for packing. In general the dumped saddle type packing should give less blocking to support openings than ring type.

Example 9-1: Evaluation of Tower Condition and Pressure Drop

Check the design of a 4-foot, 6-inch I.D. tower packed with 45 ft. of 1-inch x $\frac{1}{16}$-inch thick steel Raschig rings if the service requires a liquid rate of 2250 lbs./hr.(sq.ft.) of 10 percent caustic solution (Sp. Gr. = 1.22) and 4540 lbs./hr.(sq.ft.) of 110° F. air containing CO_2 to be scrubbed at 365 psia.

1.) Determine the operating range for the tower by referencing to Figure 9-13A or 9-13B. Use 9-13B for this example.

$$\rho_G = \left(\frac{29}{379}\right)\left(\frac{520}{570}\right)\left(\frac{365}{14.7}\right) = 1.732 \text{ lbs./cu. ft.}$$

$$\rho_L = (62.3)(1.22) = 76.1 \text{ lbs./cu. ft.}$$

$$\mu = 2 \text{ cp. at } 104° \text{ F. for liquid}$$

$$F = \frac{a}{\varepsilon^3} = 137 \text{ Table 9-23}$$

$$\frac{L}{G}[\rho_G/(\rho_L - \rho_G)]^{1/2} = \frac{2250}{4540}\left(\frac{1.732}{76.1 - 1.732}\right)^{1/2} = 0.07563$$

$$\frac{G^2}{\rho_G}\left(\frac{a}{\varepsilon^3}\right)\frac{\mu^{0.1}}{(\rho_L - \rho_G) g_c} = \frac{(4540/3600)^2 (1.07)^{0.1} (137)}{1.732 (76.1-1.732)(32.2)}$$

$$= 0.0563$$

2.) Locating 0.0756 and 0.0563 on Figure 9-13B reading the intersection indicates a condition in the *lower loading region*, and a pressure drop of approximately 0.60 in. water/ft. of packing.

3.) Expected pressure drop through bed:

$$= (45 \text{ feet})(0.60) = 27 \text{ inches water, total}$$

4.) This bed should be in three sections (two might be acceptable under some circumstances, or if different packing were used) thereby requiring two intermediate combined packing supports and redistribution plates and one bottom support plate.

Estimate pressure drop per redistribution set-up or support

$$= 1.0 \text{ inch}$$

For two redistributors plus one support plate:

Total estimated pressure drop $= (3)(1.0)$
$$= 3 \text{ inches water}$$

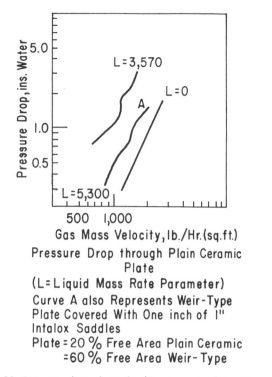

Figure 9.22. Pressure drop through plain ceramic plate. (By permission M. Leva, J. M. Lucas, H. H. Frahme, "Ind. Eng. Chem." Vol. 46, No. 6, 1954.)

5.) Total estimated pressure drop through packed portion of tower:

$$\text{Bed } \Delta P = 27.0$$
$$\text{Internals} = \underline{3.0}$$
$$30.0 \text{ inches water}$$

Say, 30 to 35 inches water (this should be 30.0 ± 15-20%)

6.) Estimated percent of flooding

Reading the abscissa of Figure 9-13B at value 0.0756 for ordinate at flooding line for dumped packing:

$$= 0.13$$

Then, actual value of 0.0563 is:

Percent of liquid flooding $= \dfrac{0.0563}{0.13} (100) = 43.3$ percent

Note that this rather low value will usually occur when operating at the low L/G values due to the greater operating spread between flooding and loading (see Figure 9-13B).

7. Estimated percent of loading (average)

Reading abscissa at 0.0756 for ordinate of line B gives ordinate = 0.078

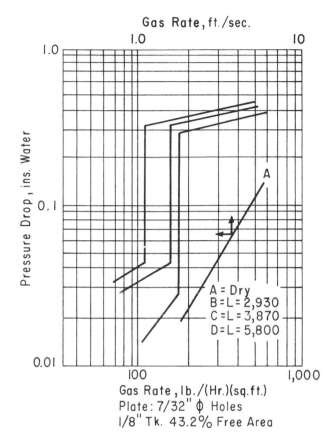

Figure 9-23. Flooding on perforated plate. By permission B. J. Lerner, C. S. Grove, Jr., "Ind. Eng. Chem.," Vol. 43, No. 1, p. 216, 1951.)

Percent of loading $- \dfrac{0.0563}{0.078} (100) = 72.1$ percent
(not very precise)

This is an acceptable value and should not be exceeded except in known systems. It is preferable to operate reasonably close to the loading condition for best efficiency of contact.

As an alternate consideration, assume various pressure drops/foot of packing (same) and determine effect on calculated column diameter. Use the same input information as original stated conditions, then:

Assumed Pressure Drop, In. H₂O/ Foot	Calculated Column Diameter, Feet
0.25	5.22
0.50	4.61
0.75	4.35

Example 9-2: Alternate Evaluation of Tower Condition and Pressure Drop

Using Example 9-1 as reference, the tower will be examined for critical liquor rate, L_c, using Figure 9-17

$$\text{Centistokes} = \left(\frac{\text{centipoise}}{\text{Sp. Gr.}}\right) \text{ for caustic sol'n.} = \frac{2}{1.22} = 1.64$$

$$\text{reading: } L_c = 16{,}000 \text{ lb./(hr.)(sq.ft.)}$$

Since actual $L' = 2250$ is less than $16{,}000$ this tower operates in the gas continuous region.

Pressure drop at flooding from Table 9-25 and Figure 9-16

$$\triangle P_f = 4 \text{ in. water/ft. (not exact figure, since table is for ceramic rings)}$$

Correction $= 0.94$

Then actual expected pressure drop at flooding:

$$\triangle P_f = (0.94)(4) = 3.76 \text{ inch water/foot}$$

For 45 feet of packing:

$$\triangle P_f \text{ total} = (45)(3.76) = 169 \text{ inches water}$$

Comparison with Figure 9-13B gives 3 inches water/foot (parameter) or a total of $(3)(45) = 135$ inches water. Neither of these values represents a condition (flooding) that should be considered for tower operation, except under known experience studies. Distillation operations sometimes operate above flooding, but other types of contacting normally require operations in the loading region (or below) for stable performance.

Example 9-3: Change of Performance with Change in Packing in Existing Tower

A tower is packed with 1-inch ceramic Raschig rings. It presently floods while drying water from a product at a production feed rate of 1,800,000 lbs./month with 0.25 mol percent being water. Flooding does not start at the bottom, but at some intermediate point up the tower. What can be done to eliminate the flooding? Is it possible to increase production rate to 2,000,000 lbs./month?

1.) Examine packing characteristics.

Size	a/ε^3	Surface area, sq. ft./cu. ft.
1 Inch Raschig Rings	158	58
1 Inch Intalox	124	78
1 Inch Berl Saddles	125	76
1 Inch Pall Ring*	45	66.3
1½ Inch Intalox	69	59.5
1½ Inch Berl Saddle	79	44

* Metal, all others ceramic.

2.) Percent of flooding for various packings, holding tower flow rates (including reflux) constant.

Refer to Flooding, Loading and Pressure Drop Chart, Figure 9-13C

$\dfrac{L}{G} (\rho_G/\rho_L)^{0.5}$ remains constant for same separation at increased production rate.

$\dfrac{G^2 \, \psi^2 \, \mu^{0.2}}{\rho_G \, \rho_L \, g_c} \left(\dfrac{a}{\varepsilon^3}\right)$ increases as G^2 at increased production rate for a fixed a/ε^3.

Packing	Percent of Flooding at 2,000,000 lb/mo. rate referenced to flooding of 1 inch ceramic Raschig rings
1 Inch R. R.	$= 100\%$
1 Inch Intalox	$\left(\dfrac{2}{1.8}\right)^2 \left(\dfrac{124}{158}\right)(100) = 96.9\%$
1 Inch Pall Rings (metal)	$\left(\dfrac{2}{1.8}\right)^2 \left(\dfrac{45}{158}\right)(100) = 35.2\%$
1½ Inch Intalox	$\left(\dfrac{2}{1.8}\right)^2 \left(\dfrac{69}{158}\right)(100) = 53.9\%$
1½ Inch Berl Saddles	$\left(\dfrac{2}{1.8}\right)^2 \left(\dfrac{79}{158}\right)(100) = 61.8\%$

The flooding of the packing is a direct function of the a/ε^3, therefore it is valid at constant separation to examine the performance as shown. The metal Pall rings appear to allow for a considerable increase in capacity. In fact the condition at 35.2 percent of flood might not be good from a contact efficiency standpoint.

3.) Selection

The 1½-inch Intalox or Berl ceramic saddles would be the preferred choice because: (1) the flooding point is sufficiently low and yet probably not too far from the load point (only flood data available, but would estimate 70 - 85 percent of load); (2) the surface area per cubic foot is essentially the same as for the existing 1-inch Raschig rings. By reference to the effective interfacial area graphs, and by using the Berl saddle data instead of Intalox as an estimate since it is not available, the separation performance would be expected to be essentially identical to the existing tower (for the Intalox); (3) the production rate can be increased; (4) the flooding can be removed from present operations using the 1½-inch Intalox or any of the other packings, but note that the a/ε^3 of the Berl saddles is not as high as the 1-inch R.R. This might mean less efficient contact, requiring more packing. However, from Figure 9-24 note that for a given L'/G' the Berl saddles are from 15 - 30 percent better wetted in any given packing volume. From Figure 9-25 the comparative effective areas, a, indicate that the Berl saddles have about the same area/cu.ft. as the existing rings. Therefore, it appears that the flooding can be stopped (lower a/ε^2) and yet the contact can be as good, or maybe a little better than it was originally.

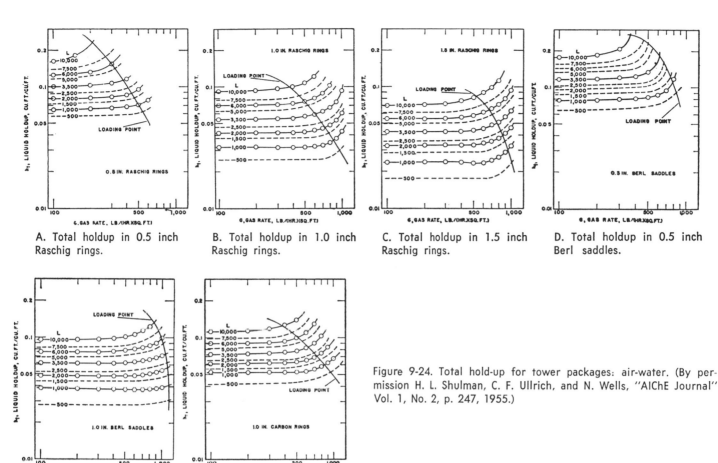

A. Total holdup in 0.5 inch Raschig rings.

B. Total holdup in 1.0 inch Raschig rings.

C. Total holdup in 1.5 inch Raschig rings.

D. Total holdup in 0.5 inch Berl saddles.

E. Total holdup in 1.0 inch Berl saddles.

F. Total holdup in 1.5 inch carbon rings.

Figure 9-24. Total hold-up for tower packages: air-water. (By permission H. L. Shulman, C. F. Ullrich, and N. Wells, "AIChE Journal" Vol. 1, No. 2, p. 247, 1955.)

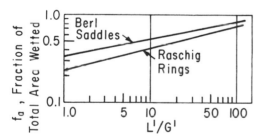

Figure 9-25. Fraction packing wetted. (By permission H. L. Shulman, C. F. Ullrich, A. Z. Proulx, J. O. Zimmerman, "AIChE Jour." Vol. 1, No. 2, p. 253, 1955.)

4.) Check support grid voidage

The packing support consists of a floor grating material with bar openings spaced to give 57.5 percent free void area of cross-section.

In order to avoid the possibility of local flooding at the support, it would be well to place a heavy hardware cloth over this grid to keep the saddles from nesting at the first layer in the opening slots. It is preferable to have them resting on a surface that cannot be blanked easily.

Select a 1-inch x 1-inch (center line) x 0.063-inch wire cloth with voidage of 87.8 percent.

Combined voidage, support grid plus cloth:

$$= (0.575)(0.878) = 50.5 \text{ percent}$$

This should be satisfactory, but a value much lower than this could not be tolerated.

Dump Intalox (or Berl) saddles into tower while tower is filled with water.

Example 9-4: Stacked Packing Pressure Drop

Consider the problem of drying air with sulfuric acid, Example 9-5. If the mass transfer relations are evaluated, a reasonably good estimate of the new packed height can be determined for using 2-inch stacked ceramic Raschig rings in place of Intalox saddles. For the present, assume the new required stacked height is 25 ft. Although the pressure drop per foot will be less and the flooding point higher than the dumped packing, it is inadvisable to go

to a smaller diameter tower because of the high superficial gas velocity.

Using the 15-inch I.D. ceramic tower, the expected pressure drop will be:

$$\Delta P = (\alpha)\,(10^{\beta L})\left(\frac{G^2}{\rho_G}\right) \qquad (9\text{-}2)$$

From Table 9-24A

$$\alpha = 0.06$$

$$\beta = 0.012$$

Liquor range checks satisfactory

$$G = 0.593 \text{ lb./(sec.)(sq.ft.)}$$

Leva[40] has shown that for liquids other than water, the L must be corrected by the ratio of the density of water to that of the fluid in the system.

$$L = 0.378 \text{ lb./(sec.)(sq. ft.)}\left(\frac{62.3}{112.6}\right) = 0.209$$

$$\rho_G = 0.087 \text{ lb./cu. ft.}$$

$$\Delta P = (0.06)\,(10^{(0.12)\,(.209)})\left(\frac{(0.593)^2}{0.087}\right)$$

$$\Delta P = 0.00258 \text{ in. water/foot packed height}$$

Total tower drop:

Packing $= (0.00258)(25) = 0.064$ in. water (approximate)

Support (estimated) $\underline{= 1.5 \quad}$ in. water

Total (approximate) $= 1.56$ in. water

Note that the weight of liquid will be greater in this arrangement at flooding, and the operating hold-up will be almost the same as the dumped Intalox. The total weight of packing will be approximately 50 percent greater than if the same 2-inch rings had been dumped in place. Two-inch rings are not usually stacked. In this small tower made up of 3-foot ceramic sections, the stacking is not too difficult a job if there are conditions which justify the extra effort and expense.

Liquid Hold-up

Liquid hold up in a tower represents the liquid held in the void spaces of the packing during operating conditions. At flooding, essentially all of the voids are filled with liquid.

Usually low hold-up is desired but reasonable hold-up is necessary for efficient tower operation. The weight of liquid held in the packing must be considered when determining the support loads at the bottom of the packing, as well as the tower itself. The higher the hold-up for any particular packing the greater will be the gas pressure drop, and the longer the tower drainage time when shut down. Smaller size packing tends to have greater hold-up than larger packing.

Figure 9-26 presents water hold-up data which is correlated by.[40]

$$h_{tw} = 0.0004\left(\frac{L'}{d_p}\right)^{0.6} \qquad (9\text{-}6)$$

where: $h_{tw} =$ water hold-up, cubic feet liquid/cu. ft. volume tower

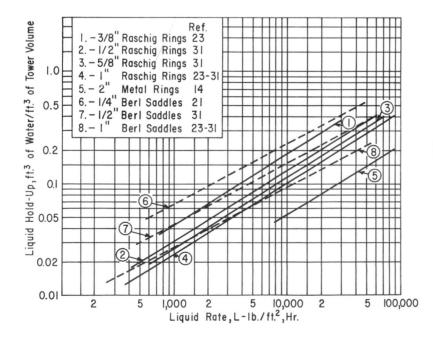

Figure 9-26. Gas-liquid hold-up data for rings and saddles. (By permission M. Leva, "Tower Packings and Packed Tower Design, 2nd Ed." U. S. Stoneware Co., 1953.)

$L' =$ Liquid rate, lbs./(hr.) (sq. ft.)

$d_p =$ Equivalent spherical packing diameter, inches (diameter of packing equivalent to sphere of same surface area as the packing piece). Values given for some packings with physical data Tables 9-1 through 9-15. Area of sphere $= \pi$ (diameter)^2.

For liquids other than water:[36, 40]

$$h_l = h_{tw} (\mu_L)^{0.1} \left(\frac{62.3}{\rho_L}\right)^{0.78} \left(\frac{73}{\sigma}\right)^n \qquad (9\text{-}7)$$

where: $h_l =$ liquid hold-up, cu.ft./cu. ft. packed tower volume

$\mu_L =$ liquid viscosity, centipoise

$\rho_L =$ liquid density, lb./cu. ft.

$\sigma =$ surface tension, dynes/cm.

Values of exponent n are given in Figure 9-27.

Total liquid hold-up in packed bed, $h_t =$ static hold-up, h_s, plus operating hold-up, h_o.[64, 66]

The static hold-up is independent of liquid and gas rates, since it represents the liquid held in the packing after a period of drainage time, usually until constant weight of material is received. This requires approximately 1 hour for a 10-inch dia. x 36-inch packed height tower. Table 9-26 adequately summarizes the data.

Total hold-up, h_t, of water is represented for Raschig rings and Berl saddles.[66]

$$h_t = \alpha L'^\beta / D_p^2 \qquad (9\text{-}8)$$

$$\beta = \gamma D_p \theta$$

Constants are given in Table 9-27

Figures 9-24A, B, C, D, E, F present the graphical interpretation of the total hold-up equation. These are more convenient to apply where the system fits (or nearly fits) the curves.

This data is valuable for determining the total weight of liquid held in the packing, and also the void fraction, in an operating column. ε is the void fraction of the dry packing minus the total hold-up, h_t.

Table 9-26

Static Hold-up in Packings*

Packing Nominal Size In Inches	Static Water Hold-up, h_s, cu.ft./ cu.ft. packing
Raschig rings (unglazed porcelain)	
½	0.0325
1	0.0150
1½	0.0089
2	0.0058
Berl saddles (unglazed porcelain)	
½	0.0317
1	0.0110
1½	0.0052
Raschig rings (carbon)	
1	0.0358
1½	0.0200
2	0.0150

*From Shulman, H. L. et al, Amer. Inst. Chem. Engr. Jour 1, No. 2, 247 (1955) and Ibid, p. 259 (1955), Ref. 64 and 66. By permission.

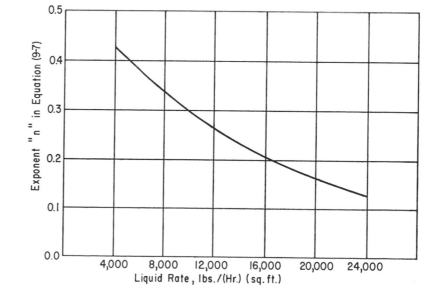

Figure 9-27. Liquid hold-up variation of surface tension exponent with liquid rate. (By permission B. W. Jesser and J. C. Elgin, "Trans." Amer. Inst. Chem. Engr. Vol. 39, No. 3, p. 295, 1943.)

Table 9-27: Total Hold-up Constants*

Packing	α	γ	θ
Porcelain Raschig ring	2.25×10^{-5}	0.965	0.376
Carbon Raschig ring	7.90×10^{-5}	0.706	0.376
Porcelain Berl saddles	2.50×10^{-5}	0.965	0.376

Porcelain (Inches)	Equivalent Spherical Dia., Feet
½ R. R.	0.0582
1 R. R.	0.1167
1½ R. R.	0.1740
2 R. R.	0.238
½ Berl saddle	0.0532
1 Berl saddle	0.1050
1½ Berl saddle	0.155

Carbon (Inches)	
1 R. R.	0.1167
1½ R. R.	0.178
2 R. R.	0.235

* From Shulman, H. L. et. al., Amer. Inst. Chem. Engr. Jour. 1, No. 2, 247 (1955) and Ibid, p. 259 (1955), Ref. 64 and 66, by permission.

Correction Factors For Liquids Other Than Water

In order to use the data in systems handling liquids other than water correction equations and charts are used.[66] The charts are more convenient to use and are presented in Figures 9-28A, B, C, D. First, determine the total or static hold-ups for water at 20° C; second, determine separately the correction for viscosity, density, and surface tension; third, multiply the water hold-up by each of the corrections to obtain hold-up for liquid of the specific system.

A second hold-up correlation reported by T. Otake and K. Okada[55] represents a survey of considerable literature, and is applicable to aqueous and non-aqueous systems for Reynolds numbers from 10, - 20,000.[40]

$$h_o = 1.295 \left(\frac{D'_p L}{\mu'} \right)^{0.676} \left[\frac{(D'_p)^3 g_c \rho^2}{\mu'^2} \right]^{-0.44} (a \, D'_p) \tag{9-9}$$

Packing Wetted Area

Wetted packing area may differ considerably from the physical area of a packing. This is of particular importance in comparing the effectiveness of different packings.

It is only recently that a coordinated group of data became available for wetted areas in Raschig ring and Berl saddle packing.[65]

Figure 9-25 represents the water-air and ammonia-water data for Berl saddles by:[65, 67]

$$f_a = \frac{a'}{a_t} = 0.35 \left[\frac{L'}{G'} \right]^{0.20} \tag{9-10}$$

and for Raschig rings by

$$f_a = \frac{a'}{a_t} = 0.24 \left[\frac{L'}{G'} \right]^{0.25} \tag{9-11}$$

where: f_a = Fraction of total packing area, a_t, that is wetted
a' = Wetted packing surface not necessarily same as effective interfacial surface area for contact, sq.ft./cu.ft.
a_t = Total packing surface, sq. ft./cu. ft.
L' = Superficial liquid rate, lb./hr. (sq. ft.)
G' = Superficial gas rate, lb./hr. (sq. ft.)

The fraction wetted area immediately indicates the effectiveness of contact for the liquid system in the packing. This packing area contact efficiency must be considered in some design problems.

Effective Interfacial Area

The effective interfacial area is used in mass transfer studies as an undivided part of individual and overall coefficients when it is difficult to separate and determine the effective area. The work of Shulman et.al.,[65] presents a well organized evaluation of other work in addition to their own. One of the difficulties in correlating tower packing performance lies in obtaining the correct values for the effective interfacial areas of the packing on which the actual absorption, desorption, chemical reaction, etc. are completed. Figures 9-29 A, B, C, D, E, F, G present a correlation for water flow based on the ammonia-water data of Fellinger[27] and are valid for absorption work.

There are differences between wetted and effective area as discussed by Shulman:[65] (1) wetted areas increase as packing size decreases; (2) effective area is smallest for the smallest packings; (3) the effective area seems to go through a maximum for the 1-inch size packing although the larger packings have almost as much area. This is better understood in terms of the hold-up data for these packings.

For vaporization in packed beds of Raschig rings and Berl saddles:[66]

$$a_{vap} = 0.85 \, (a_{abs}) \left(\frac{h_t}{h_o} \right) \tag{9-12}$$

or

$$a_{vap} = 0.85 \, (a_{abs})_w \left(\frac{h_t}{h_{ow}} \right) \tag{9-13}$$

where the subscripts *vap* and *abs* represent conditions of vaporization and absorption respectively, and subscript *w* represents a water system.

Entrainment From Packing Surface

There is not much data available on this point. Operational experience plus qualitative tests indicate that entrainment is negligible until the packing reaches the flooding condition. See discussion under distillation section.

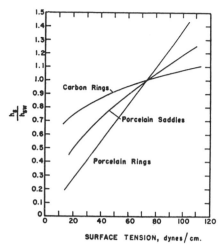

Figure 9-28A. Factors to be applied to water static holdups to determine the effect of surface tension. (By permission H. L. Shulman, C. F. Ullrich, N. Wells, A. Z. Proulx, "AIChE Journal" Vol. 1, No. 2, p. 259, 1955.)

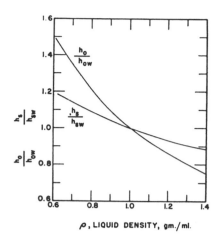

Figure 9-28C. Factors to be applied to water holdups to determine the effect of liquid density. (By permission H. L. Shulman, C. F. Ullrich, N. Wells, A. Z. Proulx, "AIChE Jour." Vol. 1, No. 2, p. 259, 1955.)

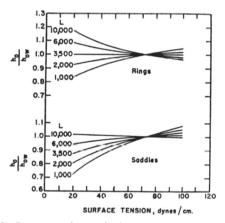

Figure 9-28B. Factors to be applied to water operating holdups to determine the effect of surface tension. (By permission H. L. Shulman, C. F. Ullrich, N. Wells, A. Z. Proulx, "AIChE Jour." Vol. 1, No. 2, p. 259, 1955.)

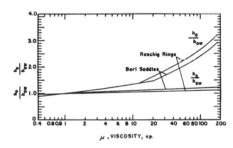

Figure 9-28D. Factors to be applied to water holdups to estimate the effect of viscosity. (By permission H. L. Shulman, C. F. Ullrich, N. Wells, A. Z. Proulx, "AIChE Jour." Vol. 1, No. 2, p. 259, 1955.)

Figure 9-28. Physical property corrections for liquid hold-up.

Example 9-5: Operation at Low Rate, Liquid Hold-up

A sulfuric acid drying tower uses 98 percent acid for drying an incoming air stream. The pilot plant tests show that 15 feet of 1-inch Intalox packing will do this job. The plant scale rates are:

Air = 500 Scfm at 90° F and 2 psig

Acid = 6 gpm at 90° F and Sp. Gr. = 1.81

Determine (1) the tower diameter (2) pressure drop (3) liquid hold-up

$$\text{air rate} = \frac{500}{359} \left(\frac{29}{60} \right) \left(\frac{460 + 60}{460 + 90} \right) \left(\frac{14.7 + 2}{14.7} \right)$$

$$= 0.725 \text{ lbs./(sec.)}$$

$$\text{liquid rate} = \left(\frac{18}{60} \right) \frac{(8.33)}{1.81} = 0.461 \text{ lb./sec.}$$

Assume for first trial:

Inside tower diameter = 12 inches

$$\text{Cross-section area} = \frac{\pi (1)^2}{4} = 0.785 \text{ sq. ft.}$$

$$\text{then: air rate, } G = \frac{0.725}{0.785} = 0.925 \text{ lb./(sec) (sq. ft.)}$$

$$= 3340 \text{ lb./(hr.) (sq. ft.)}$$

$$\text{liquid rate, } L = \frac{0.461}{0.785} = 0.588 \text{ lb./(sec.) (sq. ft.)}$$

$$= 2120 \text{ lb./(hr.) (sq. ft.)}$$

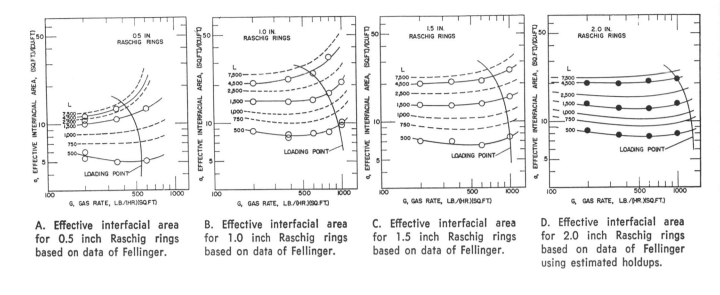

A. Effective interfacial area for 0.5 inch Raschig rings based on data of Fellinger.

B. Effective interfacial area for 1.0 inch Raschig rings based on data of Fellinger.

C. Effective interfacial area for 1.5 inch Raschig rings based on data of Fellinger.

D. Effective interfacial area for 2.0 inch Raschig rings based on data of Fellinger using estimated holdups.

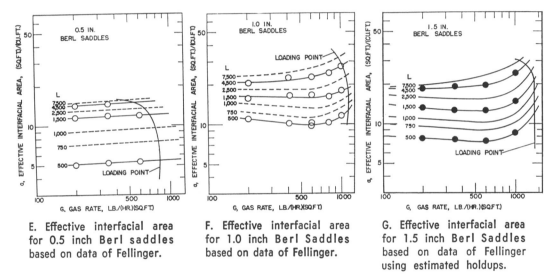

E. Effective interfacial area for 0.5 inch Berl saddles based on data of Fellinger.

F. Effective interfacial area for 1.0 inch Berl Saddles based on data of Fellinger.

G. Effective interfacial area for 1.5 inch Berl Saddles based on data of Fellinger using estimated holdups.

Figure 9-29. Effective interfacial areas for tower packings. (By permission H. L. Shulman, C. F. Ullrich, A. Z. Proulx, J. O. Zimmerman, "AIChE Journal" Vol. 1, No. 2, p. 253, 1955.) Note: for gases or vapors other than air, use abscissa, G, as: $G/\rho_{gas}/0.075)^{0.8}$

$$\rho_L = (1.81)(62.3) = 112.6 \text{ lb./cu. ft.}$$

$$\rho_G = \frac{29}{359}\left(\frac{460+60}{460+90}\right)\left(\frac{14.7+2}{14.7}\right) = 0.087 \text{ lb./cu. ft.}$$

$$\frac{L}{G}(\rho_G/\rho_L)^{\frac{1}{2}} = \frac{0.588}{0.925}\left(\frac{0.087}{112.6}\right)^{\frac{1}{2}} = 0.01975, \text{ (abscissa)}$$

$$\left(\frac{a}{\varepsilon^3}\right) \text{for 1-inch Intalox saddles} = 92 \text{ (Table 9-23)} \\ \text{(original value)}$$

$$\psi^2 = \left(\frac{1}{1.81}\right)^2 = 0.305$$

$$g_c = 32.2 \text{ (lbs.)(ft.)/(lb.)(sec.)}^2$$

$$\mu^{0.2} = (17.0)^{0.2} = 1.762 \text{ cp. at } 90° \text{ F.}$$

$$\frac{G^2}{\rho_G}\left(\frac{a}{\varepsilon^3}\right)\frac{\psi^2 \mu^{0.2}}{\rho_L g_c} = \frac{(0.925)^2 (92)(0.305)(1.762)}{(0.087)(112.6)(32.2)} \\ = 0.13411 \text{ (ordinate)}$$

Reading Figure 9-13C at the calculated ordinate and abscissa, we obtain:

(a) An indicated operating condition above the upper loading limit

(b) A condition of high pressure drop, approximately 1.5 in./foot of packing height

(c) A situation too close to flooding, thus requiring a larger tower diameter

Second Assumption: Try 15-inch Dia. Ceramic Tower

Inspection of Figures 9-13A, B or C shows that the increase on tower diameter is not reflected in the value of the abscissa. By changing the tower diameter to 15 inch, cross-section area = 1.22 sq. ft.

$$G = \frac{0.725}{1.22} = 0.593 \text{ lb./(sec.) (sq. ft.)}$$

$$L = 0.461/1.22 = 0.378 \text{ lb./(sec.) (sq. ft.)}$$

$$\frac{G^2}{\rho_G}\left(\frac{a}{\varepsilon^3}\right)\frac{\psi^2 \mu^{0.2}}{\rho_L g_c} = (0.1535)\left(\frac{0.593}{0.925}\right)^2 = 0.063$$

This indicates operation in the loading region. **The expected pressure drop is 0.5 in. water/foot.**

Total expected pressure drop:
Packing = (0.5)(15) = 7.5 inches water

Support = 1.5 inches (estimated from Figures 9-19 and 20 for a 58 percent open grid).

Total drop = 9.0 in. water (approximate)

Superficial gas velocity through tower:

$$= \frac{0.593 \text{ lb./(sec.) (sq.ft.)}}{0.087 \text{ lb./cu.ft.}}$$

$$= 6.8 \text{ ft./sec.}$$

Entrainment

This velocity is slightly high and an entrainment knockout or separator should be installed in the air stream following the tower, or in the top of the tower itself.

Liquid Hold-up in the tower:

For water, the hold-up would be, from Equation 9-6.

$$h_{tw} = 0.0004 \left(\frac{L'}{d_p}\right)^{0.6}$$

$$d_p = 0.68 \text{ (from Table 9-7)}$$

$$h_{tw} = 0.0004 \frac{[(0.378)(3600)]^{0.6}}{(0.68)} = 0.0384 \text{ cu. ft./cu. ft.,}$$
for water.

For sulfuric acid:

From Figure 9-28C, h_o/h_{ow}, for density correction multiplier = 0.6.

From Figure 9-28B, correction for surface tension = 1.0 (at 70 dynes/cm.)

From Figure 9-28D, correction for viscosity = 1.1 (at 18 cp.)

h_o, for acid = h_{ow} (0.6) (1.0) (1.1) = (0.0384) (0.66)
= 0.0254 cu. ft. acid/cu. ft. tower volume

For a packed volume of 15 feet in a 15-inch I.D. tower, the total acid hold-up:

$$= [(15)(1.22)] (0.0254)(112.6 \text{ lbs./cu. ft.})$$

Total hold-up = 52.3 lbs. acid

Weights

Weight of dry packing in tower:

$$= (42 \text{ lbs./cu.ft.}) [(15)(1.22)]$$
$$= 770 \text{ lbs.}$$

Total weight on bottom support plate when operating (not flooded)

$$= 52.3 + 770 = 822.3 \text{ lbs.}$$

Some allowance should be made for surging or uneven operation.

The maximum expected weight of liquid would be at flooding conditions:

Using percent free gas space = 77.5

Volume of liquid space = (15) (1.22) (0.775)
$$= 14.2 \text{ cu.ft.}$$

Weight of acid in this space = (14.2) (112.6)
$$= 1600 \text{ lbs.}$$

Maximum support load = 770 + 1600 = 2370 lbs.

This is the load which should be considered for the support design and selection. To allow for unusual conditions, specify support load = (1.1) (2370 = 2600 lbs. minimum.

Mass and Heat Transfer in Packed Towers

The majority of packed towers are used for mass transfer operations such as absorption, distillation and stripping; however, there are other uses such as heat transfer quenching and entrainment knockout.

The usual packings and auxiliary features associated with these towers have been presented in connection with pressure drop considerations.

Since the packed tower is a continuous contacting device as compared to the step-wise plate tower, performance capacity is expressed as the number of transfer units, N, the height of the transfer unit, H.T.U., and mass transfer coefficients $K_G a$ and $K_L a$. Figure 9-30 identifies the key symbols and constant flow material balance.

Number of Transfer Units, N_{OG}, N_{OL}

The transfer of mass between phases in a packed tower takes place either as essentially all gas film controlling, all liquid film controlling or some combination of these mechanisms (see Figure 9-31). To express the ease (low number of transfer units) or difficulty of the transfer under the conditions of operation with respect to system equilibrium, the system is evaluated as to the number of transfer units N_{OG} or N_{OL} required. These can be determined experimentally and the data used for similar systems. However, it is also important to be in a position to estimate the number of transfer units for some foreign system when data is not available.

$$N_{OG} = \frac{Z}{H_{OG}} \text{ or } N_{OL} = \frac{Z}{H_{OL}} \qquad (9\text{-}14)$$

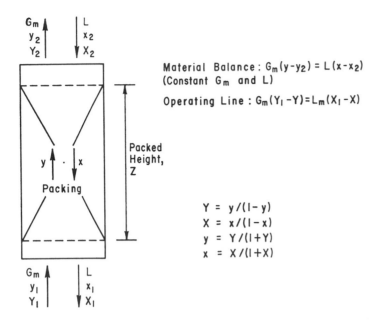

Material Balance: $G_m(y-y_2) = L(x-x_2)$
(Constant G_m and L)

Operating Line: $G_m(Y_1-Y) = L_m(X_1-X)$

$Y = y/(1-y)$
$X = x/(1-x)$
$y = Y/(1+Y)$
$x = X/(1+X)$

Figure 9-30. Counter current packed tower symbols.

where: N_{OG} = Number of transfer units, based on overall gas film coefficients

N_{OL} = Number of transfer units, based on overall liquid film coefficients

Z = Height of packing, feet

H_{OG} = Height of transfer units, based on overall gas film, coefficients, feet

H_{OL} = Height of transfer unit, based on overall liquid film coefficients, feet

The transfer process is termed gas film controlling if essentially all of the resistance to mass transfer is in the gas film. This means that the gas is usually quite soluble in, or reactive with, the liquid of the system. If the system is liquid film controlling, the gas is relatively insoluble in the liquid and the resistance to transfer is in the liquid film. Many systems are a combination of the two in various proportions. Without good data on such systems it is next to impossible to expect to accomplish an exact design of equipment, although satisfactory designs are possible. To have some guidelines, system information is presented in Table 9-28. Other data for different systems exists in the literature in a scattered fashion.

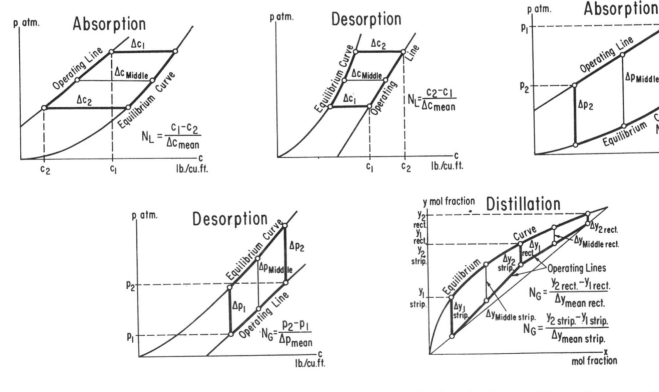

Figure 9-31. (Right) Mass transfer diagrams. The number of transfer units can be determined by the difference in concentration or vapor pressure, particularly over ranges where the equilibrium is essentially straight. (By permission J. J. Czermann, et al. Petroleum Refiner. Vol. 37, No. 4, p. 165, 1958.)

Table 9-28

System Film Control*

Gas Film

1. Absorption of ammonia in water
2. Absorption of ammonia in aqueous ammonia
3. Stripping of ammonia from aqueous ammonia
4. Absorption of water vapor in strong acids
5. Absorption of sulfur trioxide in strong sulfuric acid
6. Absorption of hydrogen chloride in water
7. Absorption of hydrogen chloride in weak hydrochloric acid
8. Absorption of 5 vol. percent ammonia in acids
9. Absorption of sulfur dioxide in alkali solutions
10. Absorption of sulfur dioxide in ammonia solutions
11. Absorption of hydrogen sulfide in weak caustic
12. Evaporation of liquids
13. Condensation of liquids

Liquid Film

1. Absorption of carbon dioxide in water
2. Absorption of oxygen in water
3. Absorption of hydrogen in water
4. Absorption of carbon dioxide in weak alkali
5. Absorption of chlorine in water

Both Gas and Liquid Film

1. Absorption of sulfur dioxide in water
2. Absorption of acetone in water
3. Absorption of nitrogen oxide in strong sulfuric acid

* From: M. Leva, *Tower Packings and Packed Tower Design*, 2nd Ed. pg. 91, U. S. Stoneware Co. (1953), by permission.

For (1) dilute solutions or (2) equal molar diffusion between phases (e.g., distillation)

$$N_{OG} = \int_{y_2}^{y_1} \frac{dy}{(y - y^*)} = \frac{y_1 - y_2}{\ln \frac{(y - y^*)_1 - (y - y^*)_2}{(y - y^*)_2}} \quad (9\text{-}15)$$

where: $(y - y^*) =$ driving force, expressed as mol fractions

$y =$ mol fraction of one component (solute) at any point in the gas phase of the contacting system

$y^* =$ Mol fraction gas phase composition in equilibrium with a liquid composition, x

$x =$ Mol fraction in the liquid at the same corresponding point in the system as y

$1, 2 =$ Inlet and outlet conditions of system

If the system has more than two components, the calculations may be based on the component which varies the most in passing through the unit, or the component for which good data is available.

A large majority of the systems have operating lines and equilibrium curves which can be assumed as straight over the range covered by the design problem. For the conditions of a straight line equilibrium curve, $y^* = mx$. Colburn[10,11] has integrated the relation above to obtain:

$$N = \frac{2.3 \log [(1 - P'')M + P'']}{1 - P''} \quad (9\text{-}16)$$

where N may be N_{OG} or N_{OL} depending on operation.

Table 9-29 identifies several important conditions that affect the values of P'' and M. These are extracted from Colburn's larger summary.[11]

Figure 9-32[10] is a plot to aid in solving the equation for N (or N_{OG} or N_{OL}).

For constant temperature absorption, with no solute in the inlet liquid, $x_2 = 0$, and the abscissa becomes y_1/y_2.

For concentrated solutions and more general application

The following equation applies for diffusion in one direction (e.g., absorption, extraction, desorption)[74]

$$N_{OG} = \int_{y_2}^{y_1} \frac{(1 - y)_M \, dy}{(1 - y)(y - y^*)} \quad (9\text{-}17)$$

$$N_{OG} = \int_{y_2}^{y_1} \frac{dy}{(y - y^*)} + \frac{1}{2} \ln \frac{(1 - y_2)}{(1 - y_1)} \quad (9\text{-}18)$$

or

$$N_{OG} = \int_{Y_2}^{Y_1} \frac{dY}{(Y - Y^*)} - \frac{1}{2} \ln \frac{1 + Y_1}{1 + Y_2} \quad (9\text{-}19)$$

or

$$N_{OG} = \int_{Y_2}^{Y_1} \frac{dY}{(Y - Y^*)} - 1.15 \log_{10} \frac{1 + Y_1}{1 + Y_2} \quad (9\text{-}20)$$

where: $(1 - y)_M =$ log mean average of concentration at the opposite ends of the diffusion process, $(1 - y)$ in main gas body, and $(1 - y^*)$ at the interface.[74]

$y =$ Concentration of solute in gas, mol fraction

$y^* =$ Concentration of solute in gas in equilibrium with liquid, mol fraction

$Y =$ Concentration of solute in gas. lb. mols solute/lb. mol solvent gas

$Y^* =$ Concentration of solute in gas in equilibrium with liquid. lb. mol solute/lb. mol solvent gas

Table 9-29

Values to Use With Transfer Equation and Figure 9-32**

Condition of Operation	P″	M
Absorption:		
1. Constant mG_m/L_m	mG_m/L_m	$(y_1 - mx_2)/(y_2 - mx_2)$
2. Varying mG_m/L_m	m_2G_{m2}/L_{m2}	$\left(\dfrac{y_1 - m_2x_2}{y_2 - m_2x_2}\right)\left(\dfrac{1 - m_2G_m/L_m}{1 - y^*_1/y_1}\right)$
Desorption (stripping):		
3. Constant L_m/mG_m	L_m/mG_m	$(x_1 - y_2/m)/(x_2 - y_2m)$
4. Varying L_m/mG_m	L_{m2}/m_2G_{m2}	$\left(\dfrac{x_1 - y_2/m_2}{x_2 - y_2/m_2}\right)\left(\dfrac{1 - L_{m2}/m_2 G_{m2}}{1 - x_1^*/x_1}\right)$
Distillation, enriching[1]		
5. Constant mG_m/L_m		Same as 1
6. Varying mG_m/L_m stripping, closed steam[2]		Same as 2
7. Constant L_m/mG_m	L_m/mG_m	$(x_1 - x_2/m)/(x_2 - x_2/m)$
8. Varying L_m/mG_m stripping, open steam[2]	L_{m2}/m_2G_{m2}	$\left(\dfrac{x_1 - x_2/m_2}{x_2 - x_2m_2}\right)\left(\dfrac{1 - L_2/m_2 G_{m2}}{1 - x_1^*/x_1}\right)$
9. Constant L_m/mG_m	L_m/mG_m	x_1/x_2
10. Varying L_m/mG_m	L_{m2}/m_2G_{m2}	$\left(\dfrac{x_1}{x_2}\right)\left(\dfrac{1 - L_{m2}/m_2G_{m2}}{1 - x_1^*/x_1}\right)$

 * Equilibrium value
  Subscripts 1 and 2 refer to the concentrated and dilute ends of the unit respectively
 (1) Concentrations and m are based on high boiler or "heavy key"
 (2) Concentrations and m are based on low boiler or "light key"
 ** By permission, A. P. Colburn, Eng. Chem. **33**, 459 (1941).

If the liquid film controls:

$$N_{OL} = \int_{x_2}^{x_1} \frac{dx}{(x^* - x)} + \tfrac{1}{2} \ln \frac{(1 - x_2)}{(1 - x_1)} \qquad (9\text{-}21)$$

$$N_{OL} = \int_{X_2}^{X_1} \frac{dX}{X^* - X} - \tfrac{1}{2} \ln \frac{1 + X_1}{1 + X_2} \qquad (9\text{-}22)$$

where: x = Concentration of solute in liquid, mol fraction

x^* = Concentration of solute in liquid in equilibrium with gas, mol fraction

X = Concentration of solute in liquid, lb. mol solute/lb. mol solvent

X^* = Concentration of solute in liquid in equilibrium with the gas, lb. mol solute/lb. mol solvent

It is usually necessary to graphically integrate the first terms of the above equations, although some problems do allow for mathematical treatment.

Example 9-6:
Number of Transfer Units For Dilute Solutions

An existing 10-inch I.D. packed tower using 1-inch Berl saddles is to absorb a vent gas in water at 85° F. Laboratory data show the Henry's Law expression for solubility to be $y^* = 1.5x$, where y^* is the equilibrium mol fraction of the gas over water at compositions of x mol fraction of gas dissolved in the liquid phase. Past experience indicates that the H_{OG} for air-water system will be acceptable. The conditions are: (refer to Figure 9-30)

$G'_1 = 200$ mols gas/hr. (sq.ft.)

$L'_2 = 500$ mols water/hr. (sq.ft.)

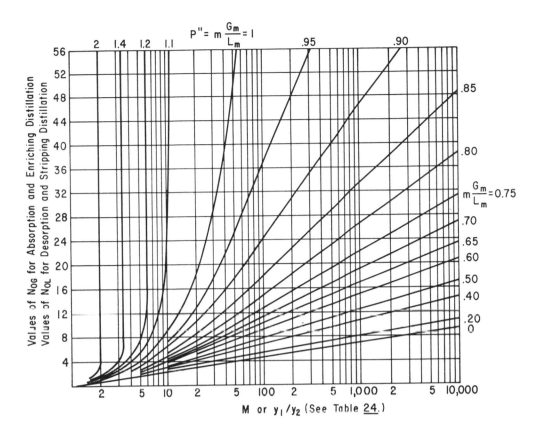

$$P'' = m\frac{G_m}{L_m} = 1$$

Values of N_{OG} for Absorption and Enriching Distillation
Values of N_{OL} for Desorption and Stripping Distillation

$m\frac{G_m}{L_m} = 0.75$

M or y_1/y_2 (See Table 24.)

Figure 9-32. Colburn plot for transfer units. (By permission A. P. Colburn, "Ind. Eng. Chem." Vol. 33, 459, 1941.)

$y_1 = 0.03$ (inlet)

$y_2 = 0.001$ (outlet)

$x_2 = 0$ (inlet)

$x_1 = ?$ (outlet)

Determine the number of transfer units, and the packed tower height.

Material Balance

Dilute solutions, assume constant L' and G'.

Gas phase change $= G_1 (y_1 - y_2) = 200 (y_1 - 0.001)$

Liquid phase change $= L_2 (x_2 - x_1) = 500 (0 - x_1)$

Since the $(-)$ sign has no significance, except to indicate the direction of mass change, use $500(x_1)$.

Now, in order to use the simplified

$$N_{OG} = \int_{y_2}^{y_1} \frac{dy}{(y - y^*)} \qquad (9\text{-}18A)$$

Assume values of y_1 and solve the equated mass change for values of x.

$$200(y_1 - 0.001) = 500(x_1)$$

Assume y	Calculated x_1	Equilibrium y^*	$\left(\dfrac{1}{y - y^*}\right)$
0.03	0.0116	0.0174	79.4
0.025	0.0096	0.0144	94.4
0.02	0.0076	0.0114	116.4
0.015	0.0056	0.0084	151.4
0.01	0.0036	0.0054	217.
0.005	0.0016	0.0024	384.
0.001	0	0	1000.

Example: Calculate x, as illustrated for point $y = 0.015$

$$200(0.015 - 0.001) = 500\, x_1$$

$$200(0.014) \qquad = 500\, x_1$$

$$x_1 = \frac{200(0.014)}{500} = 0.0056$$

Calculate the equilibrium values, y^*, as illustrated for point of $x_1 = 0.0116$

$$y^* = 1.5(0.0116) = 0.0174$$

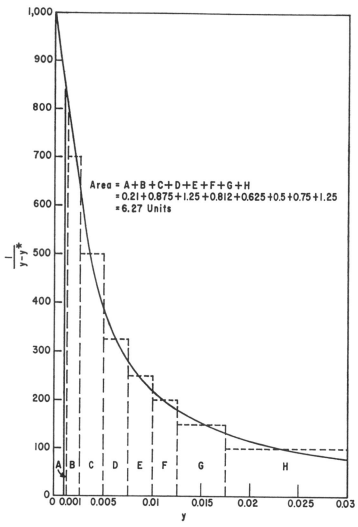

Figure 9-33. Graphical integration for example problem No. 6

Calculate $1/(y - y^*)$ for point corresponding to:
$x_1 = 0.0116$ where $y^* = 0.0174$

$$\frac{1}{y - y^*} = \frac{1}{0.03 - 0.0174} = \frac{1}{0.0126} = 79.4$$

Area Under Curve

Figure 9-33, is a summation of steps indicated, or the area can be circumscribed with a planimeter and evaluated.

Area = 6.27 units, then number of transfer units,
$N_{OG} = 6.27$

Height of Transfer Unit

From data of Mehta and Parekh for 1-inch Berl Saddles,[40]

$H_{OG} = 0.86$ feet

Height of packed section:
$Z = (6.27)\ (0.86) = 5.4$ feet

Total Packed Height Recommended

Process packed height	= 5.4 feet
Distribution packed height	= 2.00
Total	7.4 feet

Use: 8.5 to 10 feet of 1-inch Berl saddles

To complete the design, the tower should be checked for loading and flooding conditions, and the pressure drop established. However, this procedure will not be repeated as it can be found elsewhere in this section.

Example 9-7: Use of Colburn's Chart for Transfer Units— Straight Line Equilibrium Curve, Figure 9-32, Constant Temperature Operation.

Use the previous example on dilute solutions and solve by Colburn's Chart.[11]

Abscissa: $y_1/y_2 = 0.03/0.001 = 30$, since $x_2 = 0$ (no dissolved solute gas in inlet water.)

Parameter: $mG'/L' = (1.5)\ (200/500) = 0.6$

Note that m is the slope of the straight line equilibrium curve, m = 1.5

Reading chart: At $y_1/y_2 = 30$ and $mG'/L' = 0.6$
No. transfer units, N = 6.4

This compares with the value from graphical integration of 6.27 and is a good check.

If N = 6.4 were used for the tower:

$$= 6.4\ (0.86) = 5.5\text{ feet minimum for process operations}$$

Example 9-8: Number Transfer Units— Concentrated Solutions

Using the basic problems for dilute solutions, assume the following conditions for a higher concentration.

$G' = 200$ mols gas/hr. (sq.ft.)

$L' = 500$ mols water/hr. (sq.ft.)

$y_1 = 0.30$ (inlet)

$y_2 = 0.01$ (outlet)

$x_2 = 0$

$y^* = 1.54$

Material Balance

Based on inert gas

$$\text{Gas phase change} = G' (1 - y_1) \left[\frac{y}{1-y} - \frac{y_2}{1-y_2} \right]$$

$$\left[\frac{y}{1-y} - \frac{0.01}{1-0.01} \right]$$

Liquid phase change =

$$L' \left[\frac{x}{1-x} - \frac{x_1}{1-x_1} \right] = L' \left[\frac{x}{1-x} - 0 \right]$$

These changes must be equal:

$$G(1 - 0.3) \left(\frac{y}{1-y} - \frac{0.01}{0.99} \right) = L \left(\frac{x}{1-x} \right)$$

Assume values of y and solve for corresponding values of x.

$$200(0.7) \left(\frac{y}{1-y} - 0.0101 \right) = L \left(\frac{x}{1-x} \right)$$

Let $y = 0.3$

$$200(0.7) \left[\left(\frac{0.3}{1-0.3} \right) - 0.0101 \right] = 500 \left(\frac{x}{1-x} \right)$$

$$140(0.428 - 0.0101) = 500 \left(\frac{x}{1-x} \right)$$

$$\frac{x}{1-x} = \frac{58.5}{500} = 0.117$$

$$x = 0.1048$$

Calculate equilibrium y^* from values of x.
Assume that for this concentration range: (this will usually not be same as for dilute solution tower)

$y^* = 1.5x$
$y^* = 1.5 (.1048) = 0.157$
Calculate $(1 - y)$:
$1 - y = 1 - 0.30 = 0.70$
Calculate $(1 - y^*)$:
$1 - y^* = 1 - 0.157 = 0.843$
Calculate $(1 - y)_M$, arithmetic average of non-diffusing gas concentration at ends of diffusing path:

$$(1 - y)_M = \frac{(1-y) + (1-y^*)}{2} = \frac{0.7 + 0.843}{2}$$

$$= 0.7715$$

Calculate $1/(y - y^*)$:

$$\frac{1}{y - y^*} = \frac{1}{0.30 - 0.157} = 7.0$$

Calculate $(1 - y)_M / (1 - y) (y - y^*)$:

$$= 0.7715(7.0)/0.7 = 7.715$$

A plot of y versus $(1 - y)_M / (1 - y) (y - y^*)$ gives the number of transfer units as presented in the previous example.

As a second solution:

$$N_{OG} = \int_{y_2}^{y_1} \frac{dy}{y - y^*} + \tfrac{1}{2} \ln \frac{1 - y_2}{1 - y_1}$$

Assumed y	Calc. x	y^*	1-y	1-y*	$(1-y)_M$	$\dfrac{1}{y-y^*}$	$\dfrac{(1-y)_M}{(1-y)(y-y^*)}$
0.30	0.1048	0.157	0.70	0.843	0.7715	7.0	7.715
0.20	0.0631	0.0945	0.80	0.9055	0.8527	9.48	10.10
0.15	0.0446	0.0667	0.85	0.9333	0.8916	12.0	12.58
0.10	0.0276	0.0413	0.90	0.9587	0.9293	17.02	17.55
0.05	0.0142	0.0213	0.95	0.9787	0.9643	34.9	35.40
0.01	……	……	0.99	1.000	0.9950	100.0	100.50

From Figure 9-34 the area under the curve for y versus $1/(y - y^*)$ is 5.72 units $= N_{OG}$ (approximate)

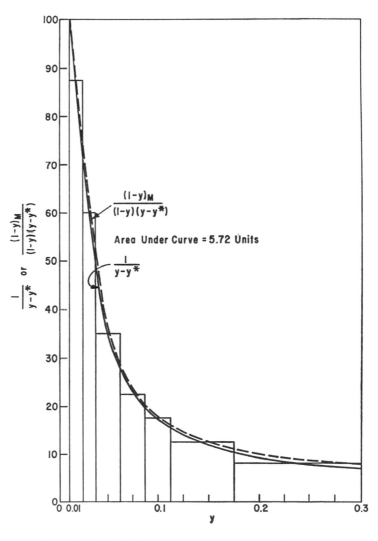

Figure 9-34. Graphical integration number transfer units.

The correction is:

$$\tfrac{1}{2} \ln \frac{1 - y_2}{1 - y_1} = \tfrac{1}{2} \ln \frac{0.99}{0.70}$$

$$= \tfrac{1}{2}(0.345) = 0.172$$

Therefore:

$$N_{OG} = 5.72 + 0.172 = 5.89 \text{ transfer units}$$

Note that the graphical integration is never exact and hence the correction often makes little difference except for cases of curved equilibrium lines.

From Figure 9-34 the area under the curve, y versus $(1 - y)_m / (1 - y)(y - y^*)$ is only slightly larger than the y versus $1/y - y^*$ for this case. In order to avoid confusion the Figure was only integrated for the latter. However, it could be performed for the former and the result should be very close to 5.89.

Gas and Liquid-phase Coefficients, k_G and k_L

Recent studies indicate that the individual film transfer coefficients may be correlated with good agreement for Raschig rings and Berl Saddles for aqueous and non-aqueous systems:[67]

$$j_D =$$

$$\left[\frac{k_G M_M P_{BM}}{G}\right]\left[\mu_{Ga}/\rho_G D_v\right]^{0.667} = 1.195 \left[\frac{D_p G'}{\mu_{Ga}(1 - \varepsilon)}\right]^{-0.36} \quad (9\text{-}23)$$

This has been shown to correlate for a wide variety of tower packings, various operating conditions, and physical properties of the solute and inert gases. The k_G calculated must be used in conjunction with the effective interfacial areas determined by Shulman,[65] Figure 9-29, to establish a reliable value for $k_G a$. Figure 9-29 should be used with the abscissa as $G/\sqrt{\rho/0.075}$ for inert gas other than air.[67]

$$k_G a = k_G (a)$$

$$\text{HTU (gas-Phase)} = G'/k_G a\, M_M P_{BM} \quad (9\text{-}24)$$

where: D_v = diffusivity of solute in gas, sq. ft./hr.

k_G = gas-phase mass transfer coefficient lb. mols/hr. (sq. ft.) (atm)

M_M = mean molecular weight of gas, lb./lb. mol

P_{BM} = mean partial pressure of inert gas in the gas phase, atm

μ_{Ga} = gas viscosity, lb./(hr.) (ft.)

ρ_G = gas density, lb./cu. ft.

G' = superficial gas rate, lb./(hr.)/(sq. ft.)

$$\frac{1}{K_G a} = \frac{1}{k_G a} + \frac{1}{H'k_L a} = \frac{1}{k_G a} + \frac{m}{k_L a} = \frac{1}{H'K_L a} \quad (9\text{-}25)$$

$$\frac{1}{K_L a} = \frac{1}{k_L a} + \frac{H'}{k_G a} = \frac{1}{K_L a} + \frac{1}{m k_G a} \quad (9\text{-}26)$$

H' = Henry's law constant, lb. mols/(cu. ft.) (atm)

k_L = liquid-phase mass transfer coefficient, lb. mols/(hr.) (sq. ft.) (lb. mols/cu. ft.)

The relation

$$\frac{\text{vaporization}}{\text{absorption}} = \frac{(k_G a)_v}{(k_G a)_a} = 0.85\, \frac{h_t}{h_o} \quad (9\text{-}27)$$

is reported to correlate $\pm$ 8 percent based on data tested, and appears to be founded on a sound investigative program.

For the liquid phase based on Raschig ring and Berl saddle data.[65]

$$\frac{k_L D_P}{D_L} = 25.1 \left[\frac{D_P L'}{\mu_{La}}\right]^{0.45} \left[\frac{\mu_{La}}{\rho_L D_L}\right]^{0.5} \quad (9\text{-}28)$$

Use of k_G and k_L

1. From physical properties of system, determine k_G and k_L. If system is known or can be assumed to be essentially all gas or all liquid film controlling, then only the controlling k need be calculated. For greater accuracy, both values are recommended, since very few systems are more than 80 percent controlled by only one k.

2. Combine effective interfacial area to calculate $k_G a$ or $k_L a$.

3. Determine $K_G a$ by:

$$\frac{1}{K_G a} = \frac{1}{k_G a} + \frac{1}{H'k_L a} = \frac{1}{H'K_L a}$$

Height of a Transfer Unit, H_{OG}, H_{OL}, HTU

An earlier concept of height equivalent to a theoretical plate (H.E.T.P.) for relating the height of packing to a unit of transfer known as the theoretical stage or plate has generally been dropped in favor of the "height of a transfer unit" HTU., and designated as H_{OG} or H_{OL} depending on whether it was determined from gas or liquid film data. H.E.T.P. data for absorption and distillation is given in the section under packed tower distillation.

$$\frac{\text{HETP}}{H_{OG}} = \frac{(mG_m/L_m) - 1}{\ln (mG_m/L_m)}$$

1. Height of Overall Transfer Unit

For small changes in concentration and total number mols of gas and liquid remain essentially constant; applicable to all but very concentrated solutions. For the latter case see References 18 or 74.

$$H_{OG} = \frac{G_M}{K_G a\, P_{ave,}} \quad (9\text{-}29)$$

$$H_{OL} = \frac{L_m}{K_L a\, \rho_L} \quad (9\text{-}30)$$

2. Height of Individual Transfer Unit

For same conditions as (1.) Some data is reported as individual gas or liquid film coefficients or transfer unit

heights. However, it is often possible to use it as overall data if the conditions are understood.

$$H_G = \frac{G_m}{k_G a \, P_{ave,}} \qquad (9\text{-}31)$$

$$H_L = \frac{L_m}{k_L a \, \rho_L} \qquad (9\text{-}32)$$

$$H_{OG} = H_G + \frac{mG_m}{L_m}(H_L) = H_G + \frac{H_L}{A'} \qquad (9\text{-}33)$$

$$H_{OL} = H_L + \frac{L_m}{mG}(H_G) = H_L + A' \, H_G \qquad (9\text{-}34)$$

where: $A' = L_m/mG_m$

For predominately liquid film controlling system, $A'H_G$ is almost negligible and $H_{OL} = H_L$; likewise for gas film controlling, H_L/A' is negligible and $H_{OG} = H_G$.

where: G_m = Gas Mass Velocity, lb. moles/(Hr.) (sq. ft.)

L_m = Liquid Mass Velocity, lb. moles/(hr.) (sq. ft.)

$K_G a$ = Overall gas mass-transfer coefficient, lb. moles/(hr.) (cu. ft.) (atm)

$K_L a$ = Overall liquid mass-transfer coefficient, lb. mole/(hr.) (cu. ft.) (lb. mole/cu. ft.)

$k_G a$ = Individual gas mass-transfer coefficient, lb. moles/(hr.) (cu. ft.) (atm)

$k_L a$ = Individual liquid mass-transfer coefficient, lb. moles/(hr.) (cu. ft.) (lb. mol./cu. ft.)

$P_{ave.}$ = Average total pressure in tower, atmospheres

H_L = Height of liquid film transfer unit, feet

H_G = Height of gas film transfer unit, feet

a = Effective interfacial area for contacting gas and liquid phases, sq. ft./cu. ft. Since this is very difficult to evaluate, it is usually retained as a part of the coefficient such as $K_G a$, $K_L a$, $k_G a$, and $k_L a$.

3. Estimation of Height of Liquid Film Transfer Units

The following relation is used in estimating liquid film transfer units.[62] For the proper systems H_L may be assumed to be equal to H_{OL}.

$$H_L = \phi \, (L'/\mu_{La})^j \, (\mu_{La}/\rho_L D_L)^{0.5}, \text{ feet} \qquad (9\text{-}35)$$

where: $\mu_{La}/\rho_L D_L$ = Schmidt number

H_L = Height of transfer unit, feet

L' = Liquid rate, lb./(hr.) (sq. ft.)

μ_L = Viscosity of liquid, lb./(ft.) (hr.)

D_L = Liquid diffusivity, sq. ft./hr.

ϕ and j are constants given in Table 9-30.

Diffusivity values are given in Table 9-31.

4. Estimation of Height of Gas Film Transfer Units

The relation[61, 62, 63]

$$H_G = \frac{\alpha G'^\beta}{L'^\gamma} \left(\frac{\mu_{Ga}}{\rho_G D_G} \right)^{0.5} \qquad (9\text{-}36)$$

Table 9-30

Liquid Film Height of Transfer Unit*

Packing	ϕ	j	Range of L' Lb./hr. (sq. ft.)
Raschig Rings (Inches)			
⅜	0.00182	0.46	400 — 15,000
½	0.00357	0.35	400 — 15,000
1	0.0100	0.22	400 — 15,000
1.5	0.0111	0.22	400 — 15,000
2	0.0125	0.22	400 — 15,000
Berl Saddles (Inches)			
½	0.00666	0.28	400 — 15,000
1	0.00588	0.28	400 — 15,000
1.5	0.00625	0.28	400 — 15,000
3 In. Partition rings, stacked staggered	0.0625	0.09	3,000 — 14,000
Spiral Rings, stacked staggered			
3-in. single spiral	0.00909	0.28	400 — 15,000
3-in. triple spiral	0.0116	0.28	3,000 — 14,000
Drip-point grids (continuous flue)			
Style 6146	0.0154	0.23	3,500 — 30,000
Style 6295	0.00725	0.31	2,500 — 22,000

* From the data of Sherwood and Holloway[62] and of Molstad, McKinney and Abbey,[51] and reprinted by permission from R. E. Treybal, *Mass Transfer Operations*, p. 237, McGraw-Hill Book Co. Inc., New York, N. Y. (1955), Ref. 66.

describes a reasonable part of the gas film data. It allows the conversion of the ammonia-air-water data of Fellinger[60] to useful interpretation for other systems. Table 9-32 gives the constants for the equation.

α, β, γ = constants peculiar to packing for dilute and moderate concentrations:[74]

$$H_{OG} = H_G + \frac{mG}{L}(H_L) = H_G + \frac{H_L}{A}$$

$$H_{OL} = H_L + \frac{L}{mG}(H_G) = H_L + A \, H_G$$

Figure 9-35 presents some of the data of Fellinger[27] as presented in Reference 40 for H_{OG} for the ammonia-air-water systems. This data may be used with the Sherwood relations to estimate H_L and H_G values for other systems.

Estimation of Diffusion Coefficients of Gases

Good reliable diffusion data is difficult to obtain, particularly over a wide range of temperature. The Gilliland relation is:[63]

$$D_V = 0.0069 \frac{T^{3/2} \sqrt{1/M_A + 1/M_B}}{P(V_A^{1/3} + V_B^{1/3})^2}, \text{ sq. ft./hr} \qquad (9\text{-}37)$$

Table 9-31

Diffusion Coefficients of Gases and Liquids in Liquids at 68° F. (Dilute Concentrations)*

	Solvent	Diffusion Coefficient, D_L Sq. ft./Hr. (Multiply all Values by 10^{-5}
Gas		
Oxygen	Water	7.0
Carbon Dioxide	Water	5.82
Nitrous Oxide	Water	5.86
Ammonia	Water	6.83
Chlorine	Water	4.74
Bromine	Water	4.66
Hydrogen	Water	19.92
Nitrogen	Water	6.37
Hydrogen Chloride	Water	10.25
Hydrogen Sulfide	Water	5.47
Acetylene	Water	6.06
Liquid		
Sulfuric Acid	Water	6.72
Nitric Acid	Water	10.15
Methanol	Water	4.97
Sodium Chloride	Water	5.23
Sodium Hydroxide	Water	5.86

Note: Additional data is given in the reference, as well as the International Critical Tables.
* From: Perry, J. H., *Chem. Engrs. Hndbk.* 3rd Ed. p. 540, McGraw-Hill Book Co., Inc. (1950). By permission.

where:

$$T = \text{Absolute temperature, °R.}$$
$$M_A, M_B = \text{Molecular weights of the two gases, A and B.}$$
$$P = \text{Total pressure, atm.}$$
$$V_A, V_B = \text{Molecular volumes of gases, obtained by Kopp's law of additive volumes, c.c./gm. mole at normal boiling point. See Table 9-33.}$$

Diffusion coefficients are used to estimate $K_G a$ values for gas film controlling systems:

$$K_G a (\text{ unknown system}) =$$

$$K_G a (\text{known system}) \left[\frac{D_V \text{ unknown}}{D_V \text{ known}} \right]^{0.56}$$

Ammonia-air-water system data, Figure 9-35, is often used by converting H_{OG} (ammonia-air) to its corresponding $K_G a$, and then substituting the above relation for the unknown $K_G a$.

Example 9-9: Design of Ammonia Absorption Tower, Figure 9-40A and B

An inert gas process vent stream contains 91 lbs./hr. (5.35 mols/hr.) ammonia. This is 5.7 percent (volume) of the total. The absorber is to operate at 150 psig and recover 99 percent of the inlet ammonia as aqua using 90° F. water. Average vapor mixture molecular weight = 11.6. Determine (a) the number of transfer units for the

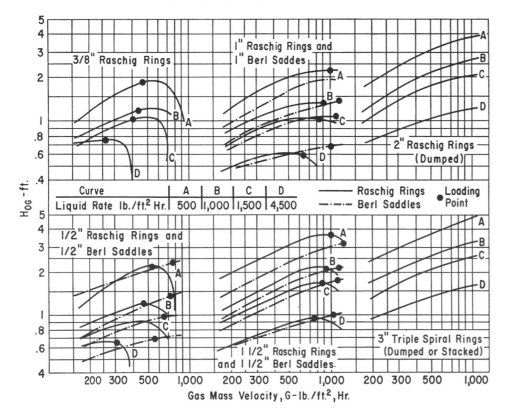

Figure 9-35. Fellinger's overall gas film mass transfer data for ammonia-water system. (By permission M. Leva, "Tower Packings and Packed Tower Design, 2nd Ed." U. S. Stoneware Co., 1953.)

Table 9-32

Gas Film Height of Transfer Unit*

Packing	α	β	γ	G'	L'
Raschig Rings (Inches)					
3/8	2.32	0.45	0.47	200- 500	500- 1,500
1	7.00	0.39	0.58	200- 800	400- 500
	6.41	0.32	0.51	200- 600	500- 4,500
1.5	17.3	0.38	0.66	200- 700	500- 1,500
	2.58	0.38	0.40	200- 700	1,500- 4,500
2	3.82	0.41	0.45	200- 800	500- 4,500
Berl Saddles (Inches)					
1/2	32.4	0.30	0.74	200- 700	500- 1,500
	0.811	0.30	0.24	200- 700	1,500- 4,500
1	1.97	0.36	0.40	200- 800	400- 4,500
1.5	5.05	0.32	0.45	200-1,000	400- 4,500
3-In. Partition Rings (Stacked (Staggered)	650	0.58	1.06	150- 900	3,000-10,000
Spiral Rings (stacked staggered) 3-in. single spiral	2.38	0.35	0.29	130- 700	3,000-10,000
3-in. triple spiral	15.6	0.38	0.60	200-1,000	500- 3,000
Drip Point Grids (continuous flue)					
Style 6146	3.91	0.37	0.39	130-1,000	3,000- 6,500
Style 6295	4.65	0.17	0.27	100-1,000	2,000-11,500

* From the data of Fellinger[27] and of Molstad et. al,[50, 51] as presented in Treybel, R. E. *Mass Transfer Operations*, pg. 239, McGraw-Hill Book Co. Inc. (1955), Ref. 74, by permission.

Table 9-33

Atomic and Molecular Volumes*

Atomic Volume		Molecular Volume	
Carbon	14.8	H_2	14.3
Hydrogen	3.7	O_2	25.6
Chlorine	24.6	N_2	31.2
Bromine	27.0	Air	29.9
Iodine	37.0	CO	30.7
Sulfur	25.6	CO_2	34.0
Nitrogen	15.6	SO_2	44.8
Nitrogen in primary amines	10.5	NO	23.6
Nitrogen in secondary amines	12.0	N_2O	36.4
Oxygen	7.4	NH_3	25.8
Oxygen in methyl esters	9.1	H_2O	18.9
Oxygen in higher esters	11.0	H_2S	32.9
Oxygen in acids	12.0	COS	51.5
Oxygen in methyl ethers	9.0	Cl_2	48.4
Oxygen in higher ethers	11.0	Br_2	53.2
Benzene ring: subtract	15	I_2	71.5
Naphthalene ring: subtract	30		

* By permission, R. E. Treybal, "Mass-Transfer Operations," pg. 27, McGraw-Hill Book Co., Inc. (1955). Also see Ref. 63 for additional data.

Entering gas, Y_1, mols NH_3/mol inert gas

$$= \frac{5.35}{(5.35/0.057)(0.943)} = 0.0607$$

Leaving gas, Y_2, mols NH_3/mol inert gas

$$= (0.01)(.0607) = 0.000607$$

To calculate the equilibrium curve at 90° F. (constant temperature) for the system aqua ammonia-ammonia-inert vapors follow the steps on page 190:

Heat of solution $(-Q) = 45.8676 + n(286.103) - a' - nb'$, in kilojoules/g. mole.

*n, g. moles H_2O	*$-Q$ p.c.u./lb. mole NH_3	$-Q$ BTU/lb. NH_3	x, mole fraction NH_3	Lb. NH_3 per 100# H_2O	*Adiabatic Temp. rise, °F.
1	6600	698	0.5	94.5	338
2.33	7820	829	0.3	40.5	238
4	8040	851	0.2	23.6	164
9	8220	873	0.1	10.5	83
19	8290	879	0.05	4.97	41.6
49	8580	906	0.02	1.93	17.1

Data on heats of solution of ammonia taken from International Critical Tables Vol. V, pg. 213[35] by Sherwood and Pigford (*Absorption and Extraction*, pg. 161, 2nd Ed., McGraw-Hill Book Co., Inc.) Ref. 63.*

absorption (b) height of the transfer unit using 1-inch Berl saddles (c) the tower diameter and (d) the water rate.

Material Balance

Assume production of 8 weight percent aqua. Then:

$$\text{Lbs. water/hour} = (0.99)(91)\left(\frac{0.92}{0.08}\right) = 1035$$

Entering Water, X_2, mols NH_3/mol $N_2O = 0$

Leaving Water as aqua, X_1, mols NH_3/mol H_2O

$$= \frac{(5.35)(0.99)}{\left(\frac{1035}{18}\right)}$$

$$= 0.0921$$

1. Assume values for Y, (0.012 for example) mols ammonia/mol of inert gas and read corresponding vapor pressure of ammonia from Figure 9-36 (curve Y) (= 102 mm). This figure was calculated from

$$Y = \frac{vp\ NH_3}{\pi - vpNH_3}$$

for a total pressure system at 164.7 psia (150 psig) and a temperature of 90° F. with vapor pressures read from published data, Figure 9-37.

2. At the values of vapor pressure at 90° F. (32.2° C) read the corresponding weight percent aqua ammonia (= 8 percent).

3. Convert this weight percent ammonia to lb. mols ammonia per lb. mol of water by

$$\frac{mols\ NH_3}{mols\ H_2O} = \frac{(wt.\ \%)\ (18)}{(100 - wt.\ \%\ NH_3)\ (17)},\ (= 0.092\ example)$$

4. Plot equilibrium curve (curve A) of Figure 9-38.

(at Y = 0.012, x = 0.092, example)

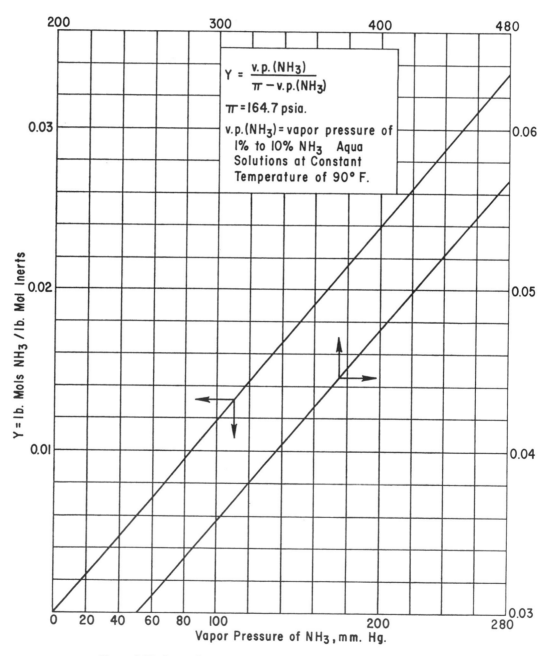

Figure 9-36. Ammonia vapor pressure—inerts data at a fixed pressure.

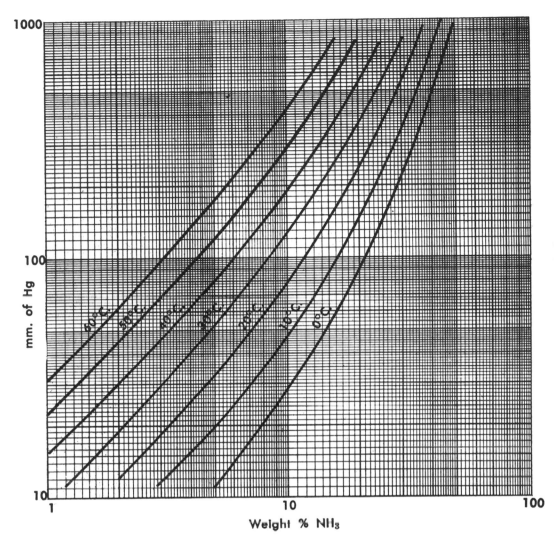

Figure 9-37. Partial pressure of ammonia over aqueous solutions of ammonia. (By permission M. Leva, "Tower Packings and Packed Tower Design, 2nd Ed." U. S. Stoneware Co., 1953.)

If the temperature rise over the temperature range is very high, then to operate at constant temperature requires internal cooling coils in the column, or other means of heat removal to maintain constant temperature operation. Usually this condition will require considerably less transfer units for the same conditions when compared to the adiabatic operation.

To calculate the equilibrium curve taking the heat of solution into account, i.e., operate adiabatically with liquid temperature variable, follow the steps:

1. Assume a temperature rise (for example, 17.8° F.) and read from Figure 9-39 (temp. rise) the lbs. NH₃/ 100 lb. H₂O (= 2, example).

2. Convert this lbs. NH₃/100 lbs. H₂O to lb. mols NH₃/ lb. mol H₂O by

$$\text{Lbs. } NH_3/100 \text{ lbs. } H_2O = \left(\frac{\text{mols } NH_3}{\text{mols } H_2O}\right)(100)\left(\frac{17}{18}\right)$$

$$(= 0.0215 \text{ lb. mols } NH_3/\text{lb. mol } H_2O)$$

3. Convert this (0.0215) lb. mols NH₃/lb. mols H₂O to weight percent NH₃ by step (3) of paragraph above (= 1.95 percent).

4. Read aqua-ammonia vapor pressure curves at wt. percent NH₃ and corrected temperature (base temperature plus rise) (= 90 + 17.8 = 107.8° F. e.g., or 41.1° C.) Read 29.5 mm Hg as vapor pressure of ammonia, Figure 9-37.

5. Read "Y" curve, Figure 9-36, at value of vapor pressure to get Y (= 0.0035 lb. mols NH₃/lb. mol inerts).

6. Plot X (= 0.0215) and Y (= 0.0035) to get equilibrium curve which takes into account this effect of heat of solution Curve B, (Figure 9-38).

Determine Number of Transfer Units, N

The number of transfer units is determined graphically by:

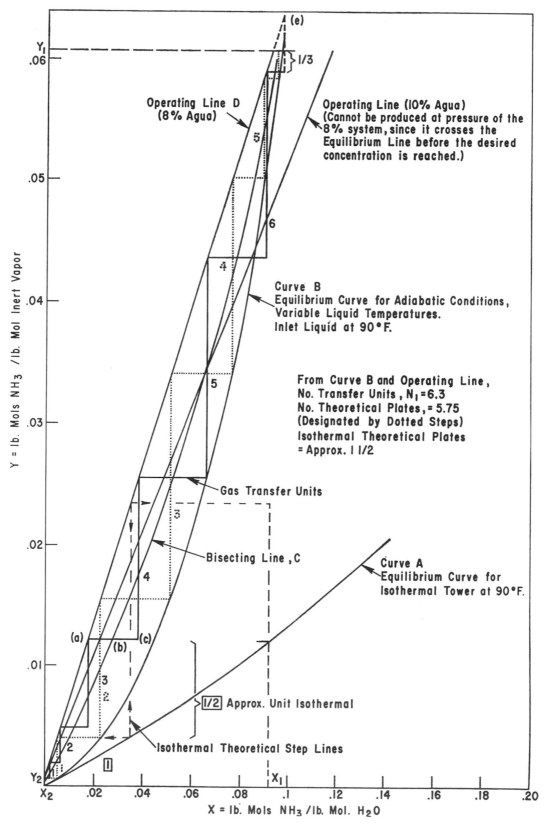

Figure 9-38. Equilibrium curves for ammonia. water: an operating system for production of 8% aqua (by weight) at total pressure of 150 psig.

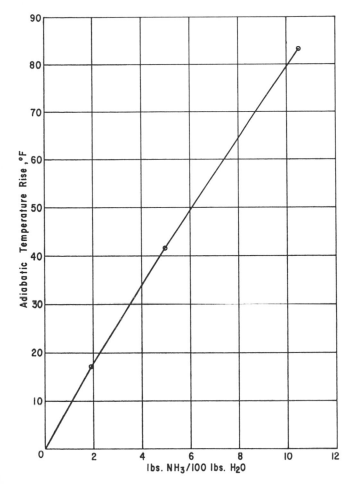

Figure 9-39. Temperature rise due to heat of solution, ammonia in water.

1. Bisecting the vertical distance (line C) of **Figure 9-38** between the 8 percent aqua operating line and the equilibrium curve B.

2. Starting at Y_2, draw horizontal line to line C. Extend this horizontal to right of C far enough to make "Y_2 to line C" equal to "line C to end," then step vertically to operating line, D. Move horizontally to line C, so that (a) (b) = (b) (c). Continue moving up the tower in this stepwise fashion.

3. At end, X_1Y_1, if steps do not end at exact point, estimate fraction of vertical step required and report as fractional transfer unit.

This problem steps off six full transfer units and approximately ⅓ of the seventh. Report as 6.33 units.

Performance Interpretation

The point X_1 represents 0.092 mols HN_3/mol H_2O which is equivalent to 8 weight percent ammonia solution.

If a weaker product were desired fewer transfer units would be required.

Point (e) is the intersection of the equilibrium curve and the operating line and represents the equilibrium condition for tower outlet liquor, and the maximum liquor concentration.

Note that the 10 percent (wt.) aqua product operating line is shown on the diagram, but such a concentration cannot be reached when operating at 150 psig. A greater pressure is required in order to lower the equilibrium curve.

Curve A represents the equilibrium condition for water entering at 90° F., the gas entering saturated with water vapor at 90° F. and isothermal tower operation.

Height of Transfer Unit

From Figure 9-35 the experimental H_{OG} may be picked based on ammonia from a mixture with air absorbing in water. Assume an 18 O.D. tower (pipe) which has an I.D. of 16.8 inches.

$$\text{At inlet, } G' = \frac{5.35\ (11.6)}{(.057)\ (1.553\ \text{sq. ft.})} = 702\ \text{lbs./hr. (sq. ft.)}$$

$$\text{At outlet, } G' = 702 - \frac{(0.99)\ (5.35)\ (17)}{1.553}$$

$$= 702 - 57.8 = 644\ \text{lbs./hr. (sq. ft.)}$$

$$\text{Avg. } G' = \frac{702 + 644}{2} = 673\ \text{lbs./hr. (sq. ft.)}$$

$$\text{At Inlet, } L' = \frac{1035}{1.553} = 666\ \text{lbs./hr. (sq. ft.)}$$

$$\text{At Outlet, } L' = 666 + 57.8 = 724$$

$$\text{Avg. } L' = \frac{666 + 724}{2} = 695\ \text{lbs./hr. (sq. ft.)}$$

$$\text{At, } L' = 695,\ G' = 673$$

$H_{OG} = 1.6$ ft. (interpolated) based on ammonia-air-water system. The system under study has inerts other than air.

Tower Height Based on Air as Inert Gas In System

$$Z = N H_{OG}$$
$$Z = (6.33)\ (1.6) = 10.1\ \text{feet packing}$$

Tower Loading, Flooding and Pressure Drop

Assume 18-inch O.D. steel pipe, 16.8-inch I.D., cross-section area is 1.553 sq.ft.

$$\rho_L = 62.3\ \text{lb./cu. ft.}$$
$$\rho_G = \frac{11.6\ (492)\ (164.7)}{359\ (550)\ (14.7)} = 0.324\ \text{lb./cu. ft.}$$
$$\frac{a}{\epsilon^3} = 125\ \text{for 1-inch Berl saddles}$$
$$\mu^{0.2} = (0.77)^{0.2} = 0.949$$

$$\frac{L}{G}\left(\frac{\rho_G}{\rho_L}\right)^{0.5} = \frac{695}{673}\left(\frac{0.324}{62.3}\right)^{0.5} 0.0744$$

$$\frac{G^2 \psi^2 \mu^{0.2}}{\rho_L \rho_G g_c}\left(\frac{a}{\varepsilon^3}\right) = \frac{(673/3600)^2 (62.3/62.3)^2 (0.949)}{(62.3)(0.324)(32.2)} \quad (125)$$

$$= 0.00635$$

Referring now to Figure 9-13C indicates that the tower would operate well below the loading zone at about 0.00635 (100)/.06 = 10.6 percent of the average loading condition. This is too low.

A new tower diameter can be assumed, or the limiting velocities can be calculated, and the diameter set from these. For illustration purposes, use the latter approach:

Average gas rate = (673) (1.553) = 1047 lbs./hr.

Inlet gas rate = (702) (1.553) = 1090 lbs./hr.

Average liquid rate = (695) (1.553) = 1080 lbs./hr.

Outlet liquid rate = (724) (1.553) = 1124 lbs./hr.

$$\frac{L}{G}\left(\frac{\rho_G}{\rho_L}\right)^{0.5} = \frac{1080}{1047}\left(\frac{0.324}{62.3}\right)^{0.5} = 0.0744$$

Since:

$$\frac{G^2 \psi^2 \mu^{0.2}}{\rho_L \rho_G g_c}\left(\frac{a}{\varepsilon^3}\right) = \frac{V_g^2 \rho_G \mu^{0.2} \psi^2}{g_c \rho_L}\left(\frac{a}{\varepsilon^3}\right)$$

where: V_g = superficial gas velocity, ft./sec.

Solve for V_g: at abscissa = 0.0744

Read Figure 9-13 at flooding, ordinate = 0.150

$$V_g^2 = \frac{(0.150)(32.2)(62.3)}{(0.324)(0.949)(1)(125)} = 7.83$$

V_g = 2.8 ft./sec. flooding velocity

Read Figure 9-13 at upper loading, ordinate = 0.084

V_g = 2.1 ft./sec. upper loading velocity

Base diameter on 50 percent of flooding

Operating velocity = 0.5 (2.8) = 1.4 ft./sec.

$$\text{Gas flow rate} = \frac{(1047)}{(0.324)(3600)} = 0.896 \text{ cu. ft./sec.}$$

Required tower cross-sectional area at 50 percent of flooding:

$$\text{Sq. ft.} = \frac{0.896}{1.4} = 0.64$$

Tower dia. = $\sqrt{(4/\pi)(0.64)}$ = 0.902 foot = 10.8 in.

If a standard 10-inch pipe is used (10.02-inch I.D.) the superficial velocity = 0.896/0.546 sq.ft. = 1.64 ft./sec.

Percent of flooding = 1.64 (100)/2.8 = 58.6 percent.

Percent of upper loading = 1.64 (100)/2.1 = 78.3 percent.

Pressure drop is approximately 0.5 in./foot packing height, Figure 9-13C.

This should be an acceptable operating condition, therefore, use tower diameter of 10-inch nominal Sch. 40 pipe. This pipe is satisfactory for 150 psig operating pressure (see Figures 9-40A and B).

Correcting Height of Transfer Unit for Inert Gases in System

Diffusivity: $D_v = 0.0069 \dfrac{T^{3/2}\sqrt{1/M_A + 1/M_B}}{P(V_A^{1/3} + V_B^{1/3})^2}$

T (for 90° F.) = 90 + 460 = 550° R at liquid inlet

T (for 90 + 72°) = 162 + 460 = 622° R max. at liquid outlet

M_A = 17 for NH$_3$

M_B = 29 for air

P = 164.7/14.7 = 11.2 atm.

V_A = 26.7 for NH$_3$ from Table 9-33 (molecular volume)

Note: The Value of V_A is from Ref. 63.
Molecular volume values vary between references.

V_B = 29.9 for air

Diffusion coefficient of NH$_3$ through air:

$$D_v = 0.0069 \frac{(550)^{3/2}\sqrt{1/17 + 1/29}}{11.2[(26.7)^{1/3} + (29.9)^{1/3}]^2} = 0.065 \text{ sq.ft./hr.}$$

Diffusion coefficient of NH$_3$ through 3:1 H$_2$ — N$_2$ mixture gas:

M_A = 17 for NH$_3$

M_B = 11.2 for inert gas mixtures, less NH$_2$

V_A = 26.7 for NH$_3$

V_B = (0.75) (14.3) + (0.25) (31.2) = 18.5 for H$_2$ — N$_2$ mixture

Diffusion of ammonia through hydrogen — nitrogen inert gas:

$$D_v = 0.0069 \frac{(550)^{3/2}\sqrt{1/17 + 1/11.2}}{11.2[(26.7)^{1/3} + (18.5)^{1/3}]^2}$$

$$D_v = 0.096 \text{ sq.ft./hr.}$$

For an ammonia-air system using mass rates in the tower the same as the H$_2$ — N$_2$ system: G' = 1047/0.546 = 1920 lb./hr. (sq.ft.) and L' = 1080/0.546 = 1980 lbs./hr. (sq.ft.)

From Figure 9-35, Extrapolated H$_{OG}$ = 0.95 (this should be maximum to expect)

Then substituting, for ammonia-air mixture:

$$H_{OG} = \frac{G'}{K_Ga P}$$

$$K_Ga = \frac{1920/(28.4 \text{ mol. wt. of mixture})}{(0.95)(11.2)}$$

$$= 6.35 \text{ mols/hr. (cu.ft.) (atm.)}$$

Converting this to ammonia-H$_2$-N$_2$ mixture:

$$K_Ga = 6.35 \left[\frac{0.096}{0.065}\right]^{0.56} = 7.9 \text{ mols/hr. (cu.ft.) (atm.)}$$

(Text continued on page 197)

		SPEC. DWG. NO.	
		A-1	

Job No._____

_____

B/M No._____

TOWER SPECIFICATIONS

Page _1_ of _2_ Pages

Unit Price _____

No. Units _1_

Item No. _T-63_

Service _Ammonia Absorber_ Size _10" Sch. 40 Pipe x approx. 30'_

No. Trays _____ Type _____ Caps _____ Feet Packing _15_ Size _1" Berl_ Sprays _____

Tower Internals Spec. Dwg. No. _2_

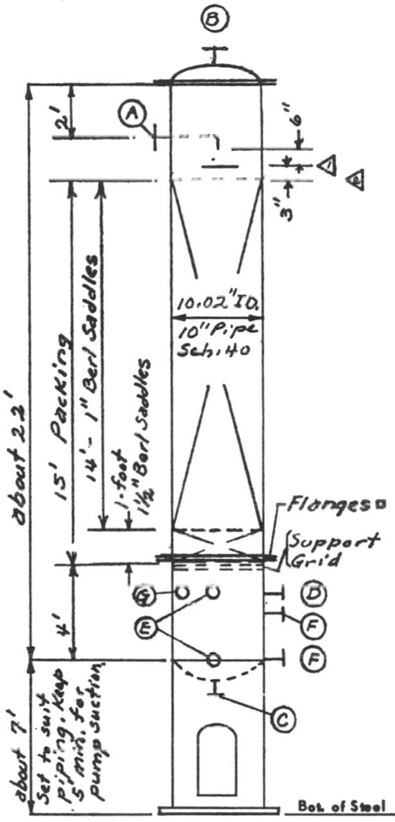

OPERATING AND MECHANICAL CONDITIONS

Oper. Press. _150_ PSIG. Oper. Temp. _90 to 162_ °F

Des. Press. _175_ PSIG. Des. Temp. _200_ °F

Code _ASME_ Stamp. Req'd. _Yes_ Density of Contents _62-64_ lbs./cu. ft.

Lethal Construction _No_ Self Supporting _Yes_

Materials: Shell _Steel_ Heads _Steel_ Skirt _Steel_

Lining; Metal _None_ Rubber or Plastic _____

Brick _____ Cement _____

Internal Corrosion Allowance _1/16" max._

Insulation? ☐ Yes ☒ No Class _____

NOZZLES

SERVICE	NO. REQ'D.	SIZE	PRESS. CL.	FACING	MARK NO.
Feed* (Water)	1		150	Raised	A
Reflux					
Vapor Out	1		150	Raised	B
Liquid Out	1		150	"	C
~~Reboiler~~ Vapor	1		150	"	D
Reboiler Liquid					
Drain					
Safety Valve					
Manhole					
Gage Glass	2	3/4	6000	Coupling	E
Level Control	2	1 1/2	150	Raised	F
Thermowell Pts.					
Pressure Taps	1	3/4	6000	Coupling	G

* Feed Points to be located in: ☒ Vapor Space ☐ Downcomer

REMARKS

1. TW Points in Vapor Located-
2. TW Points in Liquid Located-
3. Sample Points in Vapor Located-
4. Sample Points in Liquid Located-
5. Pressure Taps Located in Vapor Space as Follows:

◁ 4" Dia. Splash Plate ◁ Packing Hold-down Plate

Note *Flanges are necessary for removal of packing, or provide 10" handhole at this level.

By.	Chk'd.	App.	Rev.	Rev.	Rev.
Date					

P.O. To:_____

Figure 9-40A. Tower specifications.

	SPEC. DWG. NO.
	A- 2
	Page 2 of 2 Pages
	Unit Price
	No. Units 1
	Item No. T-63

Job No. _____

B/M No. _____

TOWER INTERNAL SPECIFICATIONS
SPRAY OR PACKED TYPE COLUMNS

Packing: _____
  (a) Size, Type & Thickness   *1" Berl Saddles, Standard Weight* Bulk Density _____
  (b) Height of Packing Sections: No. 1 ___ *1'-0" of 1½"* ___ No. 2 *14'-0" of 1"* ___ No. 3 _____
  (c) Method of Packing (Wet) (Dry) ___ *Float into tower filled with water*
  (d) Packing Arrangement (Dumped) (Stacked) ___ *Dumped*
Type of Distributor Tray *Splash Plate, 4" Dia.* _____ How Removed *Out Top*
Type of Re-Distributor Tray *None* _____ How Removed _____
Type of Packing Support(s) *75% open Hardware Cloth, 1x1 mesh* How Removed *At flanges*
Packing removal Manways Located *Use flanges at support grid*
Entrainment Separator: (Type, Size, Thickness) *None*

	Bank No.	No. of Nozzles	Size	Type	Manufacturer
Spray Nozzles					

MATERIALS OF CONSTRUCTION

Packing *Unglazed porcelain*
Distributor Tray *Carbon steel*
Re-Distributor Tray _____
Packing Support *Carbon steel*
Spray Nozzles _____

REMARKS

Packing on Supports:
  1st. Layer Arrangement *1'-0" of 1½" Berl saddles dumped*
  2nd. Layer Arrangement *14'-0" of 1" Berl saddles dumped*
  3rd. Layer Arrangement _____
  Bulk of Packing Arrangement *See 2nd Layer.*

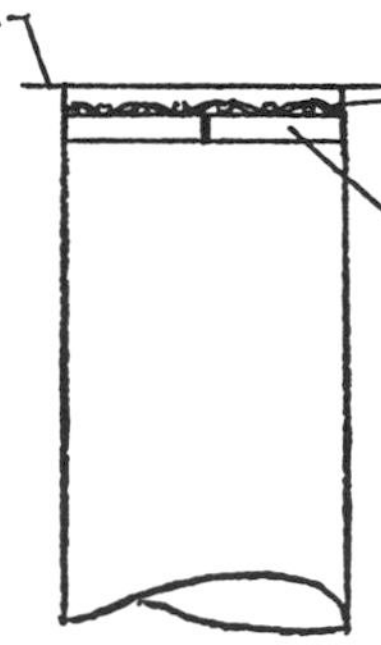

Flange—

1"x1"x.09 Mesh Cloth
Cross-bar Support for 1x1 Mesh

By	Chk'd.	App.	Rev.	Rev.	Rev.
Date					

P.O. To: _____

Figure 9-40B. Tower internal specifications; spray or packed type columns.

Then; substituting,

$$H_{OG} \text{ for this mixture)} = \frac{(1920/(11.2 \text{ Mol. wt. } H_2\text{-}N_2 \text{ mixture})}{(7.9)\ (11.2 \text{ atm.})}$$

$$= 1.875 \text{ foot}$$

Tower Packing Height for Ammonia-Hydrogen-Nitrogen Mixture

$$Z = (1.875)\ (6.33) = 11.9 \text{ ft. packing}$$

For 1-inch Berl saddles allow 2.0 ft. for good liquid distribution through the packing from the top.

Minimum packed bed depth = 11.9 + 2.0 = 13.9 ft.

Use: 15 ft (or perhaps 18 ft. to allow for variations in performance)

Expected Pressure Drop

Packing:	(15) (0.5 in./ft.)	= 7.5 in.
Support:	(Grating type), approx.	= 1.0
Total drop		= 8.5 in. water

Inlet Liquid

For this small diameter tower, bring water into center of top of packing with a turned down 90° ell, placed 6-9 inches above packing.

Mass Transfer With Chemical Reaction

Many absorption processes involve some chemical reaction; however, it is fortunate that satisfactory correlation can be made without delving into the complexities of the reaction.

In many instances the gas being absorbed is to be recovered from the solution, and hence the effluent from the absorption must be treated. Often the application of heat will release the gas, e.g., CO_2 from ethanolamine; however, in other cases chemical treatment must be used. In order to fully utilize the absorbent liquid, recycle systems must be established, and the economics of absorbent selection become of considerable importance, determining the size of the system in many cases. Since the absorption ability of the various combinations of gas and liquid vary rather widely and depend upon the system condition, it is often necessary to examine more than one absorbent for a given gas. The performance of several important systems is given in summary or reference form:

I. Carbon Dioxide or Sulfur Dioxide in Alkaline Solutions

$$K_Ga = \frac{n}{Z\ A\ \Delta p_{1m}\ f_a} \qquad (9\text{-}38)$$

where:

K_Ga = Gas coefficient, lb. mols/(hr.) (cu.ft.) (atm)

n = CO_2 (or SO_2) absorbed, lb. mols/hr.

A = Tower cross-section area. sq.ft.

Z = Height of packed section in tower, feet

Δp_{1m} = Log. mean partial pressure of gas in inlet and exit gas streams, atm.

f_a = Fraction effective packing wetted

Design Procedure for Alkali-absorbers

A. Calculate material balance, determining quantity of gas to be absorbed, and alkali required.

B. Estimate a tower diameter and establish its operating point from Figure 9-13. For initial trial set operating point at 50-60 percent of flood point system based on varying gas mass velocity at variable tower diameters for a fixed

$$\frac{L}{G}\left(\frac{\rho_G}{\rho_L}\right)^{0.5}$$

C. Estimate the effective fraction wetted packing area by Figure 9-28. As a general rule, try not to accept design if fraction wetted is less than 0.5. If it is less, adjust tower conditions to raise value, bearing in mind that this factor is based on scattered and very incomplete data.

D. Determine K_ga based on inlet alkali normality and percent conversion to carbonate (for carbon dioxide).

K_ga Data and Corrections:[42,69,72]

The necessary data required to properly design a CO_2 scrubber are separated into three sections, depending upon the CO_2 concentration in the feed gas. Corrections are necessary to convert "procedure based" information to the specific design basis of a given problem. The corrections outlined below are specific to the CO_2 concentration range being presented in the section.

Since there is not sufficient data to serve completely for all types and sizes of packing, it may be necessary to estimate K_ga values by ratioing packing surface areas and making the other appropriate correction for the problem conditions.

1. Inlet CO_2 concentration, 100 to 1000 ppm by volume K_Ga: Use Figures 9-41A, B, C, D, and E and Figure 9-42.

   a. Increases with increase in liquid rate, L, to the 0.2 power of the ratio, $K_Ga \propto \left(\dfrac{L_2}{L_1}\right)^{0.2}$

   b. Increases with increase in gas rate, G, to the 0.35 power of the rate ratio, up to a rate of 500 lb./hr. (sq.ft.). Above this rate the increase is reduced, being to the 0.15 power at rates near 1000 lb./hr. (sq. ft.)

   $$K_Ga \propto \left(\frac{G_2}{G_1}\right)^{0.35} \text{ for G = 1 to 500}$$

   $$K_Ga \propto \left(\frac{G_2}{G_1}\right)^{0.15} \text{ for G > 1000}$$

   c. Increases with increase in temperature to the 6.0 power of the absolute temperature ratio.

   d. Decreases with increase in pressure to the 0.5 power of the absolute pressure ratio.

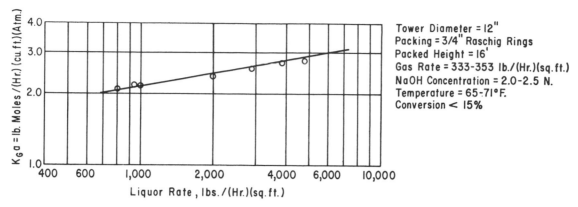

Tower Diameter = 12"
Packing = 3/4" Raschig Rings
Packed Height = 16'
Gas Rate = 333-353 lb./(Hr.)(sq.ft.)
NaOH Concentration = 2.0-2.5 N.
Temperature = 65-71°F.
Conversion < 15%

Figure 9-41A. CO_2 absorption from atmosphere: effect of liquor rate on K_Ga at atmospheric pressure.

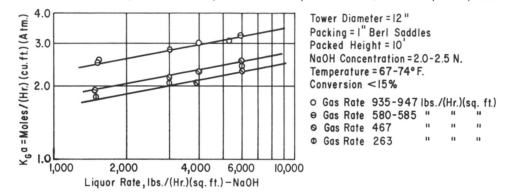

Tower Diameter = 12"
Packing = 1" Berl Saddles
Packed Height = 10'
NaOH Concentration = 2.0-2.5 N.
Temperature = 67-74°F.
Conversion < 15%

O Gas Rate 935-947 lbs./(Hr.)(sq. ft.)
⊖ Gas Rate 580-585   "   "   "
⊘ Gas Rate 467   "   "   "
Φ Gas Rate 263   "   "   "

Figure 9-41B. Absorption of CO_2 from atmosphere: effect of liquor rate on K_Ga at atmospheric pressure and various gas rates.

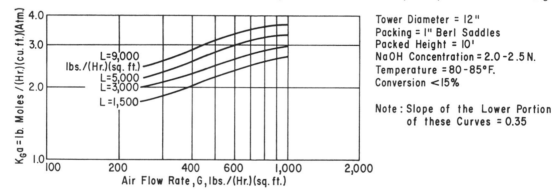

Tower Diameter = 12"
Packing = 1" Berl Saddles
Packed Height = 10'
NaOH Concentration = 2.0-2.5 N.
Temperature = 80-85°F.
Conversion < 15%

Note: Slope of the Lower Portion
of these Curves = 0.35

Figure 9-41C. CO_2 absorption from atmosphere: effect of gas rate on K_Ga at atmospheric pressure.

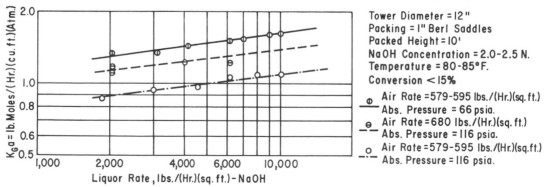

Tower Diameter = 12"
Packing = 1" Berl Saddles
Packed Height = 10'
NaOH Concentration = 2.0-2.5 N.
Temperature = 80-85°F.
Conversion < 15%

⊕ Air Rate = 579-595 lbs./(Hr.)(sq.ft.)
── Abs. Pressure = 66 psia.
⊖ Air Rate = 680 lbs./(Hr.)(sq.ft.)
-- Abs. Pressure = 116 psia.
O Air Rate = 579-595 lbs./(Hr.)(sq.ft.)
-·- Abs. Pressure = 116 psia.

Figure 9-41D. CO_2 absorption from atmosphere: effect of flow rates on K_Ga at elevated pressures.

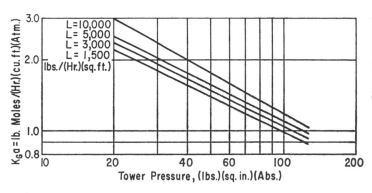

Figure 9-41E. CO_2 absorption from atmosphere: effect of tower pressure on K_Ga at various liquor rates.

Figures 9-41A—9-41E, by permission, N. A. Spector and B. F. Dodge, "Trans" AIChE, Vol. 42, p. 827, 1946.

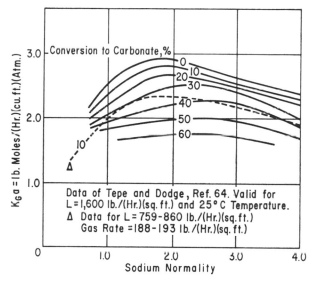

Figure 9-42. Absorption of CO_2 in NaOH. (By permission M. Leva, "Tower Packings and Packed Tower Design, 2nd ed." U. S. Stoneware Co.)

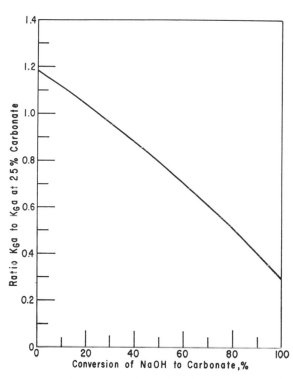

Figure 9-43. CO_2 absorption: effect of carbonate on K_Ga. (By permission M. Leva "AIChE Jour." Vol. 1, p. 224, 1955.)

2. Inlet CO_2 Concentration 1.5 to 5.0 mol per cent K_Ga: Use Figures 9-42, 43 and 44, A-F.

  a. Increases with increase in liquid rate, L, to the 0.28 power of the rate ratio, $K_Ga \propto \left(\dfrac{L_2}{L_1}\right)^{0.28}$

  b. No correction to gas rate, G, below loading. Above loading point, K_Ga increases with increase in gas rate G, to the 0.3 power of the rate ratio.

$$K_g a \propto \left(\frac{G_2}{G_1}\right)^{0.3} \text{ above loading}$$

  c. Effect of temperature and pressure same as section "1" above.

3. Inlet CO_2 concentration 5.0 to 10.0 mol per cent K_Ga: Use Figures 9-42, 43 and 44A-F.

  a. Liquor rate correction follows section "2" above

  b. Increases with increase in gas rate, G, to the 0.15 power of rate ratio.

  c. Effect of temperature and pressure same as section "1".

  e. Calculate height of packing required:

$$z = \frac{n}{K_Ga\ (A)\ (\Delta p_{1m})\ (f_a)}$$

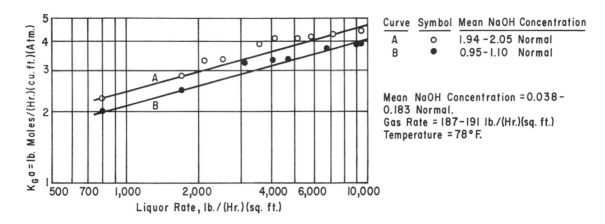

Figure 9-44A. CO_2 absorption: effect of liquor rate. (By permission J.B. Tepe and B. F. Dodge, "Trans." Amer. Inst. Chem. Engrs., Vol. 39.

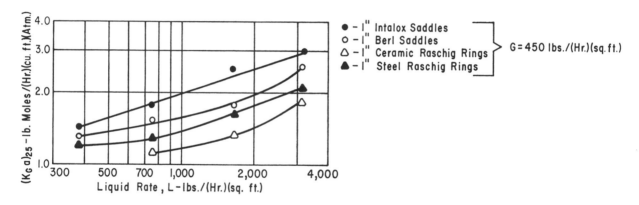

Figure 9-44B. CO_2 absorption: 1-inch packing data at constant gas rate. (By permission M. Leva, Amer. Inst. Chem. Engrs. Jour. Vol. 1, p. 224, 1955.)

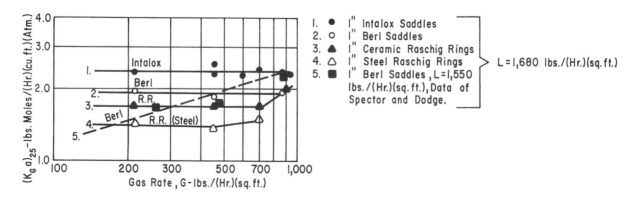

Figure 9-44C. CO_2 absorption: 1-inch packing data at constant liqquid rate. (By permission M. Leva, Amer. Inst. Chem. Engrs. Jour. Vol. 1, p. 224, 1955.)

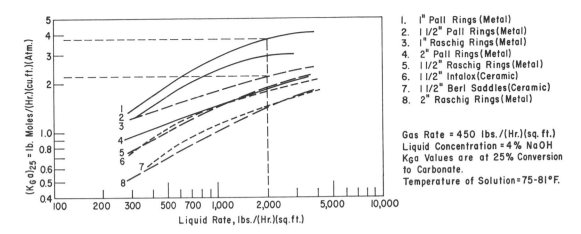

Figure 9-44D. K_Ga versus liquid rate for 4% sodium hydroxide. (Compiled from References 20 and 35.)

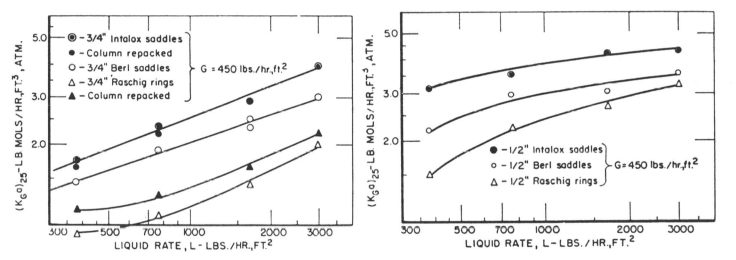

Figure 9-44E. ¾″ packing data for system carbon dioxide—sodium hydroxide: Gas rate constant. (By permission M. Leva, "AIChE Jour." Vol. 1, No. 2, p. 224, 1955.)

Figure 9-44F. ½″ packing data for system carbon dioxide—sodium hydroxide: gas rate constant. (By permission M. Leva, "AIChE Jour." Vol. 1, No. 2, p. 224, 1955.)

Calculate tower pressure drop from Figure 9-13 for packing, and Figure 9-19, 20 or 21 for support and grids.

g. Make specification sheet.

Example 9-10: Design a Packed Tower Using Caustic to Remove Carbon Dioxide From a Vent Stream

A process stream containing mostly nitrogen and carbon dioxide is to be scrubbed with 10 percent (wt.) NaOH for CO_2 removal, but not recovery. The requirements are:

Inlet gas: $CO_2 = 40.6$ mols/hr.
Inerts $= 365.4$ mols/hr.
Avg. Mol. wt. $= 20$
Temperature $= 90°$ F.

Pressure $= 35$ psig $= 49.7$ psia
Outlet gas: $CO_2 = 0.1$ mol%
Inerts $= 99.9$ mol%

Max. allowable pressure drop $= 2$ psi
Liquid Sp. Gr. $= 1.21$

From a material balance; the NaOH required based on 25% conversion to Na_2CO_3:

$$2\,NaOH + CO_2 = Na_2CO_3 + H_2O$$

Lbs. 10% NaOH required/hr. $=$

$$\frac{(40.6 \text{ mols } CO_2/hr.)\ [(2)\ (40)\ \text{lb. NaOH/Mol } CO_2]}{(0.1 \text{ wt. fraction NaOH})\ (0.25 \text{ conversion})}$$

$$= 129,000 \text{ lbs./hr.}$$

Assume 3.5 ft. I.D. Tower, Use 1½ inch Steel Raschig Rings. At operating point

$$L' = \frac{129,000}{(\pi/4)(3.5)^2} = 13,470 \text{ lb./hr. (sq.ft.)}$$

$$G' = \frac{(40.6 + 365.4)(20)}{(\pi/4)(3.5)^2} = 846 \text{ lb./hr. (sq.ft.)}$$

$$G = 0.235 \text{ lbs./sec. (sq.ft.)}$$

$$\rho_G = \frac{(20)(35 + 14.7)(520)}{(379)(14.7)(550)} = 0.1688 \text{ lbs./cu.ft.}$$

For Figure 9-13C

$$\frac{L}{G}\left(\frac{\rho_G}{\rho_L}\right)^{\frac{1}{2}} = \frac{13,470}{846}\left(\frac{0.1688}{1.21(62.3)}\right)^{\frac{1}{2}} = 0.776$$

$$\frac{G^2 \psi^2 \mu^{0.2}}{\rho_G \rho_L g_c}\left(\frac{a}{\varepsilon^3}\right) = \frac{(0.235)^2(0.825)^2(2.6)^2}{0.1688(1.21)(62.3)32.2}(110)$$

$$= 0.012$$

At flooding, ordinate = 0.0275, for abscissa = 0.776

At lower loading, ordinate = 0.012

Operating point = (0.012/0.0275)(100) = 43.8% of flood

This is only slightly lower than good practice, but since the operating point is at the lower loading point, continue with this selection. A smaller diameter tower might calculate to be a better choice. However, extreme caution must be used in designing too close to limits with packed towers. Very little of the data is exact, and often the range is not known.

Effective Wetted Packing

From Figure 9-23.

f_a = approx. 0.50 for ceramic material at L'/G' = 15.9

Since steel rings have thinner walls, it seems that the liquid should flow and wet this material a little better than ceramic.

Use f_a = 0.6

K_Ga from Figure 9-44D, uncorrected:

$$(K_Ga)_{25} = 1.9 \text{ lb. mols/hr. (cu. ft.) (atm.)}$$

The conditions for K_Ga from Figure 9-44D are 4 wt. percent NaOH, which is 1 normal, and G' = 450 lbs./hr. (sq.ft.), L' = 2000 lbs./hr. (sq.ft.), pressure = 14.7 psia. The $(K_Ga)_{25}$ is also for 25 percent conversion to carbonate.

Correct the K_Ga for pressure, normality of NaOH and liquid rate:

There is no correction for gas rate at or below the loading point. Note that from Figure 9-42 the ratio of K_Ga at 1 normal and 2.5 normal solutions and for 25 percent conversion = 2.6/2.1.

$$K_Ga = (1.91)\left(\frac{13,470}{2000}\right)^{0.28}\left(\frac{14.7}{35 + 14.7}\right)^{0.5}\left(\frac{2.6}{2.1}\right)$$

$$K_Ga = 2.18 \text{ lb. mols/hr. (cu. ft.) (atm)}$$

Note: since the solution temperature of data for Figure 9-44D is 75 — 81° F., it is assumed ambient, and no correction is made. If the operating temperature were higher or lower, then a temperature correction multiplier should be used above, with the absolute temperatures ratio being raised to the 6.0 power.

Log mean driving force, for CO_2:

Inlet = 10%

Outlet = 0.1%

$$\Delta p_{lm} = \frac{[(0.10(49.7/14.7) — 0.001(49.7/14.7)]}{\ln[0.10(49.7/14.7)/(0.001)(49.7/14.7)]}$$

$$= 0.0726 \text{ atm.}$$

Packing Height

$$Z = \frac{40.6 — 365.4(0.001)/0.999}{(2.18)(0.0726)[(\pi/4)(3.5)^2]0.6}$$

$$Z = 44.3 \text{ ft.}$$

Experience in caustic-CO_2-steel Raschig ring systems indicates that the packing must be wetted better than the value of 60 percent (0.6); therefore a value of 0.85 is suggested.

then: Revised Z = 44.3 (0.6/0.85) = 31.3 feet

Allowance for distribution at top = 2 feet

Allowance for redistribution at mid-point

$$= (2 \text{ feet})(2 \text{ sections}) = 4 \text{ feet}$$

Total packing height required = 31.3 + 2 + 4 = 37.3

Use 40 ft. of packing.

Pressure Drop

From Figure 9-13C

$$\Delta P = 0.38 \text{ inches } H_2O/\text{foot of packing}$$

Total ΔP = (38)(0.38) = 14.4″ H_2O

This is an acceptable figure

Arrangement

There are no data available on the liquid flow distribution vs height for 1½-inch raschig rings. Some information indicates that for 2-inch rings about 33 percent of the liquid is on the wall of a large tower after flowing through 20 ft. of packed height, starting with good top liquid distribution.

To insure *good* tower performance, use three—thirteen —plus feet packed sections of the 1½-inch Raschig rings. Two sections of 20 ft. of packing would also probably perform satisfactorily, and be less expensive.

If Pall rings had been used, only two packed sections would be considered, since the general liquid distribution pattern is better. This would require a re-evaluation of the performance, and a probable reduction in total packed height.

a/ε^3	1.5 inch Metal Pall Rings 25	1.5 Metal Raschig Rings 110
Abscissa of Figure 9-13C	0.00272 (by ratio)	0.012
% Flood	$\frac{0.00272}{0.0275}(100) = 9.9\%$	43.8

On the basis of this better performance of the Pall ring, a *smaller* diameter tower *must* be selected and the tower reevaluated based on the new mass flow rates with this packing. The economics require that the higher packing cost, smaller tower diameter, new total packing volume, and tower pressure drop be considered.

II. NH₃-Air-H₂O System

a. H_{OG} data of Fellinger,[27] Figure 9-35

b. K_Ga data of Dwyer and Dodge[21]

$$\frac{1}{K_Ga} = \frac{1}{\gamma G'^\propto L'^b} + \frac{1}{H'jL'^\tau}\text{lbs. moles/hr. (cu.ft.) (atm)}$$

$$(9-39)$$

Carbon Raschig rings:

Size, In.	γ	$\propto$	τ	b	j
½	0.0065	0.90	0.65	0.39	0.310
1	0.036	0.77	0.78	0.20	0.103
1½	0.014	0.72	0.78	0.38	0.093

(For average temperature of 85° F., H' = 2.74 (lb. mols/cu. ft.)/atm in dilute NH₃ solution, D = 9.8 × 10⁻⁵, μ = 1.97)

Effect of humidity of entering gas found to be minor. K_Ga increases as the 0.45 power of packing superficial area, and decreases with increase in temperature °F. as the 0.635 power of inverse water temperature ratio.

where:

H' = Henry's Law constant, (lb. mols/cu. ft.)/atm.

G' = gas rate, lb./hr. (sq. ft.)

L' = liquid rate, lb./hr. (sq. ft.)

c. K_Ga and H_{OG} data of Wen,[77] Figure 9-45

For ceramic Berl saddles:

$$K_Ga = 0.0073\, G_m^{0.655} L_m^{0.477} \qquad (9-40)$$

$$H_{OG} = 5.15\, G_m^{0.406} L_m^{-0.520} \qquad (9-41)$$

where: G_m = Gas rate, lb.mols/hr. (sq. ft.)

L_m = Liquid rate, lb. mols/hr. (sq. ft.)

For ceramic Intalox saddles:

$$K_Ga = 0.0145\, G_m^{0.688} L_m^{0.404} \qquad (9-42)$$

$$H_{OG} = 1.14\, G_m^{0.316} L_m^{-0.315} \qquad (9-43)$$

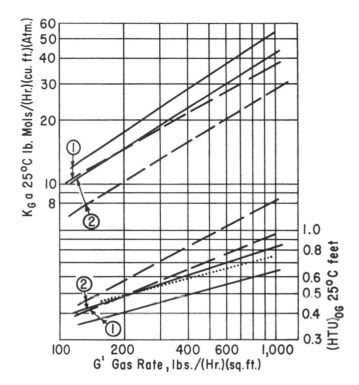

① L' = 5,000 lbs./(Hr.)(sq. ft.)
② L' = 3,000 lbs./(Hr.)(sq. ft.)
—— Intalox Saddles
– – – Berl Saddles
········ Fellinger Data, Berl Saddles

Figure 9-45. Ammonia-air-water absorption of Wen, with ceramic packing. (By permission Chin-Yung Wen, Thesis, West Virginia Univ., 1953.)

Figure 9-46 shows effect of water temperature on K_Ga and H_{OG}.

III. SO₂-H₂O System (dilute gas)

K_La data of Whitney and Vivian[79]

Data for 1-inch ceramic Raschig rings, correlates reasonably well with 3-inch spiral tile and 1-inch coke.

$$\frac{1}{K_La} = \frac{H'}{0.028(G')^{0.7}(L')^{0.25}} + \frac{1}{b(L')^{0.82}} \qquad (9-44)$$

lb. moles/hr. (cu. ft.) (lb. mole/cu. ft.)

Temperature °F.	b	H', Lb. Moles/cu. ft (atm)
50	0.034	0.163
60	0.038	0.130
80	0.048	0.090
90	0.056	0.076

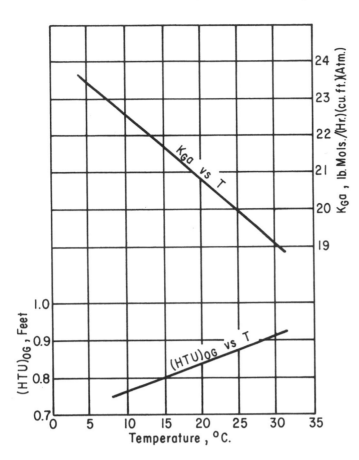

Figure 9-46. Effect of water temperature on ammonia absorption. (By permission Chin-Yung Wen, Thesis, West Virginia, Univ., 1953.)

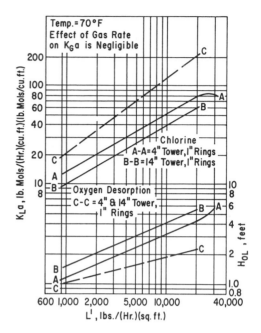

Figure 9-47. Effect of liquor rate on K_La and H_{OL} for chlorine and oxygen in water. (By permission J. E. Vivian, R. P. Whitney, "Chem. Eng. Prog." Vol. 43, p. 691, 1947.)

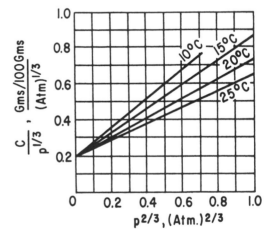

Figure 9-48. Solubility of Chlorine in water. (By permission J.E. Vivian, R. P. Whitney, "Chem. Eng. Prog." Vol. 43, p. 691, 1947.)

where:

K_La = Overall absorption coefficient,
     lb. mols/hr. (cu. ft.) lb. mols/cu. ft.

L = Liquor rate, lb./hr. (sq. ft. of tower cross-section)
     G' is average gas rate of top and bottom of tower.

$H_{OL} = L'/\rho\, K_La$, feet

     ρ = Liquid density, lb./cu. ft.

H_{OL} = Height of overall transfer unit in terms of liquid film, feet.

H' = Henry's Law constant, c/p = lb. mols/cu.ft. (atm)

Effects of temperature on k_La:

$$k_La \propto e^{0.023T}, \quad T = °C.$$

k_La is represented by the second term in the overall equation,

$$k_La = b(L')^{0.82}$$

k_La = Liquid film absorption coefficient, lb. mols/ hr. (cu. ft.) lb. mol/cu. ft.) = 1/hr.

Effect of temperature on k_Ga = nil (assumed)

Reference 71 has excellent solubility data and absorption curves for the system.

IV. Cl₂—H₂O System (for dilute gas concentrations)

Chlorine has limited solubility in water, Figure 9-48.
K_La and H_{OL} data of Vivian and Whitney,[76] Figure 9-47.
Data for 1-inch ceramic Raschig rings.

$$K_La = \frac{L'\,(C_1 - C_2)}{\rho Z \quad \Delta C_{1m}} \qquad (9\text{-}45)$$

$$H_L = \frac{L}{\rho K_La}, \text{ft.} \qquad (9\text{-}46)$$

$$K_La \propto (L')^{0.6} \qquad (9\text{-}47)$$

$$K_La \propto T^6 \text{ (of liquid, degrees absolute)}$$

where: T = absolute liquid temperature, °R.

K_La = liquid coeff., lb. mols/hr. (cu. ft.) (lb. mols/cu. ft.)

L' = liquid rate, lb./hr. (sq. ft.)

C_1 = concentration of chlorine in liquid, bottom of tower, lb. mols/cu. ft.

C_2 = concentration of chlorine in liquid, top of tower, lb. mols/cu. ft.

V. Air-Water System

The system is used in humidification and dehumidification. However, grid and slat packings are more commonly used types.

The H_{CG} data of Mehta and Parekh[49] is compiled by Leva[39, 62] for the ring and saddle packing.

Sherwood and Holloway[61] also studied the desorption of oxygen from water.

VI. Hydrogen Chloride-Water System

The recovery of hydrogen chloride as well as the production of hydrochloric acid is effectively performed in adiabatic type absorption towers. Uncooled or adiabatic towers can be used to produce 33.5 weight percent acid and cooled towers will produce 35-36 percent acid with negligible vent losses[49] when using a feed gas containing 10-100 percent HCl. Due to the heat of absorption, heat dissipation must be taken care of by increasing the temperature of dilute acid product or as a combination of this plus removal as water vapor in the vent. It is important to recognize that acid strengths greater than the constant boiling mixture are made in this tower from gases containing less than 20 percent hydrogen chloride. The lower the inlet feed gas temperature, the lower will be the acid product temperature.

Van Nuys[75] gives excellent thermodynamic data for HCl. Figure 9-49 gives the equilibrium for the 100 percent HCl gas feed in an adiabatic tower, and Table 9-34 summarizes performance for two concentrations of feed gas. From the data it can be seen that it requires fewer theoretical plates to make 32 percent acid from 10 percent feed gas than from 100 percent gas and at the same time yield a vent containing only 0.01 weight % HCl.

In general about 18 feet of 1-inch Karbate or other acid resistant Raschig rings will satisfactorily absorb HCl from a gas stream up to 100 percent and produce 32 percent HCl acid.

Figure 9-50 illustrates a falling film type absorber using water jacketed tubes in the cooler-absorber. The tails tower removes last traces of HCl in the vents. Figure 9-51 is a preliminary selection chart for this type of unit.

Distillation in Packed Towers

Packed towers are used in some distillation operations in preference to plate towers. Usually the selection requires an understanding of the fouling characteristics of

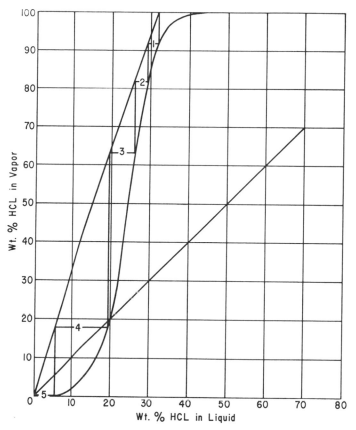

Figure 9-49. X-Y diagram for adiabatic absorption of HCl at 1 atmosphere. (By permission C. F. Oldershaw, L. Simenson, T. Brown and F. Radcliffe, Trans. Sect. "Chem. Eng. Prog." Vol. 43, No. 7, p. 371, 1947.)

Table 9-34
Adiabatic Absorption of HCl Effect of Inert Gases

Operating Conditions
Feed gas enters at equilibrium temperature at bottom of tower
Make-up water enters at equilibrium temperature at top of tower
Vent contains 0.1 wt.% HCl

Theoretical Plates	Weight % HCl in Product	
	10 Mole % HCl Feed	100 Mole % HCl Feed
2	26.5	20.5
4	32.0	30.5
6	33.8	32.8
10	34.7	34.0
∞	35.0	34.6

By permission; Oldershaw, C. F., et. al., Chem. Eng. Prog., 43, No. 7, p. 371 (1947).

fluids of the system. These towers have been used even in polymer forming operations. However, other contacting devices can be cleaned easier. For some processes the packed tower is much more effective as well as cheaper than a tray tower.

Height Equivalent to a Theoretical Plate (HETP)

Distillation operations can best be expressed in terms of equilibrium relations and theoretical plates. Therefore,

COOLER ABSORBER DIMENSIONS										
NO. OF TUBES	A OD	B	C	D	E	F	G ID	H PIPE ID	J ID	K ID
31	12¾	9	10½	92¾	12	7	4	2	2	1
38	14	10	12	91¼	13½	7½	4	3	3	1½
55	16	10	13½	89¼	15	7½	4	3	4	1½
74	18	10	14	89¼	15½	7½	4	3	4	1½
92	20	12	14¾	89¼	16½	8½	6	4	4	2
121	22	14	16½	86¼	19½	10	8	6	6	2
151	24	15	17¾	86¼	20	10	8	6	6	3
170	26	16	18¼	86¼	20½	10	10	6	6	3
206	28	16	20¼	83¼	22½	10	10	6	8	3
241	30	19	21	83¼	23½	11	12	8	8	4

TAILS TOWER DIMENSIONS							
TOWER SIZE ID	M OD	P	Q	R	S	T ID	U ID
8	9¾	21¼	20⅞	13¾	10⅞	2½	1
10	13	22	21⅜	14	10⅞	3	1
12	15½	23	21⅝	17	11⅛	4	2
16	19½	24	21⅝	18	11⅝	4	2
19	23½	30	27¹⁵⁄₁₆	22	14³⁄₁₆	6	3
24	29	31	28⅛	22	15⅝	8	4

For certain conditions, exchangers can be furnished with 12-foot long tubes. See selection chart.

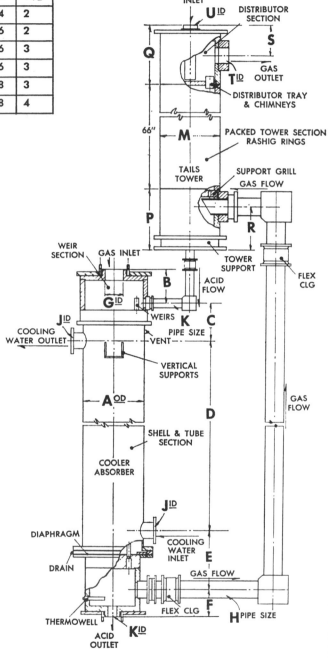

Figure 9-50. Graphite type HCl absorption tower. (By permission Falls Industries.)

TAILS TOWER SELECTION CHART

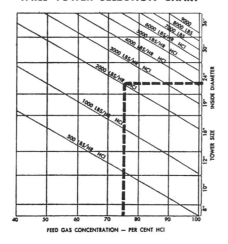

COOLER ABSORBER SELECTION CHART

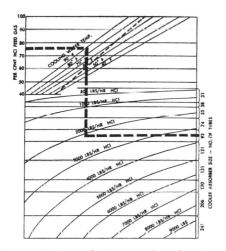

To select correct size tails tower and cooler absorber, to meet your specific requirements, follow the dotted line in the two charts. For example, using a 75% concentration of feed gas, 90° cooling water, and absorbing 2,000 lbs./hr. HCl; a 92 tube cooler absorber would be required in conjunction with a 24" diameter tower. To produce acid over 20° Be to 22° Be, use 12-foot long tubes in all instances where cooling water temperature falls to left of black dotted line in cooler absorber selection chart. Use 9-foot long tubes where temperature point is to the right of the dotted line.

Figure 9-51. Preliminary selection charts for HCl towers. (By permission, Falls Ind. Inc.)

one of the correlating factors for various packings is the height of packing equivalent to a theoretical plate for the separation. Data for effectively using this concept is extremely meager and apparently contains many uncertainties as far as general application is concerned. For this reason the use of HETP is not popular. When good correlations are developed to predict HETP without test data, then this can be an effective means of expressing packing heights in distillation. Most HETP data has been

obtained on small diameter (often laboratory size) columns using very small packing, and operated at essentially total reflux, or on moderate sized columns, but with limited systems. The scale-up of such data to industrial sizes is questionable. Murch[47] has a comprehensive survey, yet this correlation does not include an effect for pressure, nor does it, represent current industrial packing sizes or designs. The data were taken from small equipment, again raising the same question of effective scale-up to 12-inch dia. towers and larger using $\frac{3}{4}$ inch and larger packing.

$$\text{HETP} = K_1 G'^{K_2} D^{K_3} Z^{\frac{1}{8}} (\propto_{1h} \mu/\rho'), \text{ inches} \qquad (9\text{-}48)$$

where: $G' =$ vapor mass velocity, lbs./hr. (sq. ft.)

$D =$ tower diameter inches

$Z =$ packed height, feet

$\propto_{1h} =$ average relative volatility, light to heavy components*

$\mu =$ liquid viscosity, centipoises*

$\rho' =$ liquid density, grams/cc.*

*average values based on compositions at top and bottom of column.

$K_1, K_2, K_3 =$ constants from Table 9-35.

Most tower packing suppliers do not have satisfactory correlations for HETP, but rely on applications files for "similar" systems. When the designer does not have actual

Table 9-35

Constants For Murch's H.E.T.P. Relation*

Packing	Size, Inches	K_1	K_2	K_3	Remarks
Rings	$\frac{3}{8}$	2.10	—0.37	1.24	
	$\frac{1}{2}$	8.53	—0.24	1.24	Est. values
	1	0.57	—0.10	1.24	of K_2
	2	0.42	0	1.24	
Saddles	$\frac{1}{2}$	5.62	—0.45	1.11	
	1	0.76	—0.14	1.11	
McMahon	$\frac{1}{4}$	0.017	+0.50	1.00	
	$\frac{3}{8}$	0.20	+0.25	1.00	
	$\frac{1}{2}$	0.33	+0.20	1.00	
Protruded	$\frac{1}{4}$ (0.16)	0.39	+0.25	0.30	
	$\frac{3}{8}$ (0.24)	0.076	+0.50	0.30	Raschig Rings
	$\frac{3}{4}$ (0.48)	0.45	+0.30	—	of
	1	3.06	+0.12	0.30	Protruded Metal
Stedman	#128(2)	0.077	+0.48	0.24	
	#107(3)	0.363	+0.26	0.24	
	#115(6)	0.218	+0.32	0.24	

*From Murch, D.P., Ind. Eng. Chem. 45, 2616 (1953) Ref. 47. By permission.

data from similar services (often broad classes of similarity may have to be assumed to arrive at what might be termed a reasonable and safe value for HETP), then it can be helpful to contact manufacturer's technical service departments for their recommendations (which they normally will develop from application files). Keep in mind that the HETP is also unique to the packing size and configuration; therefore values obtained for one packing definitely do not accurately apply to another size or type. There is a rough relation, recognizing that the large size packing requires greater HETP than small size, but pressure drop is greater for the small packing.

There can be a significant difference between the conventional "particle" packing as represented in most of the examples of Figure 9-6, and the HETP values for the Koch Sulzer or Flexipac, and Metex Goodloe or Panapak close or compact packing forms. These later types offer HETP values varying from about five (5) inches to fourteen (14) inches. Due to the unique HETP characteristics, it is important to consult the manufacturer on the specific system involved and operating conditions. Care must be excercised in selecting these or any other type of packing since plugging with suspended solids, polymer formation on surfaces, and similar mechanical problems can influence performance and life of the packing system.

Many correlations for HETP have been limited to Raschig rings or Berl saddles[25] both being the least efficient for mass transfer and pressure drop when compared to the more sophisticated designs represented in in Figure 9-6. The guidelines given in a later paragraph are adequate for most of these applications.

Cornell, Knapp, and Fair[12, 13, 14] proposed the use of the transfer-unit concept for distillation, where:

$$H_{og} = H_g + m \left(\frac{G}{L} \right)_m H_l$$

where: H_{og} = Height of overall gas-phase transfer unit, feet
            H_g = Height of gas phase transfer unit, feet
            H_l = Height of a liquid-phase transfer unit, feet
            m = Slope of equilibrium curve
            G = Lb-moles gas/hour/sq. foot
            L = Lb-moles liquid/hour/sq. foot

$$H_l = \phi \, C_p \left(\frac{\mu_l}{\rho_l D_l} \right)^{0.5} \left(\frac{Z}{10} \right)^{0.15}$$

where: ϕ = correlation from Figure 9-52 and 9-53 for a given packing
         C_p = Correction factor for high gas rates, from Figure 9-54
         μ_l = Liquid vicosity, lb/ft. (hr.)
         ρ_l = Liquid density, lb/cu. ft.
         D_l = Liquid-diffusion coefficient, sq. ft./hr.
         Z = Height of packing, feet

For Raschig Rings:

$$H_g = \frac{\psi \, S_{cg}^{0.5}}{(Lf_1f_2f_3)^{0.6}} \left(\frac{D}{12} \right)^{1.24} \left(\frac{Z}{10} \right)^{1/3}$$

For Berl Saddles:

$$H_g = \frac{\psi \, S_{cg}^{0.5}}{(Lf_1f_2f_3)^{0.5}} \left(\frac{D}{12} \right)^{1.11} \left(\frac{Z}{10} \right)^{1/3}$$

where ψ = Parameter for a given packing, from Figures 9-55 and 56
     S_{cg} = Gas-phase Schmidt Number = $\mu_g / \rho_g D_g$

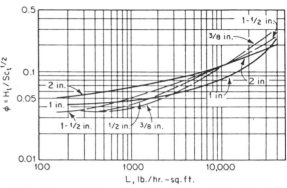

Figure 9-52. H_l correlation for various sizes of Raschig rings. Sc = Schmidt Number (N_{Sc}). (By permission, Cornell et al, Chem. Eng. Progr., 56 (8), 68, 1960.)

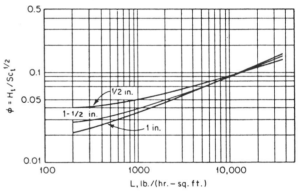

Figure 9-53. H_l correlation for various sizes of Berl Saddles. (By permission, Cornell, et al, "Chem. Eng. Progr., 56 (8), 68, 1960.)

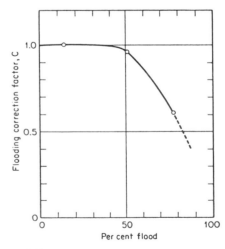

Figure 9-54. Liquid-film correction factor for operation at high percent of flood. (By permission, "Chem. Eng. Progr., 56 (8), 68, 1960.)

μ_g = Gas viscosity, lb/ft (hr)

ρ_g = Gas Density, lb/cu. ft.

D_g = Gaseous diffusion coefficient, sq. ft-hr.

D = Column diameter, inches

Z = Packed height, feet

$f_1 = (\rho_1 \, 2.42)^{0.16}$

$f_2 = (62.4/\rho_1)^{1.25}$

$f_3 = (72.8/\sigma)^{0.8}$

μ_1 = Liquid viscosity, Lb/ft. (hr.)

ρ_1 = Liquid density, Lb/cu. ft.

σ = Surface tension, dynes/cm.

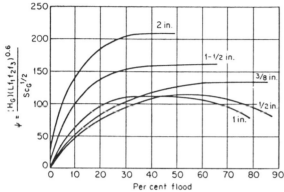

Figure 9-55. H_g correlations for various sizes of Raschig rings. (By permission, Cornell, et al, "Chem. Eng. Progr., 56 (8), 68, 1960.)

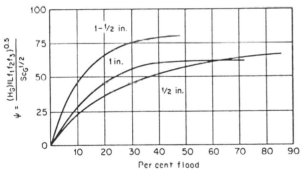

Figure 9-56. H_g correlations for various sizes of Berl Saddles. (By permission, Cornell, et al, "Chem. Eng. Progr.," 56, (8), 68, 1960.)

In Reference 14, the authors modified the equations for H_g and H_1 as follows: (a) eliminate column diameter correction above 24 inch, and (b) columns with *good* liquid distribution probable can allow elimination of the packing height correction.

Two separate investigators have evaluated the various correlation methods, and reported the Cornell, et.al. method is significantly better than others. These were 1-and 2-inch metal Pall rings and 1-inch ceramic Intalox saddles[24] and ¾, 1½ and 3 inch Raschig rings.[68]

Whitt[80] has correlated literature data of commercial size Raschig ring packing as shown in Figure 9-57. The range of plotted data is indicated, and the suggested design lines are good medians. The HTU values are for gas film controlling absorption systems, and the HETP data are for distillations at 760 mm Hg and below. These values should be usable for most pressure systems. The viscosity of the liquid ranged 0.35 to 1.0 centipoises. The equation for the HETP line is:[34]

$$\text{HETP} = 32 \left/ \left(\frac{L'}{d_o \mu}\right)^{0.5} \right. \qquad (9\text{-}49)$$

and for H.T.U.$_G$

$$\text{HTU}_G = 36 \left/ \left(\frac{L'}{d_o \mu}\right)^{0.5} \right. \qquad (9\text{-}50)$$

In general, for the same liquid and vapor rates the HETP and HTU values for Berl saddles and others with a/ε^3 lower than Raschig rings should be lower. Correlating data is not available, except tests of Teller[71] which indicate 1-inch Berl saddles have HETP values 0.75 as compared to 0.85 for 1-inch Raschig rings.

The accuracy of establishing HETP values for new conditions in the same packing referenced to known values as suggested by Planovski[57] has not been tested by other literature references.

$$(\text{HETP})_{new} = (\text{HETP})_{known} P^* G_{new}/P_{new} G^* \qquad (9\text{-}51)$$

*represents known conditions

P = system pressure, absolute

Figure 9-57. H. E. T. P. and H. T. U. correlation for tower packings. (By permission F. R. Whitt, British Chem. Eng. July p. 365, 1955.)

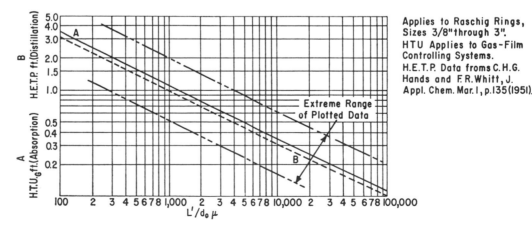

Applies to Raschig Rings, Sizes 3/8"through 3". HTU Applies to Gas-Film Controlling Systems. H.E.T.P. Data from s C.H.G. Hands and F.R.Whitt, J. Appl. Chem. Mar. 1, p.135 (1951).

The operation of packed towers under vacuum conditions is not well defined in the literature. However, the work of Hands and Whitt[33] specifically evaluates several systems operating from 20 to 760 mm Hg. ads. Their recommended limiting vapor velocity is

$$V_g = 0.065 (\rho_L/\rho_G)^{0.5}, \text{ feet/sec.} \qquad (9\text{-}52)$$

or

$$L_m = 0.334 (\text{Pressure, mm Hg. abs.})^{0.5} \qquad (9\text{-}53)$$

Operating values are recommended to be two-thirds of the limiting values. From the data it appears that entrainment (internal may be more significant than exernal) becomes a limiting factor before the flooding values predicted by Figure 9-13.

HETP Guide Lines

For industrial process equipment some general guide lines in this undefined area are (for particle packing)

A. Never use HETP less than 12 inches if tower is 12 inches Dia. or larger; for general assumption, use HETP = 1.5 to 2.0 feet.

B. Use HETP = H_{OG} or H_{OL} if other data not available

C. Use HETP = Column diameter (over 12 inches Dia.) if no other information available, up to 48″ Dia.

H.E.T.P. values appear to vary somewhat within the process system of the distillation, while certainly varying with the size and style of packing. In general the larger, more open packing designs exhibit higher H.E.T.P. values; while the smaller particle type packing and the compact styles exhibit significantly lower values for the same system. A brief guide to recent published values for various systems can be helpful in establishing the right order of magnitude for a system in design.

Transfer Unit

The transfer unit concept is also applicable to distillation in packed towers. Height of the packing required is:

$$Z = N_{OG} H_{OG} \qquad (9\text{-}54)$$

For usual applications in rectifying where the number of transfer units N_{OG} is:

$$N_{OG} = \int_{y_1}^{y_2} \frac{dy}{y^* - y} \qquad (9\text{-}54A)$$

for stripping, usually:

$$Z = N_{OL} H_{OL} \qquad (9\text{-}54B)$$

The height of the transfer unit has not been satisfactorily correlated for application to a wide variety of systems. If pilot plant or other acceptable data are available to represent the system, then the height of packing can be safely scaled-up to commercial units. If such data are not available, rough approximations may be made by determining H_G and H_L as for absorption and combining to obtain an H_{OG} (Ref. 74, pg. 330). This is only very approximate. In fact it is because of the lack of any volume of data on commercial units that many potential applications of packed towers are designed as tray towers.

$$N_{OL} = \int_{x_1}^{x_2} \frac{dx}{x - x^*} \text{ for liquid concentration gradients} \qquad (9\text{-}54\text{C})$$

Example 9-11: Transfer Units in Distillation

A benzene-toluene mixture is to be separated in a tower packed with 1-inch Berl saddles. The feed is 55.2 mol percent (liquid feed, saturated), and an overhead of 90 mol percent benzene, and bottoms of not more than 24 mol percent benzene is desired. Using the data of Ref. 51 plotted in Figure 9-58, determine the number of transfer units in the rectifying and stripping sections using a reflux ratio (reflux to product, L/D) = 1.35.

Referring to Figure 9-58 for the graphical solution:

Rectifying section operating line slope =

$$\frac{R}{R+1} = \frac{1.35}{1.35+1} = 0.576$$

Note that point 7 can be determined by the intersection of the rectifying operating line and the feed condition line 8-7.

Establish the location of the feed, bottoms and overhead compositions on the graph. Draw in the operating lines as for a distillation in a tray column.

To establish the transfer units draw in line A-B-C so that it is always half-way vertically between the equilibrium line and the operating line, making dimension 1-2 equal to 2-3. Begin drawing the transfer units at the overhead product 4, such that 4-9 equals 9-5, then drop vertically to the operating line and repeat the process always making the line A-B-C bisect the horizontal portion of the step. At the feed point re-start the stepwise process if the transfer unit step does not terminate at the feed point 7.

For this example, the number of transfer units is:

Rectifying:	2.9 ±
Stripping:	2.6 ±
Total	5.5 ± units

The reboiler for the column is in addition to this; however, the bottoms were specified as being the inlet from the reboiler. For most purposes the reboiler can be considered one additional transfer unit.

Alternate:

An alternate method to determining the number the of transfer units is the graphical integration of dy/ (y* — y). The procedure is basically the same as for absorbers, that is:

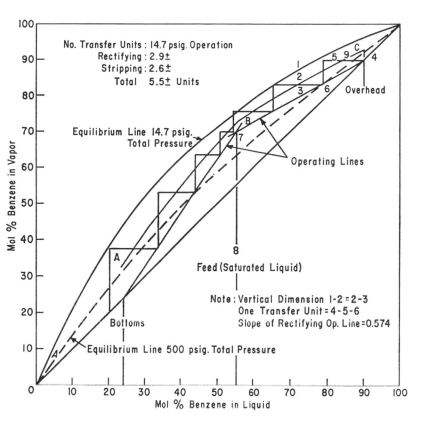

Figure 9-58. Vapor-liquid equilibrium (data only): Benzene-toluene. (By permission J. Griswold, D. Andres, V. A. Klein, "Trans." Amer. Inst. Chem. Engrs. Vol. 39, p. 223, 1943.)

(1). For assumed values of x (mol fraction of component under consideration in liquid) from bottoms to overhead, read values of y (vapor under operating conditions corresponding to x) and values of y* (vapor in equilibrium with x) from the equilibrium line.

(2). Calculate $1/(y^*-y)$ at each selected point. thus:

x	y*	y	y*—y	1/(y*—y)
0.24	0.44	0.24	0.20	5.0
0.30	0.52	0.328	0.192	5.21

(3). Plot y, from y bottoms to y overhead versus $1/(y^*-y)$. The position of y-feed can be noted on the graph, and the integration so arranged as to reveal the split between rectifying and stripping transfer units. The total number by this method should check closely with the graphical step-wise method.

Height of Transfer Unit

The height of a transfer unit for this system is not available, therefore it may be *roughly* approximated by the method of additive H_G and H_L which is questionable at best, or the approximation of 2 feet for HTU may be used. The latter is just about as reliable as the former.

Then: height of tower packing, using 1-inch Berl saddles:

From transfer units = (2) (5.5) = 11 ft.

Allowances: for top distribution:	2 ft.
Sub-total	13 ft.
Extra, 20%	2.5 ft.
Total Z,	15.5 ft.
	use 16 ft.

The tower must be designed for throughput,—diameter determined and pressure drop established.

Check Theoretical Plate Basis

HETP by approximate method:

$$HETP = K_1 G'^{K_2} d^{K_3} h^{1/3} (\alpha_{lh} \mu/\rho), \text{ Equation 9-48.}$$

From Table 9-35:

$K_1 = 0.76$

$K_2 = -0.14$

$K_3 = 1.11$

$G' = 610$ lbs./hr.(sq. ft.)

$d = 18$-inch I.D.

$h = 13$-foot (assumed)

$\alpha_{lh} = 2.6$ at top temp. of 80° C. (Ref. 51 pg. 233)

$\alpha_{1h} = 2.35$ at bottom temp. of 115° C.

α_{1h} (average) $= 2.44$

$$\mu = \frac{0.30 + 0.17}{2} = 0.24 \text{ cp. avg. viscosity}$$

$\rho = 0.85$ gm/cc. average

HETP $= 0.76 \ (610)^{-0.14} \ (18)^{1.11} \ (13)^{0.34} \ (2.44) \ (0.24)/0.85$

HETP $= 12.4$ inches

Safety factor suggested $= 2$, in any case a value not less than 1.25

Therefore use:

HETP $= 24$ inches $= 2$ feet

From Figure 9-58 it is evident that the number of theoretical plates and number of transfer units are not the same. When stepped off, the number of theoretical plates is 6+.

Height of packing $= (6) \ (2) = 12$ ft
Allowance for distribution $\quad = \quad \underline{2}$ ft
Total $\qquad\qquad\qquad\qquad\qquad$ 14 ft

Use: 14-feet packing, 1-inch Berl saddles.

Since the 16 feet of packing by the HTU method is larger, this would be the recommended safe height to use.

For comparison, note the relative increase in the number of transfer units if the operation were at a higher pressure as shown by the dotted line for 500 psig.

Cooling Water With Air

Wood or plastic filled towers for cooling water by using air are quite economical for certain heat loads and geographical locations. The costs of installation and operation must be compared with once-through water costs at any location to arrive at a proper understanding of the advisability of the installation. The four commercial tower types are:

1. Atmospheric

This tower depends upon the atmospheric wind to blow horizontally (or nearly so) through the tower (Figure 9-59). These towers must be relatively open areas to receive the available wind from any particular direction. Wind velocities of 4.5 to 6.5 mph are necessary for reasonable operation. The towers operate in cross-flow of wind to falling water and range from 30-55 percent effective.

Table 9-36
HETP Estimates for Distillation Applications

System	Pressure Range if Known	General Packing Type/Style/Make	Estimating HETP* Feet
Iso-Octane/Toluene	100mm Hg	Hy-Pak No. 2	2.0 - 2.7
Same	740mm Hg	Hy-Pak No. 1	0.7 - 2.7
Para/Ortho Xylene	740mm Hg	Metal Intalox No. 25	0.8 - 1.3
Same	740mm Hg	Metal Intalox No. 40	1.3 - 1.55
Same	740mm Hg	Metal Intalox No. 50	1.75 - 2.15
Chlorinated HC	Vacuum	Metal Intalox No. 25	2
Chlorinated HC	Vacuum	Metal Intalox No. 40	2.4
Chlorinated HC	Vacuum	Metal Intalox No. 50	3.5
Iso-Octane/Toluene	740mm Hg	Pall Ring, 1″ Metal	1.0 - 2.0
Iso-Octane/Toluene	740mm Hg	Pall Ring, 1½″ Metal	0.75 - 1.0 (3.5)**
Iso-Octane/Toluene	740mm Hg	Pall Ring, 2″ Metal	1.5 - 2.2
Methanol/Water	740mm Hg	Pall Ring, 1″ Metal	0.65 - 0.8 (1.2)**
Isopropanol/Water	740mm Hg	Pall Ring, 1″ Metal	0.6 - 1.5
Benzene/Toluene	740mm Hg	Pall Ring, 1″ Metal	1.0 - 1.5
Acetone/Water	740mm Hg	Pall Ring, 1″ Metal	0.9 - 1.2 (1.4)**
Same	—	Flexirings, 1″ Metal	1.6 - 1.8 (2.3)**
Same	—	Flexirings, 2″ Metal	1.8 - 2.2 (2.4)**
Same	—	Koch Sulzer Metal	0.45 - 0.9
Light Hydrocarbon	400 psia	Goodloe Metal	approx. 0.75
Propane/Butane	235 psia	Goodloe Metal	approx. 0.80

*Based on industrial data or commercial sized tests
**At very low gas rates
   Data for table compiled from respective manufacturer's published literature.

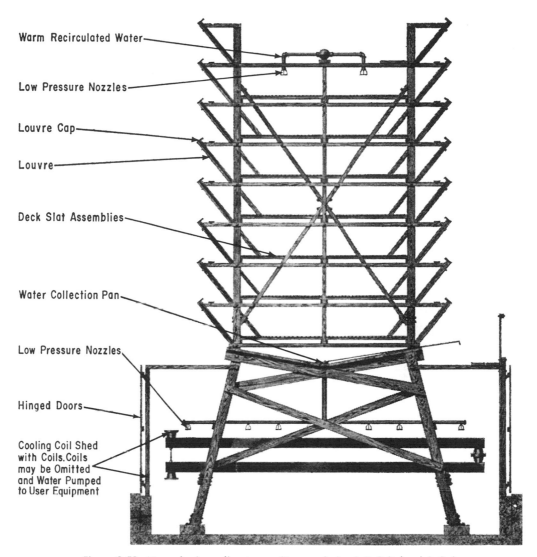

Warm Recirculated Water

Low Pressure Nozzles

Louvre Cap

Louvre

Deck Slat Assemblies

Water Collection Pan

Low Pressure Nozzles

Hinged Doors

Cooling Coil Shed
with Coils. Coils
may be Omitted
and Water Pumped
to User Equipment

Figure 9-59. Atmospheric cooling tower. (By permission J. F. Pritchard & Co.)

They are not capable of producing water at a temperature much closer than 4° F. of the entering air wet-bulb temperature. They require no fan, but do consume power to pump the water to the (relatively high) top of the tower. Ground area requirements may be large.

2. Natural Draft:

This tower depends upon natural draft action the same as a chimney to draw cool air in at the bottom and expel it out the top as warm moist air (Figure 9-60). The action of the tower depends upon the atmospheric temperature; therefore, on a hot day the action of the tower may be less than on a cool day. These towers are relatively large, and require power for pumping the water to a point in the tower which is usually lower than for an atmospheric tower. There are no fan costs.

Units have been built 310 ft. high, base diameter 210 ft. and a throat of 120 ft., widening to 134 ft. in diameter at the top.[30]

3. Forced Draft

This type of tower utilizes fans at the base to force air through the tower fill or packing (Figure 9-61). Due to the relatively low outlet air velocity there is a tendency for discharged hot air to recirculate into the fan intake and reduce tower performance. The fan handles only atmospheric air thereby reducing its corrosion problem when compared to the fan on an induced draft tower. The tower size for the forced as well as the induced draft unit is considerably less than for an atmospheric or natural draft unit due to the higher heat transfer rates.

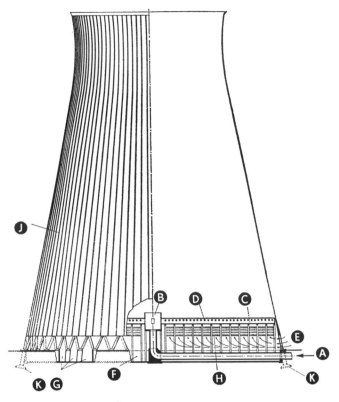

A   Hot water inlet main

B   Central Tank

C   Hot water channels

D   Asbestos distribution tubes

E   Air intake

F   Basin

G   Cold water outlet

H   Heat Exchanger

J   Tower Ribs

K   Foundation Footings

Figure 9-60. Component parts of modern natural draft tower. (By permission Hamon, Inc.)

4. Induced Draft

This tower utilizes fans at the top of the tower to draw air in the base of the tower, through the fill and out the fan discharge (Figures 9-62 and 9-63). In this type of mechanical draft tower the hot moist air discharges vertically (usually) to the atmosphere with such a velocity as to eliminate the possibility of recirculation of this air in at the base of the tower. This moist air is corrosive to the fan parts and therefore requires protection of coated plastic or special metal blades and sealed motors and reduction gears.

General Construction

The majority of cooling towers are built of redwood or cypress. However, special conditions and atmospheres dictate other types of construction.

Materials:

1. Framework
   Heart redwood
   Cypress
   Galvanized steel
   Brick or Concrete

2. Casing
   Heart redwood
   Cypress
   Corrugated asbestos board, or some combination with redwood.
   Brick or concrete block

3. Fill or Packing
   Heart redwood
   Cypress
   Asbestos-cement boards or strips
   Plastic sheet, grids or pieces

4. Drift Eliminators, same as 3.

5. Louvers, same as 3.

6. Miscellaneous Hardware
   Monel, galvanized or other corrosion resistant metals

7. Fans and Drivers
   Axial or propeller blade fans are either belt or gear driven. Some drivers are variable speed motors, and some fans have variable pitch blades. In special circumstances, steam turbine, gas or gasoline engine drivers are used. Gears should be carefully specified to avoid overload and should be specially sealed to prevent moisture entering the case.

Cooling Tower Terminology

Wet Bulb Temperature: the temperature of air at which it would saturate without a change in its heat content. It is the theoretical minimum temperature to which water may be cooled in a cooling tower. However, in actuality this temperature can never be reached, but only approached. The selection of the proper wet bulb temperature is very critical, as it is the single most important factor in tower rating. The selected temperature should be high enough to include 95 percent of the maximum readings recorded during the time most critical or important in the cooling service.

If the temperature is too high, an expensive tower will be specified; and of course, if too low, the cooling load service will be required to sacrifice performance during the times when the wet bulb exceeds the specified value. At constant inlet humidity and constant rates for liquid, L', and air, G', the effect of changing wet bulb on the

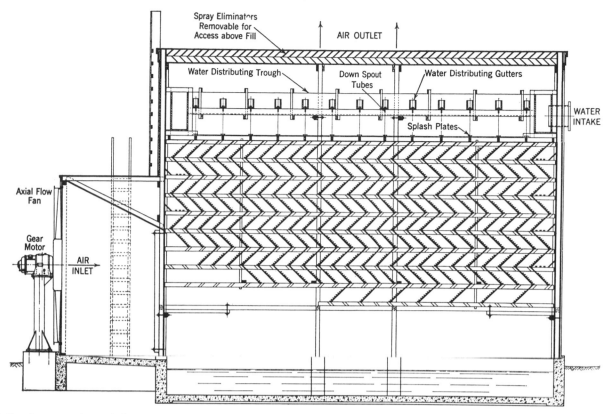

Figure 9-61. Cross section of low head forced tower showing fan house arrangement, filling, water distribution system and spray eliminators. (Courtesy Foster Wheeler Corp., Cooling Tower Dept.)

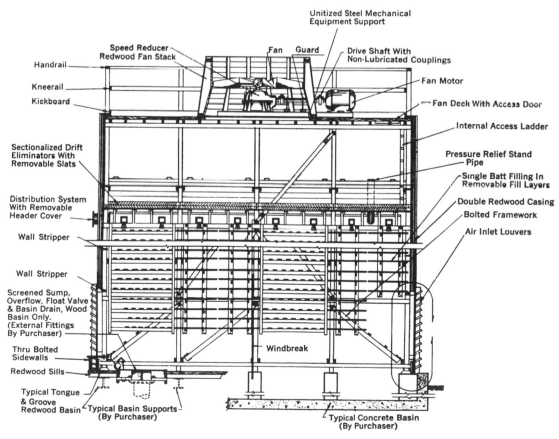

Transverse Cross Section
One Fan per Cell

Figure 9-62. Counter flow induced draft cooling tower. (By permission J. F. Pritchard & Co.)

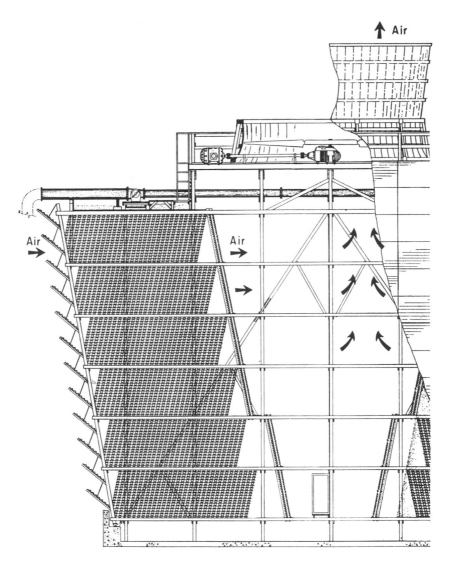

Figure 9-63. Cross-flow induced draft cooling tower. (By permission The Marley Co.)

performance factor KaV/L' is only 1.2 percent with no trend dependent on rates.[38]

Approach: the temperature difference between the tower cold water outlet temperature and the wet bulb temperature of the air. The smaller the approach the more difficult the cooling job, and the larger the required tower. For a fixed cold water temperature, changing the wet bulb temperature by one degree can make a significant difference in tower requirements. Usually an approach of 5° F. is considered minimum.

Range: the temperature difference between the warm water into the tower and the cold water out. The range determines the heat load on the tower, which in turn reflects the requirements of the cooling water service. The average reduction in KaV/L' for each 10° F. increase in hot water inlet temperature is 2 percent.[38]

Drift Loss or Windage Loss: the amount of water lost from a tower as fine droplets entrained in the leaving air. For an atmospheric type tower this is usually 0.1-0.2 percent of the total water circulated. For mechanical draft towers it is usually less.

Make-up: the water required to be added to the system to make-up for losses by evaporation, drift loss and blow-down.

Blow-down: the amount of water continuously or intermittently removed from the system to maintain a predetermined water analysis with respect to chemicals and dissolved gases. The build-up of solid or chemical concentration which will take place with continued evaporation and no blow-down can become very corrosive and harmful to metal and wood parts of the system. In addition, the deposition of salts on exposed surfaces and

	SPEC. DWG. NO.
A-	

Page	of	Pages
Unit Price		
No. Units		
Item No.		

Job No. _____

B/M No. _____

COOLING TOWER SPECIFICATIONS

PERFORMANCE

Water Circulating Rate: _____ gpm. Temp. In: _____ °F Temp. Out: _____ °F

Cooling Duty _____ Btu/Hr.; Perform. Test Code* _____

*At Option of Owner _____

SELECTION

Manufacturer: _____ Model: _____

Type: _____ No. of Cells: _____

DESIGN

Wet Bulb Temp: _____ °F; Static Pumping Hd. _____ Ft. Eff. Cool. Vol. _____ Cu. Ft.

Fill Wetted Surf. _____ Sq. Ft; Total Wetted Surf. _____ Sq. Ft; Eff. Splash Surf; _____ Cu. Ft.

No. of Fans Req'd. _____ Cfm/Fan _____ ;Static Press _____ In. H2O; Normal BHP/Fan _____

Evaporation Loss. Max. % _____ Spray Loss. Max. % _____

MATERIALS OF CONSTRUCTION

Framework _____ Casing _____ Fill _____

Fan Cylinder _____ Stairway _____

Bolts Nuts, Misc. Hardware _____ Nails _____

Water Inlet Hdrs. _____ Nozzles _____ Basin _____

Fan Blade _____ Fan Hub _____ Fan Shaft. _____

Code for Lumber Grades _____ Code for Lumber Struct. Design _____

**Exception: Wind Loading, See Inquiry or P.O. _____

AUXILIARY EQUIPMENT

Fan
Manufacturer _____ Type _____

Diameter _____ Ft.; Speed _____ RPM; Tip Speed _____ fpm.

Gear
Manufacturer _____ Type _____ Size _____

Reduction Ratio _____ Rated Cap. _____ BHP; Mechanical Eff. _____ %

Driver
Manufacturer _____ Type _____ Speed _____ RPM

Electric Power _____ BHP _____ Service Factor _____ Frame _____

REMARKS

By	Chk'd.	App.	Rev.	Rev.	Rev.
Date					

P.O. To: _____

Figure 9-64. Cooling tower specifications form.

accumulation of sludge in the basin of the tower can influence performance as well as affect the life of the tower.

Recirculation: the portion of exit or outlet air from the tower which recirculates back to the inlet of the fresh air to the tower. In order to keep this low it is important to space towers away from each other as well as from any structures which can deflect the exit moist air back to the inlet. Due to recirculation the wet bulb temperature at the tower inlet may be different than at a point 100 yards away. The recirculation of induced draft towers is usually less than forced draft due to the upward velocity of discharge of the air.

Normal recirculation in average installations for forced draft may run 3-10 percent of total inlet air, and 1-8 percent for induced draft towers, all depending upon the location and wind conditions during any day or season. Some towers can be arranged to have less than 1 percent recirculation. If conditions are suspected of being conductive to recirculation, it should definitely be allowed for in design of the tower. Recirculation increases the wet bulb temperature of entering air, increases the total air required (and hence size of all equipment) in order to maintain a given tower performance.

Specifications

Specifications for performance rating are usually set by the process engineer with the rating selection performed by the cooling tower manufacturer. Each manufacturer has packing arrangements with known specific performance characteristics and has developed size modules for standard cells (usually 6 feet x 6 feet or 8 feet x 8 feet) together with the associated fan requirements. Some of this information is tabulated in general information form in the catalog literature. Specific economical ratings must consider the performance specified in light of the local application of the tower. To do otherwise can very often lead to excessive costs for this type of equipment. An informational specification sheet to be used by the process engineer is given in Figure 9-64.

Additional detailed information is available from the Cooling Tower Institute, including ATF-105 *Acceptance Test Procedure for Water-Cooling Towers,* STD-101 *CTI Grades of Redwood Lumber*[31] STD-102 *'Structural Design Data*[70] and TSC-302 *Cooling Tower Wood Maintenance.*[16]

It is recommended that performance tests be specified and conducted in accordance with the Cooling Tower Institute procedure, as this gives the process engineer a standard of reference. Most cooling tower manufacturers are members of this Institute.

Manufacturer's bid proposals should include all of the information specified by the blanks on the specification sheet and in addition, details of construction, details re-

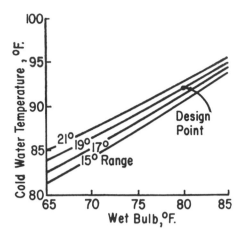

Figure 9-65. Typical performance for design GPM. (By permission J. Whitesell Chem. Eng. Jan. p. 187, 1955.)

garding driver, gear, etc., and a guaranteed performance curve showing the effect of ± 10 percent change in water quantity and lower wet bulb temperature, similar to Figure 9-65.

For rating by the manufacturer, the process engineer must specify and consider:

1. Water rate, gpm

2. Inlet water temperature, °F.

3. Outlet cold water temperature, °F.

4. Design wet bulb temperature, °F., for the location of construction of the tower.

5. Water condition (sandy, oily, etc.) and type (river, canal, harbor, sea). The contaminating chemicals and/or minerals should be identified. Type of water treatment.

6. Drift loss or mist loss, usually maximum of 0.2 percent of design water flow rate.

7. External wind force or loading for standard design. Most designs are for 30 lbs. per sq. ft., although specific geographical locations may require other specifications. Give minimum, and average wind velocities with compass direction for atmospheric and natural draft towers.

8. Geographical location; plant site location, general proximity to other structures and other factors relating to recirculation of exit air back to the inlet of the tower.

9. Type and specifications on fan driver, gear types, power voltage, phase, cycles. Motors should at least meet specifications equivalent to totally enclosed, fan cooled, or if in explosive hazardous area, TEFC Class I, Group D (except this not acceptable in hydrogen or acetylene atmosphere). Due to moisture conditions around this equipment, it should be protected against moisture penetration and corrosion.

10. Number, type, height, area requirements for cooling coils (if any) to be installed in tower basin by purchaser.

11. Power costs for fan and pump horsepower, approximate pump efficiency for water, and any special data peculiar to the economics of the installation. This will allow the manufacturer to select a tower giving consideration to the economic factors involved.

12. Items to be furnished by the purchaser, such as concrete basin, anchor bolts, electrical components, external piping, material handling to job site. If the tower manufacturer is to perform a turn-key or package job, this should be specified, as in some instances the tower manufacturer may not be in a position to do this.

13. Fire protection if unit is to be allowed to stand dry for prolonged periods, or required by insurance.

Performance

The cooling tower cools hot water with cool air by countercurrent (or cross-current) flow of the two fluids past each other in a tower filled with packing. This involves both mass and heat transfer. The water surface which exists on the tower packing is covered with an air film assumed to be saturated at the water temperature. The heat is transferred between this film and the main body of air by diffusion and convection. Detailed presentations of the development of cooling tower theory are given in References 39 and 46.

Figures 9-66 and 9-67 indicate the variables in tower performance.

The packing or fill is arranged to prevent a droplet of water from falling the full height of the tower. As it falls it hits a packing member, splashes, forms a film, drops off and falls to hit the next packing member. The counter-current stream of air sweeps across these drops and films to effectively cool the water and humidify the air. As the water flows down through the tower its temperature may drop below the dry bulb temperature of the inlet air to the tower. It can never go below the inlet air wet bulb temperature, in fact, it just *approaches* this wet bulb. One of the controlling features in tower design and performance is how close these two temperatures, inlet air wet bulb and outlet water, are expected to operate. The driving force for the cooling is the difference in enthalpies of the film of air surrounding the water and that of the main body of the air.

The number of transfer units or tower characteristic is based on overall heat and mass transfer:

$$\int_{t_2}^{t_1} \frac{dt}{h' - h} = KaV/L'$$

where: h' = Enthalpy of saturated air film at bulk water temperature BTU/lb. dry air

h = Enthalpy of the main air stream, BTU/lb. dry air

t_1 = Entering warm water temperature, °F.

t_2 = Outlet cool water temperature, °F.

t = Bulk water temperature, °F.

Cooling tower data[15, 19, 46] has been plotted as KaV/L' vs. L'/G_a and indicates that the tower characteristic KaV/L' is a function of L'/G_a and not dependent on the value of G_a only, when using high voidage splash deck grid type packings. A few representative tower fill packings are shown in Figure 9-68 and performance characteristic values

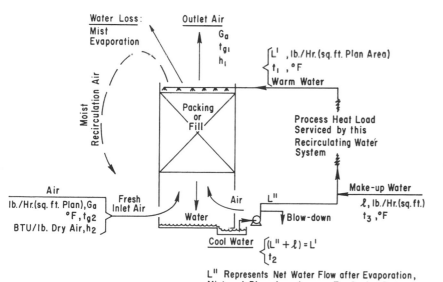

Figure 9-66. Diagram of counter current air-water cooling tower.

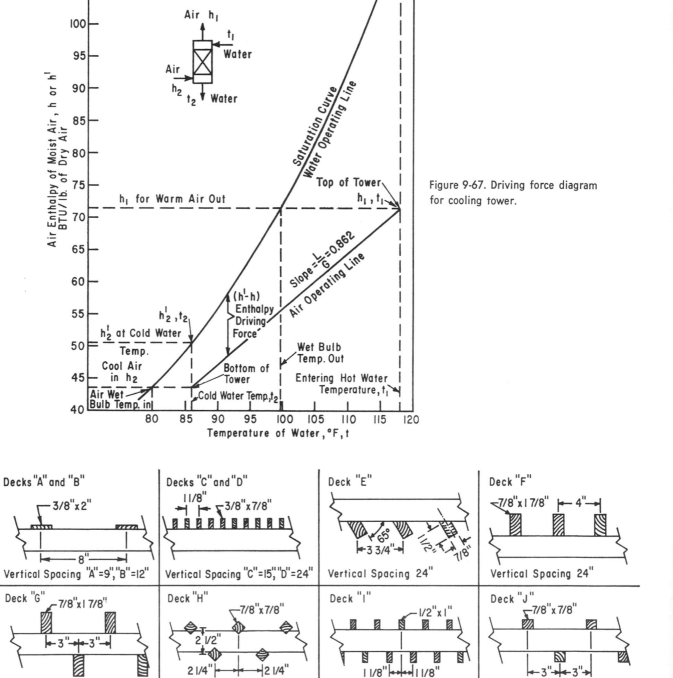

Figure 9-67. Driving force diagram for cooling tower.

Figure 9-68. Commercial cooling tower fill packing. (By permission N. W. Kelly and L. K. Swenson, Chem. Eng. Prog. Vol. 52, No. 7, p. 263, 1956.)

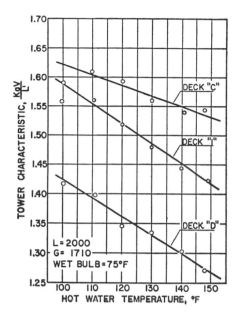

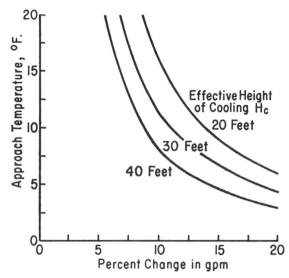

Figure 9-70. Percent change in GPM to produce 1° F change in approach.

Figure 9-69. Typical effect of hot water temperature on tower characteristic, KaV/L' at constant L', G$_a$ wet-bulb temperature, and packed height. (By permission N. W. Kelly and L. K. Swenson, "Chem. Eng. Prog." Vol. 52, No. 7, p. 263, 1956.) Note: L and G shows in chart are hourly rates.

are shown in Figure 9-69. Figures 9-70 to 9-75 illustrate counterflow tower performance. The curves are satisfactory for close estimating, while exact data should be obtained from the manufacturers.

Enthalpy of air operating line:

The enthalpy of air at any point on the operating line is:[34]

$$h_1{}^* = h_2 + (L'/G_a)\,(t_1 - t_2')\qquad(9\text{-}55)$$

The equation for the line at terminal conditions is:

$$h_1 = h_2 + (L'/G_a)\,(t_1 - t_2)\qquad(9\text{-}55A)$$

where: $h_1{}^*$ = Enthalpy of air at any temperature higher than inlet, BTU/lb. dry air; note that h_1 is exit air

h_2 = Enthalpy of inlet air to tower, equivalent to enthalpy of saturated air at wet bulb temperature, BTU/lb. dry air, from *Moist Air Tables* ASHVE Guide.

t_2' = Any water temperature lower than inlet water temperature and higher than inlet air wet bulb temperature, °F.

t_1 = Inlet water temperature, °F.

The effects of wet bulb, approach and range on mechanical draft cooling tower size is indicated in Figure 9-76.

The curves are necessarily the approximate midrange of a spread or band of the magnitude of the respective influences on the ground area. That is, the information is good for guidance as to the direction certain changes will

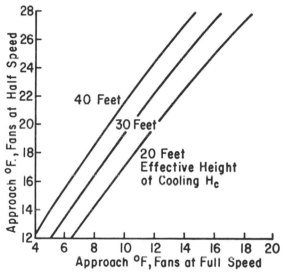

Figure 9-71. Effect of half speed operation.

take in the final selection. For example, the data is referenced to a 70° F. wet bulb and a 15° F. approach, therefore, a change in wet bulb only to 75° F. will indicate a tower requiring 90 percent of the ground area. If the approach changes too, then its correction must also be multiplied against the previous result, and the same handling applies to the wet bulb.

In examining the tower performance it is not the air temperature that sets the capacity, but the heat content or enthalpy of the air. Although the air temperature and wet bulbs at inlet may be different for two different inlet

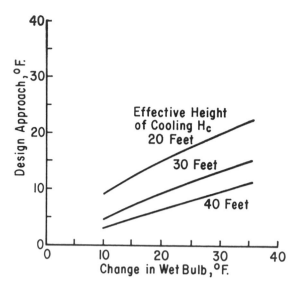

Figure 9-72. Decrease from approach for maintaining design water temperature.

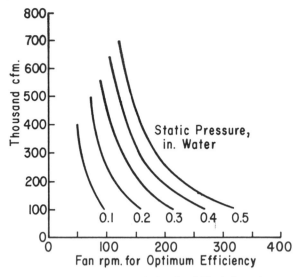

Figure 9-74. RPM correlation for 16° pitch angle.

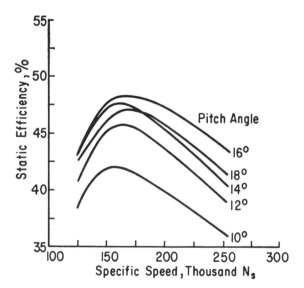

Figure 9-73. Fan efficiency versus specific speed for various blade angle settings.

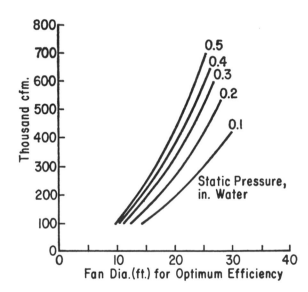

Figure 9-75. Diameter correlation for 16° pitch angle.

(Figures 9-70—9-75, by permission, J. Whitesell, "Chem. Eng." p. 187, Jan. 1955).

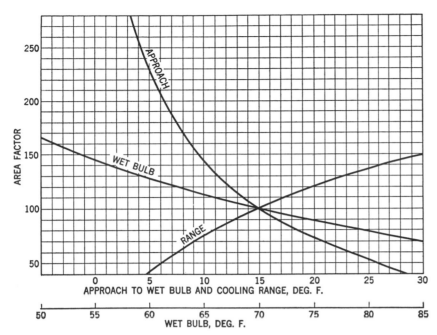

Figure 9-76. Effect of cooling tower performance variables on plan ground area required. (Courtesy Foster Wheeler Corp., Cooling Tower Dept.)

Curve showing effect of wet bulb temperature, approach to wet bulb, and cooling range on cooling tower size. The normal tower is assumed to be designed for 15 degree cooling range and a 15 degree approach to a 70 degree wet bulb. If all other factors remain the same, reducing the approach to the wet bulb to 6.3 degrees will double the size of the tower; or decreasing the cooling range to 6.1 degrees will permit the use of a tower only half as large; or designing for a 53.7 degree wet bulb instead of a 70 degree wet bulb will require a tower 1½ times as large because of the lower water absorbing capacity of colder air.

air conditions, it is still possible for the air to have the same enthalpy. Therefore, two different air streams of different conditions can produce the same effect on tower performance. The heat content or enthalpy of all air with the same wet bulb is the same, therefore it is clear that the wet bulb temperature is important and sets the performance.

Recent studies indicate that the performance of all commonly used commercial high voidage packings can be correlated by:[38]

$$KaV/L' = 0.07 + A'N'(L'/G_a)^{-n'} \qquad (9\text{-}56)$$

This relates the tower characteristic to the number of packing decks in the tower and the L'/G_a ratio. Values of A' and n are given in Table 9-37.

The simultaneous solution of Equation 9-55 involving the approach and cooling range and Equation 9-56 involving the number of packing decks (and thereby available surface area) yields the $L'G_a$ which satisfies the specified performance. The accuracy of this combined with the data is within 5 percent. Equation 9-56 is essentially a straight line on log-log paper, so two points are sufficient to determine its position. The tediousness is involved in integrating the expression for the several enthalpy conditions involving approach and range that could satisfy the problem.

Ground Area Vs. Height

The economics of forced and induced draft cooling tower operation require a study of fan and water pump

Table 9-37*

Values of A', n', B, C', and S_F

Deck Type	A'	n	S_F, Feet	B Mult. x 10⁻⁸	C' Mult. x 10⁻¹²
A	0.060	0.62	3.00	0.34	0.11
B	0.070	0.62	4.00	0.34	0.11
C	0.092	0.60	3.75	0.40	0.14
D	0.119	0.58	6.00	0.40	0.14
E	0.110	0.46	4.95	0.60	0.15
F	0.100	0.51	9.13	0.26	0.07
G	0.104	0.57	6.85	0.40	0.10
H	0.127	0.47	3.64	0.75	0.26
I	0.135	0.57	4.50	0.52	0.16
J	0.103	0.54	6.85	0.40	0.10

*From: N. W. Kelly and L. K. Swenson, *Chem. Eng. Prog.*, 52, 263 (1956) Ref. 38, By permission.

horsepower and usually dictate a fan static pressure requirement not to exceed 0.75-1.0 inch of water. For atmospheric and natural draft towers the economics of pumping water are still very important. This means that the ground area must be so selected as to keep the height down while not dropping the unit rates so low that performance becomes poor. This then, is a balance of ground area versus total deck height. Pritchard[16] presents an estimating curve indicating that as packed height varies from 12-40 feet, the

economics of ground area suggest a G_a of 2000-1400 respectively, being slightly less than a straight line function.

Pressure Losses

The tower pressure losses are: (1) tower packing or fill (70-80 percent of loss), (2) air inlet if induced draft, (3) mist eliminators at top (4) air direction change losses and entrance to packing on forced draft units. These losses are a function of air velocity, number and spacing of packing decks, liquid rate and the relation between L' and G_a.

The pressure drop for a given number and type of packing deck is expressed:[38]

$$\Delta P' = N'BG_a^2\left(\frac{0.0675}{\rho_G}\right) + N'C'\sqrt{S_F}(L)G_E^2\left(\frac{0.0675}{\rho_G}\right) \quad (9\text{-}57)$$

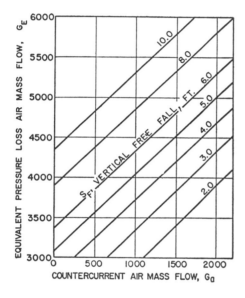

Figure 9-77. Values of equivalent air mass velocity. (By permission N. W. Kelly and L. K. Swenson, "Chem. Eng. Prog.," Vol. 52, p. 263, 1956.)

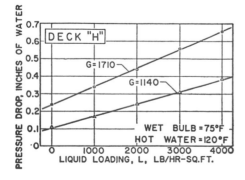

Figure 9-78. Typical effect of liquid loading on air pressure drop showing linear relationship. Total deck height is 20 feet. (By permission, N. W. Kelly and L. K. Swenson, "Chem. Eng. Prog.," Vol. 52, p. 263, 1956.)

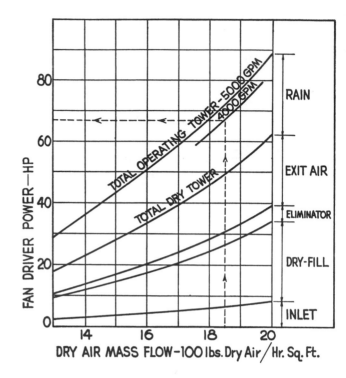

Figure 9-79. Fan power requirements for components of a typical counterflow induced draft cooling tower. (By permission E. E. Groitein, Combustion Nov., p. 38, 1957.)

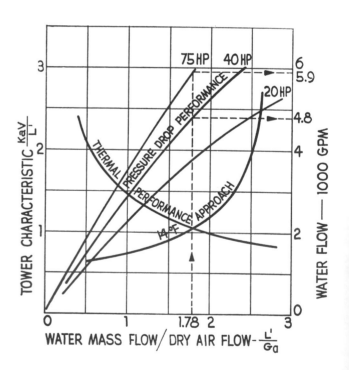

Figure 9-80. Plot illustrating combination of thermal and fan power characteristics to directly determine flow capacities of a tower of a given size. (By permission E. E. Groitein, "Combustion," Nov. p. 38, 1957.)

Values of B, C' and S_F are given in Table 9-37. Pressure drop values, $\Delta P'/N'$, per individual deck range from 0.003-0.006 inch water for low L' and G_a rates to 0.03-0.06 inch water for high L' (3500) and G_a (2000) rates.[19] Values of G_E are taken from Figure 9-77. T typical pressure drop curve is shown in Figure 9-78.

Pressure loss through wooden mist eliminators based on 0.0675 lb./cu.ft. air varies from 0.01 inch water at $G_a = 800$ to 0.07 at $G_a = 2000$ as almost a straight line function.[16] These losses are based on the face area of the eliminators.

Pressure loss for inlet louvers based on two face velocity heads and 0.075 lb./cu.ft. air is given as 0.02 inch water for 400 ft./min. face velocity to 0.32 inch water for 1600 fpm, varying slightly less than a straight line.[19]

Fan Horsepower for Mechanical Draft Tower

$$BHP = F \, p_s/(6356) \, (0.50) \qquad (9\text{-}58)$$

where: F = actual cfm at fan inlet, cubic ft./min.

p_s = total static pressure of fan, inches of water

This relation includes a 50 percent static efficiency of the fan and gear losses, assuming a gear drive.[19] If belt driven the difference will not be great.

For study purposes the effects of performance as related to fan horsepower may be patterned after Figures 9-79 and 9-80. The conditions for actual air inlet conditions for an induced draft fan must be obtained from Equation 9-55 read from a diagram similar to Figure 9-67.

Economical tower sizes usually require fan horsepower between 0.05 and 0.08 horsepower per square foot of ground plan area,[19] and motors larger than 75 HP are not often used due to inability to obtain the proper fans and gears in the space required.

Water Rates and Distribution

Water distribution must give uniform water flow over the tower packing. Many towers use a gravity feed system discharging the water through troughs and ceramic, metal or plastic nozzles. Other systems use pressure nozzles discharging upward, before falling back over the packing. This latter method requires more pumping head due to the pressure required at the nozzles. Water rates usually run from 1 to 3.5 gpm/sq.ft. of ground plan area.

Preliminary Design Estimate of New Tower

Refer to psychrometric chart, Figure 9-81, for basic considerations in establishing tower conditions.

1. Determine the inlet water temperature to the tower. This is approximately the outlet temperature from the cooling water load.

2. Determine the heat load to be performed by the tower, based on required water inlet and outlet temperatures and flow rates.

3. Establish the wet bulb temperature for the air at the geographical site of the tower. Use weather bureau records if other data is not available. Use caution, do not select a value too high.

4. Prepare a plot of the saturation curve for air-water. Establish the operating line by starting at the point set by the outlet cold water temperature and the enthalpy of air at the wet bulb temperature, and with a slope L'/G_a assumed between 0.9 and 2.7. See Figure 9-67.

5. Graphically integrate, by plotting $1/h'\text{-}h$ vs. t, reading (h'-h) from the operating-equilibrium line plot for various values of temperature. See Figure 9-82.

6. The value of the integral is equal to the number of transfer units, so set it equal to Equation 9-56 and solve for the number of decks needed, N. Select the desired deck from Figure 9-68 and the constants A' and n from Table 9-37.

7. If the number of decks required is unreasonable from a height standpoint, the procedure must be repeated using a new assumed L'/G_a, or a new approach, or a new wet bulb temperature, or some combination of these.

8. For the assumed L'/G_a and known L', calculate the required air rate G_a.

Alternate Preliminary Design of New Tower (after References 12 and 16)

1. Follow Steps (1), (2) and (3) of the procedure just outlined.

2. Refer to a plot of KaV/L' versus L'/G_a as in Figure 9-83A-G or in References 15 and 19. This saves the integration step, as this has been performed and calculated for a selection of reasonable wet bulb temperatures and temperature ranges. The curve to fit the design problem must be used.

3. Plot Equation 9-56 for two assumed L'/G_a values and an assumed number of checks on the plot of Figure 9-83C or its equivalent. The intersection with the approach curve gives the value of L'/G_a which satisfies the two Equations 9-54 and 9-56.

4. From the known liquid rate L' and the value of L'/G_a assumed, calculate the needed value of the air rate, G_a. This value converted to CFM at the fan inlet, together with the calculated pressure drop gives the fan horsepower requirements.

Performance Evaluation of Existing Tower[19]

1. Since the heat load, L', G_a and temperatures are known for an operating tower, its performance as repre-

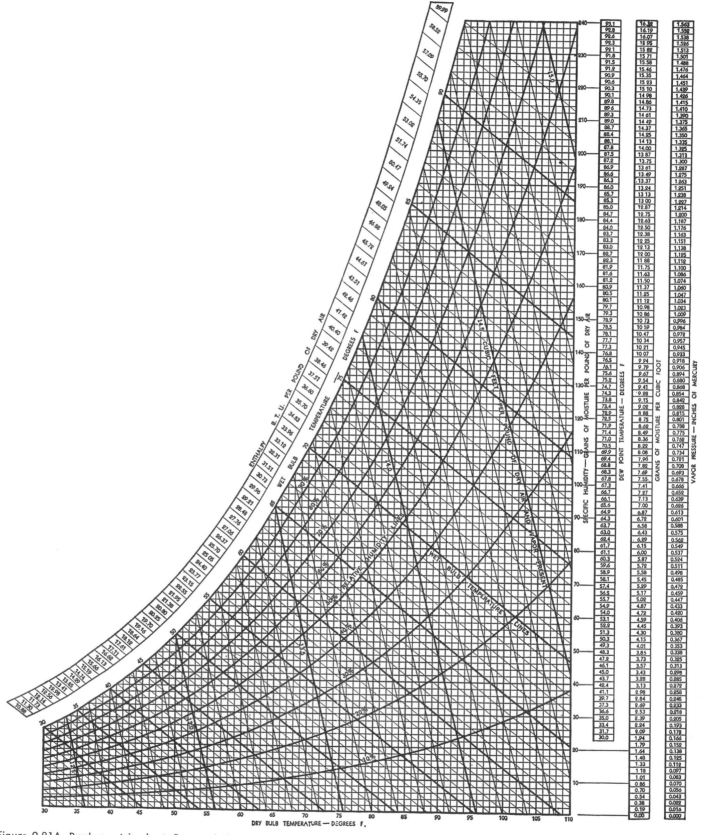

Figure 9-81A. Psychrometric chart. By permission Westinghouse Electric Corp. Sturtevant Div. Reference barometric pressure 29.92 inches HG.

If any two properties of air are known, all others may be found.

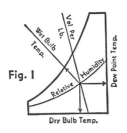

Fig. I

Numerical values of properties may be read directly.

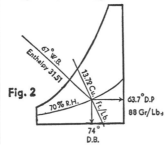

Fig. 2

SENSIBLE HEATING & COOLING is represented by a horizontal line between the limits of the process. All the properties of air change except the moisture content.

EXAMPLE:—Air initially at 90° D.B. is heated to 105° D.B.

Fig. 3

	INITIAL	FINAL		INITIAL	FINAL
Dry bulb	90°	105°	Dew point	62.4	62.4
Wet bulb	71°	75°	Vap. pres.	0.562	0.562
Rel. hum.	40%	26.0%	Enthalpy	34.83	38.46
Grains/lb.	84	84	Cu. ft./lb.	14.12	14.5

HUMIDIFYING & DEHUMIDIFYING with no change in dry bulb is represented by a vertical line between the limits of the process.

EXAMPLE:—Air at 90° D.B. and 84 GR./LB. is humidified without change of temperature to 128 GR./LB.

Fig. 4

	INITIAL	FINAL		INITIAL	FINAL
Dry bulb	90°	90°	Dew point	62.4	74.3
Wet bulb	71°	78°	Vap. pres.	0.562	0.854
Rel. hum.	40%	60%	Enthalpy	34.83	41.42
Grains/lb.	84	128	Cu. ft./lb.	14.12	14.26

EVAPORATING COOLING is accomplished by passing air thru a spray or finely divided curtain of recirculated water, and is represented by a line of constant W. B. temperature. Sens. heat is absorbed in evaporation thereby increasing the moisture content while the total heat remains constant.

EXAMPLE:—Air at 90° D.B. and 40% rel. hum. is passed thru a spray of recirculated water. The water temp. will approach the W.B. temp. of the air which remains constant.

Fig. 5

	INITIAL	FINAL		INITIAL	FINAL
Dry bulb	90°	72°	Dew point	62.4	70.5
Wet bulb	71°	71°	Vap. pres.	.562	.747
Rel. hum.	40%	95%	Enthalpy	34.83	34.83
Grains/lb.	84	112	Cu. ft./lb.	14.12	13.74

TEMPERATURES OF A MIXTURE

Find the final wet and dry bulb temperatures of a mixture of 3000 C.F.M. at 60° D.B. and 46° W.B., and 5000 C.F.M. at 80° D.B. and 63° W.B. Read from constant volume lines on chart.

Fig. 6

3000 c.f.m.   60° d.b.   46° w.b.   13.17 cu. ft./lb.
5000 c.f.m.   80° d.b.   63° w.b.   13.85 cu. ft./lb.

$\frac{3000}{13.17} = 228$ lbs./Min. $\frac{5000}{13.85} = 361$ lbs./min.

228 + 361 = 589 total wt. of air per min.

DRY BULB temperature of the mixture

$\frac{228}{589} \times 60 = 23.25°$ $\frac{361}{589} \times 80 = 49.10°$

23.25 + 49.10 = 72.35° Final D.B.

WET BULB temperature of the mixture

Enthalpy at 46° W.B. = 18.12   at 63° W.B. = 28.48

$\frac{228}{589} \times 18.12 = 7.01$ $\frac{361}{589} \times 28.48 = 17.45$

7.01 + 17.45 = 24.46 Enthalpy of Mixture
Corresponding W.B. Temp. = 57° Final W.B.

Figure 9-81B. Directions for using Figure 9-71A. (By permission Westinghouse Elec. Corp. Sturtevant Div.)

---

sented by the number of transfer units, or tower characteristic can be determined. Solve Equation 9-56 for Ka V/L', or use the modified Merkel diagram, Figure 9-84. This is the number of transfer units operating in the tower.

2. If it is desired to evaluate a change in performance on an existing tower, knowing the required conditions and numbers of decks and kind of packing, calculate KaV/L' for two assumed values of L'/G_a.

3. Following Reference 19, plot this on the appropriate curve (good up to altitudes of 3000 ft.) for KaV/L' vs L'/G_a for the proper wet bulb, range and at the intersection of the straight line plot with the approach value selected or needed, read the L'/G_a required to meet the performance conditions.

4. Calculate the new G_a, assuming that L' is the important value known. If on the other hand, it is desired to determine just how much cooling can be obtained, then for a fixed air rate, calculate the L' that can be accommodated.

Example 9-12: Wood Packing Cooling Tower With Recirculation, Induced Draft

Perform the preliminary design on a cooling tower to establish its performance and size.

Required GPM = 5,000

Inlet hot water = 110° F.

Outlet cold water = 85° F.

Wet bulb = 75° F.

Recirculation allowance = 3 percent

Use alternate design procedure:

1. Range = 110 — 85 = 25° F.

2. Wet Bulb

Since recirculation is to be considered, the ambient wet bulb of 75° F. must be corrected.

3. Solve Equation 9-56:

$$KaV/L' = 0.07 + AN (L'/G_a)^{-n}$$

Select Deck "A":

Constants:

$A' = 0.060$

$n = 0.62$

$L'/G_a = 1.00$ assumed

$N' = 30$, assumed number deck levels

$KaV/L' = 0.07 + 0.060 (30) (1.00)^{-0.62}$

$= 1.87$

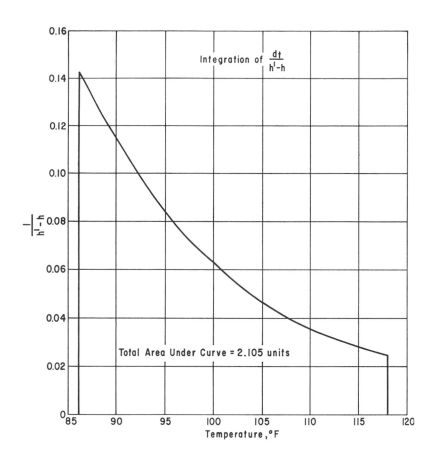

Figure 9-82. Graphical integration to determine number of transfer units.

Second solution of Equation 9-56 to determine line for plot:

$$L'/G_a = 2.0 \text{ assumed}$$

All other values remain the same.

$$Ka\ V/L' = 0.07 + 0.060\ (30)\ (2.0)^{-0.62}$$
$$= 0.07 + (0.060)\ (30)\ (0.651)$$
$$KaV/L' = 1.24$$

4. Plot points

$KaV/L' = 1.87$ and 1.24 on Figure 9-83C representing 75° F. wet bulb, and 25° F. range:

For approach $= 85° - 75°$ F. $= 10°$ F.

L'/G_a at intersection of straight line plot $= 1.13$

This is L'/G_a required for 75° F. wet bulb.

Enthalpy of exit air, $h_1 = h_2 + (L'/G_a)\ (t_1 - t_2)$

$$h_2 \text{ at } 75° \text{ F.} = 38.61 \text{ BTU/lb. dry air}$$
$$h_1 = 38.61 + 1.13\ (110 - 85)$$
$$= 66.91 \text{ BTU/lb. dry air}$$

Recirculation of 3%:

For 3% of air entering recirculated from the exit air, 97% comes from fresh air.

Enthalpy of recirculated air	$= 66.91$
Enthalpy of fresh air	$= 38.61$

Average enthalpy of inlet mixture:
$$= 0.97\ (38.61) + 0.03\ (66.91)$$
$$= 39.41 \text{ BTU/lb. dry air}$$

Refer now to "Moist Air" tables or other data of enthalpy vs. temperature:

At enthalpy $= 39.41$ BTU/lb. dry air, read Corresponding wet bulb temperature $= 76°$ F. (close)

New approach for tower design $= 85° - 76° = 9°$ F., instead of the previous 10° F.

Referring back to plot of number of decks on KaV/L' vs. L'/G_a,

Read at intersection of 9° F. approach, $L'/G_a = 1.05$

(Text continued on page 236)

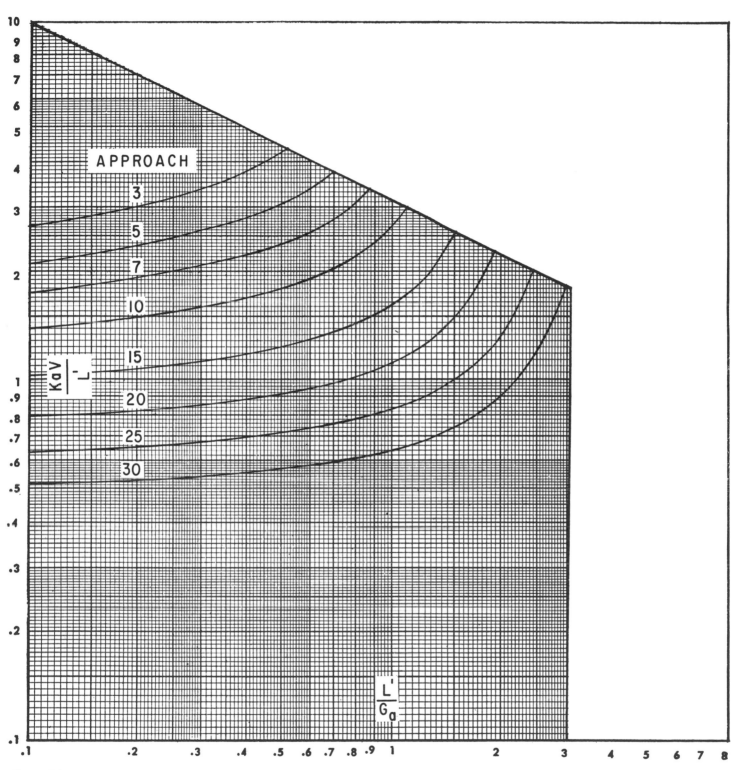

Figure 9-83A. 65° F wet bulb; 30° F range. Counterflow cooling tower performance curves.* By permission, "Counterflow Cooling Tower Performance," J. F. Pritchard Co.

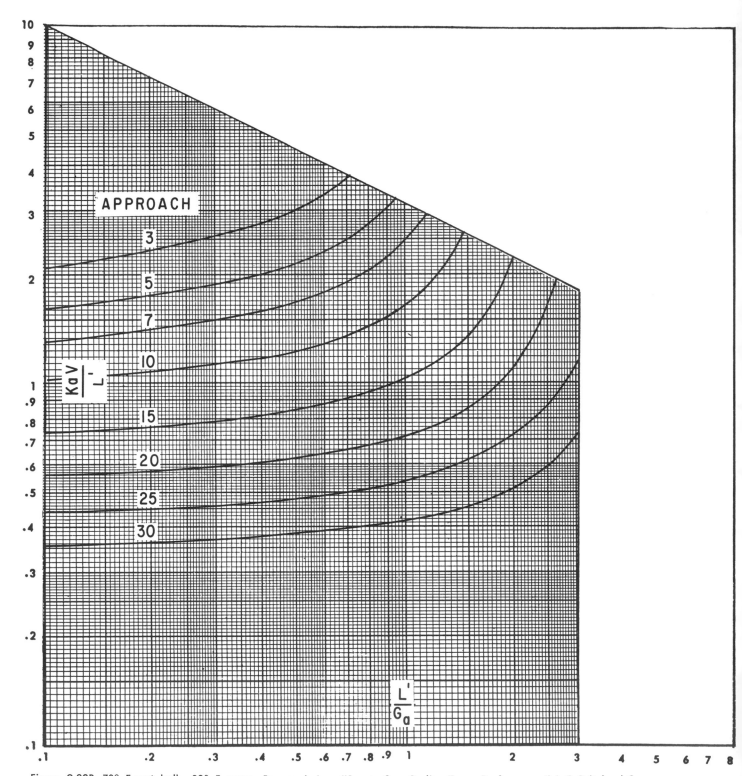

Figure 9-83B. 70° F wet bulb; 20° F range. By permission, "Counterflow Cooling Tower Performance," J. F. Pritchard Co.

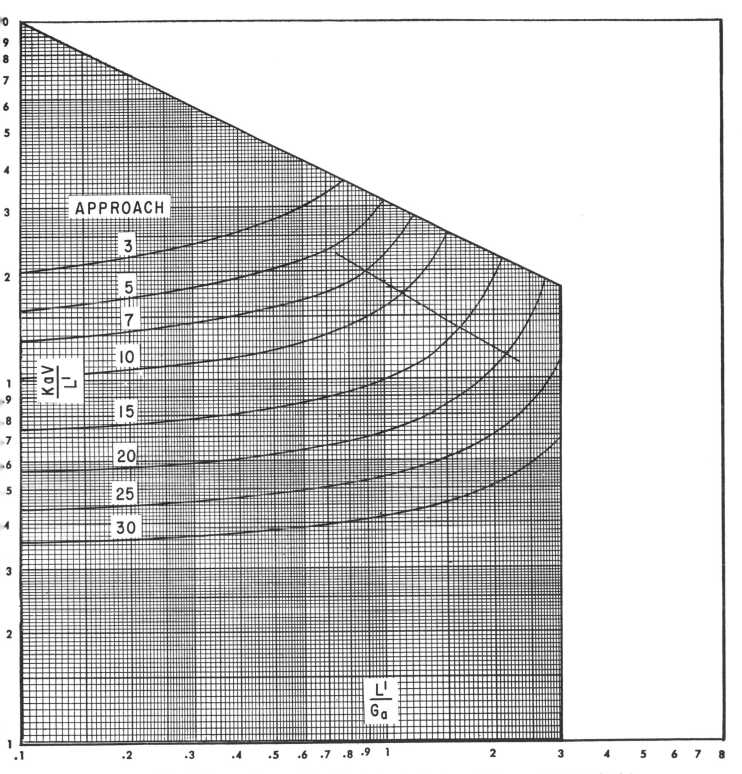

Figure 9-83C. 75° F wet bulb; 25° F range. By permission, "Counterflow Cooling Tower Performance," J. F. Pritchard Co.

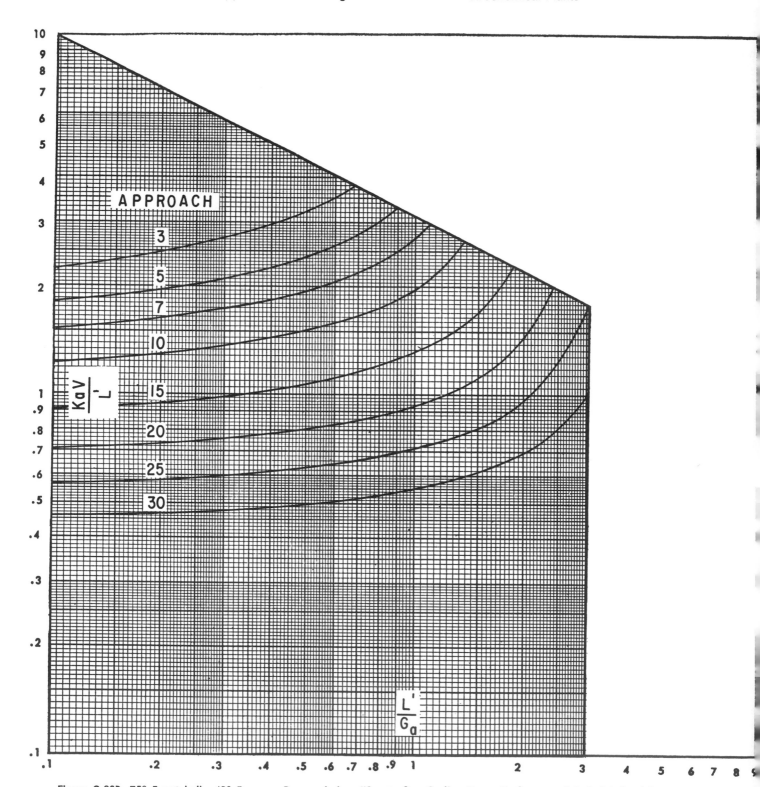

Figure 9-83D. 75° F wet bulb; 40° F range. By permission, "Counterflow Cooling Tower Performance," J. F. Pritchard Co.

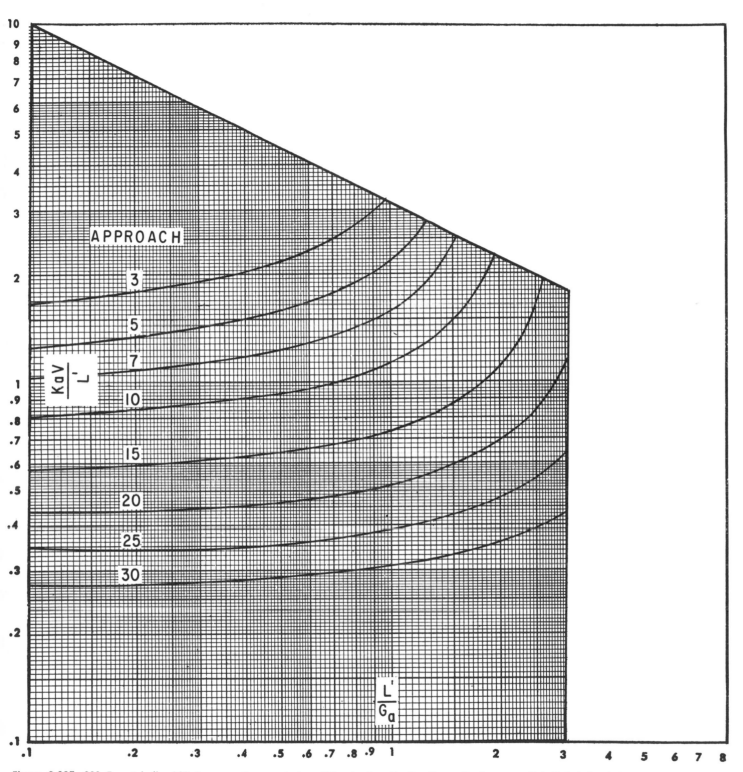

Figure 9-83E. 80° F wet bulb; 20° F range. By permission, "Counterflow Cooling Tower Performance," J. F. Pritchard Co.

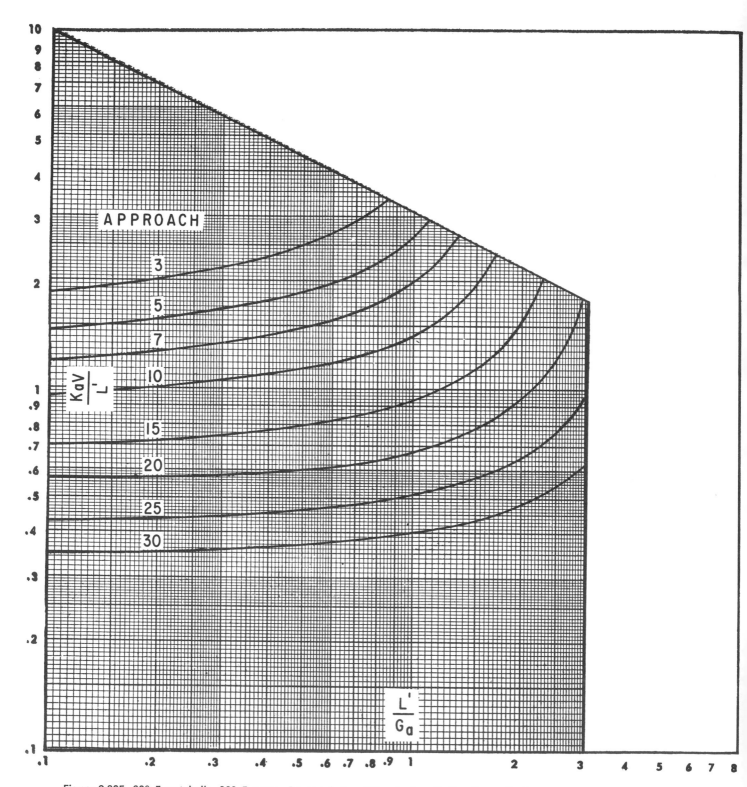

Figure 9-83F. 80° F wet bulb; 30° F range. By permission, "Counterflow Cooling Tower Performance," J. F. Pritchard Co.

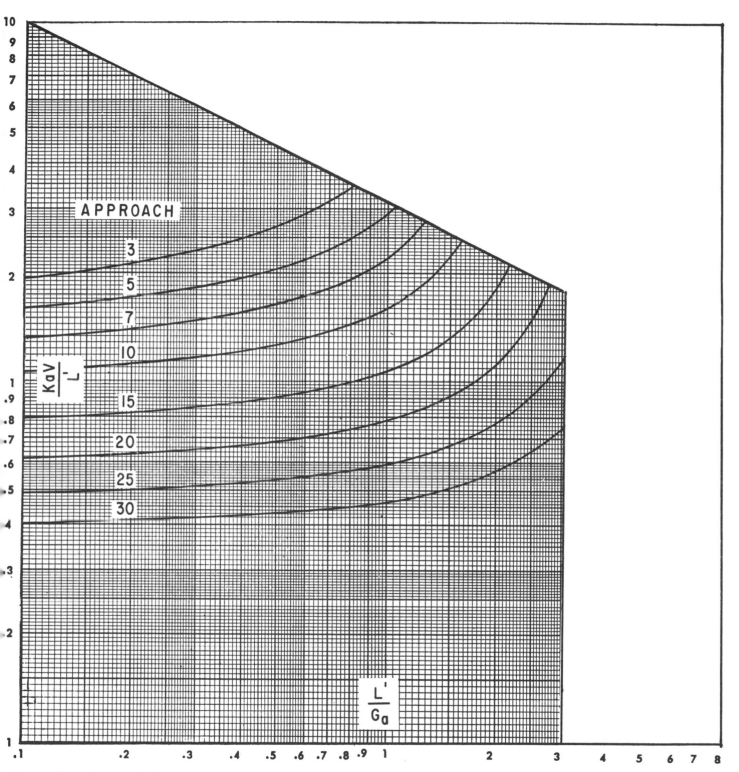

Figure 9-83G. 80° F wet bulb; 40° F range. By permission, "Counterflow Cooling Tower Performance," J. F. Pritchard Co.

Note for Use: Locate "Cold Water - Cooling Range" Point and Connect to Selected Wet Bulb Temperature of Air.(Line I.) Then, through L'/G_a Draw Line Parallel to Locate Value of KaV/L'. (Line 2.) The Graph may be used in Reverse to Examine Changing Conditions on a Given Tower.

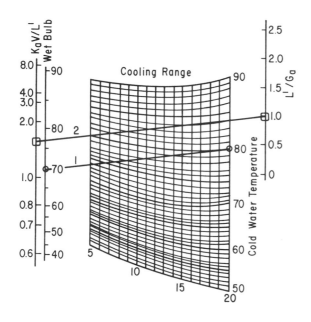

Figure 9-84. Calculation of KaV/L' Factors. (By permission M. Brooke, "Ref. Engr.," May p. C-41, 1958 as reproduced from Woods and Betts, "The Engineer" (London) Mar. 17 and 24, 1950.)

5. Estimated G_a, for ground plan area:

The assumed 30 decks on 9 inch spacing give a packed height of $(30-1) (9/12) = 21.8$ feet $= 21$ feet, 10 inches By approximate straight line interpolation given under "Ground Area Vs. Height":

$$\frac{40'-12'}{40'-21.8'} = \frac{2000-1400}{x}, G_a \text{ limit values are 2000 and}$$

$$1400$$

$x = 390$ lb./hr. (sq.ft. ground area) incremental air rate.

Suggested $G_a = 1400 + 390 = 1790$ lb./hr. (sq.ft.)
Then for $L'/G_a = 1.05$

$$L' = (1790) (1.05) = 1880 \text{ lb./hr. (sq.ft.)}$$

For 5000 gpm:

$$\text{lb./hr.} = (5000) (8.33 \text{ lb./gal.}) (60)$$
$$= 2,500,000 \text{ lb./hr.}$$

$$\text{sq. feet ground plan area} = \frac{2,500,000}{1800} = 1330$$

6. Cooling Tower Cells

Since cells are in modules of 6 feet, try combination of

$$30 \text{ feet x } 24 \text{ feet} = 720 \text{ sq.ft.}$$
$$\text{Two cells} = 1440 \text{ sq.ft.}$$

Using this area:

$$L' = \frac{2,500,000}{1440} = 1740 \text{ lb./hr. (sq. ft.)}$$

$$G_a = \frac{1740}{1.05} = 1658 \text{ lb./hr. (sq. ft.)}$$

This is about as close as can be estimated without manufacturer's data.

7. Pressure drop through packing:

$$\Delta P' = N'BG_a^2 \left(\frac{0.0675}{\rho_G}\right) + N'C \sqrt{S_F}(L)G_E^2 \left(\frac{0.0675}{\rho_G}\right)$$

$$N' = 30$$
$$B = 0.34 \times 10^{-8}$$
$$C = 0.11 \times 10^{-12}$$
$$S_F = 3.00$$
$$G_a^2 = (1658)^2 = 2,750,000$$
$$L' = 1740$$
$$G_E = 4050 \text{ at } S_F = 3.0 \text{ and } G_a = 1658 \text{ from Figure 9-77}$$
$$\rho_G = 0.07125 \text{ lb./cu. ft. avg. for tower}$$

$$\Delta P' = 30 (0.34 \times 10^{-8}) (2,750,000) \left(\frac{0.0675}{0.0712}\right) +$$

$$30 (0.11 \times 10^{-12}) \sqrt{3.0} (1740) (4050)^2 \left(\frac{0.0675}{0.0712}\right)$$
$$= 0.265 + 0.154 = 0.419 \text{ inch water}$$

This is an acceptable value.

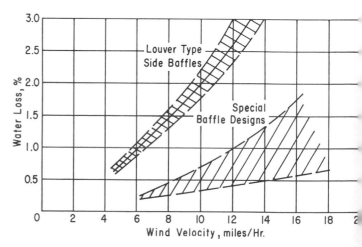

Figure 9-85. Atmospheric cooling power; water loss for various wind velocities.

Figure 9-86A. Poly grid plastic cooling tower packing (By permission Fluor Products Co. Patent pending.)

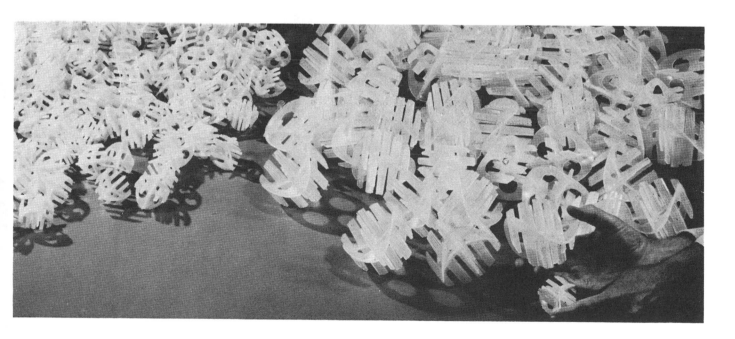

Figure 9-86B. Plastic shaped cooling and trickling tower packing. (Reproduced by permission Plastics Technical Services, Dow Chemical Co., Midland, Mich.)

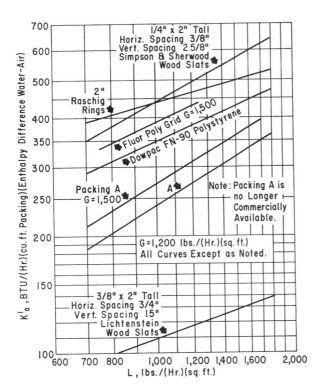

Figure 9-87. Comparison of cooling efficiency of several packing materials in terms of the coefficient of heat transfer K'a. (Courtesy Plastics Technical Service, Dow Chemical Co., Midland, Mich., with data added from A. L. Fuller et. al., "Chem. Eng. Prog," Vol. 53, No. 10, p. 501, 1957.)

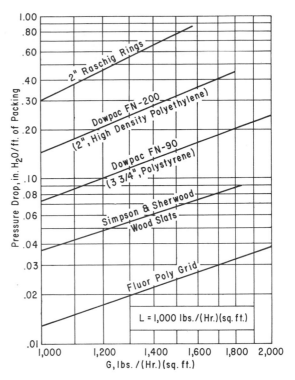

Figure 9-88. Comparison of pressure drop of several packing materials. (Courtesy Plastics Technical Service, Dow Chemical Co., Midland, Mich. with data added from A. L. Fuller et. al., "Chem. Eng. Prog," Vol. 53, No. 10, p. 501, 1957.)

8. Pressure Loss through Louvers for Induced Draft Tower

Assume louvers are along 24 feet dimension

Total louver face area
= (24) (2 cells) (2 sides) (6 feet high) = 576 sq. ft.

Sq. ft. tower ground area = (24) (30) (2) = 1440

Air rate, lbs./hr. = (1658) (1440) = 2,380,000

$$\underset{\text{(at inlet)}}{\text{CFM}} = \frac{2,380,000}{(60)(0.075 \text{ lb./cu. ft.})} = 530,000$$

Note the average value of $\rho_G = 0.07125$ could be used here.

$$\text{Face velocity through louvers} = \frac{530,000}{576} = 920 \text{ fpm}$$

Louver pressure drop approximation from paragraph "Pressure Losses"

$$\frac{0.32 - 0.02}{x} = \frac{1600 - 400}{1600 - 920}$$

$$x = 0.17 \text{ inch water}$$

Pressure loss = 0.32 — 0.17 = 0.15 inch water

Note that this value is high by 20-40% due to the approximation.

9. Pressure loss through mist eliminators

Approximation will give results on high side:

$$\frac{2000 - 800}{2000 - 1658} = \frac{0.07 - 0.01}{x}$$

$$x = 0.0171'' \text{ water}$$

Pressure loss = 0.07 — 0.02 = 0.05 inch water

10. Total estimated static pressure loss

0.42 + 0.15 + 0.05 = 0.62 inch water

This is an acceptable and reasonable value

11. Estimated fan brake horsepower

Assume gear drive

Air density at outlet = 0.067 lb./cu.ft. (close to 95 percent saturation at hot water temperature, induced draft fan condition).

$$BHP = \left(\frac{2,380,000}{0.067 \ (60)} \right) \frac{(0.62)}{(6356) \ (0.50)} = 115$$

This would be in at least two fans, one per cell.

$$BHP/cell = \frac{115}{2} = 57.5$$

Use 60 hp. motor each.

Cooling Tower Based on Ka Data

The data on cooling water with air is usually presented in the literature as Ka values. In using this information the units should be checked very carefully.

1. Height of Packing
$$Z = NL'/K'a \qquad (9\text{-}59)$$

where: $K'a$ = Enthalpy coefficient of total heat transfer, BTU/(hr.) (cu. ft. tower packing volume) (enthalpy difference between air and water)

2. Number of transfer Units
$$N = \int_{t_2}^{t_1} \frac{dt}{h' - h} \qquad (9\text{-}60)$$

3. $K'a$ Data

   Figure 9-87 presents data for several packings in water cooling service.

4. Pressure Drop

   Data is given in Figure 9-88 for water-air system.

Performance of Atmospheric and Natural Draft Towers

The evaluation of atmospheric and natural draft towers has not been completely presented in the detail comparable to mechanical draft towers. Some data is available in estimating form, but the evaluation of transfer rates is only adequate for estimating purposes.[4] The design of such towers by the process engineer must be made only after due consideration of this, and ample factor of safety should be included. Figure 9-85 presents general information on water loss due to wind on the tower.

Nomenclature

A = Tower cross-section area, sq. ft.

A' = Constant in cooling tower performance equation, or in mass transfer = L_m/mG_m.

a = Effective interfacial area for contacting gas and liquid phases, square feet/cu.ft. Since this is very difficult to evaluate, it is usually retained as a part of the coefficient such as K_Ga or K_La; in water cooling towers = area of transfer surface per unit of tower volume, sq. ft./cu. ft.

a' = Wetted packing surface, not necessarily same as effective interfacial surface area for contact, sq. ft./cu. ft.

a_t = Total specific packing surface area, sq.ft./cu.ft.

B = Constant in pressure drop equation for cooling tower.

C = Concentration, lb. moles/cu. ft.

C' = Constant in pressure drop equation for cooling towers.

c = Concentration of solution, lb. solute/cu. ft. solution.

ΔC_{lm} = Log. mean of the driving force at the top and bottom of tower.

D = Tower diameter, inches.

D_L = Diffusivity of solute in liquid, sq.ft./hr.

D_P = Equivalent spherical diameter of particle as a sphere possessing same surface area as a piece of packing, feet.

D'_p = Nominal packing size, feet.

D_v = Diffusivity of solute in gas, sq. ft./hr.

d_i = Individual packing piece inside diameter, inches.

d_o = Individual packing piece outside diameter, inches.

d_p = Equivalent spherical diameter of particle as a sphere possessing same surface area as a piece of packing, inches.

F = Packing factor = a/ε^3

F = Actual CFM at fan inlet, cubic feet/minute.

f_a = Fraction of total packing area, a_t, wetted.

G = Superficial mass gas rate, lb./(second) (sq. ft. tower cross-section).

G' = Superficial mass gas rate, lb./(hr.) (sq. ft. tower cross-section).

G'' = Gas rate, lbs./sec.

G_a = Air mass velocity, lb. dry air/(hr.) (sq.ft. of plan area).

G_E = Equivalent mass air velocity for pressure drop between air and falling water drops, lb./(hr.) (sq. ft. of plan area), See Fig. 9-67.

G_m = Gas mass velocity, lb. moles/(hr.) (sq. ft.).

g_c = Acceleration of gravity, 32.2 feet/(sec.) (sec.).

H = HTU = Height of a transfer unit, feet.

H' = Henry's Law constant, lb. moles/(cu.ft.) (atm), or other units to suit system.

H_G = Height of individual gas film transfer unit, feet.

H_L = Height of individual liquid film transfer unit, feet.

H_{OG} = Height of transfer unit, based on overall gas film coefficients, feet.

H_{OL} = Height of transfer unit, based on overall liquid film coefficients, feet.

$HETP$ = Height equivalent to a theoretical plate, feet.

h = Enthalpy of the main air stream, BTU/lb. dry air.

h' = Enthalpy of saturated air film at bulk water temperature, BTU/lb. dry air.

h_o = Operating hold-up for any liquid, cu.ft./cu.ft. packing volume.

h_s = Static hold-up for any liquid, cu. ft./cu. ft. packing volume.

h_t = Total hold-up cu.ft. liquid/cu.ft. packing volume.

h_{ow} = Operating hold-up for water, cu.ft./cu.ft. packing volume.

h_{sw} = Static hold-up for water, cu.ft./cu.ft. packing volume.

j = Constant.

K = Overall enthalpy transfer coefficient, lb./(hr.) (sq.ft. transfer area) (lb. water/lb. dry air).

K'_a = Enthalpy coefficient of total heat transfer, BTU/(hr.) (cu.ft. tower packing volume) enthalpy difference between air and water).

K_G = Gas phase mass transfer coefficient, lb. mols/(hr.) (sq.ft.) (atm).

K_Ga = Overall gas mass-transfer coefficient, lb. moles/(hr.) (cu.ft.) (atm).

K_L = Overall mass transfer coefficient based on liquid phase, lb. mols/(hr.) (sq.ft.) (lb. moles/cu.ft.).

K_La = Overall mass transfer coefficient based on liquid film controlling, lb. moles/(hr.) (cu.ft.) (lb. moles/cu.ft.).

k_G = Gas-phase mass transfer coefficient, lb. moles/(hr.) (sq.ft.) (atm).

k_{Ga} = Individual gas mass-transfer coefficient, lb. mols/(hr.) (cu.ft.) (atm).

k_L = Liquid phase mass transfer coefficient, lb. mols/(hr.) sq.ft) (lb.mols/cu.ft.).

k_{La} = Individual liquid mass transfer coefficient, lb. mols/(hr.) (cu.ft.) (lb. mol/cu.ft.).

L = Liquid superficial mass rate, lb./(sec.) (sq.ft. tower cross-section).

L' = Liquid superficial mass rate, lb./(hr.) sq.ft tower plan cross-section).

L_c = Critical liquid rate for liquid continuous system, at which the packing becomes completely wetted and tower operation is in the liquid continuous range, lb./(hr.) (sq.ft.).

L_M = Liquid mass rate, lb. moles/(hr.) (sq.ft.).

$L_{Min.}$ = Minimum liquid wetting rate in packed tower, cu.ft./(hr.) (sq.ft. cross-section).

l = Individual packing piece height (or length), inches.

M_M = Mean molecular weight of gas, lb./lb. mole.

MWR = Minimum Wetting Rate, (liquid), cu.ft/(hr.) (sq.ft. cross-section)/(sq.ft. packing surface/cu.ft. tower volume).

m = Slope of the equilibrium-solubility curve, mole fraction in gas/mols fraction in liquid.

N = Number of transfer units.

N' = Number of deck levels in cooling tower.

N_{OG} = Number of transfer units, based on overall gas film coefficients.

N_{OL} = Number of transfer units, based on overall liquid film coefficients.

n = Mols absorbed or transferred, lb. mols per hour.

n' = Constant in cooling tower performance equation.

P = Average total pressure in tower, atmospheres, or absolute units.

P_{BM} = Mean partial pressure of inert gas in the gas phase, atm.

ΔP = Pressure drop, inches water/foot packed height.

$\Delta P'$ = Air pressure loss, inches of water.

p = Partial pressure of soluble gas, atmospheres.

Δp_{lm} = Log mean partial pressure of gas in inlet and exit gas streams, atm.

p_s = Total static pressure of fan, inches of water.

S_F = Vertical free fall of water drops, feet.

T = Absolute temperature, °R, = °F. + 460.

t = Bulk water temperature, °F.

t_1 = Entering water temperature, °F.

t_2 = Outlet water temperature, °F.

V = Tower Volume, cu.ft./sq.ft. ground plan area.

V_g = Superficial gas velocity, ft./second.

V_A, V_B = Molecular volumes of gases, obtained by Kopp's Law of additive volumes, cc./gm. mole at normal boiling point.

X = Concentration of solute in liquid, lb. mols solute/lb. mols solute free solvent, (or stream).

X^* = Concentration of solute in liquid, in equilibrium with the gas, lb. mole solute/lb. mole solvent.

x = Concentration of solute in liquid, mole fraction.

x^* = Concentration of solute in gas in equilibrium with gas, mole fraction.

Y = Concentration of solute in gas, lb. moles solute/lb. moles solute free (solvent) (stream).

Y^* = Concentration of solute in liquid in equilibrium with liquid, lb. moles solute/lb. mole solute free (solvent) (stream).

y = Mole fraction of solute in gas.

y^* = Mole fraction gas phase composition in equilibrium with a liquid composition, x.

Z = Height of packed section in tower, feet.

Subscripts

A, B = Refer to different items, gases, etc.

a = Air

f = Flooding condition

G = Gas

L = Liquid

w = Water

1 = Refers to inlet, or condition 1.

2 = Refers to outlet, or condition 2.

α_{1h} = Average relative volatility, light to heavy component.

α = Constant, or relative volatility

β = Constant

γ = Constant

π = Total absolute pressures, or 3.141, as appropriate

Δ_M or Δ_{middle} = Driving force at middle position on gas or liquid basis.

Δ_m or Δ_{mean} = Mean driving force on gas or liquid basis.

ε = Void fraction of packing under operating conditions = void fraction of dry packing minus the total hold-up. (Not the free volume of dry packing).

μ = Viscosity of liquid, centipoise.

μ' = Absolute viscosity, lb./sec. feet.

μ_a = Viscosity, lb./(hr.) (ft.).

μ_{Ga} = Gas viscosity, lb./(hr.) (ft.)

ρ = Density, lb./cu.ft.

ρ' = Liquid density, grams/cubic centimeter.

ρ_G = Gas density, lb./cu. ft.

σ = Surface tension, dynes/centimeter.

ψ = Ratio of density of water to density of new liquid (dimensionless).

∞ = Proportional to.

Bibliography

1. "Acceptance Test Procedure for Water-Cooling Towers, ATP-105," Cooling Tower Institute, Palo Alto, Calif.
2. *Air Conditioning Refrigerating Data Book*, 10th Ed. (1958), American Society of Heating, Refrigerating and Air-Conditioning Engineers, Inc., 234 Fifth Ave., New York 1, N. Y.
3. Baker, T., C. H. Chilton and H. C. Vernon. "The Course of Liquor Flow Packed Towers," Trans. Amer. Inst. Chem. Engrs. 31, 296 (1935).
4. Bulletin, "Fluor Aerator Cooling Towers," The Fluor Corp. Ltd., Los Angeles, Calif. (1944).
5. Bulletin TP-54, Tower Packings, U. S. Stoneware Co., Akron, Ohio.
6. Bulletin S-29, Intalox Saddle Packing, The United States Stoneware Co., Akron, Ohio.
7. Campbell, J. M. and R. L. Huntington, "Heat Transfer and Pressure Drop in Fixed Beds of Spherical and Cylindrical Solids," *Pet. Ref.*, 30, 12, 127 (1951).

8. Chilton, C. H., "Drift or Mist Eliminator Loss," Trans. Inst. Chem. Engrs. 30, 235 (London) (1952).

9. Chilton, T. H. and A. P. Colburn, Part II, "Pressure Drop in Packed Tubes," Trans. A. I. Ch. E. 26, 178 (1931).

10. Colburn, A. P., The Simplified Calculation of Diffusional Processes, General Considerations of Two Film Resistance, Trans. A. I. Ch. E. 35, 211 (1939).

11. Colburn, A. P., "Simplified Calculation of Diffusional Processes" Ind. Eng. Chem. 33, 459 (1941).

12. Cornell, Knapp, and Fair, Chem. Engr. Prog. 56 (7) (1960) p. 68.

13. Cornell, et al, Chem, Engr. Prog., (58)(8) 1960 p. 68.

14. Fair, J., Chem Engr Prog., 76, (15) (July 1969).

15. Cooling Tower Performance, Bulletin CT-43-2, Foster Wheeler Corp., New York, N.Y.

16. "Cooling Tower Wood Maintenance, TSC-302," Cooling Tower Institute, Palo Alto, Calif.

17. Cooper, C. M., R. J. Christl and L. C. Perry, Packed Tower Performance at High Liquor Rates, Trans. Amer. Inst. Chem. Engr. 37, 979 (1941).

18. Coulson, J. M. and J. F. Richardson, Chemical Engineering, Vol. II, 719 (1955), McGraw-Hill Book Co., New York, N.Y.

19. "Counterflow Cooling Tower Performance," J. F. Pritchard and Co. of California, Kansas City, Mo. (1957).

20. Czermann, J. J., S. L. Gyokhegyi, and J. J. Hay, "Design Packed Towers Graphically," Pet. Ref. 37, No. 4, 165 (1958).

21. Dwyer, O. E., and B. F. Dodge, "Rate of Absorption of Ammonia by Water in a Packed Tower," Ind. Eng. Chem. 36, 485 (1941).

22. Eckert, J., U.S. Stoneware Co., private communication.

23. Eckert, J. S., E. H. Foote and R. L. Huntington, "Pall-Rings—New Type of Tower Packing," Chem. Engr. Progress, 54, No. 1, 70 (1958).

24. Eckert, R. G., and Walter, Hydrocarbon Processing, 43 (2) (1964) p.107.

25. Ellis, Chem. Engr. News, 31, (44) (1953) p. 4613.

26. Elgin, J. C. and F. B. Weiss, "Liquid Hold-up and Flooding in Packed Towers," Ind. Eng. Chem. 31, 435 (1939).

27. Fellinger, L., Sc. D. Thesis, Mass. Inst. Technol. (1941).

28. Furnas, C. C. and F. Bellinger, "Operating Characteristics of Packed Columns," Trans. A. I. Ch. E. 34, 251 (1938).

29. Gambill, W. R., "How To Estimate Mass Transfer Factors," Chem. Eng., Dec. p. 207 (1955).

30. Goitein, E. E., "Selection and Application of Cooling Towers," Combustion, Nov., p. 38 (1957).

31. "Grades of Redwood Lumber, Std.-101," Cooling Tower Institute, Palo Alto, Calif.

32. Griswold, J., D. Andres and V. A. Klein, "Determination of High Pressure Vapor-Liquid Equilibria. The Vapor-Liquid Equilibrium of Benzene-Toluene," Trans. Amer. Inst. Chem. Engrs. 39, 223 (1943).

33. Hands, C. H. G. and F. R. Whitt, "Design of Packed Distillation Columns II, Operating Vapor Rates for Packed Distillation Columns," J. Appl. Chem., Jan. 1, p. 19 (1951).

34. Hands, C. H. G. and F. R. Whitt, "Design of Packed Distillation Columns IV. An Empirical Method For the Estimation of Column Height Using the H.E.T.P. Concept," J. Appl. Chem., Mar. 1, p. 135 (1951).

35. International Critical Tables, Ed. W. Washburn, Editor, Vol. V, p. 213, National Research Council, McGraw-Hill Book Co., New York, N.Y.

36. Jesser, B. W. and J. C. Elgin, "Studies of Liquid Hold-up in Packed Towers," Trans. Amer. Inst. Chem. Engr., 39, No. 3 277 (1943).

37. Johnstone, H. F. and A. D. Singh, "Recovery of Sulfur Dioxide from Waste Gases," Ind. Eng. Chem., 29, 286 (1937).

38. Kelly, N. W. and L. K. Swenson, "Comparative Performance of Cooling Tower Packing Arrangement," Chem. Eng. Prog., 52, p. 265 (1956).

39. Kern, D. Q., Process Heat Transfer, 1st Ed. McGraw-Hill Book Co., Inc., New York, N. Y. (1950) p. 600.

40. Leva, M., "Tower Packings and Packed Tower Design," 2nd Ed. U. S. Stoneware Co., Akron, Ohio (1953).

41. Leva, M., Chemical Engineering Progress Sym. Series No. 10, 50, 151 (1954).

42. Leva, M., "Gas Absorption in Beds of Rings and Saddles," A. I. Ch. E. Jour., 1, No 2, p. 224 (1955).

43. Leva, M., "Flow Through Packings and Beds," Chem. Eng. 64, 261 (1957).

44. Leva, M., J. M. Lucas and H. H. Frahme, "Effect of Packing Supports on Mechanical Operation of Packed Towers," Ind. Eng. Chem. 46, No. 6, 1225 (1954).

45. Lerner, B. J., and C. S. Grove, Jr., "Critical Conditions of Two-Phase Flow in Packed Columns," Ind. Eng. Chem. 43, 1, p. 216 (1951).

46. Lichtenstein, S., "Performance and Selection of Mechanical Draft Cooling Towers," Trans. Amer. Soc. Mech. Engrs., Oct. p. 779 (1943).

47. Lobo, W. E., L. Friend, F. Hashmall and F. Zenz, "Limiting Capacity of Dumped Tower Packings," Trans. Amer. Inst. Chem. Engrs. 41, 693 (1945).

48. Mass Transfer, Inc., "Absorption, Distillation Optimization," (1978) p. 14.

49. Menta and Parekh, M. S. Thesis Chemical Engineering, Mass. Inst. Technology, Cambridge, Mass. (1939).

50. Molstad, M. C., R. G. Abbey, A. R. Thompson, and J. F. McKinney, "Performance of Drip-Point Grid Tower Packings, Trans. A. I. Ch. E. 38, 387 (1942).

51. Molstad, M. C., J. F. McKinney and R. G. Abbey, "Performance of Drip-Point Grid Tower Packings," Trans. Amer. Inst. of Chem. Engr. Vol. 39, No. 5, 605 (1943).

52. Morris, R. and J. Jackson, Absorption Towers, Butterworth Scientific Publications (1953), London, England.

53. Murch, D. P., "Height of Equivalent Theoretical Plate in Packed Fractionation Columns," Ind. Eng. Chem., 45, 2616 (1953).

54. Norton Company, "Design Information for Packed Towers," Bulletin DC-11 (1977).

55. Otake, T. and K. Okada, "Liquid Hold-up in Packed Towers, Operating Holdup Without Gas Flow," Soc. Chem. Engrs. (Japan) 17, No. 7, 176 (1953).

56. Oldershaw, C. F., L. Simenson, T. Brown and F. Radcliffe, "Absorption and Purification of Hydrogen Chloride from Chlorination of Hydrocarbons," Chem. Eng. Prog. Trans. Section, 43, No. 7, 371 (1947).

57. Planovski, Khimicheskay Prom., 45, No. 3, p. 16-20.

58. Robinson, C. S. and E. R. Gilliland, Elements of Fractional Distillation, 4th Ed. (1950) McGraw-Hill Book Co., Inc., New York, N.Y.

59. Sakiadis, B. C. and A. I. Johnson, "Generalized Correlation of Flooding Rates, Ind. Eng. Chem., 46, 1229 (1954).

60. Sarchet, B. R., "Flooding in Packed Towers," Trans. A. I. Ch. E., 38, No. 2, 293 (1942).

61. Sherwood, T. K. and F. A. L. Holloway, "Performance of Packed Towers—Experimental Studies of Absorption and Desorption," Trans. Amer. Inst. Chem. Eng., 36, 21 (1940).

62. Sherwood, T. K. and F. A. L. Holloway, "Performance of Packed Towers, Liquid Flow Data For Several Packings," Trans. Amer. Inst. Chem. Engrs., 36, 39 (1940).

63. Sherwood, T. K. and R. L. Pigford, Absorption and Extraction, 2nd Ed. (1952) McGraw-Hill Book Co., Inc., New York, N. Y. p. 161.

64. Shulman, H. L., C. F. Ullrich, and N. Wells, "Performance of Packed Columns, Total, Static and Operating Holdups," Amer. Inst. Engr. Jour. 1, No. 2, 247 (1955).

65. Shulman, H. L., C. F. Ullrich, A. Z. Proulx and J. O. Zimmerman, "Wetted and Effective Interfacial Areas, Gas- and Liquid-phase Mass Transfer Rates," A. I. Ch. E. Jour. 1, No. 2, 253 (1955).

66. Shulman, H. L., C. F. Ullrich, N. Wells and A. Z. Proulx, "Holdup for Aqueous and Nonaqueous Systems," A. I. Ch. E. Jour. Vol. 1 No. 2, 259 (1955).

67. Shulman, H. L. and J. E. Margolis, "Performance of Packed Columns," A. I. Mh.E. Jour, Vol. 3, 157 (1957).
68. Silvey and Keller, Proc. Intern. Symp. Dist. (Brighton, U.K.) (1970).
69. Spector, N. A., and B. F. Dodge, "Removal of Carbon Dioxide from Atmospheric Air," Trans. Amer. Inst. Chem. Engrs. 42, 827 (1946.)
70. "Structural Design Data, Std-102," Cooling Tower Institute, Palo Alto, California,
71. Teller, A. J., "Packing Performance Below and Above Flooding," preprint copy prior to presentation at A. I. Ch. E. meeting 1953.
72. Tepe, J. B. and B. F. Dodge, "Absorption of Carbon Dioxide By Sodium Hydroxide Solutions in a Packed Column," Trans. Amer. Inst. Chem. Engrs. 39, 255 (1943).
73. Tillson, Thesis, Mass. Inst. Technology, Cambridge, Mass. (1939).
74. Treyball, R. E. Mass Transfer Operations, McGraw-Hill Book Co., New York, N. Y. (1955).
75. Van Nuys, C. C., "Enthalpy and Heats of Dilution of the System HCl-H2O," Trans. Amer. Inst. Chem. Engr. 39, 663 (1943)
76. Vivian, J. E. and R. P. Whitney, "Absorption of Chlorine in Water," Chem. Eng. Prog., Trans. Sect., 43, 691 (1947).
77. Chin-Yung Wen, "Ammonia Absorption in Beds of Saddles," Thesis, West Virginia University (1953).
78. Whitesell, Jack, "How To Evaluate Variable in Counterflow Cooling Towers," Chem. Eng. 62, Jan., p. 187 (1955).
79. Whitney, R. P. and J. E. Vivian, "Absorption of Sulfur Dioxide in Water," Chem. Eng. Prog. 45, 323 (1949).
80. Whitt, F. R., "A Correlation For Absorption Column Packrings," British chem. Eng., July, p. 395 (1959).
81. Zenz, F. A., "What Every Engineer Should Know About Packed Tower Operations, Chem. Eng., August, p. 176 (1953).

References

Baker, W. J., "Direct Digital Control of Batch Processes Pays Off," Chem. Eng. Dec. 15, (1969) p. 121.
Bannon, R. P. and S. Marple, Jr., "Heat Recovery in Hydrocarbon Distillation," Chem. Eng. Progr. 74, 7, p. 41 (1978).
Biddulph, M. W. "Tray Efficiency is not Constant," Hydrocarbon Processing, Oct., (1977) p. 145.
Billet, R. "Cost Optimization of Towers" Chem. Eng. Progr., 66, 1, (1970) p. 41.
Billet, R. "Development and Progress in the Design and Performance of Valve Trays," British Chem. Eng., Apr. (1969).
Bolles, W. L., "Distillation, The Solution of a Foam Problem," Chem. Eng. Progr. 63, 9, (1967) p. 48.
Broughton, D. B. and K. D. Uitti, "Estimate Tower For Naphtha Cuts," Hydrocarbon Processing, Oct., 109, (1971).
Buckley, P. S., R. K. Cox and W. L. Luyben, "How to Use a Small Calculator In Distillation Column Design," Chem. Eng. Progr. 74, 6, (1978) p. 49.
Chow, A., A. M. Fayon, and Bili Bauman, "Simulations Provide Blueprint For Distillation Operation," Chem. Eng. June 7, 1731, (1976)
"Distillation Tray Features Low ΔP, High Efficiency," Chem. Engr. Jan. 20 (1975).

Douglas, J. M. "Rule-of-Thumb For Minimum Trays," Hydrocarbon Processing, Nov., (1977) p. 291.
Eckhart, R. A. and A. Rose, "New Method For Distillation Prediction," Hydrocarbon Processing, May, (1968) p. 165.
Economopoulos, A. P., "A Fast Computer Method For Distillation Calculations," Chem. Eng., Apr. 24 (1978).
Edmister, W. C., "Applied Hydrocarbon Thermodynamics, Part 49" Hydrocarbon Processing, May, 169, (1973).
Edmister, W. C., ibid, "Part 46, Dec. 93 (1972).
Ellerbe, R. W., "Batch Distillation Bases," Chem. Eng. May 28, (1973) p. 110.
Ellerbe, R. W. "Steam-Distillation Basics," Chem. Eng., Mar. 4, (1974) p. 105.
Fair, J. R. and W. L. Bolles, "Modern Design of Distillation Columns," Chem. Eng. Apr. 22, (1968) p. 178.
Frank, J. C., G. R. Geyer and H. Kehde, "Styrene-Ethylbenzene Separation with Sieve Trays," Chem. Eng. Progr. 65, 2, (1969) p. 79.
Frank, O., "Shortcuts For Distillation Design," Chem. Eng. Mar. 14, (1977) p. 111.
Gallun, S. E. and C. D. Holland, "Solve More Distillation Problems, Part 5" Hydrocarbon Processing, Jan., 137, (1976).
Garrett, G. R., R. H. Anderson and M. Van Winkle, "Calculation of Sieve and Valve Tray Efficiencies in Column Scale-up," Ind. Eng. Chem., Process Des. Dev. 16, 1, (1977) p. 79.
Garvin, R. G. and E. R. Norton, "Sieve Tray Performance Under G S Process Conditions," Chem. Eng. Progr., 64, 3, (1968) p. 99.
Geyer, G. R. and P. E. Kline, "Energy Conservation Schemes For Distillation Process," Chem. Eng. Progr., 72, 5, (1976) p. 49.
Guerreri, G., Bruno Peri, and F. Seneci, "Comparing Distillation Designs, Hydrocarbon Processing, Dec. (1972) p. 78.
Haman, S. E. M. et al, "Generalized Temperature-Dependent Parameters of the Redlich-Kwong of State for Vapor-Liquid Equilibrium Calculations," Ind. Eng. Chem. Process Des. Dev. 16, 1, (1977) p. 51.
Hanson, D. N. and J. Newman, "Calculation of Distillation Columns at the Optimum Feed Plate Location," Ind. Eng. Chem. Process Des. Dev. 16, 1, (1977) p. 223.
Hattiangadi, U. S., "How to Interpret a Negative of Minimum Reflux Ratio," Chem. Eng., May 18, (1970) p. 178.
Hess, F. E. et. al., "Solve More Distillation Problems," Hydrocarbon Processing, June, (1977) p. 183 May, (1977) p. 243.
Holland, C. D., G. P. Pendon, and S. E. Gallun, "Solve More Distillation Problems," Hydrocarbon Processing, June, 101 (1975).
Holland, C. D. and G. P. Pendon, "Solve More Distillation Problems," Hydrocarbon Processing, July, (1974) p. 148.

Kemp, D. W., and D. G. Ellis, "Computer Control of Fractionation Plants," *Chem. Eng.* Dec. 5, 115, (1975).

Kern, R. "Layout Arrangements For Distillation Columns," *Chem. Eng.,* Aug. 15, (1977) p. 153.

Kister, H. Z. and I. D. Doig, "Entrainment Flooding Prediction," Hydrocarbon Processing, Oct. (1977) p. 150.

Koppel, P. M., "Fast Way to Solve Problems For Batch Distillations," *Chem. Eng.* Oct. 16, 109, (1972).

Leach, M. J., "An Approach to Multiphase Vapor-Liquid Equilibria," *Chem. Eng.* May 23, (1977) p. 137.

Lenoir, J. M. and C. R. Koppany, "Need Equilibrium Ratios? Do it Right," *Hydrocarbon Processing,* Vol. 46, 249 (1967).

Lenoir, J. M., "Predict Hash Points Accurately," *Hydrocarbon Processing,* Jan., 95 (1975).

Lieberman, N. P., "Change Controls to Save Energy," *Hydrocarbon Processing,* Feb., (1978) p. 93.

Loud, G. D. and R. C. Waggoner, "The Effects of Interstage Backmixing on the Design of a Multicomponent Distillation Column," *Ind. Eng. Chem. Process Des & Dev.,* 17, 2, (1978) p. 149.

Luyben, W. L., "Azeotropic Tower Design by Graph," *Hydrocarbon Processing,* Jan., (1973) p. 109.

Maas, J. H., "Optimum-Feed-Stage Location in Multicomponent Distillations," *Chem. Eng.,* Apr. 16, (1973) p. 96.

Mapstone, G. E., "Reflux Versus Trays by Chart," 17, 5, (1968) p. 169.

Martinez-Ortiz, J. A., and D. B. Manley, "Direct Solution of the Isothermal Gibbs-Duhem Equation for Multicomponent Systems," *Ind. Eng. Chem. Process Des. Dev.,* 17, 3, (1978) p. 346.

McWilliams M. L., "An Equation to Relate K-Factors to Pressure and Temperature," *Chem. Eng.,* Oct. 29, (1973) p. 138.

Mix, T. J., et. al., "Energy Conservation In Distillation," *Chem. Eng. Progr.,* Apr. (1978) p. 49.

Nemunaitis, R. R., "Sieve Trays? Consider Viscosity," *Hydrocarbon Processing,* Nov., 235, (1971).

Petterson, W. C. and T. A. Wells, "Energy-Saving Schemes in Distillation," *Chem. Eng.,* Sept. 26, (1977) p. 79.

Rao, A. K., "Prediction of Liquid Activity Coefficients," *Chem. Eng.* May 9, (1977) p. 143.

Robinson, D. B., et. al. "Capability of the Peng-Robinson Programs," *Hydrocarbon Processing,* Apr. (1978) p. 95.

Ross, S. "Mechanisms of Foam Stabilization and Antifoaming Action," *Chem. Eng. Progr.* **63,** 9, (1967) p. 41.

Scheiman, A. D. "Find Minimum Reflux By Heat Balance," *Hydrocarbon Processing,* Sept. (1969) p. 187.

Shah, G. C., "Troubleshooting Distillation Columns," Chem. Eng. July 31, (1978) p. 70.

Shinskey, F. G., "Energy Conserving Control Systems For Distillation Units," *Chem. Engr. Progr.* **72,** 5, (1976) p. 73.

Silverman, N. and D. Tassios, "The Number of Roots in the Wilson Equation and its Effect on Vapor-Liquid Equilibrium Calculations," *Ind. Eng. Chem., Process Des. Dev.,* **16,** 1, (1977) p. 13.

Sommerville R. F., "New Method Gives Quick, Accurate Estimate of Distillation Costs," *Chem. Eng.,* May 1, (1972) p. 71.

Thorngren, J. T., "Valve Tray Flooding Generalized," *Hydrocarbon Processing,* **57,** 8, (1978) p. 111.

Treybal, R. E. "A Simple Method For Batch Distillation," *Chem. Eng.,* Oct. 5, (1970) p. 95.

Van Winkle, M. and W. G. Todd, "Minimizing Distillation Costs via Graphical Techniques," *Chem. Eng.,* Mar. 6, (1972) p. 105.

Wade, H. L. and C. J. Ryskamp, "Tray Flooding Sets Crude Thruput," *Hydrocarbon Processing,* Nov. (1977) p. 281.

Wheeler, D. E., "Design Criteria For Chimney Trays," *Hydrocarbon Processing,* July, (1968) p. 119.

Wichterle, I. R. Kobayashi, and P. S. Chappelear, "Caution! Pinch Point in Y-X Curve," *Hydrocarbon Processing,* Nov. 233, (1971).

Zanker, A. "Nomograph Replaces Gilliland Plot," *Hydrocarbon Processing,* May, (1977) p. 263.

A-1.
Alphabetical Conversion Factors

TO CONVERT	INTO	MULTIPLY BY	TO CONVERT	INTO	MULTIPLY BY
A			Btu/hr	gram-cal/sec	0.0700
Abcoulomb	Statcoulombs	2.998×10^{10}	Btu/hr	horsepower-hrs	3.929×10^{-4}
Acre	Sq. chain (Gunters)	10	Btu/hr	watts	0.2931
Acre	Rods	160	Btu/min	foot-lbs/sec	12.96
Acre	Square links (Gunters)	1×10^5	Btu/min	horsepower	0.02356
Acre	Hectare or sq. hectometer	.4047	Btu/min	kilowatts	0.01757
acres	sq feet	43,560.0	Btu/min	watts	17.57
acres	sq meters	4,047.	Btu/sq ft/min	watts/sq in.	0.1221
acres	sq miles	1.562×10^{-3}	Bucket (Br. dry)	Cubic Cm.	1.818×10^4
acres	sq yards	4,840.	bushels	cu ft	1.2445
acre-feet	cu feet	43,560.0	bushels	cu in.	2,150.4
acre-feet	gallons	3.259×10^5	bushels	cu meters	0.03524
amperes/sq cm	amps/sq in.	6.452	bushels	liters	35.24
amperes/sq cm	amps/sq meter	10^4	bushels	pecks	4.0
amperes/sq in.	amps/sq cm	0.1550	bushels	pints (dry)	64.0
amperes/sq in.	amps/sq meter	1,550.0	bushels	quarts (dry)	32.0
amperes/sq meter	amps/sq cm	10^{-4}			
amperes/sq meter	amps/sq in.	6.452×10^{-4}			
ampere-hours	coulombs	3,600.0	**C**		
ampere-hours	faradays	0.03731	Calories, gram (mean)	B.T.U. (mean)	3.9685×10^{-3}
ampere-turns	gilberts	1.257	Candle/sq. cm	Lamberts	3.142
ampere-turns/cm	amp-turns/in.	2.540	Candle/sq. inch	Lamberts	.4870
ampere-turns/cm	amp-turns/meter	100.0	centares (centiares)	sq meters	1.0
ampere-turns/cm	gilberts/cm	1.257	Centigrade	Fahrenheit	$(C° \times 9/5) + 32$
ampere-turns/in.	amp-turns/cm	0.3937	centigrams	grams	0.01
ampere-turns/in.	amp-turns/meter	39.37	Centiliter	Ounce fluid (US)	.3382
ampere-turns/in.	gilberts/cm	0.4950	Centiliter	Cubic inch	.6103
ampere-turns/meter	amp-turns/cm	0.01	Centiliter	drams	2.705
ampere-turns/meter	amp-turns/in.	0.0254	centiliters	liters	0.01
ampere-turns/meter	gilberts/cm	0.01257	centimeters	feet	3.281×10^{-2}
Angstrom unit	Inch	3937×10^{-9}	centimeters	inches	0.3937
Angstrom unit	Meter	1×10^{-10}	centimeters	kilometers	10^{-5}
Angstrom unit	Micron or (Mu)	1×10^{-4}	centimeters	meters	0.01
Are	Acre (US)	.02471	centimeters	miles	6.214×10^{-6}
Ares	sq. yards	119.60	centimeters	millimeters	10.0
ares	acres	0.02471	centimeters	mils	393.7
ares	sq meters	100.0	centimeters	yards	1.094×10^{-2}
Astronomical Unit	Kilometers	1.495×10^8	centimeter-dynes	cm-grams	1.020×10^{-3}
Atmospheres	Ton/sq. inch	.007348	centimeter-dynes	meter-kgs	1.020×10^{-8}
atmospheres	cms of mercury	76.0	centimeter-dynes	pound-feet	7.376×10^{-8}
atmospheres	ft of water (at 4°C)	33.90	centimeter-grams	cm-dynes	980.7
atmospheres	in. of mercury (at 0°C)	29.92	centimeter-grams	meter-kgs	10^{-5}
atmospheres	kgs/sq cm	1.0333	centimeter-grams	pound-feet	7.233×10^{-5}
atmospheres	kgs/sq meter	10,332.	centimeters of mercury	atmospheres	0.01316
atmospheres	pounds/sq in.	14.70	centimeters of mercury	feet of water	0.4461
atmospheres	tons/sq ft	1.058	centimeters of mercury	kgs/sq meter	136.0
			centimeters of mercury	pounds/sq ft	27.85
			centimeters of mercury	pounds/sq in.	0.1934
			centimeters/sec	feet/min	1.1969
			centimeters/sec	feet/sec	0.03281
B			centimeters/sec	kilometers/hr	0.036
Barrels (U.S., dry)	cu. inches	7056.	centimeters/sec	knots	0.1943
Barrels (U.S., dry)	quarts (dry)	105.0	centimeters/sec	meters/min	0.6
Barrels (U.S., liquid)	gallons	31.5	centimeters/sec	miles/hr	0.02237
barrels (oil)	gallons (oil)	42.0	centimeters/sec	miles/min	3.728×10^{-4}
bars	atmospheres	0.9869	centimeters/sec/sec	feet/sec/sec	0.03281
bars	dynes/sq cm	10^6	centimeters/sec/sec	kms/hr/sec	0.036
bars	kgs/sq meter	1.020×10^4	centimeters/sec/sec	meters/sec/sec	0.01
bars	pounds/sq ft	2,089.	centimeters/sec/sec	miles/hr/sec	0.02237
bars	pounds/sq in.	14.50	Chain	Inches	792.00
Baryl	Dyne/sq. cm.	1.000	Chain	meters	20.12
Bolt (US Cloth)	Meters	36.576	Chains (surveyors' or Gunter's)	yards	22.00
BTU	Liter—Atmosphere	10.409	circular mils	sq cms	5.067×10^{-6}
Btu	ergs	1.0550×10^{10}	circular mils	sq mils	0.7854
Btu	foot-lbs	778.3	Circumference	Radians	6.283
Btu	gram-calories	252.0	circular mils	sq inches	7.854×10^{-7}
Btu	horsepower-hrs	3.931×10^{-4}	Cords	cord feet	8
Btu	joules	1,054.8	Cord feet	cu. feet	16
Btu	kilogram-calories	0.2520	Coulomb	Statcoulombs	2.998×10^9
Btu	kilogram-meters	107.5	coulombs	faradays	1.036×10^{-5}
Btu	kilowatt-hrs	2.928×10^{-4}			
Btu/hr	foot-pounds/sec	0.2162			

A-1.
(Continued). Alphabetical Conversion Factors

TO CONVERT	INTO	MULTIPLY BY	TO CONVERT	INTO	MULTIPLY BY
coulombs/sq cm	coulombs/sq in.	64.52	degrees/sec	radians/sec	0.01745
coulombs/sq cm	coulombs/sq meter	10^4	degrees/sec	revolutions/min	0.1667
coulombs/sq in.	coulombs/sq cm	0.1550	degrees/sec	revolutions/sec	2.778×10^{-3}
coulombs/sq in.	coulombs/sq meter	1,550.	dekagrams	grams	10.0
coulombs/sq meter	coulombs/sq cm	10^{-4}	dekaliters	liters	10.0
coulombs/sq meter	coulombs/sq in.	6.452×10^{-4}	dekameters	meters	10.0
cubic centimeters	cu feet	3.531×10^{-5}	Drams (apothecaries' or troy)	ounces (avoidupois)	0.1371429
cubic centimeters	cu inches	0.06102	Drams (apothecaries' or troy)	ounces (troy)	0.125
cubic centimeters	cu meters	10^{-6}	Drams (U.S., fluid or apoth.)	cubic cm.	3.6967
cubic centimeters	cu yards	1.308×10^{-6}	drams	grams	1.7718
cubic centimeters	gallons (U. S. liq.)	2.642×10^{-4}	drams	grains	27.3437
cubic centimeters	liters	0.001	drams	ounces	0.0625
cubic centimeters	pints (U.S. liq.)	2.113×10^{-3}	Dyne/cm	Erg/sq. millimeter	.01
cubic centimeters	quarts (U.S. liq.)	1.057×10^{-3}	Dyne/sq. cm.	Atmospheres	9.869×10^{-7}
cubic feet	bushels (dry)	0.8036	Dyne/sq. cm.	Inch of Mercury at 0°C	2.953×10^{-5}
cubic feet	cu cms	28,320.0	Dyne/sq. cm.	Inch of Water at 4°C	4.015×10^{-4}
cubic feet	cu inches	1,728.0	dynes	grams	1.020×10^{-3}
cubic feet	cu meters	0.02832	dynes	joules/cm	10^{-7}
cubic feet	cu yards	0.03704	dynes	joules/meter (newtons)	10^{-5}
cubic feet	gallons (U.S. liq.)	7.48052	dynes	kilograms	1.020×10^{-6}
cubic feet	liters	28.32	dynes	poundals	7.233×10^{-5}
cubic feet	pints (U.S. liq.)	59.84	dynes	pounds	2.248×10^{-6}
cubic feet	quarts (U.S. liq.)	29.92	dynes/sq cm	bars	10^{-6}
cubic feet/min	cu cms/sec	472.0			
cubic feet/min	gallons/sec	0.1247			
cubic feet/min	liters/sec	0.4720			
cubic feet/min	pounds of water/min	62.43			
cubic feet/sec	million gals/day	0.646317		**E**	
cubic feet/sec	gallons/min	448.831			
cubic inches	cu cms	16.39	Ell	Cm.	114.30
cubic inches	cu feet	5.787×10^{-4}	Ell	Inches	45
cubic inches	cu meters	1.639×10^{-5}	Em, Pica	Inch	.167
cubic inches	cu yards	2.143×10^{-5}	Em, Pica	Cm.	.4233
cubic inches	gallons	4.329×10^{-3}	Erg/sec	Dyne — cm/sec	1.000
cubic inches	liters	0.01639	ergs	Btu	9.480×10^{-11}
cubic inches	mil-feet	1.061×10^5	ergs	dyne-centimeters	1.0
cubic inches	pints (U.S. liq.)	0.03463	ergs	foot-pounds	7.367×10^{-8}
cubic inches	quarts (U.S. liq.)	0.01732	ergs	gram-calories	0.2389×10^{-7}
cubic meters	bushels (dry)	28.38	ergs	gram-cms	1.020×10^{-3}
cubic meters	cu cms	10^6	ergs	horsepower-hrs	3.7250×10^{-14}
cubic meters	cu feet	35.31	ergs	joules	10^{-7}
cubic meters	cu inches	61,023.0	ergs	kg-calories	2.389×10^{-11}
cubic meters	cu yards	1.308	ergs	kg-meters	1.020×10^{-8}
cubic meters	gallons (U.S. liq.)	264.2	ergs	kilowatt-hrs	0.2778×10^{-13}
cubic meters	liters	1,000.0	ergs	watt-hours	0.2778×10^{-10}
cubic meters	pints (U.S. liq.)	2,113.0	ergs/sec	Btu/min	$5,688 \times 10^{-9}$
cubic meters	quarts (U.S. liq.)	1,057.	ergs/sec	ft-lbs/min	4.427×10^{-6}
cubic yards	cu cms	7.646×10^5	ergs/sec	ft-lbs/sec	7.3756×10^{-8}
cubic yards	cu feet	27.0	ergs/sec	horsepower	1.341×10^{-10}
cubic yards	cu inches	46,656.0	ergs/sec	kg-calories/min	1.433×10^{-9}
cubic yards	cu meters	0.7646	ergs/sec	kilowatts	10^{-10}
cubic yards	gallons (U.S. liq.)	202.0			
cubic yards	liters	764.6			
cubic yards	pints (U.S. liq.)	1,615.9			
cubic yards	quarts (U.S. liq.)	807.9		**F**	
cubic yards/min	cubic ft/sec	0.45	farads	microfarads	10^6
cubic yards/min	gallons/sec	3.367	Faraday/sec	Ampere (absolute)	9.6500×10^4
cubic yards/min	liters/sec	12.74	faradays	ampere-hours	26.80
			faradays	coulombs	9.649×10^4
			Fathom	Meter	1.828804
			fathoms	feet	6.0
	D		feet	centimeters	30.48
Dalton	Gram	1.650×10^{-24}	feet	kilometers	3.048×10^{-4}
days	seconds	86,400.0	feet	meters	0.3048
decigrams	grams	0.1	feet	miles (naut.)	1.645×10^{-4}
deciliters	liters	0.1	feet	miles (stat.)	1.894×10^{-4}
decimeters	meters	0.1	feet	millimeters	304.8
degrees (angle)	quadrants	0.01111	feet	mils	1.2×10^4
degrees (angle)	radians	0.01745	feet of water	atmospheres	0.02950
degrees (angle)	seconds	3,600.0	feet of water	in. of mercury	0.8826
			feet of water	kgs/sq cm	0.03048

(Continued on next page)

A-1.
(Continued). Alphabetical Conversion Factors

TO CONVERT	INTO	MULTIPLY BY
feet of water	kgs/sq meter	304.8
feet of water	pounds/sq ft	62.43
feet of water	pounds/sq in.	0.4335
feet/min	cms/sec	0.5080
feet/min	feet/sec	0.01667
feet/min	kms/hr	0.01829
feet/min	meters/min	0.3048
feet/min	miles/hr	0.01136
feet/sec	cms/sec	30.48
feet/sec	kms/hr	1.097
feet/sec	knots	0.5921
feet/sec	meters/min	18.29
feet/sec	miles/hr	0.6818
feet/sec	miles/min	0.01136
feet/sec/sec	cms/sec/sec	30.48
feet/sec/sec	kms/hr/sec	1.097
feet/sec/sec	meters/sec/sec	0.3048
feet/sec/sec	miles/hr/sec	0.6818
feet/100 feet	per cent grade	1.0
Foot — candle	Lumen/sq. meter	10.764
foot-pounds	Btu	1.286×10^{-3}
foot-pounds	ergs	1.356×10^{7}
foot-pounds	gram-calories	0.3238
foot-pounds	hp-hrs	5.050×10^{-7}
foot-pounds	joules	1.356
foot-pounds	kg-calories	3.24×10^{-4}
foot-pounds	kg-meters	0.1383
foot-pounds	kilowatt-hrs	3.766×10^{-7}
foot-pounds/min	Btu/min	1.286×10^{-3}
foot-pounds/min	foot-pounds/sec	0.01667
foot-pounds/min	horsepower	3.030×10^{-5}
foot-pounds/min	kg-calories/min	3.24×10^{-4}
foot-pounds/min	kilowatts	2.260×10^{-5}
foot-pounds/sec	Btu/hr	4.6263
foot-pounds/sec	Btu/min	0.07717
foot-pounds/sec	horsepower	1.818×10^{-3}
foot-pounds/sec	kg-calories/min	0.01945
foot-pounds/sec	kilowatts	1.356×10^{-3}
Furlongs	miles (U.S.)	0.125
furlongs	rods	40.0
furlongs	feet	660.0

G

TO CONVERT	INTO	MULTIPLY BY
gallons	cu cms	3,785.0
gallons	cu feet	0.1337
gallons	cu inches	231.0
gallons	cu meters	3.785×10^{-3}
gallons	cu yards	4.951×10^{-3}
gallons	liters	3.785
gallons (liq. Br. Imp.)	gallons (U.S. liq.)	1.20095
gallons (U.S.)	gallons (Imp.)	0.83267
gallons of water	pounds of water	8.3453
gallons/min	cu ft/sec	2.228×10^{-3}
gallons/min	liters/sec	0.06308
gallons/min	cu ft/hr	8.0208
gausses	lines/sq in.	6.452
gausses	webers/sq cm	10^{-8}
gausses	webers/sq in.	6.452×10^{-8}
gausses	webers/sq meter	10^{-4}
gilberts	ampere-turns	0.7958
gilberts/cm	amp-turns/cm	0.7958
gilberts/cm	amp-turns/in	2.021
gilberts/cm	amp-turns/meter	79.58
Gills (British)	cubic cm.	142.07
gills	liters	0.1183
gills	pints (liq.)	0.25
Grade	Radian	.01571
Grains	drams (avoirdupois)	0.03657143

TO CONVERT	INTO	MULTIPLY BY
grains (troy)	grains (avdp)	1.0
grains (troy)	grams	0.06480
grains (troy)	ounces (avdp)	2.0833×10^{-3}
grains (troy)	pennyweight (troy)	0.04167
grains/U.S. gal	parts/million	17.118
grains/U.S. gal	pounds/million gal	142.86
grains/Imp. gal	parts/million	14.286
grams	dynes	980.7
grams	grains	15.43
grams	joules/cm	9.807×10^{-5}
grams	joules/meter (newtons)	9.807×10^{-3}
grams	kilograms	0.001
grams	milligrams	1,000.
grams	ounces (avdp)	0.03527
grams	ounces (troy)	0.03215
grams	poundals	0.07093
grams	pounds	2.205×10^{-3}
grams/cm	pounds/inch	5.600×10^{-3}
grams/cu cm	pounds/cu ft	62.43
grams/cu cm	pounds/cu in	0.03613
grams/cu cm	pounds/mil-foot	3.405×10^{-7}
grams/liter	grains/gal	58.417
grams/liter	pounds/1,000 gal	8.345
grams/liter	pounds/cu ft	0.062427
grams/liter	parts/million	1,000.0
grams/sq cm	pounds/sq ft	2.0481
gram-calories	Btu	3.9683×10^{-3}
gram-calories	ergs	4.1868×10^{7}
gram-calories	foot-pounds	3.0880
gram-calories	horsepower-hrs	1.5596×10^{-6}
gram-calories	kilowatt-hrs	1.1630×10^{-6}
gram-calories	watt-hrs	1.1630×10^{-3}
gram-calories/sec	Btu/hr	14.286
gram-centimeters	Btu	9.297×10^{-8}
gram-centimeters	ergs	980.7
gram-centimeters	joules	9.807×10^{-5}
gram-centimeters	kg-cal	2.343×10^{-8}
gram-centimeters	kg-meters	10^{-5}

H

TO CONVERT	INTO	MULTIPLY BY
Hand	Cm.	10.16
hectares	acres	2.471
hectares	sq feet	1.076×10^{5}
hectograms	grams	100.0
hectoliters	liters	100.0
hectometers	meters	100.0
hectowatts	watts	100.0
henries	millihenries	1,000.0
Hogsheads (British)	cubic ft.	10.114
Hogsheads (U.S.)	cubic ft.	8.42184
Hogsheads (U.S.)	gallons (U.S.)	63
horsepower	Btu/min	42.44
horsepower	foot-lbs/min	33,000.
horsepower	foot-lbs/sec	550.0
horsepower (metric) (542.5 ft lb/sec)	horsepower (550 ft lb/sec)	0.9863
horsepower (550 ft lb/sec)	horsepower (metric) (542.5 ft lb/sec)	1.014
horsepower	kg-calories/min	10.68
horsepower	kilowatts	0.7457
horsepower	watts	745.7
horsepower (boiler)	Btu/hr	33.479
horsepower (boiler)	kilowatts	9.803
horsepower-hrs	Btu	2,547.
horsepower-hrs	ergs	2.6845×10^{13}
horsepower-hrs	foot-lbs	1.98×10^{6}
horsepower-hrs	gram-calories	641,190.
horsepower-hrs	joules	2.684×10^{6}

A-1.
(Continued). Alphabetical Conversion Factors

TO CONVERT	INTO	MULTIPLY BY	TO CONVERT	INTO	MULTIPLY BY
horsepower-hrs	kg-calories	641.1	kilograms/sq cm	inches of mercury	28.96
horsepower-hrs	kg-meters	2.737×10^5	kilograms/sq cm	pounds/sq ft	2,048.
horsepower-hrs	kilowatt-hrs	0.7457	kilograms/sq cm	pounds/sq in.	14.22
hours	days	4.167×10^{-2}	kilograms/sq meter	atmospheres	9.678×10^{-5}
hours	weeks	5.952×10^{-3}	kilograms/sq meter	bars	98.07×10^{-6}
Hundredweights (long)	pounds	112	kilograms/sq meter	feet of water	3.281×10^{-3}
Hundredweights (long)	tons (long)	0.05	kilograms/sq meter	inches of mercury	2.896×10^{-3}
Hundredweights (short)	ounces (avoirdupois)	1600	kilograms/sq meter	pounds/sq ft	0.2048
Hundredweights (short)	pounds	100	kilograms/sq meter	pounds/sq in.	1.422×10^{-3}
Hundredweights (short)	tons (metric)	0.0453592	kilograms/sq mm	kgs/sq meter	10^6
Hundredweights (short)	tons (long)	0.0446429	kilogram-calories	Btu	3.968
			kilogram-calories	foot-pounds	3,088.
	I		kilogram-calories	hp-hrs	1.560×10^{-3}
			kilogram-calories	joules	4,186.
inches	centimeters	2.540	kilogram-calories	kg-meters	426.9
inches	meters	2.540×10^{-2}	kilogram-calories	kilojoules	4.186
inches	miles	1.578×10^{-5}	kilogram-calories	kilowatt-hrs	1.163×10^{-3}
inches	millimeters	25.40	kilogram meters	Btu	9.294×10^{-3}
inches	mils	1,000.0	kilogram meters	ergs	9.804×10^7
inches	yards	2.778×10^{-2}	kilogram meters	foot-pounds	7.233
inches of mercury	atmospheres	0.03342	kilogram meters	joules	9.804
inches of mercury	feet of water	1.133	kilogram meters	kg-calories	2.342×10^{-3}
inches of mercury	kgs/sq cm	0.03453	kilogram meters	kilowatt-hrs	2.723×10^{-6}
inches of mercury	kgs/sq meter	345.3	kilolines	maxwells	1,000.0
inches of mercury	pounds/sq ft	70.73	kiloliters	liters	1,000.0
inches of mercury	pounds/sq in.	0.4912	kilometers	centimeters	10^5
inches of water (at 4°C)	atmospheres	2.458×10^{-3}	kilometers	feet	3,281.
inches of water (at 4°C)	inches of mercury	0.07355	kilometers	inches	3.937×10^4
inches of water (at 4°C)	kgs/sq cm	2.540×10^{-3}	kilometers	meters	1,000.0
inches of water (at 4°C)	ounces/sq in.	0.5781	kilometers	miles	0.6214
inches of water (at 4°C)	pounds/sq ft	5.204	kilometers	millimeters	10^6
inches of water (at 4°C)	pounds/sq in.	0.03613	kilometers	yards	1,094.
International Ampere	Ampere (absolute)	.9998	kilometers/hr	cms/sec	27.78
International Volt	Volts (absolute)	1.0003	kilometers/hr	feet/min	54.68
International volt	Joules (absolute)	$1·593 \times 10^{-19}$	kilometers/hr	feet/sec	0.9113
International volt	Joules	9.654×10^4	kilometers/hr	knots	0.5396
			kilometers/hr	meters/min	16.67
	J		kilometers/hr	miles/hr	0.6214
			kilometers/hr/sec	cms/sec/sec	27.78
joules	Btu	9.480×10^{-4}	kilometers/hr/sec	ft/sec/sec	0.9113
joules	ergs	10^7	kilometers/hr/sec	meters/sec/sec	0.2778
joules	foot-pounds	0.7376	kilometers/hr/sec	miles/hr/sec	0.6214
joules	kg-calories	2.389×10^{-4}	kilowatts	Btu/min	56.92
joules	kg-meters	0.1020	kilowatts	foot-lbs/min	4.426×10^4
joules	watt-hrs	2.778×10^{-4}	kilowatts	foot-lbs/sec	737.6
joules/cm	grams	1.020×10^4	kilowatts	horsepower	1.341
joules/cm	dynes	10^7	kilowatts	kg-calories/min	14.34
joules/cm	joules/meter (newtons)	100.0	kilowatts	watts	1,000.0
joules/cm	poundals	723.3	kilowatt-hrs	Btu	3,413.
joules/cm	pounds	22.48	kilowatt-hrs	ergs	3.600×10^{13}
			kilowatt-hrs	foot-lbs	2.655×10^6
	K		kilowatt-hrs	gram-calories	859,850.
			kilowatt-hrs	horsepower-hrs	1.341
kilograms	dynes	980,665.	kilowatt-hrs	joules	3.6×10^6
kilograms	grams	1,000.0	kilowatt-hrs	kg-calories	860.5
kilograms	joules/cm	0.09807	kilowatt-hrs	kg-meters	3.671×10^5
kilograms	joules/meter (newtons)	9.807	kilowatt-hrs	pounds of water evaporated from and at 212° F.	3.53
kilograms	poundals	70.93			
kilograms	pounds	2.205			
kilograms	tons (long)	9.842×10^{-4}			
kilograms	tons (short)	1.102×10^{-3}	kilowatt-hrs	pounds of water raised from 62° to 212° F.	22.75
kilograms/cu meter	grams/cu cm	0.001			
kilograms/cu meter	pounds/cu ft	0.06243	knots	feet/hr	6,080.
kilograms/cu meter	pounds/cu in.	3.613×10^{-5}	knots	kilometers/hr	1.8532
kilograms/cu meter	pounds/mil-foot	3.405×10^{-10}	knots	nautical miles/hr	1.0
kilograms/meter	pounds/ft	0.6720	knots	statute miles/hr	1.151
Kilogram/sq. cm.	Dynes	980,665			
kilograms/sq cm	atmospheres	0.9678			
kilograms/sq cm	feet of water	32.81			

(Continued on next page)

A-1.
(Continued). Alphabetical Conversion Factors

TO CONVERT	INTO	MULTIPLY BY
knots	yards/hr	2,027.
knots	feet/sec	1.689

L

TO CONVERT	INTO	MULTIPLY BY
league	miles (approx.)	3.0
Light year	Miles	5.9×10^{12}
Light year	Kilometers	9.46091×10^{12}
lines/sq cm	gausses	1.0
lines/sq in.	gausses	0.1550
lines/sq in.	webers/sq cm	1.550×10^{-9}
lines/sq in.	webers/sq in.	10^{-8}
lines/sq in.	webers/sq meter	1.550×10^{-5}
links (engineer's)	inches	12.0
links (surveyor's)	inches	7.92
liters	bushels (U.S. dry)	0.02838
liters	cu cm	1,000.0
liters	cu feet	0.03531
liters	cu inches	61.02
liters	cu meters	0.001
liters	cu yards	1.308×10^{-3}
liters	gallons (U.S. liq.)	0.2642
liters	pints (U.S. liq.)	2.113
liters	quarts (U.S. liq.)	1.057
liters/min	cu ft/sec	5.886×10^{-4}
liters/min	gals/sec	4.403×10^{-3}
lumens/sq ft	foot-candles	1.0
Lumen	Spherical candle power	.07958
Lumen	Watt	.001496
Lumen/sq. ft.	Lumen/sq. meter	10.76
lux	foot-candles	0.0929

M

TO CONVERT	INTO	MULTIPLY BY
maxwells	kilolines	0.001
maxwells	webers	10^{-8}
megalines	maxwells	10^{6}
megohms	microhms	10^{12}
megohms	ohms	10^{6}
meters	centimeters	100.0
meters	feet	3.281
meters	inches	39.37
meters	kilometers	0.001
meters	miles (naut.)	5.396×10^{-4}
meters	miles (stat.)	6.214×10^{-4}
meters	millimeters	1,000.0
meters	yards	1.094
meters	varas	1.179
meters/min	cms/sec	1.667
meters/min	feet/min	3.281
meters/min	feet/sec	0.05468
meters/min	kms/hr	0.06
meters/min	knots	0.03238
meters/min	miles/hr	0.03728
meters/sec	feet/min	196.8
meters/sec	feet/sec	3.281
meters/sec	kilometers/hr	3.6
meters/sec	kilometers/min	0.06
meters/sec	miles/hr	2.237
meters/sec	miles/min	0.03728
meters/sec/sec	cms/sec/sec	100.0
meters/sec/sec	ft/sec/sec	3.281
meters/sec/sec	kms/hr/sec	3.6
meters/sec/sec	miles/hr/sec	2.237
meter-kilograms	cm-dynes	9.807×10^{7}
meter-kilograms	cm-grams	10^{5}
meter-kilograms	pound-feet	7.233
microfarad	farads	10^{-6}
micrograms	grams	10^{-6}
microhms	megohms	10^{-12}

TO CONVERT	INTO	MULTIPLY BY
microhms	ohms	10^{-6}
microliters	liters	10^{-6}
Microns	meters	1×10^{-6}
miles (naut.)	feet	6,080.27
miles (naut.)	kilometers	1.853
miles (naut.)	meters	1,853.
miles (naut.)	miles (statute)	1.1516
miles (naut.)	yards	2,027.
miles (statute)	centimeters	1.609×10^{5}
miles (statute)	feet	5,280.
miles (statute)	inches	6.336×10^{4}
miles (statute)	kilometers	1.609
miles (statute)	meters	1,609.
miles (statute)	miles (naut.)	0.8684
miles (statute)	yards	1,760.
miles/hr	cms/sec	44.70
miles/hr	feet/min	88.
miles/hr	feet/sec	1.467
miles/hr	kms/hr	1.609
miles/hr	kms/min	0.02682
miles/hr	knots	0.8684
miles/hr	meters/min	26.82
miles/hr	miles/min	0.1667
miles/hr/sec	cms/sec/sec	44.70
miles/hr/sec	feet/sec/sec	1.467
miles/hr/sec	kms/hr/sec	1.609
miles/hr/sec	meters/sec/sec	0.4470
miles/min	cms/sec	2,682.
miles/min	feet/sec	88.
miles/min	kms/min	1.609
miles/min	knots/min	0.8684
miles/min	miles/hr	60.0
mil-feet	cu inches	9.425×10^{-6}
milliers	kilograms	1,000.
Millimicrons	meters	1×10^{-9}
Milligrams	grains	0.01543236
milligrams	grams	0.001
milligrams/liter	parts/million	1.0
millihenries	henries	0.001
milliliters	liters	0.001
millimeters	centimeters	0.1
millimeters	feet	3.281×10^{-3}
millimeters	inches	0.03937
millimeters	kilometers	10^{-6}
millimeters	meters	0.001
millimeters	miles	6.214×10^{-7}
millimeters	mils	39.37
millimeters	yards	1.094×10^{-3}
million gals/day	cu ft/sec	1.54723
mils	centimeters	2.540×10^{-3}
mils	feet	8.333×10^{-5}
mils	inches	0.001
mils	kilometers	2.540×10^{-8}
mils	yards	2.778×10^{-5}
miner's inches	cu ft/min	1.5
Minims (British)	cubic cm.	0.059192
Minims (U.S., fluid)	cubic cm.	0.061612
minutes (angles)	degrees	0.01667
minutes (angles)	quadrants	1.852×10^{-4}
minutes (angles)	radians	2.909×10^{-4}
minutes (angles)	seconds	60.0
myriagrams	kilograms	10.0
myriameters	kilometers	10.0
myriawatts	kilowatts	10.0

N

TO CONVERT	INTO	MULTIPLY BY
nepers	decibels	8.686
Newton	Dynes	1×10^{5}

A-1.
(Continued). Alphabetical Conversion Factors

TO CONVERT	INTO	MULTIPLY BY
O		
OHM (International)	OHM (absolute)	1.0005
ohms	megohms	10^{-6}
ohms	microhms	10^{6}
ounces	drams	16.0
ounces	grains	437.5
ounces	grams	28.349527
ounces	pounds	0.0625
ounces	ounces (troy)	0.9115
ounces	tons (long)	2.790×10^{-5}
ounces	tons (metric)	2.835×10^{-5}
ounces (fluid)	cu inches	1.805
ounces (fluid)	liters	0.02957
ounces (troy)	grains	480.0
ounces (troy)	grams	31.103481
ounces (troy)	ounces (avdp.)	1.09714
ounces (troy)	pennyweights (troy)	20.0
ounces (troy)	pounds (troy)	0.08333
Ounce/sq. inch	Dynes/sq. cm.	4309
ounces/sq in.	pounds/sq in.	0.0625
P		
Parsec	Miles	19×10^{12}
Parsec	Kilometers	3.084×10^{13}
parts/million	grains/U.S. gal	0.0584
parts/million	grains/Imp. gal	0.07016
parts/million	pounds/million gal	8.345
Pecks (British)	cubic inches	554.6
Pecks (British)	liters	9.091901
Pecks (U.S.)	bushels	0.25
Pecks (U.S.)	cubic inches	537.605
Pecks (U.S.)	liters	8.809582
Pecks (U.S.)	quarts (dry)	8
pennyweights (troy)	grains	24.0
pennyweights (troy)	ounces (troy)	0.05
pennyweights (troy)	grams	1.55517
pennyweights (troy)	pounds (troy)	4.1667×10^{-3}
pints (dry)	cu inches	33.60
pints (liq.)	cu cms.	473.2
pints (liq.)	cu feet	0.01671
pints (liq.)	cu inches	28.87
pints (liq.)	cu meters	4.732×10^{-4}
pints (liq.)	cu yards	6.189×10^{-4}
pints (liq.)	gallons	0.125
pints (liq.)	liters	0.4732
pints (liq.)	quarts (liq.)	0.5
Planck's quantum	Erg — second	6.624×10^{-27}
Poise	Gram/cm. sec.	1.00
Pounds (avoirdupois)	ounces (troy)	14.5833
poundals	dynes	13,826.
poundals	grams	14.10
poundals	joules/cm	1.383×10^{-3}
poundals	joules/meter (newtons)	0.1383
poundals	kilograms	0.01410
poundals	pounds	0.03108
pounds	drams	256.
pounds	dynes	44.4823×10^{4}
pounds	grains	7,000.
pounds	grams	453.5924
pounds	joules/cm	0.04448
pounds	joules/meter (newtons)	4.448
pounds	kilograms	0.4536
pounds	ounces	16.0
pounds	ounces (troy)	14.5833
pounds	poundals	32.17
pounds	pounds (troy)	1.21528
pounds	tons (short)	0.0005
pounds (troy)	grains	5,760.
pounds (troy)	grams	373.24177
pounds (troy)	ounces (avdp.)	13.1657
pounds (troy)	ounces (troy)	12.0
pounds (troy)	pennyweights (troy)	240.0
pounds (troy)	pounds (avdp.)	0.822857
pounds (troy)	tons (long)	3.6735×10^{-4}
pounds (troy)	tons (metric)	3.7324×10^{-4}
pounds (troy)	tons (short)	4.1143×10^{-4}
pounds of water	cu feet	0.01602
pounds of water	cu inches	27.68
pounds of water	gallons	0.1198
pounds of water/min	cu ft/sec	2.670×10^{-4}
pound-feet	cm-dynes	1.356×10^{7}
pound-feet	cm-grams	13,825.
pound-feet	meter-kgs	0.1383
pounds/cu ft	grams/cu cm	0.01602
pounds/cu ft	kgs/cu meter	16.02
pounds/cu ft	pounds/cu in.	5.787×10^{-4}
pounds/cu ft	pounds/mil-foot	5.456×10^{-9}
pounds/cu in.	gms/cu cm	27.68
pounds/cu in.	kgs/cu meter	2.768×10^{4}
pounds/cu in.	pounds/cu ft	1,728.
pounds/cu in.	pounds/mil-foot	9.425×10^{-6}
pounds/ft	kgs/meter	1.488
pounds/in.	gms/cm	178.6
pounds/mil-foot	gms/cu cm	2.306×10^{6}
pounds/sq ft	atmospheres	4.725×10^{-4}
pounds/sq ft	feet of water	0.01602
pounds/sq ft	inches of mercury	0.01414
pounds/sq ft	kgs/sq meter	4.882
pounds/sq ft	pounds/sq in.	6.944×10^{-3}
pounds/sq in.	atmospheres	0.06804
pounds/sq in.	feet of water	2.307
pounds/sq in.	inches of mercury	2.036
pounds/sq in.	kgs/sq meter	703.1
pounds/sq in.	pounds/sq ft	144.0
Q		
quadrants (angle)	degrees	90.0
quadrants (angle)	minutes	5,400.0
quadrants (angle)	radians	1.571
quadrants (angle)	seconds	3.24×10^{5}
quarts (dry)	cu inches	67.20
quarts (liq.)	cu cms	946.4
quarts (liq.)	cu feet	0.03342
quarts (liq.)	cu inches	57.75
quarts (liq.)	cu meters	9.464×10^{-4}
quarts (liq.)	cu yards	1.238×10^{-3}
quarts (liq.)	gallons	0.25
quarts (liq.)	liters	0.9463
R		
radians	degrees	57.30
radians	minutes	3,438.
radians	quadrants	0.6366
radians	seconds	2.063×10^{5}
radians/sec	degrees/sec	57.30
radians/sec	revolutions/min	9.549
radians/sec	revolutions/sec	0.1592
radians/sec/sec	revs/min/min	573.0
radians/sec/sec	revs/min/sec	9.549
radians/sec/sec	revs/sec/sec	0.1592
revolutions	degrees	360.0
revolutions	quadrants	4.0
revolutions	radians	6.283
revolutions/min	degrees/sec	6.0
revolutions/min	radians/sec	0.1047
revolutions/min	revs/sec	0.01667

(Continued on next page)

A-1.
(Continued). Alphabetical Conversion Factors

TO CONVERT	INTO	MULTIPLY BY
revolutions/min/min	radians/sec/sec	1.745×10^{-3}
revolutions/min/min	revs/min/sec	0.01667
revolutions/min/min	revs/sec/sec	2.778×10^{-4}
revolutions/sec	degrees/sec	360.0
revolutions/sec	radians/sec	6.283
revolutions/sec	revs/min	60.0
revolutions/sec/sec	radians/sec/sec	6.283
revolutions/sec/sec	revs/min/min	3,600.0
revolutions/sec/sec	revs/min/sec	60.0
Rod	Chain (Gunters)	.25
Rod	Meters	5.029
Rods (Surveyors' meas.)	yards	5.5
rods	feet	16.5

S

TO CONVERT	INTO	MULTIPLY BY
Scruples	grains	20
seconds (angle)	degrees	2.778×10^{-4}
seconds (angle)	minutes	0.01667
seconds (angle)	quadrants	3.087×10^{-6}
seconds (angle)	radians	4.848×10^{-6}
Slug	Kilogram	14.59
Slug	Pounds	32.17
Sphere	Steradians	12.57
square centimeters	circular mils	1.973×10^5
square centimeters	sq feet	1.076×10^{-3}
square centimeters	sq inches	0.1550
square centimeters	sq meters	0.0001
square centimeters	sq miles	3.861×10^{-11}
square centimeters	sq millimeters	100.0
square centimeters	sq yards	1.196×10^{-4}
square feet	acres	2.296×10^{-5}
square feet	circular mils	1.833×10^8
square feet	sq cms	929.0
square feet	sq inches	144.0
square feet	sq meters	0.09290
square feet	sq miles	3.587×10^{-8}
square feet	sq millimeters	9.290×10^4
square feet	sq yards	0.1111
square inches	circular mils	1.273×10^6
square inches	sq cms	6.452
square inches	sq feet	6.944×10^{-3}
square inches	sq millimeters	645.2
square inches	sq mils	10^6
square inches	sq yards	7.716×10^{-4}
square kilometers	acres	247.1
square kilometers	sq cms	10^{10}
square kilometers	sq ft	10.76×10^6
square kilometers	sq inches	1.550×10^9
square kilometers	sq meters	10^6
square kilometers	sq miles	0.3861
square kilometers	sq yards	1.196×10^6
square meters	acres	2.471×10^{-4}
square meters	sq cms	10^4
square meters	sq feet	10.76
square meters	sq inches	1,550.
square meters	sq miles	3.861×10^{-7}
square meters	sq millimeters	10^6
square meters	sq yards	1.196
square miles	acres	640.0
square miles	sq feet	27.88×10^6
square miles	sq kms	2.590
square miles	sq meters	2.590×10^6
square miles	sq yards	3.098×10^6
square millimeters	circular mils	1,973.
square millimeters	sq cms	0.01
square millimeters	sq feet	1.076×10^{-5}
square millimeters	sq inches	1.550×10^{-3}
square mils	circular mils	1.273

TO CONVERT	INTO	MULTIPLY BY
square mils	sq cms	6.452×10^{-6}
square mils	sq inches	10^{-6}
square yards	acres	2.066×10^{-4}
square yards	sq cms	8,361.
square yards	sq feet	9.0
square yards	sq inches	1,296.
square yards	sq meters	0.8361
square yards	sq miles	3.228×10^{-7}
square yards	sq millimeters	8.361×10^5

T

TO CONVERT	INTO	MULTIPLY BY
temperature (°C) +273	absolute temperature (°C)	1.0
temperature (°C) +17.78	temperature (°F)	1.8
temperature (°F) +460	absolute temperature (°F)	1.0
temperature (°F) −32	temperature (°C)	5/9
tons (long)	kilograms	1,016.
tons (long)	pounds	2,240.
tons (long)	tons (short)	1.120
tons (metric)	kilograms	1,000.
tons (metric)	pounds	2,205.
tons (short)	kilograms	907.1848
tons (short)	ounces	32,000.
tons (short)	ounces (troy)	29,166.66
tons (short)	pounds	2,000.
tons (short)	pounds (troy)	2,430.56
tons (short)	tons (long)	0.89287
tons (short)	tons (metric)	0.9078
tons (short)/sq ft	kgs/sq meter	9,765.
tons (short)/sq ft	pounds/sq in.	2,000.
tons of water/24 hrs	pounds of water/hr	83.333
tons of water/24 hrs	gallons/min	0.16643
tons of water/24 hrs	cu ft/hr	1.3349

V

TO CONVERT	INTO	MULTIPLY BY
Volt/inch	Volt/cm.	.39370
Volt (absolute)	Statvolts	.003336

W

TO CONVERT	INTO	MULTIPLY BY
watts	Btu/hr	3.4129
watts	Btu/min	0.05688
watts	ergs/sec	107.
watts	foot-lbs/min	44.27
watts	foot-lbs/sec	0.7378
watts	horsepower	1.341×10^{-3}
watts	horsepower (metric)	1.360×10^{-3}
watts	kg-calories/min	0.01433
watts	kilowatts	0.001
Watts (Abs.)	B.T.U. (mean)/min.	0.056884
Watts (Abs.)	joules/sec.	1
watt-hours	Btu	3.413
watt-hours	ergs	3.60×10^{10}
watt-hours	foot-pounds	2,656.
watt-hours	gram-calories	859.85
watt-hours	horsepower-hrs	1.341×10^{-3}
watt-hours	kilogram-calories	0.8605
watt-hours	kilogram-meters	367.2
watt-hours	kilowatt-hrs	0.001
Watt (International)	Watt (absolute)	1.0002
webers	maxwells	10^8
webers	kilolines	10^5

A-2.
Physical Property Conversion Factors

Acceleration of gravity = 32.172 ft./sec./sec.

= 980.6 cm./sec./sec.

Electrical conductance;

1 mho = 1 ohm^{-1}

= 10^{-6} megamho

= 10^6 micromho

Heat Value of Fuel

Lower heating value
= Higher heating value − 10.3 (9H$_2$ + H$_2$O), Btu/lb.

where: H$_2$ = weight % hydrogen in fuel

H$_2$O = weight % water vapor in fuel

GPM = (pounds/hour)/(500 × Sp.Gr.)

Velocity, feet/sec. = $\dfrac{0.321 \text{ (GPM)}}{\text{(Flow Area, sq.in.)}}$

Head, feet = 2.31 (Pressure or head, psi)/Sp.Gr.

Brake horsepower, BHP = $\dfrac{\text{(GPM) (Sp.Gr.) (Head, feet)}}{3960 \text{ (Efficiency, fraction)}}$

Weight/Volume (avoirdupois unless otherwise stated)

Density of sea water = 1.025 grams/cc.

1 gram-molecular volume of a gas at 760 mm Hg and 0° C. = 22.4 liters

1 U. S. gallon = (8.34 × Sp.Gr. of fluid), pounds

Weight of one cu.ft. liquid = (62.32 pounds × Sp.Gr. of fluid), pounds/cu.ft.

1 pound avoirdupois = 1.2153 pound apothecaries'

1 grain avoirdupois = 1 grain troy =1 grain apothecaries' weight

Air Analysis*

	By Weight %	By Volume %
Nitrogen	75.47	78.2
Oxygen	23.19	21.0

* Neglects trace gases such as argon, xenon, helium, krypton and assumes dry basis.

Gas Constants, (R), Universal

R = 0.0821 (atm) (liter)/(g-mol) (°K)

= 1.987 (g-cal.)/(g-mol) (°K)

= 1.987 Btu/(lb.-mol) (°R)

= 1.987 (Chu)/(lb.-mol) (°K)

= 8.314 joules/(g-mol) (°K)

= 1,546 (ft.) (lb.force)/(lb.-mol) (°R)

= 10.73 (lb.-force/sq.in.) (cu.ft.)/(lb.-mol) (°R)

= 18,510 (lb.-force/sq.in.) (cu.in.)/(lb.-mol) (°R)

= 0.7302 (Atm) (cu.ft.)/(lb.-mol.) (°R

= 8.314 × 10^{-7} ergs/(g-mol) (°K)

R$_i$ = R/mol.wt. gas

where: R$_i$ = individual gas constant

Avogadro Constant, N$_a$ = 6.02252 × 10^{23} molecules/mol

Density, Vapor or Gases (Ideal), ρ

$$\rho = \left(\frac{\text{mol. wt., vapor}}{359}\right)\left(\frac{14.7 + \text{P}}{14.7}\right)\left(\frac{460 + 32}{460 + °\text{F}}\right), \text{lbs./cu.ft.}$$

where, P = gage pressure at actual condition

°F = fahrenheit temperature at actual condition

$$\rho = \frac{144 \text{ P}}{\text{R}_i \text{ T}}, \text{pounds/cu.ft.}$$

where: P = absolute pressure, pounds/sq.in. abs.

T = absolute temperature, °Rankine, °R

Specific Volume, Gas or Vapor

$$\overline{V} = 1/\rho, \text{cu.ft./pound}$$

Velocity of sound in dry air @ 0° C. and 1 atm. = 1,089 ft./sec.

Density of dry air @ 0° C. and 1 atm.

= 0.001293 gm/cu.cm.

= 0.0808 lb./cu.ft.

Viscosity (Dynamic)

1 Poise = 1 gram/cm.-sec. = 1 dyne-sec./sq:cm.

= 0.1 kg/meter-sec.

1 Poise × 100 = Centipoise (μ)

Poise × 2.09 × 10^{-3} = slugs/ft.-sec.

= pounds (force)-sec./sq.ft.

Poise × 0.10 = pascal-sec.

Poise × 0.0672 = pounds (mass)/(ft.-sec.)

= poundal-sec./sq.ft.

Poise × 0.10 = Newton-sec./sq. meter

Centipoise × 0.01 = gm./cm.-sec.

Centpoise × 6.72 × 10^{-4} = pound/ft.-sec

Centipoise × 2.4 = pound/ft.-hr.

Millipoise × 1000 = poise

Micropoise × 1,000,000 = poise

Slugs/ft.-sec. × 47,900 = centipoise

(Continued on next page)

A-2.
(Continued). Physical Property Conversion Factors

Slugs/ft.-sec. $\times$ 32.2 = pounds (mass)/ft.-sec.

Pounds/ft.-sec. $\times$ 3600 = lb./ft.-hr.

Pounds (mass)/ft.-sec. $\times$ 1487 = centipoise

Pounds (mass)/ft.-sec. $\times$ 0.0311 = slugs/ft.-sec.
= pounds (force)-sec./sq.ft.

Viscosity of air @ 68° F. = 180.8 $\times$ 10^{-6} poise

Viscosity of water @ 66° F = 0.010087 poise

Viscosity (Kinematic)

Kinematic viscosity, centistokes $(\nu) = \dfrac{\text{Dynamic viscosity, centipoise}}{\text{Fluid density, gm./cu.cm.}}$

$= \dfrac{\text{Centipoise}}{\text{Sp.Gr. of liquid relative to water at 39.2° F. (4° C.)}}$

Centistokes $\times$ 0.01 = stokes, sq.cm./sec.

Centistokes $\times$ 1.076 $\times$ 10^{-5} = sq.ft./sec.

Centistokes $\times$ 0.01 = Stokes, sq.cm./sec.

Thermal Conductivity (through a homogeneous material)

$\dfrac{\text{Btu (ft.)}}{\text{(sq.ft.) (°F.) (hr.)}}$ $\times$ 4.134 $\times$ 10^{-3} = $\dfrac{\text{(g.-cal.) (cm.)}}{\text{(sq.cm.) (°C.) (sec.)}}$

$\times$ 1.200 $\times$ 10 = $\dfrac{\text{(Btu) (in.)}}{\text{(sq.ft.) (°F.) (hr.)}}$

$\times$ 3.518 $\times$ 10^{-3} = $\dfrac{\text{(kilowatt hrs.) (in.)}}{\text{(sq.ft.) (°F.) (hr.)}}$

$\dfrac{\text{(g.-cal.) (cm.)}}{\text{(sq.cm.) (°C.) (hr.)}}$ $\times$ 8.063 $\times$ 10^{-1} = $\dfrac{\text{Btu (in.)}}{\text{(sq.ft.) (°F.) (hr.)}}$

$\times$ 6.719 $\times$ 10^{-2} = $\dfrac{\text{Btu (ft.)}}{\text{(sq.ft.) (°F.) (hr.)}}$

$\dfrac{\text{(g.-cal.) (cm.)}}{\text{(sq.cm.) (°C.) (sec.)}}$ $\times$ 2.903 $\times$ 10^{3} = $\dfrac{\text{Btu (in.)}}{\text{(sq.ft.) (°F.) (hr.)}}$

$\times$ 8.063 $\times$ 10^{-1} = $\dfrac{\text{Btu (in.)}}{\text{(sq.ft.) (°F.) (sec.)}}$

$\times$ 8.506 $\times$ 10^{2} = $\dfrac{\text{(joules) (in.)}}{\text{(sq.ft.) (°F.) (sec.)}}$

Specific Gravity (Liquid)

$$s = \dfrac{\rho \text{ of liquid @ 60° F.*}}{\rho \text{ of water @ 60° F.*}}$$

* or at other specified temperature

Oil

$$s \text{ at } 60° \text{ F.}/60° \text{ F.} = \dfrac{141.5}{131.5 + \text{degrees API}}$$

Liquids Lighter Than Water

$$s \text{ @ } 60° \text{ F.}/60° \text{ F.} = \dfrac{140}{130 + \text{degrees Baume}'}$$

Liquids Heavier Than Water

$$s \text{ @ } 60° \text{ F.}/60° \text{ F.} = \dfrac{145}{145 - \text{degrees Baume}'}$$

Specific Gravity (Gases)

$$S_g = \dfrac{\text{R of air}}{\text{R of gas}} = \dfrac{53.3}{\text{R of gas}}, \text{ where R = gas constant}$$

$$S_g = \dfrac{\text{mol. wt. (gas)}}{\text{mol. wt. (air)}} = \dfrac{\text{mol. wt. (gas)}}{29}$$

Density, Liquid ρ

Density liquid, ρ = (62.3 lb./cu. ft. water) (Sp. Gr. liquid), pounds /cu. ft.

Metric

1 gram = 10 decigrams
= 100 centigrams
= 1,000 milligrams
= 1,000,000 microgram
= 0.001 kilogram
= 10^{-6} megagram

1 liter = 10 deciliters = 1.0567 liquid quarts

10 liters = 1 dekaliter = 2.6417 liquid gallons

10 dekaliters = 1 hectoliter = 2.8375 U. S. bushels

1 meter = 10 decimeters = 39.37 inches
= 100 centimeters
= 1,000 millimeters
= 1,000,000 miscrons = 1,000,000 micrometers
= 1/1,000 kilometer
= 10^{10} Angstrom units

10 millimeters = 1 centimeter = 0.3937 inches

10 centimeters = 1 decimeter = 3.937 inches

25.4 millimeters = 1 inch

Specific Heat

$\dfrac{\text{(gram-cal.)}}{\text{(gram) (°C.)}}$ $\times$ 1.8 = $\dfrac{\text{Btu}}{\text{(pound) (°C.)}}$

$\times$ 1.0 = $\dfrac{\text{Btu}}{\text{(pound) (°F.)}}$

A-2.
(Concluded). Physical Property Conversion Factors

$$\times\ 4.186 = \frac{\text{joules}}{(\text{gram})\,(^{\circ}\text{C.})}$$

$$\times\ 1055 = \frac{\text{joules}}{(\text{pound})\,(^{\circ}\text{F.})}$$

$$\times\ 1.163 \times 10^{-3} = \frac{\text{kilowatt-hours}}{(\text{kilogram})\,(^{\circ}\text{C.})}$$

$$\times\ 2.930 \times 10^{-4} = \frac{\text{kilowatt-hours}}{(\text{pound})\,(^{\circ}\text{F.})}$$

Specific heat of water at 1 atm. = 0.238 cal./gm-°C.
Btu/lb. − ° F. × 0.2390 = Btu/lb. − ° R

Heat Transfer Coefficient

PCU/(hr.) (sq. ft.) (°C.) × 1.0
= Btu/(hr.)(sq.ft.)(°F)
Kg-cal./(hr.)(sq. m.)(°C.) × 0.2048
= Btu/(hr.)(sq.ft.)(°F)
G-cal./(sec.)(sq. cm.)(°C.) × 7,380
= Btu/(hr.)(sq.ft.)(°F)
Watts/(sq. in.)(°F.) × 490 = Btu/(hr.)(sq. ft.)(°F.)

Energy Units

Pound-Centigrade-Unit(PCU) × 1.8 = Btu
  × 0.45359 = calorie
  × 1400.4 = ft.-lb.
  × 0.0005276 =
  kilowatt-hr.
  × 1899.36 = joules

Calories × 3.9683 = Btu
  × 3091.36 = ft.-lb.
  × 0.001559 = horsepower-hr.
  × 0.001163 = kilowatt-hr.
  × 4187.37 = joules

Pressure

1 mm Hg = 1,333 dynes/sq. cm.
750 mm Hg = 10 dynes/sq. cm. = 1 megabar @ °C.
and g = 980.6

A-3.
Synchronous Speeds

$$\text{Synchronous Speed} = \frac{\text{Frequency} \times 120}{\text{No. of Poles}}$$

	FREQUENCY				FREQUENCY	
Poles	60 cycle	50 cycle	25 cycle	Poles	60 cycle	50 cycle
2	3600	3000	1500	42	171.4	142.9
4	1800	1500	750	44	163.6	136.4
6	1200	1000	500	46	156.5	130.4
8	900	750	375	48	150	125
10	720	600	300	50	144	120
12	600	500	250	52	138.5	115.4
14	514.3	428.6	214.3	54	133.3	111.1
16	450	375	187.5	56	128.6	107.1
18	400	333.3	166.7	58	124.1	103.5
20	360	300	150	60	120	100
22	327.2	272.7	136.4	62	116.1	96.8
24	300	250	125	64	112.5	93.7
26	276.9	230.8	115.4	66	109.1	90.9
28	257.1	214.3	107.1	68	105.9	88.2
30	240	200	100	70	102.9	85.7
32	225	187.5	93.7	72	100	83.3
34	211.8	176.5	88.2	74	97.3	81.1
36	200	166.7	83.3	76	94.7	78.9
38	189.5	157.9	78.9	78	92.3	76.9
40	180	150	75	80	90	75

Courtesy Ingersoll-Rand Co.

A-4.
Conversion Factors

Units of Length	Multiply units in left column by proper factor below							
	in.	ft.	yd.	mile	mm.	cm.	m.	km.
1 inch	1	0.0833	0.0278	——	25.40	2.540	0.0254	——
1 foot	12	1	0.3333	——	304.8	30.48	0.3048	——
1 yard	36	3	1	——	914.4	91.44	0.9144	——
1 mile	——	5280	1760	1	——	——	1609.3	1.609
1 millimeter	0.0394	0.0033	——	——	1	0.100	0.001	——
1 centimeter	0.3937	0.0328	0.0109	——	10	1	0.01	——
1 meter	39.37	3.281	1.094	——	1000	100	1	0.001
1 kilometer	——	3281	1094	0.6214	——	——	1000	1

(1 micron = 0.001 millimeter)

Courtesy Ingersoll-Rand Co.

(Continued on next page)

A-4.
(Continued). Conversion Factors

Units of Weight	Multiply units in left column by proper factor below						
	grain	oz.	lb.	ton	gram	kg.	metric ton
1 grain	1	——	——	——	0.0648	——	——
1 ounce	437.5	1	0.0625	——	28.35	0.0283	——
1 pound	7000	16	1	0.0005	453.6	0.4536	——
1 ton	——	32,000	2000	1	——	907.2	0.9072
1 gram	15.43	0.0353	——	——	1	0.001	——
1 kilogram	——	35.27	2.205	——	1000	1	0.001
1 metric ton	——	35,274	2205	1.1023	——	1000	1

Units of Density	Multiply units in left column by proper factor below				
	lb/cu. in.	lb/cu. ft.	lb/gal.	g/cu. cm.	g/liter
1 pound/cu. in.	1	1728	231.0	27.68	27,680
1 pound/cu. ft.	——	1	0.1337	0.0160	16.019
1 pound/gal.	0.00433	7.481	1	0.1198	119.83
1 gram/cu. cm.	0.0361	62.43	8.345	1	1000.0
1 gram/liter	——	0.0624	0.00835	0.001	1

Units of Area	Multiply units in left column by proper factor below						
	sq. in.	sq. ft.	acre	sq. mile	sq. cm.	sq. m.	hectare
1 sq. inch	1	0.0069	——	——	6.452	——	——
1 sq. foot	144	1	——	——	929.0	0.0929	——
1 acre	——	43,560	1	0.0016	——	4047	0.4047
1 sq. mile	——	——	640	1	——	——	259.0
1 sq. centimeter	0.1550	——	——	——	1	0.0001	——
1 sq. meter	1550	10.76	——	——	10,000	1	——
1 hectare	——	——	2.471	——	——	10,000	1

Units of Volume	Multiply units in left column by proper factor below							
	cu. in.	cu. ft.	cu. yd.	cu. cm.	cu. meter	liter	U.S. gal.	Imp. gal.
1 cu. inch	1	——	——	16.387	——	0.0164	——	——
1 cu. foot	1728	1	0.0370	28,317	0.0283	28.32	7.481	6.229
1 cu. yard	46,656	27	1	——	0.7646	764.5	202.0	168.2
1 cu. centimeter	0.0610	——	——	1	——	0.0010	——	——
1 cu. meter	61,023	35.31	1.308	1,000,000	1	999.97	264.2	220.0
1 liter	61.025	0.0353	——	1000.028	0.0010	1	0.2642	0.2200
1 U.S. gallon	231	0.1337	——	3785.4	——	3.785	1	0.8327
1 Imperial gallon	277.4	0.1605	——	4546.1	——	4.546	1.201	1

(Continued on next page)

Units of Pressure	Multiply units in left column by proper factor below						
	lb/sq. in.	lb/sq. ft.	int. ata.	kg/cm²	mm Hg at 32°F	in. Hg at 32°F	ft. water at 39.2°F
1 pound/sq. in.	1	144	——	0.0703	51.713	2.0359	2.307
1 pound/sq. ft.	0.00694	1	——	——	0.3591	0.01414	0.01602
1 intern. atmosphere	14.696	2116.2	1	1.0333	760	29.921	33.90
1 kilogram/sq. cm.	14.223	2048.1	0.9678	1	735.56	28.958	32.81
1 millimeter-mercury— 1 torr (torricelli)—	0.0193	2.785	——	——	1	0.0394	0.0446
1 inch mercury	0.4912	70.73	0.0334	0.0345	25.400	1	1.133
1 foot water	0.4335	62.42	——	0.0305	22.418	0.8826	1

Units of Energy	Multiply units in left column by proper factor below					
	ft.-lb.	Btu	g. cal.	Joule	kw-hr.	hp-hr.
1 foot-pound	1	0.001285	0.3240	1.3556	——	——
1 Btu	778.2	1	252.16	1054.9	——	——
1 gram calorie	3.0860	0.003966	1	4.1833	——	——
1 int. Joule	0.7377	0.000948	0.2390	1	——	——
1 int. kilowatt-hour	2,655,656	3412.8	860,563	——	1	1.3412
1 horsepower-hour	1,980,000	2544.5	641,617	——	0.7456	1

Units of Specific Energy	Multiply units in left column by proper factor below				
	absolute Joule/g	int. Joule/g	cal/g	int. cal/g	Btu/lb.
1 absolute Joule/gram	1	0.99984	0.23901	0.23885	0.42993
1 int. Joule/gram	1.000165	1	0.23904	0.23892	0.43000
1 calorie/gram	4.1840	4.1833	1	0.99935	1.7988
1 int. calorie/gram	4.1867	4.1860	1.00065	1	1.8000
1 Btu/lb.	2.3260	2.3256	0.55592	0.55556	1

Units of Power (rates of energy use)	Multiply units in left column by proper factor below								
	hp	watt	kw	Btu/min.	Btu/hr.	ft-lb/sec.	ft-lb/min.	g. cal/sec.	metric hp
1 horsepower	1	745.7	0.7475	42.41	2544.5	550	33.000	178.2	1.014
1 watt	——	1	0.001	0.0569	3.413	0.7376	44.25	0.2390	0.00136
1 kilowatt	1.3410	1000	1	56.88	3412.8	737.6	44,254	239.0	1.360
1 Btu per minute	——	——	——	1	60	12.97	778.2	4.203	0.0239
1 metric hp	0.9863	735.5	0.7355	41.83	2509.6	542.5	32.550	175.7	1

Units of Refrigeration	Multiply units in left column by factor below					
	Btu(IT)/min.	Btu(IT)/hr.	kg cal/hr.	ton (U.S.) comm	ton (BRIT.) comm	frigorie/hr.
1 ton (U.S.) comm	200	12,000	3025.9	1	0.8965	3025.9
1 ton (Brit) comm	223.08	13,385	3375.2	1.1154	1	3375.2
1 frigorie/hr.	0.06609	3.9657	1	0.0003305	0.0002963	1

Note:—Btu is International Steam Table Btu(IT). 1 frigorie = 1 kg cal (**Not** IT).

A-5.
Temperature Conversion

NOTE: The center column of numbers in boldface refers to the temperature in degrees, either Centigrade or Fahrenheit, which it is desired to convert into the other scale. If converting from Fahrenheit to Centigrade degrees, the equivalent temperature will be found in the left column, while if converting from degrees Centigrade to degrees Fahrenhiet, the answer will be found in the column on the right.

Centigrade		Fahrenheit
-273.17	-459.7	
-268	-450	
-262	-440	
-257	-430	
-251	-420	
-246	-410	
-240	-400	
-234	-390	
-229	-380	
-223	-370	
-218	-360	
-212	-350	
-207	-340	
-201	-330	
-196	-320	
-190	-310	
-184	-300	
-179	-290	
-173	-280	
-169	-273	-459.4
-168	-270	-454
-162	-260	-436
-157	-250	-418
-151	-240	-400
-146	-230	-382
-140	-220	-364
-134	-210	-346
-129	-200	-328
-123	-190	-310
-118	-180	-292
-112	-170	-274
-107	-160	-256
-101	-150	-238
-96	-140	-220
-90	-130	-202
-84	-120	-184
-79	-110	-166
-73.3	-100	-148.0
-67.8	-90	-130.0
-62.2	-80	-112.0
-59.4	-75	-103.0
-56.7	-70	-94.0
-53.9	-65	-85.0
-51.1	-60	-76.0
-48.3	-55	-67.0
-45.6	-50	-58.0
-42.8	-45	-49.0
-40.0	-40	-40.0
-37.2	-35	-31.0
-34.4	-30	-22.0
-31.7	-25	-13.0
-28.9	-20	-4.0
-26.1	-15	5.0
-23.3	-10	14.0

Centigrade		Fahrenheit
-20.6	-5	23.0
-17.8	0	32.0
-17.2	1	33.8
-16.7	2	35.6
-16.1	3	37.4
-15.6	4	39.2
-15.0	5	41.0
-14.4	6	42.8
-13.9	7	44.6
-13.3	8	46.4
-12.8	9	48.2
-12.2	10	50.0
-11.7	11	51.8
-11.1	12	53.6
-10.6	13	55.4
-10.0	14	57.2
-9.4	15	59.0
-8.9	16	60.8
-8.3	17	62.6
-7.8	18	64.4
-7.2	19	66.2
-6.7	20	68.0
-6.1	21	69.8
-5.6	22	71.6
-5.0	23	73.4
-4.4	24	75.2
-3.9	25	77.0
-3.3	26	78.8
-2.8	27	80.6
-2.2	28	82.4
-1.7	29	84.2
-1.1	30	86.0
-0.6	31	87.8
0.0	32	89.6
0.6	33	91.4
1.1	34	93.2
1.7	35	95.0
2.2	36	96.8
2.8	37	98.6
3.3	38	100.4
3.9	39	102.2
4.4	40	104.0
5.0	41	105.8
5.6	42	107.6
6.1	43	109.4
6.7	44	111.2
7.2	45	113.0
7.8	46	114.8
8.3	47	116.6
8.9	48	118.4
9.4	49	120.2
10.0	50	122.0
10.6	51	123.8

Centigrade		Fahrenheit
11.1	52	125.6
11.7	53	127.4
12.2	54	129.2
12.8	55	131.0
13.3	56	132.8
13.9	57	134.6
14.4	58	136.4
15.0	59	138.2
15.6	60	140.0
16.1	61	141.8
16.7	62	143.6
17.2	63	145.4
17.8	64	147.2
18.3	65	149.0
18.9	66	150.8
19.4	67	152.6
20.0	68	154.4
20.6	69	156.2
21.1	70	158.0
21.7	71	159.8
22.2	72	161.6
22.8	73	163.4
23.3	74	165.2
23.9	75	167.0
24.4	76	168.8
25.0	77	170.6
25.6	78	172.4
26.1	79	174.2
26.7	80	176.0
27.2	81	177.8
27.8	82	179.6
28.3	83	181.4
28.9	84	183.2
29.4	85	185.0
30.0	86	186.8
30.6	87	188.6
31.1	88	190.4
31.7	89	192.2
32.2	90	194.0
32.8	91	195.8
33.3	92	197.6
33.9	93	199.4
34.4	94	201.2
35.0	95	203.0
35.6	96	204.8
36.1	97	206.6
36.7	98	208.4
37.2	99	210.2
37.8	100	212.0
40.6	105	221
43.3	110	230
46.1	115	239
48.9	120	248
51.7	125	257

Centigrade		Fahrenheit
54.4	130	266
57.2	135	275
60.0	140	284
62.8	145	293
65.6	150	302
68.3	155	311
71.1	160	320
73.9	165	329
76.7	170	338
79.4	175	347
82.2	180	356
85.0	185	365
87.8	190	374
90.6	195	383
93.3	200	392
96.1	205	401
98.9	210	410
100.0	212	414
102	215	419
104	220	428
107	225	437
110	230	446
113	235	455
116	240	464
118	245	473
121	250	482
124	255	491
127	260	500
129	265	509
132	270	518
135	275	527
138	280	536
141	285	545
143	290	554
146	295	563
149	300	572
154	310	590
160	320	608
166	330	626
171	340	644
177	350	662
182	360	680
188	370	698
193	380	716
199	390	734
204	400	752
210	410	770
216	420	788
221	430	806
227	440	824
232	450	842
238	460	860
243	470	878
249	480	896
254	490	914
260	500	932

The formulas at the right may also be used for converting Centigrade or Fahrenheit degrees into the other scales.

$$\text{Degrees Cent., } °C = \frac{5}{9}\,(°F + 40) - 40$$

$$= \frac{5}{9}\,(°F - 32)$$

$$\text{Degrees Kelvin, } °K = °C + 273.2$$

$$\text{Degrees Fahr., } °F = \frac{9}{5}\,(°C + 40) - 40$$

$$= \frac{9}{5}\,C + 32$$

$$\text{Degrees Rankine, } °R = °F + 459.7$$

A-6.
Altitude and Atmospheric Pressures

Altitude above Sea Level			Tempera-ture**		Barometer*		Atmospheric Pressure	
Feet*	Miles	Meters*	°F	°C	Inches Hg Abs.	mm Hg Abs.	PSIA	Kg/sq cm Abs.
−5000	———	−1526	77	25	35.58	903.7	17.48	1.229
−4500	———	−1373	75	24	35.00	889.0	17.19	1.209
−4000	———	−1220	73	23	34.42	874.3	16.90	1.188
−3500	———	−1068	71	22	33.84	859.5	16.62	1.169
−3000	———	−915	70	21	33.27	845.1	16.34	1.149
−2500	———	−763	68	20	32.70	830.6	16.06	1.129
−2000	———	−610	66	19	32.14	816.4	15.78	1.109
−1500	———	−458	64	18	31.58	802.1	15.51	1.091
−1000	———	−305	63	17	31.02	787.9	15.23	1.071
−500	———	−153	61	16	30.47	773.9	14.96	1.052
0	———	0	59	15	29.92	760.0	14.696	1.0333
500	———	153	57	14	29.38	746.3	14.43	1.015
1000	———	305	55	13	28.86	733.0	14.16	.956
1500	———	458	54	12	28.33	719.6	13.91	.978
2000	———	610	52	11	27.82	706.6	13.66	.960
2500		763	50	10	27.32	693.9	13.41	.943
3000	———	915	48	9	26.82	681.2	13.17	.926
3500	———	1068	47	8	26.33	668.8	12.93	.909
4000	———	1220	45	7	25.84	656.3	12.69	.892
4500	———	1373	43	6	25.37	644.4	12.46	.876
5000	0.95	1526	41	5	24.90	632.5	12.23	.860
6000	1.1	1831	38	3	23.99	609.3	11.78	.828
7000	1.3	2136	34	1	23.10	586.7	11.34	.797
8000	1.5	2441	31	−1	22.23	564.6	10.91	.767
9000	1.7	2746	27	−3	21.39	543.3	10.50	.738
10,000	1.9	3050	23	−5	20.58	522.7	10.10	.710
15,000	2.8	4577	6	−14	16.89	429.0	8.29	.583
20,000	3.8	6102	−12	−24	13.76	349.5	6.76	.475
25,000	4.7	7628	−30	−34	11.12	282.4	5.46	.384
30,000	5.7	9153	−48	−44	8.903	226.1	4.37	.307
35,000	6.6	10,679	−66		7.060	179.3	3.47	.244
40,000	7.6	12,204	−70	−57	5.558	141.2	2.73	.192
45,000	8.5	13,730	−70	−57	4.375	111.1	2.15	.151
50,000	9.5	15,255	−70	−57	3.444	87.5	1.69	.119
55,000	10.4	16,781	−70	−57	2.712	68.9	1.33	.0935
60,000	11.4	18,306	−70	−57	2.135	54.2	1.05	.0738
70,000	13.3	21,357	−67	−55	1.325	33.7	.651	.0458
80,000	15.2	24,408	−62	−52	†8.273^{-1}	21.0	.406	.0285
90,000	17.1	27,459	−57	−59	5.200^{-1}	13.2	.255	.0179
100,000	18.9	30,510	−51	−46	3.290^{-1}	8.36	.162	.0114
120,000	22.8	36,612	−26	−48	1.358^{-1}	3.45	———	———
140,000	26.6	42,714	4	−16	5.947^{-2}	1.51	———	———
160,000	30.4	48,816	28	−2	2.746^{-2}	†6.97^{-1}	———	———
180,000	34.2	54,918	19	−7	1.284^{-2}	3.26^{-1}	———	———
200,000	37.9	61,020	−3	−19	5.846^{-3}	1.48^{-1}	———	———
220,000	41.7	67,122	−44	−42	2.523^{-3}	6.41^{-2}	———	———
240,000	45.5	73,224	−86	−66	9.955^{-4}	2.53^{-2}	———	———
260,000	49.3	79,326	−129	−90	3.513^{-4}	8.92^{-3}	———	———
280,000	53.1	85,428	−135	−93	1.143^{-4}	3.67^{-3}	———	———
300,000	56.9	91,530	−127	−88	3.737^{-5}	9.49^{-4}	———	———
400,000	75.9	122,040	———	———	6.3^{-7}	1.60^{-5}	———	———
500,000	94.8	152,550	———	———	1.4^{-7}	3.56^{-6}	———	———
600,000	114	183,060	———	———	5.9^{-8}	1.50^{-6}	———	———
800,000	152	244,080	———	———	1.6^{-8}	4.06^{-7}	———	———
1,000,000	189	305,100	———	———	5.1^{-9}	1.30^{-7}	———	———
1,200,000	228	366,120	———	———	2.0^{-9}	5.08^{-8}	———	———
1,400,000	266	427,140	———	———	8.2^{-10}	2.08^{-8}	———	———
1,600,000	304	488,160	———	———	3.8^{-10}	9.65^{-9}	———	———
1,800,000	342	549,180	———	———	1.8^{-10}	4.57^{-9}	———	———
2,000,000	379	610,200	———	———	9.2^{-11}	2.34^{-9}	———	———

Data from NASA Standard Atmosphere (1962).

*Temperature and barometer are approximate for negative altitudes.

**Temperatures are average existing at 40° latitude and are rounded to even numbers.

†Negative exponent shows number of spaces the decimal point must be moved to the left.

Courtesy Ingersoll-Rand Co.

A-7.
Vapor Pressure Curves. (Courtesy Ingersoll-Rand Co.)

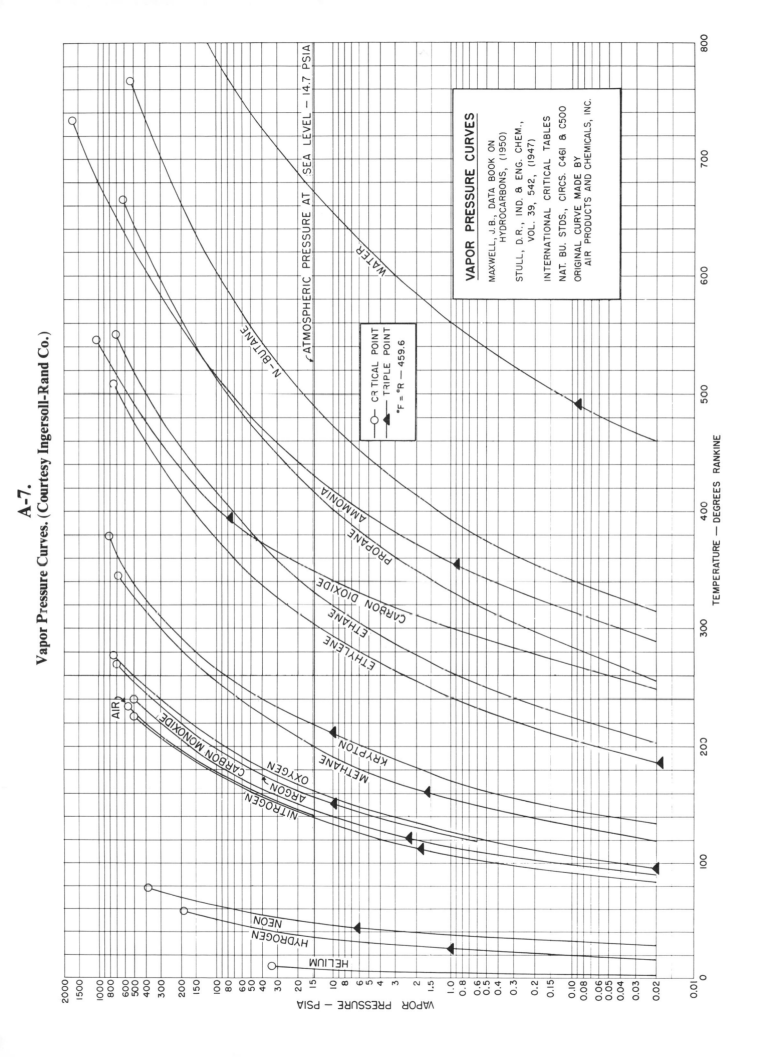

A-8.
Pressure Conversion Chart

BY FACTOR TO OBTAIN →

MULTIPLY GIVEN NUMBER OF →

GIVEN	lb/in²	in H₂O (at +39.2°F)	cm H₂O (at +4°C)	in Hg (at +32°F)	mm Hg (Torr) (at 0°C)	dyne/cm² (1μ bar)	newton/m² (PASCAL)	kgm/cm²	bar	atm. (A_n)	lb/ft²	ft H₂O (at +39.2°F)
lb/in²	1.0000	2.7680×10^1	7.0308×10^1	2.0360	5.1715×10^1	6.8948×10^4	6.8948×10^3	7.0306×10^{-2}	6.8947×10^{-2}	6.8045×10^{-2}	1.4400×10^2	2.3067
in H₂O (at +39.2°F)	3.6127×10^{-2}	1.0000	2.5400	7.3554×10^{-2}	1.8683	2.4908×10^3	2.4908×10^2	2.5399×10^{-3}	2.4908×10^{-3}	2.4582×10^{-3}	5.2022	8.3333×10^{-2}
cm H₂O (at +4°C)	1.4223×10^{-2}	0.3937	1.0000	2.8958×10^{-2}	0.7355	9.8064×10^2	9.8064×10^1	9.9997×10^{-4}	9.8064×10^{-4}	9.6781×10^{-4}	2.0481	3.2808×10^{-2}
in Hg (at +32°F)	4.9116×10^{-1}	1.3596×10^1	3.4532×10^1	1.0000	2.5400×10^1	3.3864×10^4	3.3864×10^3	3.4532×10^{-2}	3.3864×10^{-2}	3.3421×10^{-2}	7.0727×10^1	1.1330
mm Hg (Torr) (at 0°C)	1.9337×10^{-2}	5.3525×10^{-1}	1.3595	3.9370×10^{-2}	1.0000	1.3332×10^3	1.3332×10^2	1.3595×10^{-3}	1.3332×10^{-3}	1.3158×10^{-3}	2.7845	4.4605×10^{-2}
dyne/cm² (1μ bar)	1.4504×10^{-5}	4.0147×10^{-4}	1.0197×10^{-3}	2.9530×10^{-5}	7.5006×10^{-4}	1.0000	1.0000×10^{-1}	1.0197×10^{-6}	1.0000×10^{-6}	9.8692×10^{-7}	2.0886×10^{-3}	3.3456×10^{-5}
newton/m² (PASCAL)	1.4504×10^{-4}	4.0147×10^{-3}	1.0197×10^{-2}	2.9530×10^{-4}	7.5006×10^{-3}	1.0000×10^1	1.0000	1.0197×10^{-5}	1.0000×10^{-5}	9.8692×10^{-6}	2.0885×10^{-2}	3.3456×10^{-4}
kgm/cm²	1.4224×10^1	3.9371×10^2	1.00003×10^3	2.8959×10^1	7.3556×10^2	9.8060×10^5	9.8060×10^4	1.0000	9.8060×10^{-1}	9.678×10^{-1}	2.0482×10^3	3.2809×10^1
bar	1.4504×10^1	4.0147×10^2	1.0197×10^3	2.9530×10^1	7.5006×10^2	1.0000×10^6	1.0000×10^5	1.0197	1.0000	9.8692×10^{-1}	2.0885×10^3	3.3456×10^1
atm. (A_n)	1.4696×10^1	4.0679×10^2	1.0333×10^3	2.9921×10^1	7.6000×10^2	1.0133×10^6	1.0133×10^5	1.0332	1.0133	1.0000	2.1162×10^3	3.3900×10^1
lb/ft²	6.9445×10^{-3}	1.9223×10^{-1}	4.882×10^{-1}	1.4139×10^{-2}	3.591×10^{-1}	4.7880×10^2	4.7880×10^1	4.8824×10^{-4}	4.7880×10^{-4}	4.7254×10^{-4}	1.0000	1.6019×10^{-2}
ft H₂O (at +39.2°F)	4.3352×10^{-1}	1.2000×10^1	3.0480×10^1	8.826×10^{-1}	2.2419×10^1	2.9890×10^4	2.9890×10^3	3.0479×10^{-2}	2.9890×10^{-2}	2.9499×10^{-2}	6.2427×10^1	1.0000

A-9.
Vacuum Conversion

Torr	Absolute Pressure		Inches Hg (Abs.)	Psia	Vacuum* Inches Hg
	Microns Hg	Mm Hg			
		762	30.00	14.74	—
		750	29.53	14.50	0.47
		700	27.56	13.54	2.44
		650	25.59	12.57	4.41
		600	23.62	11.60	6.38
		550	21.65	10.64	8.35
		500	19.68	9.67	10.32
		450	17.72	8.70	12.28
		400	15.75	7.74	14.25
		350	13.78	6.77	16.22
		300	11.81	5.80	18.19
		250	9.84	4.84	20.16
		200	7.84	3.87	22.13
		150	5.91	2.900	24.09
		100	3.94	1.934	26.06
		50	1.97	.967	28.03
		40	1.57	.774	28.43
		30	1.181	.580	28.82
		20	0.787	.3868	
		10	0.394	.1934	
		5	.197	.0967	
		4	.158	.0774	
		3	.1181	.0580	
		2	.0787	.0387	
1.0	1000	1	.0392	.0193	
0.5	500	0.50	.0197		Low Vacuum
1×10^{-1}	100	0.10	.0039		
5×10^{-2}	50	0.050			
1×10^{-2}	10	0.010			
5×10^{-3}	5	0.005			
1×10^{-3}	1	0.001			
1×10^{-4} to 1×10^{-6}					High Vacuum
1×10^{-6} to 1×10^{-9}					Very High Vac.
1×10^{-9} and beyond					Ultra High Vac.

*Refers to 30″ Barometer

Conversion Factors:
1 millimeter = 1000 microns   1 inch Hg = 25.4 mm Hg
1 Torr = 1 mm Hg Abs.   1 atmosphere = 14.7 pounds per sq. in. = 760 mm Hg = 29.92 in. Hg

Courtesy Pfaudler Co., Div. of Sybron Corp.

A-10.
Decimal and Millimeter Equivalents of Fractions

Inches (Fractions)	Inches (Decimals)	Milli-meters	Inches (Fractions)	Inches (Decimals)	Milli-meters
1/64	.015625	.397	33/64	.515625	13.097
1/32	.03125	.794	17/32	.53125	13.494
3/64	.046875	1.191	35/64	.546875	13.891
1/16	.0625	1.588	9/16	.5625	14.288
5/64	.078125	1.984	37/64	.578125	14.684
3/32	.09375	2.381	19/32	.59375	15.081
7/64	.109375	2.778	39/64	.609375	15.478
1/8	.125	3.175	5/8	.625	15.875
9/64	.140625	3.572	41/64	.640625	16.272
5/32	.15625	3.969	21/32	.65625	16.669
11/64	.171875	4.366	43/64	.671875	17.066
3/16	.1875	4.763	11/16	.6875	17.463
13/64	.203125	5.159	45/64	.703125	17.859
7/32	.21875	5.556	23/32	.71875	18.256
15/64	.234375	5.953	47/64	.734375	18.653
1/4	.250	6.350	3/4	.750	19.050
17/64	.265625	6.747	49/64	.765625	19.447
9/32	.28125	7.144	25/32	.78125	19.844
19/64	.296875	7.541	51/64	.796875	20.241
5/16	.3125	7.938	13/16	.8125	20.638
21/64	.328125	8.334	53/64	.828125	21.034
11/32	.34375	8.731	27/32	.83475	21.431
23/64	.359375	9.128	55/64	.859375	21.828
3/8	.375	9.525	7/8	.875	22.225
25/64	.390625	9.922	57/64	.890625	22.622
13/32	.40625	10.319	29/32	.90625	23.019
27/64	.421875	10.716	59/64	.921875	23.416
7/16	.4375	11.113	15/16	.9375	23.813
29/64	.453125	11.509	61/64	.953125	24.209
15/32	.46875	11.906	31/32	.96875	24.606
31/64	.484375	12.303	63/64	.984375	25.003
1/2	.500	12.700	1	1.000	25.400

A-11.
Particle Size Measurement

Meshes/Lineal Inch US and ASTM Std. Sieve No.	Actual Opening (Inches)	Actual Opening (Microns)	Meshes/Lineal Inch US and ASTM Std. Sieve No.	Actual Opening (Inches)	Actual Opening (Microns)
10	.0787	2000	170	.0035	88
12	.0661 1/6	1680	200	.0029	74
14	.0555	1410		.0026	65
16	.0469 3/64	1190	230	.0024	62
18	.0394	1000	270	.0021	53
20	.0331 1/32	840		.0020	50
25	.0280	710	325	.0017	44
30	.0232	590		.0016	40
35	.0197 1/64	500	400	.00142	36
40	.0165	420		.00118	30
45	.0138	350	550	.00099	25
50	.0117	297	625	.00079	20
60	.0098	250		.00059	15
70	.0083	210	1,250	.000394	10
80	.0070	177	1,750	.000315	8
100	.0059	149	2,500	.000197	5
120	.0049	125	5,000	.000099	2.5
140	.0041	105	12,000	.0000394	1

* 1 micron (μ) = 1 micrometer (μm), new National Bureau of Standards terminology
1 micron = one-millionth of a meter
Inches $\times$ 25,400 = microns or micrometers
Reference ASTM E 11-70

A-12.
Viscosity Conversions. (By permission, Tube Turns Div., Chemetron Corp., Bull. TT 725.)

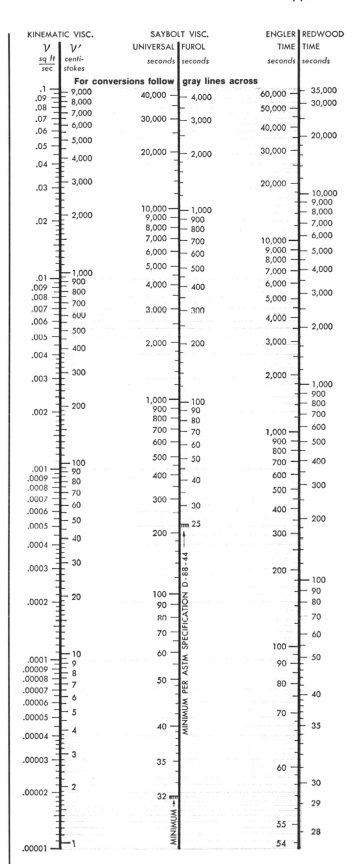

KINEMATIC VISC.		SAYBOLT VISC.		ENGLER	REDWOOD
ν $\frac{sq\ ft}{sec}$	ν' centi-stokes	UNIVERSAL seconds	FUROL seconds	TIME seconds	TIME seconds

For conversions follow gray lines across

MINIMUM PER ASTM SPECIFICATION D-88-44

into sq ft per sec (ν)

$\nu = 0.000\ 010\ 76\ \nu'$

....

converted from ASTM Spec. D-446-39

converted from ASTM Spec. D-666-44

$\nu = 0.000\ 001\ 58\ \mathrm{Engler} - \dfrac{0.00403}{\mathrm{Engler}}$

$\nu = 0.000\ 002\ 80\ \mathrm{Redwood} - \dfrac{0.00185}{\mathrm{Redwood}}$

$\nu = 32.2\ \mu\ \dfrac{(\text{lb sec per sq ft})}{\rho\ (\text{lb per cu ft})}$

into centistokes (ν')

....

$\nu' = 92\ 900\ \nu$

see Table I in ASTM Spec. D-446-39 (plotted for basic temperature 100 F)

see Table I in ASTM Spec. D-666-44 (plotted for std temp of 122 F)

$\nu' = 0.147\ \mathrm{Engler} - \dfrac{374}{\mathrm{Engler}}$

$\nu' = 0.260\ \mathrm{Redwood} - \dfrac{171.5}{\mathrm{Redwood}}$

$\nu' = \dfrac{\text{centipoises}}{\text{density}}$

To convert:

from Metric units (centistokes)

from English units (sq ft per sec)

from Saybolt Universal (seconds)

from Saybolt Furol (seconds)

from Engler (seconds)

from Redwood standard (seconds)

from absolute viscosity

To convert other units in- to kinematic viscosity in English units ν (sq ft per sec) or in Metric units ν' (centistokes), use the chart or the formulas to the right:

Liquids heavier than water (U.S. Bureau of Stds.)

$$\text{Specific gravity} = \frac{145}{145 - \text{Degrees Baumé}}$$

Liquids lighter than water (API Formula)

$$\text{Specific gravity } 60/60F = \frac{141.5}{131.5 + \text{Degrees API}}$$

To convert degrees API and Baumé into Specific Gravity, use the formulas to right:

A-13.

Viscosity Conversions. (Courtesy Kinney Vacuum Div., The New York Air Brake Co.)

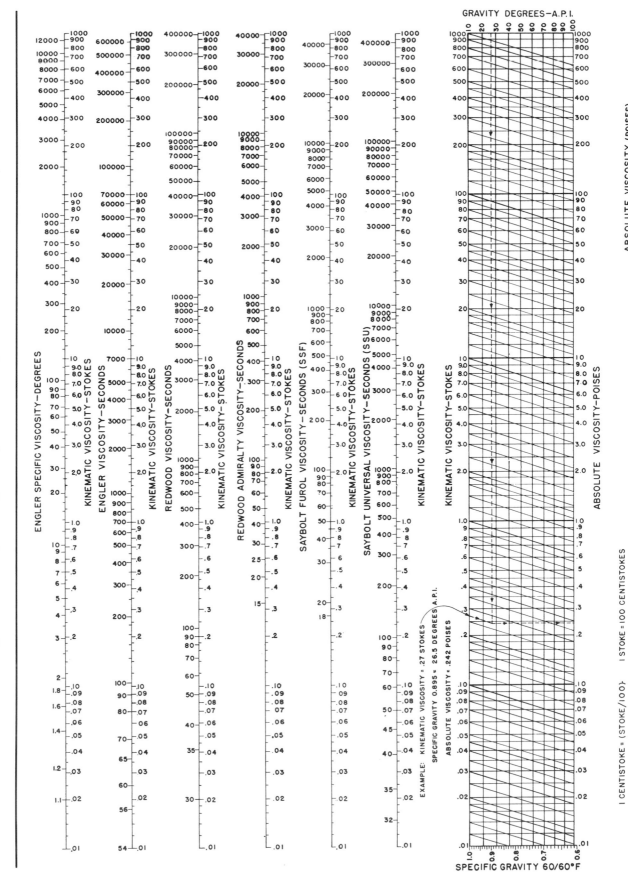

A-14.
Commercial Wrought Steel Pipe Data
(Based on ANSI B36.10 wall thicknesses)

Schedule	Nominal Pipe Size (Inches)	Outside Diameter (Inches)	Thickness (Inches)	Inside Diameter d (Inches)	Inside Diameter D (Feet)	d^2	d^3	d^4	d^5	Transverse Internal Area a (Sq. In.)	Transverse Internal Area A (Sq. Ft.)
Schedule 10	14	14	0.250	13.5	1.125	182.25	2460.4	33215.	448400.	143.14	0.994
	16	16	0.250	15.5	1.291	240.25	3723.9	57720.	894660.	188.69	1.310
	18	18	0.250	17.5	1.4583	306.25	5359.4	93789.	1641309.	240.53	1.670
	20	20	0.250	19.5	1.625	380.25	7414.9	144590.	2819500.	298.65	2.074
	24	24	0.250	23.5	1.958	552.25	12977.	304980.	7167030.	433.74	3.012
	30	30	0.312	29.376	2.448	862.95	25350.	744288.	21864218.	677.76	4.707
Schedule 20	8	8.625	0.250	8.125	0.6771	66.02	536.38	4359.3	35409.	51.85	0.3601
	10	10.75	0.250	10.25	0.8542	105.06	1076.9	11038.	113141.	82.52	0.5731
	12	12.75	0.250	12.25	1.021	150.06	1838.3	22518.	275855.	117.86	0.8185
	14	14	0.312	13.376	1.111	178.92	2393.2	32012.	428185.	140.52	0.9758
	16	16	0.312	15.376	1.281	236.42	3635.2	55894.	859442.	185.69	1.290
	18	18	0.312	17.376	1.448	301.92	5246.3	91156.	1583978.	237.13	1.647
	20	20	0.375	19.250	1.604	370.56	7133.3	137317.	2643352.	291.04	2.021
	24	24	0.375	23.25	1.937	540.56	12568.	292205.	6793832.	424.56	2.948
	30	30	0.500	29.00	2.417	841.0	24389.	707281.	20511149.	660.52	4.587
Schedule 30	8	8.625	0.277	8.071	0.6726	65.14	525.75	4243.2	34248.	51.16	0.3553
	10	10.75	0.307	10.136	0.8447	102.74	1041.4	10555.	106987.	80.69	0.5603
	12	12.75	0.330	12.09	1.0075	146.17	1767.2	21366.	258304.	114.80	0.7972
	14	14	0.375	13.25	1.1042	175.56	2326.2	30821.	408394.	137.88	0.9575
	16	16	0.375	15.25	1.2708	232.56	3546.6	54084.	824801.	182.65	1.268
	18	18	0.438	17.124	1.4270	293.23	5021.3	85984.	1472397.	230.30	1.599
	20	20	0.500	19.00	1.5833	361.00	6859.0	130321.	2476099.	283.53	1.969
	24	24	0.562	22.876	1.9063	523.31	11971.	273853.	6264703.	411.00	2.854
	30	30	0.625	28.75	2.3958	826.56	23764.	683201.	19642160.	649.18	4.508
Schedule 40	1/8	0.405	0.068	0.269	0.0224	0.0724	0.0195	0.005242	0.00141	0.057	0.00040
	1/4	0.540	0.088	0.364	0.0303	0.1325	0.0482	0.01756	0.00639	0.104	0.00072
	3/8	0.675	0.091	0.493	0.0411	0.2430	0.1198	0.05905	0.02912	0.191	0.00133
	1/2	0.840	0.109	0.622	0.0518	0.3869	0.2406	0.1497	0.09310	0.304	0.00211
	3/4	1.050	0.113	0.824	0.0687	0.679	0.5595	0.4610	0.3799	0.533	0.00371
	1	1.315	0.133	1.049	0.0874	1.100	1.154	1.210	1.270	0.864	0.00600
	1 1/4	1.660	0.140	1.380	0.1150	1.904	2.628	3.625	5.005	1.495	0.01040
	1 1/2	1.900	0.145	1.610	0.1342	2.592	4.173	6.718	10.82	2.036	0.01414
	2	2.375	0.154	2.067	0.1722	4.272	8.831	18.250	37.72	3.355	0.02330
	2 1/2	2.875	0.203	2.469	0.2057	6.096	15.051	37.161	91.75	4.788	0.03322
	3	3.500	0.216	3.068	0.2557	9.413	28.878	88.605	271.8	7.393	0.05130
	3 1/2	4.000	0.226	3.548	0.2957	12.59	44.663	158.51	562.2	9.886	0.06870
	4	4.500	0.237	4.026	0.3355	16.21	65.256	262.76	1058.	12.730	0.08840
	5	5.563	0.258	5.047	0.4206	25.47	128.56	648.72	3275.	20.006	0.1390
	6	6.625	0.280	6.065	0.5054	36.78	223.10	1352.8	8206.	28.891	0.2006
	8	8.625	0.322	7.981	0.6651	63.70	508.36	4057.7	32380.	50.027	0.3474
	10	10.75	0.365	10.02	0.8350	100.4	1006.0	10080.	101000.	78.855	0.5475
	12	12.75	0.406	11.938	0.9965	142.5	1701.3	20306.	242470.	111.93	0.7773
	14	14.0	0.438	13.124	1.0937	172.24	2260.5	29666.	389340.	135.28	0.9394
	16	16.0	0.500	15.000	1.250	225.0	3375.0	50625.	759375.	176.72	1.2272
	18	18.0	0.562	16.876	1.4063	284.8	4806.3	81111.	1368820.	223.68	1.5533
	20	20.0	0.593	18.814	1.5678	354.0	6659.5	125320.	2357244.	278.00	1.9305
	24	24.0	0.687	22.626	1.8855	511.9	11583.	262040.	5929784.	402.07	2.7921
Schedule 60	8	8.625	0.406	7.813	0.6511	61.04	476.93	3725.9	29113.	47.94	0.3329
	10	10.75	0.500	9.750	0.8125	95.06	926.86	9036.4	88110.	74.66	0.5185
	12	12.75	0.562	11.626	0.9688	135.16	1571.4	18268.	212399.	106.16	0.7372
	14	14.0	0.593	12.814	1.0678	164.20	2104.0	26962.	345480.	128.96	0.8956
	16	16.0	0.656	14.688	1.2240	215.74	3168.8	46544.	683618.	169.44	1.1766
	18	18.0	0.750	16.500	1.3750	272.25	4492.1	74120.	1222982.	213.83	1.4849
	20	20.0	0.812	18.376	1.5313	337.68	6205.2	114028.	2095342.	265.21	1.8417
	24	24.0	0.968	22.064	1.8387	486.82	10741.	236994.	5229036.	382.35	2.6552
Schedule 80	1/8	0.405	0.095	0.215	0.0179	0.0462	0.00994	0.002134	0.000459	0.036	0.00025
	1/4	0.540	0.119	0.302	0.0252	0.0912	0.0275	0.008317	0.002513	0.072	0.00050
	3/8	0.675	0.126	0.423	0.0353	0.1789	0.0757	0.03200	0.01354	0.141	0.00098
	1/2	0.840	0.147	0.546	0.0455	0.2981	0.1628	0.08886	0.04852	0.234	0.00163
	3/4	1.050	0.154	0.742	0.0618	0.5506	0.4085	0.3032	0.2249	0.433	0.00300
	1	1.315	0.179	0.957	0.0797	0.9158	0.8765	0.8387	0.8027	0.719	0.00499
	1 1/4	1.660	0.191	1.278	0.1065	1.633	2.087	2.6667	3.409	1.283	0.00891

Courtesy Crane Co., Technical Manual 410, Flow of Fluids.   *(Continued on next page)*

A-14.
(Continued). Commercial Wrought Steel Pipe Data
(Based on ANSI B36.10 wall thicknesses)

	Nominal Pipe Size Inches	Outside Diameter Inches	Thickness Inches	Inside Diameter d Inches	Inside Diameter D Feet	d^2	d^3	d^4	d^5	a Sq. In.	A Sq. Ft.
Schedule 80—cont.	1½	1.900	0.200	1.500	0.1250	2.250	3.375	5.062	7.594	1.767	0.01225
	2	2.375	0.218	1.939	0.1616	3.760	7.290	14.136	27.41	2.953	0.02050
	2½	2.875	0.276	2.323	0.1936	5.396	12.536	29.117	67.64	4.238	0.02942
	3	3.5	0.300	2.900	0.2417	8.410	24.389	70.728	205.1	6.605	0.04587
	3½	4.0	0.318	3.364	0.2803	11.32	38.069	128.14	430.8	8.888	0.06170
	4	4.5	0.337	3.826	0.3188	14.64	56.006	214.33	819.8	11.497	0.07986
	5	5.563	0.375	4.813	0.4011	23.16	111.49	536.38	2583.	18.194	0.1263
	6	6.625	0.432	5.761	0.4801	33.19	191.20	1101.6	6346.	26.067	0.1810
	8	8.625	0.500	7.625	0.6354	58.14	443.32	3380.3	25775.	45.663	0.3171
	10	10.75	0.593	9.564	0.7970	91.47	874.82	8366.8	80020.	71.84	0.4989
	12	12.75	0.687	11.376	0.9480	129.41	1472.2	16747.	190523.	101.64	0.7058
	14	14.0	0.750	12.500	1.0417	156.25	1953.1	24414.	305176.	122.72	0.8522
	16	16.0	0.843	14.314	1.1928	204.89	2932.8	41980.	600904.	160.92	1.1175
	18	18.0	0.937	16.126	1.3438	260.05	4193.5	67626.	1090518.	204.24	1.4183
	20	20.0	1.031	17.938	1.4948	321.77	5771.9	103536.	1857248.	252.72	1.7550
	24	24.0	1.218	21.564	1.7970	465.01	10027.	216234.	4662798.	365.22	2.5362
Schedule 100	8	8.625	0.593	7.439	0.6199	55.34	411.66	3062.	22781.	43.46	0.3018
	10	10.75	0.718	9.314	0.7762	86.75	807.99	7526.	69357.	68.13	0.4732
	12	12.75	0.843	11.064	0.9220	122.41	1354.4	14985.	165791.	96.14	0.6677
	14	14.0	0.937	12.126	1.0105	147.04	1783.0	21621.	262173.	115.49	0.8020
	16	16.0	1.031	13.938	1.1615	194.27	2707.7	37740.	526020.	152.58	1.0596
	18	18.0	1.156	15.688	1.3057	246.11	3861.0	60572.	950250.	193.30	1.3423
	20	20.0	1.281	17.438	1.4532	304.08	5302.6	92467.	1612438.	238.83	1.6585
	24	24.0	1.531	20.938	1.7448	438.40	9179.2	192195.	4024179.	344.32	2.3911
Schedule 120	4	4.50	0.438	3.624	0.302	13.133	47.595	172.49	625.1	10.315	0.07163
	5	5.563	0.500	4.563	0.3802	20.82	95.006	433.5	1978.	16.35	0.1136
	6	6.625	0.562	5.501	0.4584	30.26	166.47	915.7	5037.	23.77	0.1650
	8	8.625	0.718	7.189	0.5991	51.68	371.54	2671.	19202.	40.59	0.2819
	10	10.75	0.843	9.064	0.7553	82.16	744.66	6750.	61179.	64.53	0.4481
	12	12.75	1.000	10.750	0.8959	115.56	1242.3	13355.	143563.	90.76	0.6303
	14	14.0	1.093	11.814	0.9845	139.57	1648.9	19480.	230137.	109.62	0.7612
	16	16.0	1.218	13.564	1.1303	183.98	2495.5	33849.	459133.	144.50	1.0035
	18	18.0	1.375	15.250	1.2708	232.56	3546.6	54086.	824804.	182.66	1.2684
	20	20.0	1.500	17.000	1.4166	289.00	4913.0	83521.	1419857.	226.98	1.5762
	24	24.0	1.812	20.376	1.6980	415.18	8459.7	172375.	3512313.	326.08	2.2645
Schedule 140	8	8.625	0.812	7.001	0.5834	49.01	343.15	2402.	16819.	38.50	0.2673
	10	10.75	1.000	8.750	0.7292	76.56	669.92	5862.	51291.	60.13	0.4176
	12	12.75	1.125	10.500	0.8750	110.25	1157.6	12155.	127628.	86.59	0.6013
	14	14.0	1.250	11.500	0.9583	132.25	1520.9	17490.	201136.	103.87	0.7213
	16	16.0	1.438	13.124	1.0937	172.24	2260.5	29666.	389340.	135.28	0.9394
	18	18.0	1.562	14.876	1.2396	221.30	3292.0	48972.	728502.	173.80	1.2070
	20	20.0	1.750	16.5	1.3750	272.25	4492.1	74120.	1222981.	213.82	1.4849
	24	24.0	2.062	19.876	1.6563	395.06	7852.1	156069.	3102022.	310.28	2.1547
Schedule 160	½	0.840	0.187	0.466	0.0388	0.2172	0.1012	0.04716	0.02197	0.1706	0.00118
	¾	1.050	0.218	0.614	0.0512	0.3770	0.2315	0.1421	0.08726	0.2961	0.00206
	1	1.315	0.250	0.815	0.0679	0.6642	0.5413	0.4412	0.3596	0.5217	0.00362
	1¼	1.660	0.250	1.160	0.0966	1.346	1.561	1.811	2.100	1.057	0.00734
	1½	1.900	0.281	1.338	0.1115	1.790	2.395	3.205	4.288	1.406	0.00976
	2	2.375	0.343	1.689	0.1407	2.853	4.818	8.138	13.74	2.241	0.01556
	2½	2.875	0.375	2.125	0.1771	4.516	9.596	20.39	43.33	3.546	0.02463
	3	3.50	0.438	2.624	0.2187	6.885	18.067	47.41	124.4	5.408	0.03755
	4	4.50	0.531	3.438	0.2865	11.82	40.637	139.7	480.3	9.283	0.06447
	5	5.563	0.625	4.313	0.3594	18.60	80.230	346.0	1492.	14.61	0.1015
	6	6.625	0.718	5.189	0.4324	26.93	139.72	725.0	3762.	21.15	0.1469
	8	8.625	0.906	6.813	0.5677	46.42	316.24	2155.	14679.	36.46	0.2532
	10	10.75	1.125	8.500	0.7083	72.25	614.12	5220.	44371.	56.75	0.3941
	12	12.75	1.312	10.126	0.8438	102.54	1038.3	10514.	106461.	80.53	0.5592
	14	14.0	1.406	11.188	0.9323	125.17	1400.4	15668.	175292.	98.31	0.6827
	16	16.0	1.593	12.814	1.0678	164.20	2104.0	26961.	345482.	128.96	0.8956
	18	18.0	1.781	14.438	1.2032	208.45	3009.7	43454.	627387.	163.72	1.1369
	20	20.0	1.968	16.064	1.3387	258.05	4145.3	66590.	1069715.	202.67	1.4074
	24	24.0	2.343	19.314	1.6095	373.03	7204.7	139152.	2687582.	292.98	2.0346

A-14.

(Concluded). Commercial Wrought Steel Pipe Data
(Based on ANSI B36.10 wall thicknesses)

Nominal Pipe Size Inches	Outside Diameter Inches	Thickness Inches	Inside Diameter d Inches	Inside Diameter D Feet	Inside Diameter Functions (In Inches) d^2	d^3	d^4	d^5	Transverse Internal Area a Sq. In.	A Sq. Ft.
Standard Wall Pipe										
⅛	0.405	0.068	0.269	0.0224	0.0724	0.0195	0.00524	0.00141	0.057	0.00040
¼	0.540	0.088	0.364	0.0303	0.1325	0.0482	0.01756	0.00639	0.104	0.00072
⅜	0.675	0.091	0.493	0.0411	0.2430	0.1198	0.05905	0.02912	0.191	0.00133
½	0.840	0.109	0.622	0.0518	0.3869	0.2406	0.1497	0.0931	0.304	0.00211
¾	1.050	0.113	0.824	0.0687	0.679	0.5595	0.4610	0.3799	0.533	0.00371
1	1.315	0.133	1.049	0.0874	1.100	1.154	1.210	1.270	0.864	0.00600
1¼	1.660	0.140	1.380	0.1150	1.904	2.628	3.625	5.005	1.495	0.01040
1½	1.900	0.145	1.610	0.1342	2.592	4.173	6.718	10.82	2.036	0.01414
2	2.375	0.154	2.067	0.1722	4.272	8.831	18.250	37.72	3.355	0.02330
2½	2.875	0.203	2.469	0.2057	6.096	15.051	37.161	91.75	4.788	0.03322
3	3.500	0.216	3.068	0.2557	9.413	28.878	88.605	271.8	7.393	0.05130
3½	4.000	0.226	3.548	0.2957	12.59	44.663	158.51	562.2	9.886	0.06870
4	4.500	0.237	4.026	0.3355	16.21	65.256	262.76	1058.	12.730	0.08840
5	5.563	0.258	5.047	0.4206	25.47	128.56	648.72	3275.	20.006	0.1390
6	6.625	0.280	6.065	0.5054	36.78	223.10	1352.8	8206.	28.891	0.2006
8	8.625	0.277	8.071	0.6725	65.14	525.75	4243.0	34248.	51.161	0.3553
	8.625S	0.322	7.981	0.6651	63.70	508.36	4057.7	32380.	50.027	0.3474
10	10.75	0.279	10.192	0.8493	103.88	1058.7	10789.	109876.	81.585	0.5666
	10.75	0.307	10.136	0.8446	102.74	1041.4	10555.	106987.	80.691	0.5604
	10.75S	0.365	10.020	0.8350	100.4	1006.0	10080.	101000.	78.855	0.5475
12	12.75	0.330	12.090	1.0075	146.17	1767.2	21366.	258300.	114.80	0.7972
	12.75S	0.375	12.000	1.000	144.0	1728.0	20736.	248800.	113.10	0.7854
Extra Strong Pipe										
⅛	0.405	0.095	0.215	0.0179	0.0462	0.00994	0.002134	0.000459	0.036	0.00025
¼	0.540	0.119	0.302	0.0252	0.0912	0.0275	0.008317	0.002513	0.072	0.00050
⅜	0.675	0.126	0.423	0.0353	0.1789	0.0757	0.03201	0.01354	0.141	0.00098
½	0.840	0.147	0.546	0.0455	0.2981	0.1628	0.08886	0.04852	0.234	0.00163
¾	1.050	0.154	0.742	0.0618	0.5506	0.4085	0.3032	0.2249	0.433	0.00300
1	1.315	0.179	0.957	0.0797	0.9158	0.8765	0.8387	0.8027	0.719	0.00499
1¼	1.660	0.191	1.278	0.1065	1.633	2.087	2.6667	3.409	1.283	0.00891
1½	1.900	0.200	1.500	0.1250	2.250	3.375	5.062	7.594	1.767	0.01225
2	2.375	0.218	1.939	0.1616	3.760	7.290	14.136	27.41	2.953	0.02050
2½	2.875	0.276	2.323	0.1936	5.396	12.536	29.117	67.64	4.238	0.02942
3	3.500	0.300	2.900	0.2417	8.410	24.389	70.728	205.1	6.605	0.04587
3½	4.000	0.318	3.364	0.2803	11.32	38.069	128.14	430.8	8.888	0.06170
4	4.500	0.337	3.826	0.3188	14.64	56.006	214.33	819.8	11.497	0.07986
5	5.563	0.375	4.813	0.4011	23.16	111.49	536.6	2583.	18.194	0.1263
6	6.625	0.432	5.761	0.4801	33.19	191.20	1101.6	6346.	26.067	0.1810
8	8.625	0.500	7.625	0.6354	58.14	443.32	3380.3	25775.	45.663	0.3171
10	10.75	0.500	9.750	0.8125	95.06	926.86	9036.4	88110.	74.662	0.5185
12	12.75	0.500	11.750	0.9792	138.1	1622.2	19072.	223970.	108.434	0.7528
Double Extra Strong Pipe										
½	0.840	0.294	0.252	0.0210	0.0635	0.0160	0.004032	0.00102	0.050	0.00035
¾	1.050	0.308	0.434	0.0362	0.1884	0.0817	0.03549	0.01540	0.148	0.00103
1	1.315	0.358	0.599	0.0499	0.3588	0.2149	0.1287	0.07711	0.282	0.00196
1¼	1.660	0.382	0.896	0.0747	0.8028	0.7193	0.6445	0.5775	0.630	0.00438
1½	1.900	0.400	1.100	0.0917	1.210	1.331	1.4641	1.611	0.950	0.00660
2	2.375	0.436	1.503	0.1252	2.259	3.395	5.1031	7.670	1.774	0.01232
2½	2.875	0.552	1.771	0.1476	3.136	5.554	9.8345	17.42	2.464	0.01710
3	3.500	0.600	2.300	0.1917	5.290	12.167	27.984	64.36	4.155	0.02885
3½	4.000	0.636	2.728	0.2273	7.442	20.302	55.383	151.1	5.845	0.04059
4	4.500	0.674	3.152	0.2627	9.935	31.315	98.704	311.1	7.803	0.05419
5	5.563	0.750	4.063	0.3386	16.51	67.072	272.58	1107.	12.966	0.09006
6	6.625	0.864	4.897	0.4081	23.98	117.43	575.04	2816.	18.835	0.1308
8	8.625	0.875	6.875	0.5729	47.27	324.95	2234.4	15360.	37.122	0.2578

A-15.
Stainless Steel Pipe Data
(Based on ANSI B36.19 wall thicknesses)

Nominal Pipe Size	Outside Diameter	Thickness	Inside Diameter		Inside Diameter Functions (In Inches)				Transverse Internal Area	
			d	D	d^2	d^3	d^4	d^5	a	A
Inches	Inches	Inches	Inches	Feet					Sq. In.	Sq. Ft.
Schedule 5 S										
½	0.840	0.065	0.710	0.0592	0.504	0.358	0.254	0.1804	0.396	0.00275
¾	1.050	0.065	0.920	0.0767	0.846	0.779	0.716	0.659	0.664	0.00461
1	1.315	0.065	1.185	0.0988	1.404	1.664	1.972	2.337	1.103	0.00766
1¼	1.660	0.065	1.530	0.1275	2.341	3.582	5.480	8.384	1.839	0.01277
1½	1.900	0.065	1.770	0.1475	3.133	5.545	9.815	17.37	2.461	0.01709
2	2.375	0.065	2.245	0.1871	5.040	11.31	25.40	57.03	3.958	0.02749
2½	2.875	0.083	2.709	0.2258	7.339	19.88	53.86	145.9	5.764	0.04003
3	3.500	0.083	3.334	0.2778	11.12	37.06	123.6	411.9	8.733	0.06065
3½	4.000	0.083	3.834	0.3195	14.70	56.36	216.1	828.4	11.545	0.08017
4	4.500	0.083	4.334	0.3612	18.78	81.41	352.8	1529.	14.750	0.1024
5	5.563	0.109	5.345	0.4454	28.57	152.7	816.2	4363.	22.439	0.1558
6	6.625	0.109	6.407	0.5339	41.05	263.0	1685.	10796.	32.241	0.2239
8	8.625	0.109	8.407	0.7006	70.68	594.2	4995.	41996.	55.512	0.3855
10	10.750	0.134	10.482	0.8375	109.9	1152.	12072.	126538.	86.315	0.5994
12	12.750	0.156	12.438	1.0365	154.7	1924.	23933.	297682.	121.50	0.8438
Schedule 10 S										
⅛	0.405	0.049	0.307	0.0256	0.0942	0.0289	0.00888	0.00273	0.074	0.00051
¼	0.540	0.065	0.410	0.0342	0.1681	0.0689	0.02826	0.01159	0.132	0.00092
⅜	0.675	0.065	0.545	0.0454	0.2970	0.1619	0.08822	0.04808	0.233	0.00162
½	0.840	0.083	0.674	0.0562	0.4543	0.3062	0.2064	0.1391	0.357	0.00248
¾	1.050	0.083	0.884	0.0737	0.7815	0.6908	0.6107	0.5398	0.614	0.00426
1	1.315	0.109	1.097	0.0914	1.203	1.320	1.448	1.589	0.945	0.00656
1¼	1.660	0.109	1.442	0.1202	2.079	2.998	4.324	6.235	1.633	0.01134
1½	1.900	0.109	1.682	0.1402	2.829	4.759	8.004	13.46	2.222	0.01543
2	2.375	0.109	2.157	0.1798	4.653	10.04	21.65	46.69	3.654	0.02538
2½	2.875	0.120	2.635	0.2196	6.943	18.30	48.21	127.0	5.453	0.03787
3	3.500	0.120	3.260	0.2717	10.63	34.65	112.9	368.2	8.347	0.05796
3½	4.000	0.120	3.760	0.3133	14.14	53.16	199.9	751.5	11.11	0.07712
4	4.500	0.120	4.260	0.3550	18.15	77.31	329.3	1403.	14.26	0.09899
5	5.563	0.134	5.295	0.4413	28.04	148.5	786.1	4162.	22.02	0.1529
6	6.625	0.134	6.357	0.5298	40.41	256.9	1633.	10382.	31.74	0.2204
8	8.625	0.148	8.329	0.6941	69.37	577.8	4813.	40083.	54.48	0.3784
10	10.750	0.165	10.420	0.8683	108.6	1131.	11789.	122840.	85.29	0.5923
12	12.750	0.180	12.390	1.0325	153.5	1902.	23566.	291982.	120.6	0.8372

Schedule 40 S

⅛ to 12	Values are the same, size for size, as those shown on the facing page for Standard Wall Pipe (heaviest weight on 8, 10, and 12-inch sizes).

Schedule 80 S

⅛ to 12	Values are the same, size for size, as those shown on the facing page for Extra Strong Pipe.

Courtesy Crane Co., Technical Manual 410, Flow of Fluids.

A-16.
Properties of Pipe

Tabulated below are the most generally required data used in piping design. This table is believed to be the most comprehensive published up to this time. Many thicknesses traditionally included in such tables have been omitted because of their having become obsolete through disuse and lack of coverage by any Standard.

Sizes and thicknesses listed herein are covered by the following Standards:—

1) American National Standard Institute B36.10

2) American National Standard Institute B36.19

3) American Petroleum Institute Standard API 5L

4) American Petroleum Institute Standard API 5LX

5) New United States Legal Standard for Steel Plate Gauges.

ANSI American National Standards Institute

Sizes and thicknesses to which no Standard designation applies are largely the more commonly used dimensions to which Taylor Forge Electric Fusion Welded Pipe is produced for a wide variety of applications including river crossings, penstocks, power plant and other piping.

All data is computed from the *nominal* dimensions listed and the effect of tolerances is not taken into account. Values are computed by application of the following formulas:

Radius of Gyration: $R = \dfrac{\sqrt{D^2 + d^2}}{4}$

Moment of Inertia: $I = R^2 A$

Section Modulus: $Z = \dfrac{I}{0.5\ D}$

Pipe Size	Outside Diam. D	Designation	Wall Thickness	Inside Diam. d	Weight per Foot	Wt. of Water per Ft. of Pipe	Sq. Ft. Outside Surface per Ft.	Sq. Ft. Inside Surface per Ft.	Transverse Area in.² a	Area of Metal in.² A	Moment of Inertia in.⁴ I	Section Modulus in.³ Z	Radius of Gyration in. R
⅛	.405	10S	.049	.307	.186	.0320	.106	.0804	.0740	.0548	.00090	.00440	.1270
		Std.	.068	.269	.244	.0246	.106	.0705	.0568	.0720	.00106	.00530	.1215
		X-Stg.	.095	.215	.314	.0157	.106	.0563	.0364	.0925	.00122	.00600	.1146
¼	.540	10S	.065	.410	.330	.0570	.141	.1073	.1320	.0970	.00280	.01030	.1695
		Std.	.088	.364	.424	.0451	.141	.0955	.1041	.1250	.00331	.01230	.1628
		X-Stg.	.119	.302	.535	.0310	.141	.0794	.0716	.1574	.00378	.01395	.1547
⅜	.675	10S	.065	.545	.423	.1010	.177	.1427	.2333	.1245	.00590	.01740	.2160
		Std.	.091	.493	.567	.0827	.177	.1295	.1910	.1670	.00730	.02160	.2090
		X-Stg.	.126	.423	.738	.0609	.177	.1106	.1405	.2173	.00862	.02554	.1991
½	.840	10S	.083	.670	.671	.1550	.220	.1764	.3568	.1974	.01430	.03410	.2692
		Std.	.109	.622	.850	.1316	.220	.1637	.3040	.2503	.01710	.04070	.2613
		X-Stg.	.147	.546	1.087	.1013	.220	.1433	.2340	.3200	.02010	.04780	.2505
		160	.138	.464	1.310	.0740	.220	.1220	.1706	.3836	.02213	.05269	.2402
		XX-Stg.	.294	.252	1.714	.0216	.220	.0660	.0499	.5043	.02424	.05772	.2192
¾	1.050	10S	.083	.884	.857	.2660	.275	.2314	.6138	.2522	.02970	.05660	.3430
		Std.	.113	.824	1.130	.2301	.275	.2168	.5330	.3326	.03704	.07055	.3337
		X-Stg.	.154	.742	1.473	.1875	.275	.1948	.4330	.4335	.04479	.08531	.3214
		160	.219	.612	1.940	.1280	.275	.1607	.2961	.5698	.05270	.10038	.3041
		XX-Stg.	.308	.434	2.440	.0633	.275	.1137	.1479	.7180	.05792	.11030	.2840
1	1.315	10S	.109	1.097	1.404	.4090	.344	.2872	.9448	.4129	.07560	.1150	.4282
		Std.	.133	1.049	1.678	.3740	.344	.2740	.8640	.4939	.08734	.1328	.4205
		X-Stg.	.179	.957	2.171	.3112	.344	.2520	.7190	.6388	.10560	.1606	.4066
		160	.250	.815	2.850	.2261	.344	.2134	.5217	.8364	.12516	.1903	.3868
		XX-Stg.	.358	.599	3.659	.1221	.344	.1570	.2818	1.0760	.14050	.2136	.3613
1¼	1.660	10S	.109	1.442	1.806	.7080	.434	.3775	1.633	.5314	.1606	.1934	.5499
		Std.	.140	1.380	2.272	.6471	.434	.3620	1.495	.6685	.1947	.2346	.5397
			.191	1.278	2.996	.5553	.434	.3356	1.283	.8815	.2418	.2913	.5237
			.250	1.160	3.764	.4575	.434	.3029	1.057	1.1070	.2833	.3421	.5063
			.382	.896	5.214	.2732	.434	.2331	.6305	1.5340	.3411	.4110	.4716

Courtesy Taylor Forge Division, Energy Products Group, Gulf and Western Mfg. Co., by permission. *(Continued on next page)*

A-16.
(Continued). Properties of Pipe

Nominal Pipe Size	Outside Diam. D	Designation	Wall Thickness	Inside Diam. d	Weight per Foot	Wt. of Water per Ft. of Pipe	Sq. Ft. Outside Surface per Ft.	Sq. Ft. Inside Surface per Ft.	Transverse Area in.² a	Area of Metal in.² A	Moment of Inertia in.⁴ I	Section Modulus in.³ Z	Radius of Gyration in. R
1½	1.900	10S	.109	1.682	2.085	.9630	.497	.4403	2.221	.613	.2469	.2599	.6344
		Std.	.145	1.610	2.717	.8820	.497	.4213	2.036	.800	.3099	.3262	.6226
		X-Stg.	.200	1.500	3.631	.7648	.497	.3927	1.767	1.068	.3912	.4118	.6052
		160	.281	1.337	4.862	.6082	.497	.3519	1.405	1.430	.4826	.5080	.5809
		XX-Stg.	.400	1.100	6.408	.4117	.497	.2903	.950	1.885	.5678	.5977	.5489
2	2.375	10S	.109	2.157	2.638	1.583	.622	.5647	3.654	.775	.5003	.4213	.8034
		Std.	.154	2.067	3.652	1.452	.622	.5401	3.355	1.075	.6657	.5606	.7871
		X-Stg.	.218	1.939	5.022	1.279	.622	.5074	2.953	1.477	.8679	.7309	.7665
		- -	.250	1.875	5.673	1.196	.622	.4920	2.761	1.669	.9555	.8046	.7565
		160	.344	1.687	7.450	.970	.622	.4422	2.240	2.190	1.162	.9790	.7286
		XX-Stg.	.436	1.503	9.029	.769	.622	.3929	1.774	2.656	1.311	1.1040	.7027
2½	2.875	10S	.120	2.635	3.53	2.360	.753	.6900	5.453	1.038	.9878	.6872	.9755
		Std.	.203	2.469	5.79	2.072	.753	.6462	4.788	1.704	1.530	1.064	.9474
		X-Stg.	.276	2.323	7.66	1.834	.753	.6095	4.238	2.254	1.924	1.339	.9241
		160	.375	2.125	10.01	1.535	.753	.5564	3.547	2.945	2.353	1.638	.8938
		XX-Stg.	.552	1.771	13.69	1.067	.753	.4627	2.464	4.028	2.871	1.997	.8442
3	3.500	10S	.120	3.260	4.33	3.62	.916	.853	8.346	1.272	1.821	1.041	1.196
		API	.125	3.250	4.52	3.60	.916	.851	8.300	1.329	1.900	1.086	1.195
		API	.156	3.188	5.58	3.46	.916	.835	7.982	1.639	2.298	1.313	1.184
		API	.188	3.125	6.65	3.34	.916	.819	7.700	1.958	2.700	1.545	1.175
		Std.	.216	3.068	7.57	3.20	.916	.802	7.393	2.228	3.017	1.724	1.164
		API	.250	3.000	8.68	3.06	.916	.785	7.184	2.553	3.388	1.936	1.152
		API	.281	2.938	9.65	2.94	.916	.769	6.780	2.842	3.819	2.182	1.142
		X-Stg.	.300	2.900	10.25	2.86	.916	.761	6.605	3.016	3.892	2.225	1.136
		160	.438	2.624	14.32	2.34	.916	.687	5.407	4.214	5.044	2.882	1.094
		XX-Stg.	.600	2.300	18.58	1.80	.916	.601	4.155	5.466	5.993	3.424	1.047
3½	4.000	10S	.120	3.760	4.97	4.81	1.047	.984	11.10	1.46	2.754	1.377	1.372
		API	.125	3.750	5.18	4.79	1.047	.982	11.04	1.52	2.859	1.430	1.371
		API	.156	3.688	6.41	4.63	1.047	.966	10.68	1.88	3.485	1.743	1.360
		API	.188	3.624	7.71	4.48	1.047	.950	10.32	2.27	4.130	2.065	1.350
		Std.	.226	3.548	9.11	4.28	1.047	.929	9.89	2.68	4.788	2.394	1.337
		API	.250	3.500	10.02	4.17	1.047	.916	9.62	2.94	5.201	2.601	1.329
		API	.281	3.438	11.17	4.02	1.047	.900	9.28	3.29	5.715	2.858	1.319
		X-Stg.	.318	3.364	12.51	3.85	1.047	.880	8.89	3.68	6.280	3.140	1.307
		XX-Stg.	.636	2.728	22.85	2.53	1.047	.716	5.84	6.72	9.848	4.924	1.210
4	4.500	10S	.120	4.260	5.61	6.18	1.178	1.115	14.25	1.65	3.97	1.761	1.550
		API	.125	4.250	5.84	6.15	1.178	1.113	14.19	1.72	4.12	1.829	1.548
		API	.156	4.188	7.24	5.97	1.178	1.096	13.77	2.13	5.03	2.235	1.537
		API	.188	4.124	8.56	5.80	1.178	1.082	13.39	2.52	5.86	2.600	1.525
		API	.219	4.062	10.02	5.62	1.178	1.063	12.96	2.94	6.77	3.867	1.516
		Std.	.237	4.026	10.79	5.51	1.178	1.055	12.73	3.17	7.23	3.214	1.510
		API	.250	4.000	11.35	5.45	1.178	1.049	12.57	3.34	7.56	3.360	1.505
		API	.281	3.938	12.67	5.27	1.178	1.031	12.17	3.73	8.33	3.703	1.495
		API	.312	3.876	14.00	5.12	1.178	1.013	11.80	4.11	9.05	4.020	1.482
		X-Stg.	.337	3.826	14.98	4.98	1.178	1.002	11.50	4.41	9.61	4.271	1.477
		120	.438	3.624	19.00	4.47	1.178	.949	10.32	5.59	11.65	5.177	1.444
		- -	.500	3.500	21.36	4.16	1.178	.916	9.62	6.28	12.77	5.676	1.425
		160	.531	3.438	22.60	4.02	1.178	.900	9.28	6.62	13.27	5.900	1.416
		XX-Stg.	.674	3.152	27.54	3.38	1.178	.826	7.80	8.10	15.28	6.793	1.374

A-16.
(Continued). Properties of Pipe

Nominal Pipe Size	Nominal Outside Diam. D	Desig-nation	Wall Thick-ness	Inside Diam. d	Weight per Foot	Wt. of Water per Ft. of Pipe	Sq. Ft. Outside Surface per Ft.	Sq. Ft. Inside Surface per Ft.	Trans-verse Area in.² a	Area of Metal in.² A	Moment of Inertia in.⁴ I	Section Modulus in.³ Z	Radius of Gyra-tion in. R
		10S	.134	5.295	7.77	9.54	1.456	1.386	22.02	2.29	8.42	3.028	1.920
		API	.156	5.251	9.02	9.39	1.456	1.375	21.66	2.65	9.70	3.487	1.913
		API	.188	5.187	10.80	9.16	1.456	1.358	21.13	3.17	11.49	4.129	1.902
		API	.219	5.125	12.51	8.94	1.456	1.342	20.63	3.68	13.14	4.726	1.891
		Std.	.258	5.047	14.62	8.66	1.456	1.321	20.01	4.30	15.16	5.451	1.878
		API	.281	5.001	15.86	8.52	1.456	1.309	19.64	4.66	16.31	5.862	1.870
5	5.563	API	.312	4.939	17.51	8.31	1.456	1.293	19.16	5.15	17.81	6.402	1.860
		API	.344	4.875	19.19	8.09	1.456	1.276	18.67	5.64	19.28	6.932	1.849
		X-Stg.	.375	4.813	20.78	7.87	1.456	1.260	18.19	6.11	20.67	7.431	1.839
		120	.500	4.563	27.10	7.08	1.456	1.195	16.35	7.95	25.74	9.253	1.799
		160	.625	4.313	32.96	6.32	1.456	1.129	14.61	9.70	30.03	10.800	1.760
		XX-Stg.	.750	4.063	38.55	5.62	1.456	1.064	12.97	11.34	33.63	12.090	1.722
		12 Ga.	.104	6.417	7.25	14.02	1.734	1.680	32.34	2.13	11.33	3.42	2.31
		10S	.134	6.357	9.29	13.70	1.734	1.660	31.75	2.73	14.38	4.34	2.29
		8 Ga.	.164	6.297	11.33	13.50	1.734	1.649	31.14	3.33	17.38	5.25	2.28
		API	.188	6.249	12.93	13.31	1.734	1.639	30.70	3.80	19.71	5.95	2.28
		6 Ga.	.194	6.237	13.34	13.25	1.734	1.633	30.55	3.92	20.29	6.12	2.27
		API	.219	6.187	15.02	13.05	1.734	1.620	30.10	4.41	22.66	6.84	2.27
		API	.250	6.125	17.02	12.80	1.734	1.606	29.50	5.01	25.55	7.71	2.26
		API	.277	6.071	18.86	12.55	1.734	1.591	28.95	5.54	28.00	8.46	2.25
6	6.625	Std.	.280	6.065	18.97	12.51	1.734	1.587	28.90	5.58	28.14	8.50	2.24
		API	.312	6.001	21.05	12.26	1.734	1.571	28.28	6.19	30.91	9.33	2.23
		API	.344	5.937	23.09	12.00	1.734	1.554	27.68	6.79	33.51	10.14	2.22
		API	.375	5.875	25.10	11.75	1.734	1.540	27.10	7.37	36.20	10.90	2.21
		X-Stg.	.432	5.761	28.57	11.29	1.734	1.510	26.07	8.40	40.49	12.22	2.19
		- -	.500	5.625	32.79	10.85	1.734	1.475	24.85	9.63	45.60	13.78	2.16
		120	.562	5.501	36.40	10.30	1.734	1.470	23.77	10.74	49.91	15.07	2.15
		160	.719	5.187	45.30	9.16	1.734	1.359	21.15	13.36	58.99	17.81	2.10
		XX-Stg.	.864	4.897	53.16	8.14	1.734	1.280	18.83	15.64	66.33	20.02	2.06
		12 Ga.	.104	8.417	9.47	24.1	2.26	2.204	55.6	2.78	25.3	5.86	3.01
		10 Ga.	.134	8.357	12.16	23.8	2.26	2.188	54.8	3.57	32.2	7.46	3.00
		10S	.148	8.329	13.40	23.6	2.26	2.180	54.5	3.94	35.4	8.22	3.00
		8 Ga.	.164	8.297	14.83	23.4	2.26	2.172	54.1	4.36	39.1	9.06	2.99
		API	.188	8.249	16.90	23.2	2.26	2.161	53.5	5.00	44.5	10.30	2.98
		6 Ga.	.194	8.237	17.48	23.1	2.26	2.156	53.3	5.14	45.7	10.60	2.98
		API	.203	8.219	18.30	23.1	2.26	2.152	53.1	5.38	47.7	11.05	2.98
		API	.219	8.187	19.64	22.9	2.26	2.148	52.7	5.80	51.3	11.90	2.97
		3 Ga.	.239	8.147	21.42	22.6	2.26	2.133	52.1	6.30	55.4	12.84	2.96
		20	.250	8.125	22.40	22.5	2.26	2.127	51.8	6.58	57.7	13.39	2.96
		30	.277	8.071	24.70	22.2	2.26	2.115	51.2	7.26	63.3	14.69	2.95
		API	.312	8.001	27.72	21.8	2.26	2.095	50.3	8.15	70.6	16.37	2.94
8	8.625	Std.	.322	7.981	28.55	21.6	2.26	2.090	50.0	8.40	72.5	16.81	2.94
		API	.344	7.937	30.40	21.4	2.26	2.078	49.5	8.94	76.8	17.81	2.93
		API	.375	7.875	33.10	21.1	2.26	2.062	48.7	9.74	83.1	19.27	2.92
		60	.406	7.813	35.70	20.8	2.26	2.045	47.9	10.48	88.8	20.58	2.91
		API	.438	7.749	38.33	20.4	2.26	2.029	47.2	11.27	94.7	21.97	2.90
		X-Stg.	.500	7.625	43.39	19.8	2.26	2.006	45.6	12.76	105.7	24.51	2.88
		100	.594	7.437	50.90	18.8	2.26	1.947	43.5	14.96	121.4	28.14	2.85
		- -	.625	7.375	53.40	18.5	2.26	1.931	42.7	15.71	126.5	29.33	2.84
		120	.719	7.187	60.70	17.6	2.26	1.882	40.6	17.84	140.6	32.61	2.81
		140	.812	7.001	67.80	16.7	2.26	1.833	38.5	19.93	153.8	35.65	2.78
		XX-Stg.	.875	6.875	72.42	16.1	2.26	1.800	37.1	21.30	162.0	37.56	2.76
		160	.906	6.813	74.70	15.8	2.26	1.784	36.4	21.97	165.9	38.48	2.76

(Continued on next page)

A-16.
(Continued). Properties of Pipe

Pipe Size	Outside Diam. D	Designation	Wall Thickness	Inside Diam. d	Weight per Foot	Wt. of Water per Ft. of Pipe	Sq. Ft. Outside Surface per Ft.	Sq. Ft. Inside Surface per Ft.	Transverse Area in.² a	Area of Metal in.² A	Moment of Inertia in.⁴ I	Section Modulus in.³ Z	Radius of Gyration in. R
10	10.750	12 Ga.	.104	10.542	11.83	37.8	2.81	2.76	87.3	3.48	49.3	9.16	3.76
		10 Ga.	.134	10.482	15.21	37.4	2.81	2.74	86.3	4.47	63.0	11.71	3.75
		8 Ga.	.164	10.422	18.56	37.0	2.81	2.73	85.3	5.45	76.4	14.22	3.74
		10S	.165	10.420	18.65	36.9	2.81	2.73	85.3	5.50	76.8	14.29	3.74
		API	.188	10.374	21.12	36.7	2.81	2.72	84.5	6.20	86.5	16.10	3.74
		6 Ga.	.194	10.362	21.89	36.6	2.81	2.71	84.3	6.43	89.7	16.68	3.73
		API	.203	10.344	22.86	36.5	2.81	2.71	84.0	6.71	93.3	17.35	3.73
		API	.219	10.310	24.60	36.2	2.81	2.70	83.4	7.24	100.5	18.70	3.72
		3 Ga.	.239	10.272	28.05	35.9	2.81	2.69	82.9	7.89	109.2	20.32	3.72
		20	.250	10.250	28.03	35.9	2.81	2.68	82.6	8.26	113.6	21.12	3.71
		API	.279	10.192	31.20	35.3	2.81	2.66	81.6	9.18	125.9	23.42	3.70
		30	.307	10.136	34.24	35.0	2.81	2.65	80.7	10.07	137.4	25.57	3.69
		API	.344	10.062	38.26	34.5	2.81	2.63	79.5	11.25	152.3	28.33	3.68
		Std.	.365	10.020	40.48	34.1	2.81	2.62	78.9	11.91	160.7	29.90	3.67
		API	.438	9.874	48.28	33.2	2.81	2.58	76.6	14.19	188.8	35.13	3.65
		X-Stg.	.500	9.750	54.74	32.3	2.81	2.55	74.7	16.10	212.0	39.43	3.63
		80	.594	9.562	64.40	31.1	2.81	2.50	71.8	18.91	244.9	45.56	3.60
		100	.719	9.312	77.00	29.5	2.81	2.44	68.1	22.62	286.2	53.25	3.56
		- -	.750	9.250	80.10	29.1	2.81	2.42	67.2	23.56	296.2	55.10	3.54
		120	.844	9.062	89.20	27.9	2.81	2.37	64.5	26.23	324.3	60.34	3.51
		140	1.000	8.750	104.20	26.1	2.81	2.29	60.1	30.63	367.8	68.43	3.46
		160	1.125	8.500	116.00	24.6	2.81	2.22	56.7	34.01	399.4	74.31	3.43
12	12.750	12 Ga.	.104	12.542	14.1	53.6	3.34	3.28	123.5	4.13	82.6	12.9	4.47
		10 Ga.	.134	12.482	18.1	53.0	3.34	3.27	122.4	5.31	105.7	16.6	4.46
		8 Ga.	.164	12.422	22.1	52.5	3.34	3.25	121.2	6.48	128.4	20.1	4.45
		10S	.180	12.390	24.2	52.2	3.34	3.24	120.6	7.11	140.4	22.0	4.44
		6 Ga.	.194	12.362	26.0	52.0	3.34	3.23	120.0	7.65	150.9	23.7	4.44
		API	.203	12.344	27.2	52.0	3.34	3.23	119.9	7.99	157.2	24.7	4.43
		API	.219	12.312	29.3	51.7	3.34	3.22	119.1	8.52	167.6	26.3	4.43
		3 Ga.	.239	12.272	32.0	51.3	3.34	3.21	118.3	9.39	183.8	28.8	4.42
		20	.250	12.250	33.4	51.3	3.34	3.12	118.0	9.84	192.3	30.2	4.42
		API	.281	12.188	37.4	50.6	3.34	3.19	116.7	11.01	214.1	33.6	4.41
		API	.312	12.126	41.5	50.1	3.34	3.17	115.5	12.19	236.0	37.0	4.40
		30	.330	12.090	43.8	49.7	3.34	3.16	114.8	12.88	248.5	39.0	4.39
		API	.344	12.062	45.5	49.7	3.34	3.16	114.5	13.46	259.0	40.7	4.38
		Std.	.375	12.000	49.6	48.9	3.34	3.14	113.1	14.58	279.3	43.8	4.37
		40	.406	11.938	53.6	48.5	3.34	3.13	111.9	15.74	300.3	47.1	4.37
		API	.438	11.874	57.5	48.2	3.34	3.11	111.0	16.95	321.0	50.4	4.35
		X-Stg.	.500	11.750	65.4	46.9	3.34	3.08	108.4	19.24	361.5	56.7	4.33
		60	.562	11.626	73.2	46.0	3.34	3.04	106.2	21.52	400.5	62.8	4.31
		- -	.625	11.500	80.9	44.9	3.34	3.01	103.8	23.81	438.7	68.8	4.29
		80	.688	11.374	88.6	44.0	3.34	2.98	101.6	26.03	475.2	74.6	4.27
		- -	.750	11.250	96.2	43.1	3.34	2.94	99.4	28.27	510.7	80.1	4.25
		100	.844	11.062	108.0	41.6	3.34	2.90	96.1	31.53	561.8	88.1	4.22
		- -	.875	11.000	110.9	41.1	3.34	2.88	95.0	32.64	578.5	90.7	4.21
		120	1.000	10.750	125.5	39.3	3.34	2.81	90.8	36.91	641.7	100.7	4.17
		140	1.125	10.500	140.0	37.5	3.34	2.75	86.6	41.08	700.7	109.9	4.13
		- -	1.250	10.250	153.6	35.8	3.34	2.68	82.5	45.16	755.5	118.5	4.09
		160	1.312	10.126	161.0	34.9	3.34	2.65	80.5	47.14	781.3	122.6	4.07
		- -	1.375	10.000	167.2	34.0	3.34	2.62	78.5	49.14	807.2	126.6	4.05
		- -	1.500	9.750	180.4	32.4	3.34	2.55	74.7	53.01	853.8	133.9	4.01

A-16.
(Continued). Properties of Pipe

Pipe Size	Outside Diam. D	Designation	Wall Thickness	Inside Diam. d	Weight per Foot	Wt. of Water per Ft. of Pipe	Sq. Ft. Outside Surface per Ft.	Sq. Ft. Inside Surface per Ft.	Transverse Area in.² a	Area of Metal in.² A	Moment of Inertia in.⁴ I	Section Modulus in.³ Z	Radius of Gyration in. R
14	14.000	10 Ga.	.134	13.732	20	64.2	3.67	3.59	148.1	5.84	140.4	20.1	4.90
		8 Ga.	.164	13.672	24	63.6	3.67	3.58	146.8	7.13	170.7	24.4	4.89
		6 Ga.	.194	13.612	29	63.1	3.67	3.56	145.5	8.41	200.6	28.7	4.88
		API	.210	13.580	31	62.8	3.67	3.55	144.8	9.10	216.2	30.9	4.87
		API	.219	13.562	32	62.6	3.67	3.55	144.5	9.48	225.1	32.2	4.87
		3 Ga.	.239	13.522	35	62.3	3.67	3.54	143.6	10.33	244.9	35.0	4.87
		10	.250	13.500	37	62.1	3.67	3.54	143.0	10.82	256.0	36.6	4.86
		API	.281	13.438	41	61.5	3.67	3.52	141.8	12.11	285.2	40.7	4.85
		20	.312	13.375	46	60.8	3.67	3.50	140.5	13.44	314.9	45.0	4.84
		API	.344	13.312	50	60.3	3.67	3.48	139.2	14.76	344.3	49.2	4.83
		Std.	.375	13.250	55	59.7	3.67	3.47	137.9	16.05	372.8	53.2	4.82
		40	.438	13.124	63	58.5	3.67	3.44	135.3	18.66	429.6	61.4	4.80
		X-Stg.	.500	13.000	72	57.4	3.67	3.40	132.7	21.21	483.8	69.1	4.78
		60	.594	12.812	85	55.9	3.67	3.35	129.0	24.98	562.4	80.3	4.74
		- -	.625	12.750	89	55.3	3.67	3.34	127.7	26.26	588.5	84.1	4.73
		80	.750	12.500	107	51.2	3.67	3.27	122.7	31.22	687.5	98.2	4.69
		- -	.875	12.250	123	51.1	3.67	3.21	117.9	36.08	780.1	111.4	4.65
		100	.938	12.124	131	50.0	3.67	3.17	115.5	38.47	820.5	117.2	4.63
		- -	1.000	12.000	139	49.0	3.67	3.14	113.1	40.84	868.0	124.0	4.61
		120	1.094	11.812	151	47.5	3.67	3.09	109.6	44.32	929.8	132.8	4.58
		- -	1.125	11.750	155	47.0	3.67	3.08	108.4	45.50	950.3	135.8	4.57
		140	1.250	11.500	171	45.0	3.67	3.01	103.9	50.07	1027.5	146.8	4.53
		- -	1.375	11.250	186	43.1	3.67	2.94	99.4	54.54	1099.5	157.1	4.49
		160	1.406	11.188	190	42.6	3.67	2.93	98.3	55.63	1116.9	159.6	4.48
		- -	1.500	11.000	200	41.2	3.67	2.88	95.0	58.90	1166.5	166.6	4.45
16	16.000	10 Ga.	.134	15.732	23	84.3	4.19	4.12	194.4	6.68	210	26.3	5.61
		8 Ga.	.164	15.672	28	83.6	4.19	4.10	192.9	8.16	256	32.0	5.60
		- -	.188	15.624	32	83.3	4.19	4.09	192.0	9.39	294	36.7	5.59
		6 Ga.	.194	15.612	33	83.0	4.19	4.09	191.4	9.63	301	37.6	5.59
		API	.219	15.562	37	82.5	4.19	4.07	190.2	10.86	338	42.3	5.58
		3 Ga.	.239	15.522	40	82.0	4.19	4.06	189.2	11.83	368	45.9	5.57
		10	.250	15.500	42	82.1	4.19	4.06	189.0	12.40	385	48.1	5.57
		API	.281	15.438	47	81.2	4.19	4.04	187.0	13.90	430	53.8	5.56
		20	.312	15.375	52	80.1	4.19	4.03	185.6	15.40	474	59.2	5.55
		API	.344	15.312	57	80.0	4.19	4.01	184.1	16.94	519	64.9	5.54
		Std.	.375	15.250	63	79.1	4.19	4.00	182.6	18.41	562	70.3	5.53
		API	.438	15.124	73	78.2	4.19	3.96	180.0	21.42	650	81.2	5.51
		X-Stg.	.500	15.000	83	76.5	4.19	3.93	176.7	24.35	732	91.5	5.48
		- -	.625	14.750	103	74.1	4.19	3.86	170.9	30.19	893	111.7	5.44
		60	.656	14.688	108	73.4	4.19	3.85	169.4	31.62	933	116.6	5.43
		- -	.750	14.500	122	71.5	4.19	3.80	165.1	35.93	1047	130.9	5.40
		80	.844	14.312	137	69.7	4.19	3.75	160.9	40.14	1157	144.6	5.37
		- -	.875	14.250	141	69.1	4.19	3.73	159.5	41.58	1192	149.0	5.35
		- -	1.000	14.000	160	66.7	4.19	3.66	153.9	47.12	1331	166.4	5.31
		100	1.031	13.938	165	66.0	4.19	3.65	152.6	48.49	1366	170.7	5.30
		- -	1.125	13.750	179	64.4	4.19	3.60	148.5	52.57	1463	182.9	5.27
		120	1.219	13.562	193	62.6	4.19	3.55	144.5	56.56	1556	194.5	5.24
		- -	1.250	13.500	197	62.1	4.19	3.53	143.1	57.92	1586	198.3	5.23
		- -	1.375	13.250	215	59.8	4.19	3.47	137.9	63.17	1704	213.0	5.19
		140	1.438	13.124	224	58.6	4.19	3.44	135.3	65.79	1761	220.1	5.17
		- -	1.500	13.000	232	57.4	4.19	3.40	132.7	68.33	1816	227.0	5.15
		160	1.594	12.812	245	55.9	4.19	3.35	129.0	72.10	1893	236.6	5.12

(Continued on next page)

A-16.
(Continued). Properties of Pipe

Pipe Size	Outside Diam. D	Desig-nation	Wall Thick-ness	Inside Diam. d	Weight per Foot	Wt. of Water per Ft. of Pipe	Sq. Ft. Outside Surface per Ft.	Sq. Ft. Inside Surface per Ft.	Transverse Area in.² a	Area of Metal in.² A	Moment of Inertia in.⁴ I	Section Modulus in.³ Z	Radius of Gyration in. R
		10 Ga.	.134	17.732	26	107.1	4.71	4.64	246.9	7.52	300	33.4	6.32
		8 Ga.	.164	17.672	31	106.3	4.71	4.63	245.3	9.19	366	40.6	6.31
		6 Ga.	.194	17.612	37	105.6	4.71	4.61	243.6	10.85	430	47.8	6.29
		3 Ga.	.239	17.522	45	104.5	4.71	4.59	241.1	13.34	526	58.4	6.28
		10	.250	17.500	47	104.6	4.71	4.58	241.0	13.96	550	61.1	6.28
		API	.281	17.438	49	104.0	4.71	4.56	240.0	14.49	570	63.4	6.27
		20	.312	17.375	59	102.5	4.71	4.55	237.1	17.36	679	75.5	6.25
		API	.344	17.312	65	102.0	4.71	4.53	235.4	19.08	744	82.6	6.24
		Std.	.375	17.250	71	101.2	4.71	4.51	233.7	20.76	807	89.6	6.23
		API	.406	17.188	76	100.6	4.71	4.50	232.0	22.44	869	96.6	6.22
		30	.438	17.124	82	99.5	4.71	4.48	229.5	24.95	963	107.0	6.21
		X-Stg.	.500	17.000	93	98.2	4.71	4.45	227.0	27.49	1053	117.0	6.19
18	18.000	40	.562	16.876	105	97.2	4.71	4.42	224.0	30.85	1177	130.9	6.17
		- -	.625	16.750	116	95.8	4.71	4.39	220.5	34.15	1290	143.2	6.14
		60	.750	16.500	138	92.5	4.71	4.32	213.8	40.64	1515	168.3	6.10
		- -	.875	16.250	160	89.9	4.71	4.25	207.4	47.07	1730	192.3	6.06
		80	.938	16.124	171	88.5	4.71	4.22	204.2	50.23	1834	203.8	6.04
		- -	1.000	16.000	182	87.2	4.71	4.19	201.1	53.41	1935	215.0	6.02
		- -	1.125	15.750	203	84.5	4.71	4.12	194.8	59.64	2133	237.0	5.98
		100	1.156	15.688	208	83.7	4.71	4.11	193.3	61.18	2182	242.3	5.97
		- -	1.250	15.500	224	81.8	4.71	4.06	188.7	65.78	2319	257.7	5.94
		120	1.375	15.250	244	79.2	4.71	3.99	182.7	71.82	2498	277.5	5.90
		- -	1.500	15.000	265	76.6	4.71	3.93	176.7	77.75	2668	296.5	5.86
		140	1.562	14.876	275	75.3	4.71	3.89	173.8	80.66	2750	305.5	5.84
		160	1.781	14.438	309	71.0	4.71	3.78	163.7	90.75	3020	335.5	5.77
		10 Ga.	.134	19.732	28	132.6	5.24	5.17	305.8	8.36	413	41.3	7.02
		8 Ga.	.164	19.672	35	131.8	5.24	5.15	303.9	10.22	503	50.3	7.01
		6 Ga.	.194	19.612	41	131.0	5.24	5.13	302.1	12.07	592	59.2	7.00
		3 Ga.	.239	19.522	50	129.8	5.24	5.11	299.3	14.84	725	72.5	6.99
		10	.250	19.500	53	130.0	5.24	5.11	299.0	15.52	759	75.9	6.98
		API	.281	19.438	59	128.6	5.24	5.09	296.8	17.41	846	84.6	6.97
		API	.312	19.374	66	128.1	5.24	5.08	295.0	19.36	937	93.7	6.95
		API	.344	19.312	72	127.0	5.24	5.06	292.9	21.24	1026	102.6	6.95
		Std.	.375	19.250	79	126.0	5.24	5.04	291.1	23.12	1113	111.3	6.94
		API	.406	19.188	85	125.4	5.24	5.02	289.2	24.99	1200	120.0	6.93
		API	.438	19.124	92	125.1	5.24	5.01	288.0	26.95	1290	129.0	6.92
		X-Stg.	.500	19.000	105	122.8	5.24	4.97	283.5	30.63	1457	145.7	6.90
20	20.000	40	.594	18.812	123	120.4	5.24	4.93	278.0	36.15	1704	170.4	6.86
		- -	.625	18.750	129	119.5	5.24	4.91	276.1	38.04	1787	178.7	6.85
		60	.812	18.376	167	114.9	5.24	4.81	265.2	48.95	2257	225.7	6.79
		- -	.875	18.250	179	113.2	5.24	4.78	261.6	52.57	2409	240.9	6.77
		- -	1.000	18.000	203	110.3	5.24	4.71	254.5	59.69	2702	270.2	6.73
		80	1.031	17.938	209	109.4	5.24	4.80	252.7	61.44	2771	277.1	6.72
		- -	1.125	17.750	227	107.3	5.24	4.65	247.4	66.71	2981	298.1	6.68
		- -	1.250	17.500	250	104.3	5.24	4.58	240.5	73.63	3249	324.9	6.64
		100	1.281	17.438	256	103.4	5.24	4.56	238.8	75.34	3317	331.7	6.63
		- -	1.375	17.250	274	101.3	5.24	4.52	233.7	80.45	3508	350.8	6.60
		120	1.500	17.000	297	98.3	5.24	4.45	227.0	87.18	3755	375.5	6.56
		140	1.750	16.500	342	92.6	5.24	4.32	213.8	100.33	4217	421.7	6.48
		160	1.969	16.062	379	87.9	5.24	4.21	202.7	111.49	4586	458.6	6.41

A-16.
(Continued). Properties of Pipe

Nominal Pipe Size	Nominal Outside Diam. D	Desig-nation	Wall Thick-ness	Inside Diam. d	Weight per Foot	Wt. of Water per Ft. of Pipe	Sq. Ft. Outside Surface per Ft.	Sq. Ft. Inside Surface per Ft.	Trans-verse Area in.² a	Area of Metal in.² A	Moment of Inertia in.⁴ I	Section Modulus in.³ Z	Radius of Gyra-tion in. R
22	22.000	8 Ga.	.164	21.672	38	159.9	5.76	5.67	368.9	11.25	671	61.0	7.72
		6 Ga.	.194	21.612	45	159.0	5.76	5.66	366.8	13.29	790	71.8	7.71
		3 Ga.	.239	21.522	56	157.7	5.76	5.63	363.8	16.34	967	87.9	7.69
		API	.250	21.500	58	157.4	5.76	5.63	363.1	17.18	1010	91.8	7.69
		API	.281	21.438	65	156.5	5.76	5.61	361.0	19.17	1131	102.8	7.68
		API	.312	21.376	72	155.6	5.76	5.60	358.9	21.26	1250	113.6	7.67
		API	.344	21.312	80	154.7	5.76	5.58	356.7	23.40	1373	124.8	7.66
		API	.375	21.250	87	153.7	5.76	5.56	354.7	25.48	1490	135.4	7.65
		API	.406	21.188	94	152.9	5.76	5.55	352.6	27.54	1607	146.1	7.64
		API	.438	21.124	101	151.9	5.76	5.53	350.5	29.67	1725	156.8	7.62
		API	.500	21.000	115	150.2	5.76	5.50	346.4	33.77	1953	177.5	7.61
		- -	.625	20.750	143	146.6	5.76	5.43	338.2	41.97	2400	218.2	7.56
		- -	.750	20.500	170	143.1	5.76	5.37	330.1	50.07	2829	257.2	7.52
		- -	.875	20.250	198	139.6	5.76	5.30	322.1	58.07	3245	295.0	7.47
		- -	1.000	20.000	224	136.2	5.76	5.24	314.2	65.97	3645	331.4	7.43
		- -	1.125	19.750	251	132.8	5.76	5.17	306.4	73.78	4029	366.3	7.39
		- -	1.250	19.500	277	129.5	5.76	5.10	298.6	81.48	4400	400.0	7.35
		- -	1.375	19.250	303	126.2	5.76	5.04	291.0	89.09	4758	432.6	7.31
		- -	1.500	19.000	329	122.9	5.76	4.97	283.5	96.60	5103	463.9	7.27
24	24.000	8 Ga.	.164	23.672	42	190.8	6.28	6.20	440.1	12.28	872	72.7	8.43
		6 Ga.	.194	23.612	49	189.8	6.28	6.18	437.9	14.51	1028	85.7	8.42
		3 Ga.	.239	23.522	61	188.4	6.28	6.16	434.5	17.84	1260	105.0	8.40
		10	.250	23.500	63	189.0	6.28	6.15	435.0	18.67	1320	110.0	8.40
		API	.281	23.438	71	187.0	6.28	6.14	431.5	20.94	1472	122.7	8.38
		API	.312	23.376	79	186.9	6.28	6.12	430.0	23.20	1630	136.0	8.38
		API	.344	23.312	87	185.0	6.28	6.10	426.8	25.57	1789	149.1	8.36
		Std.	.375	23.250	95	183.8	6.28	6.09	424.6	27.83	1942	161.9	8.35
		API	.406	23.188	102	183.1	6.28	6.07	422.3	30.09	2095	174.6	8.34
		API	.438	23.124	110	182.1	6.28	6.05	420.0	32.42	2252	187.7	8.33
		X-Stg.	.500	23.000	125	181.0	6.28	6.02	416.0	36.90	2550	213.0	8.31
		30	.562	22.876	141	178.5	6.28	5.99	411.0	41.40	2840	237.0	8.28
		- -	.625	22.750	156	175.9	6.28	5.96	406.5	45.90	3137	261.4	8.27
		40	.688	22.624	171	174.2	6.28	5.92	402.1	50.30	3422	285.2	8.25
		- -	.750	22.500	186	172.1	6.28	5.89	397.6	54.78	3705	308.8	8.22
		- -	.875	22.250	216	168.6	6.28	5.82	388.8	63.57	4257	354.7	8.18
		60	.969	22.062	238	165.8	6.28	5.78	382.3	70.04	4652	387.7	8.15
		- -	1.000	22.000	246	164.8	6.28	5.76	380.1	72.26	4788	399.0	8.14
		- -	1.125	21.750	275	161.1	6.28	5.69	371.5	80.85	5302	441.8	8.10
		80	1.219	21.562	297	158.2	6.28	5.65	365.2	87.17	5673	472.8	8.07
		- -	1.250	21.500	304	157.4	6.28	5.63	363.1	89.34	5797	483.0	8.05
		- -	1.375	21.250	332	153.8	6.28	5.56	354.7	97.73	6275	522.9	8.01
		- -	1.500	21.000	361	150.2	6.28	5.50	346.4	106.03	6740	561.7	7.97
		100	1.531	20.938	367	149.3	6.28	5.48	344.3	108.07	6847	570.6	7.96
		120	1.812	20.376	429	141.4	6.28	5.33	326.1	126.30	7823	651.9	7.87
		140	2.062	19.876	484	134.4	6.28	5.20	310.3	142.10	8627	718.9	7.79
		160	2.344	19.312	542	127.0	6.28	5.06	293.1	159.40	9457	788.1	7.70
26	26.000	8 Ga.	.164	25.672	45	224.4	6.81	6.72	517.6	13.31	1111	85.4	9.13
		6 Ga.	.194	25.612	54	223.4	6.81	6.70	515.2	15.73	1310	100.7	9.12
		3 Ga.	.239	25.522	66	221.8	6.81	6.68	511.6	19.34	1605	123.4	9.11
		API	.250	25.500	67	221.4	6.81	6.68	510.7	19.85	1646	126.6	9.10
		API	.281	25.438	77	220.3	6.81	6.66	508.2	22.70	1877	144.4	9.09
		API	.312	25.376	84	219.2	6.81	6.64	505.8	25.18	2076	159.7	9.08

(Continued on next page)

A-16.
(Continued). Properties of Pipe

Nominal		Desig- nation	Wall Thick- ness	Inside Diam.	Weight per Foot	Wt. of Water per Ft. of Pipe	Sq. Ft. Outside Surface per Ft.	Sq. Ft. Inside Surface per Ft.	Trans- verse Area in.²	Area of Metal in.²	Moment of Inertia in.⁴	Section Modulus in.³	Radius of Gyra- tion in.
Pipe Size	Outside Diam. D			d					a	A	I	Z	R
26 cont.	**26.000**	API	.344	25.312	94	218.2	6.81	6.63	503.2	27.73	2280	175.4	9.07
		API	.375	25.250	103	217.1	6.81	6.61	500.7	30.19	2478	190.6	9.06
		API	.406	25.188	111	216.0	6.81	6.59	498.3	32.64	2673	205.6	9.05
		API	.438	25.124	120	214.9	6.81	6.58	495.8	35.17	2874	221.1	9.04
		API	.500	25.000	136	212.8	6.81	6.54	490.9	40.06	3259	250.7	9.02
		- -	.625	24.750	169	208.6	6.81	6.48	481.1	49.82	4013	308.7	8.98
		- -	.750	24.500	202	204.4	6.81	6.41	471.4	59.49	4744	364.9	8.93
		- -	.875	24.250	235	200.2	6.81	6.35	461.9	69.07	5458	419.9	8.89
		- -	1.000	24.000	267	196.1	6.81	6.28	452.4	78.54	6149	473.0	8.85
		- -	1.125	23.750	299	192.1	6.81	6.22	443.0	87.91	6813	524.1	8.80
		- -	1.375	23.250	362	184.1	6.81	6.09	424.6	106.37	8088	622.2	8.72
		- -	1.500	23.000	393	180.1	6.81	6.02	415.5	115.45	8695	668.8	8.68
30	**30.000**	8 Ga.	.164	29.672	52	299.9	7.85	7.77	691.4	15.37	1711	114.0	10.55
		6 Ga.	.194	29.612	62	298.6	7.85	7.75	688.6	18.17	2017	134.4	10.53
		3 Ga.	.239	29.522	76	296.7	7.85	7.73	684.4	22.35	2474	165.0	10.52
		API	.250	29.500	79	296.3	7.85	7.72	683.4	23.37	2585	172.3	10.52
		API	.281	29.438	89	295.1	7.85	7.70	680.5	26.24	2897	193.1	10.51
		10	.312	29.376	99	293.7	7.85	7.69	677.8	29.19	3201	213.4	10.50
		API	.344	29.312	109	292.6	7.85	7.67	674.8	32.04	3524	235.0	10.49
		API	.375	29.250	119	291.2	7.85	7.66	672.0	34.90	3823	254.8	10.48
		API	.406	29.188	130	290.7	7.85	7.64	669.0	37.75	4132	275.5	10.46
		API	.438	29.124	138	288.8	7.85	7.62	666.1	40.68	4442	296.2	10.45
		20	.500	29.000	158	286.2	7.85	7.59	660.5	46.34	5033	335.5	10.43
		30	.625	28.750	196	281.3	7.85	7.53	649.2	57.68	6213	414.2	10.39
		- -	.750	28.500	234	276.6	7.85	7.46	637.9	68.92	7371	491.4	10.34
		- -	.875	28.250	272	271.8	7.85	7.39	620.7	80.06	8494	566.2	10.30
		- -	1.000	28.000	310	267.0	7.85	7.33	615.7	91.11	9591	639.4	10.26
		- -	1.125	27.750	347	262.2	7.85	7.26	604.7	102.05	10653	710.2	10.22
		- -	1.250	27.500	384	257.5	7.85	7.20	593.9	112.90	11682	778.8	10.17
		- -	1.375	27.250	421	252.9	7.85	7.13	583.1	123.65	12694	846.2	10.13
		- -	1.500	27.000	457	248.2	7.85	7.07	572.5	134.30	13673	911.5	10.09
32	**32.000**	API	.250	31.500	85	337.8	8.38	8.25	779.2	24.93	3141	196.3	11.22
		API	.281	31.438	95	336.5	8.38	8.23	776.2	28.04	3525	220.3	11.21
		API	.312	31.376	106	335.2	8.38	8.21	773.2	31.02	3891	243.2	11.20
		API	.344	31.312	116	333.8	8.38	8.20	770.0	34.24	4287	268.0	11.19
		API	.375	31.250	127	332.5	8.38	8.18	766.9	37.25	4656	291.0	11.18
		API	.406	31.188	137	331.2	8.38	8.16	764.0	40.29	5025	314.1	11.17
		API	.438	31.124	148	329.8	8.38	8.15	760.8	43.43	5407	337.9	11.16
		API	.500	31.000	168	327.2	8.38	8.11	754.7	49.48	6140	383.8	11.14
		- -	.625	30.750	209	321.9	8.38	8.05	742.5	61.59	7578	473.6	11.09
		- -	.750	30.500	250	316.7	8.38	7.98	730.5	73.63	8990	561.9	11.05
		- -	.875	30.250	291	311.5	8.38	7.92	718.6	85.53	10368	648.0	11.01
		- -	1.000	30.000	331	306.4	8.38	7.85	706.8	97.38	11680	730.0	10.95
		- -	1.125	29.750	371	301.3	8.38	7.79	695.0	109.0	13003	812.7	10.92
		- -	1.250	29.500	410	296.3	8.38	7.72	680.5	120.7	14398	899.9	10.88
		- -	1.375	29.250	450	291.2	8.38	7.66	671.9	132.2	15526	970.4	10.84
		- -	1.500	29.000	489	286.3	8.38	7.59	660.5	143.7	16752	1047.0	10.80

A-16.
(Concluded). Properties of Pipe

Pipe Size	Outside Diam. D	Designation	Wall Thickness	Inside Diam. d	Weight per Foot	Wt. of Water per Ft. of Pipe	Sq. Ft. Outside Surface per Ft.	Sq. Ft. Inside Surface per Ft.	Transverse Area in.² a	Area of Metal in.² A	Moment of Inertia in.⁴ I	Section Modulus in.³ Z	Radius of Gyration in. R
34	34.000	API	.250	33.500	90	382.0	8.90	8.77	881.2	26.50	3773	221.9	11.93
		API	.281	33.438	101	380.7	8.90	8.75	878.2	29.77	4230	248.8	11.92
		API	.312	33.376	112	379.3	8.90	8.74	874.9	32.99	4680	275.3	11.91
		API	.344	33.312	124	377.8	8.90	8.72	871.6	36.36	5147	302.8	11.90
		API	.375	33.250	135	376.2	8.90	8.70	867.8	39.61	5597	329.2	11.89
		API	.406	33.188	146	375.0	8.90	8.69	865.0	42.88	6047	355.7	11.87
		API	.438	33.124	157	373.6	8.90	8.67	861.7	46.18	6501	382.4	11.86
		API	.500	33.000	179	370.8	8.90	8.64	855.3	52.62	7385	434.4	11.85
		- -	.625	32.750	223	365.0	8.90	8.57	841.9	65.53	9124	536.7	11.80
		- -	.750	32.500	266	359.5	8.90	8.51	829.3	78.34	10829	637.0	11.76
		- -	.875	32.250	308	354.1	8.90	8.44	816.8	90.66	12442	731.9	11.71
		- -	1.000	32.000	353	348.6	8.90	8.38	804.2	103.6	14114	830.2	11.67
		- -	1.125	31.750	395	343.2	8.90	8.31	791.6	116.1	15703	923.7	11.63
		- -	1.250	31.500	437	337.8	8.90	8.25	779.2	128.5	17246	1014.5	11.58
		- -	1.375	31.250	479	332.4	8.90	8.18	766.9	140.9	18770	1104.1	11.54
		- -	1.500	31.000	521	327.2	8.90	8.11	754.7	153.1	20247	1191.0	11.50
36	36.000	- -	.164	35.672	63	433.2	9.42	9.34	999.3	18.53	2975	165.3	12.67
		- -	.194	35.612	74	431.8	9.42	9.32	996.0	21.83	3499	194.4	12.66
		- -	.239	35.522	91	429.6	9.42	9.30	991.0	26.86	4293	238.5	12.64
		API	.250	35.500	96	429.1	9.42	9.29	989.7	28.11	4491	249.5	12.64
		API	.281	35.438	107	427.6	9.42	9.28	986.4	31.49	5023	279.1	12.63
		API	.312	35.376	119	426.1	9.42	9.26	982.9	34.95	5565	309.1	12.62
		API	.344	35.312	131	424.6	9.42	9.24	979.3	38.56	6127	340.4	12.60
		API	.375	35.250	143	423.1	9.42	9.23	975.8	42.01	6664	370.2	12.59
		API	.406	35.188	154	421.6	9.42	9.21	972.5	45.40	7191	399.5	12.58
		API	.438	35.124	166	420.1	9.42	9.19	968.9	48.93	7737	429.9	12.57
		API	.500	35.000	190	417.1	9.42	9.16	962.1	55.76	8785	488.1	12.55
		- -	.625	34.750	236	411.1	9.42	9.10	948.3	69.50	10872	604.0	12.51
		- -	.750	34.500	282	405.3	9.42	9.03	934.7	83.01	12898	716.5	12.46
		- -	.875	34.250	329	399.4	9.42	8.97	921.2	96.60	14906	828.1	12.42
		- -	1.000	34.000	374	393.6	9.42	8.90	907.9	109.9	16851	936.2	12.38
		- -	1.125	33.750	419	387.8	9.42	8.83	894.5	123.3	18766	1042.6	12.34
		- -	1.250	33.500	464	382.1	9.42	8.77	881.3	136.5	20624	1145.8	12.29
		- -	1.375	33.250	509	376.4	9.42	8.70	868.2	149.6	22451	1247.3	12.25
		- -	1.500	33.000	553	370.8	9.42	8.64	855.3	162.6	24237	1346.5	12.21
42	42.000	- -	.250	41.500	112	586.4	10.99	10.86	1352.6	32.82	7126	339.3	14.73
		- -	.375	41.250	167	579.3	10.99	10.80	1336.3	49.08	10627	506.1	14.71
		- -	.500	41.000	222	572.3	10.99	10.73	1320.2	65.18	14037	668.4	14.67
		- -	.625	40.750	276	565.4	10.99	10.67	1304.1	81.28	17373	827.3	14.62
		- -	.750	40.500	331	558.4	10.99	10.60	1288.2	97.23	20689	985.2	14.59
		- -	.875	40.250	385	551.6	10.99	10.54	1272.3	113.0	23896	1137.9	14.54
		- -	1.000	40.000	438	544.8	10.99	10.47	1256.6	128.8	27080	1289.5	14.50
		- -	1.125	39.750	492	537.9	10.99	10.41	1240.9	144.5	30193	1437.8	14.45
		- -	1.250	39.500	544	531.2	10.99	10.34	1225.3	160.0	33233	1582.5	14.41
		- -	1.375	39.250	597	524.4	10.99	10.27	1209.9	175.5	36240	1725.7	14.37
		- -	1.500	39.000	649	517.9	10.99	10.21	1194.5	190.8	39181	1865.7	14.33

A-17.
Equation of Pipes

The table below gives the number of pipes of one size required to equal in delivery other larger pipes of same length and under same conditions. The upper portion above the diagonal line of stars pertains to "standard" steam and gas pipes, while the lower portion is for pipes of the ACTUAL internal diameters given. The figures given in the table opposite the intersection of any two sizes is the number of the smaller-sized pipes required to equal one of the larger. Thus, it requires 29 standard 2-inch pipes to equal one standard 7-inch pipe.

STANDARD STEAM AND GAS PIPES

Dia.	½	¾	1	1½	2	2½	3	4	5	6	7	8	9	10	11	12	13	14	15	16	17	Dia.
½	* * *	2.27	4.88	15.8	31.7	52.9	96.9	205	377	620	918	1292	1767	2488	3014	3786	4904	5927	7321	8535	9717	½
¾	2.60	* * *	2.05	6.97	14.0	23.3	42.5	90.4	166	273	405	569	779	1096	1328	1668	2161	2615	3226	3761	4282	¾
1	7.55	2.90	* * *	3.45	6.82	11.4	20.9	44.1	81.1	133	198	278	380	536	649	815	1070	1263	1576	1837	2092	1
1½	24.2	9.30	3.20	* * *	1.26	3.34	6.13	13.0	23.8	39.2	58.1	81.7	112	157	190	239	310	375	463	539	614	1½
2	54.8	21.0	7.25	2.26	* * *	1.67	3.06	6.47	11.9	19.6	29.0	40.8	55.8	78.5	95.1	119	155	187	231	269	307	2
2½	102	39.4	13.6	4.23	1.87	* * *	1.83	3.87	7.12	11.7	17.4	24.4	33.4	47.0	56.9	71.5	92.6	112	138	161	184	2½
3	170	65.4	22.6	7.03	3.11	1.66	* * *	2.12	3.89	6.39	9.48	13.3	20.9	23.7	31.2	39.1	50.6	61.1	75.5	88.0	100	3
4	376	144	49.8	15.5	6.87	3.67	2.21	* * *	1.84	3.02	4.48	6.30	8.61	12.1	14.7	18.5	23.9	28.9	35.7	41.6	47.4	4
5	686	263	90.9	28.3	12.5	6.70	4.03	1.83	* * *	1.65	2.44	3.43	4.69	6.60	8.00	10.0	13.0	15.7	19.4	22.6	25.8	5
6	1116	429	148	46.0	20.4	10.9	6.56	2.97	1.63	* * *	1.48	2.09	2.85	4.02	4.86	6.11	7.91	9.56	11.8	13.8	15.6	6
7	1707	656	226	70.5	31.2	16.6	10.0	4.54	2.49	1.51	* * *	1.41	1.93	2.71	3.28	4.12	5.34	6.45	7.97	9.31	10.6	7
8	2435	936	322	101	44.5	23.8	14.3	6.48	3.54	2.18	1.43	* * *	1.35	1.93	2.33	2.92	3.79	4.57	5.67	6.60	7.52	8
9	3335	1281	440	137	60.8	32.5	19.5	8.85	4.85	2.98	1.95	1.37	* * *	1.41	1.71	2.14	2.77	3.35	4.14	4.83	5.50	9
10	4393	1688	582	181	80.4	42.9	25.8	11.7	6.40	3.93	2.57	1.80	1.32	* * *	1.21	1.52	1.97	2.38	2.94	3.43	3.91	10
11	5642	2168	747	233	103	55.1	33.1	15.0	8.22	5.05	3.31	2.32	1.70	1.28	* * *	1.26	1.63	1.88	2.43	2.83	3.22	11
12	7087	2723	938	293	129	69.2	41.6	18.8	10.3	6.34	4.15	2.91	2.13	1.61	1.26	* * *	1.30	1.57	1.93	2.26	2.58	12
13	8657	3326	1146	358	158	84.5	50.7	23.0	12.6	7.75	5.07	3.56	2.60	1.98	1.53	1.22	* * *	1.24	1.49	1.74	1.98	13
14	10600	4070	1403	438	193	103	62.2	28.2	15.4	9.48	6.21	4.35	3.18	2.41	1.88	1.50	1.22	* * *	1.24	1.44	1.64	14
15	12824	4927	1698	530	234	125	75.3	34.1	18.7	11.5	7.52	5.27	3.85	2.92	2.27	1.81	1.48	1.21	* * *	1.17	1.35	15
16	14978	5758	1984	619	274	146	88.0	39.9	21.8	13.4	8.78	6.15	4.51	3.41	2.66	2.12	1.73	1.42	1.18	* * *	1.14	16
17	17537	6738	2322	724	320	171	103	46.6	25.6	15.7	10.3	7.20	5.27	3.99	3.11	2.47	2.03	1.66	1.37	1.17	* * *	17
18	20327	7810	2691	840	317	198	119	54.1	29.6	18.2	11.9	8.35	6.11	4.63	3.60	2.87	2.35	1.92	1.59	1.36	1.16	18
20	26676	10249	3532	1102	487	260	157	70.9	38.9	23.9	15.6	10.9	8.02	6.07	4.73	3.76	3.08	2.52	2.08	1.78	1.52	20
24	42624	16376	5644	1761	778	416	250	113	62.1	38.2	25.0	17.5	12.8	9.70	7.55	6.01	4.92	4.02	3.32	2.84	2.43	24
30	75453	28990	9990	3117	1378	736	443	201	110	67.6	44.2	31.0	22.7	17.2	13.4	10.7	8.72	7.14	5.88	5.03	4.30	30
36	120100	46143	15902	4961	2193	1172	705	319	175	108	70.4	49.3	36.1	27.3	21.3	16.9	13.9	11.3	9.37	8.01	6.85	36
42	177724	68282	23531	7341	3245	1734	1044	473	259	159	104	73.0	53.4	40.5	31.5	25.1	20.5	16.8	13.9	11.9	10.1	42
48	249351	95818	33020	10301	4554	2434	1465	663	363	223	146	102	75.0	56.8	44.2	35.2	28.8	23.5	19.4	16.6	14.2	48
Dia.	½	¾	1	1½	2	2½	3	4	5	6	7	8	9	10	11	12	13	14	15	16	17	

By permission, Buffalo Tank Div., Bethlehem Steel Corp.

A-18.
(Continued). Circumferences and Areas of Circles
(Advancing by eighths)

Dia.	Circum.	Area*
11.	34.558	95.033
1/8	34.950	97.205
1/4	35.343	99.402
3/8	35.736	101.62
1/2	36.128	103.87
5/8	36.521	106.14
3/4	36.914	108.43
7/8	37.306	110.75
12.	37.699	113.10
1/8	38.092	115.47
1/4	38.485	117.86
3/8	38.877	120.28
1/2	39.270	122.72
5/8	39.663	125.19
3/4	40.055	127.68
7/8	40.448	130.19
13.	40.841	132.73
1/8	41.233	135.30
1/4	41.626	137.89
3/8	42.019	140.50
1/2	42.412	143.14
5/8	42.804	145.80
3/4	43.197	148.49
7/8	43.590	151.20
14.	43.982	153.94
1/8	44.375	156.70
1/4	44.768	159.48
3/8	45.160	162.30
1/2	45.553	165.13
5/8	45.946	167.99
3/4	46.338	170.87
7/8	46.731	173.78
15.	47.124	176.71
1/8	47.517	179.67
1/4	47.909	182.65
3/8	48.302	185.66
1/2	48.695	188.69
5/8	49.087	191.75
3/4	49.480	194.83
7/8	49.873	197.93
16.	50.265	201.06
1/8	50.658	204.22
1/4	51.051	207.39
3/8	51.444	210.60
1/2	51.836	213.82
5/8	52.229	217.08
3/4	52.622	220.35
7/8	53.014	223.65
17.	53.407	226.98
1/8	53.800	230.33

Dia.	Circum.	Area*
17 1/4	54.192	233.71
3/8	54.585	237.10
1/2	54.978	240.53
5/8	55.371	243.98
3/4	55.763	247.45
7/8	56.156	250.95
18.	56.549	254.47
1/8	56.941	258.02
1/4	57.334	261.59
3/8	57.727	265.18
1/2	58.119	268.80
5/8	58.512	272.45
3/4	58.905	276.12
7/8	59.298	279.81
19.	59.690	283.53
1/8	60.083	287.27
1/4	60.476	291.04
3/8	60.868	294.83
1/2	61.261	298.65
5/8	61.654	302.49
3/4	62.046	306.35
7/8	62.439	310.24
20.	62.832	314.16
1/8	63.225	318.10
1/4	63.617	322.06
3/8	64.010	326.05
1/2	64.403	330.06
5/8	64.795	334.10
3/4	65.188	338.16
7/8	65.581	342.25
21.	65.973	346.36
1/8	66.366	350.50
1/4	66.759	354.66
3/8	67.152	358.84
1/2	67.544	363.05
5/8	67.937	367.28
3/4	68.330	371.54
7/8	68.722	375.83
22.	69.115	380.13
1/8	69.508	384.46
1/4	69.900	388.82
3/8	70.293	393.20
1/2	70.686	397.61
5/8	71.079	402.04
3/4	71.471	406.49
7/8	71.864	410.97
23.	72.257	415.48
1/8	72.649	420.00
1/4	73.042	424.56
3/8	73.435	429.13

Dia.	Circum.	Area*
23 1/2	73.827	433.74
5/8	74.220	438.36
3/4	74.613	443.01
7/8	75.006	447.69
24.	75.398	452.39
1/8	75.791	457.11
1/4	76.184	461.86
3/8	76.576	466.64
1/2	76.969	471.44
5/8	77.362	476.26
3/4	77.754	481.11
7/8	78.147	485.98
25.	78.540	490.87
1/8	78.933	495.79
1/4	79.325	500.74
3/8	79.718	505.71
1/2	80.111	510.71
5/8	80.503	515.72
3/4	80.896	520.77
7/8	81.289	525.84
26.	81.681	530.93
1/8	82.074	536.05
1/4	82.467	541.19
3/8	82.860	546.35
1/2	83.252	551.55
5/8	83.645	556.76
3/4	84.038	562.00
7/8	84.430	567.27
27.	84.823	572.56
1/8	85.216	577.87
1/4	85.608	583.21
3/8	86.001	588.57
1/2	86.394	593.96
5/8	86.786	599.37
3/4	87.179	604.81
7/8	87.572	610.27
28.	87.965	615.75
1/8	88.357	621.26
1/4	88.750	626.80
3/8	89.143	632.36
1/2	89.535	637.94
5/8	89.928	643.55
3/4	90.321	649.18
7/8	90.713	654.84
29.	91.106	660.52
1/8	91.499	666.23
1/4	91.892	671.96
3/8	92.284	677.71
1/2	92.677	683.49

*Approximate area, sufficiently accurate for practical purposes, including estimating.

(Continued on next page)

A-18.
Circumferences and Areas of Circles
(Advancing by eighths)

Dia.	Circum.	Area*
1/64	.04909	.00019
1/32	.09818	.00077
3/64	.14726	.00173
1/16	.19635	.00307
3/32	.29452	.00690
1/8	.39270	.01227
5/32	.49087	.01917
3/16	.58905	.02761
7/32	.68722	.03758
1/4	.78540	.04909
9/32	.88357	.06213
5/16	.98175	.07670
11/32	1.0799	.09281
3/8	1.1781	.11045
13/32	1.2763	.12962
7/16	1.3744	.15033
15/32	1.4726	.17257
1/2	1.5708	.19635
17/32	1.6690	.22166
9/16	1.7671	.24850
19/32	1.8653	.27688
5/8	1.9635	.30680
21/32	2.0617	.33824
11/16	2.1598	.37122
23/32	2.2580	.40574
3/4	2.3562	.44179
25/32	2.4544	.47937
13/16	2.5525	.51849
27/32	2.6507	.55914
7/8	2.7489	.60132
29/32	2.8471	.64504
15/16	2.9452	.69029
31/32	3.0434	.73708
1.	3.1416	.7854
1 1/16	3.3379	.8866
1 1/8	3.5343	.9940
1 3/16	3.7306	1.1075
1 1/4	3.9270	1.2272
1 5/16	4.1233	1.3530
1 3/8	4.3197	1.4849
1 7/16	4.5160	1.6230
1 1/2	4.7124	1.7671
1 9/16	4.9087	1.9175
1 5/8	5.1051	2.0739
1 11/16	5.3014	2.2365
1 3/4	5.4978	2.4053
1 13/16	5.6941	2.5802
1 7/8	5.8905	2.7612
1 15/16	6.0868	2.9483
2.	6.2832	3.1416
1/16	6.4795	3.3410

Dia.	Circum.	Area*
2 1/8	6.6759	3.5466
3/16	6.8722	3.7583
1/4	7.0686	3.9761
5/16	7.2649	4.2000
3/8	7.4613	4.4301
7/16	7.6576	4.6664
1/2	7.8540	4.9087
9/16	8.0503	5.1572
5/8	8.2467	5.4119
11/16	8.4430	5.6727
3/4	8.6394	5.9396
13/16	8.8357	6.2126
7/8	9.0321	6.4918
15/16	9.2284	6.7772
3.	9.4248	7.0686
1/8	9.6211	7.3662
3/16	9.8175	7.6699
1/4	10.014	7.9798
5/16	10.210	8.2958
3/8	10.407	8.6179
7/16	10.603	8.9462
1/2	10.799	9.2806
5/8	10.996	9.6211
11/16	11.192	9.9678
3/4	11.388	10.321
13/16	11.585	10.680
7/8	11.781	11.045
15/16	11.977	11.416
4.	12.174	11.793
1/16	12.370	12.177
1/8	12.566	12.566
3/16	12.763	12.962
1/4	12.959	13.364
5/16	13.155	13.772
3/8	13.352	14.186
7/16	13.548	14.607
1/2	13.744	15.033
9/16	13.941	15.466
5/8	14.137	15.904
11/16	14.334	16.349
3/4	14.530	16.800
13/16	14.726	17.257
7/8	14.923	17.728
15/16	15.119	18.190
5.	15.315	18.665
1/8	15.512	19.147
1/4	15.708	19.635
3/16	15.904	20.129
1/4	16.101	20.629
5/16	16.297	21.135
	16.493	21.648
	16.690	22.166

*Approximate area, sufficiently accurate for practical purposes, including estimating.

By permission, Buffalo Tank Div., Bethlehem Steel Corp.

A-18.
Circumferences and Areas of Circles
(Advancing by eighths)

Dia.	Circum	Area*	Dia.	Circum.	Area*	Dia.	Circum.	Area*	Dia.	Circum.	Area*
29 5/8	93.070	689.30	36.	113.097	1017.9	42 1/4	132.732	1402.0	48 5/8	152.760	1857.0
3/4	93.462	695.13	1/8	113.490	1025.0	3/8	133.125	1410.3	3/4	153.153	1866.5
7/8	93.855	700.98	1/4	113.883	1032.1	1/2	133.518	1418.6	7/8	153.545	1876.1
30.	94.248	706.86	3/8	114.275	1039.2	5/8	133.910	1427.0	49.	153.938	1885.7
1/8	94.640	712.76	1/2	114.668	1046.3	3/4	134.303	1435.4	1/8	154.331	1895.4
1/4	95.033	718.69	5/8	115.061	1053.5	7/8	134.696	1443.8	1/4	154.723	1905.0
3/8	95.426	724.64	3/4	115.454	1060.7	43.	135.088	1452.2	3/8	155.116	1914.7
1/2	95.819	730.62	7/8	115.846	1068.0	1/8	135.481	1460.7	1/2	155.509	1924.4
5/8	96.211	736.62	37.	116.239	1075.2	1/4	135.874	1469.1	5/8	155.902	1934.2
3/4	96.604	742.64	1/8	116.632	1082.5	3/8	136.267	1477.6	3/4	156.294	1943.9
7/8	96.997	748.69	1/4	117.024	1089.8	1/2	136.659	1486.2	7/8	156.687	1953.7
31.	97.389	754.77	3/8	117.417	1097.1	5/8	137.052	1494.7	50.	157.080	1963.5
1/8	97.782	760.87	1/2	117.810	1104.5	3/4	137.445	1503.3	1/8	157.472	1973.3
1/4	98.175	766.99	5/8	118.202	1111.8	7/8	137.837	1511.9	1/4	157.865	1983.2
3/8	98.567	773.14	3/4	118.596	1119.2	44.	138.230	1520.5	3/8	158.258	1993.1
1/2	98.960	779.31	7/8	118.988	1126.7	1/8	138.623	1529.2	1/2	158.650	2003.0
5/8	99.353	785.51	38.	119.381	1134.1	1/4	139.015	1537.9	5/8	159.043	2012.9
3/4	99.746	791.73	1/8	119.773	1141.6	3/8	139.408	1546.6	3/4	159.436	2022.8
7/8	100.138	797.98	1/4	120.166	1149.1	1/2	139.801	1555.3	7/8	159.829	2032.8
32.	100.531	804.25	3/8	120.559	1156.6	5/8	140.194	1564.0	51.	160.221	2042.8
1/8	100.924	810.54	1/2	120.951	1164.2	3/4	140.586	1572.8	1/8	160.614	2052.8
1/4	101.316	816.86	5/8	121.344	1171.7	7/8	140.979	1581.6	1/4	161.007	2062.9
3/8	101.709	823.21	3/4	121.737	1179.3	45.	141.372	1590.4	3/8	161.399	2073.0
1/2	102.102	829.58	7/8	122.129	1186.9	1/8	141.764	1599.3	1/2	161.792	2083.1
5/8	102.494	835.97	39.	122.522	1194.6	1/4	142.157	1608.2	5/8	162.185	2093.2
3/4	102.887	842.39	1/8	122.915	1202.3	3/8	142.550	1617.0	3/4	162.577	2103.3
7/8	103.280	848.83	1/4	123.308	1210.6	1/2	142.942	1626.0	7/8	162.970	2113.5
33.	103.673	855.30	3/8	123.700	1217.7	5/8	143.335	1634.9	52.	163.363	2123.7
1/8	104.065	861.79	1/2	124.093	1225.4	3/4	143.728	1643.9	1/8	163.756	2133.9
1/4	104.458	868.31	5/8	124.486	1233.2	7/8	144.121	1652.9	1/4	164.148	2144.2
3/8	104.851	874.85	3/4	124.878	1241.0	46.	144.513	1661.9	3/8	164.541	2154.5
1/2	105.243	881.41	7/8	125.271	1248.8	1/8	144.906	1670.9	1/2	164.934	2164.8
5/8	105.636	888.00	40.	125.664	1256.6	1/4	145.299	1680.0	5/8	165.326	2175.1
3/4	106.029	894.62	1/8	126.056	1264.5	3/8	145.691	1689.1	3/4	165.719	2185.4
7/8	106.421	901.26	1/4	126.449	1272.4	1/2	146.084	1698.2	7/8	166.112	2195.8
34.	106.814	907.92	3/8	126.842	1280.3	5/8	146.477	1707.4	53.	166.504	2206.2
1/8	107.207	914.61	1/2	127.235	1288.2	3/4	146.869	1716.5	1/8	166.897	2216.6
1/4	107.600	921.32	5/8	127.627	1296.2	7/8	147.262	1725.7	1/4	167.290	2227.0
3/8	107.992	928.06	3/4	128.020	1304.2	47.	147.655	1734.9	3/8	167.683	2237.5
1/2	108.385	934.82	7/8	128.413	1312.2	1/8	148.048	1744.2	1/2	168.075	2248.0
5/8	108.778	941.61	41.	128.805	1320.3	1/4	148.440	1753.5	5/8	168.468	2258.5
3/4	109.170	948.42	1/8	129.198	1328.3	3/8	148.833	1762.7	3/4	168.861	2269.1
7/8	109.563	955.25	1/4	129.591	1336.4	1/2	149.226	1772.1	7/8	169.253	2279.6
35.	109.956	962.11	3/8	129.983	1344.5	5/8	149.618	1781.4	54.	169.646	2290.2
1/8	110.348	969.00	1/2	130.376	1352.7	3/4	150.011	1790.8	1/8	170.039	2300.8
1/4	110.741	975.91	5/8	130.769	1360.8	7/8	150.404	1800.1	1/4	170.431	2311.5
3/8	111.134	982.84	3/4	131.161	1369.0	48.	150.796	1809.6	3/8	170.824	2322.1
1/2	111.527	989.80	7/8	131.554	1377.2	1/8	151.189	1819.0	1/2	171.217	2332.8
5/8	111.919	996.78	42.	131.947	1385.4	1/4	151.582	1828.5	5/8	171.609	2343.5
3/4	112.312	1003.8	1/8	132.340	1393.7	3/8	151.975	1837.9	3/4	172.002	2354.3
7/8	112.705	1010.8				1/2	152.367	1847.5	7/8	172.395	2365.0

A-18.
(Continued). Circumferences and Areas of Circles
(Advancing by eighths)

Dia.	Circum.	Area*	Dia.	Circum.	Area*
55.	172.788	2375.8	61 1/4	192.423	2946.5
1/8	173.180	2386.6	3/8	192.815	2958.5
1/4	173.573	2397.5	1/2	193.208	2970.6
3/8	173.966	2408.3	5/8	193.601	2982.7
1/2	174.358	2419.2	3/4	193.993	2994.8
5/8	174.751	2430.1	7/8	194.386	3006.9
3/4	175.144	2441.1	62.	194.779	3019.1
7/8	175.536	2452.0	1/8	195.171	3031.3
56.	175.929	2463.0	1/4	195.564	3043.5
1/8	176.322	2474.0	3/8	195.957	3055.7
1/4	176.715	2485.0	1/2	196.350	3068.0
3/8	177.107	2496.1	5/8	196.742	3080.3
1/2	177.500	2507.2	3/4	197.135	3092.6
5/8	177.893	2518.3	7/8	197.528	3104.9
3/4	178.285	2529.4	63.	197.920	3117.2
7/8	178.678	2540.6	1/8	198.313	3129.6
57.	179.071	2551.8	1/4	198.706	3142.0
1/8	179.463	2563.0	3/8	199.098	3154.5
1/4	179.856	2574.2	1/2	199.491	3166.9
3/8	180.249	2585.4	5/8	199.884	3179.4
1/2	180.642	2596.7	3/4	200.277	3191.9
5/8	181.034	2608.0	7/8	200.669	3204.4
3/4	181.427	2619.4	64.	201.062	3217.0
7/8	181.820	2630.7	1/8	201.455	3229.6
58.	182.212	2642.1	1/4	201.847	3242.2
1/8	182.605	2653.5	3/8	202.240	3254.8
1/4	182.998	2664.9	1/2	202.633	3267.5
3/8	183.390	2676.4	5/8	203.025	3280.1
1/2	183.783	2687.8	3/4	203.418	3292.8
5/8	184.176	2699.3	7/8	203.811	3305.6
3/4	184.569	2710.9	65.	204.204	3318.3
7/8	184.961	2722.4	1/8	204.596	3331.1
59.	185.354	2734.0	1/4	204.989	3343.9
1/8	185.747	2745.6	3/8	205.382	3356.7
1/4	186.139	2757.2	1/2	205.774	3369.6
3/8	186.532	2768.8	5/8	206.167	3382.4
1/2	186.925	2780.5	3/4	206.560	3395.3
5/8	187.317	2792.2	7/8	206.952	3408.2
3/4	187.710	2803.9	66.	207.345	3421.2
7/8	188.103	2815.7	1/8	207.738	3434.2
60.	188.496	2827.4	1/4	208.131	3447.2
1/8	188.888	2839.2	3/8	208.523	3460.2
1/4	189.281	2851.0	1/2	208.916	3473.2
3/8	189.674	2862.9	5/8	209.309	3486.3
1/2	190.066	2874.8	3/4	209.701	3499.4
5/8	190.459	2886.6	7/8	210.094	3512.5
3/4	190.852	2898.6	67.	210.487	3525.7
7/8	191.244	2910.5	1/8	210.879	3538.8
61.	191.637	2922.5	1/4	211.272	3552.0
1/8	192.030	2934.5	3/8	211.665	3565.2

(Continued). Circumferences and Areas of Circles
(Advancing by eighths)

Dia.	Circum.	Area*	Dia.	Circum.	Area*	Dia.	Circum.	Area*
86¼	270.962	5842.6	92½	290.597	6720.1	98¾	310.232	7658.9
3/8	271.355	5859.6	5/8	290.990	6738.2	7/8	310.625	7678.3
1/2	271.748	5876.5	3/4	291.383	6756.4	99.	311.018	7697.7
5/8	272.140	5893.5	7/8	291.775	6774.7	1/8	311.410	7717.1
3/4	272.533	5910.6	93.	292.168	6792.9	1/4	311.803	7736.6
7/8	272.926	5927.6	1/8	292.561	6811.2	3/8	312.196	7756.1
87.	273.319	5944.7	1/4	292.954	6829.5	1/2	312.588	7775.6
1/8	273.711	5961.8	3/8	293.346	6847.8	5/8	312.981	7795.2
1/4	274.104	5978.9	1/2	293.739	6866.1	3/4	313.374	7814.8
3/8	274.497	5996.0	5/8	294.132	6884.5	7/8	313.767	7834.4
1/2	274.889	6013.2	3/4	294.524	6902.9	100.	314.16	7854
5/8	275.282	6030.4	7/8	294.917	6921.3	1/8	314.55	7873
3/4	275.675	6047.6	94.	295.310	6939.8	1/4	314.95	7893
7/8	276.067	6064.9	1/8	295.702	6958.2	3/8	315.34	7913
88.	276.460	6082.1	1/4	296.095	6976.7	1/2	315.73	7933
1/8	276.853	6099.4	3/8	296.488	6995.3	5/8	316.12	7952
1/4	277.246	6116.7	1/2	296.881	7013.8	3/4	316.52	7972
3/8	277.638	6134.1	5/8	297.273	7032.4	7/8	316.91	7992
1/2	278.031	6151.4	3/4	297.666	7051.0	101.	317.30	8012
5/8	278.424	6168.8	7/8	298.059	7069.6	1/8	317.69	8032
3/4	278.816	6186.2	95.	298.451	7088.2	1/4	318.09	8052
7/8	279.209	6203.7	1/8	298.844	7106.9	3/8	318.48	8071
89.	279.602	6221.1	1/4	299.237	7125.6	1/2	318.87	8091
1/8	279.994	6238.6	3/8	299.629	7144.3	5/8	319.27	8111
1/4	280.387	6256.1	1/2	300.022	7163.0	3/4	319.66	8131
3/8	280.780	6273.7	5/8	300.415	7181.8	7/8	320.05	8151
1/2	281.173	6291.2	3/4	300.807	7200.6	102.	320.44	8171
5/8	281.565	6308.8	7/8	301.200	7219.4	1/8	320.84	8191
3/4	281.958	6326.4	96.	301.593	7238.2	1/4	321.23	8211
7/8	282.351	6344.1	1/8	301.986	7257.1	3/8	321.62	8231
90.	282.743	6361.7	1/4	302.378	7276.0	1/2	322.01	8252
1/8	283.136	6379.4	3/8	302.771	7294.9	5/8	322.41	8272
1/4	283.529	6397.1	1/2	303.164	7313.8	3/4	322.80	8292
3/8	283.921	6414.9	5/8	303.556	7332.8	7/8	323.19	8312
1/2	284.314	6432.6	3/4	303.949	7351.8	103.	323.59	8332
5/8	284.707	6450.4	7/8	304.342	7370.8	1/8	323.98	8352
3/4	285.100	6468.2	97.	304.734	7389.8	1/4	324.37	8372
7/8	285.492	6486.0	1/8	305.127	7408.9	3/8	324.76	8393
91.	285.885	6503.9	1/4	305.520	7428.0	1/2	325.16	8413
1/8	286.278	6521.8	3/8	305.913	7447.1	5/8	325.55	8434
1/4	286.670	6539.7	1/2	306.305	7466.2	3/4	325.94	8454
3/8	287.063	6557.6	5/8	306.698	7485.3	7/8	326.33	8474
1/2	287.456	6575.5	3/4	307.091	7504.5	104.	326.73	8495
5/8	287.848	6593.5	7/8	307.483	7523.7	1/8	327.12	8515
3/4	288.241	6611.5	98.	307.876	7543.0	1/4	327.51	8536
7/8	288.634	6629.6	1/8	308.269	7562.2	3/8	327.91	8556
92.	289.027	6647.6	1/4	308.661	7581.5	1/2	328.30	8577
1/8	289.419	6665.7	3/8	309.054	7600.8	5/8	328.69	8597
1/4	289.812	6683.8	1/2	309.447	7620.1	3/4	329.08	8618
3/8	290.205	6701.9	5/8	309.840	7639.5	7/8	329.48	8638

*Approximate area, sufficiently accurate for practical purposes, including estimating.

(Continued on next page)

(Continued). Circumferences and Areas of Circles
(Advancing by eighths)

Dia.	Circum.	Area*	Dia.	Circum.	Area*	Dia.	Circum.	Area*
67½	212.058	3578.5	73¾	231.692	4271.8	80.	251.327	5026.5
5/8	212.450	3591.7	7/8	232.085	4286.3	1/8	251.720	5042.3
3/4	212.843	3605.0	74.	232.478	4300.8	1/4	252.113	5058.0
7/8	213.236	3618.3	1/8	232.871	4315.4	3/8	252.506	5073.8
68.	213.628	3631.7	1/4	233.263	4329.9	1/2	252.898	5089.6
1/8	214.021	3645.0	3/8	233.656	4344.5	5/8	253.291	5105.4
1/4	214.414	3658.4	1/2	234.049	4359.2	3/4	253.684	5121.2
3/8	214.806	3671.8	5/8	234.441	4373.8	7/8	254.076	5137.1
1/2	215.199	3685.3	3/4	234.834	4388.5	81.	254.469	5153.0
5/8	215.592	3698.7	7/8	235.227	4403.1	1/8	254.862	5168.9
3/4	215.984	3712.2	75.	235.619	4417.9	1/4	255.254	5184.9
7/8	216.377	3725.7	1/8	236.012	4432.6	3/8	255.647	5200.8
69.	216.770	3739.3	1/4	236.405	4447.4	1/2	256.040	5216.8
1/8	217.163	3752.8	3/8	236.798	4462.2	5/8	256.433	5232.8
1/4	217.555	3766.4	1/2	237.190	4477.0	3/4	256.825	5248.9
3/8	217.948	3780.0	5/8	237.583	4491.8	7/8	257.218	5264.9
1/2	218.341	3793.7	3/4	237.976	4506.7	82.	257.611	5281.0
5/8	218.733	3807.3	7/8	238.368	4521.5	1/8	258.003	5297.1
3/4	219.126	3821.0	76.	238.761	4536.5	1/4	258.396	5313.3
7/8	219.519	3834.7	1/8	239.154	4551.4	3/8	258.789	5329.4
70.	219.911	3848.5	1/4	239.546	4566.4	1/2	259.181	5345.6
1/8	220.304	3862.2	3/8	239.939	4581.3	5/8	259.574	5361.8
1/4	220.697	3876.0	1/2	240.332	4596.3	3/4	259.967	5378.1
3/8	221.090	3889.8	5/8	240.725	4611.4	7/8	260.359	5394.3
1/2	221.482	3903.6	3/4	241.117	4626.4	83.	260.752	5410.6
5/8	221.875	3917.5	7/8	241.510	4641.5	1/8	261.145	5426.9
3/4	222.268	3931.4	77.	241.903	4656.6	1/4	261.538	5443.3
7/8	222.660	3945.3	1/8	242.295	4671.8	3/8	261.930	5459.6
71.	223.053	3959.2	1/4	242.688	4686.9	1/2	262.323	5476.0
1/8	223.446	3973.1	3/8	243.081	4702.1	5/8	262.716	5492.4
1/4	223.838	3987.1	1/2	243.473	4717.3	3/4	263.108	5508.8
3/8	224.231	4001.1	5/8	243.866	4732.5	7/8	263.501	5525.3
1/2	224.624	4015.2	3/4	244.259	4747.8	84.	263.894	5541.8
5/8	225.017	4029.2	7/8	244.652	4763.1	1/8	264.286	5558.3
3/4	225.409	4043.3	78.	245.044	4778.4	1/4	264.679	5574.8
7/8	225.802	4057.4	1/8	245.437	4793.7	3/8	265.072	5591.4
72.	226.195	4071.5	1/4	245.830	4809.0	1/2	265.465	5607.9
1/8	226.587	4085.7	3/8	246.222	4824.4	5/8	265.857	5624.5
1/4	226.980	4099.8	1/2	246.615	4839.8	3/4	266.250	5641.2
3/8	227.373	4114.0	5/8	247.008	4855.2	7/8	266.643	5657.8
1/2	227.765	4128.2	3/4	247.400	4870.7	85.	267.035	5674.5
5/8	228.158	4142.5	7/8	247.793	4886.2	1/8	267.428	5691.2
3/4	228.551	4156.8	79.	248.186	4901.7	1/4	267.821	5707.9
7/8	228.944	4171.1	1/8	248.579	4917.2	3/8	268.213	5724.7
73.	229.336	4185.4	1/4	248.971	4932.7	1/2	268.606	5741.5
1/8	229.729	4199.7	3/8	249.364	4948.3	5/8	268.999	5758.3
1/4	230.122	4214.1	1/2	249.757	4963.9	3/4	269.392	5775.1
3/8	230.514	4228.5	5/8	250.149	4979.5	7/8	269.784	5791.9
1/2	230.907	4242.9	3/4	250.542	4995.2	86.	270.177	5808.8
5/8	231.300	4257.4	7/8	250.935	5010.9	1/8	270.570	5825.7

*Approximate area, sufficiently accurate for practical purposes, including estimating.

A-18.
(Continued). Circumferences and Areas of Circles
(Advancing by eighths)

Dia.	Circum.	Area*	Dia.	Circum.	Area*	Dia.	Circum.	Area*
123⅝	388.38	12004	130.	408.41	13273	136¼	428.04	14580
¾	388.77	12028	⅛	408.80	13299	⅜	428.44	14607
⅞	389.17	12052	¼	409.19	13324	½	428.83	14633
124.	389.56	12076	⅜	409.59	13350	⅝	429.22	14660
⅛	389.95	12101	½	409.98	13375	¾	429.61	14687
¼	390.34	12125	⅝	410.37	13401	⅞	430.01	14714
⅜	390.74	12150	¾	410.76	13426	137.	430.40	14741
½	391.13	12174	⅞	411.16	13452	⅛	430.79	14768
⅝	391.52	12199	131.	411.55	13478	¼	431.19	14795
¾	391.92	12223	⅛	411.94	13504	⅜	431.58	14822
⅞	392.31	12248	¼	412.34	13529	½	431.97	14849
125.	392.70	12272	⅜	412.73	13555	⅝	432.36	14876
⅛	393.09	12297	½	413.12	13581	¾	432.76	14903
¼	393.49	12321	⅝	413.51	13607	⅞	433.15	14930
⅜	393.88	12346	¾	413.91	13633	138.	433.54	14957
½	394.27	12370	⅞	414.30	13659	⅛	433.93	14984
⅝	394.66	12395	132.	414.69	13685	¼	434.33	15012
¾	395.06	12419	⅛	415.08	13711	⅜	434.72	15039
⅞	395.45	12444	¼	415.48	13737	½	435.11	15067
126.	395.84	12469	⅜	415.87	13763	⅝	435.50	15094
⅛	396.23	12494	½	416.26	13789	¾	435.90	15121
¼	396.63	12518	⅝	416.66	13815	⅞	436.29	15148
⅜	397.02	12543	¾	417.05	13841	139.	436.68	15175
½	397.41	12568	⅞	417.44	13867	⅛	437.08	15203
⅝	397.81	12593	133.	417.83	13893	¼	437.47	15230
¾	398.20	12618	⅛	418.23	13919	⅜	437.86	15258
⅞	398.59	12643	¼	418.62	13946	½	438.25	15285
127.	398.98	12668	⅜	419.01	13972	⅝	438.65	15313
⅛	399.38	12693	½	419.40	13999	¾	439.04	15340
¼	399.77	12718	⅝	419.80	14025	⅞	439.43	15367
⅜	400.16	12743	¾	420.19	14051	140.	439.82	15394
½	400.55	12768	⅞	420.58	14077	⅛	440.22	15422
⅝	400.95	12793	134.	420.97	14103	¼	440.61	15449
¾	401.34	12818	⅛	421.37	14130	⅜	441.00	15477
⅞	401.73	12843	¼	421.76	14156	½	441.40	15504
128.	402.13	12868	⅜	422.15	14183	⅝	441.79	15532
⅛	402.52	12893	½	422.55	14209	¾	442.18	15559
¼	402.91	12919	⅝	422.94	14236	⅞	442.57	15587
⅜	403.30	12944	¾	423.33	14262	141.	442.97	15615
½	403.70	12970	⅞	423.72	14288	⅛	443.36	15642
⅝	404.09	12995	135.	424.12	14314	¼	443.75	15670
¾	404.48	13020	⅛	424.51	14341	⅜	444.14	15697
⅞	404.87	13045	¼	424.90	14367	½	444.54	15725
129.	405.27	13070	⅜	425.29	14394	⅝	444.93	15753
⅛	405.66	13096	½	425.69	14420	¾	445.32	15781
¼	406.05	13121	⅝	426.08	14447	⅞	445.72	15809
⅜	406.44	13147	¾	426.47	14473	142.	446.11	15837
½	406.84	13172	⅞	426.87	14500	⅛	446.50	15865
⅝	407.23	13198	136.	427.26	14527	¼	446.89	15893
¾	407.62	13223	⅛	427.65	14553	⅜	447.29	15921
⅞	408.02	13248						

A-18.
(Continued). Circumferences and Areas of Circles
(Advancing by eighths)

Dia.	Circum.	Area*	Dia.	Circum.	Area*	Dia.	Circum.	Area*
105.	329.87	8659	111¼	349.50	9720	117½	369.14	10844
⅛	330.26	8679	⅜	349.90	9742	⅝	369.53	10867
¼	330.65	8700	½	350.29	9764	¾	369.92	10890
⅜	331.05	8721	⅝	350.68	9786	⅞	370.32	10913
½	331.44	8741	¾	351.07	9808	118.	370.71	10936
⅝	331.83	8762	⅞	351.47	9830	⅛	371.11	10960
¾	332.22	8783	112.	351.86	9852	¼	371.49	10983
⅞	332.62	8804	⅛	352.25	9874	⅜	371.89	11007
106.	333.01	8825	¼	352.65	9897	½	372.28	11030
⅛	333.40	8845	⅜	353.04	9919	⅝	372.67	11053
¼	333.80	8866	½	353.43	9941	¾	373.07	11076
⅜	334.19	8887	⅝	353.82	9963	⅞	373.46	11099
½	334.58	8908	¾	354.22	9985	119.	373.85	11122
⅝	334.97	8929	⅞	354.61	10007	⅛	374.24	11146
¾	335.37	8950	113.	355.00	10029	¼	374.64	11169
⅞	335.76	8971	⅛	355.39	10052	⅜	375.03	11193
107.	336.15	8992	¼	355.79	10074	½	375.42	11216
⅛	336.54	9014	⅜	356.18	10097	⅝	375.81	11240
¼	336.94	9035	½	356.57	10119	¾	376.21	11263
⅜	337.33	9056	⅝	356.96	10141	⅞	376.60	11287
½	337.72	9077	¾	357.36	10163	120.	376.99	11310
⅝	338.12	9098	⅞	357.75	10185	⅛	377.39	11334
¾	338.51	9119	114.	358.14	10207	¼	377.78	11357
⅞	338.90	9140	⅛	358.54	10230	⅜	378.17	11381
108.	339.29	9161	¼	358.93	10252	½	378.56	11404
⅛	339.69	9183	⅜	359.32	10275	⅝	378.96	11428
¼	340.08	9204	½	359.71	10297	¾	379.35	11451
⅜	340.47	9225	⅝	360.11	10320	⅞	379.74	11475
½	340.86	9246	¾	360.50	10342	121.	380.13	11499
⅝	341.26	9268	⅞	360.89	10365	⅛	380.53	11522
¾	341.65	9289	115.	361.28	10387	¼	380.92	11546
⅞	342.04	9310	⅛	361.68	10410	⅜	381.31	11570
109.	342.43	9331	¼	362.07	10432	½	381.70	11594
⅛	342.83	9353	⅜	362.46	10455	⅝	382.10	11618
¼	343.22	9374	½	362.86	10477	¾	382.49	11642
⅜	343.61	9396	⅝	363.25	10500	⅞	382.88	11666
½	344.01	9417	¾	363.64	10522	122.	383.28	11690
⅝	344.40	9439	⅞	364.03	10545	⅛	383.67	11714
¾	344.79	9460	116.	364.43	10568	¼	384.06	11738
⅞	345.18	9481	⅛	364.82	10590	⅜	384.45	11762
110.	345.58	9503	¼	365.21	10613	½	384.85	11786
⅛	345.97	9525	⅜	365.60	10636	⅝	385.24	11810
¼	346.36	9546	½	366.00	10659	¾	385.63	11834
⅜	346.75	9568	⅝	366.39	10682	⅞	386.02	11858
½	347.15	9589	¾	366.78	10705	123.	386.42	11882
⅝	347.54	9611	⅞	367.18	10728	⅛	386.81	11907
¾	347.93	9633	117.	367.57	10751	¼	387.20	11931
⅞	348.33	9655	⅛	367.96	10774	⅜	387.60	11956
111.	348.72	9677	¼	368.35	10798	½	387.99	11980
⅛	349.11	9698	⅜	368.75	10821			

A-18.
(Continued). Circumferences and Areas of Circles
(Advancing by eighths)

Dia.	Circum.	Area*	Dia.	Circum.	Area*
161 1/4	506.58	20421	167 1/2	526.22	22035
3/8	506.98	20453	5/8	526.61	22068
1/2	507.37	20484	3/4	527.00	22101
5/8	507.76	20516	7/8	527.40	22134
3/4	508.15	20548	168.	527.79	22167
7/8	508.55	20580	1/8	528.18	22200
162.	508.94	20612	1/4	528.57	22233
1/8	509.33	20644	3/8	528.97	22266
1/4	509.73	20675	1/2	529.36	22299
3/8	510.12	20707	5/8	529.75	22332
1/2	510.51	20739	3/4	530.15	22366
5/8	510.90	20771	7/8	530.54	22399
3/4	511.30	20803	169.	530.93	22432
7/8	511.69	20835	1/8	531.32	22465
163.	512.08	20867	1/4	531.72	22499
1/8	512.47	20899	3/8	532.11	22532
1/4	512.87	20931	1/2	532.50	22566
3/8	513.26	20964	5/8	532.89	22599
1/2	513.65	20996	3/4	533.29	22632
5/8	514.04	21028	7/8	533.68	22665
3/4	514.44	21060	170.	534.07	22698
7/8	514.83	21092	1/8	534.47	22731
164.	515.22	21124	1/4	534.86	22765
1/8	515.62	21157	3/8	535.25	22798
1/4	516.01	21189	1/2	535.64	22832
3/8	516.40	21221	5/8	536.04	22865
1/2	516.79	21254	3/4	536.43	22899
5/8	517.19	21287	7/8	536.82	22932
3/4	517.58	21319	171.	537.21	22966
7/8	517.97	21351	1/8	537.61	22999
165.	518.36	21383	1/4	538.00	23033
1/8	518.76	21416	3/8	538.39	23066
1/4	519.15	21448	1/2	538.78	23100
3/8	519.54	21481	5/8	539.18	23133
1/2	519.94	21513	3/4	539.57	23167
5/8	520.33	21546	7/8	539.96	23201
3/4	520.72	21578	172.	540.36	23235
7/8	521.11	21610	1/8	540.75	23268
166.	521.51	21642	1/4	541.14	23302
1/8	521.90	21675	3/8	541.53	23336
1/4	522.29	21707	1/2	541.93	23370
3/8	522.68	21740	5/8	542.32	23404
1/2	523.08	21772	3/4	542.71	23438
5/8	523.47	21805	7/8	543.10	23472
3/4	523.86	21838	173.	543.50	23506
7/8	524.26	21871	1/8	543.89	23540
167.	524.65	21904	1/4	544.28	23575
1/8	525.04	21937	3/8	544.68	23609
1/4	525.43	21969	1/2	545.07	23643
3/8	525.83	22002	5/8	545.46	23677

Dia.	Circum.	Area*
173 3/4	545.85	23711
7/8	546.25	23745
174.	546.64	23779
1/8	547.03	23813
1/4	547.42	23848
3/8	547.82	23882
1/2	548.21	23917
5/8	548.60	23951
3/4	549.00	23985
7/8	549.39	24019
175.	549.78	24053
1/8	550.17	24087
1/4	550.57	24122
3/8	550.96	24156
1/2	551.35	24191
5/8	551.74	24225
3/4	552.14	24260
7/8	552.53	24294
176.	552.92	24329
1/8	553.31	24363
1/4	553.71	24398
3/8	554.10	24432
1/2	554.49	24467
5/8	554.89	24501
3/4	555.28	24536
7/8	555.67	24571
177.	556.06	24606
1/8	556.46	24640
1/4	556.85	24675
3/8	557.24	24710
1/2	557.63	24745
5/8	558.03	24780
3/4	558.42	24815
7/8	558.81	24850
178.	559.21	24885
1/8	559.60	24920
1/4	559.99	24955
3/8	560.38	24990
1/2	560.78	25025
5/8	561.17	25060
3/4	561.56	25095
7/8	561.95	25130
179.	562.35	25165
1/8	562.74	25200
1/4	563.13	25236
3/8	563.53	25271
1/2	563.92	25307
5/8	564.31	25342
3/4	564.70	25377
7/8	565.10	25412

*Approximate area, sufficiently accurate for practical purposes, including estimating.

(Continued on next page)

A-18.
(Continued). Circumferences and Areas of Circles
(Advancing by eighths)

Dia.	Circum.	Area*	Dia.	Circum.	Area*
142 1/2	447.68	15949	148 3/4	467.31	17379
5/8	448.07	15977	7/8	467.71	17408
3/4	448.46	16005	149.	468.10	17437
7/8	448.86	16033	1/8	468.49	17466
143.	449.25	16061	1/4	468.88	17496
1/8	449.64	16089	3/8	469.28	17525
1/4	450.03	16117	1/2	469.67	17555
3/8	450.43	16145	5/8	470.06	17584
1/2	450.82	16173	3/4	470.46	17614
5/8	451.21	16201	7/8	470.85	17643
3/4	451.61	16229	150.	471.24	17672
7/8	452.00	16258	1/8	471.63	17702
144.	452.39	16286	1/4	472.03	17731
1/8	452.78	16314	3/8	472.42	17761
1/4	453.18	16342	1/2	472.81	17790
3/8	453.57	16371	5/8	473.20	17820
1/2	453.96	16399	3/4	473.60	17849
5/8	454.35	16428	7/8	473.99	17879
3/4	454.75	16456	151.	474.38	17908
7/8	455.14	16485	1/8	474.77	17938
145.	455.53	16513	1/4	475.17	17967
1/8	455.93	16542	3/8	475.56	17997
1/4	456.32	16570	1/2	475.95	18026
3/8	456.71	16599	5/8	476.35	18056
1/2	457.10	16627	3/4	476.74	18086
5/8	457.50	16656	7/8	477.13	18116
3/4	457.89	16684	152.	477.52	18146
7/8	458.28	16713	1/8	477.92	18175
146.	458.67	16742	1/4	478.31	18205
1/8	459.07	16770	3/8	478.70	18235
1/4	459.46	16799	1/2	479.09	18265
3/8	459.85	16827	5/8	479.49	18295
1/2	460.24	16856	3/4	479.88	18325
5/8	460.64	16885	7/8	480.27	18355
3/4	461.03	16914	153.	480.67	18385
7/8	461.42	16943	1/8	481.06	18415
147.	461.82	16972	1/4	481.45	18446
1/8	462.21	17000	3/8	481.84	18476
1/4	462.60	17029	1/2	482.24	18507
3/8	462.99	17058	5/8	482.63	18537
1/2	463.39	17087	3/4	483.02	18567
5/8	463.78	17116	7/8	483.41	18597
3/4	464.17	17145	154.	483.81	18627
7/8	464.56	17174	1/8	484.20	18658
148.	464.96	17203	1/4	484.59	18688
1/8	465.35	17232	3/8	484.99	18719
1/4	465.74	17262	1/2	485.38	18749
3/8	466.14	17291	5/8	485.78	18779
1/2	466.53	17321	3/4	486.16	18809
5/8	466.92	17350	7/8	486.56	18839

Dia.	Circum.	Area*
155.	486.95	18869
1/8	487.34	18900
1/4	487.73	18930
3/8	488.13	18961
1/2	488.52	18991
5/8	488.91	19022
3/4	489.30	19052
7/8	489.70	19083
156.	490.09	19113
1/8	490.48	19144
1/4	490.88	19174
3/8	491.27	19205
1/2	491.66	19235
5/8	492.05	19266
3/4	492.45	19297
7/8	492.84	19328
157.	493.23	19359
1/8	493.62	19390
1/4	494.02	19421
3/8	494.41	19452
1/2	494.80	19483
5/8	495.20	19514
3/4	495.59	19545
7/8	495.98	19576
158.	496.37	19607
1/8	496.77	19638
1/4	497.16	19669
3/8	497.55	19701
1/2	497.94	19732
5/8	498.34	19763
3/4	498.73	19794
7/8	499.12	19825
159.	499.51	19856
1/8	499.91	19887
1/4	500.30	19919
3/8	500.69	19950
1/2	501.09	19982
5/8	501.48	20013
3/4	501.87	20044
7/8	502.26	20075
160.	502.66	20106
1/8	503.05	20138
1/4	503.44	20169
3/8	503.83	20201
1/2	504.23	20232
5/8	504.62	20264
3/4	505.01	20295
7/8	505.41	20327
161.	505.80	20358
1/8	506.19	20390

*Approximate area, sufficiently accurate for practical purposes, including estimating.

A-18.
(Concluded). Circumferences and Areas of Circles
(Advancing by eighths)

Area*	Circum.	Dia.	Area*	Circum.	Dia.	Area*	Circum.	Dia.
34967	662.88	211.	32966	643.63	204 7/8	31025	624.40	198 3/4
35008	663.28	1/8	33006	644.03	205.	31064	624.79	7/8
35050	663.67	1/4	33046	644.43	1/8	31103	625.18	199.
35091	664.07	3/8	33087	644.82	1/4	31142	625.58	1/8
35133	664.46	1/2	33127	645.21	3/8	31181	625.97	1/4
35174	664.85	5/8	33168	645.61	1/2	31220	626.36	3/8
35216	665.24	3/4	33208	646.00	5/8	31260	626.76	1/2
35257	665.63	7/8	33249	646.39	3/4	31299	627.15	5/8
35299	666.02	212.	33289	646.78	7/8	31338	627.54	3/4
35340	666.43	1/8	33329	647.17	206.	31377	627.94	7/8
35382	666.82	1/4	33369	647.57	1/8	31416	628.32	200.
35423	667.21	3/8	33410	647.96	1/4	31455	628.72	1/8
35465	667.61	1/2	33450	648.35	3/8	31495	629.11	1/4
35507	668.00	5/8	33491	648.75	1/2	31534	629.51	3/8
35549	668.39	3/4	33531	649.14	5/8	31574	629.90	1/2
35591	668.78	7/8	33572	649.53	3/4	31613	630.29	5/8
35633	669.16	213.	33613	649.93	7/8	31653	630.69	3/4
35674	669.57	1/8	33654	650.31	207.	31692	631.08	7/8
35716	669.96	1/4	33694	650.71	1/8	31731	631.46	201.
35758	670.35	3/8	33735	651.10	1/4	31770	631.86	1/8
35800	670.75	1/2	33775	651.50	3/8	31810	632.26	1/4
35842	671.14	5/8	33816	651.89	1/2	31849	632.65	3/8
35884	671.53	3/4	33857	652.29	5/8	31889	633.05	1/2
35926	671.93	7/8	33898	652.68	3/4	31928	633.43	5/8
35968	672.30	214.	33939	653.07	7/8	31968	633.83	3/4
36010	672.71	1/8	33980	653.45	208.	32007	634.29	7/8
36052	673.10	1/4	34020	653.85	1/8	32047	634.60	202.
36094	673.50	3/8	34061	654.25	1/4	32086	635.00	1/8
36137	673.89	1/2	34102	654.64	3/8	32126	635.40	1/4
36179	674.28	5/8	34143	655.04	1/2	32166	635.79	3/8
36221	674.67	3/4	34184	655.42	5/8	32206	636.18	1/2
36263	675.07	7/8	34225	655.82	3/4	32246	636.57	5/8
36305	675.44	215.	34266	656.28	7/8	32286	636.97	3/4
36347	675.85	1/8	34307	656.59	209.	32326	637.36	7/8
36390	676.25	1/4	34348	656.99	1/8	32366	637.74	203.
36432	676.64	3/8	34389	657.39	1/4	32405	638.15	1/8
36475	677.04	1/2	34431	657.78	3/8	32445	638.54	1/4
36517	677.42	5/8	34472	658.17	1/2	32485	638.93	3/8
36560	677.82	3/4	34513	658.56	5/8	32525	639.32	1/2
36602	678.28	7/8	34554	658.96	3/4	32565	639.72	5/8
36644	678.58	216.	34595	659.35	7/8	32605	640.11	3/4
36686	678.99	1/8	34636	659.73	210.	32645	640.50	7/8
36729	679.39	1/4	34677	660.14	1/8	32685	640.88	204.
36771	679.78	3/8	34719	660.53	1/4	32725	641.28	1/8
36814	680.17	1/2	34760	660.92	3/8	32766	641.67	1/4
36856	680.56	5/8	34802	661.31	1/2	32806	642.07	3/8
36899	680.96	3/4	34843	661.71	5/8	32846	642.46	1/2
36941	681.36	7/8	34885	662.10	3/4	32886	642.85	5/8
			34926	662.49	7/8	32926	643.24	3/4

*Approximate area, sufficiently accurate for practical purposes, including estimating.

A-18.
(Continued). Circumferences and Areas of Circles
(Advancing by eighths)

Dia.	Circum.	Area*	Dia.	Circum.	Area*	Dia.	Circum.	Area*
180.	565.49	25447	186 1/4	585.12	27245	192 1/2	604.76	29103
1/8	565.88	25482	3/8	585.52	27281	5/8	605.15	29141
1/4	566.27	25518	1/2	585.91	27318	3/4	605.54	29179
3/8	566.67	25553	5/8	586.30	27354	7/8	605.94	29217
1/2	567.06	25589	3/4	586.70	27391	193.	606.33	29255
5/8	567.45	25624	7/8	587.09	27428	1/8	606.72	29293
3/4	567.84	25660	187.	587.48	27465	1/4	607.11	29331
7/8	568.24	25695	1/8	587.87	27501	3/8	607.51	29369
181.	568.63	25730	1/4	588.27	27538	1/2	607.90	29407
1/8	569.02	25765	3/8	588.66	27574	5/8	608.29	29445
1/4	569.42	25801	1/2	589.05	27611	3/4	608.68	29483
3/8	569.81	25836	5/8	589.44	27648	7/8	609.08	29521
1/2	570.20	25872	3/4	589.84	27685	194.	609.47	29559
5/8	570.59	25908	7/8	590.23	27722	1/8	609.86	29597
3/4	570.99	25944	188.	590.62	27759	1/4	610.26	29636
7/8	571.38	25980	1/8	591.01	27796	3/8	610.65	29674
182.	571.77	26016	1/4	591.41	27833	1/2	611.05	29713
1/8	572.16	26051	3/8	591.80	27870	5/8	611.43	29751
1/4	572.56	26087	1/2	592.19	27907	3/4	611.83	29789
3/8	572.95	26122	5/8	592.58	27944	7/8	612.22	29827
1/2	573.34	26158	3/4	592.98	27981	195.	612.61	29865
5/8	573.74	26194	7/8	593.37	28018	1/8	613.00	29903
3/4	574.13	26230	189.	593.76	28055	1/4	613.40	29942
7/8	574.52	26266	1/8	594.16	28092	3/8	613.79	29980
183.	574.91	26302	1/4	594.55	28130	1/2	614.18	30019
1/8	575.31	26338	3/8	594.94	28167	5/8	614.57	30057
1/4	575.70	26374	1/2	595.33	28205	3/4	614.97	30096
3/8	576.09	26410	5/8	595.73	28242	7/8	615.36	30134
1/2	576.48	26446	3/4	596.12	28279	196.	615.75	30172
5/8	576.88	26482	7/8	596.51	28316	1/8	616.15	30210
3/4	577.27	26518	190.	596.90	28353	1/4	616.54	30249
7/8	577.66	26554	1/8	597.29	28390	3/8	616.93	30287
184.	578.05	26590	1/4	597.68	28428	1/2	617.32	30326
1/8	578.45	26626	3/8	598.08	28465	5/8	617.72	30364
1/4	578.84	26663	1/2	598.47	28503	3/4	618.11	30403
3/8	579.23	26699	5/8	598.86	28540	7/8	618.50	30442
1/2	579.63	26736	3/4	599.25	28578	197.	618.89	30481
5/8	580.02	26772	7/8	599.64	28615	1/8	619.29	30519
3/4	580.41	26808	191.	600.04	28652	1/4	619.68	30558
7/8	580.80	26844	1/8	600.44	28689	3/8	620.08	30596
185.	581.20	26880	1/4	600.83	28727	1/2	620.47	30635
1/8	581.59	26916	3/8	601.22	28764	5/8	620.86	30674
1/4	581.98	26953	1/2	601.62	28802	3/4	621.25	30713
3/8	582.37	26989	5/8	602.01	28839	7/8	621.64	30752
1/2	582.77	27026	3/4	602.40	28877	198.	622.04	30791
5/8	583.16	27062	7/8	602.79	28915	1/8	622.44	30830
3/4	583.55	27099	192.	603.19	28953	1/4	622.83	30869
7/8	583.95	27135	1/8	603.58	28990	3/8	623.22	30908
186.	584.34	27172	1/4	603.97	29028	1/2	623.62	30947
1/8	584.73	27208	3/8	604.36	29065	5/8	624.01	30986

*Approximate area, sufficiently accurate for practical purposes, including estimating.

A-19.
Capacities of Cylinders and Spheres

Diam. in Feet	Cu. Ft. per Foot of Cylinder	Gallons per Foot of Cylinder	42 Gallon Barrels per Foot of Cylinder	Sphere Surface in Sq. Ft.	Sphere Volume in Cu. Ft.
1/64	.0002	.00143	.000034	.00077	.000002
1/32	.0008	.00574	.000137	.00307	.000016
1/16	.0031	.02295	.000546	.01227	.000128
3/32	.0069	.05164	.00123	.02761	.000431
1/8	.0123	.09180	.00219	.04909	.00102
5/32	.0192	.14344	.00342	.07670	.00200
3/16	.0276	.20655	.00492	.11045	.00345
7/32	.0376	.28114	.00669	.15033	.00548
1/4	.0491	.36720	.00874	.19635	.00818
9/32	.0621	.46474	.01107	.24850	.01165
5/16	.0767	.57375	.01366	.30680	.01598
11/32	.0928	.69424	.01653	.37122	.02127
3/8	.1104	.82620	.01967	.44179	.02761
13/32	.1296	.96964	.02309	.51849	.03511
7/16	.1503	1.1245	.02677	.60132	.04385
15/32	.1726	1.2909	.03074	.69029	.05393
1/2	.1963	1.4688	.03497	.78540	.06545
17/32	.2217	1.6581	.03948	.88664	.07850
9/16	.2485	1.8589	.04426	.99402	.09319
19/32	.2769	2.0712	.04932	1.1075	.10960
5/8	.3068	2.2950	.05464	1.2272	.12783
21/32	.3382	2.5302	.06024	1.3530	.14798
11/16	.3712	2.7769	.06612	1.4849	.17014
23/32	.4057	3.0351	.07227	1.6230	.19442
3/4	.4418	3.3048	.07869	1.7671	.22089
25/32	.4794	3.5859	.08538	1.9175	.24967
13/16	.5185	3.8785	.09235	2.0739	.28085
27/32	.5591	4.1826	.09959	2.2365	.31451
7/8	.6013	4.4982	.10710	2.4053	.35077
29/32	.6450	4.8252	.11489	2.5802	.38971
15/16	.6903	5.1637	.12295	2.7612	.43143
31/32	.7371	5.5137	.13128	2.9483	.47603
1	.7854	5.8752	.13989	3.1416	.52360
1 1/16	.8866	6.6325	.15794	3.5466	.62804
1 1/8	.9940	7.4358	.17704	3.9761	.74551
1 3/16	1.1075	8.2849	.19726	4.4301	.87680
1 1/4	1.2272	9.1800	.21857	4.9087	1.0227
1 5/16	1.3530	10.121	.24097	5.4119	1.1838
1 3/8	1.4849	11.108	.26447	5.9396	1.3612
1 7/16	1.6230	12.141	.28906	6.4918	1.5553
1 1/2	1.7671	13.219	.31474	7.0686	1.7671
1 9/16	1.9175	14.344	.34152	7.6699	1.9974
1 5/8	2.0739	15.514	.36938	8.2958	2.2468
1 11/16	2.2365	16.731	.39835	8.9462	2.5161
1 3/4	2.4053	17.993	.42840	9.6211	2.8062
1 13/16	2.5802	19.301	.45955	10.321	3.1177
1 7/8	2.7612	20.655	.49178	11.045	3.4515
1 15/16	2.9483	22.055	.52512	11.793	3.8082
2	3.1416	23.501	.55954	12.566	4.1888
2 1/16	3.3410	24.992	.59506	13.364	4.5939
2 1/8	3.5466	26.530	.63167	14.186	5.0243
2 3/16	3.7583	28.114	.66937	15.033	5.4808
2 1/4	3.9761	29.743	.70817	15.904	5.9641
2 5/16	4.2000	31.418	.74806	16.800	6.4751
2 3/8	4.4301	33.140	.78904	17.721	7.0144
2 7/16	4.6664	34.907	.83112	18.665	7.5829

A-19.
(Continued). Capacities of Cylinders and Spheres

Diam. in Feet	Cu. Ft. per Foot of Cylinder	Gallons per Foot of Cylinder	42 Gallon Barrels per Foot of Cylinder	Sphere Surface in Sq. Ft.	Sphere Volume in Cu. Ft.
2 1/2	4.9087	36.720	.87428	19.635	8.1812
2 9/16	5.1572	38.579	.91854	20.629	8.8103
2 5/8	5.4119	40.484	.96390	21.648	9.4708
2 11/16	5.6727	42.434	1.0103	22.691	10.164
2 3/4	5.9396	44.431	1.0578	23.758	10.889
2 13/16	6.2126	46.474	1.1065	24.850	11.649
2 7/8	6.4918	48.562	1.1562	25.967	12.443
2 15/16	6.777	50.696	1.2071	27.109	13.272
3	7.0686	52.877	1.2590	28.274	14.137
3 1/16	7.3662	55.103	1.3120	29.465	15.039
3 1/8	7.6699	57.375	1.3661	30.680	15.979
3 3/16	7.9798	59.693	1.4213	31.919	16.957
3 1/4	8.2958	62.057	1.4775	33.183	17.974
3 5/16	8.6179	64.466	1.5349	34.472	19.031
3 3/8	8.9462	66.922	1.5934	35.785	20.129
3 7/16	9.2806	69.424	1.6529	37.122	21.268
3 1/2	9.621	71.971	1.7136	38.485	22.449
3 5/8	10.321	77.204	1.8382	41.282	24.942
3 3/4	11.045	82.620	1.9671	44.179	27.612
3 7/8	11.793	88.220	2.1005	47.173	30.466
4	12.566	94.003	2.2382	50.265	33.510
4 1/8	13.364	99.970	2.3802	53.456	36.751
4 1/4	14.186	106.12	2.5267	56.745	40.194
4 3/8	15.033	112.45	2.6775	60.132	43.846
4 1/2	15.904	118.97	2.8327	63.617	47.713
4 5/8	16.800	125.67	2.9922	67.201	51.800
4 3/4	17.721	132.56	3.1562	70.882	56.115
4 7/8	18.665	139.63	3.3245	74.662	60.663
5	19.635	146.88	3.4971	78.540	65.450
5 1/8	20.629	154.32	3.6742	82.516	70.482
5 1/4	21.648	161.93	3.8556	86.590	75.766
5 3/8	22.691	169.74	4.0414	90.763	81.308
5 1/2	23.758	177.72	4.2315	95.033	87.114
5 5/8	24.850	185.89	4.4261	99.402	93.189
5 3/4	25.967	194.25	4.6250	103.87	99.541
5 7/8	27.109	202.79	4.8282	108.43	106.17
6	28.274	211.51	5.0359	113.10	113.10
6 1/8	29.465	220.41	5.2479	117.86	120.31
6 1/4	30.680	229.50	5.4643	122.72	127.83
6 3/8	31.919	238.77	5.6850	127.68	135.66
6 1/2	33.183	248.23	5.9102	132.73	143.79
6 5/8	34.472	257.87	6.1397	137.89	152.25
6 3/4	35.785	267.69	6.3735	143.14	161.03
6 7/8	37.122	277.69	6.6118	148.49	170.14
7	38.485	287.88	6.8544	153.94	179.59
7 1/8	39.871	298.26	7.1014	159.48	189.39
7 1/4	41.282	308.81	7.3527	165.13	199.53
7 3/8	42.718	319.56	7.6085	170.87	210.03
7 1/2	44.179	330.48	7.8686	176.71	220.89
7 5/8	45.664	341.59	8.1330	182.65	232.12
7 3/4	47.173	352.88	8.4019	188.69	243.73
7 7/8	48.707	364.35	8.6751	194.83	255.71
8	50.265	376.01	8.9527	201.06	268.08
8 1/8	51.849	387.85	9.2346	207.39	280.85
8 1/4	53.456	399.88	9.5209	213.82	294.01
8 3/8	55.088	412.09	9.8116	220.35	307.58
8 1/2	56.745	424.48	10.107	226.98	321.56
8 5/8	58.426	437.06	10.406	233.71	335.95
8 3/4	60.132	449.82	10.710	240.53	350.77
8 7/8	61.862	462.76	11.018	247.45	366.02
9	63.617	475.89	11.331	254.47	381.70
9 1/8	65.397	489.20	11.648	261.59	397.83
9 1/4	67.201	502.70	11.969	268.80	414.40
9 3/8	69.029	516.37	12.295	276.12	431.43
9 1/2	70.882	530.24	12.625	283.53	448.92
9 5/8	72.760	544.28	12.959	291.04	466.88
9 3/4	74.662	558.52	13.298	298.65	485.30
9 7/8	76.589	572.92	13.641	306.35	504.21
10	78.540	587.52	13.989	314.16	523.60
10 1/4	82.516	617.26	14.697	330.06	563.86
10 1/2	86.590	647.74	15.422	346.36	606.13
10 3/4	90.763	678.95	16.166	363.05	650.47
11	95.033	710.50	16.926	380.13	696.91
11 1/4	99.402	743.58	17.704	397.61	745.51
11 1/2	103.87	776.59	18.500	415.48	796.33
11 3/4	108.43	811.14	19.313	433.74	849.40
12	113.10	846.03	20.143	452.39	904.78
12 1/4	117.86	881.65	20.992	471.44	962.51
12 1/2	122.72	918.00	21.857	490.87	1022.7
12 3/4	127.68	955.08	22.740	510.71	1085.2
13	132.73	992.91	23.641	530.93	1150.3
13 1/4	137.89	1031.5	24.559	551.55	1218.0
13 1/2	143.14	1070.8	25.494	572.56	1288.2
13 3/4	148.49	1110.8	26.447	593.96	1361.2
14	153.94	1151.5	27.418	615.75	1436.8
14 1/4	159.48	1193.0	28.405	637.94	1515.1
14 1/2	165.13	1235.3	29.411	660.52	1596.3
14 3/4	170.87	1278.2	30.434	683.49	1680.3
15	176.71	1321.9	31.474	706.86	1767.1
15 1/4	182.65	1366.3	32.532	730.62	1857.0
15 1/2	188.69	1411.5	33.607	754.77	1949.8
15 3/4	194.83	1457.4	34.700	779.31	2045.7
16	201.06	1504.0	35.811	804.25	2144.7
16 1/4	207.39	1551.4	36.938	829.58	2246.8
16 1/2	213.82	1599.5	38.084	855.30	2352.1
16 3/4	220.35	1648.4	39.247	881.41	2460.6
17	226.98	1697.9	40.427	907.92	2572.4
17 1/4	233.71	1748.2	41.625	934.82	2687.6
17 1/2	240.53	1799.3	42.840	962.11	2806.2
17 3/4	247.45	1851.1	44.073	989.80	2928.2
18	254.47	1903.6	45.323	1017.9	3053.6
18 1/4	261.59	1956.8	46.591	1046.3	3182.6
18 1/2	268.80	2010.8	47.876	1075.2	3315.2
18 3/4	276.12	2065.5	49.178	1104.5	3451.5
19	283.53	2120.9	50.499	1134.1	3591.4
19 1/4	291.04	2177.1	51.836	1164.2	3735.0
19 1/2	298.65	2234.0	53.191	1194.6	3882.4
19 3/4	306.35	2291.7	54.564	1225.4	4033.7
20	314.16	2350.1	55.954	1256.6	4188.8
20 1/4	322.06	2409.2	57.362	1288.2	4347.8
20 1/2	330.06	2469.0	58.787	1320.3	4510.9
20 3/4	338.16	2529.6	60.229	1352.7	4677.9
21	346.36	2591.0	61.689	1385.4	4849.0
21 1/4	354.66	2653.0	63.167	1418.6	5024.3
21 1/2	363.05	2715.8	64.662	1452.2	5203.7
21 3/4	371.54	2779.3	66.175	1486.2	5387.4
22	380.13	2843.6	67.705	1520.5	5575.3
22 1/4	388.82	2908.6	69.252	1555.3	5767.5
22 1/2	397.61	2974.3	70.817	1590.4	5964.1
22 3/4	406.49	3040.8	72.399	1626.0	6165.1
23	415.48	3108.0	73.999	1661.9	6370.6
23 1/4	424.56	3175.9	75.617	1698.2	6580.6
23 1/2	433.74	3244.6	77.252	1734.9	6795.2
23 3/4	443.01	3314.0	78.904	1772.1	7014.4
24	452.39	3384.1	80.574	1809.6	7238.2
24 1/4	461.86	3455.0	82.261	1847.5	7466.8
24 1/2	471.44	3526.6	83.966	1885.7	7700.1
24 3/4	481.11	3598.9	85.689	1924.4	7938.2
25	490.87	3672.0	87.428	1963.5	8181.2
25 1/4	500.74	3745.8	89.186	2003.0	8429.1
25 1/2	510.71	3820.3	90.960	2042.8	8682.0
25 3/4	520.77	3895.6	92.753	2083.1	8939.9
26	530.93	3971.6	94.563	2123.7	9202.8
26 1/4	541.19	4048.4	96.390	2164.8	9470.8
26 1/2	551.55	4125.8	98.235	2206.2	9744.0
26 3/4	562.00	4204.1	100.10	2248.0	10022
27	572.56	4283.0	101.98	2290.2	10306
27 1/4	583.21	4362.7	103.87	2332.8	10555
27 1/2	593.96	4443.1	105.79	2375.8	10889
27 3/4	604.81	4524.3	107.72	2419.2	11189
28	615.75	4606.1	109.67	2463.0	11494
28 1/4	626.80	4688.8	111.64	2507.2	11805
28 1/2	637.94	4772.1	113.62	2551.8	12121
28 3/4	649.18	4856.2	115.62	2596.7	12443
29	660.52	4941.0	117.64	2642.1	12770
29 1/4	671.96	5026.6	119.68	2687.8	13103
29 1/2	683.49	5112.9	121.74	2734.0	13442
29 3/4	695.13	5199.9	123.81	2780.5	13787

(Continued on next page)

By permission, Buffalo Tank Div., Bethlehem Steel Corp.

A-19.
(Continued). Capacities of Cylinders and Spheres

Diam. in Feet	Cu. Ft. per Foot of Cylinder	Gallons per Foot of Cylinder	42 Gallon Barrels per Foot of Cylinder	Sphere Surface in Sq. Ft.	Sphere Volume in Cu. Ft.
54	2290.2	17132	407.91	9160.9	82448
54¼	2311.5	17291	411.69	9245.9	83598
54½	2332.8	17451	415.49	9331.3	84759
54¾	2354.3	17611	419.32	9417.1	85931
55	2375.8	17772	423.15	9503.3	87114
55¼	2397.5	17934	427.01	9589.9	88307
55½	2419.2	18097	430.88	9676.9	89511
55¾	2441.1	18260	434.77	9764.3	90726
56	2463.0	18423	438.68	9852.0	91952
56¼	2485.0	18589	442.61	9940.2	93189
56½	2507.2	18755	446.55	10029	94437
56¾	2529.4	18921	450.51	10118	95697
57	2551.8	19088	454.49	10207	96967
57¼	2574.2	19256	458.48	10297	98248
57½	2596.7	19425	462.50	10387	99541
57¾	2619.4	19594	466.53	10477	100845
58	2642.1	19764	470.57	10568	102160
58¼	2664.9	19935	474.64	10660	103487
58½	2687.8	20106	478.72	10751	104825
58¾	2710.9	20279	482.82	10843	106175
59	2734.0	20452	486.94	10936	107536
59¼	2757.2	20625	491.08	11029	108909
59½	2780.5	20800	495.23	11122	110293
59¾	2803.9	20975	499.40	11216	111690
60	2827.4	21151	503.59	11310	113097
60¼	2851.0	21327	507.79	11404	114517
60½	2874.8	21505	512.02	11499	115948
60¾	2898.6	21683	516.26	11594	117392
61	2922.5	21862	520.51	11690	118847
61¼	2946.5	22041	524.79	11786	120314
61½	2970.6	22221	529.08	11882	121793
61¾	2994.8	22402	533.39	11979	123285
62	3019.1	22584	537.72	12076	124788
62¼	3043.5	22767	542.06	12174	126304
62½	3068.0	22950	546.43	12272	127832
62¾	3092.6	23134	550.81	12370	129372
63	3117.2	23319	555.21	12469	130924
63¼	3142.0	23504	559.62	12568	132489
63½	3166.9	23690	564.05	12668	134066
63¾	3191.9	23877	568.50	12768	135656
64	3217.0	24065	572.97	12868	137258
64¼	3242.2	24253	577.46	12969	138873
64½	3267.5	24442	581.96	13070	140500
64¾	3292.8	24632	586.48	13171	142141
65	3318.3	24823	591.02	13273	143793
65¼	3343.9	25014	595.57	13376	145459
65½	3369.6	25206	600.14	13478	147137
65¾	3395.3	25399	604.73	13581	148828
66	3421.2	25592	609.34	13685	150533
66¼	3447.2	25787	613.97	13789	152250
66½	3473.2	25982	618.61	13893	153980
66¾	3499.4	26177	623.27	13998	155723
67	3525.7	26374	627.95	14103	157479
67¼	3552.0	26571	632.64	14208	159249
67½	3578.5	26769	637.35	14314	161031
67¾	3605.0	26967	642.08	14420	162827
68	3631.7	27167	646.83	14527	164636
68¼	3658.4	27367	651.59	14634	166459
68½	3685.3	27568	656.38	14741	168295
68¾	3712.2	27769	661.18	14849	170144
69	3739.3	27972	665.99	14957	172007
69¼	3766.4	28175	670.83	15066	173883
69½	3793.7	28379	675.68	15175	175773
69¾	3821.0	28583	680.55	15284	177677
70	3848.5	28788	685.44	15394	179594
70¼	3876.0	28994	690.34	15504	181525
70½	3903.6	29201	695.27	15615	183470
70¾	3931.4	29409	700.21	15725	185429
71	3959.2	29617	705.16	15837	187402
71¼	3987.1	29826	710.14	15948	189388
71½	4015.2	30035	715.13	16061	191389
71¾	4043.3	30246	720.14	16173	193404
72	4071.5	30457	725.17	16286	195432
72¼	4099.8	30669	730.21	16399	197475
72½	4128.2	30881	735.27	16513	199532
72¾	4156.8	31095	740.35	16627	201603
73	4185.4	31309	745.45	16742	203689
73¼	4214.1	31524	750.56	16856	205789
73½	4242.9	31739	755.70	16972	207903
73¾	4271.8	31956	760.85	17087	210032
74	4300.8	32173	766.01	17203	212175
74¼	4329.9	32390	771.20	17320	214332
74½	4359.2	32609	776.40	17437	216505
74¾	4388.5	32828	781.62	17554	218692
75	4417.9	33048	786.86	17671	220893
75¼	4447.4	33269	792.11	17789	223110
75½	4477.0	33490	797.38	17908	225341
75¾	4506.7	33712	802.67	18027	227587
76	4536.5	33935	807.98	18146	229847
76¼	4566.4	34159	813.30	18265	232123
76½	4596.3	34383	818.64	18385	234414
76¾	4626.4	34608	824.00	18506	236719
77	4656.6	34834	829.38	18627	239040
77¼	4686.9	35061	834.87	18748	241376
77½	4717.3	35288	840.19	18869	243727
77¾	4747.8	35516	845.62	18991	246093

A-19.
(Continued). Capacities of Cylinders and Spheres

Diam. in Feet	Cu. Ft. per Foot of Cylinder	Gallons per Foot of Cylinder	42 Gallon Barrels per Foot of Cylinder	Sphere Surface in Sq. Ft.	Sphere Volume in Cu. Ft.
30	706.86	5287.7	125.90	2827.4	14137
30¼	718.69	5376.2	128.00	2874.8	14494
30½	730.62	5465.4	130.13	2922.5	14856
30¾	742.64	5555.4	132.27	2970.6	15224
31	754.77	5646.1	134.43	3019.1	15599
31¼	766.99	5737.5	136.61	3068.0	15979
31½	779.31	5829.7	138.80	3117.2	16366
31¾	791.73	5922.6	141.01	3166.9	16758
32	804.25	6016.2	143.24	3217.0	17157
32¼	816.86	6110.6	145.49	3267.5	17563
32½	829.58	6205.7	147.75	3318.3	17974
32¾	842.39	6301.5	150.04	3369.6	18392
33	855.30	6398.1	152.34	3421.2	18817
33¼	868.31	6495.4	154.65	3473.2	19247
33½	881.41	6593.4	156.99	3525.7	19685
33¾	894.62	6692.2	159.34	3578.5	20129
34	907.92	6791.7	161.71	3631.7	20580
34¼	921.32	6892.0	164.09	3685.3	21037
34½	934.82	6992.9	166.50	3739.3	21501
34¾	948.42	7094.7	168.92	3793.7	21972
35	962.11	7197.1	171.36	3848.5	22449
35¼	975.91	7300.3	173.82	3903.6	22934
35½	989.80	7404.2	176.29	3959.2	23425
35¾	1003.8	7508.9	178.78	4015.2	23924
36	1017.9	7614.2	181.29	4071.5	24429
36¼	1032.1	7720.4	183.82	4128.2	24942
36½	1046.3	7827.2	186.36	4185.4	25461
36¾	1060.7	7934.8	188.92	4242.9	25988
37	1075.2	8043.1	191.50	4300.8	26522
37¼	1089.8	8152.2	194.10	4359.2	27063
37½	1104.5	8262.0	196.71	4417.9	27612
37¾	1119.2	8372.5	199.35	4477.0	28168
38	1134.1	8483.8	201.99	4536.5	28731
38¼	1149.1	8595.8	204.66	4596.3	29302
38½	1164.2	8708.5	207.35	4656.7	29880
38¾	1179.3	8822.0	210.05	4717.3	30466
39	1194.6	8936.2	212.77	4778.4	31059
39¼	1210.0	9051.1	215.50	4839.8	31660
39½	1225.4	9166.8	218.26	4901.7	32269
39¾	1241.0	9283.2	221.03	4963.9	32886
40	1256.6	9400.3	223.82	5026.5	33510
40¼	1272.4	9518.2	226.62	5089.6	34143
40½	1288.2	9636.8	229.45	5153.0	34783
40¾	1304.2	9756.1	232.29	5216.8	35431
41	1320.3	9876.2	235.15	5281.0	36087
41¼	1336.4	9997.0	238.02	5345.6	36751
41½	1352.7	10119	240.92	5410.6	37423
41¾	1369.0	10241	243.83	5476.0	38104
42	1385.4	10364	246.76	5541.8	38792
42¼	1402.0	10488	249.70	5607.9	39489
42½	1418.6	10612	252.67	5674.5	40194
42¾	1435.4	10737	255.65	5741.5	40908
43	1452.2	10863	258.65	5808.8	41630
43¼	1469.1	10990	261.66	5876.5	42360
43½	1486.2	11117	264.70	5944.7	43099
43¾	1503.3	11245	267.75	6013.2	43846
44	1520.5	11373	270.82	6082.1	44602
44¼	1537.9	11504	273.90	6151.4	45367
44½	1555.3	11634	277.01	6221.1	46140
44¾	1572.8	11765	280.13	6291.2	46922
45	1590.4	11897	283.27	6361.7	47713
45¼	1608.2	12030	286.42	6432.6	48513
45½	1626.0	12163	289.60	6503.9	49321
45¾	1643.9	12297	292.79	6575.5	50139
46	1661.9	12432	296.00	6647.6	50965
46¼	1680.0	12567	299.22	6720.1	51800
46½	1698.2	12704	302.47	6792.9	52645
46¾	1716.5	12841	305.73	6866.1	53499
47	1734.9	12978	309.01	6939.8	54362
47¼	1753.5	13117	312.30	7013.8	55234
47½	1772.1	13256	315.62	7088.2	56115
47¾	1790.8	13396	318.95	7163.0	57006
48	1809.6	13536	322.30	7238.2	57906
48¼	1828.5	13678	325.66	7313.8	58815
48½	1847.5	13820	329.05	7389.8	59734
48¾	1866.5	13963	332.45	7466.2	60663
49	1885.7	14106	335.86	7543.0	61601
49¼	1905.0	14251	339.30	7620.1	62549
49½	1924.4	14396	342.75	7697.7	63506
49¾	1943.9	14541	346.23	7775.6	64473
50	1963.5	14688	349.71	7854.0	65450
50¼	1983.2	14835	353.22	7932.7	66437
50½	2003.0	14983	356.74	8011.8	67433
50¾	2022.8	15132	360.28	8091.4	68439
51	2042.8	15281	363.84	8171.3	69456
51¼	2062.9	15432	367.42	8251.6	70482
51½	2083.1	15582	371.01	8332.3	71519
51¾	2103.3	15734	374.62	8413.4	72565
52	2123.7	15887	378.25	8494.9	73622
52¼	2144.2	16040	381.90	8576.7	74689
52½	2164.8	16193	385.56	8659.0	75766
52¾	2185.4	16348	389.24	8741.7	76854
53	2206.2	16503	392.94	8824.7	77952
53¼	2227.0	16659	396.65	8908.2	79060
53½	2248.0	16816	400.39	8992.0	80179
53¾	2269.1	16974	404.14	9076.3	81308

A-19.
(Continued). Capacities of Cylinders and Spheres

Diam. in Feet	Cu. Ft. per Foot of Cylinder	Gallons per Foot of Cylinder	42 Gallon Barrels per Foot of Cylinder	Sphere Surface in Sq. Ft.	Sphere Volume in Cu. Ft.
102	8171.3	61125	1455.4	32685	555647
102¼	8211.4	61425	1462.5	32846	559743
102½	8251.6	61726	1469.7	33006	563859
102¾	8291.9	62028	1476.8	33168	567994
103	8332.3	62330	1484.0	33329	572151
103¼	8372.8	62633	1491.3	33491	576327
103½	8413.4	62936	1498.5	33654	580523
103¾	8454.1	63241	1505.7	33816	584740
104	8494.9	63546	1513.0	33979	588977
104¼	8535.8	63852	1520.3	34143	593235
104½	8576.7	64159	1527.6	34307	597513
104¾	8617.8	64466	1534.9	34471	601812
105	8659.0	64774	1542.2	34636	606131
105¼	8700.3	65083	1549.6	34801	610471
105½	8741.7	65392	1557.0	34967	614831
105¾	8783.2	65703	1564.3	35133	619213
106	8824.7	66014	1571.8	35299	623615
106¼	8866.4	66325	1579.2	35466	628037
106½	8908.2	66638	1586.6	35633	632481
106¾	8950.1	66951	1594.1	35800	636945
107	8992.0	67265	1601.5	35968	641431
107¼	9034.1	67580	1609.0	36136	645938
107½	9076.3	67895	1616.6	36305	650465
107¾	9118.5	68211	1624.1	36474	655014
108	9160.9	68528	1631.6	36644	659584
108¼	9203.3	68846	1639.2	36813	664175
108½	9245.9	69164	1646.8	36984	668787
108¾	9288.6	69483	1654.4	37154	673421
109	9331.3	69803	1662.0	37325	678076
109¼	9374.2	70124	1669.6	37497	682752
109½	9417.1	70445	1677.3	37668	687450
109¾	9460.2	70767	1684.9	37841	692169
110	9503.3	71090	1692.6	38013	696910
110¼	9546.6	71413	1700.3	38186	701672
110½	9589.9	71737	1708.0	38360	706457
110¾	9633.4	72062	1715.8	38533	711262
111	9676.9	72388	1723.5	38708	716090
111¼	9720.5	72715	1731.3	38882	720939
111½	9764.3	73042	1739.1	39057	725810
111¾	9808.1	73370	1746.9	39232	730704
112	9852.0	73698	1754.7	39408	735619
112¼	9896.1	74028	1762.6	39584	740556
112½	9940.2	74358	1770.4	39761	745515
112¾	9984.4	74689	1778.3	39938	750496
113	10029	75020	1786.2	40115	755499
113¼	10073	75353	1794.1	40293	760525
113½	10118	75686	1802.0	40471	765572
113¾	10162	76019	1810.0	40649	770642
114	10207	76354	1818.0	40828	775735
114¼	10252	76689	1825.9	41007	780849
114½	10297	77025	1833.9	41187	785986
114¾	10342	77362	1841.9	41367	791146
115	10387	77699	1850.0	41548	796328
115¼	10432	78038	1858.0	41728	801533
115½	10477	78376	1866.1	41910	806760
115¾	10523	78716	1874.2	42091	812010
116	10568	79057	1882.3	42273	817283
116¼	10614	79398	1890.4	42456	822579
116½	10660	79739	1898.6	42638	827897
116¾	10705	80082	1906.7	42822	833238
117	10751	80425	1914.9	43005	838603
117¼	10797	80769	1923.1	43189	843990
117½	10843	81114	1931.3	43374	849400
117¾	10890	81460	1939.5	43558	854833
118	10936	81806	1947.8	43744	860290
118¼	10982	82153	1956.0	43929	865769
118½	11029	82501	1964.3	44115	871272
118¾	11075	82849	1972.6	44301	876798
119	11122	83199	1980.9	44488	882347
119¼	11169	83548	1989.2	44675	887920
119½	11216	83899	1997.6	44863	893516
119¾	11263	84251	2006.0	45051	899136
120	11310	84603	2014.3	45239	904779
120¼	11357	84956	2022.8	45428	910445
120½	11404	85309	2031.2	45617	916136
120¾	11452	85664	2039.6	45806	921850
121	11499	86019	2048.1	45996	927587
121¼	11547	86374	2056.5	46186	933349
121½	11594	86731	2065.0	46377	939134
121¾	11642	87088	2073.5	46568	944943
122	11690	87446	2082.1	46759	950776
122¼	11738	87805	2090.6	46951	956633
122½	11786	88165	2099.2	47144	962514
122¾	11834	88525	2107.7	47336	968419
123	11882	88886	2116.3	47529	974348
123¼	11931	89247	2124.9	47723	980301
123½	11979	89610	2133.6	47916	986278
123¾	12028	89973	2142.2	48111	992280
124	12076	90337	2150.9	48305	998306
124¼	12125	90701	2159.6	48500	1004356
124½	12174	91067	2168.3	48695	1010431
124¾	12223	91433	2177.0	48891	1016530
125	12272	91800	2185.7	49087	1022654
125¼	12321	92167	2194.5	49284	1028802
125½	12370	92536	2203.2	49481	1034975
125¾	12420	92905	2212.0	49678	1041172

(Continued on next page)

A-19.
(Continued). Capacities of Cylinders and Spheres

Diam. in Feet	Cu. Ft. per Foot of Cylinder	Gallons per Foot of Cylinder	42 Gallon Barrels per Foot of Cylinder	Sphere Surface in Sq. Ft.	Sphere Volume in Cu. Ft.
78	4778.4	35745	851.06	19113	248475
78¼	4809.0	35974	856.53	19236	250872
78½	4839.8	36204	862.01	19359	253284
78¾	4870.7	36435	867.51	19483	255712
79	4901.7	36667	873.02	19607	258155
79¼	4932.7	36899	878.56	19731	260613
79½	4963.9	37133	884.11	19856	263087
79¾	4995.2	37367	889.68	19981	265577
80	5026.5	37601	895.27	20106	268083
80¼	5058.0	37837	900.87	20232	270604
80½	5089.6	38073	906.49	20358	273141
80¾	5121.2	38310	912.13	20485	275693
81	5153.0	38547	917.79	20612	278262
81¼	5184.9	38785	923.46	20739	280846
81½	5216.8	39024	929.15	20867	283447
81¾	5248.9	39264	934.86	20995	286063
82	5281.0	39505	940.59	21124	288696
82¼	5313.3	39746	946.33	21253	291344
82½	5345.6	39988	952.09	21382	294009
82¾	5378.1	40231	957.87	21512	296690
83	5410.6	40474	963.67	21642	299387
83¼	5443.3	40718	969.48	21773	302100
83½	5476.0	40963	975.32	21904	304830
83¾	5508.8	41209	981.16	22035	307576
84	5541.8	41455	987.03	22167	310339
84¼	5574.8	41702	992.92	22299	313118
84½	5607.9	41950	998.82	22432	315914
84¾	5641.2	42199	1004.7	22565	318726
85	5674.5	42448	1010.7	22698	321555
85¼	5707.9	42698	1016.6	22832	324401
85½	5741.5	42949	1022.6	22966	327263
85¾	5775.1	43201	1028.6	23100	330142
86	5808.8	43453	1034.6	23235	333038
86¼	5842.6	43706	1040.6	23371	335951
86½	5876.5	43960	1046.7	23506	338881
86¾	5910.6	44214	1052.7	23642	341828
87	5944.7	44469	1058.8	23779	344791
87¼	5978.9	44725	1064.9	23916	347772
87½	6013.2	44982	1071.0	24053	350770
87¾	6047.6	45239	1077.1	24190	353785
88	6082.1	45497	1083.3	24328	356818
88¼	6116.7	45756	1089.4	24467	359868
88½	6151.4	46016	1095.6	24606	362935
88¾	6186.2	46276	1101.8	24745	366019
89	6221.1	46537	1108.0	24885	369121
89¼	6256.1	46799	1114.3	25025	372240
89½	6291.2	47062	1120.5	25165	375377
89¾	6326.4	47325	1126.8	25306	378531
90	6361.7	47589	1133.1	25447	381704
90¼	6397.1	47854	1139.4	25588	384893
90½	6432.6	48119	1145.7	25730	388101
90¾	6468.2	48385	1152.0	25873	391326
91	6503.9	48652	1158.4	26016	394569
91¼	6539.7	48920	1164.8	26159	397830
91½	6575.5	49189	1171.2	26302	401109
91¾	6611.5	49458	1177.6	26446	404405
92	6647.6	49728	1184.0	26590	407720
92¼	6683.8	49998	1190.4	26735	411053
92½	6720.1	50270	1196.9	26880	414404
92¾	6756.4	50542	1203.4	27026	417773
93	6792.9	50814	1209.9	27172	421160
93¼	6829.5	51088	1216.4	27318	424566
93½	6866.1	51362	1222.9	27465	427990
93¾	6902.9	51637	1229.5	27612	431432
94	6939.8	51913	1236.0	27759	434893
94¼	6976.7	52190	1242.6	27907	438372
94½	7013.8	52467	1249.2	28055	441870
94¾	7051.0	52745	1255.8	28204	445386
95	7088.2	53024	1262.5	28353	448920
95¼	7125.6	53303	1269.1	28502	452474
95½	7163.0	53583	1275.8	28652	456046
95¾	7200.6	53864	1282.5	28802	459637
96	7238.2	54146	1289.2	28953	463247
96¼	7276.0	54428	1295.9	29104	466875
96½	7313.8	54711	1302.6	29255	470523
96¾	7351.8	54995	1309.4	29407	474189
97	7389.8	55280	1316.2	29559	477874
97¼	7428.0	55565	1323.0	29712	481579
97½	7466.2	55851	1329.8	29865	485302
97¾	7504.5	56138	1336.6	30018	489045
98	7543.0	56425	1343.5	30171	492807
98¼	7581.5	56714	1350.3	30326	496588
98½	7620.1	57003	1357.2	30481	500388
98¾	7658.9	57292	1364.1	30635	504208
99	7697.7	57583	1371.0	30791	508047
99¼	7736.6	57874	1377.9	30946	511906
99½	7775.6	58166	1384.9	31103	515784
99¾	7814.8	58458	1391.9	31259	519682
100	7854.0	58752	1398.9	31416	523599
100¼	7893.3	59046	1405.9	31573	527536
100½	7932.7	59341	1412.9	31731	531492
100¾	7972.2	59636	1419.9	31889	535468
101	8011.8	59933	1427.0	32047	539464
101¼	8051.6	60230	1434.0	32206	543480
101½	8091.4	60528	1441.1	32365	547516
101¾	8131.3	60826	1448.2	32525	551572

A-19.
(Concluded). Capacities of Cylinders and Spheres

Diam. in Feet	Cu. Ft. per Foot of Cylinder	Gallons per Foot of Cylinder	42 Gallon Barrels per Foot of Cylinder	Sphere Surface in Sq. Ft.	Sphere Volume in Cu. Ft.	Diam. in Feet	Cu. Ft. per Foot of Cylinder	Gallons per Foot of Cylinder	42 Gallon Barrels per Foot of Cylinder	Sphere Surface in Sq. Ft.	Sphere Volume in Cu. Ft.
126	12469	93274	2220.8	49876	1047394	138	14957	111887	2664.0	59828	1376055
126¼	12519	93645	2229.6	50074	1053641	138¼	15011	112293	2673.6	60045	1383547
126½	12568	94016	2238.5	50273	1059913	138½	15066	112699	2683.3	60263	1391067
126¾	12618	94388	2247.3	50471	1066209	138¾	15120	113107	2693.0	60481	1398613
127	12668	94761	2256.2	50671	1072531	139	15175	113514	2702.7	60699	1406187
127¼	12718	95134	2265.1	50870	1078877	139¼	15229	113923	2712.5	60917	1413788
127½	12768	95508	2274.0	51071	1085248	139½	15284	114333	2722.2	61136	1421416
127¾	12818	95883	2282.9	51271	1091645	139¾	15339	114743	2732.0	61356	1429072
128	12868	96259	2291.9	51472	1098066	140	15394	115154	2741.8	61575	1436755
128¼	12918	96635	2300.8	51673	1104513	140¼	15449	115565	2751.6	61795	1444466
128½	12969	97013	2309.8	51875	1110985	140½	15504	115978	2761.4	62016	1452204
128¾	13019	97390	2318.8	52077	1117481	140¾	15559	116391	2771.2	62237	1459970
129	13070	97769	2327.8	52279	1124004	141	15615	116805	2781.1	62458	1467763
129¼	13121	98148	2336.9	52482	1130551	141¼	15670	117219	2790.9	62680	1475584
129½	13171	98528	2345.9	52685	1137124	141½	15725	117634	2800.8	62902	1483433
129¾	13222	98909	2355.0	52889	1143723	141¾	15781	118050	2810.7	63124	1491310
130	13273	99291	2364.1	53093	1150347	142	15837	118467	2820.6	63347	1499214
130¼	13324	99673	2373.2	53297	1156996	142¼	15893	118885	2830.6	63570	1507146
130½	13376	100056	2382.3	53502	1163671	142½	15948	119303	2840.5	63794	1515107
130¾	13427	100440	2391.4	53707	1170371	142¾	16005	119722	2850.5	64018	1523095
131	13478	100824	2400.6	53913	1177098	143	16061	120142	2860.5	64242	1531111
131¼	13530	101209	2409.7	54119	1183850	143¼	16117	120562	2870.5	64467	1539156
131½	13581	101595	2418.9	54325	1190627	143½	16173	120983	2880.6	64692	1547228
131¾	13633	101982	2428.1	54532	1197431	143¾	16230	121405	2890.6	64918	1555329
132	13685	102369	2437.4	54739	1204260	144	16286	121828	2900.7	65144	1563458
132¼	13737	102757	2446.6	54947	1211116	144¼	16343	122251	2910.7	65370	1571615
132½	13789	103146	2455.9	55155	1217997	144½	16399	122675	2920.8	65597	1579800
132¾	13841	103536	2465.1	55363	1224904	144¾	16456	123100	2931.0	65824	1588014
133	13893	103926	2474.4	55572	1231838	145	16513	123526	2941.1	66052	1596256
133¼	13945	104317	2483.7	55781	1238797	145¼	16570	123952	2951.2	66280	1604527
133½	13998	104709	2493.1	55990	1245783	145½	16627	124379	2961.4	66508	1612826
133¾	14050	105102	2502.4	56200	1252795	145¾	16684	124807	2971.6	66737	1621154
134	14103	105495	2511.8	56410	1259833	146	16742	125235	2981.8	66966	1629511
134¼	14155	105889	2521.2	56621	1266898	146¼	16799	125665	2992.0	67196	1637896
134½	14208	106284	2530.6	56832	1273988	146½	16856	126095	3002.3	67426	1646310
134¾	14261	106679	2540.0	57044	1281106	146¾	16914	126525	3012.5	67656	1654752
135	14314	107075	2549.4	57256	1288249	147	16972	126957	3022.8	67887	1663224
135¼	14367	107472	2558.9	57468	1295420	147¼	17029	127389	3033.1	68118	1671724
135½	14420	107870	2568.3	57680	1302616	147½	17087	127822	3043.4	68349	1680253
135¾	14473	108268	2577.8	57893	1309840	147¾	17145	128256	3053.7	68581	1688811
136	14527	108667	2587.3	58107	1317090	148	17203	128690	3064.0	68813	1697398
136¼	14580	109067	2596.8	58321	1324366	148¼	17262	129125	3074.4	69046	1706015
136½	14634	109468	2606.4	58535	1331670	148½	17320	129561	3084.8	69279	1714660
136¾	14687	109869	2615.9	58750	1339000	148¾	17378	129998	3095.2	69513	1723334
137	14741	110271	2625.5	58965	1346357	149	17437	130435	3105.6	69746	1732038
137¼	14795	110674	2635.1	59180	1353741	149¼	17495	130873	3116.0	69981	1740771
137½	14849	111078	2644.7	59396	1361152	149½	17554	131312	3126.5	70215	1749533
137¾	14903	111482	2654.3	59612	1368590	149¾	17613	131751	3136.9	70450	1758325
						150	17671	132192	3147.4	70686	1767146

A-20.
Tank Capacities, Horizontal Cylindrical—
Contents of Tanks with Flat Ends
When Filled to Various Depths

To ascertain the contents of a tank over one-half full: Let h = depth of unfilled portion. Find from the table the quantity corresponding to a depth h. Subtract this quantity from the contents of a full tank.

Diameter of tank inches	Full tank	3″	6″	9″	12″	15″	18″	21″	24″	27″	30″	33″	36″	39″	42″	45″	48″	51″	54″	57″	60″
12″	5.88	1.15	2.94																		
18″	13.22	1.45	3.86	6.61																	
24″	23.50	1.70	4.60	8.05	11.75																
30″	36.72	1.91	5.23	9.27	13.72	18.36															
36″	52.88	2.12	5.79	10.34	15.43	20.85	26.44														
42″	71.97	2.28	6.31	11.31	16.97	23.07	29.47	35.99													
48″	94.01	2.45	6.78	12.20	18.38	25.10	32.20	39.54	47.00												
54″	118.98	2.60	7.22	13.04	19.68	26.97	34.72	42.80	51.08	59.49											
60″	146.89	2.75	7.64	13.82	20.91	28.72	37.06	45.82	54.87	64.11	73.44										
66″	177.73	2.89	8.04	14.56	22.07	30.37	39.28	48.65	58.39	68.41	78.59	88.86									
72″	211.52	3.02	8.42	15.26	23.17	31.92	41.36	51.32	61.71	72.45	83.41	94.54	105.76								
78″	248.24	3.15	8.78	15.94	24.21	33.41	43.34	53.86	64.87	76.27	87.97	99.90	111.97	124.13							
84″	287.90	3.26	9.12	16.57	25.21	34.85	45.24	56.29	67.87	79.91	92.30	104.98	117.85	130.87	143.95						
90″	330.49	3.43	9.46	17.20	26.20	36.21	47.05	58.61	70.75	83.39	96.43	109.81	123.45	137.28	151.23	165.25					
96″	376.02	3.50	9.79	17.80	27.13	37.52	48.81	60.84	73.52	86.73	100.39	114.44	128.79	143.40	158.17	173.06	188.01				
102″	424.50	3.61	10.10	18.37	28.01	39.00	50.49	62.99	76.18	89.94	104.20	118.89	133.92	149.25	164.81	180.53	196.37	212.25			
108″	476.10	3.71	10.39	18.94	28.90	40.03	52.14	65.09	78.74	93.04	107.87	123.17	138.87	154.89	171.19	187.71	204.37	221.14	238.05		
114″	530.25	3.78	10.74	19.49	29.75	41.22	53.73	67.10	81.24	96.05	111.43	127.31	143.63	160.33	177.33	194.60	212.05	229.65	247.37	265.13	
120″	587.54	3.91	10.98	20.02	30.57	42.39	55.26	69.06	83.65	98.95	114.87	131.32	148.25	165.58	183.27	201.24	219.46	237.87	256.43	275.08	293.77

Contents in U.S. gallons per 1 foot of length.
By permission, The Permutit Co., Inc., Data Book, 1953.

A-21.
Tank Capacities, Horizontal Cylindrical—
Contents of Standard Dished Heads
When Filled to Various Depths

Radius = Diameter

To ascertain the contents of a head over one-half full: Let h = depth of unfilled portion. Find from the table the quantity corresponding to a depth h. Subtract this quantity from the contents of a full head.

Diameter of head inches	Full head	3″	6″	9″	12″	15″	18″	21″	24″	27″	30″	33″	36″	39″	42″	45″	48″	51″	54″	57″	60″
12″	0.40	0.05	0.20																		
18″	1.36	0.07	0.32	0.68																	
24″	3.22	0.08	0.41	0.95	1.61																
30″	6.30	0.10	0.49	1.18	2.10	3.15															
36″	10.88	0.11	0.56	1.39	2.54	3.92	5.44														
42″	17.28	0.12	0.63	1.59	2.94	4.64	6.57	8.64													
48″	25.79	0.13	0.68	1.75	3.31	5.29	7.62	10.19	12.89												
54″	36.72	0.14	0.74	1.90	3.64	5.91	8.60	11.65	14.95	18.36											
60″	50.37	0.14	0.82	2.07	3.98	6.49	9.54	13.03	16.87	20.96	25.18										
66″	67.04	0.15	0.83	2.19	4.25	6.98	10.35	14.30	18.68	23.43	28.42	33.52									
72″	87.04	0.16	0.88	2.32	4.52	7.47	11.15	15.48	20.38	25.74	31.46	37.43	43.52								
78″	110.66	0.17	0.93	2.44	4.79	7.97	11.94	16.65	22.02	27.97	34.39	41.46	48.20	55.33							
84″	138.22	0.18	0.98	2.59	5.07	8.44	12.69	17.78	23.60	30.11	37.19	44.75	52.67	60.83	69.11						
90″	170.01	0.18	1.00	2.68	5.33	8.91	13.44	18.86	25.12	32.18	39.90	48.22	56.99	66.14	75.52	85.00					
96″	206.32	0.20	1.07	2.83	5.59	9.36	14.14	19.90	26.60	34.17	42.52	51.53	61.13	71.22	81.66	92.34	103.16				
102″	247.48	0.22	1.14	3.01	5.89	9.87	14.92	21.01	28.11	36.18	45.19	54.91	65.31	76.29	87.73	99.56	111.59	123.74			
108″	293.77	0.20	1.13	3.03	6.04	10.21	15.50	21.93	29.47	38.03	47.56	57.97	69.14	81.05	93.53	106.47	119.76	133.26	146.88		
114″	345.51	0.21	1.16	3.12	6.25	10.55	16.06	22.80	30.70	39.73	49.81	60.88	72.85	85.61	99.05	113.07	127.56	142.41	157.51	172.75	
120″	402.27	0.21	1.19	3.23	6.47	10.93	16.68	23.70	31.96	41.43	52.04	63.73	76.40	89.95	104.32	119.39	135.04	151.15	167.62	184.32	201.13

Contents in U.S. gallons for one head only. This table
is only approximate, but close enough for practical use.
By permission, The Permutit Co., Inc., Data Book, 1953.

A-22.
Miscellaneous Formulas
(Courtesy of Chicago Bridge and Iron Co.)

1. **Area of Roofs.**

   Umbrella Roofs:

   D = diameter of tank in feet.

   Surface area in square feet $\{$ = 0.842 D² (when radius = diameter)
   = 0.882 D² (when radius = 0.8 diameter)

   Conical Roofs:

   Surface area in square feet $\{$ = 0.787 D² (when pitch is ¾ in 12)
   = 0.792 D² (when pitch is 1½ in 12)

2. **Average weights.**

   Steel — 490 pounds per cubic foot—specific gravity 7.85

   Wrought iron —485 pounds per cubic foot—specific gravity 7.77

   Cast iron — 450 pounds per cubic foot—specific gravity 7.21

   1 cubic foot air or gas at 32° F., 760 m.m. barometer = molecular weight x 0.0027855 pounds.

3. Expansion in steel pipe = 0.78 inch per 100 lineal feet per 100 degrees Fahr. change in temperature = 0.412 inch per mile per degree Fahr. temperature change.

4. Linear coefficients of expansion per degree increase in temperature:

	Per Degree Fahrenheit	Per Degree Centigrade
STRUCTURAL STEEL—A-7		
70° to 200° F.	0.0000067	—
21.1° to 93° C.	—	0.0000121
STAINLESS STEEL—TYPE 304		
32° to 932° F.	0.0000102	—
0° to 500° C.	—	0.0000184
ALUMINUM		
−76° to 68° F.	0.0000120	—
−60° to 20° C.	—	0.0000216

5. To determine the net thickness of shells for horizontal cylindrical pressure tanks:

   $$T = \frac{6\,PD}{S}$$

   P = working pressure in pounds per square inch

   D = diameter of cylinder in feet

   S = allowable unit working stress in pounds per square inch

   T = Net thickness in inches

   Resulting net thickness must be corrected to gross or actual thickness by dividing by joint efficiency.

6. To determine the net thickness of heads for cylindrical pressure tanks:

   (6a) Ellipsoidal or Bumped Heads:

   $$T = \frac{6\,PD}{S}$$

   T, P and D as in formula 5

   (6b) Dished or Basket Heads:

   $$T = \frac{10.6P(MR)}{S}$$

   T, S and P as in formula 5

   MR = principal radius of head in feet

   Resulting net thickness of heads is both net and gross thickness if one piece seamless heads are used, otherwise net thickness must be corrected to gross thickness as above.

   Formulas 5 and 6 must often be modified to comply with various engineering codes, and state and municipal regulations. Calculated gross plate thicknesses are sometimes arbitrarily increased to provide an additional allowance for corrosion.

7. **Heads for Horizontal Cylindrical Tanks:**

   Hemi-ellipsoidal Heads have an ellipsoidal cross section, usually with minor axis equal to one half the major axis—that is, depth = ¼ D, or more.

   Dished or Basket Heads consist of a spherical segment normally dished to a radius equal to the inside diameter of the tank cylinder (or within a range of 6 inches plus or minus) and connected to the straight cylindrical flange by a "knuckle" whose inside radius is usually not less than 6 per cent of the inside diameter of the cylinder nor less than 3 times the thickness of the head plate. Basket heads closely approximate hemi-ellipsoidal heads.

   Bumped Heads consist of a spherical segment joining the tank cylinder directly without the transition "knuckle." The radius = D, or less. This type of head is used only for pressures of 10 pounds per square inch or less, excepting where a compression ring is placed at the junction of head and shell.

   Surface Area of Heads:

   (7a) Hemi-ellipsoidal Heads:

   $$S = \pi R^2 [1 + K^2(2-K)]$$

   S = surface area in square feet

   R = radius of cylinder in feet

   K = ratio of the depth of the head (not including the straight flange) to the radius of the cylinder

   The above formula is not exact but is within limits of practical accuracy.

   (7b) Dished or Basket Heads:

   Formula (7a) gives surface area within practical limits.

   (7c) Bumped Heads:

   $$S = \pi R^2 (1 + K^2)$$

   S, R, and K as in formula (7a)

   Volume of Heads:

   (7d) Hemi-ellipsoidal Heads:

   $$V = \tfrac{2}{3} \pi K R^3$$

   R = radius of cylinder in feet

   K = ratio of the depth of the head (not including the straight flange) to the radius of the cylinder

   (7e) Dished or Basket Heads:

   Formula (7d) gives volume within practical limits.

   (7f) Bumped Heads:

   $$V = \tfrac{1}{2} \pi K R^3 (1 + \tfrac{1}{3} K^2)$$

   V, K and R as in formula (7d)

   Note: K in above formulas may be determined as follows: Hemi-ellipsoidal heads—K is known

   Dished Heads—$K = M - \sqrt{(M-1)(M+1-2m)}$

   Bumped Heads—$K = [M - \sqrt{M^2-1}]$

   MR = principal radius of head in feet

   mR = radius of knuckle in feet

   R = radius of cylinder in feet

   $$M = \frac{MR}{R} \qquad m = \frac{mR}{R}$$

   For bumped heads m = o

8. Total volume or length of shell in cylindrical tank with ellipsiodal or hemispherical heads:

   V = Total volume

   L = Length of cylindrical shell

   KD = Depth of head

   $$V = \frac{\pi D^2}{4} (L + 1\tfrac{1}{3} KD)$$

   $$L = (V \div \frac{\pi D^2}{4}) - 1\tfrac{1}{3} KD$$

   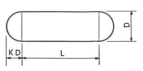

A-22.
(Continued). Miscellaneous Formulas

9. Volume or contents of partially filled horizontal cylindrical tanks:

(9a) Tank cylinder or shell (straight portion only)

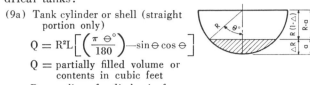

$$Q = R^2L\left[\left(\frac{\pi\,\Theta^\circ}{180}\right) - \sin\Theta\cos\Theta\right]$$

Q = partially filled volume or contents in cubic feet

R = radius of cylinder in feet

L = length of straight portion of cylinder in feet

The straight portion or flange of the heads must be considered a part of the cylinder. The length of flange depends upon the diameter of tank and thickness of head but ranges usually between 2 and 4 inches.

a = $\triangle$ R = depth of liquid in feet

$\triangle = \dfrac{a}{R}$ = a ratio

Cos Θ = 1 − $\triangle$, or $\dfrac{R\text{-}a}{R}$

$\leftrightarrow$ = degrees

(9b) Hemi ellipsoidal Heads:

$$Q = \tfrac{3}{4}\,V\,\triangle^2\,(1 - \tfrac{1}{3}\,\triangle)$$

Q = partially filled volume or contents in cubic feet

V = total volume of one head per formula (7d)

$\triangle = \dfrac{a}{R}$ = a ratio

a = $\triangle$ R = depth of liquid in feet

R = radius of cylinder in feet

(9c) Dished or Basket Heads:

Formula (9b) gives partially filled volume within practical limits, and formula (7d) gives V within practical limits.

(9d) Bumped Heads:

Formula (9b) gives partially filled volume within practical limits, and formula (7f) gives V.

Note: To obtain the volume or quantity of liquid in partially filled tanks, add the volume per formula (9a) for the cylinder or straight portion to twice (for 2 heads) the volume per formula (9b), (9c) or (9d) for the type of head concerned.

10. Volume or contents of partially filled hemi-ellipsoidal heads with major axis vertical:

Q = Partially filled volume or contents in cubic feet

V = Total volume of one head per formula (7d)

R = Radius of cylinder in feet

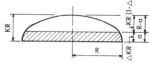

(10a) Upper Head:

$$Q = 1\tfrac{1}{2}\,V\,\triangle\,(1 - \tfrac{1}{3}\triangle^2)$$

$\triangle = \dfrac{a}{KR}$ = a ratio

a = $\triangle$ KR = depth of liquid in feet

(10b) Lower Head:

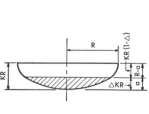

$$Q = 1\tfrac{1}{2}\,V\,\triangle^2(1 - \tfrac{1}{3}\triangle)$$

$\triangle = \dfrac{a}{KR}$ = a ratio

a = $\triangle$ KR = depth of liquid in feet

A-23.
Decimal Equivalents in Inches, Feet and Millimeters

In. Equiv. for Decimal of In.	Decimals	Millimeter Equiv. for Decimal of In.	In. Equiv. for Decimal of Ft.
1/64	.0156	0.397	3/16
1/32	.0313	0.794	3/8
3/64	.0469	1.191	9/16
1/16	.0625	1.588	3/4
5/64	.0781	1.984	15/16
3/32	.0938	2.381	1 1/8
7/64	.1094	2.778	1 5/16
1/8	.1250	3.175	1 1/2
9/64	.1406	3.572	1 11/16
5/32	.1563	3.969	1 7/8
11/64	.1719	4.366	2 1/16
3/16	.1875	4.763	2 1/4
13/64	.2031	5.159	2 7/16
7/32	.2188	5.556	2 5/8
15/64	.2344	5.953	2 13/16
1/4	.2500	6.350	3
17/64	.2656	6.747	3 3/16
9/32	.2813	7.144	3 3/8
19/64	.2969	7.541	3 9/16
5/16	.3125	7.938	3 3/4
21/64	.3281	8.334	3 15/16
11/32	.3438	8.731	4 1/8
23/64	.3594	9.128	4 5/16
3/8	.3750	9.525	4 1/2
25/64	.3906	9.922	4 11/16
13/32	.4063	10.319	4 7/8
27/64	.4219	10.716	5 1/16
7/16	.4375	11.113	5 1/4
29/64	.4531	11.509	5 7/16
15/32	.4688	11.906	5 5/8
31/64	.4844	12.303	5 13/16
1/2	.5000	12.700	6
33/64	.5156	13.097	6 3/16
17/32	.5313	13.494	6 3/8
35/64	.5469	13.891	6 9/16
9/16	.5625	14.288	6 3/4
37/64	.5781	14.684	6 15/16
19/32	.5938	15.081	7 1/8
39/64	.6094	15.478	7 5/16
5/8	.6250	15.875	7 1/2
41/64	.6406	16.272	7 11/16
21/32	.6563	16.669	7 7/8
43/64	.6719	17.066	8 1/16
11/16	.6875	17.463	8 1/4
45/64	.7031	17.859	8 7/16
23/32	.7188	18.256	8 5/8
47/64	.7344	18.653	8 13/16
3/4	.7500	19.050	9
49/64	.7656	19.447	9 3/16
25/32	.7813	19.844	9 3/8
51/64	.7969	20.241	9 9/16
13/16	.8125	20.638	9 3/4
53/64	.8281	21.034	9 15/16
27/32	.8438	21.431	10 1/8
55/64	.8594	21.828	10 5/16
7/8	.8750	22.225	10 1/2
57/64	.8906	22.622	10 11/16
29/32	.9063	23.019	10 7/8
59/64	.9219	23.416	11 1/16
15/16	.9375	23.813	11 1/4
61/64	.9531	24.209	11 7/16
31/32	.9688	24.606	11 5/8
63/64	.9844	25.003	11 13/16
1	1.0000	25.400	12

A-24.
(Continued).

AREA OF PLANE FIGURES

Triangle: Base x ½ perpendicular height.
$$\sqrt{s(s-a)(s-b)(s-c)},$$
s = ½ sum of the three sides a, b and c.

Trapezium: Sum of area of the two triangles.

Trapezoid: ½ sum of parallel sides x perpendicular height.

Parallelogram: Base x perpendicular height.

Regular Polygon: ½ sum of sides x inside radius.

Circle: $\pi r^2 = 0.78540 \times$ dia.$^2 = 0.07958 \times$ circumference^2

Sector of Circle: $\dfrac{\pi r^2 A^\circ}{360} =$ arc x ½ radius.

Segment of Circle: $\dfrac{r^2}{2}\left(\dfrac{\pi A^\circ}{180} - \sin A^\circ\right)$

Circle of same area as square: diameter = side x 1.12838

Square of same area as circle: side = diameter x 0.88623

Ellipse: Long diameter x short diameter x 0.78540

Parabola: Base x ⅔ perpendicular height.

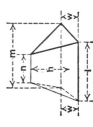

Irregular plane surface

Divide any plane surface A, B, C, D, along a line a–b into an even number, n, of parallel and sufficiently small strips, d, whose ordinates are $h_1, h_2, h_3, h_4, h_5 \ldots h_{n-1}, h_n, h_{n+1}$, and considering contours between three ordinates as parabolic curves, then for section ABCD,

$$\text{Area} = \frac{d}{3}\Big[h_1 + h_{n+1} + 4(h_2 + h_4 + h_6 \ldots + h_n) + 2(h_3 + h_5 + h_7 \ldots + h_{n-1})\Big]$$

or, approximately, Area = Sum of ordinates x width, d.

VOLUME OF A WEDGE

This formula is useful in obtaining the contents of special, wedge-shaped, tank bottoms.

$$\text{Volume} = \frac{wh}{6}(l + m + n)$$

A-24.

PROPERTIES OF THE CIRCLE

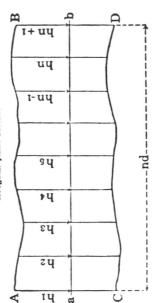

Circumference = 6.28318 r = 3.14159 d
Diameter = 0.31831 circumference
Area = 3.14159 r²

Arc $a = \dfrac{\pi r A^\circ}{180^\circ} = 0.017453\, r\, A^\circ$

Angle $A^\circ = \dfrac{180^\circ a}{\pi r} = 57.29578\, \dfrac{a}{r}$

Radius $r = \dfrac{4b^2 + c^2}{8b}$

Chord $c = 2\sqrt{2br - b^2} = 2\,r\sin\dfrac{A}{2}$

Rise $b = r - \tfrac{1}{4}\sqrt{4r^2 - c^2} = \dfrac{c}{2}\tan\dfrac{A}{4}$
$= 2\,r\sin^2\dfrac{A}{4} = r + y - \sqrt{r^2 - x^2}$
$y = b - r + \sqrt{r^2 - x^2}$
$x = \sqrt{r^2 - (r + y - b)^2}$

Diameter of circle of equal periphery as square = 1.27324 side of square
Side of square of equal periphery as circle = 0.78540 diameter of circle
Diameter of circle circumscribed about square = 1.41421 side of square
Side of square inscribed in circle = 0.70711 diameter of circle

CIRCULAR SECTOR

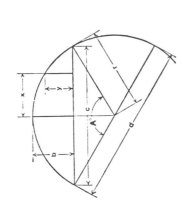

r = radius of circle   y = angle ncp in degrees

Area of Sector ncpo = ½ (length of arc nop × r)

$= \text{Area of Circle} \times \dfrac{y}{360}$

$= 0.0087266 \times r^2 \times y$

CIRCULAR SEGMENT

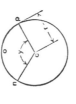

r = radius of circle   x = chord   b = rise

Area of Segment nop = Area of Sector ncpo − Area of triangle ncp

$= \dfrac{(\text{Length of arc nop} \times r) - x\,(r - b)}{2}$

Area of Segment nsp = Area of Circle − Area of Segment nop

VALUES FOR FUNCTIONS OF π

π = 3.14159265359, log = 0.4971499

π^2 = 9.8696044, log = 0.9942998 $\dfrac{1}{\pi}$ = 0.3183099, log = $\overline{1}$.5028501 $\sqrt{\dfrac{1}{\pi}}$ = 0.5641896, log = $\overline{1}$.7514251

π^3 = 31.0062767, log = 1.4914497 $\dfrac{1}{\pi^2}$ = 0.1013212, log = $\overline{1}$.0057002 $\dfrac{\pi}{180}$ = 0.0174533, log = $\overline{2}$.2418774

$\sqrt{\pi}$ = 1.7724539, log = 0.2485749 $\dfrac{1}{\pi^3}$ = 0.0322515, log = $\overline{2}$.5085503 $\dfrac{180}{\pi}$ = 57.2957795, log = 1.7581226

A-24.
(Continued).

TRIGONOMETRIC FORMULAS

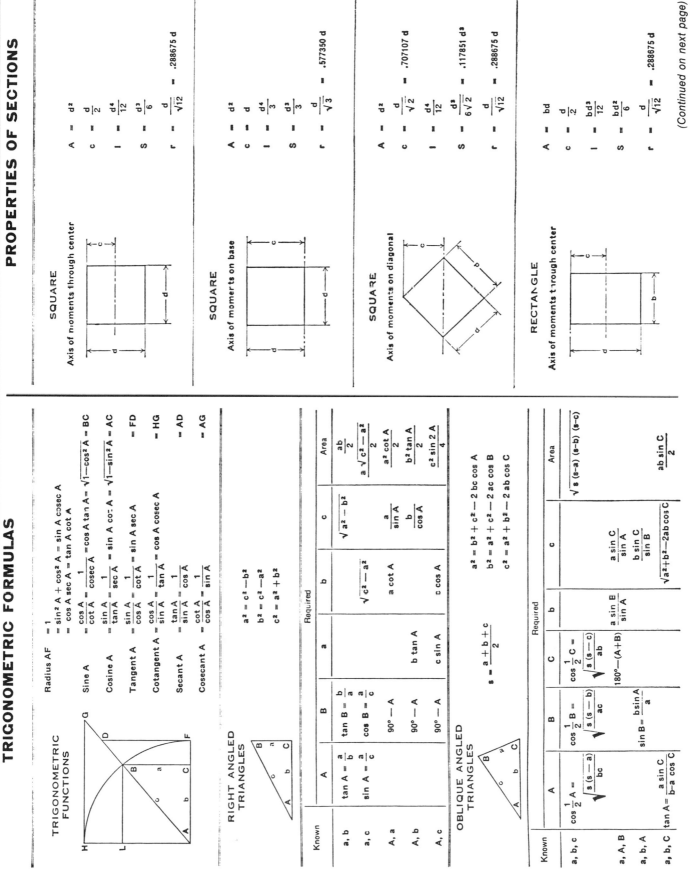

TRIGONOMETRIC FUNCTIONS

Radius AF = 1
$= \sin^2 A + \cos^2 A = \sin A \cosec A$
$= \cos A \sec A = \tan A \cot A$

$\text{Sine } A = \dfrac{\cos A}{\cot A} = \dfrac{1}{\cosec A} = \cos A \tan A = \sqrt{1-\cos^2 A} = BC$

$\text{Cosine } A = \dfrac{\sin A}{\tan A} = \dfrac{1}{\sec A} = \sin A \cot A = \sqrt{1-\sin^2 A} = AC$

$\text{Tangent } A = \dfrac{\sin A}{\cos A} = \dfrac{1}{\cot A} = \sin A \sec A = FD$

$\text{Cotangent } A = \dfrac{\cos A}{\sin A} = \dfrac{1}{\tan A} = \cos A \cosec A = HG$

$\text{Secant } A = \dfrac{\tan A}{\sin A} = \dfrac{1}{\cos A} = AD$

$\text{Cosecant } A = \dfrac{\cot A}{\cos A} = \dfrac{1}{\sin A} = AG$

RIGHT ANGLED TRIANGLES

$a^2 = c^2 - b^2$
$b^2 = c^2 - a^2$
$c^2 = a^2 + b^2$

Known	A	B	a	b	c	Area
a, b	$\tan A = \dfrac{a}{b}$	$\tan B = \dfrac{b}{a}$			$\sqrt{a^2-b^2}$	$\dfrac{ab}{2}$
a, c	$\sin A = \dfrac{a}{c}$	$\cos B = \dfrac{a}{c}$		$\sqrt{c^2-a^2}$		$\dfrac{a\sqrt{c^2-a^2}}{2}$
A, a		$90°-A$		$\sqrt{c^2-a^2}$	$\dfrac{a}{\sin A}$	$\dfrac{a^2 \cot A}{2}$
A, b		$90°-A$	$b \tan A$		$\dfrac{b}{\cos A}$	$\dfrac{b^2 \tan A}{2}$
A, c		$90°-A$	$c \sin A$	$c \cos A$		$\dfrac{c^2 \sin 2A}{4}$

OBLIQUE ANGLED TRIANGLES

$$s = \dfrac{a+b+c}{2}$$

$$a^2 = b^2 + c^2 - 2bc \cos A$$
$$b^2 = a^2 + c^2 - 2ac \cos B$$
$$c^2 = a^2 + b^2 - 2ab \cos C$$

Known	A	B	C	a	b	c	Area
a, b, c	$\cos \tfrac{1}{2}A = \sqrt{\dfrac{s(s-a)}{bc}}$	$\cos \tfrac{1}{2}B = \sqrt{\dfrac{s(s-b)}{ac}}$	$\cos \tfrac{1}{2}C = \sqrt{\dfrac{s(s-c)}{ab}}$				$\sqrt{s(s-a)(s-b)(s-c)}$
a, A, B			$180°-(A+B)$		$\dfrac{a \sin B}{\sin A}$	$\dfrac{a \sin C}{\sin A}$	
a, b, A		$\sin B = \dfrac{b \sin A}{a}$				$\dfrac{b \sin C}{\sin B}$	
a, b, C	$\tan A = \dfrac{a \sin C}{b - a \cos C}$					$\sqrt{a^2+b^2-2ab \cos C}$	$\dfrac{ab \sin C}{2}$

A-24.
(Continued)

PROPERTIES OF SECTIONS

SQUARE
Axis of moments through center

$A = d^2$
$c = \dfrac{d}{2}$
$I = \dfrac{d^4}{12}$
$S = \dfrac{d^3}{6}$
$r = \dfrac{d}{\sqrt{12}} = .288675\,d$

SQUARE
Axis of moments on base

$A = d^2$
$c = d$
$I = \dfrac{d^4}{3}$
$S = \dfrac{d^3}{3}$
$r = \dfrac{d}{\sqrt{3}} = .577350\,d$

SQUARE
Axis of moments on diagonal

$A = d^2$
$c = \dfrac{d}{\sqrt{2}} = .707107\,d$
$I = \dfrac{d^4}{12}$
$S = \dfrac{d^3}{6\sqrt{2}} = .117851\,d^3$
$r = \dfrac{d}{\sqrt{12}} = .288675\,d$

RECTANGLE
Axis of moments through center

$A = bd$
$c = \dfrac{d}{2}$
$I = \dfrac{bd^3}{12}$
$S = \dfrac{bd^2}{6}$
$r = \dfrac{d}{\sqrt{12}} = .288675\,d$

(Continued on next page)

A-24. (Continued).

PROPERTIES OF SECTIONS

RECTANGLE
Axis of moments on base

$$A = bd$$
$$c = d$$
$$I = \frac{bd^3}{3}$$
$$S = \frac{bd^2}{3}$$
$$r = \frac{d}{\sqrt{3}} = .577350\,d$$

RECTANGLE
Axis of moments on diagonal

$$A = bd$$
$$c = \frac{bd}{\sqrt{b^2 + d^2}}$$
$$I = \frac{b^3 d^3}{6\,(b^2 + d^2)}$$
$$S = \frac{b^2 d^2}{6\sqrt{b^2 + d^2}}$$
$$r = \frac{bd}{\sqrt{6\,(b^2 + d^2)}}$$

RECTANGLE
Axis of moments any line through center of gravity

$$A = bd$$
$$c = \frac{b \sin a + d \cos a}{2}$$
$$I = \frac{bd\,(b^2 \sin^2 a + d^2 \cos^2 a)}{12}$$
$$S = \frac{bd\,(b^2 \sin^2 a + d^2 \cos^2 a)}{6\,(b \sin a + d \cos a)}$$
$$r = \sqrt{\frac{b^2 \sin^2 a + d^2 \cos^2 a}{12}}$$

HOLLOW RECTANGLE
Axis of moments through center

$$A = bd - b_1 d_1$$
$$c = \frac{d}{2}$$
$$I = \frac{bd^3 - b_1 d_1^3}{12}$$
$$S = \frac{bd^3 - b_1 d_1^3}{6d}$$
$$r = \sqrt{\frac{bd^3 - b_1 d_1^3}{12\,A}}$$

A-24. (Continued).

PROPERTIES OF SECTIONS

EQUAL RECTANGLES
Axis of moments through center of gravity

$$A = b\,(d - d_1)$$
$$c = \frac{d}{2}$$
$$I = \frac{b\,(d^3 - d_1^3)}{12}$$
$$S = \frac{b\,(d^3 - d_1^3)}{6d}$$
$$r = \sqrt{\frac{d^3 - d_1^3}{12\,(d - d_1)}}$$

UNEQUAL RECTANGLES
Axis of moments through center of gravity

$$A = bt + b_1 t_1$$
$$c = \frac{\frac{1}{2} bt^2 + b_1 t_1 (d - \frac{1}{2} t_1)}{A}$$
$$I = \frac{bt^3}{12} + bty^2 + \frac{b_1 t_1^3}{12} + b_1 t_1 y_1^2$$
$$S = \frac{I}{c} \qquad S_1 = \frac{I}{c_1}$$
$$r = \sqrt{\frac{I}{A}}$$

TRIANGLE
Axis of moments through center of gravity

$$A = \frac{bd}{2}$$
$$c = \frac{2d}{3}$$
$$I = \frac{bd^3}{36}$$
$$S = \frac{bd^2}{24}$$
$$r = \frac{d}{\sqrt{18}} = .235702\,d$$

TRIANGLE
Axis of moments on base

$$A = \frac{bd}{2}$$
$$c = d$$
$$I = \frac{bd^3}{12}$$
$$S = \frac{bd^2}{12}$$
$$r = \frac{d}{\sqrt{6}} = .408248\,d$$

/>

A-24.
(Continued).

PROPERTIES OF SECTIONS

PARABOLA

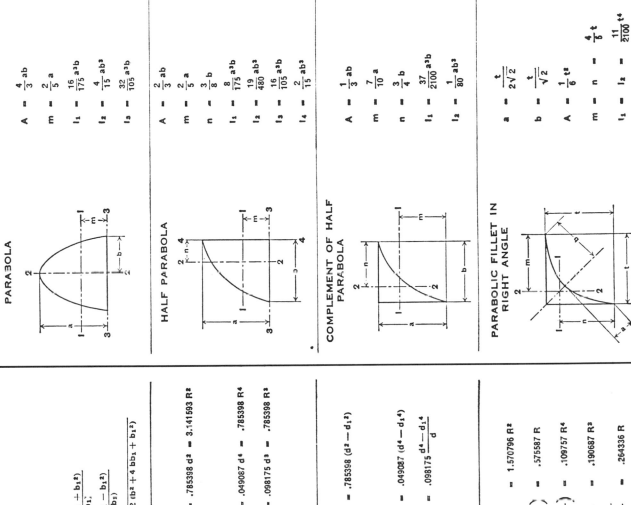

$A = \dfrac{4}{3}\,ab$

$m = \dfrac{2}{5}\,a$

$I_1 = \dfrac{16}{175}\,a^3b$

$I_2 = \dfrac{4}{15}\,ab^3$

$I_3 = \dfrac{32}{105}\,a^3b$

HALF PARABOLA

$A = \dfrac{2}{3}\,ab$

$m = \dfrac{2}{5}\,a$

$n = \dfrac{3}{8}\,b$

$I_1 = \dfrac{8}{175}\,a^3b$

$I_2 = \dfrac{19}{480}\,ab^3$

$I_3 = \dfrac{16}{105}\,a^3b$

$I_4 = \dfrac{2}{15}\,ab^3$

COMPLEMENT OF HALF PARABOLA

$A = \dfrac{1}{3}\,ab$

$m = \dfrac{7}{10}\,a$

$n = \dfrac{3}{4}\,b$

$I_1 = \dfrac{37}{2100}\,a^3b$

$I_2 = \dfrac{1}{80}\,ab^3$

PARABOLIC FILLET IN RIGHT ANGLE

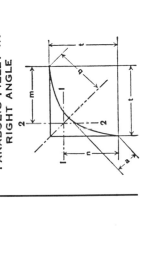

$a = \dfrac{t}{2\sqrt{2}}$

$b = \dfrac{t}{\sqrt{2}}$

$A = \dfrac{1}{6}\,t^2$

$m = n = \dfrac{4}{5}\,t$

$I_1 = I_2 = \dfrac{11}{2100}\,t^4$

(Continued on next page)

A-24.
(Continued).

PROPERTIES OF SECTIONS

TRAPEZOID
Axis of moments through center of gravity

$A = \dfrac{d(b + b_1)}{2}$

$c = \dfrac{d(2b + b_1)}{3(b + b_1)}$

$I = \dfrac{d^3(b^2 + 4bb_1 + b_1^2)}{36(b + b_1)}$

$S = \dfrac{d^2(b^2 + 4bb_1 - b_1^2)}{12(2b + b_1)}$

$r = \dfrac{d}{6(b + b_1)}\sqrt{2(b^2 + 4bb_1 + b_1^2)}$

CIRCLE
Axis of moments through center

$A = \dfrac{\pi d^2}{4} = \pi R^2 = .785398\,d^2 = 3.141593\,R^2$

$c = \dfrac{d}{2} = R$

$I = \dfrac{\pi d^4}{64} = \dfrac{\pi R^4}{4} = .049087\,d^4 = .785398\,R^4$

$S = \dfrac{\pi d^3}{32} = \dfrac{\pi R^3}{4} = .098175\,d^3 = .785398\,R^3$

$r = \dfrac{d}{4} = \dfrac{R}{2}$

HOLLOW CIRCLE
Axis of moments through center

$A = \dfrac{\pi(d^2 - d_1^2)}{4} = .785398\,(d^2 - d_1^2)$

$c = \dfrac{d}{2}$

$I = \dfrac{\pi(d^4 - d_1^4)}{64} = .049087\,(d^4 - d_1^4)$

$S = \dfrac{\pi(d^4 - d_1^4)}{32d} = .098175\,\dfrac{d^4 - d_1^4}{d}$

$r = \dfrac{\sqrt{d^2 + d_1^2}}{4}$

HALF CIRCLE
Axis of moments through center of gravity

$A = \dfrac{\pi R^2}{2} = 1.570796\,R^2$

$c = R\left(1 - \dfrac{4}{3\pi}\right) = .575587\,R$

$I = R^4\left(\dfrac{\pi}{8} - \dfrac{8}{9\pi}\right) = .109757\,R^4$

$S = \dfrac{R^3(9\pi^2 - 64)}{24(3\pi - 4)} = .190687\,R^3$

$r = R\,\dfrac{\sqrt{9\pi^2 - 64}}{6\pi} = .264336\,R$

A-24.
(Continued).

PROPERTIES OF SECTIONS

* HALF ELLIPSE

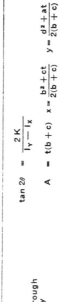

$$A = \frac{1}{2}\pi ab$$

$$m = \frac{4a}{3\pi}$$

$$I_1 = a^3 b\left(\frac{\pi}{8} - \frac{8}{9\pi}\right)$$

$$I_2 = \frac{1}{8}\pi ab^3$$

$$I_3 = \frac{1}{8}\pi a^3 b$$

* QUARTER ELLIPSE

$$A = \frac{1}{4}\pi ab$$

$$m = \frac{4a}{3\pi}$$

$$n = \frac{4b}{3\pi}$$

$$I_1 = a^3 b\left(\frac{\pi}{16} - \frac{4}{9\pi}\right)$$

$$I_2 = ab^3\left(\frac{\pi}{16} - \frac{4}{9\pi}\right)$$

$$I_3 = \frac{1}{16}\pi a^3 b$$

$$I_4 = \frac{1}{16}\pi ab^3$$

* ELLIPTIC COMPLEMENT

$$A = ab\left(1 - \frac{\pi}{4}\right)$$

$$m = \frac{a}{6\left(1-\frac{\pi}{4}\right)}$$

$$n = \frac{b}{6\left(1-\frac{\pi}{4}\right)}$$

$$I_1 = a^3 b\left(\frac{1}{3} - \frac{\pi}{16} - \frac{1}{36\left(1-\frac{\pi}{4}\right)}\right)$$

$$I_2 = ab^2\left(\frac{1}{3} - \frac{\pi}{16} - \frac{1}{36\left(1-\frac{\pi}{4}\right)}\right)$$

* To obtain properties of half circle, quarter circle and circular complement substitute a = b = R.

A-24.
(Concluded).

PROPERTIES OF SECTIONS

REGULAR POLYGON

Axis of moments through center

n = Number of sides

$$\phi = \frac{180°}{n}$$

$$a = 2\sqrt{R^2 - R_1^2}$$

$$R = \frac{a}{2\sin\phi}$$

$$R_1 = \frac{a}{2\tan\phi}$$

$$A = \frac{1}{4}na^2\cot\phi = \frac{1}{2}nR^2\sin2\phi = nR_1^2\tan\phi$$

$$I_1 = I_2 = \frac{A(6R^2 - a^2)}{24} = \frac{A(12R_1^2 + a^2)}{48}$$

$$r_1 = r_2 = \sqrt{\frac{6R^2 - a^2}{24}} = \sqrt{\frac{12R_1^2 + a^2}{48}}$$

ANGLE

Axis of moments through center of gravity

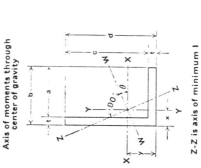

$$\tan 2\theta = \frac{2K}{I_y - I_x}$$

$$A = t(b+c) \qquad x = \frac{b^2 + ct}{2(b+c)} \qquad y = \frac{d^2 + at}{2(b+c)}$$

$$K = \text{Product of Inertia about X-X \& Y-Y}$$

$$= \frac{abcdt}{4(b+c)}$$

$$I_x = \frac{1}{3}\left(t(d-y)^3 + by^3 - a(y-t)^3\right)$$

$$I_y = \frac{1}{3}\left(t(b-x)^3 + dx^3 - c(x-t)^3\right)$$

$$I_z = I_x\sin^2\theta + I_y\cos^2\theta + K\sin2\theta$$

$$I_w = I_x\cos^2\theta + I_y\sin^2\theta - K\sin2\theta$$

K is negative when heel of angle, with respect to c. g., is in 1st or 3rd quadrant, positive when in 2nd or 4th quadrant.

Z-Z is axis of minimum I

BEAMS AND CHANNELS

Transverse force oblique through center of gravity

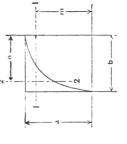

$$I_3 = I_x\sin^2\phi + I_y\cos^2\phi$$

$$I_4 = I_x\cos^2\phi + I_y\sin^2\phi$$

$$= M\left(\frac{y}{I_x}\sin\phi + \frac{x}{I_y}\cos\phi\right)$$

where M is bending moment due to force F. Extreme fiber assumed same as for case $\phi = 0$. If not, locate extreme fiber and find f by usual method.

A-25.
Wind Chill Equivalent Temperatures on Exposed Flesh at Varying Velocity

	WIND VELOCITY (MILES PER HOUR)										
	45	35	25	20	15	10	5	3	2	1	0
	90	89.5	89	88.5	88	88.75	87.5	87	86	84.5	83
	82	81	80.5	80	79.5	78	76	74	72.5	70	60
	72	71	69.5	68	67	65	60	57	53.5	47.5	23
	63	61	59	57	55	52	44.5	39	34.5	20	−11
Temperature, F	51	49	47	45	42.5	38	28	18.5	11	0	−27
	41	39	36	34	30.5	25	11	0	−9	−23.5	−38
	30	28	25	23	18	11	−5	−16.5	−40	Below −40	Below −40
	20	18	14	11	6	−2	−19	−40	Below −40	do	do
	10	7.5	3	0	−6	−15	−35	Below −40	do	do	do
	0	−2.5	−8	−12	−18	−29	Below −40	do	do	do	do
	−11	−14	−18	−23	−30	Below −40	do	do	do	do	do
	−21	−24	−30	−35	Below −40	do	do	do	do	do	do
	−32	−35	−40	−40				do	do	do	

Instructions for use of the table:

(1) First obtain the temperature and wind velocity forecast data.
(2) Locate the number at the top corresponding to the expected wind speed (or the number closest to this).
(3) Read down this column until the number corresponding to the expected temperature (or the number closest to this) is reached.
(4) From this point follow across to the right on the same line until the last number is reached under the column marked zero (0) wind speed.
(5) This is the equivalent temperature reading. Example: weather information gives the expected temperature (at a given time, such as midnight) to be 35°F, and the expected wind speed (at the same time, midnight) to be 20 miles per hour (mph). Locate the 20 mph column at the top, follow down this column to the number nearest to 35°F. The nearest number is 34°F. From this point, move all the way to the right on the same line and find the last number, which is −38°F. This means that with a temperature of 35°F, and a windspeed of 20 mph the rate of cooling of all exposed flesh is the same as −38°F, with no wind.

Reproduced by permission of the Department of the Army.

do means ditto.

A-26.
Impurities in Water

U. S. Systems of Expressing Impurities

1 grain per gallon .... = 1 grain calcium carbonate ($CaCO_3$) per U. S. gallon of water
1 part per million .... = 1 part calcium carbonate ($CaCO_3$) per 1,000,000 parts of water
1 part per hundred thousand.. = 1 part calcium carbonate ($CaCO_3$) per 100,000 parts of water

Foreign Systems of Expressing Impurities

1 English degree (or °Clark).. = 1 grain calcium carbonate ($CaCO_3$) per British Imperial gal. of water
1 French degree .... = 1 part calcium carbonate ($CaCO_3$) per 100,000 parts of water
1 German degree .... = 1 part calcium oxide (CaO) per 100,000 parts of water

Conversions

CONVERSION TABLE (Expressed to 3 Significant Figures)	Parts CaCo₃ per Million (ppm)	Parts CaCo₃ per Hundred Thousand (Pts./100,000)	Grains CaCo₃ per U.S. Gallon (gpg)	English Degrees or ° Clark	French Degrees — °French	German Degrees — °German	Milli-equivalents per Liter or Equivalents per Million
1 Part per Million	1.	.1	.0583	.07	.1	.0560	.020
1 Part per Hundred Thousand	10.0	1.	.583	.7	1.	.560	.20
1 Grain per U. S. Gallon	17.1	1.71	1.	1.2	1.71	.958	.343
1 English or Clark Degree	14.3	1.43	.833	1.	1.43	.800	.286
1 French Degree	10.	1.	.583	.7	1.	.560	.20
1 German Degree	17.9	1.79	1.04	1.24	1.79	1.	.357
1 Milli-equivalent per Liter or 1 Equivalent per Million	50.	5.	2.92	3.50		2.80	1.

By permission, The Permutit Co., Inc., Data Book, 1953.

A-27.
Water Analysis Conversions for
Units Employed: Equivalents

WATER ANALYSIS UNITS CONVERSION TABLE (Expressed to 3 Significant Figures)	Parts per Million (ppm)	Milligrams per Liter (mgm/L)	Grams per Liter (grms/L)	Parts per Hundred Thousand (Pts./100,000)	Grains U.S. Gallon (grs/U.S. gal)	Grains per British Imp. Gallon	Kilograins per Cubic Foot (Kgr/cu. ft.)
1 Part per Million	1.	1.	.001	.1	.0583	.07	.0004
1 Milligram per Liter	1.	1.	.001	.1	.0583	.07	.0004
1 Gram per Liter	1000.	1000.	1.	100.	58.3	70.	.436
1 Part per Hundred Thousand	10.	10.	.01	1.	.583	.7	.00436
1 Grain per U.S. Gallon	17.1	17.1	.017	1.71	1.	1.2	.0075
1 Grain per British Imp. Gallon	14.3	14.3	.014	1.43	.833	1.	.0062
1 Kilograin per Cubic Foot	2294.	2294.	2.294	229.4	134.	161.	1.

NOTE: In practice, water analysis samples are measured by volume, not by weight and corrections for variations in specific gravity are practically never made. Therefore, parts per million are assumed to be the same as milligrams per liter and hence the above relationships are, for practical purposes, true.

By permission, The Permutit Co., Inc., Data Book, 1953.

A-28.
Parts Per Million to Grains Per U. S. Gallon

A. To convert parts per million of hardness to grains per U. S. gallon, divide by the factor 17.1.

Example:

1. $\dfrac{242 \text{ parts/million}}{17.1} = 14.1 \text{ grains/U. S. gallon}$

B. To convert grains per U. S. gallons to parts per million of hardness, multiply by the factor 17.1.

2. 24.3 grains/U. S. gallon $\times$ 17.1 = 416 parts/million

Equivalents

Water analyses may also be expressed as:

(1) Equivalents per million (epm) . . . . = $\dfrac{\text{No. of ppm of substance present}}{\text{Equivalent weight of substance}}$

(2) Milli equivalents per liter (meq/l) . . . . = Equivalents per million

(3) Parts per million expressed as $CaCO_3$ . . . . = No. of ppm $CaCO_3$ equivalent to No. of ppm of substance present

(4) Fiftieths of equivalents per million (epm/50) . . = $\dfrac{\text{No. of ppm of substance present} \times 50}{\text{Equivalent weight of substance}}$

NOTES: Numerically (1) and (2) are equal.   Section xxiii contains equivalent weights of a number of substances.
Numerically (3) and (4) are equal.   Section xxiii contains factors for converting various substances to $CaCO_3$.
    Section xxiii contains factors for various chemical conversions.

By permission, The Permutit Co., Inc., Data Book, 1953.

A-29.

Formulas, Molecular and Equivalent Weights, and Conversion Factors to CaCO₃ of Substances Frequently Appearing in the Chemistry of Water Softening

Substance	Formula	Molecular weight	Equivalent weight	Multiplying Factor Considering molecular wt. of CaCO₃ as 100.	
				Substance to CaCO₃ equivalent	CaCO₃ equivalent to substance
Aluminum	Al	27.0	9.0	5.56	0.18
Aluminum Chloride	AlCl₃	133.	44.4	1.13	0.89
Aluminum Chloride	AlCl₃.6H₂O	241.	80.5	0.62	1.61
Aluminum Sulfate	Al₂(SO₄)₃·18H₂O	666.4	111.1	0.45	2.22
Aluminum Sulfate	Al₂(SO₄)₃ (anhydrous)	342.1	57.0	0.88	1.14
Aluminum Hydrate	Al(OH)₃	78.0	26.0	1.92	0.52
Alumina	Al₂O₃	101.9	17.0	2.94	0.34
Sodium Aluminate	Na₂Al₂O₄	163.9	27.3	1.83	0.55
Ammonium Alum	Al₂(SO₄)₃·(NH₄)₂SO₄·24H₂O	906.6	151.1	0.33	3.02
Potassium Alum	Al₂(SO₄)₃K₂SO₄·24H₂O	948.8	156.1	0.32	3.12
Ammonia	NH₃	17.0	17.0	2.94	0.34
Ammonium (Ion)	NH₄	18.0	18.0	2.78	0.36
Ammonium Chloride	NH₄Cl	53.5	53.5	0.94	1.07
Ammonium Hydroxide	NH₄OH	35.1	35.1	1.43	0.70
Ammonium Sulfate	(NH₄)₂SO₄	132.	66.1	0.76	1.32
Barium	Ba	137.4	68.7	0.73	1.37
Barium Carbonate	BaCO₃	197.4	98.7	0.51	1.97
Barium Chloride	BaCl₂·2H₂O	244.3	122.2	0.41	2.44
Barium Hydroxide	Ba(OH)₂	171.	85.7	0.59	1.71
Barium Oxide	BaO	153.	76.7	0.65	1.53
Barium Sulfate	BaSO₄	233.4	116.7	0.40	2.33
Calcium	Ca	40.1	20.0	2.50	0.40
Calcium Bicarbonate	Ca(HCO₃)₂	162.1	81.1	0.62	1.62
Calcium Carbonate	CaCO₃	100.08	50.1	1.00	1.00
Calcium Chloride	CaCl₂	111.0	55.5	0.90	1.11
Calcium Hydrate	Ca(OH)₂	74.1	37.1	1.35	0.74
Calcium Hypochlorite	Ca(ClO)₂	143.1	35.8	0.70	1.43
Calcium Oxide	CaO	56.1	28.0	1.79	0.56
Calcium Sulfate	CaSO₄ (anhydrous)	136.1	68.1	0.74	1.36
Calcium Sulfate	CaSO₄·2H₂O (gypsum)	172.2	86.1	0.58	1.72
Calcium Nitrate	Ca(NO₃)₂	164.1	82.1	0.61	1.64
Calcium Phosphate	Ca₃(PO₄)₂	310.3	51.7	0.97	1.03
Carbon	C	12.0	3.00	16.67	0.06
Chlorine (Ion)	Cl	35.5	35.5	1.41	0.71
Copper (Cupric)	Cu	63.6	31.8	1.57	0.64
Copper Sulfate (Cupric)	CuSO₄	160.	80.0	0.63	1.60
Copper Sulfate (Cupric)	CuSO₄·5H₂O	250.	125.	0.40	2.50
Iron (Ferrous)	Fe″	55.8	27.9	1.79	0.56
Iron (Ferric)	Fe‴	55.8	18.6	2.69	0.37
Ferrous Carbonate	FeCO₃	116.	57.9	0.86	1.16
Ferrous Hydroxide	Fe(OH)₂	89.9	44.9	1.11	0.90
Ferrous Oxide	FeO	71.8	35.9	1.39	0.72
Ferrous Sulfate	FeSO₄ (anhydrous)	151.9	76.0	0.66	1.52
Ferrous Sulfate	FeSO₄·7H₂O	278.0	139.0	0.36	2.78
Ferrous Sulfate	FeSO₄ (anhydrous)	151.9	151.9	oxidation	
Ferric Chloride	FeCl₃	162.	54.1	0.93	1.08
Ferric Chloride	FeCl₃·6H₂O	270.	90.1	0.56	1.80
Ferric Hydroxide	Fe(OH)₃	107.	35.6	1.41	0.71
Ferric Oxide	Fe₂O₃	160.	26.6	1.88	0.53
Ferric Sulfate (Ferrisul)	Fe₂(SO₄)₃	399.9	66.7	0.75	1.33
Ferrous or Ferric	Fe or Fe	55.8	55.8	oxidation	
Ferrous Sulfate	FeSO₄	151.9	151.9	oxidation	
Fluorine	F	19.0	19.0	2.66	0.38
Hydrogen (Ion)	H	1.01	1.01	50.0	0.02
Iodine	I	127.	127.	0.40	2.54
Lead	Pb	207.	104.	0.48	2.08
Magnesium	Mg	24.3	12.2	4.10	0.24
Magnesium Oxide	MgO	40.3	20.2	2.48	0.40
Magnesium Bicarbonate	Mg(HCO₃)₂	146.3	73.2	0.68	1.46
Magnesium Carbonate	MgCO₃	84.3	42.2	1.19	0.84
Magnesium Chloride	MgCl₂	95.2	47.6	1.05	0.95
Magnesium Hydrate	Mg(OH)₂	58.3	29.2	1.71	0.58
Magnesium Nitrate	Mg(NO₃)₂	148.3	74.2	0.67	1.48
Magnesium Phosphate	Mg₃(PO₄)₂	262.9	43.8	1.14	0.88
Magnesium Sulfate	MgSO₄	120.4	60.2	0.83	1.20
Manganese (Manganous)	Mn″	54.9	27.5	1.82	0.55
Manganese (Manganic)	Mn‴	54.9	18.3	2.73	0.37
Manganese Chloride	MnCl₂	125.8	62.9	0.80	1.26
Manganese Dioxide	MnO₂	86.9	21.7	2.30	0.43
Manganese Hydrate	Mn(OH)₂	89.0	44.4	1.13	0.89
Manganic Oxide	Mn₂O₃	158.	26.3	1.90	0.53
Manganous Oxide	MnO	70.9	35.5	1.41	0.71

By permission, The Permutit Co., Inc., Data Book, 1953.

(Continued on next page)

A-29.

(Concluded). Formulas, Molecular and Equivalent Weights, and Conversion Factors to CaCO₃ of Substances Frequently Appearing in the Chemistry of Water Softening

Substance	Formula	Molecular weight	Equivalent weight	Substance to CaCO₃ equivalent	CaCO₃ equivalent to substance
				Multiplying Factor — Considering molecular wt. of CaCO₃ as 100.	
Nitrate (Ion)	NO_3	62.0	62.0	0.81	1.24
Nitric Acid	HNO_3	63.0	63.0	0.79	1.26
Nitrogen (Valence 3)	N'''	14.0	4.67	10.8	0.093
Nitrogen (Valence 5)	N'''''	14.0	2.80	17.9	0.056
Oxygen	O	16.0	8.00	6.25	0.16
Phosphorus (Valence 3)	P'''	31.0	10.3	4.76	0.21
Phosphorus (Valence 5)	P'''''	31.0	6.20	8.33	0.12
Potassium	K	39.1	39.1	1.28	0.78
Potassium Carbonate	K_2CO_3	138.	69.1	0.72	1.38
Potassium Chloride	KCl	74.6	74.6	0.67	1.49
Potassium Hydroxide	KOH	56.1	56.1	0.88	1.12
Silver Chloride	AgCl	143.3	143.3	0.35	2.87
Silver Nitrate	$AgNO_3$	169.9	169.9	0.29	3.40
Silica	SiO_2	60.1	30.0	1.67	0.60
Silicon	Si	28.1	7.03	7.14	0.14
Sodium	Na	23.0	23.0	2.18	0.46
Sodium Bicarbonate	$NaHCO_3$	84.0	84.0	0.60	1.68
Sodium Bisulfate	$NaHSO_4$	120.			
Sodium Bisulfite	$NaHSO_3$	104.			
Sodium Carbonate	Na_2CO_3	106.	53.0	0.94	1.06
Sodium Carbonate	$Na_2CO_3 \cdot 10H_2O$	286.	143.	0.35	2.86
Sodium Chloride	NaCl	58.5	58.5	0.85	1.17
Sodium Hypochlorite	NaClO	74.5	37.3	0.67	1.49
Sodium Hydrate	NaOH	40.0	40.0	1.25	0.80
Sodium Nitrate	$NaNO_3$	85.0	85.0	0.59	1.70
Sodium Nitrite	$NaNO_2$	69.0	34.5	0.73	1.38
Sodium Oxide	Na_2O	62.0	31.0	1.61	0.62
Tri-sodium Phosphate	$Na_3PO_4 \cdot 12H_2O$ (18.7% P_2O_5)	380.2	126.7	0.40	2.53
Tri-sodium Phos. (anhydrous)	Na_3PO_4(43.2% $\cdot P_2O_5$)	164.0	54.7	0.91	1.09
Di-sodium Phosphate	$Na_2HPO_4 \cdot 12H_2O$ (19.8% P_2O_5)	358.2	119.4	0.42	2.39
Di-sodium Phos. (anhydrous)	Na_2HPO_4 (50% P_2O_5)	142.0	47.3	1.06	0.95
Mono-sodium Phosphate	$NaH_2PO_4 \cdot H_2O$ (51.4% P_2O_5)	138.1	46.0	1.09	0.92
Mono-sod. phos. (anhydrous)	NaH_2PO_4 (59.1% P_2O_5)	120.0	40.0	1.25	0.80
Meta-Phosphate (Hagan)	$NaPO_3$ (69% P_2O_5)	102.0	34.0	1.47	0.68
Sodium Sulfate	$Na_2SO_4 \cdot 10H_2O$	322.1	161.1	0.31	3.22
Sodium Sulfate	Na_2SO_4	142.1	71.0	0.70	1.42
Sodium Thiosulfate	$Na_2S_2O_3$	158.1	158.1	0.63	1.59
Sodium Tetrathionate	$Na_2S_4O_6$	270.2	135.1	0.37	2.71
Sodium Sulfite	Na_2SO_3	126.1	83.0	0.79	1.27
Sulfur (Valence 2)	S''	32.1	16.0	3.13	0.32
Sulfur (Valence 4)	S''''	32.1	8.02	6.25	0.16
Sulfur (Valence 6)	S''''''	32.1	5.34	9.10	0.11
Sulfur Dioxide	SO_2	64.1	32.0		
Tin	Sn	119.			
Water	H_2O	18.0	9.00	5.56	0.18
Zinc	Zn	65.4	32.7	1.54	0.65
ACID RADICALS					
Bicarbonate	HCO_3	61.0	61.0	0.82	1.22
Carbonate	CO_3	60.0	30.0	1.67	.60
Carbon Dioxide	CO_2	44.0	22.0	2.27	.44
Chloride	Cl	35.5	35.5	1.41	.71
Iodide	I	126.9	126.9	0.40	2.54
Nitrate	NO_3	62.0	62.0	0.81	1.24
Hydrate	OH :	17.0	17.0	2.94	0.34
Phosphate	PO_4	95.0	31.7	1.58	0.63
Phosphorous Oxide	P_2O_5	142.0	23.7	2.11	0.47
Sulfide	S	32.1	16.0	3.11	0.32
Sulfate	SO_4	96.1	48.0	1.04	0.96
Sulfur Trioxide	SO_3	80.1	40.0	1.25	0.80
ACIDS					
Hydrogen	H	1.0	1.0	50.00	0.02
Acetic Acid	$HC_2H_3O_2$	60.1	60.1	0.83	1.20
Carbonic Acid	H_2CO_3	62.0	31.0	1.61	0.62
Hydrochloric Acid	HCl	36.5	36.5	1.37	0.73
Phosphoric Acid	H_3PO_4	98.0	32.7	1.53	0.65
Sulfurous Acid	H_2SO_3	82.1	41.1	1.22	0.82
Sulfuric Acid	H_2SO_4	98.1	49.0	1.02	0.98
Hydrogen Sulfide	H_2S	—	—	—	—
Manganous Acid	H_2MnO_3	104.9	52.5	0.95	1.05

A-30.
Grains Per U.S. Gallons—
Pounds Per 1000 Gallons

A. To convert grains per U. S. gallons to pounds per 1000 gallons multiply by the factor 0.143.

B. To convert pounds per 1000 gallons to grains per U. S. gallons multiply by the factor 7.0.

Example:

1. 4.5 grains/U. S. gallon $\times$ 0.143 = 0.644 lbs./1000 gals.
2. 0.5 lbs./1000 gallons $\times$ 7.0 = 3.5 grains/U. S. gal.

A-31.
Parts Per Million—
Pounds Per 1000 Gallons

A. To convert parts per million to pounds per 1000 gallons divide by the factor 120.

B. To convert pounds per 1000 gallons to parts per million multiply by the factor 120.

Example:

1. $\dfrac{39 \text{ parts/million}}{120}$ = 0.325 lbs./1000 gals.

2. 0.167 lbs./1000 gals. $\times$ 120 = 20 parts/million

A-32.
Coagulant, Acid, and Sulfate—1 ppm Equivalents

1 Ppm Name of Chemical	1 Ppm. Formula of Chemical	ppm Alkalinity Reduction	ppm SO_3 as $CaCO_3$ Increase	ppm Na_2SO_4 Increase	ppm CO_2 Increase	ppm Total Solids Increase
Filter Alum	$Al_2(SO_4)_3 \cdot 18H_2O$	0.45	0.45	0.61	0.40	0.16
Ammonia Alum	$Al_2(SO_4)_3 \cdot (NH_4)_2SO_4 \cdot 24H_2O$	0.33	0.44	0.63	0.29	0.27
Potash Alum	$Al_2(SO_4)_3 \cdot K_2SO_4 \cdot 24H_2O$	0.32	0.43	0.60	0.28	0.30
Copperas (ferrous sulfate)	$FeSO_4 \cdot 7H_2O$	0.36	0.36	0.51	0.31	0.13
Chlorinated Copperas	$FeSO_4 \cdot 7H_2O + (\frac{1}{2}Cl_2)$	0.54	0.36	0.51	0.48	0.18
Ferric Sulfate (100% $Fe_2(SO_4)_3$)	$Fe_2(SO_4)_3$	0.75	0.75	1.07	0.66	0.27
Sulfuric Acid—98%	H_2SO_4	1.00	1.00	1.42	0.88	0.36
Sulfuric Acid—93.2% (66° Be)	H_2SO_4	0.95	0.95	1.35	0.84	0.34
Sulfuric Acid—77.7% (60° Be)	H_2SO_4	0.79	0.79	1.13	0.70	0.28
Salt Cake—95%	Na_2SO_4	—	0.66	0.95	—	1.00

By permission, The Permutit Co., Inc., Data Book, 1953.

A-33.
Alkali and Lime—1 ppm Equivalents

Name 1 Ppm	Formula 1 Ppm	Alkalinity A Increase ppm	Free CO_2 Reduction ppm	T.H. as $CaCO_3$ Increase ppm
Sodium Bicarbonate	$NaHCO_3$	0.60	—	—
Soda Ash (56% Na_2O = 99.16% Na_2CO_3)	Na_2CO_3	0.94	0.41	—
Caustic Soda (76% Na_2O = 98.06% NaOH)	NaOH	1.23	1.08	—
Chemical Lime (Quicklime—Usually 90% CaO)	CaO	1.61	1.41	1.61
Hydrated Lime (Usually 93% $Ca(OH)_2$)	$Ca(OH)_2$	1.26	1.11	1.26

By permission, The Permutit Co., Inc., Data Book, 1953.

A-34.
Sulfuric, Hydrochloric Acid Equivalent

Name		Formula	Specific Gravity 60°/60°F.	Concentration	Grams/Liter	$CaCO_3$ Equivalent to one lb. Acid	
						Lbs.	Grains
Sulfuric Acid	60° Be	H_2SO_4	1.7059	77.67%	1325	.7926	5548
Sulfuric Acid	66° Be	H_2SO_4	1.8354	93.19%	1710	.9509	6657
Sulfuric Acid	98%	H_2SO_4	1.8407	98.00%	1804	1.0000	7000
Hydrochloric Acid	18% Be	HCl	1.1417	27.92%	319	.3831	2682

By permission, The Permutit Co., Inc., Data Book, 1953.

Author Index

Abbey, R.G., 187
Akers, W.W., 36
Andres, D., 211

Bogart, M.J.P., 22
Bolles, W.L., 65, 70, 72, 88, 90, 91, 92, 93, 95, 96, 97, 98, 99, 100, 101, 103, 105
Biston, W., 37
Bradford, J.B., 18
Broaddus, J.E., 88
Brooke, M., 236
Brown, G.G., 48, 66, 67, 108, 118
Brown, T., 205
Bryant, P.A., 48

Chueh, P.L., 3
Cicalese, J.J., 104
Colburn, A.P., 31, 33, 182, 183, 184
Cornell, W., 208
Czermann, J.J., 180

Dauphine, T.C., 100, 101, 104, 105
Davies, J.A., 93
Dodge, B.F., 199, 201
Drickamer, H.G., 18

Eckert, J., 168
Edmister, W.C., 48, 49, 52, 54
Eduljee, H.E., 102
Elgin, J.C., 175

Faasen, J.W., 9
Fair, J.R., 208
Fellinger, L., 189
Frahme, H.H., 169, 171
Fuller, A.L., 238

Guatreaux, M.F., 18
Gilliland, E.R., 11, 13, 24, 34, 187
Griswald, J., 211
Groitein, E.E., 224
Grove, C.S., Jr., 171

Hands, C.H.G., 210
Hanson, D.N., 108
Henke, G.E., 37
Hodson, J.R., 106, 107, 112
Holland, C.D., 11, 37
Holloway, F.A.L., 187
Huang, Chen-Jung, 106, 107, 112
Hughmark, G.A., 109, 110, 111, 117
Hull, R.J., 56, 57, 58
Hunt, C.D A., 108, 119

Jackson, J., 157, 158, 162

Kelly, N.W., 220, 221, 223, 224
Kister, T., 4
Klein, J.H., 109
Klein, V.A., 211
Knapp, W., 208
Kremser, A., 48
Kwong, J.N.S., 3

Lerner, B.J., 171
Leva, M., 135, 138, 151, 154, 160, 167, 174, 181, 188, 191, 199, 200, 201
Lucas, J.M., 169, 171

McKinney, J.F., 187
Molstad, M.C., 187, 188
Montross, C.F., 33, 34
Morris, R., 157, 158, 162
Murch, D.P., 207
Myers, H.S., 116, 120

O'Connell, H.E., 18, 59, 109, 110, 111,
Okada, K., 176
Oldershaw, C.F., 205
Olney, R.B., 102
Otake, T., 176

Perry, J.H., 188, 115
Pigford, R.L., 189
Prausnitz, J.M., 37
Proulx, A.Z., 173, 177, 178

Radcliffe, F., 205
Raymond, K., 56, 57, 58
Redlich, O., 3, 4
Renon, H., 4
Robinson, C.S.R., 11, 13, 24

Sarchet, B.R., 158
Sheibel, E.G., 33, 34
Sherwood, T.K., 159, 187, 188
Shiras, R.N., 30
Shulman, H.L., 173, 175, 176, 177, 178
Simenson, L., 205
Simkin, D.J., 102
Smith, B.D., 4, 5, 6
Smoker, E.H., 9
Souders, M., Jr., 66, 67, 108, 118
Spector, N.A., 199
Strand, C.P., 102
Sullivan, W., 37
Sutherland, S., 116, 117, 120
Swenson, L.K., 220, 221, 223, 224

Teller, A.J., Dr., 18, 145
Tepe, J.B., 201
Treybal, R.E., 187, 189

Ulbrich, C.F., 173, 177, 178
Underwood, A.J.V., 30

Van Winkle, M., 29, 35
Vivian, J.E., 204

Wade, D.E., 36
Wang, J.C., 37
Wells, N., 173, 177
Wen, Chin-Yung, 203, 204
Whitesell, J., 218, 222
Whitney, R.P., 204
Whitt, F.R., 209, 210
Wilke, C.R., 108
Wilson, G.M., 4

Zenz, F.A., 110, 159, 167, 168, 169
Zimmerman, J.O., 173, 178

Subject Index

Absorption and stripping, hydrocarbon, 48
  design procedures, 48, 50
  Edmister method, 52, 53
  effective absorption/stripping
    factors chart, 54
  equilibrium curve, 58
  example calculation, 55
  flow diagram of system, 49
  Kremiser-Brown-Sherwood meth-
    od, 48
Absorption, components in fixed tray
  tower, 48
Absorption/desorption, packed
  tower, 180
Absorption factor, 49
  chart, 52, 54
Absorption, heats of, 57
Absorbers, intercooling, 56, 57
Activity, 3, 4
Air-water system, 205
Akers and Wade method, 36
  example, 39
Algebraic plate-to-plate, 29, 36
  Akers and Wade method, 36, 39
  Colburn method, pinch tempera-
    tures, 31
  Scheibel-Montross adjacent keys,
    33, 34
  Underwood method, 29, 30
  with digital computer, 36, 37
Ammonia
  air-water system, 203
    data chart, 203
  aqua, 188
  equilibrium curve, 192
  partial pressure over water, 191
  temperature, water absorption,
    effect of, 204
  vapor pressure, 190
Ammonia-water mass transfer data,
  188
  absorption tower, 188
  air-water system, 203
Ammonia-water system, 26, 28
  Ponchon distillation diagram, 27
Area requirements, cooling towers,
  223
Atmospheric cooling tower, 212, 213,
  239

Atomic and molecular volumes, 189
Azeotropes
  diagrams, 4, 5
  heterogenous, 4, 5
  maximum, 4, 5, 6
  minimum, 4, 5, 6
  system types, 4, 5

Batch distillation, 18, 20, 22, 23
Bell and spigot tower, 132, 133
Berl saddles, dimensions, 136
Bibliography, distillation, 126
Bibliography, packed towers, 240
Binary distillation, 3, 6
  operating line equations, 3, 6, 13
Bubble cap standard type detail, 72-
    76, 78-86, 87
  dimensions, 89
  shroud ring, 89
  slot sizes, 89
  slots, 89
Bubble cap trays, 62
  area distribution table, 69
  classification of tray areas, 70
  design, 65, 70, 89
  diagram, dynamic operation, 66
  layout details, 71
  layouts, 72, 73, 74, 77, 78-86, 87
  mechanical design details, 71
  mechanical guide, 70
  standard types, 75, 76
Bubble cap tray performance, 89
  entrainment, 91
  flooding, 91
  liquid gradients, effects of, 91
  overdesign, 91
  pulsing, blowing, coning, 91
  qualitative effects of loads, chart,
    90
  stability, 91
  tray capacity, 90
  tray flexibility, 90
  vapor on slot opening, effect of,
    chart, 90

Carbon dioxide absorption data, 198-
  200
  absorption example, 201
Carbon dioxide in alkaline solution,
  mass transfer, 197

Chempak,® dimensions, 138
Chlorine-water system (dilute), 204
  solubility chlorine in water, 204
Colburn minimum reflux method, 31
  graph, 33
Column, distillation, see Towers.
Computer
  multicomponent mixture calcula-
    tions, 37, 42
Condensers
  duty, 2, 4
  partial, 6, 7, 8
  total, 6, 7, 41
Cooling towers
  general construction, 214
  performance
    atmospheric and natural draft,
      239
    curves, counterflow, 229-235
    diagram counter flow, 219
    evaluate performance, existing
      unit, 225
    fan performance, 222, 225
    hot water, effects of, 221
    pressure loss, 224
    psychrometric chart, 226, 227
    typical curve, 218
    variables, effects of, 221, 222,
      224
    water rates, 225
  terminology, 214
  types, 212
    atmospheric, 212
    forced draft, 213
    induced draft, 214
    natural draft, 213
Cooling water with air, 212
Costs, tower packing, 138
Cross-partition rings dimensions, 137

Dauphine pressure drop, bubble caps,
  100
Design procedures, absorption and
  stripping
  absorption: number trays for fixed
    recovery, 53
  component absorption, fixed tray
    tower, 48
  lean oil requirement for fixed re-
    covery, 52

stripping rate for fixed recovery, 51
trays for specified absorption,
    number of, 50
trays for stripping recovery,
    number of, 50
Design procedures, cooling towers
comparison of packings, 238
drift loss (water), 236
driving force diagram, 220
evaluation of existing tower, 225
ground area requirements, 223
operation diagram, 219
performance, 219
power requirements, 224, 225
pressure loss, 224
transfer unit design, 239
variables, effects of, 221, 222, 224
water rates, 225
Design procedures, distillation
actual number trays, 35
batch, no trays, binary mixture, 18
batch, no trays, multicomponent
    mixture, 20
batch, with trays, constant product,
    multicomponent, 22
binary, Ponchon non-ideal heat
    effects, graphical, 24
column minimum reflux, pinch
    temperature, 31
feed tray location, 35
graphical design, binary systems,
    11, 13
heat balances, 41
minimum reflux, 9, 10
minimum trays, total reflux, 34
multicomponent systems, 29
open steam, with trays, binary, 23
relative volatility, 10
Scheibel-Montross, adjacent keys,
    33
steam, continuous differential,
    multicomponent, 21
steam, continuous flash multi-
    component, 21
steam, continuous flash, two liquid
    phases, multicomponent, 22
theoretical trays, operating reflux,
    34
theoretical trays at actual reflux, 11
total trays required, 8
tray-by-tray multicomponent sys-
    tems, 36
tray-by-tray using computer, 37
Underwood algebraic, adjacent
    keys, 29, 30
Underwood algebraic, split keys, 30
Design Procedures, hydraulics for
    bubble cap trays
bubble cap, 65, 89
    design, 89
    dynamic operation diagram, 66
    recommended layout pitch, 87
    system design components, 66
    tower diameter, 66, 67, 68
    tray area classification, 70

tray area distribution, 69
tray design guide, 70
tray layouts, 72, 73, 74, 78-86, 87
downcomer, 88
example design, 103
free height in downcomer, 103
liquid entrainment, 102
liquid height over straight weir,
    chart, 92, equation 93
pressure drop, total design, 93
seal pan, 89
slot seals, table, 91
tray drainage holes, 88
trays, 65
weir correction factor, segment,
    chart, 92
weirs, 87
Design procedures, hydraulics for
    sieve trays. See also Pressure
    drop.
design hole velocity, 111
entrainment, chart, 108
tower diameter, 108, 112
tray spacing, 108
tray stability, 112
typical performance chart, 112
Design procedure, hydraulics, per-
    forated trays, 116
capacity, 117
diameter, 117
efficiency, 118
entrainment, 118
flooding, 118
pressure drop, 117
tray activation, chart, 120
tray designs and layout, 118
tray spacing, 117
Design Procedures, packed tower per-
    formance
absorption/desorption, 180
air-water system, 205
ammonia-air-water system, 203
ammonia-water mass transfer data,
    188
ammonia-water system, 188
chlorine-water system (dilute gas),
    204
design criteria and guide, 166
distillation, 180
dumped packing, 166, 167
entrainment from packing, 176
flooding chart, 159, 160
gas and liquid-phase film coeffi-
    cients, 186
height of transfer unit, 186, 187
HETP design guidelines, 210
hydrogen chloride-water system,
    205
interfacial area, effective, 176, 177
liquid continuous, packed, 169
liquid hold-up, 173, 174, 176
    chart, 174, 175, 177
mass transfer
    carbon dioxide/alkaline solution,
    197, 201

sulfur dioxide/alkaline solution,
    197, 201
mass transfer, 179, 180, 182
minimum wetting rates, 157, 158
packing factors, 160, 161, 162
packing support on flood, effect
    of, 170
packing versus tower size, 157
pressure drop correlation at flood,
    chart, 169
pressure drop design charts, 159,
    160
recommended capacity and pres-
    sure drop, 162, 166
specification design forms, 195, 196
transfer units, equation and chart,
    182, 183
wetted area, packing, 176
Diffusion coefficients, gases, 187
table, 188
Distillate product, 2
Distillation
Akers and Wade tray-by-tray, 36
batch, 18
benzene-toluene example, 11, 13
binary system material balance, 6
column reflux method, 31, 33
condenser duty, 41
conditions of operation, 6
constant molal overflow, 7, 41
continuous, binary diagram, 3, 6
digital computer tray-by-tray, 37,
    42
distillate, 2
distillate-to-feed ratio, 46
equilibrium basics, 1
feed, 2
feed tray location, 35
graphical design, binary, 11
heat balance, 23, 24, 41
ideal systems, 1
minimum plates, 8
multicomponent calculations, 37,
    42
operating characteristics, diagrams,
    8
operating line equation, 3, 6, 7, 13
operating reflux versus trays,
    graph, 35
pinch temperatures, 31
Ponchon-Savarit method (binary),
    24, 26, 27
process performance, 1
product, 2
reboiler duty, 41
rectifying section, 2
reflux, 7-11, 29
reflux ratio versus trays, 17, 35
relative volatility, 10
schematic arrangement, 2, 49
step-wise determination of trays,
    13, 15, 36
stripping and rectification, 3, 6, 13
stripping section, 2
theoretical tray at actual reflux, 17

theoretical trays, 11, 17, 36
thermal condition of feed, 7, 13
total reflux, 8
total trays, determination, Fenske, 8
tray efficiency, 18, 19
trays, (plates) 8, 9, 10, 13, 36
Underwood algebraic method, 29, 30
unequal molal overflow, 23
Distillation columns, mechanical design, 61, 108, 122-125
Distillation, differential
batch, 18, 19, 20, 22
binary mixtures, 18
steam, multicomponent and binary, 21, 22
Distillation, packed tower, 180, 205
HETP, 205
HETP estimates, 212
transfer unit concept 208, 209
Distributor, packed tower liquid
performance effects, table, 151
physical details, 152, 153, 154
Distillation, steam, 21
continuous differential, 21
continuous flash, 22
open line, 23
Distillation trays. *See also* trays.
bubble cap tray mechanical guide, 70, 73, 74, 76, 77
bubble cap standards, 73, 74, 75, 76
downcomer, 88
residence time, downcomer, 102
seal pan, 89
selection, guide for, 69
types by liquid paths, 69
weirs, 87
Distillation trays application features
ballast, 64
bubble caps, 62
flexitray, 64
multiple downcomer, sieve, 64
nutter, 64
perforated without downcomers, 63
sieve, 63
turbogrid, 64
Distillation, unequal molal overflow, 23, 24
graphical solutions, 25, 26, 27
Ponchon, Savarit method, 24, 25, 27
rigorous methods, 36, 37
Distribution in packed towers
liquid, 140
patterns, table, 154
performance effects, table, 151
physical details, 152, 153
Downcomer, 88
residence time, 102
segmental design chart, 88
Drainage. *See* tray liquid drainage.
Drift loss, cooling tower, 236

Drip-point tile, dimensions
dimensions, 139
pressure drop charts, 163-166

Edmister, absorption and stripping, 48
absorption/stripping factors chart, 54
design methods, 52
Efficiency
perforated trays, 118
Efficiency, tray
absorption, stripping, 19, 58
fractionation, 18, 19
graph, 19
Entrainment
bubble cap trays, 91, 102
sieve trays, 108
Entrainment from packing, 176
Equation of state, 3
viral, 3
Equilibrium
absorption, 58
activity, 3
activity coefficients, 4
binary system diagram, 3
charts, 36
empirical techniques, 2
fugacity, 3, 4
ideal, 1, 9
non-ideal systems, 2
Rault's Law, 1
Equilibrium curve
ammonia-water, 192
Example calculations, distillation
absorption of hydrocarbons, 55
binary distillation, 19
bubble cap tray design, 103
component absorption in fixed tray tower, 59
determine number trays for absorption, 57
graphical design binary system, 11
minimum theoretical trays at total reflux, 15
multicomponent batch distillation, 20
multicomponent examination of reflux ratio and distillate to feed ratio, 46
multicomponent mixture using digital computer, 42
multicomponent steam flash, 21
operating reflux ratio, 34
perforated tray without downcomers, 119
Ponchon unequal molal overflow, 25
Schiebel-Montross minimum reflux, 34
sieve tray design, with downcomer, 112
thermal condition of feed, 13
tray-to-tray design multicomponent mixture, 37

Example calculations, cooling towers
Wood packing cooling tower with recirculation, induced draft, 227
Example calculations, packed towers
alternate evaluation of tower condition and pressure drop, 171
design a packed tower using caustic to remove carbon dioxide from vent stream, 201
design of ammonia absorption tower, 188
evaluation of tower condition and pressure drop, 170
operation at low rate liquid hold-up, 177
performance change with packing change in existing tower, 172
stacked packing pressure drop, 173
transfer units, concentrated solutions, number of, 184
transfer units for dilute solutions, number of, 182
transfer units in distillation, 210
Colburn's chart for transfer units, use of, 184

Fan performance, cooling tower, 222, 224
Feed
calculations, 13
"q" line, 7, 8, 30
thermal condition, 7, 8, 10, 12, 13, 15, 30
tray location, 2, 35
Fenske equation, 8
total trays, 8
Flooding
bubble cap trays, 91
perforated trays, 118
sieve trays, 111
Flooding point (region), packed tower correlation, 169
data examination, 158, 159
design charts, 159, 160
Forced draft cooling tower, 213
Fractionation, continuous
binary mixture diagram, 3
graphical design, binary system, 11, 13
material balance, constant molal overflow, 7

Gilliland actual reflux versus trays, 11, 34
graph, 11
plot for example, 39

Haveg towers, dimensions, 134
Heat balance, distillation system, 41
Heat transfer, packed tower, 179
HETP (Height equivalent to theoretical plate)
correlation, 207, 209
design, guidelines for, 210
distillation, 205

distillation, estimates for, 212
related to HTU, 186
Hold-up, liquid, packed tower,
173-177
correlation factors, liquids other
than water, 176
Holes, sieve or perforated trays
charts, 113
size, spacing, 109
Horsepower (fan), cooling tower, 225
Horton and Franklin, absorption/
shipping, 53
HTU. *See also* mass transfer,
correlation, 209
Hydraulic/mechanical design distillation columns, 61
Hydrogen chloride-water
adiabatic tower, standard, 206, 207
design, 205
inert gases, effect of, 205
X-Y diagram, 205
Hy-Pak, ® dimensions, 138

Ideal systems, 1
Induced draft cooling tower, 214, 215,
216
Intalox® saddles, dimensions
ceramic, 137
syar Intalox, ceramic, 138
Interficial area, packings, 176, 177
charts, 178

K-charts, 50
Kremser-Brown-Sherwood absorption method, 48

Lean oil, 48, 50
component recovery, requirements
for, 52, 53
Lessing rings, dimensions, 136
Liquid continuous system, packed
tower, 169
Liquid distribution, packed towers
liquid, 140
patterns, table, 154
performance effects, table, 151
physical dimension details, 152, 153
Liquid gradient, bubble cap tray, 93,
96-100
sieve tray, 109
Loading point (region) packing performance, 158

McCabe-Thiele diagram, 3, 13, 28
Mass transfer, packed tower
air-water system, 205
ammonia-air water, 203
ammonia-water, 188
chemical reaction, 197
carbon dioxide, 197, 201
sulfur dioxide, 197
chlorine-water system, 204
counter-current operation, 180
diagrams, 180
equations, table, 182
film coefficients, 186

gas film height transfer unit, 189
height of transfer unit, 186
hydrogen chloride-water system,
205
temperature on ammonia absorption, effect of, 204
transfer units, 179, 183
Mechanical specification design, 121,
122, 123
composite assembly, 125
fabrication tolerances, 124
Multicomponent distillation, 29

Natural draft cooling tower, 213
214, 239
Nomenclature
absorption and stripping, Part 2, 60
distillation process performance,
Part 1, 46
tray hydraulic design, Part 3, 121
Nomenclature, packed towers, 239
Non-ideal systems, 2
Ponchon binary graphical method,
24

Operating line equations, distillation
rectifying section, 6, 14
stripping section, 6, 15

Packed column. *See* Packed towers
Packed towers, 129
Packed tower design criteria and
guide, 166
Packed tower, mechanical details
assembly, 156
bed-limiter, 155
bell and spigot tower, 132, 133
brick-lining, 130, 131
grid supports, 129, 131, 154
hold-down plate, 155
internal details, 129, 154
liquid distributor, 139, 154
mechanical cross-section, 129, 154
packing, 129
packing support, 129
shell, 132
Packed tower performance
absorption, 180
desorption, 180
distillation, 180
Packing, cooling tower
comparison of efficiency, 238
comparison of pressure drop, 238
types, 237
Packing, cooling tower (air-water),
220
Packing factors, 160-162
Packing installation, 155
assembly, 156
dumped, 156
stacked, 155
Packing, performance data, 134
dumped packing pressure drop,
166, 167
flooding, 169
interfacial area, 176, 177

liquid hold-up, 173, 174, 175, 176,
177
loading point, 158
pressure drop charts, design, 159,
160
wetted area, 176
Packing selection and performance
contact efficiency, 156
HETP, 156
HTU, 156
materials of selection, 157
packing size versus column
diameter, 157
particle versus compact packing,
157
pressure drop, 157, 158
Packing service application, 140
Packing size selection, 157
Packing supports, 138, 146, 147, 148,
149
Packing, tower; physical details
ballast ring, 143
Berl saddles, ceramic, 136, 142
Berl saddles, metal, 136
Cascade mini-ring, ® 144
Chempak, ® metal, 138
cross-partition rings, 137
142
Dowpac, plastic, 138
Flexiring, 143
Goodloe, 145
Hy-Pak, metal, 138, 143
Intalox saddles, ceramic, 137, 142
Lessing rings, ceramic, 136
Lessing rings, metal, 136, 142
Metalox, 143
pall rings, metal, 138, 142
pall rings, plastic, 143
Panapak, 144
Raschig rings, carbon, 135, 142
Raschig rings, metal, 135, 142
Raschig rings, porcelain, 132, 142
Raschig rings, stoneware, 132, 142
spiral packing rings, 137, 142
Spraypak, 145
Sulzer, 145, 146
Super Intalox, ® ceramic, 138
Super Intalox, ® plastic, 144
Teller rosette, plastic, 138, 145
tile, drip point, ceramic, 139
Packing type applications, table, 141
Pall rings, dimensions, 138
Perforated tray layout, 118
Perforated trays, (no downcomers),
116
arrangement, 116
Performance curves, cooling tower,
229-235
Ponchon-Savarit method, non-ideal,
graphical distillation, 24
Pressure drop (hydraulic), bubble cap
tray
downcomer, 101
segmental, 101
circular, 101

downcomer seal, 101
downcomer velocities, table, 102
dry cap, 100
free height in downcomer, 103
liquid gradient, 93
  charts, 96-99, 100
liquid height over weir, 93
liquid height in downcomer, 101
riser and reversal, 95, 100
slot opening, 93
  chart, 94
throw over weir, 103
total tray, 93, 101
tray spacing, 101
wet cap, 100

Pressure drop (hydraulic), perforated
    trays
dry tray, 117
dump point, 118
effective head, 117
entrainment, 118
hole size and spacing, 117
percent open area, 117
total wet tray, 117
tray spacing, 117

Pressure drop (hydraulic), sieve stray
design hole velocity, 110
downcomer, 108, 110
dry tray pressure drop, 109
dynamic liquid seal, 110
flooding, 111
free height, downcomer, 110
height of liquid over weir, 109
hole size and spacing, 109
hydraulic gradient, 109
liquid height in downcomer, 110
maximum hole velocity, 110
orifice coefficient, 109
stability, 112
static liquid seal, or submergence,
    109
tray spacing, 108
weep point, 110
wet tray, 110

Pressure drop packing supports, 169,
    170, 171

Pressure drop, tower packings
correlation at flooding, 169
design charts, 159, 160
dumped packing
  at flooding, 167
  below loading region, 166
  loading and flooding, 167
table constants, below flooding, 168
typical charts, 158
upper break-point (flood), water,
    168

Psychrometric chart, 226, 227

Raoult's Law, 1, 4, 5, 10
Raschig rings packing, dimensions
  carbon, 135
  metal, 135
  porcelain, 132
  stoneware, 132
Reboiler duty, 2, 41, 42
Recirculation, cooling tower, 218
Rectifying section, distillation, 2, 6
Redistributor, packing, 150, 154
  wall-wiper, 154
Reflux
  actual, 11, 12, 13, 17, 26, 34
  column method (minimum), 31
    graph, 33
  Gilliland method, graph, 11
  graph, 35
  minimum, 8, 9, 10, 12, 13, 17, 29
  ratio, 7, 10, 17, 25
  total, 8, 15, 34, 38
Relative volatility, 10
  calculation, 16
Residence time in downcomers, 102
Rich oil, 48
Rosette redistributor, 150

Schiebel-Montross adjacent key
    method, 33
Seal pan, 89
Sieve trays (no downcomers). See
    Perforated trays.
Sieve trays with downcomers, 62, 63,
    106
  mechanical illustration assembly,
    106
  operation illustration, 63, 107
  selection guide, 107
Specification design sheets, 121-123
Specifications cooling tower, packed
    towers, 195, 196, 217, 218
Spiral packing rings, dimensions, 137
Souders-Brown tower diameter, 67
Sodium hydroxide, absorption of
    carbon
  dioxide, 199-201
  example calculation, 201
Steam distillation, 21, 22, 23
Stripping factor, 49, 50, 51
  chart, 52, 54
Stripping section, distillation, 2, 6
Submergence, sieve trays, 109
Sulfur dioxide in alkaline solution,
    mass transfer, 197
Supports, tower packing, 138,
    146-149

Tellerette, plastic, 138
Thermal condition of feed, distil-
    lation, 7, 8
  calculation, 13
  diagram, 8

Tower diameter
  bubble cap systems, 66, 67
  "C" factor chart, 67
  chart solving for diameter, 68
  sieve tray, 108
  Souders-Brown chart, 67
Transfer unit, 210
  correlation for packing, 208
  example for distillation, 210
Transfer units, 179
  for cooling tower
    chart, 236
    graphical integration, 228
Trays, absorption and stripping
  efficiency, 19, 49, 50, 52, 58
  theoretical, 49
Tray layout, sieve trays, 112
Tray liquid drainage, 88
  time to drain, 88
Tray spacing, 101, 112
Trays (plates), distillation, separa-
    tion performance
  actual versus operation reflux,
    graph, 35
  AICHE Method, 18
  batch distillation, 22, 23
  efficiency, 18, 19
  example, 15
  infinite, 8, 9, 10, 29
  minimum, 8, 16, 34, 38
  step-wise determination, 15
  theoretical, 11, 12, 17, 34
  total, 8
Trays types or designs, 62
  bubble caps, 62
  Glitsch ballast, 65
  Koch Flexitray, 64
  Linde Multiple Downcomer, 65
  nutter float valve, 64
  perforated without downcomers, 63
  ripple, 65
  sieve with downcomers, 63

Underwood algebraic method, 29, 30
  adjacent keys, 29
  example calculations, 38
  split keys, 30

Volumes, atomic and molecular, 188

Wall-wiper redistributor, 154
Water loss, cooling tower, 236
Weep point, sieve trays, 110, 111
Weirs, 87, 109
Wet bulb temperature, 214, 221
Wetted area, packing, 176
Wetting rates, packing, 157
  minimum, 158
  table, 157, 158